INTRODUCTION TO THE
AMERICAN OFFICIAL SOURCES
FOR THE ECONOMIC AND SOCIAL HISTORY
OF THE WORLD WAR

ECONOMIC AND SOCIAL HISTORY
OF THE WORLD WAR

James T. Shotwell, Ph.D., LL.D., *General Editor.*

AMERICAN SERIES

For List of Editors, Publishers and Plan of Series
see end of this volume.

INTRODUCTION TO THE
AMERICAN OFFICIAL SOURCES
FOR THE ECONOMIC AND SOCIAL
HISTORY OF THE WORLD WAR

COMPILED BY
WALDO G. LELAND AND
NEWTON D. MERENESS

NEW HAVEN : YALE UNIVERSITY PRESS
LONDON : HUMPHREY MILFORD : OXFORD UNIVERSITY PRESS
FOR THE CARNEGIE ENDOWMENT FOR INTERNATIONAL
PEACE : DIVISION OF ECONOMICS AND HISTORY
1926

EDITOR'S PREFACE

In the autumn of 1914, when the scientific study of the effects of war upon modern life passed suddenly from theory to history, the Division of Economics and History of the Carnegie Endowment for International Peace proposed to adjust the program of its researches to the new and altered problems which the war presented. The existing program, which had been prepared as the result of a conference of economists held at Berne in 1911, and which dealt with the facts then at hand, had just begun to show the quality of its contributions; but for many reasons it could no longer be followed out. A plan was therefore drawn up at the request of the Director of the Division in which it was proposed, by means of an historical survey, to attempt to measure the economic cost of the war and the displacement which it was causing in the processes of civilization. Such an 'Economic and Social History of the World War,' it was felt, if undertaken by men of judicial temper and adequate training, might ultimately, by reason of its scientific obligations to truth, furnish data for the forming of sound public opinion, and thus contribute fundamentally toward the aims of an institution dedicated to the cause of international peace.

The need for such an analysis, conceived and executed in the spirit of historical research, was increasingly obvious as the war developed, releasing complex forces of national life not only for the vast process of destruction, but also for the stimulation of new capacities for production. This new economic activity, which under normal conditions of peace might have been a gain to society, and the surprising capacity exhibited by the belligerent nations for enduring long and increasing loss—often while presenting the outward semblance of new prosperity—made necessary a reconsideration of the whole field of war economics. A double obligation was therefore placed upon the Division of Economics and History. It was obliged to concentrate its work upon the problem thus presented, and to study it as a whole; in other words, to apply to it the tests and disciplines of history. Just as the war itself was a single event, though penetrating by seemingly unconnected ways to the remotest parts of the world, so the analysis of it must be developed according to a plan at once all embracing and yet adjustable to the practical limits of the available data.

During the actual progress of the war, however, the execution of this plan for a scientific and objective study of war economics proved impossible in any large and authoritative way. Incidental studies and surveys of portions of the field could be made and were made under the direction of the Division, but it was impossible to undertake a general history for obvious reasons. In the first place, an authoritative statement of the resources of belligerents bore directly on the conduct of armies in the field. The result was to remove as far as possible from scrutiny those data of the economic life of the countries at war which would ordinarily, in time of peace, be readily available for investigation. In addition to this difficulty of consulting documents, collaborators competent to deal with them were for the most part called into national service in the belligerent countries and so were unavailable for research. The plan for a war history was therefore postponed until conditions should arise which would make possible not only access to essential documents, but also the coöperation of economists, historians, and men of affairs in the nations chiefly concerned, whose joint work would not be misunderstood either in purpose or in content.

Upon the termination of the war, the Endowment once more took up the original plan, and it was found with but slight modification to be applicable to the situation. Work was begun in the summer and autumn of 1919. In the first place, a final conference of the Advisory Board of Economists of the Division of Economics and History was held in Paris, which limited itself to planning a series of short preliminary surveys of special fields. Since, however, the purely preliminary character of such studies was further emphasized by the fact that they were directed more especially towards those problems which were then fronting Europe as questions of urgency, it was considered best not to treat them as part of the general survey, but rather as of contemporary value in the period of war settlement. It was clear that not only could no general program be laid down *a priori* by this conference as a whole, but that a new and more highly specialized research organization than that already existing would be needed to undertake the Economic and Social History of the War, one based more upon national grounds in the first instance, and less upon purely international coöperation. Until the facts of national history could be ascertained, it would be impossible to proceed with comparative analysis; and the different national histories were themselves of almost baffling intricacy and variety. Consequently the former European Committee of Research was dissolved, and in its place it was decided to erect an Editorial Board in each of the larger countries and to nominate special editors in the smaller ones, who should concentrate, for the present at least, upon their own economic and social war history.

The nomination of these boards by the General Editor was the first step taken in every country where the work has begun. And if any justification was needed for the plan of the Endowment, it at once may be found in the lists of those, distinguished in scholarship or in public affairs, who have accepted the responsibility of editorship. This responsibility is by no means light, involving as it does, the adaptation of the general editorial plan to the varying demands of national circumstances or methods of work; and the measure of success attained is due to the generous and earnest coöperation of those in charge in each country.

Once the editorial organization was established there could be little doubt as to the first step which should be taken in each instance toward the actual preparation of the history. Without documents there can be no history. The essential records of the war, local as well as central, have therefore to be preserved and to be made available for research in so far as is compatible with public interest. But this archival task is a very great one, belonging of right to the governments and other owners of historical sources and not to the historian or economist who proposes to use them. It is an obligation of ownership; for all such documents are public trust. The collaborators on this section of the war history, therefore, working within their own field as researchers, could only survey the situation as they found it and report their findings in the form of guides or manuals; and perhaps, by stimulating a comparison of methods, help to further the adoption of those found to be most practical. In every country, therefore, this was the point of departure for actual work; although special monographs have not been written in every instance.

The first stage of the work upon the war history, dealing with little more than the externals of archives, seemed for a while to exhaust the possibilities of research, and had the plan of the history been limited to research based upon official documents, little more could have been done, for once documents have been labelled 'secret' few government officials can be found with sufficient courage or initiative to break open the seal. Thus vast masses of source material essential for the historian were effectively placed beyond his reach, although much of it was quite harmless from any point of view. While war conditions thus continued to hamper research, and were likely to do so for many years to come, some alternative had to be found.

Fortunately, such an alternative was at hand in the narrative, amply supported by documentary evidence, of those who had played some part in the conduct of affairs during the war, or who, as close observers in privileged positions, were able to record from first or at least second-hand knowledge the economic history of different phases of the Great War, and of its effect upon society. Thus a series of monographs was planned consisting for the most part of unofficial yet authoritative statements, descriptive or historical, which may best be described as about half-way between memoirs and blue-books. These monographs make up the main body of the work assigned so far. They are not limited to contemporary war-time studies; for the economic history of the war must deal with a longer period than that of the actual fighting. It must cover the years of "deflation" as well, at least sufficiently to secure some fairer measure of the economic displacement than is possible in purely contemporary judgments.

With this phase of the work, the editorial problems assumed a new aspect. The series of monographs had to be planned primarily with regard to the availability of contributors, rather than of source material as in the case of most histories; for the contributors themselves controlled the sources. This in turn involved a new attitude toward those two ideals which historians have sought to emphasize, consistency and objectivity. In order to bring out the chief contribution of each writer it was impossible to keep within narrowly logical outlines; facts would have to be repeated in different settings and seen from different angles, and sections included which do not lie within the strict limits of history; and absolute objectivity could not be obtained in every part. Under the stress of controversy or apology, partial views would here and there find their expression. But these views are in some instances an intrinsic part of the history itself, contemporary measurements of facts as significant as the facts with which they deal. Moreover, the work as a whole is planned to furnish its own corrective; and where it does not, others will.

In addition to the monographic treatment of source material, a number of studies by specialists is already in preparation, dealing with technical or limited subjects, historical or statistical. These monographs also partake to some extent of the nature of first-hand material, registering as they do the data of history close enough to the source to permit verification in ways impossible later. But they also belong to that constructive process by which history passes from analysis to synthesis. The process is a long and difficult one, however, and work upon it has only just begun. To quote an apt characterization, in the first stages of a history like this one is only "picking cotton." The tangled threads of events have still to be woven into the pattern of history; and for this creative and constructive work different plans and organizations may be needed.

In a work which is the product of so complex and varied coöperation as this, it is impossible to indicate in any but a most general way the apportionment of responsibility of editors and authors for the contents of the different monographs. For the plan of the History as a whole and its effective execution the General Editor is responsible; but the arrangement of the detailed programs of study has been largely the work of the different Editorial Boards and divisional editors, who have also read the manuscripts prepared under their direction. The acceptance of a monograph in this series, however, does not commit the editors to the opinions or conclusions of the authors. Like other editors, they are asked to vouch for the scientific merit, the appropriateness and usefulness of the volumes admitted to the series; but the authors are naturally free to make their individual contributions in their own way. In like manner, the publication of the monographs does not commit the Endowment to agreement with any specific conclusions which may be expressed therein. The responsibility of the Endowment is to History itself—an obligation not to avoid but to secure and preserve variant narratives and points of view, in so far as they are essential for the understanding of the war as a whole.

J. T. S.

COMPILERS' PREFACE

THE purpose of this volume is to present a summary account of those records and official publications of the various branches and offices of the Federal Government which constitute the primary sources for the history of the social and economic activities of the national government during the period of American participation in the World War.

The period covered is from the declaration of war in April, 1917, to the completion of demobilization in 1920. This period is, however, sometimes extended, at the one end to the commencement of hostilities in Europe in 1914, and at the other end to the later phases of reconstruction in 1922.

To have enlarged the scope of the volume to include the records and publications of state and local governments, and of the many non-governmental organizations which contributed in important and essential ways to the conduct of the war, would have increased the task of the compilers far beyond the limited time and attention which they have been able to devote to it. They have, however, endeavored to give some indication of the vast masses of material of all sorts which are being accumulated by the various state war history organizations.

To have omitted all mention of these collections would have been to ignore one of the most interesting and characteristic phases of the war itself, namely, the systematic and comprehensive effort to collect and preserve, while it could still be done on a large scale, the documents which are essential to writing the history of all aspects of the emergency, especially its social and economic aspects. It is believed, therefore, that the information presented in the section on State War History Collections, incomplete and sketchy as it is, for it has been gathered mainly by correspondence, will be found to be interesting and suggestive.

In making use of the present volume it should always be borne in mind that it is in no sense a bibliography of the war. Very few unofficial publications are mentioned, and they are included only because, on account of their authorship or for other reasons, they supplement in an especially useful way the official publications of some governmental unit.

The plan of the compilers has been to select those branches or offices of the government which conducted important social or economic activities, to give a brief account of their organization and functions, to list their significant publications and to describe their records and files.

It has not, however, been possible to adhere uniformly to this plan, and in numerous cases the description of the records and files is very summary or is omitted altogether. These omissions are due to various causes: the files of some of the emergency offices are physically inaccessible, being packed in boxes and stored; the files of other offices are regarded as confidential and no examination of them is permitted. In many cases, however, the files consist of masses of administrative material, which are of such vast physical bulk that the investigator would find great difficulty in exploring them, and from which the important data have already been compiled and presented in published or mimeographed form, or in official memoranda. In such cases the publications of the office suffice for the needs of most investigators.

The compilers have been fortunate in securing the collaboration of several persons who were especially competent to report on certain important establishments. Thus the material for the account of the Food Administration was gathered by Professor Everett S. Brown, now of the University of Michigan, who was attached to the Food Administration during its entire existence. Professor J. G. Randall, of the University of Illinois, who compiled the material for the report on the Shipping Board, was the historian of that organization during the last year of the war; the material for the accounts of the Department of Commerce and of the War Trade Board was gathered by Dr. James A. Robertson, who until recently was on the staff of the Bureau of Foreign and Domestic Commerce; while Miss Laura Thompson, librarian of the Department of Labor, performed the difficult task of dealing with the activities of that Department and of the various boards and units that composed the War Labor Administration. The basis of the report on the War Industries Board was furnished through the courtesy of the War Department, by Miss Adelaide R. Hasse, who in 1921 and 1922 was in charge of the classification and final arrangement of the files of that important organization. The section dealing with the Department of State has been recast and enlarged by Dr. Tyler Dennett, editor of that Department, and Mrs. Jeannette P. Nichols has rendered much valuable assistance of a bibliographical character and has aided in preparing the sections devoted to the Department of the Interior and to certain bureaus of the Department of Agriculture.

The obligations of the compilers are further due to many officials who have freely given valuable assistance or who have reviewed the sections relating to their respective offices and approved them or made suggestions for their improvement, and also to the executive officers of many state war history organizations who have supplied information respecting the collections in their custody.

Finally, mention should be made of the coöperation of the National Association of State War History Organizations (now dissolved), which permitted the use of a considerable body of pertinent information that had been gathered for it, and acknowledgment should be made to Mrs. R. S. Bowman for assistance in the preparation of the manuscript for the press.

While the compilers hold themselves jointly responsible for the present volume, it is only fair to state that the labor of writing by far the larger part of it devolved upon Mr. Mereness.

WALDO G. LELAND
NEWTON D. MERENESS

Washington,
June 27, 1925.

CONTENTS

UNITED STATES SUPREME COURT

EXECUTIVE DEPARTMENTS

DEPARTMENT OF STATE

DEPARTMENT OF THE TREASURY

DEPARTMENT OF WAR

DEPARTMENT OF THE NAVY

DEPARTMENT OF THE INTERIOR

CONTENTS

DEPARTMENT OF LABOR AND WAR LABOR ADMINISTRATION

INDEPENDENT BOARDS AND COMMISSIONS

INTERSTATE COMMERCE COMMISSION

FEDERAL TRADE COMMISSION

CONTENTS

CONTENTS

THE STATES

STATE WAR HISTORY COLLECTIONS

INTRODUCTION

THE military participation of the United States in the World War was made possible only by a complete mobilization of the economic and social forces of the entire nation, a mobilization on so vast a scale as to require a thorough readjustment of the machinery of normal existence.

For two years, 1917 and 1918, all the energies of the country were directed to effecting this readjustment, while for the two succeeding years they were directed to the restoration, so far as that was possible, of the normal conditions of life. During these four years the life of the individual American was profoundly affected by the necessity of considering, under unaccustomed conditions, such elementary problems as those of food and clothing, shelter, light and heat, and transportation. War, the most wasteful of all processes, the outcome of political ineptitude and failure, demanded for its conduct the most rigorous economies and the utmost attainable efficiency.

The social and economic history of the war years and of those immediately succeeding them is chiefly the history of the processes of mobilization and demobilization and of the effects of these processes upon human conduct and relationships. To write this history will be the task of more than one generation of historians; its sources are of the utmost variety and of such appalling physical bulk that their mastery in the near future is hardly to be looked for. Foremost among these sources are the publications and records of the national government, to the description of which the present volume is devoted.

Although the national government directed the processes of mobilization it was itself affected by them in many important ways. The executive departments and the independent boards and commissions which constitute the permanent establishment assumed many new functions and underwent numerous and in some cases fundamental reorganizations. By the side of the permanent establishment there was progressively organized an emergency establishment composed of such units as the Council of National Defense, the War Trade Board, the War Industries Board, the Food, Fuel, and Railroad Administrations, the boards and committees that made up the War Labor Administration, the War Finance Corporation, the Capital Issues Committee, and still others. It is not unfair to say that anything like a definitive form of war government was not evolved until shortly before the end of hostilities, and that the process of reorganization, conducted by methods of trial and error, operated continuously throughout the period of the war. Such a process was infinitely complicated and to trace its history in such detail that the precise form assumed by the national government at any given moment may be stated, is not a simple task, nor indeed is it the task of the present volume. Some understanding, however, of these changing forms and functions is essential to the intelligent use of the records, both published and manuscript, which the government produced, and there has therefore been included in the following pages a brief account of the organization and activities of each governmental unit, to serve as an introduction to the description of its publications and records.

The problem of the national government during the emergency had two distinct aspects: on the one hand, the urgent needs of the countries associated with the United States in carrying on the war must be met by supplies of money, food, and material, while at the same time the enemy countries must be shut off from all supplies; on the other hand, a military force must be raised and equipped, transported to the area of hostilities, supplied and reinforced while in that area, and finally returned to the United States and dispersed. The first step in the solution of this problem was to ascertain the requirements of the situation; the second was to learn what resources existed for meeting those requirements; the third was to devise means of augmenting those resources to the point of adequacy, either by their actual increase or by more economical and efficient methods of utilization.

The problem and the method of its attack have been thus stated in the most general terms in order to furnish if possible a key to the significance of the material described in the succeeding sections of this volume. The Draft records, for example, constitute the survey of the man power of the country; the records of the Department of Agriculture contain almost daily censuses of agricultural resources, while those of the Food Administration show the methods of so utilizing those resources as to make them meet, as nearly as possible, the needs of the situation. In the records of the War Trade Board we see how the stocks of essential commodities were increased by imports, or conserved by prohibiting their exportation, and how the channels of trade were so controlled as to insure a flow of supplies to the allied countries while shutting it off from those under enemy control. The records of the War Industries Board contain the surveys that were continually made of the industrial resources of the country, and show how the government endeavored to develop and coördinate manufacturing facilities in order to increase production and to prevent waste. The records of the Railroad Administration, of the Shipping Board, and of the Emergency Fleet Corporation reveal the efforts of the government to provide adequate means of transportation, by both land and sea, for the enormous movement of commodities and men; and the records of the various units of the War Labor Administration and of the Department of Labor show how the necessary man power was procured and maintained.

Certain categories of records common to many of the governmental units may be rapidly noted. In point of view of physical bulk the correspondence files occupy the first place, but they are largely of administrative character, and, fortunately for the investigator, are not of prime importance. Exceptions exist, of course, as in the case of the Department of State, where the records are chiefly in the form of correspondence with the diplomatic and consular agents of the United States abroad, or with foreign governments and their representatives, or with American citizens who protested against the regulations and practice of other countries in such matters as the enforcement of the commercial blockade. Of more than administrative interest is the correspondence also of those branches of the government that came in closest contact with the individual citizen, particularly of such units as the Food Administration and the Council of National Defense. For the future historian, however, perhaps the most valuable category of material includes the great mass of statistical information that was assiduously gathered in many offices of the government. These compilations bear upon all phases of economic life and activity; they show the stocks of commodities on hand at different periods, the varying rate of production, the movement of raw materials, the supply of labor, the state of the crops, the movement of money, and many other important states and processes. Similar to these are the records of the numerous investigations conducted by different bureaus into such matters as costs of production, prices, wages, conditions of living, etc. Of less direct interest for the purposes of the present survey are the technical studies made by the Forestry Service, the Bureau of Standards, the Department of Agriculture, and other scientific branches of the government for such purposes as devising and promoting economical methods of production and consumption, testing the suitability of materials, developing new sources of supply, and encouraging the use of substitutes for the commodities most urgently needed for war purposes. Finally, mention should be made of the "histories" that were prepared by many offices of their own activities during the period of the war. These histories are sometimes very comprehensive (that prepared by the Construction Division of the Army fills more than five hundred manuscript volumes), and contain in convenient form much information of value.

The best approach to the manuscript records of the government is through its publications. A surprising amount of material has been made public, in annual and special reports, and in various other ways. Fundamental sources, such as executive orders, decisions of boards and commissions, etc., were published currently. The final reports of certain of the emergency units, such as the War Trade Board, the War Industries Board, and the Fuel Administration, contain a large amount of documentary and statistical material; the annual reports of the Departments of Agriculture, Labor, and Commerce, and of other branches of the permanent establishment contain much material of first importance, and the bulletins of such units as the Federal Reserve Board and the Bureau of Labor Statistics are indispensable. In addition to printed material the government put forth much statistical information in mimeographed form, particularly in cases where it was important that the information should be made public without delay. The daily market reports of the Department of Agriculture, for example, were published in this fashion.

The records of the economic mobilization are widely scattered. The records of emergency branches were, upon the dissolution of those branches, transferred to various offices of the permanent establishment. Thus the records of the War Industries Board and of the Council of National Defense are in the custody of the Department of War, those of the Fuel Administration are with the Bureau of Mines, and the records of the War Trade Board have been transferred to the Department of State. So far as their physical preservation is concerned the records to which this volume is devoted share the same fate and incur the same grave risks as the great mass of the nation's archives. In the absence of any archival establishment or central depository they are stored wherever space can be found for them. Some of the most valuable are in semi-permanent buildings which were erected during the war and which seem destined to continue in use until they are destroyed by fire or succumb to the disintegrating influences of time.

In the last report of the Council of National Defense the director dealt with the problem of housing the war records in the following words:

The necessity for the provision of adequate permanent fireproof housing of the files and records now in the custody of the Council of National Defense cannot be too strongly urged. These records must not be considered merely an interesting chronology. They are infinitely more. They are the records concerning the most complete industrial and national readjustment that this country has ever known. For years to come and perhaps for generations these records will be searched to learn how the Nation can readjust itself to meet extreme and unusual crises. Never before in human history did a nation go through an industrial metamorphosis like that described in these records. If the conservation of human experience is in any sense one of the sacred trusts of civilization, it is exceedingly important that Congress should make provision for the permanent preservation of these records and the keeping of the same intact and accessible.

The failure to heed such a recommendation does not reflect credit upon the government of a civilized people.

BIBLIOGRAPHICAL NOTE

THE best treatment of the reorganization which the national government underwent in order to meet the new demands of the war emergency is the exceedingly clear and well-written volume by William F. Willoughby, *Government Organization in War Time and After* (New York,

1917, 370 pages). A shorter but still comprehensive account is the article by Frederic L. Paxson, on "The American War Government, 1917-1918," in the *American Historical Review* (vol. XXVI, pp. 54-76). Two general manuals, compiled early in the war, contain a considerable body of information about the various branches of the government and their activities, as well as about non-governmental organizations. The first of these, *National Service Handbook*, was published by the Committee on Public Information in the summer of 1917 and represents the situation as it existed at that time; the other compilation was prepared by the Library of Congress at about the same time and contains a certain amount of bibliographical information: *The United States at War; Organization, Literature.*

A suggestive and valuable though summary study of the processes of economic mobilization was made by the Historical Branch of the General Staff and printed as one of its publications and also as an article in the *Historical Outlook* for January, 1919: *Economic Mobilization of the United States for the War of 1917.*

Two special studies may be mentioned: *War Powers of the Executive in the United States*, by Clarence A. Berdahl (Urbana, Ill., 1921, 296 pages, published in University of Illinois Studies in the Social Sciences, vol. IX, nos. 1 and 2), and the second part of *Labor Problems and Labor Administration in the United States during the World War*, devoted to the development of the War Labor Administration, by Gordon S. Watkins (Urbana, Ill., 1919, published in University of Illinois Studies in the Social Sciences, vol. VIII, no. 4).

There are two official catalogues of the publications of all branches of the national government. The *Monthly Catalogue, United States Public Documents*, is issued every month by the Superintendent of Public Documents and includes the output of the Government Printing Office during the month. The arrangement is alphabetical by names of the various departments and offices. For most of the war period the monthly catalogue must still be used. The *Catalogue of the Public Documents of the . . . th Congress and of all Departments of the Government from . . . to . . .*, commonly styled the *Comprehensive Index*, is the most convenient and complete list for purposes of consultation, but the latest volume yet issued (1925) covers only the material published during the two years from July 1, 1915, to June 30, 1917. A useful manual dealing with the printed output of the government is *Guide to Government Publications*, compiled by Walter I. Swanton and published by the Bureau of Education as *Bulletin, 1918, No. 2*. Several of the departments issue from time to time check lists of their publications which may be had upon request.

Mention should also be made of certain of the libraries of the executive branch, especially those of the Departments of Commerce and Labor, where are to be found probably as good collections as exist of material of all sorts bearing upon the work of the respective departments. Finally, it is perhaps unnecessary to remind the reader of the other volumes appearing in this Series.

INTRODUCTION TO AMERICAN OFFICIAL SOURCES OF WAR HISTORY

CONGRESS

THE records of Congress are fundamental sources for the history of the war period. They consist of the records of debates and proceedings in the Senate and the House of Representatives, of bills and resolutions introduced into Congress and of the legislation ultimately enacted, of the records of investigations by committees and of the committee reports, and of communications, petitions, reports, and other documents received by Congress. This survey covers the records of the Sixty-Fifth and Sixty-Sixth Congresses, the sessions of which were as follows:

Sixty-Fifth Congress:
  Special session of the Senate, March 5-16, 1917;
  First session, April 2-October 6, 1917;
  Second session, December 3, 1917-November 21, 1918;
  Third session, December 2, 1918-March 4, 1919.

Sixty-Sixth Congress:
  First session, May 19-November 19, 1919;
  Second session, December 1, 1919-June 5, 1920;
  Third session, December 6, 1920-March 4, 1921.

While most of the war and reconstruction measures were enacted by these two Congresses, several acts passed by earlier Congresses had an important bearing upon the conduct of the war. Among these were the acts establishing the Federal Reserve Banks, December 23, 1913, the Bureau of War Risk Insurance, September 2, 1914, the Federal Trade Commission, September 26, 1914, the Council of National Defense, August 29, 1916, and the United States Shipping Board, September 7, 1916; and the national defense act of June 3 of the same year.

The records of Congress are, for the most part, printed, and certain of them, such as the *Record, Journal, Reports,* and *Documents* are widely distributed among the libraries of the United States. Other records, such as *Bills and Resolutions* and *Hearings* are printed only for the use of Congress, and complete sets are exceedingly rare.

Proceedings

Congressional Record: Proceedings and Debates of the . . . Congress of the United States of America:

(Permanent bound edition)

Volume 55, Sixty-Fifth Congress, first session, Parts 1-8;
Volume 56, Sixty-Fifth Congress, second session, Parts 1-12;
Volume 57, Sixty-Fifth Congress, third session, Parts 1-5;
Volume 58, Sixty-Sixth Congress, first session, Parts 1-9;
Volume 59, Sixty-Sixth Congress, second session, Parts 1-9;
Volume 60, Sixty-Sixth Congress, third session, Parts 1-5.

These forty-eight bound Parts contain 46,726 pages of debates, exclusive of the "Appendixes" which are composed of the remarks "extended" to the *Record, i.e.,* speeches which are not delivered in Congress but which are printed by consent. The debates on the floor are reported stenographically, but as printed in the *Record* they have been subjected to processes of revision and "correction" which considerably decrease the value of that publication as a verbatim report. The last Part of each volume of the *Record* contains, in addition to the Appendix and Index, a "History of Bills and Resolutions." This is a list in numerical order, *i.e.,* in order of introduction, of all bills and of all joint, concurrent, and simple resolutions introduced in the Senate and the House of Representatives, showing by whom introduced and the action taken on each.

Journal of the Senate:

Sixty-Fifth Congress, first session, 1917, 458 pages;
Sixty-Fifth Congress, second session, 1919, 546 pages;
Sixty-Fifth Congress, third session, 1919, 280 pages;
Sixty-Sixth Congress, first session, 1919, 482 pages;
Sixty-Sixth Congress, second session, 1920, 513 pages;
Sixty-Sixth Congress, third session, 1921, 262 pages.

Journal of the House of Representatives:

Sixty-Fifth Congress, first session, 1917, 623 pages;
Sixty-Fifth Congress, second session, 1918, 856 pages;
Sixty-Fifth Congress, third session, 1919, 443 pages;
Sixty-Sixth Congress, first session, 1919, 960 pages;
Sixty-Sixth Congress, second session, 1920, 720 pages;
Sixty-Sixth Congress, third session, 1920 [1921], 409 pages.

Bills and Resolutions

Each bill or resolution introduced in Congress receives a serial number and is printed. As the printing is only for the convenience of Congress there is no published set of the bills and resolutions. What is believed to be the only complete collection of this exceedingly valuable source is that which has been brought together and bound by the Library of Congress, where it is to be found for the Sixty-Fifth and Sixty-Sixth Congresses as follows:

Sixty-Fifth Congress:
   Senate: Bills, nos. 1-5680, 16 volumes;
          Resolutions, nos. 1-487, 1 volume;
          Joint Resolutions, nos. 1-230, 1 volume;
          Concurrent Resolutions, nos. 1-32, 1 volume.
   House: Bills, nos. 1-16239, 44 volumes;
          Resolutions, nos. 1-625, 1 volume;
          Joint Resolutions, nos. 1-445, 1 volume;
          Concurrent Resolutions, nos. 1-74 (nos. 73, 74 missing), 1 volume.

Sixty-Sixth Congress:
   Senate: Bills, nos. 1-5052, 17 volumes;
          Resolutions, nos. 1-475, 1 volume;
          Joint Resolutions, nos. 1-264, 1 volume;
          Concurrent Resolutions, nos. 1-40, 1 volume.
   House: Bills, nos. 1-16170, 45 volumes;
          Resolutions, nos. 1-712, 1 volume;
          Joint Resolutions, nos. 1-481, 1 volume;
          Concurrent Resolutions, nos. 1-78, 1 volume.

A complete list of bills and resolutions is printed in the "History of Bills and Resolutions," which is included in the last Part of each volume of the *Congressional Record*, noted above.

Laws

The laws are printed as they are enacted. The original of each law, with the signature of the President, President of the Senate, and Speaker of the House of Representatives, is deposited in the Department of State. Laws are first printed in "slip form," or separately, and are listed from month to month in the *Monthly Catalogue of United States Public Documents*. At the close of each session they are published in collected form in the edition known as *Session Laws;* at the close of each Congress all the laws of that Congress are recompiled and published as *Statutes at Large* as follows:

Statutes at Large:

Volume 40, April, 1917-March, 1919 (Washington, 1919, pp. cccxxxvii, 2335). Part 1, Public acts and resolutions; Part 2, Private acts and resolutions, concurrent resolutions, treaties, proclamations, amendments to the Constitution.

Volume 41, May, 1919-March, 1921 (Washington, 1921, pp. ccciii, 2142). Parts 1 and 2 as above.

Numerous compilations of laws passed by the Sixty-Fifth and Sixty-Sixth Congresses relating to special subjects, such as food, liquor, insurance, naturalization, finance, interstate and foreign commerce, etc., have been printed for Congress or for various executive branches. The more useful of these are noted below in their appropriate places.

Several lists of laws and guides to legislation have been published, the more important of which are the following:

Monthly Compendium, edited by W. Ray Loomis:

Sixty-Fifth Congress, complete (no. 15, April 1, 1919) (Washington, 1919, 241 pages). Includes measures of Sixty-Fourth Congress bearing on the war.

Sixty-Sixth Congress, complete (no. 16, March, 1921) (Washington, 1921, 360 pages).

First Session of the War Congress, by Charles Merz (Committee on Public Information, "War Information Series," no. 10, Washington, 1917, 48 pages). A summary of every public measure enacted into law during the first session of the Sixty-Fifth Congress.

Summary of the War Legislation of the Sixty-Fifth Congress, compiled by Leo F. Stock (in *Historical Outlook,* volume X, pp. 401-419, Philadelphia, October, 1919).

Reports

Reports of Senate and House committees are printed and are numbered serially for each chamber and each Congress. At the end of each session the reports of that session are bound together in two or more volumes, of which those containing reports on public legislation are numbered while those containing reports on private legislation are lettered, "A," "B," etc. Reports are usually brief except those prepared by investigating committees which are sometimes of great length. They are listed as printed in the *Monthly Catalogue*, and are included in both the *Document Index*, printed at the close of each session, and in the *Comprehensive Index*, published at the close of each Congress. The most convenient list for use and reference is that in the *Document Index*.

Documents

What are known as "Senate Documents" and "House Documents" are exceedingly miscellaneous in character. They include reports made to Congress by the executive departments, commissions, bureaus, etc., records of some of the more important investigations by Congressional committees, reports on special subjects, unofficial publications ordered to be reprinted as "Documents" upon vote by Congress, etc. Most of the "Documents" are also issued as publications of other branches of the government and will be described in their appropriate connections. The "Documents" are listed as they are printed in the *Monthly Catalogue*, are listed a second time, classified according to subject and author and also in numerical order, in the sessional *Document Index*, and are listed a third time, classified under subject and author, in the *Comprehensive Index*.

Hearings

The records of hearings held by committees of Congress as a part of the process of considering proposed legislation or of conducting investigations, constitute one of the most valuable categories of Congressional material. They consist of queries, replies, and statements, together with material offered as exhibits. This latter includes correspondence, maps, charts, diagrams, photographs, tables of statistics, and other documents which are often historical sources of great value. As practically all, and especially the economic, phases of the war have been the subject of legislation or the object of investigation the scope of the hearings is all-inclusive and the physical bulk of their printed reports is very great. Witnesses from every part of the country, intimately connected with every kind of war activity, were heard by the various committees, and their statements, together with the exhibits submitted by them, constitute a composite record unique in its character and value. The necessity of testing such a record, however, and of using it with caution, is obvious. Many witnesses were propagandists, striving to make certain views prevail; others represented special interests or had political or other bias; most were obliged, by the method of query and answer to rely at times upon memory or upon inadequate information; and the queries put by members of the committees were frequently marked by a *tendenz*. In spite of these limitations, however, the hearings contain a mass of information and opinion submitted by men of business, by manufacturers, by bankers, by educators, by economists, by representatives of labor and agriculture, by railroad men, by shippers, and by experts in nearly every line of activity connected with carrying on the war, which should have the greatest value for the investigator.

The reports of hearings are printed for the use of the several committees but they are not distributed in any systematic fashion. The most complete sets of them to be found are those in the library of the Superintendent of Documents and the library of the Senate. The set in the Library of Congress is reasonably complete for the period 1917-1921 but the different reports are dispersed among the library's collections in accordance with its scheme of classification by subject. Those in the library of the Senate are listed in *Catalogue of the Library of the United States Senate* (Washington, 1920, pp. 452-605). The *Monthly Catalogue* lists the reports of hearings as they are printed; they are also included in the *Comprehensive Index*.

The most informing list of the hearings held by the committees of the Sixty-Fifth and Sixty-Sixth Congresses is one compiled from the set in the library of the Senate by Dr. Newton D. Mereness for the National Association of State War History Organizations, a manuscript copy of which has been deposited with the Division of Documents of the Library of Congress. The following list, composed of the more important and representative hearings relating to the economic and social aspects of the war, is made up of abridged items selected from the list compiled by Dr. Mereness.

HEARINGS BEFORE COMMITTEES OF CONGRESS

SENATE

Committee on Agriculture and Forestry

April 23-May 10, 1917. "Hearing . . . relative to proposals for increasing the production, improving the distribution, and promoting the conservation of food supplies in the United States." (570 pages.) Contents include discussion of problem of farm labor, shortage of food products, wages, and prices in Philadelphia, statements respecting food situation from agricultural colleges and commissions.

June 19, 1917. "Hearing relative to S. 2463 entitled, 'A bill to provide further for the national security and defense by encouraging the production, conserving the supply and controlling the distribution of food products and fuel.' " (60 pages.) Herbert Hoover discussed proposed measures of food control.

February 14-March 30, 1918. "Hearing . . . relative to increasing the production of grain and meat supplies of the United States." (634 pages.) Discussion of live-stock and wheat situations chiefly in the Middle West.

June 13-September 5, 1918. "Hearing . . . on a House amendment to the food-production bill of 1919 (H.R. 11945) . . ." (357 pages.) Arguments for and against war-time prohibition, cost of producing wheat and beef cattle.

September 17-29, 1918. "Hearing before the subcommittee . . . on S.Res. 221 in favor of government control . . . of packing houses and packing plants during the continuance of the war." (204 pages.)

January 13-February 13, 1919. "Hearings . . . on S. 5305, a bill to stimulate the production, sale, and distribution of live stock and live-stock products." (2 volumes, 2108 pages.) Proposed government control of the meat-packing industry. Witnesses: representatives of packers, stockyards, Department of Agriculture, Federal Trade Commission, etc.

August 18, 1919-January 9, 1920. "Hearings . . . on S. 2199 and 2202, bills to stimulate the production, sale and distribution of live stock and live-stock products." (1983 pages.)

October 3, 18, 20, 21, 1919. "Hearings before the subcommittee . . . pursuant to S.Res. 197, directing the committee to investigate the shortage and prices of sugar." (164 pages.)

February 16-18, 1920. "Hearing . . . on S. 3844, a bill to provide for discontinuing the purchase and sale of grain by the government." (134 pages.)

Committee on Banking and Currency

June 11-27, 1918. "Hearings . . . on S. 3928, a bill to amend the Federal Reserve Act." (367 pages.) Depreciation of the American dollar in all neutral countries; statements by bankers, economists, financial editors, etc.

March 3, 1920. "Hearing . . . on S. 3942, a bill to encourage the development of the agricultural resources of the United States through federal and state coöperation, giving preference in the matter of employment and the establishment of rural homes to those who have served with the military and naval forces." (30 pages.) Development of semi-arid lands.

Committee on Commerce

July 23-August 13, 1917. "Hearings before the subcommittee . . . on H.R. 4960, a bill to define, regulate and punish trading with the enemy." (236 pages.)

December 21, 1917-April 5, 1918. "Hearings . . . on S.Res. 170, directing the committee to investigate all matters connected with the building of merchant vessels under the direction of the United States Shipping Board Emergency Fleet Corporation." (2515 pages.) Organization, operations, and problems of the Shipping Board. *E.g.*, Part 8, containing testimony of Matthew C. Brush, president of the American International Shipbuilding Corporation, includes a large number of photographs of Hog Island, charts showing places in United States from which materials were shipped to Hog Island, charts showing routes of steel from mills to fabricators, and fabricators to Hog Island, etc.

June 10, 1919-March 13, 1920. "Hearings . . . relative to the establishment of an American Merchant Marine." (2089 pages.)

October 10, 11, 21, 1919. "Hearings before the subcommittee . . . on S. 3170, a bill to provide for the establishment, operation, and maintenance of foreign trade zones in ports of entry of the United States, to expedite and encourage foreign commerce, etc." (129 pages.)

Committee on Education and Labor

January 3-24, 1919. "Hearings . . . pursuant to S.Res. 382, directing the committee to recommend to the Senate methods of promoting better social and industrial conditions." (224 pages.) Establishment of national tribunal to adjust labor difficulties, development of United States Employment Service, regularization of employment, promotion of better living conditions.

January 21 and February 20, 1919. "Hearing before a subcommittee . . . on H.R. 152, a bill to fix the compensation of certain employees." (129 pages.) Wages and cost of living of federal employees, with tables showing prices of food and salaries.

January 29, 1919. "Hearing . . . on S. 5397, a bill to provide for the commencement or prosecution of public works in order to provide increased opportunities for employment during the period of demobilization and industrial readjustments." (98 pages.) Unemployment, stimulation of construction activities.

September 11, 1919. "Hearing . . . on S. 17, a bill to promote the education of native illiterates, of persons unable to understand and use the English language, and of other resident persons of foreign birth; to provide for coöperation with the States in the education of such persons in the English language, the fundamental principles of government and citizenship, etc." (74 pages.)

Committee on Finance

May 11-15, 1917. "Hearings and briefs . . . on H.R. 4280, an act to defray war expenses." (665 pages.) Taxes on incomes, excess profits, beverages, cigars and tobacco, public utilities, advertising, insurance, manufactures, admissions, dues.

September 6-December 5, 1918. "Hearings . . . on H.R. 12863, to provide revenue for war purposes." (795 pages.) Taxes on incomes, beverages, cigars, tobacco, admissions and dues, excise taxes and special taxes; statements by representatives of trade organizations and business associations.

December 8, 1919-January 12, 1920. "Hearings . . . on H.R. 8078, a bill to regulate the importation of coal-tar products and to promote the establishment of the manufacture thereof in the United States, etc." (627 pages.) The dyestuff industry, statistical tables, correspondence.

January 6-13, 1921. "Hearings . . . on H.R. 15275, imposing temporary duties upon certain agricultural products to meet present emergencies, to provide revenue, and for other purposes." (290 pages.) Emergency tariff.

Committee on Immigration

January 3-26, 1921. "Hearing . . . on H.R. 14461, a bill to provide for the protection of the citizens of the United States by the temporary suspension of immigration." (13 parts, 713 pages.)

Committee on Interstate Commerce

January 2-18, 1917. "Hearings . . . on the tentative bill to amend the act providing for mediation, conciliation, and arbitration in controversies between certain employers and their employees, and the tentative bill to authorize the President in certain emergencies to take possession of railroad, telephone, and telegraph lines." (329 pages.) Railway disputes, and the impending strike of railway employees.

May 3, 10, 1917. "Hearings before the subcommittee . . . on S. 1854, a bill to save daylight and to provide standard time." (66 pages.)

June 22-July 3, 1917. "Hearings . . . on S. 2354 and S.Res. 77 to provide further for the national security and defense by regulating the production, sale and distribution of coal." (398 pages.) Coal prices, wages, cost of producing coal, car shortage.

September 21, 1917. "Hearing . . . on S. 2756, a bill to provide further for the national security and defense by regulating the production, sale, and distribution of iron ore, iron, steel, and other commodities." (70 pages.)

December 29, 1917-January 25, 1918. "Hearing . . . pursuant to S. Res. 171 authorizing the committee to inquire into and report upon the recommendations of the Interstate Commerce commission regarding conditions affecting interstate transportation." (1338 pages.) Governmental control and operation of railroads. Witnesses: railroad executives, representatives of railroad brotherhoods, and of shippers' organizations.

June 24, 1918. "Hearing . . . on S.J.Res. 159, to extend the time within which the President may relinquish control of any railroad or system of transportation." (57 pages.)

July 9, 1918. "Hearing . . . on H.J.Res. 309 to authorize the President, in time of war, to supervise or take possession and assume control of any telegraph, telephone, marine cable, or radio system." (57 pages.)

January 3-February 21, 1919. "Hearings . . . on the extension of time for relinquishment by the government of railroads to corporate ownership and control." (3 volumes, 4191 pages.) Volumes 2 and 3 contain the hearings (November 20, 1917-December 19, 1918) before the joint subcommittee charged with the investigations of the conditions relating to interstate and foreign commerce and the necessity for further legislation relating thereto.

May 4, 7, 1920. "Hearing . . . on S. 4373, a bill to amend sections 27, and 210 of the transportation act, 1920." (116 pages.) Car shortage.

September 23, 24, 1919. "Hearing . . . on S. 2906, a bill further to regulate commerce among the States and with foreign nations, etc." (46 pages.) Prevention of strikes.

May 29, 30, 1919. "Hearings . . . on relinquishment of government control of telephone and telegraph lines." (124 pages.)

Committee on Judiciary

February 23-April 13, 1918. "Hearings before the subcommittee . . . on S. 3529, a bill to repeal the act of February 25, 1907, to incorporate the National German-American Alliance." (698 pages.)

September 27, 1918-March 10, 1919. "Report and Hearings of the subcommittee . . . pursuant to S.Res. 307 and 439 relating to charges made against the United States Brewers' Association and allied interests of financing German and Bolshevik propaganda." (3 volumes, 4240 pages.) This report and hearing are also published as Senate Document 62, 66th Congress, 1st Session. Exhibits: letters, newspaper articles, and proceedings of organization meetings, report of the American Embargo Conference; a list of the principal subscribers to the American Embargo Conference; a list of members of the German University League; telegrams by W. R. Hearst giving instructions for editorials in the *New York American;* copies of the news sheet prepared by the German information service; copies of messages signed "International News" or "Hale"; a letter by the manager of the Hearst papers to Senator Overman; evidence *re* German insurance pools; a list of foreign language newspapers (by States) published in the United States; a list of Industrial Unions of the Industrial Workers of the World.

June 14-July 12, 1919. "Hearings before the subcommittee . . . on bills to prohibit the liquor traffic and to provide for the enforcement of such prohibition and the War Prohibition Act." (345 pages.)

May 22, 1920. "Hearing before a subcommittee . . . on S. 4344, a bill to authorize an association of producers of agricultural products." (69 pages.)

December 21, 1920-February 16, 1921. "Hearings before a subcommittee . . . on S.J.Res. 171, providing for the recommendation of amnesty and pardon for political prisoners in the United States." (198 pages.)

January 19-March 3, 1921. "Hearings before a subcommittee . . . on 'Report upon the Illegal Practices of the United States Department of Justice,' made by a committee of lawyers on behalf of the National Popular Government League, and a memorandum describing the personnel of the committee." (788 pages.)

Committee on Manufactures

December 14, 1917-January 16, 1918. "Hearings before a subcommittee . . . on S.Res. 163 directing the committee to investigate the causes of the shortage of coal and sugar." (1048 pages.) The sugar industry.

December 26, 1917-February 18, 1919. "Hearings before the subcommittee . . . pursuant to S.Res. 163, directing the committee to investigate the causes of the shortage of coal and sugar." (1788 pages.) Organization and operation of the Fuel Administration, activities of the Federal Trade Commission, prices, wages, measures for increasing production, transportation, distribution, control of exports to Canada, conservation, transition from peace basis to war basis, investigations of coal mining.

April 9-May 27, 1920. "Hearing before a subcommittee . . . pursuant to S.Res. 317 directing the committee to ascertain in every practicable way the cause for the increased price of shoes in the United States." (118 pages.)

May 4-17, 1920. "Hearings before a subcommittee . . . pursuant to S.Res. 164, authorizing the committee to investigate the newspaper print industry." (518 pages.) Witnesses: editors, publishers, and paper manufacturers.

January 15-February 15, 1921. "Hearings . . . on S. 4828, a bill to promote the general welfare by gathering information respecting the ownership, production, distribution, costs, sales, and profits in the coal industry and by the publication of same, and to recognize and declare coal and its production and distribution charged with public interest and use." (3 volumes, 2235 pages.)

Committee on Military Affairs

December 8, 1916-February 1, 1917. "Hearing before a subcommittee . . . on S. 1695, a bill to provide for the military and naval training of the citizen forces of the United States." (1178 pages.) Universal military training. Witnesses: military men, educators, editors, labor representatives, propagandists, clergymen, etc.

April 21, 1917. "Hearings . . . on S. 1871, a bill to authorize the President to increase temporarily the military establishment of the United States." (46 pages.) Conscription *vs.* voluntary enlistments. Witnesses: propagandists and others opposing conscription.

December 12, 1917-March 29, 1918. "Hearings . . . for the purpose of inquiring from the different branches of the service of the War Department as to the progress made in the matter of providing for ordnance, small arms, and munitions." (2560 pages.) Contracts, deliveries, etc. Witnesses: military men, executives of manufacturing concerns, officers of manufacturers' associations, government officials.

May 29-August 16, 1918. "Hearings before the subcommittee . . . relative to aircraft production." (1226 pages.) The production of the Liberty engine, cause of delays and disappointments in the aviation program, measures for expediting production.

July 12-November 18, 1918. "Hearings before a subcommittee . . . relative to matters pertaining to the Quarter Masters Corps." (796 pages.) Contracts, the condition of the subsistence department, etc. Exhibits: a list of nearly 300 large contracts, with name of contractor, character of the work, location, estimated amount, and estimated fee; correspondence with contractors; a table of cotton goods purchased subsequent to January 19, 1918 (58 pages), containing name of the contractor, mill or f.o.b. point, quantity, description of article and price, memorandum of Senator McKellar's trip to Newport News and Norfolk, a tabulation of bids on enameled ironware; a table showing average prices paid for specification cloths.

August 6-9, 1918. "Hearings . . . on S. 4856, a bill to amend the selective service act." (103 pages.) Substitution of ages 18 and 45 for 21 and 30, question of deferring groups of annual classes as the exigencies of the service may permit.

January 25, 1919. "Hearings . . . on S. 4972, a bill to regulate the collection and expenditure of money, other than by the government of the United States, or by its authority, for the use and benefit of the armed forces of the United States and its allies." (96 pages.) War charity organizations, report of January 1, 1919, by E. P. Kilroe, assistant district attorney, New York, on an investigation of war charities, correspondence.

January 21-March 1, 1920. "Hearing . . . on S. 3792, a bill to reorganize and increase the efficiency of the United States army." (62 pages.) Accompanying the report of this hearing is a report by Albert G. Love, M.D., and Charles B. Davenport, prepared under the direction of the Surgeon General and entitled: "Defects found in drafted men, statistical information compiled from the draft records, showing the physical condition of the men registered and examined in pursuance of the requirements of the selective service act." (359 pages.)

Committee on Mines and Mining

May 2-9, 1918. "Hearings . . . on H.R. 11259 to provide further for the national security and defense by encouraging the production, conserving the supply, and controlling the distribution of those ores, metals, and minerals which have formerly been largely imported, or of which there is or may be an inadequate supply." (672 pages.)

Committee on Public Buildings and Grounds

April 8 and 10, 1918. "Hearing . . . on H.R. 10265, a bill to authorize the Secretary of Labor to provide housing, local transportation, and other community facilities for war needs." (65 pages.) Restriction of production by manufacturing plants due to lack of housing for laborers.

December 6-17, 1918. "Hearings before a subcommittee . . . pursuant to S.Res. 371 providing for an investigation of the costs, construction, operation, maintenance, and future disposition of government buildings, etc." (291 pages.) Operations of the U.S. Housing Corporation.

December 6-14, 1920. "Joint hearings before the Committees on Agriculture and Forestry on S.J.Res. 212, directing the War Finance Corporation and the Federal Reserve Board to take certain action for the relief of the present depression in the agricultural sections of the country." (275 pages.)

August 7-December 11, 1919. "Hearings before a subcommittee . . . pursuant to S.Res. 210, directing the Committee to investigate and report to the Senate concerning the cost of construction and maintenance of public buildings of the government, their location, and the plan of the government as to their future disposition." (737 pages.) U.S. Housing Corporation.

Select Committee on Reconstruction and Production

July 20, 1920-February 15, 1921. "Hearings . . . pursuant to S.Res. 350, authorizing the appointment of a committee to inquire into the general building situation and to report to the Senate before December 1, 1920, such measures as may be deemed necessary to stimulate and foster the development of construction work in all its forms." (3 volumes, 2360 pages.) Coal, transportation, and housing.

Committee on Agriculture

May 1-June 11, 1917. "Hearings . . . on H.J.Res. 75, H.R. 4125, H.R. 4188, and H.R. 4630, relative to the production, distribution, and conservation of food supplies." (538 pages.) Alcoholic beverages, barley, bread, canning, brewers' grains, cheese, cold storage, corn and corn flour, cotton, drying vegetables, eggs, elevators, farm labor, fertilizer, food prices, oats, potatoes, poultry, wheat, etc.

February 11, 1918. "Hearings . . . on H.R. 8718, a bill to provide further for the national security and common defense by the conservation of foodstuffs, feeds, and materials necessary for the production, manufacture, and preservation of foodstuffs, feeds, etc." (43 pages.) Shortage of food for the allies, conservation of food.

March 13, 1918. "Hearings . . . on the spring wheat situation." (86 pages.)

April 23, 1918. "Hearings . . . on estimates of appropriations required to enforce the food-production act of August 10, 1917." (211 pages.)

August 15, 20, 1919. "Hearings . . . on amendments proposed to the food-control act." (92 pages.) High cost of living.

February 3-5, 1919. "Hearings . . . on the wheat price guaranteed by Congress." (226 pages.)

Committee on Appropriations

February 5, 1919. "Hearing before a subcommittee . . . in charge of deficiency appropriations for the fiscal year 1919 and prior fiscal years." (197 pages.) Deficit in government operation of railroads.

June 3, 1919. "Hearing before a subcommittee . . . in charge of the deficiency appropriation for the fiscal year 1919 and prior fiscal years." (369 pages.) An appropriation for the government control of railroads.

Committee on Education

February 14, 15, 1919. "Hearing . . . on H.R. 15402 to promote the education of native illiterates, of persons unable to understand and use the English language, and of other resident persons of foreign birth." (72 pages.)

March 2-May 15, 1920. "Hearings . . . of charges against the Federal Board for Vocational Education." (31 parts, 2159 pages.) Charges published in the New York *Evening Post;* "Hard boiled order" to agents with regard to applications of disabled soldiers for treatment under the rehabilitation act; hostile attitude of the board toward the soldiers.

Committee on Immigration and Naturalization

January 14-20, 1919. "Hearings . . . on H.R. 13325, 13669, 13904, and 14577, prohibiting immigration." (298 pages.)

June 12-20, September 25, 1919. "Hearings . . . relative to percentage plans for restriction of immigration." (296 pages.)

October 16-27, 1919. "Hearings . . . on H.R. 9949 relative to education and Americanization." (222 pages.)

March 30, April 9, 10, May 25, 1920. "Hearings . . . relative to the administration of immigration laws." (154 pages.) The deportation of aliens; Industrial Workers of the World.

Committee on Interstate and Foreign Commerce

April 23, 1917. "Hearings . . . on H.R. 3349, a bill to authorize the President in time of war to give direction to exports from the United States, so as to insure their wise, economic, and profitable distribution to other countries." (16 pages.)

January 8-29, 1918. "Hearings . . . on H.R. 8172, a bill to provide for the operation of transportation systems while under federal control, for the just compensation of their owners, and for other purposes." (950 pages.)

December 19, 20, 1918, and January 31-February 14, 1919. "Hearings . . . on H.R. 13324, for the government control of the meat-packing industry." (2 volumes, 5 parts, 2443 pages.)

May 30-June 5, 1919. "Hearings . . . on H.R. 421 relative to the return of the wire systems to their owners." (3 parts, 228 pages.)

September 16-October 4, 1919. "Hearings . . . on H.R. 4378 providing for the return of the railroads to private ownership." (3 volumes, 3669 pages.)

Committee on the Judiciary

July 9, 1918. "Hearings . . . on H.R. 12443, to prevent profiteering in rents during the war." (43 pages.)

April 6-May 14, 1920. "Hearings . . . on H.Res. 469 authorizing an investigation of the action of the Attorney-General relating to the price of Louisiana sugar." (305 pages.)

Committee on Merchant Marine and Fisheries

January 25, 28, 1918. "Hearings . . . on S. 3389, to authorize and empower the United States Shipping Board Emergency Fleet Corporation to purchase, lease, requisition, and otherwise acquire improved or unimproved land, houses, and buildings." (80 pages.) Housing for employees of shipyards.

July 24-August 7, 1919. "Hearings . . . relative to the operations of the United States Shipping Board." (794 pages.)

Committee on Post Offices and Post Roads

January 14-28, 1919. "Hearings . . . on H.J.Res. 368, relative to government control of the telegraph and telephone systems." (3 parts, 438 pages.)

Committee on Public Lands

May 27-June 28, 1919. "Hearings . . . on H.R. 487, a bill to provide employment and rural homes for those who served with the military and naval forces through the reclamation of lands to be known as the 'National soldier settlement act.' " (798 pages.)

Committee on Rules

March 5, 1920. "Hearings . . . on resolutions relative to relief for farmers of western States and for central and eastern Europe." (41 pages.)

Committee on Ways and Means

February 18-22, 1918. "Hearing . . . on H.R. 9499, a bill establishing the War Finance Corporation." (170 pages.)

June 7-July 17, August 5, 14, 15, 1918. "Hearings . . . on the proposed revenue act of 1918." (2242 pages.) Income, excess profits, and estate taxes, miscellaneous taxes, postal rates.

Select Committee on Expenditures in the War Department

July 23, 1919-January 10, 1921. "Hearings before the committee as a whole." (13 parts, 2312 pages.) Part 13 contains a tabulated list of war contracts of $100,000 and over.

July 31-September 12, 1919. "Hearings before subcommittee No. 1 (Aviation) . . ." (2 volumes, 2325 pages.) A list of contracts aggregating $100,000 or over made by or under Air Service from April 6, 1917, to June 1, 1919, in the United States; a statement of shipments from factories of all types of airplane engines for the United States army during the 11-year period from 1908 to 1918 inclusive; analysis of the cost of railroads constructed by the Spruce Production Division and the United States Spruce Production Corporation.

July 11, 1919-January 17, 1920. "Hearings before subcommittee No. 2 (Camps) . . ." (2 volumes, 3022 pages; a third volume, 561 pages, contains an abstract of testimony contained in volumes 1 and 2.) Copies of contracts; schedule of rental rates per day; summary of estimates for cantonments for the National Guard and the National Army; names of contractors and dates camp sites were approved, contracts executed, and work started; statement of emergency construction contracts in which the fee granted was not reached under the construction accomplished; statement of emergency construction contracts in which fee granted was reached under the construction accomplished, etc.

June 19, 1919-February 4, 1921. "Hearings before subcommittee No. 3 (Foreign Expenditures) . . ." (4 volumes, 4583 pages.) Memorandum of basis for compiling estimated present value of A.E.F. property in France available for sale to French government; a statement of claims; a list of claims disallowed by the commission; an abstract of supplies on hand at quartermaster depots of the Services of Supply, 1919, and stocks on hand at supply depots, post camps, hospital centers, etc. April 30, 1919. There are many other exhibits.

July 8, 1919-February 5, 1921. "Hearings before subcommittee No. 4 (Quartermaster Corps)." (1347 pages.)

July 17-February 2, 1921. "Hearings before subcommittee No. 5 (Ordnance)." (4 volumes, 5260 pages.) Statistical tables *re* the procurement location and cost of ordnance supplies; a table containing data *re* Ordnance Department lumber contracts; detailed report of ferrous sales; a statistical table *re* acids, chemicals, and explosives; copies of ordnance contracts; data *re* U.S. Nitrate Plant No. 4, Ancor, Ohio.

Select Committee on the United States Shipping Board

August 20, 1919-February 19, 1921. "Hearings . . . U.S. Shipping Board operations." (5 volumes, 5268 pages.)

Special Committee to Investigate the National Security League

December 19, 1918-February 22, 1919. "Hearings . . . on H.Res. 469 and 476 to investigate and make report as to the officers, membership, financial support, expenditures, general character, activities, and purpose of the National Security League." (2 volumes, 30 parts, 2086 pages.) Exhibits: list of pamphlets issued by the National Security League in 1917 and 1918; a "Record of Congress" prior to the call for mobilization of the National Guard, June 18, 1916; a list of contributions to the National Security League.

Joint Committees

November 20, 1916-December 19, 1917. "Hearings before the joint subcommittee on Interstate and Foreign Commerce pursuant to Public J.Res. 25 . . . creating a joint subcommittee to investigate the conditions relating to interstate and foreign commerce and the necessity of further legislation relating thereto." (14 parts, 2448 pages.) State and federal regulation of railroads, public ownership. Testimony of railroad executives, and members of state railroad commissions.

April 20, May 1, 2, 1918. "Hearings before the joint committee of the Senate and House on S. 4284 and H.R. 11367, bills to provide vocational rehabilitation and return to civil employment of disabled persons discharged from the military or naval forces of the United States." (168 pages.)

December 10, 1918. "Joint hearings before members of the Senate and House Committees on Education and Labor on S. 4922, a bill to provide for the promotion of vocational rehabilitation of persons disabled in industry or otherwise and their return to civil employment." (86 pages.)

June 19-July 23, 1919. "Hearings before the joint committees of the House and Senate on S. 688 and 1442 and H.R. 4305, bills providing for the establishment of a national employment system." (992 pages.)

January 28, 1920. "Joint hearings before the House and Senate Committees on Agriculture and Forestry on cost of living." (44 pages.)

SENATE AND HOUSE FILES

Each house of Congress has its file-room where are preserved the original papers received by members and committees. These consist for the greater part of petitions, resolutions, letters, and other communications from individuals, groups of citizens, clubs, societies, labor unions, churches, etc. They are variously addressed to the Vice-President, the Speaker, the Senate, the House of Representatives, the various committees, and to individual members. Their principal value, which for the purpose of this survey does not seem to be considerable, consists in such reflection of public opinion as they offer and in such evidence as they present of organized propaganda. The only guide to this material is through the references to petitions, memorials, etc., in the *Journal* and the *Record*. The physical bulk of this material is not great—about 108 boxes in the House files, not more than 15 in the Senate files, for the two Congresses with which this report deals. The subject matter of these documents is very varied—support of or opposition to the war, food control, war-time prohibition, high cost of living, compulsory military service, methods of taxation, etc. The following items, selected from the Senate files, are sufficiently illustrative.

March 29, 1917. A local union of the Mine Workers of America, in opposition to the declaration of war and to compulsory military training.

April 6, 1917. The Deutscher Liederkrantz of New York, pledging support to the government and offering its clubhouse as a hospital unit.

April 7, 1917. The Farmers' Club of East Wallop, Enfield, Connecticut, respecting shortage of skilled farm labor and favoring its exemption from the first call for military service.

April 14, 1917. Citizens of Elkhart, Indiana, in favor of compulsory military training.

April 19, 1917. The Kiwanis Club of Muskegon, Michigan, opposing the prohibition of efficiency methods in government shops.

May 20, 1917. Citizens of Laurel, Maryland, in favor of national prohibition as a war measure.

May 22, 1917. The Merchants' Association of New York, favoring the measures for food control proposed by the administration.

May 24, 1917. A business men's association of Buffalo, New York, in favor of legislation to prohibit speculation in food products and to fix maximum prices for farm products, fuel, oil, and gas.

June 12, 1917. A citizen of Pittsburgh, Pennsylvania, complaining of the high cost of living, the difficulty of buying Liberty bonds, etc., and asking for legislation to control profiteering and to enforce national prohibition during the war.

August 27, 1917. Citizens of Massachusetts, in favor of placing aliens, subjects of countries associated with the United States, on the same footing for military duty, as citizens of the United States.

February 1, 1918. Farmers of Orange Township, Iowa, in favor of prohibiting the raising of tobacco during the war.

February 8, 1918. The Woman's Committee of the Connecticut Council of Defense, in favor of measures to compel the planting of tobacco land to food crops.

February 11, 1918. The Lumbermen's Exchange of Philadelphia, in favor of establishing a board of war control with a director of munitions.

January 17, 1919. A local union of the United Automobile, Aircraft, and Vehicle Workers of America, demanding the immediate withdrawal of forces from Russia.

February 4, 1919. Workers in the Rock Island Arsenal, asking that all government equipment be manufactured, so far as possible, in government shops.

February 10, 1919. The executive committee of the Associated Industries of Massachusetts, opposing the continuation of the United States Employment Service beyond July 1, 1919.

February 12, 1919. A citizen of Grand Rapids, Michigan, favoring legislation which should provide for the completion of public improvements, temporarily prohibit immigration, provide monthly payments to unemployed discharged soldiers and service men, and provide for the reclamation of land and the settlement thereon of those who served in the war.

UNITED STATES SUPREME COURT

THE United States Supreme Court has handed down several decisions interpreting war statutes and affecting industrial and social conditions during the war and the period of reconstruction. The decisions from October, 1917, to April, 1921, are reported in volumes 246-255 of *United States Reports*. Each report contains a statement of the case, a statement of the points at issue, a brief review of the arguments presented by the contending attorneys, the opinion of the Court in full, also the dissenting opinion, if any. The complete records and briefs in each and every case constitute a voluminous mass of material, in some instances several volumes for a single case. They are to be found in the office of the Clerk of the Court, in the Law Division of the Library of Congress, and in the library of the Law Association of Philadelphia. The following cases are within the scope of this survey:

Board of Trade of the City of Chicago *et al. vs.* the United States. Decided March 4, 1918. (*U.S. Reports*, Vol. 246, pp. 227-255.) Brief for the Board of Trade, 65 pages; brief for the United States, 28 pages. Question: was the "Call rule" of the Board of Trade, which, in purchases of grain to arrive, limited price-fixing by its members to certain hours, a violation of the Sherman anti-trust act?

United States *vs.* United Shoe Machinery Company *et al.* Decided May 20, 1918. (*U.S. Reports*, Vol. 247, pp. 32-91.) Records and briefs, 7 volumes. Defendant was charged with monopolizing a part of the interstate and foreign commerce of the United States in machines used for the manufacture of shoes.

Allanwilde Transport Corporation *vs.* Vacuum Oil Company. Decided January 13, 1919. (*U.S. Reports*, Vol. 248, pp. 377-387.) Brief on behalf of claimant, 61 pages; brief on behalf of libelants, 44 pages. A charter of a sailing vessel and the bill of lading provided that the freight should be prepaid and that the freight earned should be retained, vessel lost or not lost. The vessel endeavored in good faith to make the voyage, was driven back by a storm for repairs, and then an act of the government denied clearance to sailing vessels destined for the war zone. Must the freight be refunded?

International Paper Company *vs.* the schooner *Gracie D. Chambers*.

Decided January 13, 1919. (*U.S. Reports*, Vol. 248, pp. 387-392.) Brief for the company, 25 pages; brief for the schooner, 21 pages. Similar to Allanwilde Corporation *vs.* Vacuum Oil Company.

Standard Varnish Works *vs.* steamship *Bris*. Decided January 13, 1919. (*U.S. Reports*, Vol. 248, pp. 392-398.) Brief for appellant, 26 pages; brief for claimants 57 pages. War measures taken by the government soon after the shipment made it impossible to carry to destination such goods as constituted the cargo and they were redelivered at the port of shipment. Must the freight be refunded?

Ex parte Whitney Steamboat Company. Decided March 3, 1919. (*U.S. Reports*, Vol. 249, pp. 115-119.) Records, 83 pages. Relative to an attachment of a vessel in the service of the United States Shipping Board.

Frohwerk *vs.* United States. Decided March 10, 1919. (*U.S. Reports*, Vol. 249, pp. 204-210.) Statement, brief, and argument for Frohwerk, 334 pages; brief for the United States, 23 pages. A case arising under the espionage act, 13 counts. Frohwerk was charged with being in a conspiracy with Carl Gleeser while they were engaged in the preparation and publication of the *Missouri Staats Zeitung* to violate the act.

Debs *vs.* United States. Decided March 10, 1919. (*U.S. Reports*, Vol. 249, pp. 211-217.) Transcript of record, 311 pages; brief for Debs, 87 pages; brief for the United States, 91 pages. Debs was charged with violating the espionage act by speaking in public with intent to oppose the war and obstruct recruiting; charged with expressing his approval, an hour before his speech, of a document known as an "Anti-War Proclamation and Program."

Northern Pacific Railway Company *et al. vs.* State of North Dakota. Decided June 2, 1919. (*U.S. Reports*, Vol. 250, pp. 135-152.) Brief for the company, 48 pages; brief for the State, 75 pages. A case arising under the act of March 21, 1918, for the federal control of the railroads. Had a State the right to control intra-state rates?

Dakota Central Telephone Company *et al. vs.* State of South Dakota. Decided June 2, 1919. (*U.S. Reports*, Vol. 250, pp. 163-188.) Brief for the telephone companies, 179 pages; brief for the State, 72 pages. A case arising from the federal control of telephone lines. Does the police power reserved to the States include the authority to determine local telephone rates?

State of Kansas *vs.* Burleson. Decided June 2, 1919. (*U.S. Reports*, Vol. 250, pp. 188-190.) Similar to Dakota Central Telephone Company *et al. vs.* State of South Dakota.

Burleson *vs.* Dempcy. Decided June 2, 1919. (*U.S. Reports*, Vol. 250, pp. 191-194.) Brief for Burleson, 44 pages; brief for Dempcy, 67 pages. Decided on authority of Dakota Central Telephone Company *et al. vs.* State of South Dakota.

McLeod *et al. vs.* New England Telephone Company. Decided June 2, 1919. (*U.S. Reports*, Vol. 250, pp. 195-198.) Brief for McLeod *et al.*, 45 pages; brief for the company, 54 pages. Decided on authority of Dakota Central Telephone Company *et al. vs.* State of South Dakota.

The *Lake Monroe.* Decided June 2, 1919. (*U.S. Reports*, Vol. 250, pp. 246-256.) Records and briefs, 132 pages. A case arising under the Shipping Board act of September 7, 1916. Upon petition of the United States an order was granted to show cause why a writ of prohibition or mandamus should not be issued in order to prevent the United States District Court for the District of Massachusetts, sitting in admiralty, from directing the seizure, attachment, or arrest of the *Lake Monroe*, owned and operated by the government of the United States, to satisfy a claim of the master and past owner of a fishing schooner for damages arising out of a collision between the two vessels.

Rumely *vs.* McCarthy. Decided June 2, 1919. (*U.S. Reports*, Vol. 250, pp. 283-289.) Brief and argument for Rumely, 57 pages; brief for McCarthy, 18 pages. A case in which a conspiracy to omit making a report of enemy property had been charged.

Commercial Cable Company *vs.* Burleson *et al.* and the Commercial Pacific Cable Company *vs.* Burleson *et al.* Decided June 9, 1919. (*U.S. Reports*, Vol. 250, pp. 360-363.) Brief for the companies, 93 pages; brief for Burleson, 48 pages. The companies sought to enjoin the Postmaster General and his appointees from retaining possession of the marine cables. They denied that the President had the power to take them under federal control, and held that if he had the power he was not justified in exerting it under the existing conditions.

Stilson *vs.* United States. Decided November 10, 1919. (*U.S. Reports*, Vol. 250, pp. 583-589.) Transcript of record, 278 pages; brief for Stilson, 15 pages; brief for the United States, 19 pages. A case arising under the espionage and selective service acts.

Abrams *et al. vs.* United States. Decided November 10, 1919. (*U.S. Reports*, Vol. 250, pp. 616-631.) Transcript of record, 268 pages; brief for Abrams *et al.*, 51 pages; brief for the United States, 38 pages. Abrams *et al.* had been charged with inciting a general strike of workers in the ammunition factories and convicted of a conspiracy to violate the espionage act.

Hamilton, Collector of Internal Revenue for the Collection District of Kentucky, *vs.* Kentucky Distilleries and Warehouse Company. Decided December 15, 1919. (*U.S. Reports*, Vol. 251, pp. 146-168.) Brief for the United States, 41 pages; brief for the company, 66 pages. A case arising under the war-time prohibition act. Was a reasonable time allowed by the act for disposing of liquors in bond? Did the act require the taking of property without compensation and thereby violate the Fifth Amendment?

United States *vs.* Standard Brewery. Decided January 15, 1920. (*U.S. Reports*, Vol. 251, pp. 210-220.) Brief for the United States, 18 pages; brief for the brewery, 39 pages. A case arising under the war-time prohibition act. That act prohibited the use of grains, fruits, and other products in the manufacture of "beer, wine, or other intoxicating malt or vinous liquor for beverage purposes" until the conclusion of the war. Does the word "intoxicating" qualify the terms preceding and thus exclude from the prohibition beer that is not intoxicating? If so, what percentage of alcohol renders beer intoxicating?

Jacob Ruppert *vs.* Cafferty *et al.* Decided January 5, 1920. (*U.S. Reports*, Vol. 251, pp. 264-310.) Brief for Ruppert, 78 pages; brief for the United States, 56 pages. Did the action of the President, under the food control act, in at first permitting the production of malt liquors containing not more than 2.75 per cent alcohol, in next extending the prohibition to all malt liquors irrespective of alcoholic content, and in afterwards limiting the prohibition to intoxicating malt liquors imply that 2.75 per cent beer was considered non-intoxicating or raise any equity in favor of an owner of beer that was manufactured after the President's authority over the subject had ceased?

United States *vs.* United States Steel Corporation *et al.* Decided March 1, 1920. (*U.S. Reports*, Vol. 251, pp. 417-466.) Record and briefs, 16 volumes. Was the United States Steel Corporation engaged in illegal restraint of trade and the exercise of a monopoly?

Schaefer *et al. vs.* the United States. Decided March 1, 1920. (*U.S. Reports*, Vol. 251, pp. 466-501.) Briefs for Schaefer *et al.*, 37 pages; briefs for the United States, 28 pages. Was the espionage act constitutional?

United States *vs.* A. Schrader's Sons, Inc. Decided March 1, 1920. (*U.S. Reports*, Vol. 252, pp. 85-100.) Brief for the United States, 19 pages; brief for Schrader's Sons, 61 pages. A manufacturer of patented articles sold them to its customers, who were manufacturers and jobbers in several States, under their agreements to observe certain retail prices fixed by the vendor. Did this constitute a combination engaged in illegal restraint of trade?

United States at the Relation of Kansas City Southern Railroad Company *vs.* Interstate Commerce Commission. Decided March 8, 1920. (*U.S. Reports*, Vol. 252, pp. 178-188.) Brief for the United States, 106 pages; brief for the Interstate Commerce Commission, 34 pages; brief for the railroads, 52 pages. The valuation act of March 1, 1913, requires the Interstate Commerce Commission to ascertain the present cost of condemnation and damages or of purchase of the lands, rights of way, and terminals of carriers in excess of their original cost or present value, apart from improvements. Was the Commission justified in refusing to receive and act upon evidence to this end by the supposed impossibility of performing the statutory duty or the difficulties involved in so doing?

Pierce *et al. vs.* United States. Decided March 8, 1920. (*U.S. Reports*, Vol. 252, pp. 239-273.) Transcript of record, 292 pages; brief for Pierce *et al.*, 27 pages; brief for the United States, 21 pages. A case arising under the espionage act. Pierce *et al.* were charged with circulating pamphlets headed "The Price We Pay" and attempting by this means to cause insubordination, disloyalty, and the refusal of duty in the military and naval forces during the war.

Pennsylvania Railroad Company *vs.* Kittanning Iron and Steel Manufacturing Company. Decided June 1, 1920. (*U.S. Reports*, Vol. 253, pp. 319-325.) Brief for the railroad, 20 pages; brief for the company, 8 pages. Relative to demurrage. A consignee who was a party to the average agreement plan was prevented from unloading a number of cars of frozen ore during the free time on account of their accumulation and delivery by the carrier in numbers exceeding the facilities of the consignee for thawing and unloading. Was the consignee relieved from demurrage by the clause governing frozen shipments?

Duplex Co. *vs.* Deering. Decided January 3, 1921. (*U.S. Reports*, Vol. 254, pp. 443-488.) Relative to a secondary boycott for the purpose of compelling a manufacturer of printing presses to unionize its factory.

Director General of Railroads *et al. vs.* The Viscose Company. Decided January 3, 1921. (*U.S. Reports*, Vol. 254, pp. 498-504.) A case arising under the act for the federal control of railroads and the transportation act of 1920, and involving a question of jurisdiction of the Interstate Commerce Commission with regard to the classification of commodities.

United States *vs.* Cohen Grocery Company. Decided February 28, 1921. (*U.S. Reports*, Vol. 255, pp. 81-97.) Brief for the United States, 59 pages; brief and argument for the company, 55 pages. Was section 4 of the food control act, in that it forbids and attaches a penalty to the exaction of an excessive price for a commodity, repugnant to the Fifth and Sixth Amendments? Other cases much the same as this are: Tedrow *vs.* Lewis and Son Co. (*U.S. Reports*, Vol. 255, pp. 98-99); Kennington *et al. vs.* Palmer *et al., ibid.,* pp. 100-101; Kinnane *vs.* Detroit Creamery Co., *ibid.,* Vol. 255, pp. 102-104; Weed and Co. *vs.* Lockwood, *ibid.,* pp. 104-106.

Smith *vs.* Kansas City Title Company. Decided February 28, 1921. (*U.S. Reports*, Vol. 255, pp. 180-215.) A case in which the constitutionality of the authorizing the creation of federal land banks was called into question.

Stroehr *vs.* Wallace. Decided February 28, 1921. (*U.S. Reports*, Vol. 255, pp. 239-251.) A case arising under the trading with the enemy act in which the Court upheld a certain seizure by the Alien Property Custodian.

Milwaukee Publishing Company *vs.* Burleson. Decided March 7, 1921. (*U.S. Reports*, Vol. 255, pp. 407-438.) Was the Postmaster General empowered by the espionage act to deny the mails to newspapers and other publications which violated its prohibitions?

DEPARTMENT OF STATE

War-Time Functions

In its conduct of foreign affairs during the period of the war the Department of State coöperated with or exercised a varying amount of supervision over activities of the War Trade Board, the United States Shipping Board, the Alien Property Custodian, the Committee on Public Information, the American Red Cross, the Council of National Defense, the War Industries Board, the Food Administration, the War, Navy, and Treasury Departments, and the Department of Justice. The Secretary of State was represented on the War Trade Board by its chairman. He was a member of the Committee on Public Information and of the Central Committee of the American Red Cross. For the coördination of the activities of other organizations with those of the State Department liaison officers were designated. The department coöperated with the War Trade Board in the operation of the trading with the enemy act and in the creation of export and import embargoes, with the United States Shipping Board in securing foreign tonnage, with the War Industries Board in the procurement from other countries of materials necessary for American military operations, with the Treasury Department in making loans to the allies, and with the Department of Justice in the detection and apprehension of enemy agents.

Publications and Records

Executive Orders and Proclamations

As the Secretary of State attests and promulgates all Executive Orders and Proclamations a complete file of this important material for the period of the war is among the records of the Department. They were published, as issued, by the Committee on Public Information in the successive numbers of the *Official Bulletin*. The Proclamations, but not the Orders, are published with the *United States Statutes at Large*. Both Proclamations and Orders are listed in the *Monthly Catalogue of Public Documents* and are filed according to classification in the library of the Superintendent of Documents. The Library of Congress, Manuscript Division, has them in bound volumes in chronological order, and there is a copy in the library of the United States Senate. Complete sets are no longer obtainable.

Diplomatic and Consular Correspondence

Diplomatic Correspondence with Belligerent Governments relating to Neutral Rights and Commerce (Washington, 1915-1918, 4 volumes, 1122 pages). Contraband of war, restraints on commerce, violations of neutrality by belligerent warships, defensive armament, internment of ships, submarines, and armed merchant-men, status of consuls, maritime danger zones.

The diplomatic correspondence relating to the World War, which had been compiled for publication under the title "A History of the World War as Shown by the Records in the Department of State," will be published as appendixes to the volumes of *Foreign Relations* for the years current with the war.

Some materials which were printed by the department but never published are in the department library and available for consultation by qualified students with such restrictions as to use as are warranted by the subject in question. The department does not permit the use of correspondence from other governments without the permission of the government with which the document in question originated.

List of Articles Embargoed by Neutral European Countries. (Department of State, December 15, 1914.)

A Report by the Secretary of State. (Senate Document No. 396, 66th Congress, third session. 18 pages.) Information received by the Department of State in response to the instructions sent to consular officers of the United States in foreign countries where American cotton is consumed. February, 1921.

The reports of the Bureau of Foreign and Domestic Commerce which were issued during the war period by the Department of Commerce were drawn in large part from consular correspondence supplied by the Department of State. When the files of the department, including those of the War Trade Board, become available for research much material in addition to what has been printed will be found.

Petitions and Protests from Business Organizations

Covering the period from the outbreak of the war until the United States entered it, there is in the Bureau of Indexes and Archives a large mass of correspondence from chambers of commerce and heads of business concerns in all parts of the country petitioning or protesting against the blockade and seizures, correspondence, also, regarding contraband. Some of this material was a form of pro-German propaganda, but the greater part of it is a product of industrial distress. The protests are particularly vigorous from States producing cotton, copper, tobacco, and naval stores, but they came also from importers and from representatives of industries that were only indirectly affected and the substance of their general contention was that bankruptcy would ensue if relief were not afforded. The following, with names omitted, are illustrative:

July 29, 1914. A.B. to the Secretary of Agricultural. Believes that Europe could use 150,000,000 bushels of American wheat in a year at good prices, and asks if there is any way that "our Government could arrange with the Powers abroad that . . . our wheat would be free of capture and confiscation, irrespective of the flag the freighter may carry."

August 6, 1914, P.S. Company to the State Department. Suggests government insurance of importers and manufacturers of foodstuffs expecting cargoes in neutral bottoms from neutral ports as a means of preventing a great increase in the cost of food supplies.

November 6, 1914. A.B. to the State Department. Urges the State Department to see that American tanners are not prevented from obtaining leather from Canada and Australia.

November 7, 1914. The A.R. Company to J. P. Tumulty. ". . . We respectfully ask if you will see that representations are made to England to keep them from declaring Magnesite as a contraband of war, as this would be a serious crippling to our Company, our Austrian Company, and all of the Steel Works of the United States. I urgently ask if you will not do me the favor, of having the State Department take this up at once, in the most vigorous way they can."

January 16, 1915. A.B. to the President of the United States. Urges that an embargo be placed on all exports which in any way affect the prices of foodstuffs that the poor of the American people may cease wondering how they are going to live with the high cost of food at a time when the country is blessed with the banner crops of its entire history.

January 20, 1915. A.B. to President Wilson. "The present industrial condition of the United States warrants that you immediately place an embargo on the exportation of wheat and all other food products, that are now held at abnormal values, caused by the wild demand of foreign countries. We will soon have our larders depleted, and this, the greatest producing Nation on Earth, will be on the brink of starvation."

January 25, 1915. A.B. to Woodrow Wilson. Nearly all the people the writer had met while travelling in Iowa were strongly in favor of an embargo upon the shipment of contraband of war and food to the warring nations of Europe.

February 6, 1915. The H.G. Company to the State Department. "Inasmuch as the shipping conditions or importation of goods from Germany is becoming more acute every hour, we are considerably alarmed . . . Our merchandise is all manufactured in the Kingdom of Saxony . . . and the sole life of our business is dependable upon its safe arrival in the United States . . . We insist that our communication be taken up by wire with Mr. Gerard, as well as our Consul at Chemnitz, and some definite policy outlined to us."

March 10, 1915. M.C. Company to Department of State. Earnestly and strenuously protest against the British blockade preventing them from importing merchandise from Germany.

March 10, 1915. R.J.M. Company to President Wilson. "As all merchandise ordered by this Company becomes *ipso facto* American property at the time of ordering . . . As all our stock is held by natural born American citizens, we respectfully ask that this Government make the proper and necessary representation to the respective French and British Governments, in order to properly inspire the protection of American import rights involved."

March 12, 1915. A. and Company, dealers in art calendars, to the State Department. If prevented from receiving importations from Germany business will be entirely disrupted.

March 15, 1915. A. and Company to Woodrow Wilson. A vigorous protest against the British regulation of traffic in cotton between the United States and the neutral countries of Europe.

March 18, 1915. A representative of the B.K. Mills to President Wilson. A protest against the action of France and England in putting aniline dyestuffs on the list of contraband of war. "We turn out a million dollars worth of high grade ladies' hosiery per year and employ 500 to 600 people . . . In one month to six weeks, we will be obliged to shut down our mill and throw all our people out of employment unless the American public is satisfied to wear hosiery in the gray without being dyed or in the bleached. It will mean a tremendous loss to us and to all other concerns in the hosiery business, if this condition is not relieved."

March 26, 1915. The A.B.G. Company to Hon. William J. Bryan. Protest against the embargo placed by England and France which affected the importation of chemicals. "We state unhesitatingly that if such restraint of trade is allowed to stand, we, as well as other concerns, will be on the brink of bankruptcy within a very short time, being dependent upon Germany for the necessary chemicals of our product, namely, Potash, Selenium, Cadmium, Sulphide, Arsenic, Manganese Oxide, Tin Oxide, as well as German Clay, it being the only clay that can be used in glass manufacturing."

March 30, 1915. A.B. to the State Department. Enters his emphatic protest against the interference with commerce which has completely shut off his supply of woolens from Germany and Austria. Wants to know if there is any way of getting redress for the losses incurred and states that "a continuance of present conditions means the closing of the department."

May 17, 1915. The Merchants Association of New York to the Secretary of State. Requests that efforts be made to have the British blockade order so modified as to permit the importation of azaleas from Belgium. "The Fall shipments of Belgian plants represent a value of approximately $450,000, dutiable at 25 per cent ad valorem. If this embargo continues over the Fall season, the U.S. will lose $112,500 in revenue . . . and the florists of the U.S. will suffer immeasurably by having no Azaleas to force and sell for the Christmas and Easter seasons."

July 15, 1915. N.B.S. Company to Robert Lansing. "It seems rather hard for us here to believe and understand . . . that we here in America cannot secure non-contraband goods in neutral vessels simply because these goods originated either in Austria or Germany."

July 24, 1915. N.S. Company to Robert Lansing. "We have considerable trade with Denmark in field seeds and grass seeds, which are non-contraband articles, but the provision now required in obtaining the bill of lading makes it impossible for us to export any of these goods, for the reason that when the goods are paid for here our control on them ceases. We are unable to tell at any time the ultimate disposition of goods when they pass into another owner's hands."

September 13, 1915. T.B. to Hon. F. N. Simmons, wants the State Department to use its good offices with the British and French Governments to get permission for cargoes of licorice root to come from Turkey to the United States by way of the Dardanelles. "As you know chewing tobacco cannot be manufactured without Licorice and if the manufacture of tobacco stops the Government revenue will be seriously affected."

DEPARTMENT OF THE TREASURY

Functions

THE Treasury Department, administered under the direction and control of the Secretary of the Treasury, is charged with the formulation of national financial policies, the management of the national finances, the enforcement of government regulation of banking, and the supervision of the Public Health Service. During the war the department assisted in the execution of the espionage act of June 15, 1917, and the trading with the enemy act of October 6, 1917; rendered decisions interpreting the revenue laws which drew revenue from many new sources but principally from the incomes of individuals and corporations; established the War Loan Organization and determined the dates, terms, and amounts of the Liberty loans, and the methods of marketing Liberty bonds and war savings stamps; organized the Foreign Loan Bureau and determined the procedure in extending credits to the allies; administered the federal farm loan act with a view to financing the farmers in war time; organized the Bureau of War Risk Insurance to administer acts of Congress providing for marine insurance, insurance of officers and crews of merchant vessels, insurance of soldiers and sailors, and allotments and allowances to their families; and was responsible for the administration of the Public Health Service, in direct charge of the Surgeon General, for the protection of the health of the military forces in civilian territory.

Division of Customs. The Division of Customs was in charge of an assistant secretary who rendered decisions interpreting customs laws. Besides collecting the customs duties, the division was required by the espionage and trading with the enemy acts (1) to make use of certificates of citizenship and identification cards, and to guard and search vessels for preventing enemy agents or unauthorized persons from entering into or departing from the United States; (2) check import entries and export declarations with licenses therefor issued by the War Trade Board; maintain a general surveillance over tugs and motor boats for the prevention of damage to shipping by the illegal lading or unlading of stowaways and merchandise, or by unlicensed communications, and supervise the anchorage and movement of vessels for the same purpose. The division collected and compiled special statistics for the use of the War Trade Board, the United States Shipping Board, and the Department of Commerce in the prosecution of the war.

Internal Revenue Service. This service was in charge of the Bureau of Internal Revenue assisted by field forces. The bureau, organized in several divisions, was under the direction of the Commissioner of Internal Revenue assisted by deputy commissioners, a supervisor of collectors, and a chief revenue agent. The field forces were under the immediate supervision of sixty-four internal revenue collectors and thirty-one internal revenue agents. The main business of the service during the war and the period of readjustment was the collection of the taxes imposed by the war revenue act of October 3, 1917, and the revenue act of February 24, 1919, more than two-thirds of which consisted of taxes on incomes of individuals and corporations, and the balance largely of taxes on distilled spirts, alcoholic beverages, tobacco, public utilities, and sales. To assist in analyzing and interpreting the war revenue act of 1917, representative business and professional men were appointed to serve as "excess profits advisers." Subsequently members of this group, supplemented by a number of public accountants, auditors, and accounting clerks, were organized into a special unit known as Excess Profits Tax Reviewers and charged with the auditing of certain classes of particularly difficult returns and the rendering of decisions in certain appeal cases. The unit was superseded by an Advisory Tax Board which served until October, 1919, when, the more difficult cases having been decided, it was dissolved. The interpretations of the war-time revenue acts, as rendered by the Commissioner of Internal Revenue, with the assistance mentioned and with the approval of the Secretary of the Treasury, are contained in the *Treasury Decisions, Internal Revenue.*

An incidental function of the Internal Revenue Service during the war was undertaken for the conservation of man power and war materials through the enforcement of the laws prohibiting or limiting the consumption of food products by distilleries and breweries and the suppression, in some instances, of the illicit manufacture and sale of intoxicants and narcotic drugs.

War Loan Organization. The Secretary of the Treasury was the directing force of each of five campaigns for the sale of Liberty bonds. For the general supervision of activities a War Loan Organization was created with a director, a Bureau of Publicity, a Speakers' Bureau, the twelve federal reserve banks as centers of the organization in their respective districts, Liberty loan committees in every part of the country, and, for the mobilization of women in the service, a National Woman's Liberty Loan Committee. Activities for the sale of war-savings certificates were directed by a branch of the War Loan Organization, the National War-Savings Committee, which organized state, county, city, and town committees.

Bureau of Foreign Loans. Loans to foreign governments, for which Congress appropriated ten billion dollars, were under the supervision of a Bureau of Foreign Loans, which was in charge of an assistant secretary of the Treasury.

Federal Farm Loan System. The federal farm loan act of July 17, 1916, established a federal farm loan system embracing (1) a Federal Farm Loan Board, with a bureau which was organized in four divisions: (a) Division of Charters and Reports, (b) Appraisement Division, (c) Bond Division, and (d) Division of Statistics and Economics; (2) twelve federal land banks, one for each of twelve federal land bank districts into which the continental United States exclusive of Alaska is divided; (3) joint-stock land banks; (4) thousands of national farm loan associations. The Federal Farm Loan Board, of which the Secretary of the Treasury is chairman, organized and chartered the federal land banks, chartered the joint-stock land banks and national farm loan associations, controls the issue of bonds, fixes the rate of interest, and requires reports from the banks. Each of the federal land banks is required to have a subscribed capital stock of not less than $750,000 in shares of $5 each. They may issue and sell farm loan bonds and act in the capacity of financial agents of the government. A joint-stock land bank may be formed by any number of persons, not less than ten, and be chartered when capital stock of at least $250,000 has been subscribed. These banks may loan on farm mortgage security and issue farm loan bonds but do not act as financial agents of the government. Loans are made by the federal land banks only to members of national farm loan associations. Such an association may be formed by ten or more persons who are owners or about to become owners of farm land qualified as security for a mortgage loan and desiring to borrow an aggregate of not less than $20,000. Only borrowers on farm land mortgages may be members of an association and before a member can obtain a loan the association must subscribe for capital stock to the amount of five per cent of the loan applied for. An amendment, January 18, 1918, to the federal farm loan act was a war measure authorizing the Secretary of the Treasury to purchase bonds of federal land banks to the amount of $100,000,000 a year during the fiscal years 1918 and 1919. The bonds so purchased were to be redeemed or repurchased after the war, but the provisions of the amendment were extended to the fiscal years 1920 and 1921 by a joint resolution of May 26, 1920.

The federal land banks were organized in February and March, 1917, and from their first operations were important war agencies in that they increased the volume and decreased the cost of agricultural production. In his report for 1918 the Secretary of the Treasury affirms that the federal farm loan system, "granting long-time loans at reasonable rates of interest, has unquestionably saved the farmers of the United States from many exactions, foreclosures, and denial of financial accommodations . . . It has constituted the great governmental agency for financing the basic industry of the United States—that of agriculture."

Bureau of War Risk Insurance. This bureau was originally designed as an instrument for the maintenance of the foreign commerce of the United States when, in 1914, it was "greatly impeded and endangered through the absence of adequate facilities for the insurance of American vessels and their cargoes against the risks of war." It was established by the war risk insurance act of September 2, 1914, to provide for insurance of United States vessels, their cargoes and freight, against loss or damage by the risks of war, whenever it should appear to the Secretary of the Treasury that adequate insurance on reasonable terms could not otherwise be secured.

The insurance of merchant seamen against loss of life or personal injury by risks of war, and compensation to them if taken prisoners, was provided for by an amendment of June 12, 1917.

An amendment of October 6, 1917, vastly enlarged the sphere of the bureau's activities by creating a division of military and naval insurance. This division not only offered insurance policies against death or total permanent disability to all men in active military or naval service of the United States and to all women in the Nurse Corps, but also provided for medical, surgical, and hospital service, artificial limbs, trusses, and similar appliances for the injured, provided compensation to the families of those who died or were disabled while in the service, provided for the allotment to his family of a portion of the monthly pay of each enlisted man, and provided, in addition, for monthly allowances to the families of enlisted men.

Minor functions included the administration of the insurance clauses of the trading with the enemy act of October 6, 1917, and of the soldiers' and sailors' civil relief act of March 8, 1918. By an act of August 9, 1921, the bureau was converted into the Veterans' Bureau, which is independent of the Treasury Department and has the additional function of vocational rehabilitation which was transferred to it from the Federal Board for Vocational Education. Immediately prior to this change the bureau was operating in eleven divisions, namely, Marine and Seamen's Division, Allotment and Allowance Division, Insurance Division, Compensation and Insurance Claims Division, Medical Division, Legal Division, Finance and Administrative Division, Liaison Division, School Teachers' Retirement Division, Personnel Division, and Trading with the Enemy Division.

United States Public Health Service. The United States Public Health Service is an evolution from the Marine Hospital Service, provision for which was made in the act of July 16, 1798, for the relief of sick and disabled seamen. The hospital service was developed by an act of April 29, 1878, into an agency to prevent the introduction of contagious and infectious diseases into the United States. Its functions were extended by an act of March 27, 1890, to prevent the spread of contagious diseases from one State to another. Further development, promoted by legislation, was followed by a change in name to the Public Health and Marine Hospital Service in 1902, and to the Public Health Service in 1912.

When the United States entered the war, the service, constituting a bureau of the Treasury Department in direct charge of the Surgeon General, was organized in seven divisions, namely, Scientific Research, Domestic (inter-state) Quarantine, Foreign and Insular (maritime) Quarantine, Sanatory Reports and Statistics, Maritime Hospitals and Relief, Personnel and Accounts, and Miscellaneous. A Division of Venereal Diseases was added in July, 1918.

The personnel and facilities of the Public Health Service were placed at the disposal of the military forces by executive order of April 3, 1917. All sanitary or public health activities carried on by any executive bureau or office, especially created for or concerned in the prosecution of the war, were placed under the supervision of the Public Health Service by executive order of July 1, 1918. An Inter-departmental Social Hygiene Board, consisting of the Secretary of War, the Secretary of the Navy, the Secretary of the Treasury, as *ex-officio* members, the Surgeon General of the army, the Surgeon General of the navy, and the Surgeon General of the Public Health Service, was created by the Chamberlain-Kahn act of July 9, 1918, for the performance of four duties: (1) to recommend rules and regulations for the expenditure of $1,000,-000 allotted to the States to assist them in caring for civilians whose detention or isolation should be found necessary for the protection of the military forces of the United States against venereal diseases; (2) to select certain educational institutions to which $400,000 should be allotted for the purpose of discovering more effective medical measures for the prevention and treatment of venereal diseases and more effective educational measures for the prevention of those diseases; (3) to recommend to the Secretary of War, the Secretary of the Navy, and the Secretary of the Treasury general measures to promote the correlation and efficiency of the work in venereal disease control in their departments; (4) to direct the expenditure of $100,000 to be used for any purpose for which appropriations were made by the act. A Reserve of the Public Health Service, subject to call to active duty by the Surgeon General in time of national emergency, was organized under a joint resolution of Congress, dated October 27, 1918.

The war activities of the Public Health Service were directed primarily toward the maintenance of the maximum man power of the United States by promoting the efficiency of the public health administration throughout the country, especially in and about zones surrounding military camps and important industrial centers engaged in war work. The work in the extra-cantonment zones was carried on in coöperation with state and local health officers and the American Red Cross to prevent the breeding of mosquitoes, protect drinking water, safeguard the milk supply, provide sanitary housing, and control communicable diseases. The service labored to promote industrial hygiene in the war industries; engaged in scientific research to determine relations of industrial fatigue to efficiency; supervised the production and use of serums, toxins, and analogous products; conducted a vigorous campaign for the control of venereal diseases; furnished a mobile corps of nearly 1100 physicians to render medical attention where most needed during the pandemic of influenza in the fall of 1918; coöperated with the Bureau of War Risk Insurance in providing medical, hospital, and sanatorium care for the beneficiaries of that bureau; prepared and distributed numerous articles of information regarding public health matters.

The after-the-war program, prepared in May, 1919, embraces measures for the promotion of industrial and rural hygiene, measures for the prevention of diseases of infancy and childhood, national development of safe water supplies, measures for the proper disposal of sewage, national development of measures for the control of malaria and malaria-bearing mosquitoes in industrially, agriculturally, and economically important areas of the United States, measures for the control of venereal diseases, a campaign against tuberculosis, railway sanitation, municipal sanitation, establishment of health standards, health education, collection of morbidity reports, and organization and training for duty in emergency of the Reserve of the Public Health Service.

Publications

Annual Report of the Secretary of the Treasury on the State of the Finances for the fiscal year ended June 30, 1917 (Washington, 1917, 350 pages, 15 statistical tables). Embraces reports relative to operations for the sale of Liberty bonds and war savings certificates, operations of the federal reserve system, the customs service, and the Public Health Service, reports relative to loans to foreign governments, war risk insurance, and the immensity of the task of the internal revenue service.

Annual Report of the Secretary of the Treasury . . . June 30, 1918 (Washington, 1918, 540 pages, 15 statistical tables). Contains a statement showing the cost of the war, and material relative to the war loan organization, Liberty loans, Liberty bonds, war savings certificates, War Finance Corporation, Capital Issues Committee, loans to foreign governments, foreign exchange, federal reserve system, internal revenue, customs, federal farm loan system, war risk insurance, and Public Health Service.

Annual Report of the Secretary of the Treasury . . . June 30, 1919 (Washington, 1919, 719 pages, 15 statistical tables). Reviews the international financial situation and contains material relative to currency and credit expansion, cost of the war, Liberty loans, Liberty bonds, war savings certificates, war loan organization, loans to foreign governments, federal farm loan system, federal reserve system, War Finance Corporation, Capital Issues Committee, internal revenue, customs, war risk insurance, and Public Health Service.

Treasury Decisions under Customs and Other Laws (Vols. 32-37, Washington, 1918-1920). Decisions interpreting acts of Congress and executive proclamations for the years 1917-1919, also a few circulars of instruction to collectors and surveyors of the customs.

Annual Report of the Commissioner of Internal Revenue for the fiscal year ended June 30, 1917 (Washington, 1917, 265 pages). Income tax, estate tax, munition manufacturers' tax, and illicit distilling. Among a number of statistical tables is one showing the receipts from the several sources of internal revenue.

Annual Report of the Commissioner of Internal Revenue . . . June 30, 1918 (Washington, 1918, 188 pages). New era of taxation, war revenue, and statistical work. The report deals separately with each object of internal tax and eighty-six statistical tables exhibit, in various phases, the returns of the war revenue act of October 3, 1917.

Annual Report of the Commissioner of Internal Revenue . . . June 30, 1919 (Washington, 1919, 244 pages). Revenue act of 1918, Advisory Tax Board, regulations, administrative rulings, solicitor of internal revenue, field service, observance and enforcement of internal revenue laws, bureau organization, objects of taxation, statistical tables.

Treasury Decisions under Internal Revenue Laws of the United States (Vols. 19-21, Washington, 1918-1920). Decisions interpreting acts of Congress relating to the internal revenue for the years 1917-1919, also some regulations and rulings of the Treasury Department relative to internal revenue.

Digest of Treasury Decisions relating to Internal Revenue (Washington, 1921, 666 pages). Alphabetically arranged. Covers the period from September, 1916, to the close of the year 1920.

Digest of Income Tax Rulings, Nos. 1-1159 (Washington, 1920, 335 pages). Administrative rulings are published at frequent intervals both in separate and cumulative bulletins.

Regulations 45, relating to the Income Tax and Excess Profits Tax under the Revenue Act of 1918 (Washington, 1919, 164 pages). Regulations are published for the instruction of the field officers and the information of the public.

Internal Revenue Laws in Force May 1, 1920 (Washington, 1920, 1035 pages). An appendix contains laws of a general nature and miscellaneous provisions applicable to the administration of the internal revenue laws.

Statistics of Income (Washington, 1918, 391 pages). Compiled from the returns for 1916; a social and sectional analysis of income tax returns.

For a thorough study of the nation's finances during the war and the period of readjustment the following publications are essential:

Estimates of Appropriations Required for the Service of the Fiscal Year ending June 30, 1918 (Washington, 1916, 1041 pages). Transmitted to the Speaker of the House of Representatives by the Secretary of the Treasury, December 4, 1916.

Digest of Appropriations for the Support of the Government of the United States for the Service of the Fiscal Year ending June 30, 1918, and on Account of Deficiencies for Prior Years Made by the Second Session of the Sixty-Fourth Congress and First Session of the Sixty-Fifth Congress (Washington, 1918, 674 pages).

The same for the fiscal years 1919 and 1920.

Combined Statement of the Receipts and Disbursements, Balances, etc., of the United States during the Fiscal Year ended June 30, 1918 (Washington, 1919, 199 pages). Transmitted to the Speaker of the House of Representatives by the Secretary of the Treasury.

The same for the fiscal years 1919 and 1920.

Daily Statement of the United States Treasury. The daily issues of three pages each are bound in one volume for each month. The *Statement* embraces data relative to assets and liabilities, daily receipts and cumulative monthly receipts from the individual income taxes, the corporation income tax, and the excess profits tax.

Annual Report of the Comptroller of the Currency, December 3, 1917

(Washington, 1918, 2 volumes: Vol. 1, 234 pages; Vol. 2, 908 pages). The first volume contains a brief review of financial and business conditions in 1917; an appeal to banks not to take advantage of war conditions to exact high interest rates; and a statement declaring that national banks are not authorized to subscribe to the Red Cross for relief purposes. The second volume is statistical.

Annual Report of the Comptroller of the Currency, December 2, 1918 (Washington, 1919, 2 volumes: Vol. 1, 222 pages; Vol. 2, 854 pages). The first volume contains some observations on the patriotism and splendid condition of the national banks in war time and their part in the sale of Liberty bonds. The second volume is statistical.

Annual Report of the Comptroller of the Currency, December 1, 1919 (Washington, 1920, 2 volumes: Vol. 1, 222 pages; Vol. 2, 909 pages). The first volume contains a discussion of problems relative to national banks in the reconstruction period, and of diminished production with price inflation, and some data relative to Liberty bonds and the federal farm loan system.

The Bureau of Publicity of the **War Loan Organization** issued a number of leaflets and pamphlets to arouse and inform the public, such as handbooks for speakers, manuals for Boy Scouts, lessons in thrift, and how to win the war. There are addresses by the Secretary of the Treasury, reports of conferences, reports of Liberty loan campaigns and subscriptions to loans by federal reserve districts, the National Woman's Liberty Loan Committee, and the War Loan Organization, and a few miscellaneous publications. Special attention is directed to the following:

The Liberty Loan Legislation (Washington, 1921, 38 pages). Embraces first Liberty bond act, consolidated second Liberty bond act amended and supplemented, and miscellaneous provisions of the Liberty loan acts not included in the consolidated second Liberty bond act.

Addresses by W. G. McAdoo, Secretary of the Treasury: *Financing the War,* delivered in Chicago, Illinois, May 17, 1917 (Washington, 1917, 11 pages); *The Second Liberty Loan,* delivered at the annual convention of the American Bankers' Association, at Atlantic City, September 28, 1917 (Washington, 1917, 16 pages); *The Second Libery Loan and the American Farmer,* delivered at Sioux City, Iowa, October 4, 1917 (Washington, 1917, 13 pages); *The Third Liberty Loan,* delivered at Richmond, Virginia, April 8, 1918 (Washington, 1918, 16 pages); *The Fourth Liberty Loan,* delivered to Liberty loan organizations and workers of the second federal reserve district, at New York, September 24, 1918.

Report of Liberty Loan Conference at the Treasury Department December 10, 11, and 12 [*1917*] (36 pages). A consideration of organization, sales management, and other matters pertaining to Liberty loan campaigns.

Results of Fourth Liberty Loan (Washington, 1919, 8 pages). Contains statistics of subscriptions by districts, States, and the larger cities.

Results of Victory Liberty Loan Subscriptions (Washington, 1919, 7 pages). Contains statistics of subscriptions by districts, States, and the larger cities.

Figuregram for the Fifth or Victory Liberty Loan in the Fourth Federal Reserve District (Cleveland, 1919, 88 pages). Contains statistical data for all four loans.

Subscriptions to the Fourth Liberty Loan in the . . . Eighth Federal Reserve District (Saint Louis, 1919, 7 volumes of 16 to 76 pages each). One volume for each of seven States comprising the district: Illinois, Indiana, Kentucky, Tennessee, Mississippi, Arkansas, and Missouri.

Report of National Woman's Liberty Loan Committee for the Victory Loan Campaign (Washington, 1920, 164 pages). Contains a report for each State. There is also a report of this committee for the first and second campaigns (Washington, 1918, 43 pages); for the third campaign (Washington, 1918, 32 pages); and for the fourth campaign (Washington, 1918, 32 pages).

The publications of the **Federal Farm Loan Board** consist of annual reports, circulars of information, and one bulletin.

First Annual Report of the Federal Farm Loan Board (Washington, 1918, 31 pages). Covers the period from the organization of the board to November 30, 1917. Chiefly a report relative to the organization of the farm loan system: district and bank sites, selection of directors, stock subscriptions, problems encountered, interest rate and sale of bonds, joint-stock land banks, question as to the utility of farm loan associations, and statistical data.

Second Annual Report of the Federal Farm Loan Board, for the year ended November 30, 1918. A report of the first year of operation: drought conditions, character of loan applications, limits of amount of loans, title examination, interest rate, and statistical data.

Third Annual Report of the Federal Farm Loan Board, for the year ended November 30, 1919 (Washington, 1920, 30 pages). Contents: appraisal system, national farm loan associations, land speculation, earnings of banks, purposes of loans, general assistance to agriculture, and statistical data.

Circulars:

No. 1. National Farm Loan Associations: Organization, Management, Powers, and Limitations.

No. 2. How Farmers May Form a National Farm Loan Association.

No. 3. The Improved Farm Mortgage: A Story Illustrating the Practical Application of the Federal Farm Loan Act.

No. 4. The Federal Farm Loan Act. A copy.

No. 5. The Farm Loan Primer: . . . Brief Form Answers to the Questions Most Frequently Asked about the Federal Farm Loan Act.

No. 6. Farm Loan Bonds.

No. 7. Killing off Mortgages: A Description of the Methods of Amortization and their Benefits to Borrowers.

No. 10. Rules and Regulations of the Farm Loan Board.

No. 11. Amendments to the Federal Farm Loan Act.

Land Title Registration by Certificate (Washington, 1918, 85 pages). Contains a report on land title registration laws in the United States and a comparative study of land title registration statutes, and favors the Torrens system simplified and adapted to constitutional requirements along lines approved by United States Supreme Court decisions.

The **Bureau of War Risk Insurance** issued a number of bulletins and circulars of information, a booklet of regulations, financial statements, one informing annual report relative to organization and operations, and decisions interpreting the acts under which the bureau operated. The more important publications are named in the following list.

Annual Report of the Director of the Bureau of War Risk Insurance for the fiscal year ended June 30, 1920 (Washington, 1920, 107 pages). Consists mainly of an account of the organization and functions of the bureau and each of its divisions. The *Annual Report* for 1914 (House Document No. 1340, 63rd Congress, 3rd Session, 5 pages) is merely a statement of receipts and expenses. The *Reports* for 1915 (Ho. Doc. No. 544, 64th Cong., 1st Sess., 15 pages), 1916 (Ho. Doc. No. 1795, 64th Cong., 2nd Sess., 5 pages) and 1917 (Ho. Doc. No. 518, 65th Cong., 2nd Sess., 5 pages), are of the same character, and no report was published for 1918 or 1919.

War Risk Insurance Soldiers' Compensation and Insurance Laws and Soldiers' and Sailors' Civil Rights Act (Washington, 1922, 76 pages). Contains a copy of the original war risk insurance act, amendments of August 11, 1916, March 3, June 12, and October 6, 1917, May 20, June 25, and July 11, 1918, February 25 and December 24, 1919, the soldiers' and sailors' civil rights act of March 8, 1918, the vocational rehabilitation act of June 27, 1918, and the act of August 9, 1921, establishing the Veterans' Bureau.

Special Regulations No. 72: Allotments, Family Allowances, Compensation, and Insurance under War Risk Insurance Act and Act of March 2, 1899, as Amended by Public No. 66, Sixty-Fifth Congress, 1918 (Washington, 1918, 58 pages). Issued by the War Department and covers such matters as preparation and disposition of applications for allotments and insurance, for changes and discontinuance of allotments, compensation for death or disability, government insurance, and the like.

Opinions of the Judge Advocate General of the Army, 1918 (Washington, 1919, Vol. 2, 1182 pages), contains a number of opinions relative to the operation of the war risk insurance act.

Compilation of War Risk Insurance Letters, Treasury Decisions, and War Department Circulars relating to War Risk Insurance (Washington, 1919, 155 pages). Interpretation of the war risk insurance act and regulations for its operation.

Premium Rates and Policy Values for United States Government Life Insurance (Washington, 1919, 103 pages). Shows the cost and value of government insurance for enlisted men of all ages.

Bulletins:

No. 1. Terms and Conditions of Soldiers' and Sailors' Insurance (7 pages).

No. 2. What the United States Government does for its Fighting Men and their Families, a Brief Explanation of their Rights, their Privileges, and their Duties under the War Risk Insurance Act (4 pages).

No. 3. Family Allowances, Allotments, Compensation, and Insurance for the Military and Naval Forces of the United States. Provided under Act of Congress approved October 6, 1917 (69 pages).

No. 4. Uncle Sam's Insurance for Soldiers and Sailors, Answers to Questions You will ask (7 pages).

Military and Naval Insurance and Military and Naval Compensation Claims as a Result of the World War (Washington, 1920, 162 pages).

A report containing classified statistics concerning the deaths and disabilities resulting from the war with relation to the payment of military and naval insurance and compensation as provided by the war risk insurance act.

The publications of the **Public Health Service** consist of annual reports, public health reports, bulletins, miscellaneous publications, and a "Keep Well" series of small pamphlets. Particular attention is directed to the following:

Annual Report of the Surgeon General of the Public Health Service of the United States for the Fiscal Year 1917 (Washington, 1917, 387 pages). Surveys of extra-cantonment areas, annual conference with state and territorial health authorities, prevalence of disease in the United States.

Annual Report of the Surgeon General of the Public Health Service of the United States for the Fiscal Year 1918 (Washington, 1918, 373 pages). Sanitary surveys of navy yards and of plants making war materials, medical and surgical care of industrial workers, industrial fatigue, mine sanitation, extra-cantonment sanitation for the protection of the military forces.

Annual Report of the Surgeon General of the Public Health Service of the United States for the Fiscal Year 1919 (Washington, 1919, 346 pages). Activities of the Public Health Service in combating the influenza epidemic, extra-cantonment zone sanitation, prevalence of disease in extra-cantonment zones, the campaign against venereal diseases.

Public Health Reports (weekly). Each number, usually of 30 to 40 pages, contains information relative to the prevalence of disease and one or more articles on miscellaneous subjects such as:

"War Program of the Public Health Service, Intended especially for Extra-Cantonment Areas and War Industry Centers" (September 27, 1918, 8 pages).

"War Activities of the United States Health Service" (June 6, 1919, 27 pages).

"Program of the Public Health Service, Intended especially to Meet After-the-War Needs" (May 9, 1919, 8 pages).

"Trachoma and the Army—the Dangers incident to enlisting Recruits affected with the Disease" (July 13, 1917, 4 pages).

"Mitigation of Heat Hazards in Industries" (December 14, 1917, 11 pages).

"Extra-Cantonment Zone Sanitation, Camp Shelby" (December 21, 1917, 16 pages).

"Industrial Efficiency" (January 11, 1918, 7 pages).

"Morbidity Statistics of War Industries Needed" (February 1, 1918, 6 pages).

"A State-Wide Plan for the Prevention of Venereal Diseases" (February 22, 1918, 16 pages).

"Suggestions for State Board of Health Regulations for the Prevention of Venereal Diseases" (March 29, 1918, 7 pages).

"Progress in Venereal Disease Control" (May 24, 1918, 6 pages).

"Regulations for Allotment of Funds for Venereal-Disease Prevention Work" (September 13, 1918, 4 pages).

"Methods of Field Study of Industrial Fatigue" (March 15, 1918, 7 pages).

"The Dietary Deficiency of Cereal Foods with reference to their Content in Anti-Neuritic Vitamine" (May 3, 1918, 22 pages).

"Influenza Studies" (August 8, 1918, 41 pages).

"A Comparison of the Mortality Rates by Weeks during the Influenza Epidemic of 1889-1890 and during the Primary Stage of the Influenza Epidemic of 1918 in twelve Cities in the United States" (January 31, 1919, 8 pages).

Laws and Comptroller's Decisions pertaining to the United States Public Health Service (Washington, 1922, 133 pages). A supplement to the *Public Health Reports.*

Transactions of the Sixteenth Annual Conference of State and Territorial Health Officers with the United States Public Health Service, held at Washington, D. C., June 3 and 4, 1918 (Washington, 1919, 149 pages). This is *Public Health Bulletin No. 96.* The principal subjects discussed are: relation to public health of industrial hygiene and sanitation, especially in war industries; sanitation of extra-cantonment areas, especially as related to the work of state and local health authorities; venereal diseases—their control, with reference to the relation of the United States Public Health Service to States and cities in handling this problem; use of records of drafted men for public health purposes; trachoma, its bearing on the public health and the military forces; hookworm disease, the importance of its prevalence and control among the military forces; effects on the public health of the forthcoming shortage in the medical profession; railroad water supplies; public health work in war time.

Transactions of the Seventeenth Annual Conference of State and Ter-

ritorial Health Officers with the United States Public Health Service, held at *Washington, D. C., June 4 and 5, 1919* (Washington, 1920, 124 pages). This is *Public Health Bulletin No. 105.* Mainly a discussion of an after-the-war program.

Studies of the Medical and Surgical Care of Industrial Workers, by C. D. Selby (Washington, 1919, 115 pages). This is *Public Health Bulletin No. 99.* Deals with relation of medical service to industry, relation of medical departments to industrial organizations, special practitioners in industry, activities of industrial medical departments, etc.

Publications of the United States Public Health Service (Washington, 1921, 104 pages). Contains complete lists of the publications in book form.

DEPARTMENT OF WAR

THE non-military activities of the Department of War during the period of the emergency centered around the major problems of procurement, equipment and supply, shelter, transportation, training, and the maintenance of morale. The organization of the department underwent an almost constant process of modification until there had been evolved, toward the close of the period, an effective machine of fitted parts. The closely related bureaus, which competed with each other for essential supplies in 1917, were by the end of 1918 subordinated to the General Staff, which had developed the means of coördinating the economic activities of the entire system. The stages of their evolution are set forth in detail in the *Report of the Chief of Staff, 1919* (see below).

General Publications

The following publications of a more or less general character, which do not appropriately come under any one of the subordinate parts of this section of the survey, should be noted.

Report of the Secretary of War, 1917 (Washington, 1918, 123 pages). Enlargement of the army; training camps; cantonments; army contracts; Commission on Training Camp Activities; supplies; expenditures; estimates and appropriations.

Report of the Secretary of War, 1918 (Washington, 1919, 143 pages). Education; morale; settlement of war contracts; liquidation of international obligations; sales and liquidation abroad; settlement of claims in the United States; appropriations, expenditures, and balances.

America's Munitions, 1917-1918 (Washington, 1919, 892 pages). This volume constitutes the final report of Benedict Crowell, assistant secretary of war and director of munitions. It is a compilation of considerable value, by various hands, illustrated with tables, graphic charts, photographs, etc., and organized in seven "Books" devoted to Ordnance, Air Service, Engineer Corps, Chemical Warfare, Quartermaster Activities, Construction Division, Signal Corps. With a few changes it is reproduced in Volumes IV and V of *How America Went to War* (New Haven, 1921), by Benedict Crowell and Robert F. Wilson.

The volume is marked by a tone of optimism and of satisfaction with the performance which it records.

A Report of the Activities of the War Department in the Field of Industrial Relations during the War (Washington, 1919, 90 pages). Early policies; establishment of labor boards and commissions to adjust controversies; administrative agencies; relations with the National War Labor Board and the War Labor Policies Board.

Report of the Chairman on Training Camp Activities, 1918 (Washington, 1918, 23 pages). Athletics, social hygiene, law enforcement, music, the Liberty theater.

Report to the Secretary of War on the Activities of Welfare Organizations Serving with the A.E.F., by Raymond B. Fosdick, chairman of the Commission on Training Camp Activities, War Department (Washington, 1919, 14 pages). Too many welfare organizations in the field; much of the work should be done by the army itself.

ADJUTANT GENERAL'S OFFICE

The Adjutant General's Office is the office of record under the Secretary of War and the principal depository of records of the Department of War. The correspondence in this office is filed in nine principal classes: general; finance and accounting; personnel; administration; supplies and equipment; transportation; buildings and grounds; medicine, hygiene, and sanitation; rivers and harbors. In the general class are papers relative to political and religious matters, civil educational institutions, welfare organizations, insurance, statistics, industrial plants, and commercial enterprises. The finance and accounting class embraces appropriations, estimates for appropriations, reimbursements, apportionment and supply of funds, contracts, and accounting for property, supplies, and stores. In the class designated as supplies, equipment, and services are included such matters as the selection, purchase, manufacture, and distribution of supplies and equipment. The transportation class comprises subjects pertaining to the transportation of persons or supplies, by land or by water, transportation accounts and contracts. The buildings and grounds class embraces the general subject of the construction, repair, and protection of buildings, and matters pertaining to particular buildings and grounds. Medicine, hygiene, and sanitation embrace all matters affecting the health and sanitation of the army: admission of patients to hospitals, hygiene of air and ground, treatment and prevention of diseases, etc. The filing system is fully set forth in *War Department Correspondence File*, compiled under the direction of the Adjutant General of the Army by Marcel S. Keene, Clay S. Worick, Ralph G. Hersey, and H. M. McLarin (Washington, 1918, 454 pages).

The records in the World War Records Section of the Adjutant General's Office are classified as: (1) personnel records; (2) organization records; and (3) miscellaneous records. By far the greater portion of the records in all three classes are of a military nature. Those of importance for the purpose of this survey are distributed in all three classes, particularly in the second and third classes. In a few instances they are somewhat segregated, but those on several subjects are much scattered. They pertain to such subjects as: the selective service or draft; conscientious objectors; industrial and farm furloughs; Students' Army Training Corps; War Camp Community Service; civilian welfare agencies working with the military service; activities of chaplains and other religious workers; educational activities in the army; economic mobilization; and services of supply.

The selective service or draft records are described below as records of the Provost Marshal General's Office. Those of economic mobilization and the services of supply are described under the Historical Branch, General Staff.

GENERAL STAFF

Organization

General Orders No. 14, February 9, 1918, organized the General Staff in five divisions: (1) Executive, (2) War Plans, (3) Purchase and Supply, (4) Storage and Traffic, and (5) Operations. General Orders No. 80, August 26, 1918, charged the Chief of Staff, as the immediate adviser of the Secretary of War on all matters relating to the military establishment, with responsibility for the planning, development, and execution of the army program and organized the work in four divisions: (1) Operations, (2) Purchase, Storage, and Traffic, (3) Military Intelligence, and (4) War Plans, each directed by an assistant chief of staff.

When the United States entered the war the bureau system prevailed in the department and supplies were procured chiefly by the Quartermaster Corps, Ordnance Department, Medical Department, Corps of Engineers, and Signal Corps. The independent handling of the supply problem by each of these bureaus developed a competition for manufactured articles, raw materials, and labor that resulted in high prices, congestion of contracts, congestion of traffic, inefficiency with respect to manufacturing facilities, and inefficiency with respect to the distribution of labor. To remedy the situation, to provide for systematic expansion, and to keep pace with the developments in military science, a redistribution of functions was necessary, and this was accomplished by (1) detaching the construction and transportation functions from the Quartermaster Corps, (2) creating the Construction Division, the Motor Transport Corps, the Transportation Service, the Bureau of Aircraft Production, and the Tank Corps, and (3) vesting in the Purchase, Storage, and Traffic Division of the General Staff the supervision and coördination of purchases and financial operations of the several bureaus.

Publications

Report of the Chief of Staff, U.S. Army, to the Secretary of War, 1917 (Washington, 1917, 30 pages). Quartermaster Corps, building and transportation; Signal Corps and the creation of an air fleet; magnitude of the task of the Ordnance Department.

Report of the Chief of Staff . . . 1918 (Washington, 1918, 24 pages). Organization and operations of the Purchase, Storage, and Traffic Division.

Report of the Chief of Staff . . . 1919 (Washington, 1919, 261 pages). An outline of the evolution of the plans and the development of the organization of the General Staff during the war. Nearly one-half of the report is devoted to the Purchase, Storage, and Traffic Division.

The War with Germany, a Statistical Summary, by Leonard P. Ayres, Chief of the Statistical Branch of the General Staff (Washington, 1919, 154 pages). Statistics relative to food, clothing, equipment, ordnance, airplanes, motors, and transportation.

The Library of Congress has a photostatic copy of a "Weekly Statistical Report," January 12, 1918, to December 13, 1919, compiled by the Statistical Branch of the General Staff. It has also a copy of statistical tables by this branch relative to tonnage for the Expeditionary Forces.

PURCHASE, STORAGE, AND TRAFFIC DIVISION

General Orders No. 102, War Department, August 4, 1917, created the Embarkation Service to take charge of embarkation matters for all supply bureaus of the army. General Orders No. 167, War Department, December 28, 1917, created the Storage and Traffic Division to be composed mainly of the Embarkation Service, the Inland Traffic Service, and what had been the Storage Division of the Quartermaster Corps. General Orders No. 5, War Department, January 11, 1918, appointed a Director of Purchase charged with reviewing and systematizing the supply activities of the several bureaus. General Orders No. 36, War Department, April 16, 1918, combined the Purchase and Supply Division with the Storage and Traffic Division to form the Purchase, Storage, and Traffic Division.

Publications

Compilation of Supply Circulars and Supply Bulletins of the Purchase, Storage, and Traffic Division, General Staff, War Department, April 24, 1918, to May 1, 1919 (Washington, 1919, 291 pages). The twenty-three "articles" of which this volume is composed are as follows:

1. Supply circulars.
2. Organization of the Purchase, Storage, and Traffic Division, General Staff.
3. Organization of Purchase and Storage Service.
4. Organization of Finance and Accounting Service.
5. Organization of Real Estate Service.
6. Transportation Service.
7. Organization of ports of embarkation.
8. War Department construction work.
9. Boards of Review.
10. Requirements of supply bureaus of the army.
11. Calculation of reserves.
12. Consolidation of procurement of articles or material procured by more than one supply bureau.
13. Inter-bureau requisitions.
14. Compulsory orders.
15. Contract regulations.

16. Contract provisions.
17. Termination of contracts.
18. Sale of war supplies.
19. War claims.
20. Negotiations with foreign governments.
21. Report on orders and contracts and requests for information.
22. Standardization, classification, and cataloguing of army material.
23. Standardization of baling, boxing, crating, and marking specifications.

Report of the Chief of Staff, U.S. Army, to the Secretary of War, 1919 (Washington, 1919, pp. 108-213). Antecedents of the Purchase, Storage, and Traffic Division; establishment and original organization; Embarkation Service; Inland Traffic Service; Storage Branch, Finance Department; reorganization, August, 1918; development of the Office of Director of Purchase and Storage; readjustments subsequent to the armistice; steps toward discontinuance of operating activities.

Report of the Quartermaster General, 1918 (Washington, 1919, 63 pages). Readjustment of military services; consolidation of procurement; development of organization within the Quartermaster Corps; problem of supply; distribution of supplies; clothing and equipage; vehicles and harness; hardware and metals; motor transport service; subsistence; depots; finance and accounts.

Report of the Quartermaster General, 1919 (Washington, 1920, 169 pages). Growth of the Supply Division; storage and requirements; reorganizations of January 26, April 16, and June 14, 1918; the zone system; establishment, organization, and development of the Office of Director of Purchase and Storage; purchase divisions; storage divisions; requirements; remount service; clothing and equipage; summary of contracted deliveries, actual deliveries, shipments overseas, losses at sea, and stocks on hand of principal items of clothing and equipage from June 30, 1918, to June 30, 1919; subsistence; motors and vehicles; raw materials and paints; medical and hospital supplies; machinery and engineering materials; storage; salvage; procurement; material control; distribution; finance; boards of review.

The Quartermaster Corps in the Year 1917 in the World War, by Henry G. Sharpe (New York, 1921, 424 pages). Clothing and equipage; depots; warehousing; transportation; remount service; financial problems and accounting. [Unofficial.]

Records

Questionnaire to firms. In the Historical Branch of the Purchase and Storage Division were assembled several file cases and several volumes of historical and statistical data. An index contains the names and addresses of the firms with which the division did business. To each of these the branch sent a form letter asking for the following information:

1. State kind of articles you supplied the War Department.
2. Quantity of each article contracted for.
3. Quantity of each article actually delivered.
4. Total value of all contracts.
5. Value of all deliveries.
6. Statement as to whether articles manufactured by your firm for the government were the same articles as your peace-time production.
7. Show increased production over normal production.
8. Include statement showing rapidity with which orders were filled after being received from the War Department.
9. Give statement showing the amount of time cut off in the production of certain articles from the average time required to make these articles under peace conditions.
10. State whether your plant was in any way changed to meet government requirements. If there was any change in plant, go into some detail as to nature of change, amount of money necessary to make the change, etc.
11. State if there was any development in your plant of any new process or method of manufacture. If so, please treat this subject very fully.
12. State number of men called into the army from your plant and show number of women employed to take their places.
13. Show increase by months in personnel from April 2, 1917, to November, 1, 1918.
14. State fully any difficulty with labor which you may have had during this period, and manner of settlement.
15. Statement as to difficulty in securing capable and efficient labor.
16. Statement as to the practicability of the employment of women to take the place of men in your factory.
17. If there are any criticisms to be made as to the purchase, inspection, or payment methods used by the army, make these criticisms without reserve. What is wanted is an exact historical file, and frankness will be appreciated.
18. Give statement showing your methods of procurement and purchase of raw material, showing how you were affected by the War Trade Board, War Industries Board, Council of National Defense, etc.
19. Show how the allocation of raw materials on priority demands affected your operations.
20. Trace in a few words any economic or sociological changes in your city or plant, which were due in any way to the war program.

The replies to this questionnaire are in the files. Some firms answered on the questionnaire form itself; others answered on separate sheets. Statistical questions were answered briefly but to some other questions, such as those inviting criticism, a paragraph or more was occasionally devoted. A few firms answered the questionnaire in a narrative of several pages.

Histories of Supply Depots. Purchasing or the placing of orders, was the function of the central organization in Washington. Procurement, which involved the necessary operations for completing the contracts, such as inspection, following up production, and acceptance of the products, was the function of the thirteen procurement zones into which the United States was divided. The operations of each zone were centered in its depot, named for the city in which it was located, and of each zone depot the Branch secured a history by some resident or residents of the zone designated for the purpose. Nine of these histories, consisting of narratives of operations, orders, and statistics of supplies procured, are as follows (in MS.) :

History of the Atlanta General Supply Depot, April, 1917-May, 1919 (87 pages). List of property leased; procurement division; clothing and equipage branch; purchasing branch, inspection division; storage division; warehousing division; distribution division; list of immense quantities of supplies on hand.

History of the General Supply Depot, Baltimore, Maryland. Brief narrative relative to the port storage and water transportation offices, and the general supply depot; special orders; office circulars; travel orders.

History of the Zone Supply Office, Boston (238 pages). General history; reports of warehouses; receiving section; distribution division; salvage division; purchase branch; list of contractors with amount of contracts.

History of the General Supply Depot, Zone Seven, Chicago (10 volumes). Vol. 1, narrative history of the depot exclusive of packing house products; Vol. 2, narrative history of packing house products, purchases, and operations; Vol. 3, photographic records of depot operations; Vols. 4-7, office orders; Vols. 8 and 9, depot orders; Vol. 10, enlistment assignment orders.

War History, Office of Zone Supply Officer, New York, 1917-1919 (5 volumes). Vol. 1, organization, summary of operations, administrative division; Vol. 2, clothing and equipage division; Vol. 3, subsistence division; Vol. 4, motors and vehicles division; Vol. 5, general supplies division, raw materials division, base sorting plant, finance division.

History of the General Supply Depot, St. Louis (2 volumes). Brief narrative of operations; statistics.

Historical Report of the San Francisco Depot, Fort Mason, General Supply Depot, Zone 13, for period April 1, 1917, to April 30, 1919 (72 pages). Finance division; subsistence division; dehydrated vegetables; clothing and equipage division; manufacture of clothing and textiles; supplies division; purchase branch; salvage division; transportation branch; army transport service.

Historical Record, Office of Depot Quartermaster, Seattle, from April 6, 1917, to January 1, 1919 (60 pages). Résumé; organization; subsistence division; supplies division; clothing and equipage subdivision; warehouse and storage subdivision; property accounting subdivision; salvage branch; fuel and storage branch; transportation division; finance division; army transport service.

Historical Data pertaining to the Zone Supply Office, Washington, D. C. Office orders.

Histories of Quartermaster and other supply units. There is a history of nearly every unit and every branch of activity of the Quartermaster Corps during the war. Particular attention is directed to the following (in MS.):

History of the Office of the Director of Purchase, by Malcolm Kenneth Gordon (105 pages).

History of the Office of the Director of Storage (5 volumes). Expansion of the Quartermaster Corps; functions of traffic and storage service; distribution of supplies in the United States; conservation and reclamation; organization of the warehousing division; storage problems; inauguration of the zone system; reserve supply system; quartermaster depots; coördination of field and headquarters services; typical zone supply office; amount of clothing and equipage required; overseas supply divisions; domestic distribution division; operations control division.

History of the Subsistence Division, Office of the Director of Purchase (6 volumes). Organization; purchasing branch; allotment branch; inspection branch; service branch; planning branch; adjustment and accounts branch.

History of General Army Inventory (2 volumes).

Historical Report of the Chief Quartermaster, including a Brief Narrative of the Quartermaster Corps, American Expeditionary Forces, 1917-1919 (555 pages).

Historical Sketch of the General Supplies Division (119 pages).

Notes on the Purchase, Manufacture and Inspection of United States Army Shoes and Shoe Lasts, by Charles G. Keene (207 pages).

History of the Salvage Division, Quartermaster Corps (279 pages).

Historical Outline Showing the Organization and Operation of the Fuel and Forage Division, Office of the Quartermaster General of the Army, and of the Raw Materials Division, Office of the Director of Purchase and Storage (138 pages).

History of Motors and Vehicles Division, Quartermaster Corps, by Walter Alexander (98 pages).

Historical and Statistical Data relative to the Machinery and Engineering Materials Division (183 pages).

History of the Purchase of Precision Instruments, by Major George A. Bentley (64 pages).

History of the Bakers and Cooks Branch, Quartermaster Corps (19 pages).

Narrative Account of the Activities of the Remount Division and the Remount Service during the War (12 pages).

Historical Data relative to the Port Supply Officer, Port of New York (88 pages).

History of Port of Embarkation, Newport News, Virginia (548 pages).

History of Camp Joseph E. Johnston (877 pages).

Organization, Personnel, and Operations of the Quartermaster's Depot, Jeffersonville, Indiana. April 6, 1917-November 11, 1918 (361 pages).

Narrative of Proceedings at the Quartermaster's Depot, Jeffersonville, Indiana, with reference to the work of adjusting claims following the termination of contracts for war supplies (26 pages).

Official History, Camp Supply Depot, Camp Lewis, American Lake, Washington (70 pages).

The History of Camp Meigs (73 pages).

History of Auxiliary Remount Depot, No. 304, Camp Meade, Maryland (18 pages).

History of Auxiliary Remount Depot, No. 330, Camp Kearney, California (4 pages).

History of Auxiliary Remount Depot, No. 324, Camp McArthur, Waco, Texas (16 pages).

History of Ft. Reno Remount Depot, Oklahoma (12 pages).

Procedure and Methods Employed in the Various Procurement Zones for the Adjustment and Cancellation of War Contracts (13 pages).

Historical Report of Office of the Port Utilities Officer, Port of Embarkation, Hoboken, N. J. (199 pages).

History of the Medical Supply Depot, U.S.A., New York, prior to the entrance of the United States into the European War and during that period (22 pages).

History of Camp Alexander, Newport News, Virginia (35 pages).

WAR PLANS DIVISION

Under General Orders No. 14, War Department, February 9, 1918, the War College Division of the General Staff was organized in four branches: (1) War Plans Branch; (2) Training and Instruction Branch; (3) Legislation, Regulations, Rules Branch; (4) Historical Branch. Under General Orders No. 80, War Department, issued August 26, 1918, the designation of the War College Division was changed to War Plans Division.

TRAINING AND INSTRUCTION BRANCH

Functions

Instructions were issued in April, 1917, for the establishment of the first series of officers' training camps. A Training Committee of the War College Division was appointed in June. Late in the same year a major general in the regular army was designated as director of training. Central officers' schools were established at permanent replacement camps in June, 1918. A Committee on Education and Special Training was appointed in February, 1918, to study the needs of the various branches of the service for skilled men and technicians, to secure the coöperation of the educational institutions of the country, to represent the War Department in its relations with such institutions, and to administer such plans of special training in them as might be adopted. To accomplish the purpose for which this committeee was appointed, National Army training detachments were organized at schools and colleges throughout the country. As junior officers in the army were early in the war supplied largely from college graduates and undergraduates and as a serious shortage of officer material developed in the summer of 1918, orders were issued in August of that year for raising and maintaining by volunteer induction and drafting a Students' Army Training Corps, units of which were authorized at educational institutions which met the prescribed requirements.

Publications

Committee on Education and Special Training, a Review of its Work during 1918, by the Advisory Board (Washington, 1919, 144 pages). History and general operations; military administration; business administration.

Special Descriptive Circulars and Special Bulletins, published in 1918 by the Collegiate Section of the Committee on Education and Special Training for the guidance of instructors and other officers in the work of the Students' Army Training Corps (160 pages).

Final Report of the War Issues Course of the Students' Army Training Corps, by Frank Aydelotte, Director War Issues Course (Washington, 1919, 112 pages). Purpose and methods; Vocational Section; Collegiate Section; results.

Records

A "Report of Line Officers' Training Schools from the Declaration of War to the Discontinuance of Schools," by Henry C. Cabell (22 pages), has been mimeographed.

Two file cases contain records of officers' training camps, consisting of weekly reports, progress reports, strength reports, training schedules, and regulations.

Records of activities of the Committee on Education and Special Training and of the Students' Army Training Corps consist of various reports and miscellaneous correspondence.

HISTORICAL BRANCH

Organization and Functions

The Historical Branch of the General Staff was created in June, 1918. In August, 1921 (General Order No. 41, War Department), it was transferred to the Army War College as the Historical Section, and a year later its collections of material were consolidated with the records of the Adjutant General's Office. Its functions were to publish monographs on subjects of military importance, to supervise the historical work of the War Department and the military establishment, and to compile a general history of American participation in the war.

Publications

Economic Mobilization in the United States for the War of 1917 (Washington, 1918, 39 pages). State of industrial preparedness; Council of National Defense; shipping; food control; fuel control; War Industries Board; war trade; war finance; railroad control; labor and employment; demobilization.

A Handbook of Economic Agencies of the War of 1917 (Washington, 1919, 539 pages). This compilation is of prime importance. It sets forth, in brief form, accounts of the functions and organization of about 3000 agencies which took part in the economic mobilization.

Organization of the Services of Supply, American Expeditionary Forces (Washington, 1921, 130 pages). Organization of the line of communication; organization of headquarters, Services of Supply; the General Purchasing Board; Chemical Warfare Service; Engineer Corps; Medical Corps; Motor Transport Corps; Ordnance Department; Quartermaster Corps; Signal Corps; Transportation Corps; Renting, Requisition, and Claims Service.

A Journal of the Great War, by Charles G. Dawes (Boston, 2 volumes, 1921). Volume II contains the daily reports and the final report of the general purchasing agent, A.E.F.

Records

The records of interest for the purposes of this survey which were accumulated by the Historical Branch, but which have been transferred to the Adjutant General's Office, are in two principal groups: (1) economic mobilization, (2) Services of Supply, A.E.F.

Economic Mobilization. The Historical Branch, in the collection of data for the *Handbook of Economic Agencies,* sent questionnaires to government organizations and to the industrial agencies listed in the *Handbook.* The material which was furnished in response to the questionnaires was assembled in 3000 *dossiers* in the files of the Economic Mobilization Section. It comprises historical accounts of the organization and war activities of the various bureaus or agencies, copies of reports made by them, files of bulletins containing detailed information relative to their work, etc. Some of the material in these files has already been noted elsewhere. The following are some of the more important *dossiers,* with mention of their contents.

Chemical Alliance, Committee on Acids. A brief sketch of the organization and its war service; 30 weekly bulletins.

Economic Cables, A.E.F. These are mostly cables during 1917 and 1918 to and from Pershing and Harbord relative to beef, pork, meat, bacon, grease, petroleum, glycerin, lubricating oils, wheat, sugar, food conditions of allied, neutral, and enemy countries, etc. (140 pages).

Committee on Chemicals, Council of National Defense. A report on its war service telling of its creation, purpose, and functions performed (3 pages).—Weekly reports to the chairman of the Raw Materials Committee from May 19 to November 10, 1917.

Ordnance Department. Report of schools on industrial ordnance reservations under jurisdiction of Community Organization Branch. The schools were located at Amatol and May's Landing, New Jersey; Jacksonville, Tennessee; Muscle Shoals and U.S.N. No. 1, Alabama; Nitro, West Virginia; Perryville, Maryland; and Penniman, Virginia. The report tells of sites and buildings, books and equipment, principals and teachers, course of study, community activities, and attendance. Filed with the report is a paper entitled, "A Plan for Providing Education for Children Resident on Federal Government Reservations under the Control of the Ordnance Department of the United States Army."

War Industries Board, Conservation Division. A thick folder of papers relating to conservation plans and practices in each of the following industries: baking, delivery, shoe, clothing, garment, packing, paint and varnish, wool, hat and cap, dry goods, baby vehicle, tin, trunk and travelling goods, furnace, automobile tire, cotton thread, spool, stove, metal bedstead, waist, beds (Davenport), refrigerator, shoe carton, agricultural implement, felt, corset, casket, vacuum cleaner, chain, wagon and truck, and horse-drawn spring vehicle.

Chemical Alliance, Dyestuffs Section. A report by the secretary covering the activities of the section during 1918 (3 pages).—Fourteen of a total of twenty-two bulletins issued during 1918.—Proceedings of a joint meeting of the Dyestuff and Intermediate Section of the Chemical Alliance, the American Dye Institute, and the American Dyestuff Manufacturers Association, September 26, 1918, which discussed the subject of restricting imports of dyes for a number of years after the war.

Edgewood Arsenal, Md. A non-technical report relative to the inception of the arsenal and each of its various projects (83 pages).

General War Service Committee of the Electrical Manufacturing Industry. Two printed reports relative to organization and activities (12 pages and 15 pages).

Army Ordnance, Industrial Service Section. Final report of the Emergency Production Branch.—Summary of report of the Western Cartridge Company, Alton, Ill.—Summary of report of the Scovill Manufacturing Company, Waterbury, Conn.—Summary of report of the Winchester Repeating Arms Company, New Haven, Conn.—Summary of report of the United States Cartridge Company, Lowell, Mass.—Report on labor conditions at Remington Arms-U.M.C. plant, Ilion, N. Y.

Department of Labor, Employment Service. Organization and functions (25 pages).

Engineering Council. A report on the war activities of the council (6 pages).

War Industries Board, Explosives Division. A paper relative to the principal explosives used in the war (17 pages).

Department of Agriculture, Fertilizer Control. Notes on the work of the Fertilizer Control Board, by E. A. Goldenweiser, statistician (21 pages).

Chemical Alliance, Committee on Fertilizers. A report (10 pages).

Department of Agriculture and Food Administration. Monthly surveys as of October 1 and November 1, 1918, by the Central Bureau of Planning and Statistics. Contents of October survey: Part I, Agriculture: production activities, conservation activities, investigations for army and navy, coöperation with army and navy; Part II, Food Administration: cereals, meats, dairy products, fish, sugar export program. (*Foreword:* "The Department of Agriculture attempts to increase production by internal economy, better methods and greater production per unit, while the Food Administration deals with the requirements made upon our food supply by both this country and the allies and the relation of these requirements to our supply, with a view of creating an adequate supply to meet the more urgent needs of the allied nations. This is accomplished through price regulation, restriction of demand, and conservation. The war activities of the Department of Agriculture indicated in this report are mostly the coöperative ones, carried on primarily for the benefit of the army and navy. The Food Administration's activities are expressed by statements showing the production and requirements of the principal agricultural commodities.") October survey, 61 pages; November survey, 60 pages.

War Trade Board, Bureau of Foreign Agents. A historical memorandum (7 pages), and reports by the bureau relative to its operations from its organization, November 2, 1917, to October, 1918.

Forest Products Laboratory, Madison, Wis. A list of reports from April 1, 1917, to April 1, 1919 (112 pages).—An account of the war work of the laboratory (13 pages).

Fuel and Petroleum Statistics. A list of fuel and petroleum statistics, issued by the Statistical Clearing House, Central Bureau of Planning and Statistics, to show the principal sources of statistics on fuel and petroleum (46 pages).

Hardware Manufacturers' Organization for War Service. Booklet describing the reasons for and the methods and purposes of the organization.—Roster, issued September 1, 1918, containing lists of industries organized, list of members, and an explanation of the operations of the organization.—Bulletins Nos. 2 to 30, except Nos. 3, 17, and 24, issued from June 10 to December 21, 1918.—Report of the activities of the organization to the Chamber of Commerce of the United States by the chairman of the War Service Committee.

National Association of Importers of Hides and Skins, War Trade Committee. One hundred and nine one-page bulletins, January 24 to December 28, 1918, issued for the information of importers.

Chief of Engineers, Historical Data Section. A copy of a paper presented by Major W. C. Cattell, Engineer Corps, at a meeting of the Conference of Army and Navy Historical Workers, January 17, 1919. In this paper Major Cattell expressed what he conceived to be the purpose of the historical work of his department. Similar papers were read at other meetings of the conference.

Ordnance Department, Industrial Service Section, Housing Branch. A report, dated December 31, 1918 (34 pages). An account of the organization and activities of the Housing Branch at Aberdeen Proving Grounds, Aberdeen, Md.; Frankford Arsenal, Bridesburg, Pa.; Eddystone Rifle Plant, Eddystone, Pa.; Rock Island Arsenal, Rock Island, Ill.; Watertown Arsenal, Watertown, Mass.; Watervliet Arsenal, Troy, N. Y.; and at Bridgeport, Conn., Hammond, Ind., and Perryville, Md.

Construction Division, Industrial Service Section. A history of the section (23 pages).

Army Ordnance, Industrial Service Section. Final reports: New York (223 pages); Chicago (15 pages); Rochester, N. Y. (18 pages); Detroit, Mich. (4 pages); Bridgeport, Conn. (6 pages); Boston (9 pages); Pittsburgh, Pa. (3 pages).

Interior Department. A summary of war work by the Bureau of Mines, Geological Survey, Bureau of Education, Indian Office, Reclamation Service, Patent Office, General Land Office, and Government Hospital for the Insane (9 pages).—Separate papers relative to the war work of the Bureau of Mines (48 pages), the Bureau of Education (9 pages), and other bureaus.

United States Pig Lead Producers. "A Brief History of the War Service Committees of the United States Pig Lead Producers," prepared at the request of the Historical Branch, War Plans Division (27 pages).

Division of Military Aeronautics, Supply Section, Oil and Lubrication Branch. A history of the branch (15 pages).

War Industries Board. Lumber Section. A history of the section (9 pages).

Machine Tool Industry. An account of the activities of the machine-tool building industry during the war, by Fred H. Colvin, principal associate editor, *American Machinist* (7 pages).

United States Food Administration, Meat Division, Packers' Committee. Historical notes on war service work of the committee.

Joint Information Board on Minerals and Derivatives. A list or index of statistical and other information compiled in the office of the secretary of the board with the aid of various government organizations represented in the board (178 pages). The purpose was to indicate briefly the nature of the information available in Washington on minerals and derivatives and where it might be obtained. A large part of the information listed was collected in response to war needs. Information in standard printed works was not listed.—Minutes of meetings of this board are in the same folder.

National Adjustment Commission. A thick folder of papers and a printed report by the chairman.

Navy Department. Four numbers of a Monthly Survey (20 to 50 pages each) contain summary statements of progress in construction of naval vessels, aircraft and ordnance, and in the accumulation of ammunition and other material.—Another folder contains accounts of war activities of each of the several bureaus of the department.

Optical Glass. Report on the production of optical glass by the Bureau of Standards, Department of Commerce (10 pages).—Report on the activities of the Optical Instrument Section in connection with the war work of the Bureau of Standards (16 pages).

Ordnance. Mimeographed copy of a "Directory of Field Establishments" containing information relative to arsenals, armories, disbursing offices, field depots, general supply ordnance depots, inland traffic service, plants, proving grounds, and schools (165 pages).

Ordnance, Carriage Division. Organization and war work (21 pages).

Ordnance, Production Division. Functions and operations of the Production Division of the Ordnance Department from its establishment January 14, 1918, to its discontinuance October 23, 1918 (25 pages).

Ordnance, Gun Division. Organization and operation of the Gun Division of the Ordnance Department during the war (23 pages).

Ordnance, Procurement Division. Accounts of each of the following sections of the Procurement Division, Ordnance Department: General Control, Legal, Credits, Raw Materials, Packing Container, Explosives, Loading, Artillery, Small Arms, Equipment, Motor Equipment, Projectile, Fuse, Trench Warfare, and Miscellaneous (58 pages).

Ordnance, Supply Division. A history of the Supply Division, Ordnance Department, for the years 1917 and 1918 (53 pages).

Ordnance, Engineering Division. A history of the Engineering Division, Ordnance Department, chiefly for the year 1918 (63 pages).

Ordnance, minor divisions and sections. The historical papers relative to the organization and operations of the Ordnance Department embrace also those dealing with the Inspection Division, Property Division, Civilian Personnel Division, Small Arms Division, Equipment Division, and the Finance Section of the General Administration Bureau.

Ordnance, District Offices. Historical data relative to the organization and functions of the district ordnance offices, located at Boston, Mass.; Bridgeport, Conn.; New York and Rochester, N. Y.; Philadelphia, Pa.; Chicago, Ill.; Cleveland and Cincinnati, Ohio; Pittsburgh, Pa.; Detroit, Mich.; and Ottawa, Canada (74 pages).

Construction Division, Patriotic Promotion Section of the Administration Division. History of the Section, by its Chief, Major Newman H. Raymond (68 pages). The purpose in organizing this section was to give the employees of the Construction Division correct information with regard to the causes of the war, why the United States was in it, and the duty of the government on the various questions growing out of it. In this paper Major Raymond tells of the effects of meetings at Norfolk and Camp Eustis, Va.; Camp Grant, Ill.; Fort Dodge, Iowa; Curtis Bay, Camp Holabird, and Aberdeen, Md.; and Azalea, N. C.

Central Bureau of Planning and Statistics. A paper on its organization and functions (13 pages); proceedings of several weekly conferences of the Statistical Group and Central Bureau Staff.

["The Central Bureau of Planning and Statistics came into existence early in June of 1918, for the express purpose of preparing for the attention of the

President a conspectus of all the present war activities of the government, on which conspectus could be based a periodical checking up of actual operations and results. . . . In developing the conspectus, the Central Bureau of Planning and Statistics found it necessary to inform itself with regard to the statistical data available in the various governmental departments, and in doing so it discovered that the preparation of the conspectus involved a second and supplemental service of vital importance to the government. Investigations made in July of 1918 by representatives of the Central Bureau disclosed the fact that in the gathering and compiling of statistical data there was very considerable duplication. The industries, notably the ship-building industry, were being burdened with the answering of innumerable questionnaires, many of which sought information of a character necessitating a vast amount of clerical labor and the interruption of highly important war work. Moreover, the same questions, addressed to the same firms and individuals, would frequently appear in a number of questionnaires; and questionnaires would be sent out by one governmental agency in quest of information which had already been compiled and brought up to the minute by another. . . . The program of the Central Bureau was therefore expanded to include not only (1) the preparation of a periodic survey or conspectus of all the war activities of the government, but also (2) the organization and maintenance of a Clearing House of Statistical Information."]

Central Bureau of Planning and Statistics, Statistical Clearing House. Two bulletins: (1) List of Food Statistics, giving the most important sources of statistical information on food and telling briefly what governmental bureaus and responsible private agencies had collected on each commodity (463 pages); (2) List of Fuel and Petroleum Statistics, showing the principal sources, both original and secondary, of statistics on fuel and petroleum and the offices in Washington from which the tabulations may be obtained (46 pages). A copy of each of these bulletins is in the Library of Congress.

Weekly Statistical News, September 10, 1918, to June 12, 1919. A periodical (about 15 pages in each number), issued by the Central Statistical Clearing House for the information of government statistical agencies.

War Industries Board, Resources and Conversion Section. A report by the Regional Advisor, Region No. 3 (New York), on the activities of his office (11 pages).—Reports for other regions are in the same folder.

Council of National Defense, State Councils Section. Bulletins, form letters, and news articles, signed by the chief of the section and addressed to the several State Councils of Defense. They contain chiefly information and recommendations.

Council of National Defense, Commission on Training Camp Activities. Bulletins issued by the chief of the State Councils Section and sent to the State Councils of Defense.

War Industries Board, Division of Statistics. Bulletins Nos. 3-8 (February-May, 1918) on war contracts. The material in these bulletins was derived from answers to the following questions addressed to firms having war contracts.

1. At what per cent of its full capacity is your plant operating?
2. If you are behind on your scheduled deliveries on war orders, do you attribute this to labor troubles, inability to secure labor, inability to secure materials, car shortage, coal shortage, or other causes?
3. How much other war business and of what sort could you handle in your present plant in addition to that which you now have?

Silk Association of America. Forty-Sixth Annual Report containing an account of the coöperation of the association with the government during the war (126 pages).

Small arms and ammunition. A paper relative to the organization and operation of the Committee on Small Arms and Ammunition of the Munitions Standards Board (17 pages).

Smithsonian Institution. A memorandum relative to the war work performed under the various branches of the Smithsonian Institution (10 pages).

Southern Pine Emergency Bureau. An account of the formation, organization, and activities of the Southern Pine Emergency Bureau (9 pages).—A printed report on the distribution of orders to June 30, 1918 (8 pages).

Spruce Production Corporation. Final report of the Contract Board for the cancellation of contracts (28 pages).—Final report of the Sales Board (8 pages).—General Orders of the War Department relative to spruce production, etc. (56 pages).

Spruce Production Division. War Department bulletins relative to spruce production (196 pages).—History of the division (300 pages).

Services of Supply, A.E.F. The records of the Services of Supply, A.E.F., were shipped from France in about 3000 filing drawers and distributed among the appropriate services of the War Department (Quartermaster, Ordnance, Engineer Corps, etc.). The histories of the various services, prepared under the supervision of the Historical Branch, and the records of the General Purchasing Agent were deposited with the Historical Branch. They include the following documents:

History of Transportation Corps, A.E.F. A detailed study of organization, personnel, railroad and port operation, and engineering activity, supported by copies of original documents from D.G.T. files.

Report of Commanding General, S.O.S., to Commanding General, A.E.F., Tours, May 25, 1918. Review of activities of S.O.S., supported by special reports from chiefs of supply services.

Report of Board on Ports appointed by Commanding General, A.E.F., en route to France. Recommends the use of Atlantic ports of France, specifying those immediately available and troops and equipment necessary.

Memorandum from Major General J. G. Harbord to Commanding General, A.E.F., May, 1919. Refers to conditions when Commanding General, A.E.F., and Staff arrived in France in June, 1917. Specific reference deals with railroad situation and the rail lines of communication then available. This memorandum was dictated personally by General Harbord while he was Commanding General, S.O.S.

History of G-1, S.O.S.

History of G-2, S.O.S.

History of G-4, S.O.S.

History of the Ordnance Department, S.O.S.

History of the Signal Corps, S.O.S.

History of the Corps of Engineers, S.O.S.

History of the Motor Transport Corps.

Report of the General Purchasing Agent.

Report of the American member of the Military Board of Allied Supply.

A collection of histories of each geographical section of the S.O.S. except Base Section No. 9. These histories were prepared by section historians, under the supervision of the section commanders, for the Historical Section, General Staff, S.O.S. They include a description of the section and the activities therein of the various services as well as non-technical descriptions of the important projects.

ORDNANCE DEPARTMENT

Organization and Functions

The function of the Ordnance Department was to supply the army with matériel and for the performance of this function it was organized in the following divisions: (1) Administrative, (2) Estimates and Requirements, (3) Engineering, (4) Procurement, (5) Inspection, (6) Supply, (7) Nitrate, (8) Office of Director of Arsenals. For the supervision of productive operations in the field, the United States and Canada were divided into thirteen ordnance districts, each under a district chief responsible to the Chief of Ordnance and with headquarters in one of the principal cities. The operations of the divisions in Washington were for the most part administrative or technical; the operations of the district offices were primarily of an economic character.

Publications

Report of the Chief of Ordnance to the Secretary of War, 1917 (Washington, 1917, 47 pages). Equipment; receipts and expenditures.

Report of the Chief of Ordnance . . . 1918 (Washington, 1918, 30 pages). Reorganization; Procurement Division; Production Division; Supply Division; expenditures.

Report of the Chief of Ordnance . . . 1919 (Washington, 1919, 97 pages). A review of operations from April, 1917, to November, 1918; the ordnance problem; estimated requirements; Ordnance Claims Board; Ordnance Salvage Board; ordnance schools; industrial service; district offices.

Ordnance and the World War, a Contribution to the History of American Preparedness, by Major General William Crozier (New York, 1920, 292 pages). A reply to criticisms with regard to progress made in the procurement of ordnance and ordnance stores during the early months of the war. [Unofficial.]

Estimates and Requirements Division (Washington, 1919, 70 pages). Organization and operation of the division during the war.

Definition of "Cost" pertaining to Contracts (Washington, 1917, 12 pages).

Price List of Ordnance and Ordnance Stores (Washington, 1917, 54 pages).

Ordnance Property Regulations (Washington, 1917, 135 pages). Purchase of ordnance property; manufacture of ordnance property; sales of ordnance property.

Cost of Manufacture of Guns, etc., in Government Arsenals. Letter from the Secretary of War transmitting statement submitted by the Chief of Ordnance of the costs of all types and experimental manufacture of guns and other articles and the average cost of the several classes of guns and other articles manufactured by the government at the several arsenals (1918, House Document 1373, 65th Congress, 3rd Session, 128 pages).

Cost of Guns, etc. Letter from the Acting Secretary of War transmitting a letter submitting statements of the cost of guns and other articles manufactured by the government at the several arsenals during the fiscal year 1919 (House Document 496, 66th Congress, 2nd Session, 158 pages).

History of District Offices (Washington, 1920). In 12 pamphlets, one for each office; the introduction (22 pages) is the same in all pamphlets. The remainder of each pamphlet is devoted to a brief narrative of the operations of the particular district, showing what ordnance was produced, by what firms, where these were located, etc. Some of the major operations were for the production of the following:

Baltimore District: shrapnel in the city of Baltimore; amatol at Perryville, Md.; guncotton at Hopewell, Va.

Boston District: cartridges at Lowell, Mass.; howitzer carriages at Worcester, Mass.

Bridgeport District: machine guns, aircraft guns, rifles, and bayonets.

Chicago District: big guns at Madison, Wis.; shells at Chicago.

Cincinnati District: tanks, explosives, and small-arms ammunition.

Cleveland District: railway mounts at Alliance, Ohio; gun carriages at Toledo; tanks at Dayton; shell fuses at Cleveland.

Detroit District: howitzer recuperators, shells, tanks, artillery caissons, and helmets.

New York District: equipment, cannon, small arms, and explosives.

Philadelphia District: gun forgings, railway mounts, rifles, explosives, and helmets.

Pittsburgh District: guns, shells, and optical glass.

Rochester District: optical glass, small arms, and picric acid.

St. Louis District: shells, small arms, picric acid, and kelp.

"History of the Aberdeen Proving Ground," by Major F. P. Lindh (in *American Machinist*, Vol. 50, Nos. 10, 11, and 13, March, 1919). [Unofficial.]

Munitions Manufacture in the Philadelphia Ordnance District, by William Bradford Williams (Philadelphia, 1921, 674 pages). Production; inspection; achievements of some of the manufacturers; settlement of claims. [Unofficial.]

Ordnance Schools during the Period of the War (Washington, 1919, 48 pages). Supply schools; inspection division training schools; motor instruction schools; welding schools; education and training in the Ordnance Department.

The Manufacture of Optical Glass and of Optical Systems, a War-

Time Problem (Washington, 1921, 309 pages). Characteristics of optical glass; raw materials; furnaces and furnace operations; etc.

Report on the Fixation and Utilization of Nitrogen, prepared by the Nitrate Division with the assistance of the Fixed Nitrogen Research Laboratory, Department of Agriculture (Washington, 1922, 353 pages). Includes a discussion of the nitrogen situation of the world together with pertinent world statistics; a discussion of the history, chemistry, and construction and operating costs of the various nitrogen fixation processes; and a history and description of the United States government nitrate plants.

Records

Ordnance Department Correspondence File, "a subjective decimal classification for arranging and filing Ordnance Department correspondence in conjunction with the War Department Correspondence File" (Washington, 1918, 62 pages).

In the Historical Branch of the Ordnance Department were assembled the data from which to prepare a list of the firms in each State to which ordnance contracts were awarded, together with statistics showing the kind and amount of ordnance produced by each firm.

CONSTRUCTION DIVISION

Organization and Functions

On May 16, 1917, the officer in charge of the Construction and Repair Division of the Quartermaster Corps was detailed to the exclusive work of cantonment construction; the unit thus established was officially designated, in an order of February 12, 1918, as the Cantonment Division; and, by an order of March 13 following, the Cantonment Division, together with the Construction and Repair Division of the Quartermaster Corps, was constituted the Construction Division of the Army.

The business of the Cantonment Division was the construction of the sixteen cantonments for the National Army and sixteen tent camps for the National Guard troops. The functions of the Construction Division were to secure funds for, design, build, maintain, repair, and operate the utilities of all construction projects recommended by a line command or staff service and approved by the

Secretary of War, within the continental and territorial limits of the United States, except fortifications and construction authorized by river and harbor legislation.

The division was organized in seven subdivisions, namely: Administrative, Procurement, Contracts, Engineering, Building, Accounting, and Utilities. The Building Division and the Utilities Division were essentially executive in character; the other five were more of the nature of advisory bodies. The Building Division managed all new construction; the Utilities Division all maintenance, repair, and operation of utilities. These two divisions selected the personnel and formed the local organizations through which the work in the field was performed, awarded contracts, and requisitioned materials, but they secured their authority and funds, the assignment of their personnel, plans for their work, and expert advice from the other divisions. For example, personnel and funds were secured through, or on the advice of, the Administrative Division; estimates, plans, and specifications through the Engineering Division; the approval and interpretation of their contracts from the Contracts Division; their building materials and equipment, except when provided by the contractor, from the Procurement Division; and their system of disbursing, accounting, and auditing from the Accounting Division. The chief of the division was directly under the Chief of Staff but was governed rather by the Operations Division of the General Staff.

Publications

Annual Report of the Chief of the Construction Division for the Fiscal Year ended June 30, 1918 (Washington, 1919, 107 pages). Cantonment construction.

Annual Report of the Chief of the Construction Division . . . 1919 (Washington, 1920, 319 pages). New construction; contracts; lists of contractors; value of orders placed.

Annual Report of the Chief of the Construction Division to the Secretary of War, 1920 (Washington, 1920, 83 pages). History of the division.

National Army Cantonments, Plans, and Photographs, June, 1918 (Washington, 1918). A compilation of plans of the sixteen national army cantonments, together with photographs showing typical buildings and their construction, selected from photographs sent from the various cantonments.

The Work of the Construction Division of the Army (Philadelphia, 1920, 43 pages; reprinted from *Journal of the Engineers Club of Philadelphia*, March, 1920). An article written with the permission of the Secretary of War, by Lieutenant Colonel E. B. Morden, U.S.A., the constructing quartermaster at Philadelphia; with a foreword by Brigadier General R. C. Marshall, Jr., U.S.A., chief of the Construction Division of the Army; and with a graphical data section compiled under the supervision of Colonel G. R. Solomon, U.S.A., chief of the Engineering Branch of the Construction Division.

The Constructor, a semi-monthly publication issued by the Construction Division from July 5 to November 5, 1918, "for the purpose of coordinating and solidifying the various branches and sections." Among leading articles are the following: "Lumber Yard Operated by Construction Division to save Government Quarter Million Dollars Annually"; "The Necessity for Cost Accounting"; "Labor"; "Engineering for the Construction Division of the Army"; "Conservation of Waste Products at Camps"; "Coöperation in the Management of Camp Utilities"; "Building up and Maintaining Morale of Workers"; "Pertinent Paragraphs about the Construction Division."

Records

The Construction Division has compiled and preserved a record of its organization, functions, and operations during the war in 573 typewritten volumes. A general history in one volume (265 pages), is composed of three parts: (1) cantonment construction from May, 1917, to March, 1918; (2) other emergency construction from October 5, 1917, to November 11, 1918; (3) demobilization. The histories of the seven branches or subdivisions constitute Appendix I, and the histories or completion reports of the construction projects constitute Appendix II. A résumé, in 17 volumes of 200 pages each, covers both the general history and the completion reports. The Historical Section, Army War College, has a copy of the general history and of most of the completion reports.

The history of the Administration Division (Appendix I-1) surveys the operations of the Office Service Section, Organization and Methods Section, Industrial Service Section, Labor Procurement Section, Patriotic Promotion Section, and Protection and Investigation Section. The history of the Engineering Division (Appendix I-2, 2 volumes) surveys the operations of the Camp Planning Section, the Expediting Section, the Hospital Section, the Camp Transportation Facilities Section, the Electrical Power and Illuminating Section, the Heating, Plumbing, Bakery, and Laundry Equipment Section, the Mechanical Equipment Section, the Refrigeration Section, the Sewage and Sanitation Section, and the Water Supply Section. The history of the Building Division (Appendix I-5) is presented under the following heads: southern camps and quartermaster shops, northern camps and general hospitals, storage and terminals, ordnance depots, manufacturing and proving plants, equipment and materials. The histories of the Contracts Division, Procurement Division, Accounting Division, and Utilities or Maintenance and Repair Divisions are brief.

A general report contains organization charts, lists of projects, and tabulated statements relative to appropriations, expenditures, allotments, labor, and procurement of materials.

The history or completion report of each of the several hundred projects deals with the following matters: attitude and activities of local people, equipment and tools, fire prevention, heating, labor and labor difficulties, housing and feeding laborers, materials, railways and railway construction, roads and road construction, sanitation, sewage, drainage, and water supply. The narrative is followed by plans and photographs. For a list of projects see "Project Directory," as of December 1, 1919, in *Report of Chief of Construction Division, 1919*, pp. 285-305.

TRANSPORTATION SERVICE

Organization and Functions

The Transportation Service, a combination of the Embarkation Service and the Inland Traffic Service, grew out of conditions demanding a means of preventing the congestion of traffic, especially at ports of embarkation, which resulted from the decentralized system of the Transportation Division, Quartermaster Corps. The Embarkation Service was formed under General Orders, No. 102, War Department, August 4, 1917, to coördinate shipments of munitions and supplies as well as troop movements to Europe, to supervise movements of supplies from points of origin to ports of embarkation, to control the employment of trans-Atlantic transports, and to arrange with the navy for convoy service. The Inland Traffic Service was established as a branch of the Purchase, Storage, and Traffic Division, in January, 1918, to exercise control over matters pertaining to routing and inland transportation of all troops and property by whatever means of transport, and the director of the service was *ex officio* chairman of the Priorities Committee of the War Department. The Embarkation Service and Inland Traffic Service were combined in March, 1919, to form the Transportation Service, which, in the following month, was charged with all transportation activities of the War Department except those pertaining to the Motor Transport Corps. It was organized in four main divisions, the Administrative Division, the Water Transportation Division, the Rail Transportation Division, and the Animal Drawn Transportation Division. The chief of the service was in liaison with the Chief of Naval Operations; the Water Transportation Division, in liaison with the United States Shipping Board; and the Railroad Transportation Division, in liaison with the United States Railroad Administration.

Publications

Annual Report of the Chief of Transportation Service, 1919 (Washington, 1919, 190 pages). Conditions leading to the organization of the service; results obtained by Embarkation and Inland Traffic services; troop movement; return troop movement; Rail Transportation Division, organization and operations; Water Transportation Division; statistics.

Annual Report of the Chief of Transportation Service, 1920 (Washington, 1920, 64 pages). Field organization; marine operations; statistics.

The Road to France: The Transportation of Troops and Military Supplies, 1917-1918, by Benedict Crowell, Assistant Secretary of War and Director of Munitions, 1917-1920, and Robert Forrest Wilson, formerly Captain, U.S. Army (New Haven and London, 1921, 2 volumes, 675 pages). Troop movement; war freight problem and its solution; the Embarkation Service; the process of embarkation; troop ships; the new merchant marine; quest for cargo tonnage; the Shipping Control Committee; convoying; marine camouflage. [Unofficial.]

Records

The records of the Transportation Service embrace correspondence, reports, memoranda, and statistical data relative to every major operation of the organization. The following items are sufficient for illustration:

A copy of the survey of all vessels under the American flag made at the beginning of the war by a Joint Board of Maritime Affairs to determine their suitability for use by the government.

Memoranda and correspondence relative to the survey of German and Austrian interned vessels, preparation for repairing damage done by the Germans, and their conversion for use as transports.

Correspondence and memoranda leading up to the acquisition by the War Department of the steamships *Northern Pacific* and *Great Northern,* together with reports and data pertaining to these vessels.

Memoranda and correspondence covering the establishment of the ports of embarkation and port terminals.

Memoranda and correspondence relative to the shipment of heavy supplies, such as motor vehicles and railway engines.

Memoranda and correspondence relative to the shipment of explosives and gasolene, and reports pertaining to each vessel used for these purposes.

Correspondence and agreements with the British government and commercial lines of other countries pertaining to the use of vessels for the Army Transport Service.

Data relative to the dispatch of the first convoy of American vessels and subsequent convoys of mixed ships.

Correspondence relative to the chartering of American commercial vessels for the return of the troops from France, together with charters and data pertaining to the individual vessels acquired in this manner.

Correspondence and memoranda relative to the construction by commercial shipbuilders of harbor boats, mine planters, barges, and tankers.

Correspondence and memoranda pertaining to special problems in life saving, including ideas and inventions of private individuals.

Charts showing transports in the service.

Lists of vessels in the transport service.

Records of each vessel showing investigation of accidents, technical data, passenger lists, manifests, etc.

Correspondence and memoranda relative to the organization of the

Inland Traffic Service, and the movement of troops and supplies in co-ordination with the United States Railroad Administration.

Data relative to troop and equipment movements and the movement of supplies by freight and by express.

Correspondence and data relative to the establishment of shuttle train movements at large camps, munition plants, and manufacturing establishments making war material.

Correspondence and data relative to tank cars for the movement of acids and oils.

MOTOR TRANSPORT CORPS

Creation, Organization, and Functions

The War Department procured its first automotive machine in 1903. It had 89 such machines when disturbances on the Mexican border, in 1916, afforded an occasion for demonstrating the efficiency and necessity of the motor truck for army transportation. Following the entrance of the United States into the World War, the Ordnance Department, Corps of Engineers, Signal Corps, and Medical Corps of the army entered into a wasteful competition in the procurement of a confusing variety of automotive equipment. A remedy was attempted April 18, 1918, by the issue of Special Orders No. 91 and General Orders No. 38. Special Orders No. 91 appointed a board of officers "to make a study of types of motor vehicles to be used in all branches of the service and to recommend to the Chief of Staff all special designs of adopted types necessitated by the peculiar requirements of the various bureaus, with a view to reducing the number of types and securing a maximum interchangeability of parts." General Orders No. 38 established a Motor Transport Service as a part of the Quartermaster Corps to coöperate with the standardization board and to have charge of the purchase, procurement, maintenance, repair, and storage of all motor vehicles except tractors of the caterpillar type. Four months later, August 15, 1918, the Motor Transport Corps was created for "the existing emergency" by General Orders No. 75, with functions enumerated as follows: (1) technical supervision of all motor vehicles except tractors of the caterpillar type and tanks; (2) design, production, procurement, reception, storage, maintenance and replacement of motor vehicles, and accounting for same; (3) design, production, procurement, storage and supply of spare and repair parts, tools, accessories and supplies of motor vehicles, and accounting for same; (4) establishment and operation of all Motor Transport garages, parks, depots, and repair shops; (5) procurement, organization, and technical training of Motor Transport Corps personnel; (6) salvage and evacuation of damaged motor vehicles; (7) operation, in accordance with instructions from the proper commanding officer, of groups of motor vehicles of the first class, *i.e.*, cargo-carrying and passenger-carrying motor vehicles used for general transportation purposes; (8) preparation of plans for hauling cargo and personnel over military roads; (9) procurement, supply, replacement, and preliminary training of personnel for the operation of motor vehicles other than those of the first class. The control of procurement and purchases was returned to the Quartermaster Corps by Circular No. 87, Purchase, Storage, and Traffic Division, September 5, 1918.

The Motor Transport Corps was organized in four divisions: (1) Executive Division, charged with the issue of orders, bulletins, and circulars, the preparation of estimates, with action upon surveys and property questions, and with the training of personnel; (2) Service Division, charged with the collection and compilation of historical data and statistics, with the consideration of questions of policy and efficiency, and with changes in design and specifications of motor vehicles; (3) Operations Division, charged with the registration of all motor vehicles belonging to the army, with the reception, assignment, transfer, and storage of serviceable and unserviceable motor vehicles, with the control of motor convoys, and with the marking, mapping, and publishing of approved road routes and traffic control regulations; (4) Maintenance Division, charged with repair of motor vehicles for the army, with requisitioning and distributing spare parts, materials, and equipment, with the operation of repair shops, depots, and garages, and with the salvaging of vehicles and parts.

For field service the continental United States was divided into six districts, Eastern, Southeastern, South Central, Southwestern, North Central, and Northwestern.

Publications

Report of the Chief of the Motor Transport Corps to the Secretary of War, 1919 (Washington, 1920, 37 pages). Evolution of the Motor Transport Corps; organization; field service; executive division; service division; operating division; maintenance division; documents; statistics.

Report of the Chief of the Motor Transport Corps . . . 1920 (Washington, 1920, 12 pages). Training; supply; repair; salvage; standardization.

Manual of the Motor Transport Corps, A.E.F., Services of Supply, October, 1918 (n.p., n.d.). Supply system; repair system; salvage system; organization of transport work.

Regulations (Tentative) for Motor Truck Transportation, Quartermaster Corps, U.S. Army, 1917 (Washington, 1917, 54 pages).

Records

The records of greatest historical value have been segregated to some extent and classified under the following heads:

Initial procurement of motor trucks, automobiles, motorcycles, and bicycles for the army. Reports of progress and delivery. Schedules for delivery overseas.

Standardization of motor vehicles and material. History of the development of the Standard "B" Truck.

Organization of repair shops in each of the districts of the United States and in the areas overseas. Organization, training, and equipping of repair units.

Projects for delivery of motor vehicles overland from the factories to seaports, resulting in the establishment of motor convoys. These records contain reports of the convoys and histories of the two special trans-continental convoys from Washington, D. C., to California.

Early procurement of supplies of spare parts and equipment for repair shops overseas. This function was later performed by the Director of Purchase and Storage.

Investigations and proceedings with regard to requirements and methods of supply of motor equipment and repair material overseas.

Tests of all kinds of motor vehicles.

Development of occupational requirements. Organization of training schools for Motor Transport personnel as chauffeurs and mechanics. Development of motion pictures, charts, and instruction books for training purposes.

An official history of the Motor Transport Corps in two manuscript volumes (2000 pages) has been prepared. About 800 pages deal with the activities of the corps in the United States; the other 1200 pages are based on a third volume, more technical in character, entitled, "History of the Motor Transport Corps in A.E.F."

CORPS OF ENGINEERS

The major operations of the Corps of Engineers during the war were with the American Expeditionary Forces in France and an account of those operations is contained in the *Historical Report of the Chief Engineer, Including all Operations of the Engineer Department, American Expeditionary Forces, 1917-1919* (Washington, 1919, 437 pages). There are sixty-eight appendices to this history which were not published.

Among other unpublished records are thirty-six temporarily bound volumes of monthly reports on operations of engineer organizations both in the United States and in France, voluminous reports on the Engineer Depot at Camp Humphreys, and historical narratives or historical and statistical data relative to each engineer organization.

SIGNAL CORPS

A review of the operations of the Signal Corps during the entire period of the war is contained in the *Report of the Chief Signal Officer to the Secretary of War, 1919* (Washington, 1919, 547 pages). This report was based upon two unpublished histories: "A History of the Signal Corps in the A.E.F." (2000 typed pages), and "A History of the Signal Corps in the United States."

AIR SERVICE

Creation, Organization, and Functions

"To increase the efficiency of the aviation service of the Army," Congress, by act of July 18, 1914, created the Aviation Section of the Signal Corps. To advise the Secretary of the Navy and the Chief Signal Officer of the Army with respect to the purchase and production of aircraft, Congress, by act of October 1, 1917, created an Aircraft Board. A separation of the Aviation Section from the Signal Corps was begun in April, 1918, and by executive order of

May 21, 1918, the aviation service was organized in two divisions, (1) Division of Military Aeronautics, and (2) Bureau of Aircraft Production. The Division of Military Aeronautics was charged with the supervision of the operation and maintenance of all military aircraft. The Bureau of Aircraft Production, the chief of which was the chairman of the Aircraft Board, was given complete and exclusive jurisdiction and control over the production of airplanes, airplane engines, and aircraft production for the use of the army. The bureau was organized in seven divisions: Executive, Engineering, Production, Spruce Production, Procurement, Finance, and Advisory and Consulting. To expedite the financing of spruce production, the United States Spruce Production Corporation was formed in August, 1918. In March, 1919, the principal functions of the Division of Military Aeronautics and the Bureau of Aircraft Production were merged to form the Air Service, and by the army reorganization act of June 4, 1920, the Air Service was made a coordinate branch of the line. The Bureau of Aircraft Production, the United States Spruce Production Corporation, and the Air Service Claims Board were retained as parts of the reorganized service only so long as was required for the completion of their financial business.

Publications

Report of the Director of Military Aeronautics, U.S. Army, to the Secretary of War, 1918 (Washington, 1918, 12 pages). Traces the development of the organization of the Air Service from 1914.

Report of the Bureau of Aircraft Production, 1918 (Washington, 1918, 11 pages). Organization and operations of the bureau.

Report of the Director of Air Service to the Secretary of War, 1920 (Washington, 1920, 49 pages). Division of Military Aeronautics, Bureau of Aircraft Production, United States Spruce Production Corporation, and Claims Board.

History of Spruce Production Division, United States Army (n.p., n.d., 126 pages). Labor question; traffic problem; legal problem; costs; accomplishments.

History of the Supply Section, Division of Military Aeronautics (Washington, 1919, 45 pages). Liabilities incurred; achievements in the United States; overseas construction; Traffic Section; Finance Branch; Motor Transport Branch.

Aircraft Production Facts, by G. W. Mixter and H. H. Emmons (Washington, 1919, 106 pages). Production of aviation engines; production of airplanes; kite balloons and the balloon cloth problem.

Records

The Air Service has prepared for publication a history of the Bureau of Aircraft Production in two volumes, and many supporting documents have been assembled. The preparation of a history of the Division of Military Aeronautics was begun, but little progress had been made with it, other than the assembly of documents, when it was discontinued. A provisional history of the Air Service, A.E.F., was compiled in France in 269 volumes and the working of this into a finished product was under way in 1920 but was discontinued in 1921.

The records of the Air Service, A.E.F., comprise orders, bulletins, correspondence, memoranda, and records of training, supply and property, and include the original files of the headquarters of the various tactical and strategical units, and the records of supply depots, instruction centers, etc. The following items taken from an incomplete list illustrate their classification:

Records of the Second Aviation Instruction Center.
Records of the Third Aviation Instruction Center.
Records of the Seventh Aviation Instruction Center
Records of Headquarters 1st Air Depot, Zone of Advance.
Records of Airplanes Acceptance and Replacement Department.
Records of Headquarters, Second Pursuit Group, 1st Army.
Records of Headquarters, Seventh Corps, Air Service.
Records of Headquarters, Fourth Pursuit Group.
Records of Headquarters, Fifth Pursuit Group.
Records of Headquarters, Observation Group, 1st Army.
Records of Headquarters, Air Service, 2nd Army.
Records of the Information Group Headquarters, Air Service, A.E.F.
Records of Air Service Representative, G.H.Q., A.E.F.
Records of Air Service Headquarters, Paris (26 file cases).
Records of Air Service Headquarters, Tours (18 file cases).
Special Orders pertaining to the Third Aviation Instruction Center, Headquarters Zone of Advance, and various other stations.
Records of the Second Aviation Instruction Center, Tours.
Records from Air Service Production Center No. 2, Romorantin.

Records of the Design and Projects Division.

Miscellaneous records of Air Service stations.

Cablegrams filed chronologically and by subjects in bound volumes.

CHEMICAL WARFARE SERVICE

Creation, Organization, and Functions

The Chemical Warfare Service was created under General Order No. 62, War Department, June 28, 1918, by a consolidation in one bureau of functions that had previously been performed by the Bureau of Mines, the Experiment Station at American University, the Chemical Service Section of the National Army, the Gas Defense Training Section of the Corps of Engineers, the Gas and Flame Troops of the Corps of Engineers, the Ordnance Department, and the Sanitary Corps of the Medical Department.

The principal divisions of the service within the United States were originally: (1) Research Division, at American University, Yale University, the University of Ohio, and the University of Wisconsin; (2) Development Division, in charge of development of manufacturing processes for products approved by the Research Division, at Cleveland, Ohio; (3) Gas Defense Division, in charge of the production of gas masks and other defensive appliances, at Long Island City, N. Y.; (4) Gas Offense Division, in charge of the production of toxic gases and other substances used offensively in gas warfare, at Baltimore and Edgewood, Md.; (5) Medical Division, at Washington, D. C.; (6) Proving Grounds in New Jersey. There were also important activities in California, Massachusetts, Michigan, Tennessee, and West Virginia.

Publications

Report of the Chemical Warfare Service, 1918 (Washington, 1918, 7 pages). Creation, organization, and functions of the service.

Report of the Director of Chemical Warfare Service, 1919 (Washington, 1920, 72 pages). Organization, functions, statistics.

Annual Report of the Chief of the Chemical Warfare Service for the Fiscal Year ending June 30, 1920 (Washington, 1920, 42 pages).

Chemical Warfare, by Amos A. Fries, Chief, Chemical Warfare Service, and Clarence J. West, National Research Council (New York, 1921,

445 pages). Chlorine, phosgene, mustard gas, arsenic derivatives, carbon monoxide, development of the gas mask, absorbents, peace-time uses of gas.

Records

The Chemical Warfare Service has compiled several volumes of historical material of which those most pertinent to this survey are as follows:

History of the Chemical Warfare Service, by Wilder D. Bancroft (300 pages). A résumé of activities in the United States other than those of the Defense Division. Indexed.

History of the Administration Division, Chemical Warfare Service, U.S.A. (10 pages).

Final Report of the Development Division, Chemical Warfare Service, U.S.A. Defense Section (6 volumes); Offense Section (2 volumes).

Final Report of the Gas Defense Division, Chemical Warfare Service, U.S.A. (59 volumes). Many documents are annexed to the text; maps and charts; index.

Final Report of the Gas Offense Division, Chemical Warfare Service, U.S.A. (12 volumes). Maps, charts, and documents; index.

Vol.   1. Shell Programs and Gas Production; History of Outside Plants; Description of Chemical Processes.

Vol. 1A. Chlorine Plant.

Vol.   2. Water Supply System; Sewer System; Steam and Air Lines; Roads; Railroads.

Vol.   3. Chemical Plants; Temporary Structures.

Vol.   4. Filling Plants.

Vol.   5. Base Hospital; Permanent Barracks.

Vol.   6. Bush River Power House; Transmission and Distribution Lines.

Vol.   7. Cost Data on Electrical Installations A.

Vol.   8. Cost Data on Electrical Installations B.

Vol.   9. General Historical Sketches.

Vol. 10. Kingsport Plant.

Vol. 11. Hastings Plant.

History of the Proving Division, Chemical Warfare Service, U.S.A. Brief.

History of the Training Division, Chemical Warfare Service, U.S.A. Six parts, maps, charts, and index.

History of the Chemical Warfare Service, A.E.F. Fifteen parts with maps and charts.

The voluminous files of the Chemical Warfare Service contain daily, weekly, monthly, and annual reports on a variety of operations; progress reports, efficiency reports, financial reports; reports relative to manufacturers, procurement orders, sales, and shipping; correspondence relative to such matters as the manufacture, lining, filling, shipping, storage, and assembling the component parts of gas shells; and correspondence relative to inventions, the business standing of firms, and the offers of firms to furnish supplies.

MEDICAL DEPARTMENT

Expansion and Functions

The Medical Corps, Dental Corps, Veterinary Corps, Sanitary Corps, and Army Nurse Corps, constituting the Medical Department, were enlarged during the war by the absorption of the major part of the medical, surgical, and nursing professions in the United States. The principal functions of the department were five in number: (1) the physical examination of the men who voluntarily enlisted or were drafted into the military service; (2) the expansion of hospital facilities from those required by an army of less than 100,000 to the needs of an army twenty times as large; (3) the procurement and distribution of medical and hospital supplies, a large portion of which prior to 1914 had been imported; (4) the protection of the fighting forces from preventable diseases; (5) treatment of the sick and wounded.

Publications

Report of the Surgeon General, U.S. Army, to the Secretary of War, 1918 (Washington, 1918, 735 pages). Physical examinations; conditions at each of the mobilization camps; Division of Sanitation; medical and hospital supplies; Division of Laboratories and Infectious Diseases; Dental Service; Division of Veterinary Corps; Division of Army Nurse Corps.

Report of the Surgeon General, U.S. Army . . . 1919 (Washington, 1919, 2 volumes, 2167 pages). Descriptive and statistical matter regarding each camp in the United States; statistics on influenza and pneumonia; information regarding sanitation activities; reports of hospitals.

Defects Found in Drafted Men, by Albert G. Love, M.D., and Charles

B. Davenport (Washington, 1919, 359 pages). Statistical information compiled from the draft records showing the physical condition of the men registered and examined in pursuance of the requirements of the selective service act.

Regulations Governing Physical Examinations, prepared by the Surgeon General and prescribed by the President under act of May 18, 1917 (Washington, 1917, 12 pages).

The Medical Department of the United States Army in the World War:

Vol. 1. *The Surgeon General's Office,* prepared under the direction of Major General M. W. Ireland, M.D., Surgeon General of the Army, by Colonel Charles Lynch, M.C., Lieutenant Colonel Frank W. Weed, M.C., and Loy McAfee, A.M., M.D. (Washington, 1923, 1389 pages).

Vol. 5. *Military Hospitals in the United States,* prepared under the direction of Major General M. W. Ireland, M.D., Surgeon General of the Army, by Lieutenant Colonel Frank W. Weed, M.C., U.S. Army (Washington, 1923, 857 pages).

Vol. 11. *Surgery.* Part 2, by Lieutenant Colonel Edward K. Dunham, M.C., and six others (Washington, 1924, 827 pages).

Vol. 15. *Statistics.* Part 1, Army Anthropology, prepared under the direction of M. W. Ireland, M.D., Surgeon General of the Army, by Charles B. Davenport and Albert G. Love, Major, M.C., U.S.A. (Washington, 1921, 633 pages).

Other volumes of this history have been announced as follows:

Vol. 2. Administration, American Expeditionary Forces (Central Administration); Hospitalization.

Vol. 3. Finance and Supply (United States; American Expeditionary Forces).

Vol. 4. Camps, Posts, and Ports.

Vol. 6. Sanitation (United States; American Expeditionary Forces).

Vol. 7. Instruction and Training.

Vol. 8. Field Operations, American Expeditionary Forces.

Vol. 9. Communicable and Other Diseases.

Vol. 10. Neuropsychiatry.

Vol. 12. Roentgenology.

Vol. 13. Physical Reconstruction; Nursing Service.

Vol. 14. Gas Poisoning.

Vol. 15. Statistics. Part 2. Medical and Casual Statistics.

Unofficial Hospital Histories

The Story of U.S. Army Base Hospital No. 5, by a "Member of the Unit" (Cambridge, 1919, 118 pages).

Base Hospital No. 9, A.E.F.: A History of the Work of the New York Hospital Unit during Two Years of Active Service, by Raymond Shiland Brown (New York, 1920, 221 pages).

History of the Pennsylvania Hospital Unit (Base Hospital No. 10, U.S.A.) in the Great War (New York, 1921, 253 pages).

History and Roster of the United States Army General Hospital No. 16 (New Haven, 1919, 39 pages).

History of Base Hospital No. 18, American Expeditionary Forces (Johns Hopkins Unit) (Baltimore, 1919, 134 pages).

A History of Base Hospital No. 32, by Benjamin D. Hitz (Indianapolis, 1922, 237 pages).

A History of United States Army Base Hospital No. 36 (Detroit College of Medicine and Surgery Unit) (Detroit, 1917, 232 pages).

American Red Cross Base Hospital No. 38, by W. M. L. Coplin (Philadelphia, 1923, 248 pages).

On Active Service with Base Hospital No. 46, U.S.A., March 20, 1918, to May 25, 1919 (n.p., n.d., 191 pages).

History of Base Hospital Number Fifty-Three, Advance Section, Service of Supply, by W. Lee Hart (Langres, 1919, 63 pages).

Records

Among the records of the Medical Corps are histories of each post hospital, camp hospital, port hospital, base hospital, general hospital, evacuation hospital, mobile hospital, and hospital center, reports of sanitary inspectors, data regarding the activities of sanitarians in the department, division, or camp, and data regarding the procurement and distribution of medical and hospital supplies.

OFFICE OF THE PROVOST MARSHAL GENERAL

Organization and Functions

The Office of the Provost Marshal General was charged with the administration of the selective service system prescribed by the act of Congress of May 18, 1917, "to authorize the President to increase temporarily the military establishment of the United States." Briefly stated, it was the function of the Provost Marshal General to direct the process of selecting men for induction into military service from their registration to their delivery at the mobilization camps or other points designated by the Secretary of War. This included the physical examination of registrants; their classification in groups to be called into service; the consideration and disposal of applications for exemption for family, industrial, or other reasons; appeals from the rulings of local boards; and the entraining of men for the mobilization camps.

The system was operated in accordance with a principle of "supervised decentralization." Actual selection of the men in most instances was by the local registration boards, the number of which finally stood at 4648. For approximately every thirty local boards, there was a district board which reviewed decisions of the local boards upon appeal and heard and determined as courts of first instance all questions of accepting or excluding men engaged in necessary industries, agriculture, or other essential occupations or employments. Coöperating with the local and district boards were industrial advisers, government appeal agents, legal and medical advisory boards, and boards of instruction. The members of the local and district boards were nominated by the governors of their respective States and appointed by the President. Supervision of the system in each State, as directed by the Provost Marshal General, was through the state headquarters in which the adjutant general of the State usually represented the governor.

The Office of the Provost Marshal General was organized in twelve divisions, namely: Administrative, Alien, Appeals, Auxiliary Agencies and Statistics, Classification, Finance, Information, Inspection and Investigation, Law, Medical Mobilization, Publication, and Registration.

Publications

Report of the Provost Marshal General to the Secretary of War on the First Draft under the Selective Service Act, 1917 (Washington, 1918, 159 pages). Part I, the selective service act and its administration; Part II, the results of calling and selection by the boards; rejection for physical disqualification; dependency; industrial necessity as a ground for discharge.

Second Report of the Provost Marshal General to the Secretary of War on the Operations of the Selective Service System to December 20, 1918 (Washington, 1919, 607 pages). Registration; selection; religious-creed members; conscientious objectors; "work or fight" order; classification of registrants; quotas; organization of the selective service system; statistical data.

Final Report of the Provost Marshal General . . . to July 15, 1919 (Washington, 1920, 288 pages). Statistical tables.

The Spirit of Selective Service, by Major General E. H. Crowder, U.S. Army, Provost Marshal General (New York, 1920, 367 pages). The volunteer system; universal service; the permanency of the selective service idea; the preservation of Americanism.

The Conscientious Objector, by Walter Guest Kellogg, Major, Judge Advocate, U.S.A., Chairman of the Board of Inquiry (New York, 1919, 141 pages). The Board of Inquiry; the objector's point of view; the farm furlough; the insincere objector; propaganda among objectors; the policy of the States; the nationality of the objector; the case for and against.

Selective Service Rules, Regulations, and Instructions (Washington, 1917-1919, 3 volumes). Office compilation. Registration regulations; regulations governing physical examinations; rules and regulations for local and district boards; instructions to disbursing officers; instructions to local boards; regulations governing the apportionment of quotas and credits; the registrants' questionnaire; instructions for medical advisory boards; a manual for legal advisory boards; boards of instruction; classification rules and principles; the process of selection; induction and mobilization; forms.

Records

The Library of Congress has a compilation of "Circular Letters and Telegrams" of the Selective Service Organization that were addressed by the Provost Marshal General to governors, draft executives, and local boards (2 volumes, 1124 pages; subject index).

The entire body of selective service records, consisting of those of the Provost Marshal General's Office, 51 state and territorial headquarters, 155 district boards, 4648 local boards, 1319 medical advisory boards, 3646 legal advisory boards, and 23,908,576 registrants, weigh approximately 8000 tons.

Records of Registrants. The registration cards are filed alphabetically. The folders, each containing the records of one registrant, are filed numerically. The number of the folder of any given registrant is the same as the order number on his registration card. The records within each folder consist of the questionnaire, affidavits, the report of the local medical board, and, usually, some correspondence regarding claims to exemption or the reverse. In some instances there are letters by government officers or other agencies asking that the registrant be retained in the industry in which he was engaged. Whenever a registrant left a hospital or there was some other important change in his condition, report was made to his local board.

Board Records. A large portion of the board records are on forms. They consist of (1) instructions from the President or the Provost Marshal General coming through the adjutant general of a State to the local and district boards; (2) form reports transmitted by the boards through the same channels; (3) records of appeals from the local boards to the district boards and through the adjutant general to the President; (4) information from state headquarters addressed to local and district boards regarding the application of the selective service laws and regulations; (5) correspondence between local boards and between local and district boards; (6) minute books, containing the daily records of a board's proceedings; (7) docket books, containing detailed information regarding registrants.

Experience Reports and Narratives. November 12, 1917, and October 25, 1918, the Provost Marshal General called upon the local boards for "Experience Reports." In the second of these requests it was stated: "Those Experience Reports of last year were highly valued . . . They furnished the flesh and blood for the dry bones of the statistics. Some day the historian of the Great War will thumb them with zest as a prime source of information for posterity." On November 28, 1918, the local and district boards were called upon for narratives of some of the most typical human incidents of the draft in their communities, "incidents pathetic, humorous, patriotic, selfish—what you will, as long as they are the most interesting incidents typical of the administration of the selective service draft." The response to this third request was quite general and these reports on the human element, together with the experience reports, are, for historical purposes, one of the most important sections of the selective service records.

FINANCE SERVICE

Functions

The Finance Service was organized as an independent bureau, under a Director of Finance, in October, 1918. Its functions as prescribed in General Orders No. 72, War Department, June 5,

1919, amended by General Orders No. 104, War Department, August 18, 1919, are in part as follows: action as the responsible authority over the finances of the military establishment, including the disbursing of funds, the classification and compilation of estimates of appropriations, the administrative examination and recording of money accounts, the auditing of property accounts. Fourteen zone finance officers, stationed at Boston, New York, Philadelphia, Baltimore, Washington, Atlanta, Jeffersonville, Chicago, St. Louis, Omaha, New Orleans, Fort Sam Houston, El Paso, and San Francisco, are under the supervision of the Director of Finance.

Publications

Annual Report of the Director of Finance, United States Army, to the Secretary of War, 1919 (Washington, 1919, 48 pages). Organization; detailed statement of expenditures.

Report of the Director of Finance . . . 1920 (Washington, 1920, 48 pages). Payment of troops; detailed statement of expenditures.

Three special financial operations were: (1) the sale of surplus supplies, authorized by the army appropriations act of July 9, 1918; (2) the adjustment of war contracts by the Board of Contract Adjustment, appointed under the act of March 2, 1919, "to provide relief in case of contracts connected with the prosecution of the war"; (3) the disposition of claims and property in France under the supervision of the United States Liquidation Commission which was created by General Orders No. 24, February 11, 1919. Reports of these operations are as follows:

Report of the Sales of Surplus Supplies, submitted by Benedict Crowell, Acting Secretary of War (Washington, 1920, 780 pages).

Report to Congress of Claims Adjusted under War Contracts Act (House Document 364, 66th Congress, 2nd Session).

Decisions of the War Department Board of Contract Adjustment (Washington, 1919-1921, 6 volumes).

Final Report of the United States Liquidation Commission—War Department (Washington, 1920, 191 pages).

DEPARTMENT OF JUSTICE

Functions

THE war activities of the Department of Justice consisted of: (1) the prosecution of cases involving the violation of neutrality and criminal operations in attempting to aid one of the belligerents, for example, a plot to promote strikes of employees in munition factories, conspiracies to prevent or hinder the foreign commerce of the United States in munitions of war, attempts to export rubber, antimony, and nickel without filing manifests, etc.; (2) the enforcement of war statutes, particularly the espionage act, which, embracing more than its title implies, provided for the protection of shipping, the selective service act, the sabotage act, and the trading with the enemy act; (3) the interpretation of war statutes, principally in opinions of the Attorney General; (4) the regulation of the conduct of alien enemies in conformity with the President's proclamations of April 6 and November 16, 1917; (5) the protection of the government from fraud in war contracts.

Organization

To cope with the situation arising from the war a special War Emergency Division was organized in the department to handle the cases arising under the war statutes, the number of special agents of the Division of Investigation (the secret service) was increased fivefold, and the American Protective League, which at one time had a membership of 250,000, was organized with the approval of the Attorney General and operated under the direction of the Division of Investigation.

Publications

Annual Reports of the Attorney General of the United States (1917, pp. 50-74; 1918, pp. 14-57, 633-676; 1919, pp. 21-32, 629-634). Circulars and instructions concerning the various war activities and a brief survey of those activities, including a list of some of the cases that were prosecuted, are published.

The Web, by Emerson Hough (Chicago, 1919, 511 pages). Published by authority of the national directors of the American Protective League; a fervent history of the achievements of that organization. [Unofficial; contains documentary material.]

Official Opinions of the Attorney General (Vol. 31, 677 pages, October 24, 1916, to August 9, 1919; Vol. 32, 653 pages, August 21, 1919, to June 23, 1921). The opinions of the Attorney General interpreting war statutes or affecting industrial and social conditions during the war and the period of reconstruction. Those enumerated in the following list are within the scope of this survey:

January 2, 1918. Opinion on question asking if the President, through the United States Food Administration, had power to requisition cottonseed cake to be used to preserve the cattle herds of Texas. (Vol. 31, pp. 198-201.)

August 31, 1918. Opinion that the Food Administration Grain Corporation, as an authorized agent of the President, might lawfully extend its operations to include the buying, selling, and storing of rye, barley, oats, rice, corn, and other cereals in order to coördinate the flow of such commodities to the seaboard and assure to the civil population and the army and navy of the United States as well as the allies a sufficient amount thereof. (Vol. 31, pp. 344-349.)

January 9, 1919. Opinion that the agreement negotiated by the United States Food Administration with the leading refiners of sugar in the United States which provided that until December 31, 1919, the refiners should purchase their entire requirements of raw sugar from the United States Sugar Equalization Board and that during such period the refiners should observe a fixed maximum price on all sugar manufactured by them, was authorized by the food control act and not prohibited by the Sherman antitrust act. (Vol. 31, pp. 376-380.)

November 3, 1917. Opinion on questions affecting importations of distilled spirits which arose under the food control act and other acts. (Vol. 31, pp. 180-184.)

March 18, 1919. Opinion relative to authority for seizure and forfeiture of distilled spirits and wines imported into the United States in violation of certain acts of Congress. (Vol. 31, pp. 392-397.)

August 21, 1919. Opinion that the sale of warehouse certificates on whiskey held in bond and subject to the payment of tax before removal, was not a sale of whiskey for beverage purposes within the meaning of the war prohibition act and therefore not prohibited. (Vol. 32, pp. 28-29.)

December 2, 1919. Opinion that liquors shipped into the United States prior to September 1, 1917, and placed in bonded warehouses under the provisions of the joint resolution of October 6, 1917, might, by virtue of sect. 600 (b) of the revenue act of 1918, be lawfully exported, although more than one year had elapsed from their entry into the United States, the prohibition of the exporting of liquors under the Eighteenth Amendment not having yet become effective. A modification of the opinion of March 18, 1919. (Vol. 32, pp. 62-63.)

January 7, 1920. Opinion relative to the exportation of liquor under the Eighteenth Amendment. (Vol. 32, pp. 191-193.)

July 20, 1917. Opinion with regard to overtime pay for laborers and mechanics engaged on government contracts. (Vol. 31, pp. 144-145.)

March 21, 1918. Opinion on question asking if the United States Employees' Compensation Commission had, under sect. 32 of the federal workmen's compensation act of September 7, 1916, power to decide whether employees of the United States Shipping Board Emergency Fleet Corporation were entitled to the benefits of that act. (Vol. 31, pp. 252-255.)

December 18, 1918. Opinion that neither the federal control of railroads nor the order of the Director General of Railroads requiring that an action to recover damages against a government controlled railroad be brought directly against the Director General has deprived the United States Employees' Compensation Commission of the power to require a beneficiary to assign his right of action to the United States or prosecute said action as a condition of settlement. (Vol. 31, pp. 365-367.)

April 1, 1919. Opinion that the proposed plan of the Industrial Board of the Department of Commerce to stabilize prices in the basic industries by means of agreements with the leading manufacturers and producers would be a violation of law. (Vol. 31, pp. 411-419.)

August 11, 1920. Opinion with regard to the authority of the United States Shipping Board to conduct litigation. (Vol. 32, pp. 276-284.)

July 28, 1919. Opinion that the United States Tariff Commission was not prohibited from furnishing the War Trade Board with trade secrets which came into its possession in the course of the exercise of its official functions. (Vol. 31, pp. 541-543.)

June 7, 1917. Opinion in reference to questions raised by the Solicitor of the Treasury in regard to the validity of a proposed agreement between the Federal Farm Loan Board and certain investment houses for the sale of bonds of the federal land banks. (Vol. 31, pp. 122-124.)

June 30, 1919. Opinion that under the federal farm loan act of July 17, 1916, joint-stock land banks are not permitted to make loans either through national farm loan associations or through agents, and cannot therefore loan to corporations. (Vol. 31, pp. 494-496.)

December 21, 1920. Opinion that the board of directors of a national farm loan association has no power to use the funds of the association for the purpose of contributing to the expenses of the promotion of another voluntary association and to its upkeep, including salaries of paid representatives in Washington. (Vol. 32, pp. 370-371.)

July 27, 1918. Opinion on question with regard to limitation imposed by the War Finance Corporation act of April 5, 1918, to advances made by the War Finance Corporation to banks, bankers, or trust companies. (Vol. 31, pp. 332-336.)

May 10, 1920. Opinion that the board of directors of the War Finance Corporation was vested with the power to suspend further loans and operations but not with the power to use funds on hand to retire a part of its outstanding capital stock. (Vol. 32, pp. 181-184.)

October 29, 1921. Opinion with regard to advances by the War Finance Corporation for raising and marketing live stock. (Vol. 33, pp. 44-49.)

May 15, 1920. Opinion that the Interstate Commerce Commission may, under the transportation act of February 28, 1920, recommend that loans be made to railroads to pay maturing obligations or refund maturing securities originally issued for capital account. (Vol. 32, pp. 191-193.)

May 21, 1919. Opinion with regard to authority of the Secretary of War to lease caterpillar tractors, dies, and gauges for commercial purposes. (Vol. 31, pp. 457-459.)

September 27, 1919. Opinion with regard to authority of the Secretary of War to transfer to the Secretary of Agriculture available war material not needed by the War Department but suitable for use in the improvement of highways. (Vol. 32, pp. 45-48.)

July 23, 1919. Opinion that a provision in a contract for furnishing ordnance material, which authorizes an allowance of plus or minus five per cent of the articles ordered, does not foreclose the government from insisting upon delivery of the full amount specified by the contract nor enable the contractor to force acceptance of a greater amount. (Vol. 31, pp. 537-541.)

June 4, 1920. Opinion that under the Dent act, March 2, 1919, the Secretary of War is authorized to reopen final awards made under that act and issue new final awards correcting errors of omission in the original awards made through the mutual mistake of the contractors and the government. (Vol. 32, pp. 199-202.)

July 1, 1919. Opinion with regard to validity of claims on account of losses incurred in producing or preparing to produce manganese, chrome, pyrites, or tungsten in compliance with the request or demand of certain designated governmental agencies. (Vol. 31, pp. 496-497.)

August 21, 1919. Opinion that the provision in sect. 5 of the war minerals relief act of March 2, 1919, authorizing the adjustment of losses incurred in producing or preparing to produce manganese, chrome, pyrites, or tungsten in compliance with the request of certain governmental agencies, is not limited to the production within the United States. (Vol. 32, pp. 7-11.)

September 3, 1919. Opinion that the producers of ferro-manganese do not come within the purview of sect. 5 of the war minerals relief act of March 2, 1919, and therefore have no claim under it for losses sustained. (Vol. 32, pp. 34-41.)

October 26, 1920. Opinion with regard to the character of the request or demand for the production of manganese, chrome, pyrites, or tungsten, which, under the war minerals relief act of March 2, 1919, would entitle a person to relief for losses sustained. (Vol. 32, pp. 323-325.)

March 12, 1918. Opinion with regard to tax on freight of articles in course of exportation. (Vol. 31, pp. 239-242.)

June 5, 1918. Opinion on question whether the tax imposed by sect. 600 of the war revenue act of October 3, 1917, upon articles sold by a manufacturer, producer, or importer applies to the sales in foreign commerce by a manufacturer, producer, or importer located in the United States. (Vol. 31, pp. 299-301.)

December 11, 1919. Opinion with regard to tax on sales of articles to be shipped abroad. (Vol. 32, pp. 84-86.)

January 7, 1920. Opinion with regard to tax on tickets for Chautauqua entertainments. (Vol. 32, pp. 88-92.)

May 19, 1919. Opinion that corporations are not entitled to deduct from their gross income for the purposes of the income tax the amount of contributions made to religious, charitable, scientific, or educational corporations or associations, even though such contributions are made to the Red Cross or other war-relief agencies. (Vol. 32, pp. 617-620.)

June 8, 1917. Opinion on question whether Liberty loan bonds, issued under the act of April 24, 1917, are subject to income tax when received by a stockholder of a corporation in payment of a corporation dividend and whether a corporation owning these bonds is to that extent exempt from excise taxes, franchise taxes, and other corporation taxes of the United States and of the several States. (Vol. 31, pp. 125-126.)

March 2, 1918. Opinion in reply to a request from the Postmaster General with regard to the validity of articles 9 and 10 of the Treasury regulations relating to the redemption of War Savings certificates and stamps of deceased owners. (Vol. 31, pp. 234-235.)

February 1, 1919. Opinion that the Bureau of War Risk Insurance might, before the formal termination of the war, convert war-time insurance into other forms of insurance authorized by the war risk insurance act. (Vol. 31, pp. 382-384.)

July 18, 1919. Opinion that under a provision of the war risk insurance act of October 6, 1917, an enlisted man who was in active service at the time of the publication of the terms and conditions of the contract of insurance covering total permanent disability, and who sustained such disability 120 days from such publication, without having applied for such insurance, was entitled to be treated as having been automatically insured. (Vol. 31, pp. 534-537.)

August 21, 1919. Opinion with regard to conditions under which personal injury or disease should be deemed to have been suffered or contracted "in the line of duty" within the meaning of sect. 300 of the war risk insurance act. (Vol. 32, pp. 12-16.)

September 2, 1919. Opinion that the Secretary of the Treasury was not authorized to provide hospital and sanatorium facilities for discharged sick and disabled soldiers, sailors, marines, or army and navy nurses who were not entitled to compensation under the war risk insurance act. (Vol. 32, pp. 31-34.)

December 8, 1919. Opinion with regard to the eligibility of aliens to benefits under the war risk insurance act. (Vol. 32, pp. 67-78.)

June 2, 1920. Opinion interpreting the phrase "in the line of duty" in the war risk insurance act. (Vol. 32, pp. 193-199.)

September 1, 1920. Opinion with regard to the right of enemy aliens to enjoy the benefits of the war risk insurance act. (Vol. 32, pp. 289-294.)

January 4, 1921. Opinion with regard to conversion of term insurance under the war risk insurance act. (Vol. 32, pp. 379-390.)

May 4, 1921. Opinion with regard to beneficiaries of war risk insurance injured on federal controlled railroads. (Vol. 32, pp. 531-536.)

May 4, 1921. Opinion with regard to the effect of the termination of the war upon certain provisions of the war risk insurance act. (Vol. 32, pp. 538-540.)

June 4, 1919. Opinion with regard to the sale of an enemy-owned patent by the Alien Property Custodian to the War Department. (Vol. 31, pp. 463-467.)

November 15, 1919. Opinion that where a suit was filed pursuant to the provisions of sect. 30 of the trading with the enemy act for the recovery of specific enemy property, such property must be retained by the Alien Property Custodian or by the Treasurer of the United States until the litigation was determined; and that where a suit was instituted to recover a debt, funds to the amount of the debt plus probable costs must, if available, be retained by the government. (Vol. 32, pp. 57-61.)

June 21, 1920. Opinion that before the return of enemy trusts to their former owners the Treasury Department might ascertain the taxes due on the income which accrued on such property during the time it was held by the Alien Property Custodian and require them to be paid. (Vol. 32, pp. 249-254.)

June 13, 1921. Opinion that the Alien Property Custodian has no right to accept in full settlement of the purchase price of property which was sold under the provision of the trading with the enemy act and the executive orders pertaining thereto, an amount less than the accepted bid of the purchaser. (Vol. 32, pp. 577-581.)

Bulletins. The Department issued 204 bulletins, of four to fifty pages each, containing decisions of United States district courts and United States circuit courts of appeals, together with instructions to juries, which interpret the selective service act, espionage act, and trading with the enemy act. Among these bulletins is also one containing an opinion of the Appellate Division of the Supreme Court of New York relating to war powers of States over liquor traffic, and about shipping and about manufacturing facilities engaged in war work. The department library has a complete set of these bulletins. The library of the Superintendent of Documents has all except No. 176. The following are illustrative:

Bulletin No. 2. Decision of the United States Circuit Court of Appeals for the second circuit relating to the constitutionality of the selective service act and the jurisdiction of courts over decisions of draft and exemption boards. (No date, 14 pages.)

Bulletin No. 36. Charge to the jury of the United States District Court, northern district of California, relative to section 13, federal penal code and Sherman act, also conspiracy to destroy railroads and munition plants. (January 10, 1917, 19 pages.)

Bulletin No. 52. Charge to the jury of the United States District Court, northern district of New York, relative to distribution of a pamphlet, "The Price We Pay," purporting to be a campaign document of the Socialist Party, and sections 3 and 4, title 1, of the espionage act, also sect. 37 of the penal code. (No date, 41 pages.)

Bulletin No. 100. Opinion of the Supreme Court of the State of Washington relative to restrictions upon occupations other than those specified in Presidential regulations. (May 10, 1918, 5 pages.)

Bulletin No. 154. Charge to the jury of the United States District Court for the eastern district of Michigan relative to sect. 13 of the federal penal code, definition of "military enterprise," and the application of the Sherman act to a conspiracy to destroy plants, tunnels, and other railroad facilities used for the production and transportation of munitions of war by a nation with which we are at peace. (December 21, 1917, 10 pages.)

Emergency Legislation passed prior to December, 1917, dealing with the control and taking of private property for public use, benefit or welfare, Presidential proclamations and executive orders thereunder, to and including January 31, 1918, to which is added a reprint of analogous legislation since 1775 (Washington, 1918, 1150 pages). Collected and annotated by J. Reuben Clark, Jr., Major, Judge Advocate General's Reserve Corps, assigned to special duty with the Attorney General of the United States.

Red Radicalism as described by its own leaders (Washington, 1920, 93 pages). Exhibits collected by A. Mitchell Palmer, Attorney General, including various communistic manifestoes, constitutions, plans, and purposes of proletariat revolution, and its seditious propaganda. Exhibit No. 1 is a report of the international secretary of the Communistic Party of America, describing its antecedents, birth, and projects. Exhibit No. 3 consists of a manifesto, program, and constitution of the party, together with a form of application for membership.

Report of the Attorney General to the Senate upon the investigation activities of the Department of Justice (November 14, 1919, 187 pages). Tells of activities of persons advising anarchy and sedition.

Report of the Attorney General to the Senate on prosecutions under the espionage act (March 9, 1922, 78 pages). Contains lists of cases involving violations of war-time legislation.

Civil Liberty in War Time (Washington, 1919, 22 pages), by John Lord O'Brian, Chief of the War Emergency Division of the Department of Justice. Discussion of the war-time operation of the legal system of the United States.

Agreement, November 26, 1917, between Thomas W. Gregory, Attorney General, and the several manufacturers of news print paper (Washington, 1919, 7 pages). Provides that after April 1, 1918, the just and reasonable maximum prices and terms of contracts for the sale of all or any news print paper should be determined and fixed by the Federal Trade Commission.

POST OFFICE DEPARTMENT

Functions

Operation of the telegraph and telephone systems. By a joint resolution, dated July 16, 1918, Congress authorized the President to take possession and assume control of the telegraph, telephone, and marine cable systems. Six days later the President issued a proclamation taking over the telegraph and telephone systems and directing that the control and operation of the same be exercised by the Postmaster General, and November 2 he issued a similar proclamation with regard to the cables. To assist in the management, operation, and control of the telegraph and telephone systems the Postmaster General appointed a committee, known as the Wire Control Board, consisting of the First Assistant Postmaster General, a member of the United States Tariff Commission, and the Solicitor for the Post Office Department, the first with the Postmaster General to have charge of the administration and organization of the service, the second with the Postmaster General to have charge of its operation, and the third with the Postmaster General to attend to the finances. For the unification of the two cable systems the operating head of one of the systems was appointed manager of both. He declined to comply with the Postmaster General's instructions and was succeeded by the president of the company owning the other system. By an order of the Postmaster General, dated April 29, 1919, the cables were returned to their owners. By an act, approved July 11, 1919, Congress repealed the joint resolution of July 16, 1918, and directed that the telegraph and telephone systems be returned to their owners at midnight July 31.

Military mail. An important service for sustaining morale was the establishment and administration of 151 military branch post offices in camps, cantonments, aviation fields, and naval training stations, the buildings as well as barracks for the accommodation of the post office clerks having been provided by the War Department. Until June, 1918, the Post Office Department had sole charge of the mail service to the troops of the American Expeditionary Forces, but after July 1, 1918, it delivered the outgoing mail, distributed according to army directions, to the military authorities at the ports of embarkation in this country, and received the incoming mail from the military authorities at a port of debarkation in France.

Coöperation with other branches of the government. The Post Office Department coöperated with the Treasury Department in the sale of Liberty bonds and war savings stamps; with the Department of Justice in the enforcement of the espionage and the trading with the enemy acts by censorship of the mails, registering alien enemies, and reporting disloyal utterances; and with the Alien Property Custodian by listing enemy-owned property.

Publications

Annual Report of the Postmaster General for the Fiscal Year ended June 30, 1918 (Washington, 1918, 149 pages). War activities, war savings and thrift stamps, domestic military mail, mail to American Expeditionary Forces, restrictions on parcel post for American Expeditionary Forces, magazines for soldiers and sailors, censorship of mails.

Annual Report of the Postmaster General for the Fiscal Year ended June 30, 1919 (Washington, 1919, 223 pages). War activities, military mail, postal telegraphs and telephones.

Government Control and Operation of Telegraph, Telephone, and Marine Cable Systems, August 1, 1918, to July 31, 1919 (Washington, 1921, 100 pages). Acts of Congress, proclamations of the President, general orders of the Postmaster General, reports on administration of the wires.

A Report of the Postmaster General to the Senate relative to the movements of mail to and from the American troops and auxiliaries abroad (July 12, 1918, 7 pages).

DEPARTMENT OF THE NAVY

Functions

THE more important war functions of the Navy Department within the scope of this survey were: (1) construction or procurement of vessels and other construction work at navy yards, wharves, naval bases, naval stations, and naval plants; (2) coast patrol; (3) protection of merchant ships and the solution of the submarine problem; (4) coöperation with the War Department in transporting troops and supplies to France; (5) production or procurement of ordnance; (6) procurement of general supplies; (7) training of men for the various services; (8) medical, surgical, and sanitary service.

Construction and procurement of vessels. Some progress was made in the construction, at the navy yards, of capital ships provided for in the three-year program of the act of August 29, 1916, but naval construction during the period of the war was concentrated upon destroyers, submarine chasers, and submarines. Six of the largest shipyards in the country were engaged in destroyer building and two government plants were constructed for that purpose. Hundreds of wooden submarine chasers were built. Sixty submarine hunters, of the "Eagle" type, were constructed at a new private plant, and a number of mine sweepers at navy yards and private plants. Through the Aircraft Board certain plants were designated to work exclusively, and others partly, for the navy in the production of seaplanes and kite balloons. A naval aircraft factory was erected in the navy yard at Philadelphia, and a New England supply of spruce lumber for aircraft construction was developed under the direction of an officer of the navy.

The commandeering of vessels needed by the government was authorized by the act of March 4, 1917, but on account of the needs of commerce the Navy Department took over only such as military necessity required. A number of vessels were taken over by voluntary agreements whereby the government paid only nominal sums but agreed to reimburse the owner in case his vessel was lost. Others were taken over on terms providing for a "just compensation" which was determined by a board of appraisal composed of three naval officers and three civilians.

It was the function of the Bureau of Engineering to design, construct, maintain, and repair all steam and internal combustion engines, electric motors and generators used for propelling vessels of the navy, also storage batteries and electric motors for submarines.

Notable repair work was done on more than a hundred German ships which were in United States ports when war was declared. Instead of making new cylinders to replace those purposely broken by the German crews the breaks were repaired by electric welding.

During the period of the war the navy yards at New York, Philadelphia, Norfolk, and Mare Island were equipped for the construction of battle cruisers and dreadnaughts, while at the other navy yards the facilities for the construction of smaller ships were increased. The enlargement of the capacity of thirty private plants for the construction of destroyers, mine sweepers, and accessories was financed by the government. Huge dry docks were built at Norfolk and Philadelphia. Aid was given to the State of Massachusetts in the construction of a dry dock in Boston. The torpedo station at Newport and the gun factory at Washington were enlarged. A powder factory was built at Indianhead, and a plant for making mines at Norfolk. Various buildings were erected for the submarine base at New London. Plants were erected at Charleston, W. Va., for making projectiles and armor plate. The capacity of each of the four permanent training stations was expanded and barracks and other buildings were erected for temporary stations. Numerous hospitals, storehouses, and ammunition depots were built.

Coast patrol. For the more efficient direction of patrol activities, the coasts were divided into several naval districts, each under a commandant, and each district was divided into sections each of which served as a base for the patrol vessels assigned to it. These vessels attended to the upkeep of anti-submarine nets, swept for mines in channels leading to the principal ports, and scrutinized the goings and comings of all vessels approaching the shore. Ships of the Coast Guard, Coast and Geodetic Survey, Lighthouse Service, and Fish Commission assisted in the service and many others were purchased, loaned, or commandeered. Besides directing patrol activities, the commandant was charged with the supervision of industrial developments and housing facilities within his district.

Submarine defense. The protection of merchant ships and the solution of the submarine problem, or the devising of defensive and offensive measures against the submarine, constituted the major efforts of the Naval Consulting Board, which was organized, as a preparedness measure, in October, 1915. At a meeting of scientists and industrial managers held under its auspices plans were prepared for the investigation of every field that might contribute to the development of a means of preventing the destruction of vessels and of defeating the submarine. Subsequently a general invitation was extended throughout the country to submit ideas for investigation. Thousands responded and a few meritorious inventions were derived from this source. An experimental station was established at New London for testing anti-submarine devices. Among the more important results were the development of means for detecting submarines and of more effective depth-bomb tactics. Continuing studies initiated by the board, the Ship-Protection Committee of the United States Shipping Board devised means of protecting merchant ships to such an extent as to reduce marine insurance rates.

Transportation of troops and supplies. The Naval Overseas Transportation Service was established in January, 1918, to assist the army in transporting troops, munitions, guns, food, fuel, and supplies to France and before the cessation of hostilities it was operating a fleet of 378 cargo-carrying ships aggregating a deadweight tonnage of 3,800,000. The fleet was composed of ships belonging to the Shipping Board, army, and private owners, and of Dutch merchant vessels taken over by the Navy Department. It was operated by 4672 officers and 29,175 men under the supervision of an organization having port headquarters at New York, Baltimore, and Newport News. Going abroad under convoy this fleet transported to French and other European ports approximately six million tons of cargo. Piers, wharves, and warehouses were built by Americans in French ports to afford the necessary unloading facilities and to house the cargoes.

Ordnance. To meet the demand for guns at the beginning of the war the Bureau of Ordnance assisted in developing increased capacity and output in some of the old plants and erected new plants until guns, chiefly 3-inch, 4-inch, and 5-inch in caliber, were produced at the rate of 450 to 500 per month. A notable achievement of the bureau was the designing and construction of the 14-inch naval guns on railway mountings that were so effective on the western front. A non-recoil aircraft gun was designed and constructed for operation on seaplanes.

Powder for the navy was produced by private plants operating at full capacity and by the naval powder plant at Indianhead. A shortage of high explosives for aerial bombs, depth charges, and the northern mine barrage was met by the substitution of TNX for TNT or xylol for toluol. Mines were manufactured at the Norfolk navy yard and mine-loading plants were established near Yorktown and at Iona Island, Hudson River. Torpedoes were manufactured at naval and private plants in excess of 400 a month. During the last few months of the war depth charges were produced in quantities in excess of the needs of the navy and merchant fleet. The armor plant at Charleston, W. Va., was designed for an annual capacity of 20,000 tons of armor plate, 10,000 tons of gun forgings, and 10,000 tons of projectiles.

A Labor Section was created in the Industrial Division of the Bureau of Ordnance to keep in touch with conditions at all industrial plants of the navy and at private plants doing work for it for the purpose of forecasting unrest or preventing the spread of unrest when discovered, by remedying conditions or by bringing about an adjustment of differences between employer and employee. The chief of the Industrial Division acted as liaison officer between the War Labor Policies Board, the War Labor Board, and the various other organizations dealing with labor conditions.

Supplies. For the purchase of supplies the organization of the Purchase Division of the Bureau of Supplies and Accounts was expanded until it embraced nine commodities sections (chemicals and explosives, cotton goods, woolens and uniforms, provisions, non-ferrous metals, steel, lumber, hardware and hand tools, and miscellaneous materials), a priorities section, requisition section, navy order section, open purchase section, emergency purchase section, contract section, legal section, award section, stock up-keep section, and schedule, correspondence, printing, mailing list, automotive, and salvage sections. The chief function of each commodity section was to acquire for the producing industry a knowledge of the raw-material supply, labor supply, fuel and power supply, financial conditions, capacity of the industry for production, probable war demands, substitution of materials previously available, expansion of producing capacity, reduction of consuming capacity, transportation facilities, application of priority in manufacture, previous and present costs of production, and pre-war profit standards. The mailing list section kept an up-to-date classified list of all the acceptable contractors in the country from which were obtained the names of all important suppliers of any principal item of naval purchase. The schedule and printing sections tabulated all naval requirements and assembled them in convenient form for the determining of prices.

For the coördination of government purchasing the Paymaster General of the navy, who was chief of the Bureau of Supplies and Accounts, was a member of the Requirements Division of the War Industries Board. In each of about forty commodities sections of that board there was an officer representing the navy and from him as well as from the board were received reports of operations of those sections. Requests of the Navy Department for priority orders or contracts for supplies were considered and passed upon by the Priorities Committee of the War Industries Board along with similar requests of other departments and governmental agencies.

In all cases in which supplies on the market were equal to the demand the principle of competitive bidding was strictly adhered to. To accelerate bidding mimeographed copies of schedules of supplies were mailed to producers on the bureau's classified mailing list, to which more than four thousand names were added during the war. In the emergency section the time required to secure bids was further shortened by use of the telegraph and telephone.

In some instances in which the supply of a material was less than the demand or the manufacturers controlling the supply refused to sell at a satisfactory price the material was secured by mandatory and commandeering orders. When this was done a fair price was usually determined by the report of an accounting officer sent to the producing plant to investigate the cost of manufacture, by investigations of the Federal Trade Commission or by the Price Fixing Committee of the War Industries Board.

Training. For the training of seamen and firemen the capacity of each of the four permanent naval training stations was greatly enlarged. A training camp was provided in each naval district. The navy trade schools, also, were expanded and a number of schools for special training were established. There were training schools for members of the hospital corps, a school for training in the use of submarine devices, schools in which entire crews were assembled and trained for submarine operations, and a school for training salvage crews. A student navy training corps was organized and nearly one hundred educational institutions of college rank assisted the navy in training radio operators, engineers, aviators, mechanics, nurses, cooks, and various tradesmen. A commission on training camp activities was organized for the navy in conjunction with that for the army to coördinate the efforts of the several welfare organizations.

Medical, surgical, and sanitary service. As directed in an executive order, dated April 3, 1917, the medical department of the navy was assisted during the war by the sanitary officers of the United States Public Health Service, especially in the selection and inspection of sites for camps and hospitals, in sanitary and laboratory work, and in other branches of the service rendered by the medical organization of each naval district. For each naval district and each hospital base there was, besides a central hospital service, a general dispensary service at outlying stations for patrol, aero, radio, and other forces. Emergency hospital buildings were erected at Portsmouth, N. H., Newport, R. I., League Island Navy Yard, Norfolk, Va., Charleston, S. C., and Pensacola, Fla. A committee on standardization of medical and surgical supplies and equipment prepared lists of staple medical and surgical supplies selected to meet war conditions as a means of making possible a larger output of those for which there was greatest need. State and county committees were organized to further an effective mobilization of medical resources.

Publications

Annual Reports of the Navy Department, 1917, 1918, and 1919 (Washington, 1918, 1919, and 1920, having a total of 5390 pages). A general report each year by the Secretary and a detailed report by each bureau chief. That for the Bureau of Supplies and Accounts contains statistical or tabulated statements with regard to cost, property investments, and supply accounts. These statements constitute nearly one-half of the reports for the three years.

Our Navy at War, by Josephus Daniels, Secretary of the Navy (Washington, 1922, 374 pages). [Unofficial.]

Digest Catalogue of Laws and Joint Resolutions, the Navy and the World War (Publication No. 3 of the Historical Section, Office of Records and Library, Navy Department, Washington, 1920, 64 pages).

History of the Bureau of Engineering, Navy Department, during the World War (Publication No. 5 of the Historical Section, Office of Naval Records and Library, Navy Department, Washington, 1922, 176 pages).

Activities of the Bureau of Yards and Docks, Navy Department, World War, 1917-1918 (Washington, 1921, 522 pages). Naval training camps, Marine Corps projects, emergency hospital construction, general development of yards and stations, shipbuilding and repair facilities, shipyard and industrial plant extensions, dry docks, power plants, public works at ordnance stations, armor and projectile plants, storage, radio stations, submarine bases, shore facilities for aviation, helium production plant, housing the navy, Construction Division of the bureau.

Navy Ordnance Activities, World War, 1917-1918 (Washington, 1920, 323 pages). Arming vessels, guns, mounts, small arms, ammunition, depth charges, the northern barrage, inventions and research, aviation ordnance, fire control and optics, torpedoes, turrets, naval railway batteries, tractor batteries, intelligence, Industrial Division.

German Submarine Activities on the Atlantic Coast of the United States and Canada (Publication No. 1 of the Historical Section, Office of Records and Library, Navy Department, Washington, 1920, 163 pages).

Naval Consulting Board of the United States, by Lloyd N. Scott, late Captain, U.S.A. and liaison officer to the Naval Consulting Board (Washington, 1920, 288 pages). Origin and organization, Special Problems Committee, Ship Protection Committee, inventions, accomplishments. [Unofficial.]

Naval Consulting Board—Bulletins: No. 1. "The submarine and kindred problems" (New York, 1917, 15 pages) ; No. 2. "The enemy submarine" (New York, 1918, 47 pages), the submarine and its operations, protection of ships, offensive against submarines; No. 3. "Problems of aeroplane improvement" (New York, 1918, 32 pages).

Records

The Historical Section of the Office of Naval Records and Library has a number of reports and historical narratives relative to war activities, and in most instances some of the more detailed records, those from which the reports were prepared, are in the bureau files of the department. The following is a list of such of the reports and narratives as are pertinent to this survey:

History of War Activities under the Bureau of Construction and Repair, by Admiral D. W. Taylor.

Activities of the Bureau of Medicine and Surgery during the European War, by Admiral W. C. Braisted.

Bureau of Supplies and Accounts, by Rear Admiral Samuel Mc-Gowan.

History of the Training Division, Bureau of Navigation, by Lieutenant Commander L. P. Clephane.

U.S. Coast Guard Activities during the European War, by D. P. Foley.

Office of Naval Intelligence, its History and Aims, by Admiral A. P. Niblack.

The Office of Naval Intelligence before and during the World War, by Captain Edward McCauley.

Relation of the Council of National Defense to the Navy Department during the War, by D. M. Reynolds.

Chemistry in War, by Lieutenant Commander Henry E. Rhodes.

History of the Naval Overseas Transportation Service, by Lieutenant Commander Clephane.

History of the First Naval District.

History of the Second Naval District.

History of the Third Naval District.

History of the Fourth Naval District.

History of the Fifth Naval District.

History of the Sixth Naval District.

History of the Seventh Naval District.

Historical Account of the U.S. Naval Air Station at Pensacola, Eighth District.

Historical Account of Ninth, Tenth, and Eleventh Naval Districts.

Historical Narrative of the Twelfth Naval District during the World War.

Historical Narrative of Puget Sound Navy Yard and the Thirteenth Naval District.

Historical Narrative of the Fourteenth Naval District.

Historical Narrative of Activities of the Fifteenth Naval District.

Historical Data on the Sixteenth Naval District, Philippines.

DEPARTMENT OF THE INTERIOR

UNITED STATES GEOLOGICAL SURVEY

Organization

THE United States Geological Survey has three field branches and three office branches. The field branches are the Geologic, the Topographic, and the Water Resources. The office branches are the Administrative, the Land Classification, and the Publication. The Geologic Branch has four divisions: Geology, with eleven sections; Chemical and Physical Research, Mineral Resources, and Alaskan Mineral Resources. The permanent organization of the Topographic Branch embraces four divisions: Atlantic, Central, Rocky Mountain, and Northwestern. In January, 1917, the Division of Military Surveys was added, and subsequently, to meet the situation arising from the war, the branch was reorganized in five departments: Northeastern, Eastern, Southeastern, Central, and Southern. The Water Resources Branch has four divisions: Surface Waters, Ground Waters, Water Utilization, Enlarged and Stock-Raising Homesteads, and Quality of Water.

War Functions

During the war the three field branches and the Publications Branch were engaged in investigations for the promotion of war industries or in rendering assistance directly to the military and naval forces.

Division of Geology. Geologists of this division limited their field studies to a search for new deposits of minerals, both metallic and non-metallic, required in the manufacture of munitions, for high grade ores, for ores more easily available, and especially—to meet the shipping emergency as well as the industrial demands of the war—for those indispensable ores for which the United States had been dependent upon overseas transportation. Section 1, Eastern Areal Geology, searched for reported deposits of manganese, chromite, tungsten, salt, high-calcium lime, and white clays. Section 2, Western Areal Geology, searched for chromite, nitrates, potash, and sulphur. Section 7, Geology of Iron and Steel Alloy Metals, was engaged in special field studies of deposits of chromium, manganese, tungsten, zirconium, molybdenum, and iron. Section 8, Geology of Non-metalliferous Deposits, investigated reported deposits of potash and nitrates. Section 11, Geology of Oil and Gas Fields, made structural examinations of prospective oil regions and coöperated with the Bureau of Mines, the War Department, and the Navy Department in a search for natural gas rich in helium.

Division of Chemical and Physical Research. Geologists of this division tested rocks for platinum and labored in various ways for an increased production of potash, mica, and sodium salts.

Division of Mineral Resources. This division rendered a service of prime importance in supplying information relative to minerals —production, imports, consumption, sources of supply—to the War Industries Board, War Trade Board, U.S. Shipping Board, and other war boards or military establishments represented on the Joint Information Board on Minerals and Derivatives which the Geological Survey took the initiative in organizing in February, 1918. Before the armistice was signed the work of the four divisions of the Geologic Branch amounted in effect to a census or quantitative appraisal of the resources of the United States in the more important war mineral commodities. Much was contributed to the knowledge of the mineral resources of foreign countries as well.

Topographic Branch. This branch made topographical surveys along the national borders in conformity with a program of the General Staff of the army for national defense. Subsequently the entire field work of the branch was made to conform to a program for military surveys drawn up by the General Staff, and 110 of the branch's engineers were commissioned in the Engineer Officers' Reserve Corps for military duty in France and at home.

Water Resources Branch. The engineers of this branch coöperated with surveys in several States in the preparation of summary reports on the underground water supplies and soil-drainage features of areas along the Atlantic and Gulf coasts and Mexican border for the use of the War Department in the selection of cantonment sites. A country-wide survey of the power situation was made to determine where water power could be substituted for steam-generated power. Assistance was rendered the Reclamation Service in the measurement of streams that were expected to furnish water to reclaimed lands.

Publications

Thirty-Eighth Annual Report of the Director of the United States Geological Survey to the Secretary of the Interior for the Fiscal Year ended June 30, 1917 (Washington, 1917, 176 pages). Search for commercial deposits of war minerals; topographic surveys; military surveys; coöperation with federal bureaus, the War Department, and the Navy Department in war work.

Thirty-Ninth Annual Report of the Director of the United States Geological Survey . . . June 30, 1918 (Washington, 1918, 163 pages). Special war activities; contributions to economic geology; coöperation with other agencies of the Federal Government.

Fortieth Annual Report of the Director of the United States Geological Survey . . . June 30, 1919 (Washington, 1919, 200 pages). Searches for deposits of war minerals; investigation of specific water-power problems; readjustment program.

A List of the Publications of the United States Geological Survey, August, 1921 (Washington, 1921, 192 pages). Annual reports, monographs, professional papers, bulletins, mineral resources, water-supply papers, folios of the Geologic Atlas of the United States, special publications.

World Atlas of Commercial Geology (Washington, 1921, two parts). Perhaps the most important printed product of the Geological Survey having an economic significance. Part I, "Distribution of Mineral Production" (72 pages, 72 plates), is a study of the distribution of mineral raw materials and their relation to the promotion of trade and the control of industry. Part II, "Water Power of the World" (39 pages, 8 plates), is a general statement of the water-power resources of the world and the extent of their development.

Mineral Resources of the United States, 1917 (Washington, 1921, Part I, "Metals," 980 pages; Part II, "Nonmetals," 1293 pages). The effects of the war on the mineral industries are shown and the economic limits to domestic independence in minerals and the international control of minerals are discussed.

Mineral Resources of the United States, 1918 (Washington, 1921, Part I, "Metals," 1096 pages; Part II, "Nonmetals," 1557 pages). An inventory of the mineral resources of the country.

Mineral Resources of the United States, 1919 (Washington, 1922, Part I, "Metals," 807 pages; Part II, "Nonmetals," 565 pages). Reflects the reaction in the mineral industries from intensive production for war purposes.

Our Mineral Supplies (Washington, 1919, *Bulletin No. 666*, 278 pages). Discusses the sources of supply, uses, and demands for each of thirty-three war minerals.

Contributions to Economic Geology (Washington, 1918, *Bulletin No. 660*, 304 pages). This bulletin comprises eleven papers, among which is one on manganese deposits in Arkansas, one on possibilities for manganese deposits in Arkansas, one on possibilities for manganese ore in the Shenandoah Valley, Va., and one on tin resources of the Kings Mountain District, N. C.

Contributions to Economic Geology (Washington, 1919, *Bulletin No. 690*, 147 pages). This bulletin comprises six papers, among which are two on manganese deposits in Montana.

Helium-Bearing Natural Gas, by G. Sherburne Rogers (Washington, 1921, *Professional Paper No. 121*, 113 pages).

A number of important articles containing detailed material relative to the war work and readjustment program of the Geological Survey were contributed by members of the staff to the *Annals* of the American Academy of Political and Social Science, *Transactions* of the American Institute of Mining and Metallurgical Engineers, *Bulletins* of the Pan-American Union, *Engineering and Mining-Journal*, and the mining and scientific press generally.

Records

As much of the survey's work on mineral resources was directly contributory to the work of the War Industries Board, War Trade Board, Shipping Board, Fuel Administration, and the army and the navy, material collected relative to it was turned over to the archives of those organizations. But the Geological Survey itself has on file in its records an important body of source material in the data turned in by the Joint Information Board on Minerals and Derivatives, which was conducted under the auspices of the Geological Survey and had a membership of representatives from some twenty federal war organizations. This data includes material on mineral commodities, collected and revised about every month, as to the occurrence and distribution of foreign as well as domestic mineral deposits, their production and export, their uses, consumption, and essential and non-essential classifications, together with substitutes for them. The records also include voluminous files of quarterly, monthly, and weekly reports on the production, consumption, movements, and commitments in the trade in minerals. A mimeographed copy of an index to this material entitled "List of Statistical and Other Information on Minerals and Mineral Derivatives Issued by Joint Information Board on Minerals and Derivatives" (October, 1918, 178 pages), is in the Library of Congress. The survey files also contain, in addition to correspondence, bibliographies and abstracts which serve as bases of research on foreign mineral deposits, and translations of important literature, especially on oil. For these files there is a card index.

Among many periodical statements in mimeographed issues the following are of economic importance:

Monthly Power Report, usually 7 pages, issued for February, March, April, July, September, and October in 1919 and monthly since January, 1920. It tabulates by States the "Production of electric power and consumption of fuels by public utility power plants in the United States," and is used to lower production costs in power plants.

Monthly and Weekly Statements of Copper Production, issued October, 1918, to December, 1918. Statistical tables exhibiting production, stocks on hand, and distribution of copper supplies.

Monthly Statement of Petroleum Production and Consumption, issued since January, 1917, for general circulation, showing quantities of oil moved, consumed, delivered, and in storage at the end of each month for each of the major oil fields east of the Rocky Mountains, also giving estimates of the California field.

Monthly Statement of Railroad Movement of Coal and Coke, issued August 1, 1916, to June, 1917.

Monthly and Weekly Statements of Spelter Production, weekly from December 8, 1917, to January 25, 1919: monthly subsequently. Tabulates the production, stock, and commitments, and in some cases the imports and exports, with occasional notes of explanation.

Weekly Statement of Bituminous Coal and Coke Production, issued since July, 1917, as an authoritative index of industrial conditions in this industry, of service both to the government and the trade.

Weekly Statement of Lead Production, issued December 1, 1917, to

January 11, 1919. Tabulates production, stocks, and commitments, with occasional notes of explanation, to serve the government and the trade.

There were also quarterly and later monthly statements showing the production, stocks, and commitments of chrome ore and manganese.

There were in addition the press notices, issued with great frequency and irregularity, conveying information of a popular as well as of a statistical character.

BUREAU OF MINES

Functions

The Bureau of Mines was established by act of Congress, May 16, 1910, to conduct scientific investigations relative to mining and mineral substances as a means of increasing health, safety, and efficiency in the mineral industries. During the war the bureau functioned mainly as a war agency. It coöperated with the War Department and the National Research Council in a study of poison gases and gas masks; with the War Department in the production of nitric acid and sodium cyanide for war purposes and ammonia for agricultural purposes; with the War and Navy Departments in an investigation of helium as a non-inflammable gas for balloons; with the chemical and fertilizer committees of the Council of National Defense in the study of problems relative to the manufacture of sulphuric acid; with the Geological Survey and the Bureau of Soils, Department of Agriculture, in an investigation of the sources of potash and methods of manufacture; with the Geological Survey in a study of the petroleum industry to determine if the war needs could be met; and in various ways with the Fuel Administration, the War Industries Board, the War Trade Board, the Shipping Board, the Emergency Fleet Corporation, the Bureau of Standards, and the Capital Issues Committee.

From the outbreak of the war in Europe the bureau labored for an increased domestic production of such war materials as had up to that time been largely imported, and in the deficiency bill of March 28, 1918, Congress made a specific appropriation for investigations, by the bureau, "concerning the mining, preparation, treatment, and utilization of ores and other mineral substances which are particularly needed for carrying on the war, in connection with military and manufacturing purposes, and which have heretofore been largely imported, with a view to developing domestic sources of supply and substitutes for such ores and mineral products as are particularly needed." A war minerals control act, for a similar purpose, was approved October 5, 1918, but hostilities ceased so soon thereafter that it did not go into effect.

Authority to supervise and regulate, by means of licenses, the manufacture, distribution, storage, use, and possession of explosives was vested in the director of the Bureau of Mines by the explosives act of October 6, 1917.

Organization

The war work of the bureau was conducted chiefly in four divisions: (1) War Gas, (2) War Minerals, (3) Explosives Regulation, and (4) Petroleum, all of which, except the last, were organized for the purpose.

War Gas Division. In its line of duty to conduct investigations with a view to promoting the health and safety of miners, the bureau had from its origin devoted attention to poisonous and explosive gases, the use of rescue apparatus and masks, and the exploring of noxious atmospheres and methods of resuscitating persons overcome by bad air; and the day on which the United States entered the war a committee on gases was formed by the National Research Council to coöperate with the bureau in this work. November 7, 1917, the Secretary of the Interior appointed a board of scientists to advise the director regarding the prosecution of further gas investigations and experiments with gases, and the work of the bureau in this field, with headquarters at the American University, was assuming large proportions when by executive order, June 25, 1918, it was transferred to the Chemical Warfare Service of the army. An organization of the bureau for supervising the construction of gas masks had been turned over to the Surgeon General's Office in August, 1917, and a staff of engineers working on the development of processes for manufacturing gases had been transferred to the Bureau of Ordnance, War Department, in December, 1917.

War Minerals Division. The director of the Bureau of Mines was a member of the military committee of the National Research Council and of the committees on mineral products of the Council of National Defense. Representatives of the bureau served on the War Minerals Committee, other members of which were representatives of the American Institute of Mining Engineers, the Mining and Metallurgical Society of America, the Association of State Geologists, and the U.S. Geological Survey. A representative of the bureau was also a member of the Joint Information Board on Minerals and Derivatives, which functioned as a clearing house of information for all branches of the government interested in mineral problems. The war minerals investigations conducted by the bureau were in charge of a chief executive with a general staff of ten members, each in charge of one of the sections devoted respectively to the following: (1) priority matters; (2) shipping problems; (3) matters relating to highways and roads; (4) matters of organization and planning, and excess-profits taxes; (5) mining methods; (6) mining costs and ore markets; (7) matters relating to the work of the Capital Issues Committee; (8) political and commercial control of minerals; (9) informational matters and non-metallic minerals; (10) files and editing of manuscripts. There were engineers in charge of researches on the different minerals, and all investigations were closely associated with the work done at the mining experiment stations of the bureau under the direction of the bureau's division chiefs and the supervisor of the experiment stations. Among the more important minerals relative to which investigations were made were: manganese, essential for making high grade steel for munitions and industrial use; graphite, for making crucibles; tin, for plating utensils and for bearing-metal; mercury, used as fulminate to explode shells; potash for fertilizer and for making explosives; tungsten and molybdenum, for high-speed tool steel; antimony, for hardening bullet lead; chromite for tool steel, for tanning leather, and as a refractory lining in furnaces; magnesite for refractory linings; mica, as insulating material; platinum for the manufacture of sulphuric acid and for electrical apparatus.

Explosives Regulation Division. This division, the function of which was the administration of the explosives act, was in charge of a chief with a staff of five members, each of whom was head of one of the five main branches or sections devoted respectively to: (1) administration and questions of policy; (2) investigation of applications for an issuance of manufacturer's, exporter's, and importer's licenses; (3) examination and appointment of field employees; (4) investigation and prosecution of violations of the act; (5) construction and location of magazines and proper storage of explosives and ingredients. In each of the States and in Alaska there was an inspector with an advisory committee, the members of which were designated as assistant inspectors. The state inspectors were appointed by the President with the approval of the Senate. The members of the advisory committees were appointed by the director of the Bureau of Mines with the approval of the Secretary of the Interior. It was the duty of each inspector, under the direction of the director of the Bureau of Mines, to see that the act was "faithfully executed and observed."

Petroleum Division. The work of this division is classified under three heads: (1) production technology, (2) engineering technology, and (3) chemical technology, but the entire division is under the direction of the chief petroleum technologist. During the war the division, coöperating with the Fuel Administration and with different bureaus of the War Department and Navy Department, was concerned chiefly with questions relating to war-time conditions and to greater efficiency in the utilization of liquid fuels.

Publications

Seventh Annual Report by the Director of the Bureau of Mines to the Secretary of the Interior for the Fiscal Year ended June 30, 1917 (Washington, 1917, 106 pages). Summary of special war work: nitrate supply, raw materials for sulphuric acid, war gases, gas masks, nickel supply, manganese supply, quicksilver, potash, petroleum products, explosives.

Eighth Annual Report by the Director of the Bureau of Mines . . . June 30, 1918 (Washington, 1918, 124 pages). Use of gases in warfare, war minerals investigation, explosives regulation.

Ninth Annual Report by the Director of the Bureau of Mines . . . June 30, 1919 (Washington, 1919, 120 pages). War minerals investigations, activities of the explosives division, helium investigations, war minerals relief commission.

Publications of the Bureau of Mines (August, 1921, 31 pages). A list of all publications issued by the bureau, consisting of 209 bulletins, 291 technical papers, 10 annual reports of the director, handbooks, and circulars.

General Information and Rulings for the Enforcement of the Law Regulating the Manufacture, Distribution, Storage, Use, or Possession of Explosives and Their Ingredients, by F. S. Peabody, assistant to the director in charge of explosives (Washington, 1918, 44 pages).

Bulletins:

178. *War Work of the Bureau of Mines,* by Van H. Manning, 4 parts: (A) War Gas Investigations (39 pages); (B) War Minerals, Nitrogen Fixation, and Sodium Cyanide (21 pages); (C) Petroleum Investigations and Production of Helium (25 pages); (D) Explosives and Miscellaneous Investigations (20 pages).

112. *Mining and Preparing Domestic Graphite for Crucible Use,* by G. H. Dubb and F. G. Moses (80 pages).

160. *Rock Quarrying for Cement Manufacture,* by Oliver Bowles (160 pages).

173. *Manganese: Uses, Preparation, Mining Costs, Manufacture of Ferro-Alloys,* by C. M. Weld and others (209 pages).

184. *The Manufacture of Sulphuric Acid in the United States,* by A. E. Wells and D. E. Fogg (216 pages).

198. *Regulation of Explosives in the United States,* by C. E. Monroe (45 pages).

Technical Papers:

179. *Preparedness Census of Mining Engineers, Metallurgists, and Chemists,* by Albert H. Fay (19 pages).

199. *Five Ways of Saving Fuel in Heating Houses,* by Henry Kreisinger (10 pages).

205. *Saving Coal in Boiler Plants,* by Henry Kreisinger (21 pages).

243. *Development of Liquid Oxygen Explosives during the War,* by George S. Rice.

Political and Commercial Geology of the World's Mineral Resources, edited by J. E. Spurr (New York, 1920, 562 pages). Includes 38 technical papers written by research workers in the War Minerals Division.

Records

From July, 1919, to July, 1922, the Reference and Information Files of the Bureau of Mines were a receiving station for war material collected by the several divisions and committees of the bureau, together with some turned over by the Fuel Administration. Subsequently this collection, which had been maintained as a composite whole and classified on the commodity basis, was divided. The foreign minerals material was taken by the Foreign Minerals Reserve of the Geological Survey, while the domestic material was distributed among the four technical divisions of the Bureau of Mines: (1) Mineral Technology, (2) Fuels, (3) Mining, (4) Petroleum and Natural Gas. That delivered to the Mining and Fuels Divisions has become a part of the inactive or dead files of the Administrative Division of the Department of the Interior. That delivered to the other two divisions has been retained in their immediate custody. The material consists of general correspondence, circular letter questionnaires and responses to them relative to war conditions, statistical data, and reports of investigations and other operations. Especially important are reports to those branches of the government with which the bureau coöperated during the war and the correspondence with state bureaus to stimulate domestic mineral production. In the bureau library is a mimeographed copy of a *War Minerals Investigation Series*, September, 1918-May, 1919, embracing 18 papers, varying in length from 8 to 45 pages, written on technical subjects by research workers of the division for general circulation.

UNITED STATES RECLAMATION SERVICE

Functions

The United States Reclamation Service was established by the reclamation act of June 17, 1902, which created a reclamation fund out of the proceeds of the sales of public lands in Arizona, California, Colorado, Idaho, Kansas, Montana, Nebraska, Nevada, New Mexico, North Dakota, Oklahoma, Oregon, South Dakota, Utah, Washington, and Wyoming for the construction and maintenance of irrigation works to reclaim arid and semi-arid lands in those States. An act of June 12, 1906, extended the provisions of the reclamation act to Texas. The control, direction, and management of the service, subject to the approval of the Secretary of the Interior, is vested in a Reclamation Board consisting of a director, chief engineer, chief counsel, comptroller, and supervisor of irrigation.

During the war all construction work was suspended which did not promise increased crop production before the restoration of peace and efforts were made to stimulate crop production on the various reclamation projects under way. Farmers cultivating land included in reclamation projects under way were supplied with seed, and, in cases where transportation was lacking, storage cellars were built for the preservation of perishable crops. Determined efforts were made by the Secretary of the Interior and the Reclamation Service to procure legislation to provide work and homes for returning soldiers by the development of new reclamation projects. The sundry civil act of July 1, 1918, appropriated $100,000 for investigations relative to the plan; surveys were made for the purpose of locating feasible projects, and steps were taken by many of the States to coöperate with the federal government. But the bill on which the fate of the program depended, the Mondell bill of February, 1919, entitled, "A bill providing for coöperation between the United States and state governments in the rural settlement of soldiers, sailors, and marines, and to promote the reclamation of lands," failed to pass.

Publications

Reclamation Record, issued monthly since January, 1908, to water-right users on reclamation projects. The twelve numbers of each year are bound in a volume of about 600 pages and indexed. The material is of a popular nature. Much of it relates to irrigation matters. For the period of the war and readjustment there is conservation propaganda and propaganda for the promotion of the plan to provide work and homes for soldiers on reclaimed lands. The March number for 1918 contains an article on the "Activities of the Interior Department War Work Association."

Development of Unused Lands, a report by the Reclamation Service. (House Document No. 262, 66th Congress, 1st Session, Washington, 1919, 184 pages). Part I, "Investigation of Swamp and Cut-Over

Lands"; Part II, "Investigations of Wet and Practically Unused Lands in the Southern Division"; Part III, "Investigations of Lands Needing Drainage and Cut-Over Lands in the Northern Division and Cut-Over Lands in the Western Division." These investigations were made for the purpose of locating feasible projects for the reclamation of lands for soldiers.

Work and Homes for Returning Soldiers, Sailors, and Marines, a report (No. 1081, 65th Congress, 3rd Session) by the House Committee on Irrigation of Arid Lands on the Mondell bill for the rural settlement of soldiers, sailors, and marines and to promote the reclamation of lands. 34 pages. There is also a report by the Senate Committee on Public Lands on the same bill. Report No. 780, 65th Congress, 3rd Session. 34 pages.

Summary of Soldier Settlements in English-Speaking Countries, by Elwood Mead, Constructing Engineer, U.S. Reclamation Service (Washington, 1918, 28 pages). A summary of soldier-settlement legislation in Great Britain, Canada, Australia, New Zealand, and Union of South Africa.

Work and Homes for Our Fighting Men, by Franklin K. Lane *et al.* (Washington, 1919, 23 pages). A program for the reclamation of lands for soldiers.

Records

The records of the Reclamation Service which come within the scope of this survey are (1) "Reclamation Circular Letters" and (2) "Miscellaneous Data on Soldiers' Settlement Project."

The Reclamation Circular Letters are issued in mimeograph at irregular but frequent intervals. Those for the years 1917-1921 are bound in five volumes, numbered and cross-indexed. They are issued exclusively for the instruction of employees in the field service and in them, for the years 1917 and 1918, are found the rules of procedure for those employees relative to (1) coöperation for food conservation on reclamation projects, (2) coöperation for increased food production on lands included in reclamation projects, and (3) coöperation in war emergency food surveys.

The Miscellaneous Data on Soldiers' Settlement Project include (1) articles and newspaper stories general and popular in character, drafted by officials of the Reclamation Service at the request of the Secretary of the Interior for release to newspapers and periodicals with a view to creating sentiment in favor of the Mondell bill; (2) "Soldiers' Settlement" letter files, 1918-1922, containing approximately 73,000 inquiries from ex-soldiers regarding homesteads, reclaimed or otherwise, from all classes and all States, but chiefly from those States in which the unemployment problem was greatest; (3) post card files, 1919-1922, containing approximately 120,000 replies to the "Soldiers' Settlement Questionnaire" card, "Hey, There! Do You Want a Home on a Farm?"

UNITED STATES BUREAU OF EDUCATION

Organization

The United States Bureau of Education has six administrative divisions and ten field divisions. The administrative divisions are: (1) Executive Management, (2) Mails and Files, (3) Publications, (4) Statistics, (5) Library, (6) Administration of Schools for Natives in Alaska. The field divisions are: (1) Higher Education, (2) City School Administration, (3) Rural Schools, (4) Civic Education, (5) Home Education, (6) Education in Industries and Home Making, (7) Commercial Education, (8) School Hygiene and Physical Education, (9) Community Organization, (10) Racial Groups. An Americanization Division, established as a war measure in May, 1918, a School Board Service Division, established in October, 1918, to meet conditions arising from the war, and an Educational Extension Division, established in December, 1918, were discontinued in 1919.

War Work

During the war the bureau, laboring to maintain the schools as nearly as possible at their normal efficiency, coöperated with the Department of Labor in combating efforts to suspend child-labor and compulsory school-attendance laws. At the same time it cooperated with the Council of National Defense, the War Department, and the American Council on Education in mobilizing the intellectual resources of the nation, with the Committee on Public Information and other government organizations in disseminating war-time propaganda, and with the Food Administration in efforts to increase crop production and the conservation of food. The bureau drafted and circulated a program of education for the war, advocated a revision of courses of study as a war measure, conducted a nation-wide publicity campaign to enable school boards to procure the requisite number of competent teachers, developed a project for the Americanization of foreign-born American citizens through education, and made studies relative to the readjustment of education after the war. The titles of the bureau's publications during the war and the period of readjustment indicate the nature of most of its war-time activities.

Publications

REPORTS

Report of the Commissioner of Education for the year ended June 30, 1917 (Washington, 1917). Vol. I (102 pages) contains a chapter on "Education and the War."

Report of the Commissioner of Education . . . June 30, 1918 (Washington, 1918, 155 pages). Discusses higher education and the war, Federal Board for Vocational Education, vocational training in army hospitals, the Students' Army Training Corps, medical education and the war, the public schools and the war, Americanization through education, and the United States School Garden Army.

Report of the Commissioner of Education . . . June 30, 1919 (Washington, 1919, 226 pages). Reviews the work of the Americanization, School Board Service, and Educational Extension Divisions.

PERIODICALS

Americanization, a monthly magazine of 16 pages issued by the Americanization Division from September 15, 1918, to November 1, 1919. It summarized the activities of the division and of unofficial agencies working for Americanization and served as a vehicle for propaganda of that kind.

National School Service, a monthly magazine, 16 to 24 pages, issued in coöperation with the Committee on Public Information from September 1, 1918, to May 1, 1919. It was a vehicle for all sorts of official propaganda on such subjects as thrift, health, the Red Cross, Liberty loans, and food conservation.

School Life, a paper of 16 pages issued semi-monthly from August 1, 1918, to July 1, 1921, and monthly from September to December, 1921; publication resumed in September, 1922.

Geographic News Bulletin, a magazine, 12 to 16 pages, published for the Bureau by the National Geographic Society from October 6, 1919, to May 9, 1921. It conveyed information regarding the changes wrought by the war in the customs and political boundaries of various nationalities and presented this material in a popular form adaptable for collateral reading assignments to classes in history, geography, and current events.

BULLETINS

Americanization as a War Measure (Bulletin, 1918, No. 18; Washington, 1918, 62 pages). A report of a conference of governors of States, members of the Council of National Defense, members of State Councils of Defense, members of chambers of commerce, and representatives of industries, held in Washington April 3, 1918.

The United States School Garden Army (Bulletin, 1919, No. 26; Washington, 1919, 6 pages).

The American Spirit in Education, by C. R. Mann, Chairman Advisory Board of the Committee on Education and Special Training, War Department (Bulletin, 1919, No. 30; Washington, 1919, 63 pages). Development of vocational education, industrial reorganization, technical education, Students' Army Training Corps.

The Federal Executive Departments as Sources of Information for Libraries (Bulletin, 1919, No. 74; Washington, 1919, 204 pages). Deals with the organization, functions, and publications of each of the ten executive departments of the federal government.

Community Americanization, by F. C. Butler, Director of Americanization, Bureau of Education (Bulletin, 1919, No. 76; Washington, 1920, 82 pages). A handbook for workers. Discusses general principles and educational and social phases of the problem of Americanization.

State Americanization, the Part of the State in the Education and Assimilation of the Immigrant, by F. C. Butler, Director of Americanization, Bureau of Education (Bulletin, 1919, No. 77; Washington, 1920, 26 pages). Discusses state legislation, the State and the community, and presents a plan for a state Americanization survey.

Biennial Survey of Education, 1916-1918 (Bulletins, 1919, Nos. 88, 89, 90, 91; Washington, 1921, 4 volumes). This publication is of considerable value for its statistical data for the years covered. Vol. I (756 pages) is by various authorities on special fields, such as higher education, secondary education, medical education, engineering education, commercial education, agricultural education, vocational education, educational work of the churches, rural education, home education, and home economics. Vol. II (558 pages) contains a survey of changes in education in the British Empire, Europe, Latin America, and Japan; Vol. III (901 pages) contains 206 tables based upon statistical surveys of education in the United States classified as to state and city systems, universities, colleges, and professional schools. Vol. IV (797 pages) contains 278 tables based upon statistical surveys of normal schools, public and private high schools, private commercial and business schools, summer schools, and schools for nurse-training, the blind, the deaf, the feeble-minded, and the delinquent. A similar study for the years 1918-1920 is published as Bulletin, 1923; No. 29 (597 pages).

Training Teachers for Americanization (Bulletin, 1920, No. 12; Washington, 1920, 62 pages). Presents a course of study for normal schools.

The National Crisis in Education: an Appeal to the People (Bulletin, 1920, No. 29; Washington, 1920, 191 pages). The report of the proceedings of the National Citizens Conference on Education, held in Washington May 19-21, 1920. Describes the effects of the war on the schools and embodies a statement of reconstruction conditions, as to shortage of teachers, adjustment to new conditions, relation of education to material wealth, the new interest in education, and education for citizenship.

Training for Foreign Service (Bulletin, 1921, No. 27; Washington, 1922, 154 pages). A series of articles by specialists on training required for foreign service in economics, in government, and in foreign languages.

Teacher Placement by Public Agencies (Bulletin, 1921, No. 42; Washington, 1921, 8 pages). Tells of measures taken to procure teachers, the supply of whom is less than the demand.

Engineering Education after the War (Bulletin, 1921, No. 50; Washington, 1922, 27 pages). Discusses the schedule of studies for courses in civil engineering, mechanical engineering, electrical engineering, and chemical engineering proposed by the Committee on Educational and Special Training during the war.

Special Publications

Lessons in Community and National Life, edited by C. H. Judd and L. C. Marshall (Washington, 1918). These lessons were published in coöperation with the Food Administration to furnish the schools with a course of study on the social organization of the United States and the effects of the war. They were circulated originally as small pamphlets during the period from October, 1917, to May, 1918, and the series was adapted to various school ages in the following manner:—for the upper classes of the high schools, Series A, 264 pages, 29 lessons; for the first class of the high schools and the upper grades of the elementary schools, Series B, 264 pages, 31 lessons; for the intermediate grades of the elementary schools, Series C, 264 pages, 32 lessons. The subject matter of these lessons varied with the age to which they were adapted, and included such topics as production and wise consumption, machine industry and community life, national control and food conservation, the war labor administration, private control of industry, impersonality of modern life, industries and institutions, and social control. Data on the methods by which these lessons were circulated is on file in the Mails and Files Division.

Proceedings of the Americanization Conference, held in Washington, May 12-15, 1919, under the auspices of the Americanization Division, Bureau of Education (Washington, 1919, 410 pages). A discussion of technical methods of teaching English, reörganization of educational administration for the purposes of Americanization, training teachers for Americanization problems, Americanization methods in industry, securing interest and coöperation, and the best fields for the service of various local agencies working for Americanization.

Flag Exercises for the Schools of the Nation (Washington, 1919, 11 pages). An appeal for the observance of daily flag exercises in the public schools.

Home Gardening for City Children of the Fifth, Sixth, and Seventh Grades, by Ethel Gowans (Washington, 1919, 72 pages). Contains directions for gardening and questions to create interest in the subject.

CIRCULARS

A number of circulars dealing with war problems were issued at irregular intervals. The following are illustrative and the most important within the scope of this survey:

Suggestions for the conduct of educational institutions during the continuance of the war (Circular, May 22, 1917, 8 pages).

Report of a conference held at Washington, May 3, 1917, under the auspices of the Committee on Science, Engineering, and Education of the Advisory Commission of the Council of National Defense (Higher Education Circular No. 1; May 8, 1917, 10 pages). A discussion of work of American colleges and universities during the war.

Report of the work of the Education Section of the Committee on Engineering and Education of the Advisory Commission of the Council of National Defense (Higher Education Circular No. 2; June 8, 1917, 7 pages). A discussion of the work of American colleges and universities during the war.

Report of a joint conference of the Education Section of the Committee on Engineering and Education of the Advisory Commission of the Council of National Defense and a commission representing the universities of Canada (Higher Education Circular No. 3; July, 1917, 6 pages). A discussion of the work of American colleges and universities during the war.

Contribution of higher institutions to the war and to reconstruction (Higher Education Circular, No. 4; August 30, 1917, 6 pages).

Report of the work of the University Section of the Committee on Engineering and Education of the Advisory Commission of the Council of National Defense (Higher Education Circular, No. 5; December 15, 1917, 13 pages).

Report on the contribution of higher institutions to the National service (Higher Education Circular, No. 6; January, 1918, 21 pages).

Effect of the war on student enrollment (Higher Education Circular, No. 9; April, 1918, 3 pages).

Effect of the war on college budgets (Higher Education Circular, No. 10; April, 1918, 3 pages).

Opportunities at college for returning soldiers (Higher Education Circular, No. 12; 29 pages).

Secondary schools and the war (Secondary School Circular, No. 1; January, 1918, 4 pages).

Organization of high schools in war time (Secondary School Circular, No. 2; April, 1918, 6 pages).

Science teaching in the secondary schools in the war emergency (Secondary School Circular, No. 3; September, 1918, 19 pages).

Industrial arts in secondary schools in the war emergency (Secondary School Circular, No. 4; September, 1918, 31 pages).

Lessons from the war and their application in the training of teachers (Industrial Education Circular, No. 1; 1919, 20 pages).

The army trade test (Industrial Education Circular, No. 4; 1919, 28 pages).

Home economics teaching under present economic conditions (Home Economics Circular, September 5, 1917).

Effect of war conditions on clothing and textile courses (Home Economics Circular, No. 7; October, 1918, 7 pages).

Opportunities for history teachers: the lessons of the Great War in the class room (Teachers' Leaflet, No. 1; 1917, 22 pages).

Education in patriotism, a synopsis of the agencies at work (Teachers' Leaflet, No. 2; April, 1918, 10 pages).

Government policies involving the schools in war time (Teachers' Leaflet, No. 3; April, 1918, 6 pages).

Outline of an emergency course of instruction on the war (Teachers' Leaflet, No. 4; August, 1918, 31 pages).

Constitution of a community association (Community Center Circular, No. 1; January, 1919, 12 pages).

Community buildings as soldiers' memorials (Community Center Circular, No. 2; January, 1919, 12 pages).

What libraries learned from the war (Library Leaflet, No. 14; January, 1922, 6 pages).

Records

The records of the Bureau of Education are chiefly available in the Mails and Files Division, in which are filed huge quantities of material collected by the Educational Extension Division, the Council of National Defense, and other agencies engaged in educational activities during the war. Because of lack of storage facilities much of this material has been destroyed; that which remains is classified by subjects but has no index. The records of the School Board Service Division show how that division worked to supply the demand for teachers of technical subjects in the higher institutions by circularizing available candidates and informing school boards of opportunities to fill vacancies. Some engineering school material includes mimeographed questionnaires calling for detailed information relative to facilities for technical instruction, but the greater part of this material has been transferred to the War Plans Division, War Department. A number of other questionnaires indicate the nature, and extent of the information which was solicited from educational institutions.

The Mails and Files Division has kept separate file boxes containing material of the following sorts: (1) Circulars on the war and education, including mimeographs and carbons of correspondence and press releases, and propaganda for the maintenance of school attendance and for the adequate supply of teachers; (2) Educational Extension Division bulletins and summaries bearing on collaboration with state extension work, the distribution of war films, and allied propaganda; (3) School Garden Army, showing coöperation with the Hoover program for food conservation; (4) addresses of the Secretary of the Interior on Americanization.

With other mimeographed material are copies of reports of occasional conferences, two of which are: (1) "Report of a Conference of Specialists in Industrial Education, in Philadelphia, February 22, 1918" (10 pages), dealing with the examination and certification of industrial teachers; (2) "Corporation School Conference," report of a meeting in Washington, June 18, 1918, aiming to coordinate corporation schools with elementary and technical public schools, and to work out the relationship between the public schools and commerce and industry. A monograph issued in mimeograph by the Educational Extension Division and entitled "Relations of Labor and Industry in Reconstruction" (29 pages) contains a bibliography of governmental publications relating to labor. The library of the Bureau of Education has mimeographed bibliographies on publications relating to the war and reconstruction, domestic and foreign education as affected by the war, teaching of

German and modern languages, education of illiterates, Americanization, education in civics and patriotism, military education, thrift, new tendencies in the education of women, reëducation of crippled soldiers, etc.

DEPARTMENT OF AGRICULTURE

Departmental Functions and Organization

THE war-time functions of the Department of Agriculture were essentially of the same nature as those which had developed under progressive legislation since the creation of the department, May 15, 1862, namely, to acquire and to diffuse useful information on subjects connected with agriculture, and to procure, propagate, and distribute new and valuable seeds and plants. On the eve of the war the functions of the department were: (1) scientific study of the fundamental problems of agriculture, (2) dissemination of information developed through experiments and discovery, and (3) administration of acts of Congress relative to agriculture. To meet the war emergency, the functioning of the system as organized had only to be enlarged and stimulated, and this need was provided by the food production act of August 10, 1917, entitled, "An act to provide further for the national security and defense by stimulating agriculture and facilitating the distribution of agricultural products." This act made appropriations to be used by the department for the prevention, control, and eradication of the diseases and pests of live stock, for the enlargement of live-stock production, for the conservation and utilization of meat, poultry, dairy, and other animal products, for procuring, storing, and furnishing seeds for cash at cost to farmers in restricted areas where emergency conditions prevailed, for the prevention, control, and eradication of insects and plant diseases injurious to agriculture, for the conservation and utilization of plant products, for the further development of the extension service coöperating with agricultural colleges in the States, for making surveys of the food supply of the United States, for gathering and disseminating information concerning farm products, for extending and enlarging the market news services, for preventing waste of food in storage, in transit, or while held for sale, for the development of the information work of the department, for the enlargement of facilities for dealing with the farm labor problem, and for the extension of the work of the Bureau of Crop Estimates and the Bureau of Chemistry.

In distinction from the United States Food Administration, which controlled and regulated the commercial distribution of foods that had reached the markets or were in the hands of consumers, the Department of Agriculture directed activities relative to production, the distribution of products to markets, and the conservation of perishable products through canning, drying, preserving, and pickling. Each, however, rendered assistance to the other.

The department was organized during the war in the following divisions: Office of the Secretary, States Relations Service, Forest Service, Bureau of Plant Industry, Bureau of Animal Industry, Bureau of Markets, Bureau of Crop Estimates, Bureau of Chemistry, Bureau of Farm Management, Weather Bureau, Bureau of Entomology, Bureau of Biological Survey, Bureau of Soils, Bureau of Public Roads, Library, Division of Publications, Office of Information, and Office of Exhibits. A National Agricultural Advisory Committee served both the Department and the United States Food Administration, and an Agricultural Commission to Europe was appointed in August, 1918.

OFFICE OF THE SECRETARY

War Measures

The Secretary of Agriculture, who is responsible for the promotion of agriculture in its broadest sense and for the general policies of the department, formulated a war program in a conference at St. Louis, Mo., April 9 and 10, 1917, with the state commissioners of agriculture and presidents of state agricultural colleges, a program in which was the genesis of the food production and food administration acts of August 10, 1917. In conformity with his purposes to effect closer coöperation of the department with state departments of agriculture, state agricultural colleges, farmers' organizations, and representative farmers, there was organized in connection with each state council of defense a division of food production and conservation composed of representatives of state boards of agriculture, state agricultural colleges, farmers' organizations, and business agencies. Community organization was also encouraged. The Secretary was a member of the

Council of National Defense and of the War Trade Council. In March, 1918, he and the United States Food Administrator created the National Agricultural Advisory Committee, and in August of the same year, he appointed the Agricultural Commission to Europe. The Assistant Secretary of Agriculture, as well as the Secretary, represented the department on several occasions at hearings before committees of Congress.

Publications

Annual Reports of the Department of Agriculture for the year ended June 30, 1917 (Washington, 1918, 499 pages). Report of the Secretary to the President relative to business and executive matters; reports of bureau and division chiefs to the Secretary relative to operations. The report of the Secretary, pages 3-44, is devoted wholly to the war program of the department.

Annual Reports of the Department of Agriculture . . . 1918 (Washington, 1919, 520 pages). In his report for this year (pages 3-54), the Secretary discusses such matters as the agricultural effort, plans for 1918, meat supply, stockyards and packing houses, market news service, farm labor supply, and seed-grain loans in drouth areas.

Annual Reports of the Department of Agriculture . . . 1919 (Washington, 1920, 560 pages). The Secretary (pages 3-46) reviews post-war conditions, yields, and exports, and discusses farm land problems, crop and live-stock reporting service, coöperative associations, roads, and need for broad survey of rural conditions.

Yearbook of the United States Department of Agriculture, 1917 (Washington, 1917, 583 pages). Report of the Secretary; brief review of the work of the bureaus and offices of the department; agricultural statistics; papers on such subjects as status of the peanut industry, federal aid to highways, sources of nitrogenous fertilizers, phosphate rock as a fertilizer asset, fertilizers from public wastes, world's supply of wheat, and pig clubs as a means of stimulating the swine industry. See also the *Yearbooks* for 1918 and 1919. Lists of pertinent articles in the successive *Yearbooks* are given below under the various bureaus.

Program of Work of the United States Department of Agriculture for the fiscal year, 1919 (Washington, 1919, 617 pages). Pages 1-548 cover regular activities; pages 549-617 cover emergency activities for the year beginning July 1, 1918, and are of prime importance for the study of the entire war program of the department.

Circulars

A number of important department circulars, printed at the Government Printing Office, were issued by the Office of the Secretary during the war. Those contributed by bureau chiefs are listed among the publications of the bureaus in which they were prepared. Others are as follows:

75. *Food Needs for 1918: Agricultural program for the period beginning with the autumn of 1917* (1917, 14 pages).

78. *Method of Sale of Nitrate of Soda to Farmers by the United States Government* (January, 1918, 11 pages).

82. *Rules and Regulations of the Secretary of Agriculture under the Food Products Inspection Law of August 10, 1917* (October 31, 1917, 8 pages).

84-93. *The Agricultural Situation for 1918.* A series of statements prepared under the direction of the Secretary of Agriculture, Parts I to XI.

84. Part I. *Hogs: Hog production should be increased* (January, 1918, 24 pages).

85. Part II. *Dairying: Dairy products should be maintained* (January 31, 1918, 24 pages).

86. Part III. *Sugar: More beet and cane sugar should be produced* (February 28, 1918, 34 pages).

87. Part IV. *Honey: More honey needed* (January 31, 1918, 8 pages).

88. Part V. *Cotton: Maintaining the supply of cotton* (February 18, 1918, 34 pages).

89. Part VI. *Rice: Produce more rice for consumption and export* (March 1, 1918, 24 pages).

90. Part VII. *Wheat: More wheat is needed for home use and for the allies* (March 6, 1918, 32 pages).

91. Part VIII. *Corn: A large acreage of corn needed* (March 4, 1918, 17 pages).

92. Part IX. *Potatoes: An ample supply of potatoes needed* (March 15, 1918, 39 pages).

93. Part X. *Wool: War makes more sheep and wool necessary* (March 15, 1918, 14 pages).

107. Part XI. *Poultry: One hundred hens on every farm; one hundred eggs from every hen* (March 25, 1918, 24 pages).

103. *Agricultural Production for 1918 with Special Reference to Spring Planting and Live Stock* (February 19, 1918, 22 pages).

105. *Method of Sale of War Emergency Seed Corn to Farmers in certain States by the United States Department of Agriculture* (February 27, 1918, 8 pages).

108. *Food Needs for 1919: Part of agricultural program for the period beginning with the autumn of 1918; Fall-sown wheat and rye* (June 23, 1918, 13 pages).

112. *The Farm Labor Problem: Man-power sufficient if properly mobilized by coöperation and community action* (April 18, 1918, 10 pages).

115. *Finding Labor to Harvest the Food Crops* (August 2, 1918, 8 pages).

116. *General Regulations governing Licenses operating Stock Yards, or handling or dealing in Live Stock in or in connection with Stock Yards* (July 26, 1918, with amendment September 24, 1918, 16 pages).

120. *Rules and Regulations of the Secretary of Agriculture under the Food Products Inspection Law of October 1, 1918* (October 4, 1918, 8 pages).

123. *Food Needs for 1919: Part of agricultural program for the period beginning with the autumn of 1918: Live-stock production for 1919* (October, 1918, 14 pages).

125. *Agricultural Production for 1919 with special reference to Crops and Live Stock* (January 23, 1919, 27 pages).

130. *Address of D. F. Houston,* Secretary of Agriculture, before the Trans-Mississippi Readjustment Congress, Omaha, Neb., February 20, 1919 (19 pages).

133. *Address of D. F. Houston,* Secretary of Agriculture, before the Governors' Conference, Annapolis, Md., December 16, 1918 (15 pages).

Records

The department library has some mimeographed records which originated in the Secretary's office; among them are the following papers:

A statement by the Secretary of Agriculture designed to stimulate the production of food products (February 16, 1918, 8 pages).

The war program suggested by the United States Department of Agriculture for the increase of pork production in 1918 (7 pages).

Suggestions to Southern farmers in view of the cotton crisis (n.d., 9 pages).

Memorandum of information explaining some of the provisions of the President's proclamation of May 14, 1918, licensing the farm equipment industry (n.d., 2 pages).

Plan for extending the system of employment exchanges in coöperation with the Department of Agriculture and the Council of National Defense (Department of Labor, revision of July 7, 1918, 8 pages).

Report by a committee of a conference of representatives of the Food Administration, the Department of Agriculture, state food administrators, and state and municipal food and drug control officials to project a plan for the conservation of eggs (May, 1918, 6 pages).

An important war duty of the South for 1918, a statement by Clarence Ousley, Assistant Secretary of Agriculture (n.d., 1 page).

A letter by Clarence Ousley, Assistant Secretary of Agriculture, to agricultural advisers of district draft boards (September 11, 1918, 3 pages).

Plans and activities of the United States Department of Agriculture, 1913-1919 (July 1, 1919, 67 pages).

Summary of activities of the Department of Agriculture affected by reduced appropriations, by E. T. Meredith, Secretary of Agriculture (June 5, 1920, 25 pages).

STATES RELATIONS SERVICE

Functions and Organization

An agricultural college is maintained in each State out of the proceeds of an endowment provided by acts of Congress of 1862, 1890, and 1907; an agricultural experiment station at each of the colleges was provided for by acts of 1887 and 1906, and extension work by the colleges in coöperation with the Department of Agriculture was provided for by act of May 8, 1914, such work to consist of instruction and practical demonstrations in agriculture and home economics to persons in the rural communities. To administer the coöperation of the Department of Agriculture with these institutions and farmer organizations the States Relations Service was organized July 1, 1915, with a director, Office of Experiment Stations, Office of Extension Work in the South (15 States), Office of Extension Work in the North and West (33 States), and Office of Home Economics, to conduct investigations relative to foods, clothing, household equipment, and management. The local operators of the system were the county agricultural agent, acting as adviser and demonstrator to the farmers, and the county home demonstration agent, a woman, acting as expert adviser to the housewives in matters of domestic science and household economy. Besides the rural workers, home demonstration agents were employed in about 200 cities. These were supervised and aided in each State by an extension director, state leaders, and extension specialists in the various branches of agriculture and home economics. Similar officers in the States Relations Service and in the several department bureaus also joined in the work of the state and county forces.

War Activities

During the war there was a large increase in the number of counties in which the extension system was organized, and the number of extension workers coöperatively employed by the Department of Agriculture, the state colleges of agriculture, and local and county authorities increased from 2500 to 6200. These workers organized the farmers, they organized thousands of community clubs of farmers, of women, and of boys, and they organized as many people as possible to undertake some type of work which would enable them to increase food production or conserve the supply of grain, fruits, vegetables, and meats. They assisted in overcoming the shortage of seed corn in 1918, and in increasing the acreage of wheat, of other cereals, and of potatoes; were active in the campaign to increase the number of live stock; reduced the acreage of cotton in the face of high prices for that commodity; promoted the conservation of fruits, vegetables, and fish by canning, drying, and pickling; and carried the lessons of wheat, meat, sugar, and fat conservation to every family within reach.

Publications

REPORTS

Report of the Director of the States Relations Service for the fiscal year ended June 30, 1917 (Washington, 1917, 35 pages). Work of the county agricultural agents, home economics, work of specialists from state agricultural colleges and department bureaus, boys' agricultural clubs.

Report of the Director of the States Relations Service, 1918 (Washington, 1918, 37 pages). Expansion of the extension system, work of the county agricultural agents, assistance rendered by specialists, home demonstrations, girls' clubs, boys' clubs, home economics, and dietary survey.

Report of the Director of the States Relations Service, 1919 (Washington, 1919, 37 pages). War-time cooking experiments, effects on agriculture of war-time activities, efforts to maintain the war-time service.

Coöperative Extension Work in Agriculture and Home Economics, 1917 (Washington, 1919, 416 pages). Extension work in the South, extension work in the North and West, farm management demonstration, work of extension specialists, extension schools, farmers' institutes and meetings, state reports, statistics.

Coöperative Extension Work in Agriculture and Home Economics, 1918 (Washington, 1919, 158 pages). War work in the South, expansion for war service in the North and West.

Work and Expenditures of the Agricultural Experiment Stations, 1917 (Washington, 1918, 335 pages). The experiment stations and the war.

Work and Expenditures of the Agricultural Experiment Stations, 1918 (Washington, 1920, 80 pages). The experiment stations in war time, modification of the working program as a result of war conditions, special war services of station workers.

Work and Expenditures of the Agricultural Experiment Stations, 1919 (Washington, 1921, 94 pages). Effects of the war on agricultural research.

Statistics of Coöperative Extension Work, 1919-1920 (Washington, 1920, 16 pages). Table III exhibits the sources of funds for coöperative agricultural extension work, 1918-1919 and 1919-1920; table IV, the total of funds from all sources for the same work, by projects, for the two years ending June 30, 1920.

FARMERS' BULLETINS

The following *Farmers' Bulletins*, relating to foods, issued by the Department of Agriculture were contributions from the States Relations Service during the period of the war.

839. *Home Canning by the One-Period Cold Pack Method,* by O. H. Benson. Issued in June, 1917, and reprinted in May, 1918 (39 pages).

853. *Home Canning of Fruits and Vegetables as Taught to Canning Club Members in the Southern States,* by Mary E. Creswell and Ola Powell (July, 1917, 41 pages).

871. *Fresh Fruits and Vegetables as Conservers of other Staple Foods,* by Caroline L. Hunt (July, 1917, 11 pages).

881. *Preservation of Vegetables by Fermentation and Salting,* by L. A. Round and H. L. Lang (August, 1917, 15 pages).

955. *Use of Wheat Flour Substitutes in Baking,* by Hannah L. Wessling (March, 1918, 22 pages).

DEPARTMENT OF AGRICULTURE CIRCULARS

66. *Organization and Results of Boys' and Girls' Club Work* (Northern and Western States), 1918, by O. H. Benson and Gertrude Warren (Washington, 1920, 38 pages).

EXPERIMENT STATION RECORD

In *Experiment Station Record,* a monthly publication consisting largely of abstracts of station and department publications, are editorials on the following subjects:

Agriculture and the war in Europe. November, 1916 (Vol. 35, pp. 601-605).

Effect of the war on agricultural conditions (*ibid.*, pp. 605-610).

The experiment stations and the war. May, 1917 (Vol. 36, pp. 601-604).

The response of the experiment stations to the present emergency. July, 1917 (Vol. 37, pp. 1-4).

The adjustment of theory and practice to war conditions (*ibid.*, pp. 4-7).

The Federal Food Production act. September, 1917 (*ibid.*, pp. 301-307).

Attendance at the agricultural colleges as affected by the war. December, 1917 (*ibid.*, pp. 701-708).

The opportunity for individual service. January, 1918 (Vol. 38, pp. 1-4).

Helping to win the war (*ibid.*, pp. 4-6).

Closer relation of station and extension forces (*ibid.*, pp. 6-7).

An agricultural program. February, 1918 (*ibid.*, pp. 101-102).

Agriculture under reconstruction. April, 1918 (*ibid.*, pp. 401-405).

The place of experiment stations in a reconstruction program (*ibid.*, pp. 405-408).

The return of station workers from war service. April, 1919 (Vol. 40, pp. 401-403).

The influence of the war on station work in the future (*ibid.*, pp. 403-407).

YEARBOOK

In the *Yearbook* for 1920 is an article entitled, "Food for Farm Families" (pp. 471-484), which is based on data assembled by a dietary survey made by the Office of Home Economics in coöperation with the Bureau of Markets.

CIRCULARS AND LEAFLETS

To promote thrift and conservation a number of circulars and leaflets were issued and widely distributed either by the States Relations Service alone or by it in coöperation with the United States Food Administration or Treasury Department. Among them are the following circulars contributed by the service in 1918.

106. *Use Potatoes to Save Wheat.* March 12, 1918 (6 pages).

110. *Use Peanut Flour to Save Wheat.* April 15, 1918 (4 pages).

111. *Use Barley—Save Wheat.* April 18, 1918 (4 pages).

113. *Use Soy-Bean Flour to Save Wheat, Meat, and Fat.* May 2, 1918 (4 pages).

117. *Use Corn Meal and Corn Flour to Save Wheat.* August 14, 1918 (4 pages).

118. *Use Oats to Save Wheat.* August 14, 1918 (4 pages).

119. *Use Rice Flour to Save Wheat.* August 14, 1918 (4 pages).

Of twenty *United States Food Leaflets*, 4 pages each, prepared and distributed in coöperation with the United States Food Administration in 1917 and 1918, ten are as follows:

Do you know corn meal?
Do you know oat meal?
Make a little meat go a long way.
Plenty of potatoes.
Milk, best food we have.
Save fuel when you cook.
Let fireless cooker help you cook.
Save sugar, use other sweets.
Use more fish.
Wheatless breads and cakes.

Of twenty *Thrift Leaflets*, 4 pages each, prepared in coöperation with the Treasury Department in 1919, thirteen are as follows:

Is thrift worth while, Mr. American?
Seven steps toward saving.
Wise spending saves clothing for family.
Saving time and money by simple housecleaning.
Saving labor and materials by easier laundry methods.
Saving materials and money by special cleaning.
Thrift in lighting.
Thrift in choice, use, and care of kitchen utensils.
Thrift in use of fuel for cooking.
Saving fuel in heating.
Saving food by proper care.
Thrift on farm.
Business methods for the home.

A *Food Thrift Series*, issued in 1917, comprises five numbers as follows:

1. *Help feed yourself, make home gardens and back yards productive* (4 pages).
2. *Watch your kitchen waste* (8 pages).
3. *Let nothing spoil* (8 pages).
4. *Appeal to women* (8 pages).
5. *Wheatless meals* (8 pages).

Mimeographed Material

A number of mimeographed papers that were issued by the States Relations Service as instructions or suggestions to home demonstration agents and other extension workers have been assembled in the department library. Among them are the following:

Household waste and ways to avoid it. May 9, 1917 (13 pages).

Extension work with women. Women as farm laborers. 1917 (5 pages).

Suggested program for rural home demonstration work with special reference to conservation, by Florence E. Ward. February 1, 1918 (Part I, 25 pages; part II, 17 pages).

Suggested program for urban home demonstration work with special reference to conservation, by Florence E. Ward. n.d. (23 pages).

To home demonstration agents in the North and West, by Florence E. Ward. August 1, 1918 (6 pages).

Suggestions for clothing, fuel, money, and strength conservation campaigns under the leadership of a home demonstration agent. 1918 (7 pages).

Suggestions for home demonstration agents regarding fuel conservation in house lighting. 1918 (5 pages).

Suggestions for organization of food emergency work with women in accordance with project on home economics extension work by means of home demonstration agents and emergency home demonstration agents. 1918 (14 pages).

Suggestions for organization of war emergency work with women in accordance with project on home economics extension work by means of home demonstration agents and emergency home demonstration agents, by Florence E. Ward and Emma A. Winslow (14 pages).

Some of the more important results of boys' and girls' club work, northern and western States, for 1917 (regular and emergency) (11 pages).

Boys' agricultural clubs; some 1917 results. July 1, 1918 (5 pages).

To state and county home demonstration agents regarding shortage of wheat, by H. L. Wessling. May 14, 1918 (5 pages).

Memorandum for home demonstration agents. August 6, 1918 (11 pages).

Rural women's clubs, by Emma Reed Davisson. September 1, 1918 (11 pages).

What the South must do. 1918 (1 page).

The South must produce its own food and feed. 1918 (1 page).

Retail equivalent values of a bale of cotton. 1918 (1 page).

Suggestions for home demonstration agents regarding methods of teaching thrift, by Winifred S. Gibbs. December 27, 1918 (3 pages).

Memorandum for home demonstration agents regarding the textile and fuel situations. December 12, 1918 (1 page).

Suggestions for the formulation of a practical thrift program by home demonstration leaders. December 15, 1918.

Suggestions for demonstration and community activities to reduce the consumption of coal, by Edith Charlton Salisbury (9 pages).

Suggestions for committee work, demonstration and volunteer classes conducted by rural and urban home demonstration agents, by Edith Charlton Salisbury (9 pages).

Suggestions on farm bureau office administration for home demonstration agents (9 pages).

Steps preparatory to cottage cheese campaign in cities (4 pages).

The war emergency community kitchen, by Margaret Huntington Hooker (23 pages).

Sugar saving campaign, by Edith Charlton Salisbury (6 pages).

Standardization of recipes: adaptation; substitution variation, by Anna Barrows (12 pages).

Suggestions for training volunteer leaders for a country wide preservation campaign (5 pages).

Helps for home demonstration agents in teaching home drying, by Grace E. Frysinger (12 pages).

Helps for home demonstration agents in teaching home salting, brining, and fermentation, by Grace E. Frysinger (12 pages).

Helps for home demonstration agents in teaching home canning, by Grace E. Frysinger (14 pages).

Memorandum to state leaders of home demonstration agents. October 1, 1919 (4 pages).

Organization list of county agent work. December 1, 1919 (35 pages).

Records

The important war records of the States Relations Service are the reports of county agents, home demonstration agents, and other field workers, and the data assembled in three surveys: (1) War emergency food survey; (2) National dietary survey; and (3) War emergency fertilizer survey. Filed with the data are samples of the printed questionnaires asking information as to stocks on hand and in transit, production, producing capacity, and importation of the various classified articles. The most extensive survey was that of the food supplies of retail concerns, as of August 31, 1917, covering the entire United States. The dietary survey was limited to 1000 American homes and 500 boarding houses, college clubs, and other institutions.

FOREST SERVICE[1]

An investigation of forestry subjects was begun by the Depart-

[1] The material for this report on the Forest Service was compiled by Mr. Herbert A. Smith, assistant forester in charge of the Branch of Public Relations.

ment of Agriculture in 1876. A Division of Forestry was established in 1881. The name was changed to Bureau of Forestry in 1902. The administration of the national forests was transferred from the Department of the Interior to the Department of Agriculture in 1905, and in the same year the Bureau of Forestry was succeeded by the Forest Service.

Functions and Organization

The primary functions of the service are: (1) to administer, protect, develop, improve, and maintain the national forests; (2) to promote the full use of their resources, prevent waste, and especially to preserve the forest cover on the watersheds. A secondary function is the promotion of the application of forestry to private timberlands. The administrative work is directed by seven branches in Washington: Operation, Forest Management, Grazing, Lands, Engineering, Research, and Public Relations. Each of the eight field districts into which the country is divided has a headquarters office similarly organized. Each of the 146 national forests is administered by a supervisor with a corps of forest rangers and guards.

The **Branch of Forest Management** is charged with the administration of national forest timber sales, timber surveys, timber and fire trespass, reforestation, administrative use, free use, and insect control.

The **Branch of Grazing** is charged with the supervision of the grazing business so as to utilize the range to its full capacity, to secure its use to settlers and others most entitled to use it, and to improve the range and the quality of the stock produced.

The **Engineering Section** is charged with the administration of water-power uses, with road and trail work, and with the execution of surveys.

The **Branch of Research** embraces the Office of Forest Experiment Stations, the Office of Forest Products and the Office of Forest Economics in Washington, the Forest Products Laboratory at Madison, Wis., and the forest experiment stations in the chief timber regions. It conducts investigations on timber growing, on forest-grown products, and in woodworking industries, collects statistics, and makes economic studies bearing on forestry, forest products, and national-forest management.

War Activities

The ordinary resources of the Forest Service were completely mobilized for the purposes of the war, and a greatly expanded research organization worked on problems connected with the best use of the country's wood supplies. Coöperating with the War Department, Navy Department, War Industries Board, Shipping Board, Emergency Fleet Corporation, Railroad Administration, War Trade Board, and other war agencies, its activities covered nearly every use of wood for war purposes: aircraft, wooden ships, military vehicles, boxes, crates, and other containers, lumber, structural timber, wood for offensive and defensive gas warfare, pulp and pulp products, fiber boards, wooden pipe, implement handles, wooden limbs, rosin for shrapnel, naval stores, tannin, and noseplugs for shells. It made a survey of the timber resources of the United States, and furnished information regarding foreign and domestic timber resources, their location, quality, production, means of increasing production, manufacturing processes, strength properties of woods, best substitutes, and various economic questions. Where time was an important factor it effected the substitution of kiln-dried woods for woods dried in the air. With the aid of coöperating States, other forestry agencies, and the Boy Scouts, the necessary supply of black walnut for gunstocks and airplane propellers was located. The service assisted in increasing the production of meats, hides, and wool by opening new ranges for grazing. It coöperated with the Fuel Administration in a campaign to conserve coal by stimulating the use of wood as a substitute.

Publications

Brief statements covering the transformation of the Forest Service from peace-time to war-time operations and the results are contained in the following reports and articles.

Report of the Forester, 1917 (Washington, 1917, 36 pages). Changes to meet war conditions, increase of stock on forest ranges, increased cost of road construction.

Report of the Forester, 1918 (Washington, 1918, 36 pages). The Forest Service in war time, timber resources and the war, increase of stock on forest ranges, war research work.

Report of the Forester, 1919 (Washington, 1919, 34 pages). Effect of the war on the Forest Service, the war and water power, investigations in forest products, forest investigations.

The following publications deal with specific investigations.

The Kiln Drying of Woods for Airplanes, by Harry D. Tiemann. Report No. 65, U.S. National Advisory Committee for Aeronautics (Washington, 1919, 31 pages).

Glues Used in Airplane Parts, by S. W. Allen and T. R. Truax. Report No. 66, U.S. National Advisory Committee for Aeronautics (Washington, 1920, 28 pages).

Supplies and Production of Aircraft Woods, by W. N. Sparhawk. Report No. 67, U.S. National Advisory Committee for Aeronautics (Washington, 1919, 62 pages).

The Effect of Kiln Drying on the Strength of Airplane Woods, by T. R. C. Wilson. Report No. 68, U.S. National Advisory Committee for Aeronautics (Washington, 1920, 69 pages).

Data on the Design of Plywood for Aircraft, by Armin Elmendorf. Report No. 84, U.S. National Advisory Committee for Aeronautics (Washington, 1920, 15 pages).

Moisture Resistant Finishes for Airplane Woods, by M. E. Dunlap. Report No. 85, U.S. National Advisory Committee for Aeronautics (Washington, 1920, 8 pages).

The Strength of One-Piece, Solid, Built-Up, and Laminated Wood Airplane Wing Beams, by John H. Nelson. Report No. 35, U.S. National Advisory Committee for Aeronautics (Washington, 1919, 12 pages).

Wood in Aircraft Construction. Aircraft Design Data, Note No. 12, U.S. Navy Department, Bureau of Construction and Repair (Washington, 1919, 149 pages).

Information for Inspectors of Airplane Woods. U.S. War Department, Signal Office (Washington, 1918, 72 pages).

Summary Report on Driving Tests on Treenails, at the Yard of the American Shipbuilding Company, Brunswick, Ga. U.S. Department of Agriculture, Forest Service (Washington, 1918, 31 pages).

Emergency Fuel from the Farm Woodlot, by A. F. Hawes. Circular No. 79, U.S. Department of Agriculture, Office of the Secretary (Washington, 1917, 8 pages).

Farm Woodlands and the War, by Henry S. Graves. U.S. Department of Agriculture *Yearbook* for 1918 (Washington, 1919, pp. 317-326).

The Seasoning of Wood, by Harold S. Betts. U.S. Department of Agriculture Bulletin No. 552 (Washington, 1917, 28 pages).

Mechanical Properties of Woods Grown in the United States, by J. A. Newlin and T. R. C. Wilson. U.S. Department of Agriculture Bulletin No. 556 (Washington, 1917, 47 pages).

Increased Yield of Turpentine and Rosin from Double Chipping, by A. W. Schorger and R. L. Pettigrew. U.S. Department of Agriculture Bulletin No. 567 (Washington, 1917, 9 pages).

Increased Cattle Production on Southwestern Ranges, by James T. Jardine and L. C. Hurtt. U.S. Department of Agriculture Bulletin No. 588 (Washington, 1917, 32 pages).

Lumber Used in the Manufacture of Wooden Products, by J. C. Nellis. U.S. Department of Agriculture Bulletin No. 605 (Washington, 1918, 18 pages).

The Use of Wood for Fuel. U.S. Department of Agriculture Bulletin No. 753 (Washington, 1919, 40 pages).

Pulpwood Consumption and Wood-Pulp Production in 1917, by Franklin H. Smith. U.S. Department of Agriculture Bulletin No. 758 (Washington, 1919, 19 pages).

Production of Lumber, Lath, and Shingles in 1917, by Franklin H. Smith and Albert H. Pierson. U.S. Department of Agriculture Bulletin No. 768 (Washington, 1919, 44 pages).

Utilization of Black Walnut, by Warren D. Brush, U.S. Department of Agriculture Bulletin No. 909 (Washington, 1921, 89 pages).

Prices of Lumber, by R. C. Bryant, No. 43 of bulletins issued by the War Industries Board under the general title: *History of Prices during the War* (Washington, 1919, 112 pages).

Records

A general survey of the investigative program of the Forest Service during the war is contained in a mimeographed circular entitled "Activities of the Branch of Research on War Problems." June 5, 1918 (17 pages). The lines of activities dealt with comprise: (1) raw materials; (2) tests and investigations of material, processes, and products; (3) education, *i.e.*, assistance in training men for specialized tasks in the service of the government and of the forest and wood-using industries; (4) coöperation. These activities are taken up successively under the following headings: aircraft, wooden ships, vehicles, pulp and paper, miscellaneous derived products, boxes and containers, lumber, and miscellaneous activities.

The progress of investigative work at the Forest Products Laboratory is set forth in the successive "Monthly Reports of the Laboratory" (manuscript). Of these, the reports covering the months from June, 1918, to January, 1919, inclusive, were mimeographed for general distribution.

The Forest Products Laboratory issued, February 1, 1919, a mimeographed list of "Reports Prepared for General Distribution, January, 1917-February, 1919." These reports are classified under the headings: airplane woods, glues, veneers, coatings, wooden ships, pulp and paper products, and miscellaneous investigations.

The Forest Products Laboratory mimeographed, April, 1919, a list of all reports issued by it from April 1, 1917, to April 1, 1919. The list comprises approximately 2600 titles, on 112 pages, arranged alphabetically by names of authors.

Under dates of July 15, 1918, and September 16, 1918, the Forest Service issued mimeographed lists entitled "Reports on National Defense Studies," in which are entered all available manuscript reports covering war investigations other than those of the Forest Products Laboratory. The list of July 15 contains thirty-five entries classified under "Specifications, Uses of Wood, Timber Tests, Supply and Production of Timber, Supply and Production of Tannin, Grading of Lumber, and Wood Fuel Production." The list of September 16 contains nineteen entries, all relating to "Supplies and Production of Timber."

In connection with the work of the Commission for Negotiating Peace, the Forest Service prepared an extensive report, with maps, on the forest resources of the world and a report on the water-power resources of the world. Copies of these reports are in the State Department, the American Geographical Society of New York, and the Forest Service. The forest material has been revised and published as *Forest Resources of the World*, by Raphael Zon and William N. Sparhawk (New York, 1923, 2 vols., 997 pages). The report on water-power resources of the world has been published by the U.S. Geological Survey in *World Atlas of Commercial Geology*, as Part II, "Water Power of the World," by Herman

Stabler, E. B. Jones, O. C. Merrill, and N. C. Grover (Washington, 1921, 39 pages, 8 maps).

Among some mimeographed papers in the department library the following were issued by the Forest Service.

Forest regiment to be organized [for service in France] (2 pages).

National forests to supply wood for fuel next winter. 1917 (2 pages).

National forests receipts increase. 1917 (2 pages).

Lumberjack regiment recruited to full strength: additional men wanted for possible second regiment. 1917 (1 page).

National forests helping increase of meat supply. 1917 (2 pages).

More men needed for lumbermen's regiment. 1918 (2 pages).

National forests to carry more live stock. 1918 (2 pages).

Boy Scouts to help government find black walnut. 1918 (2 pages).

Need for black walnut service urgent. 1918 (2 pages).

Maple furniture waste used for scrubbing-brush blocks (1 page).

List of largest users of black walnut logs (1 page).

To members of the Forest Service regarding national defense, by Henry S. Graves. March 19, 1917 (3 pages).

"Wood Fuel Items." These items were issued at intervals during the emergency fuel situation: December 15, 1917 (6 pages); December 22 (4 pages); December 27 (4 pages); January 4, 1918 (3 pages). Fourteen numbers were issued, the last on October 25, 1918.

"Weekly Bulletin," November 15, 1918, to December 1, 1919. The first number announced the purpose of the bulletin as follows, "It is planned to get out, for the benefit of all members of the Forest Service and for the information of those now engaged in war duties, a brief weekly summary of the more important matters which come up in the Washington office." There are from seven to eleven pages in each number and among the topics discussed are: the Forest Service and the Draft; the shipbuilding problem; the Forest Regiments make good; timber supplies for war needs; a way to help; forest research and the war; employment under war-time conditions.

BUREAU OF PLANT INDUSTRY

Functions

The Bureau of Plant Industry dates from the agricultural appropriations act of March 2, 1901, under which it was organized. The bureau is charged with the study and economic solution of plant problems, especially in relation to crop production and utilization. These activities include the improvement of useful plants by breeding and cultural methods, the investigation of destructive plant diseases and the development of methods for their control, the introduction and acclimatization of new plants from other parts of the world, the extension of the use of valuable crops, the development of improved methods for crop utilization, and the meeting of emergencies incident to crop production.

War Activities

War conditions stimulated the bureau's activities for increasing crop production. A survey was made of the losses by disease of wheat, barley, rye, oats, corn, potatoes, beans, cotton, sugar beets, and peaches, a campaign was conducted to reduce these losses, and special efforts were made to increase the production of wheat, rye, sugar, long staple cotton, and castor beans. The development of home vegetable gardening was promoted; instructions were given in the salvaging of fruit and vegetable crops; the pathological defects of airplane timber were investigated. In certain activities the bureau coöperated with the extension division of the States Relations Service, in others, with the Bureau of Markets. Much personal service was performed by members of the staff in connection with the crop-production activities at some of the training camps.

Publications

REPORTS

Report of the Chief of the Bureau of Plant Industry, for the fiscal year ended June 30, 1917 (Washington, 1917, 32 pages). Wilt-resistant variety of cotton, potato crop affected by shortage of potash, a new bacterial disease of wheat, rusts of cereals from barberry infection, hemp crop increasing, Egyptian cotton in Arizona, seed corn.

Report of the Acting Chief of the Bureau of Plant Industry, 1918 (n.p., n.d., 30 pages). American Egyptian cotton, community cotton production, investigation of the quality of seeds, work of the Committee on Seed Stocks, flax straw for paper making, progress in eradicating the common barberry, fiber for binder twine.

Report of the Chief of the Bureau of Plant Industry, 1919 (Washington, 1919, 40 pages). Cotton, utilization of excess war materials for fertilizer, control of cereal smuts, other diseases of wheat.

Farmers' Bulletins

The following *Farmers' Bulletins*, prepared wholly or in part by scientists of the Bureau of Plant Industry and issued by the Government Printing Office, are within the scope of this survey.

616. *Winter-Wheat Varieties for the Eastern United States,* by Clyde E. Leighty (December 12, 1914, 14 pages).

647. *The Home Garden in the South,* by H. C. Thompson (March 20, 1915, 28 pages).

663. *Drug Plants under Cultivation,* by W. W. Stockberger (June 5, 1915, 39 pages).

669. *Fiber Flax,* by Frank C. Miles (May 25, 1915, 19 pages).

677. *Growing Hay in the South for Market,* by C. V. Piper, H. B. McClure, and Lyman Carrier (June 16, 1915, 22 pages).

678. *Growing Hard Spring Wheat,* by Carleton R. Ball and J. Allen Clark (June 10, 1915, 16 pages).

680. *Varieties of Hard Spring Wheat,* by Carleton R. Ball and J. Allen Clark (October 7, 1915, 20 pages).

686. *Uses of Sorghum Grain,* by Carleton R. Ball and Benton E. Rothgeb (September 22, 1915, 15 pages).

688. *The Culture of Rice in California,* by Charles E. Chambliss and E. L. Adams (September 18, 1915, 20 pages).

726. *Natal Grass: a Southern Perennial Hay Crop,* by S. M. Tracy (June 8, 1916, 16 pages).

729. *Corn Culture in the Southeastern States,* by C. H. Kyle (July 19, 1916, 20 pages).

732. *Marquis Wheat,* by Carleton R. Ball and J. Allen Clark (May 29, 1916, 7 pages).

749. *Grains for the Montana Dry Lands,* by N. C. Donaldson (August 12, 1916, 22 pages).

751. *Peanut Oil,* by H. C. Thompson and H. S. Bailey (August 4, 1916, 16 pages).

756. *Culture of Rye in the Eastern Half of the United States,* by Clyde E. Leighty (October 11, 1916, 16 pages).

758. *Muscadine Grape Syrup,* by Charles Dearing (September 6, 1916, 11 pages).

768. *Dwarf Broom Corns,* by Benton E. Rothgeb (November 18, 1916, 16 pages).

769. *Growing Grain on Southern Idaho Dry Farms,* by L. C. Aicher (October, 1916, 23 pages).

773. *Corn Growing under Droughty Conditions,* by C. P. Hartley and L. L. Zook (December, 1916, 24 pages).

785. *Seed-Flax Production,* by Charles H. Clark (February, 1917, 19 pages).

786. *Fall-Sown Grains in Maryland and Virginia,* by T. R. Stanton (February, 1917, 23 pages).

787. *Sea Island Cotton,* by W. A. Orton (December 30, 1916, 40 pages).

800. *Grains for the Dry Lands of Central Oregon,* by L. R. Breithaupt (April, 1917, 22 pages).

818. *The Small Vegetable Garden: Suggestions for Utilizing Limited Areas* (April, 1917, 44 pages).

823. *Sugar-Beet Sirup,* by C. O. Townsend and H. C. Gore (May, 1917, 13 pages).

827. *Shallu, or "Egyptian Wheat": Variety of Sorghum,* by Benton E. Rothgeb (June, 1917, 8 pages).

833. *Methods of Controlling or Eradicating the Wild Oat in the Hard Spring-Wheat Area,* by H. R. Cates (July, 1917, 16 pages).

841. *Drying Fruits and Vegetables in the Home, with Recipes for Cooking* (June, 1917, 29 pages).

847. *Potato Storage and Storage Houses,* by William Stuart (July, 1917, 27 pages).

856. *Control of Diseases and Insect Enemies of the Home Vegetable Garden,* by W. A. Orton and F. H. Chittenden (November, 1917, 70 pages).

868. *How to Increase the Potato Crop by Spraying,* by F. H. Chittenden and W. A. Orton (September, 1917, 22 pages).

878. *Grains for Western North and South Dakota,* by F. Ray Babcock, John H. Martin, and Ralph W. Smith (October, 1917, 21 pages).

879. *Home Storage of Vegetables,* by James H. Beattie (August, 1917, 22 pages).

883. *Grains for the Utah Dry Lands,* by Jenkin W. Jones and Aaron F. Bracken (October, 1917, 21 pages).

884. *Saving Vegetable Seeds for the Home and Market Gardens,* by W. W. Tracy, Sr. (September, 1917, 16 pages).

885. *Wheat Growing in the Southeastern States,* by Clyde E. Leighty (August, 1917, 14 pages).

892. *Spring Oat Production,* by C. W. Warburton (November, 1917, 22 pages).

894. *Rye Growing in the Southeastern States,* by Clyde E. Leighty (October, 1917, 16 pages).

895. *Growing Winter Wheat on the Great Plains,* by E. C. Chilcott and John S. Cole (September, 1917, 12 pages).

900. *Homemade Fruit Butters,* by C. P. Close (September, 1917, 7 pages).

903. *Commercial Evaporation and Drying of Fruits,* by James H. Beattie and H. P. Gould (September, 1917, 60 pages).

915. *How to Reduce Weevil Waste in Southern Corn,* by C. H. Kyle (February, 1918, 7 pages).

934. *Home Gardening in the South,* by H. C. Thompson (February, 1918, 44 pages).

936. *The City and Suburban Vegetable Garden,* by H. M. Conolly (February, 1918, 52 pages).

937. *The Farm Garden in the North,* by James H. Beattie (February, 1918, 53 pages).

939. *Cereal Smuts and the Disinfection of Seed Grains,* by Harry B. Humphrey and Alden A. Potter (April, 1918, 28 pages).

948. *The Rag-Doll Seed Tester: Its Use in Determining What Ears of Corn are Fit for Seed,* by George J. Burt, H. Howard Biggar, and Clement E. Trout (February, 1918, 7 pages).

951. *Hog Pastures for the Southern States,* by Lyman Carrier and F. G. Ashbrook (May, 1918, 20 pages).

953. *Potato Culture under Irrigation,* by William Stuart, C. F. Clark, and George W. Dewey (June, 1918, 23 pages).

958. *Standard Broom Corn,* by Benton E. Rothgeb (May, 1918, 20 pages).

965. *Growing Grain Sorghums in the San Antonio District of Texas,* by C. R. Letteer (June, 1918, 12 pages).

968. *Cultivation and Utilization of Barley,* by Harry V. Harlan (June, 1918, 39 pages).

970. *Sweet-Potato Storage,* by H. C. Thompson (May, 1918, 27 pages).

972. *How to Use Sorghum Grain,* by Carleton R. Ball and Benton E. Rothgeb (June, 1918, 18 pages).

973. *The Soy Bean: Its Culture and Uses,* by W. J. Morse (July, 1918, 32 pages).

984. *Farm and Home Drying of Fruits and Vegetables,* by Joseph S. Caldwell (June, 1918, 61 pages).

999. *Sweet-Potato Growing,* by Fred E. Miller (February, 1919, 30 pages).

1033. *Muscadine Grape Paste,* by Charles Dearing (March, 1919, 15 pages).

1034. *Growing Sugar Cane for Sirup,* by P. A. Yoder (March, 1919, 35 pages).

1041. *The Eelworm Disease of Wheat and Its Control,* by Luther P. Byars (March, 1919, 10 pages).

1058. *Destroy the Common Barberry,* by E. C. Stakman (May, 1919, 12 pages).

1062. *Buckwheat,* by Clyde E. Leighty (October, 1919, 24 pages).

1063. *Take-All and Flag Smut, Two Wheat Diseases New to the United States,* by Harry B. Humphrey and Aaron G. Johnson (August, 1919, 8 pages).

DEPARTMENT OF AGRICULTURE BULLETINS

Four bulletins written to meet war-time conditions and published by the Government Printing Office in the series entitled *United States Department of Agriculture Bulletins* are as follows:

486. *Sugar-Cane Culture for Sirup Production in the United States,* by P. A. Yoder (March 19, 1917, 45 pages).

533. *Extension of Cotton Production in California,* by O. F. Cook (March 3, 1917, 16 pages).

721. *The Beet-Sugar Industry in the United States,* by C. O. Townsend (November 22, 1918, 56 pages).

734. *Nematode Galls as a Factor in the Marketing and Milling of Wheat* (November 13, 1918, 16 pages).

Yearbook

In the *Yearbook of the United States Department of Agriculture* for 1917 and 1918 (Washington, 1918 and 1919) are eight articles contributed by the Bureau of Plant Industry that were particularly appropriate because of the war. They are:

"The soy-bean industry in the United States," by W. J. Morse (1917, pp. 101-111).

"Present status of the peanut industry," by H. C. Thompson (1917, pp. 113-126).

"Production of drug-plant crops in the United States," by W. W. Stockberger (1917, pp. 169-176).

"Cereal diseases and the national food supply," by Harry B. Humphrey (1917, pp. 481-495).

"The seed supply of the nation," by R. A. Oakley (1917, pp. 497-536).

"The black stem rust and the barberry," by E. C. Stakman (1918, pp. 75-100).

"The place of rye in American agriculture," by Clyde E. Leighty (1918, pp. 169-184.)

"Sisal and henequen binder-twine fibers," by H. T. Edwards (1918, pp. 357-366).

Records

The manuscript, mimeographed, and multigraphed records of the Bureau of Plant Industry consist of correspondence, reports, circulars, memorandums, and miscellaneous data. The main office has a typewritten report entitled "Participation in the Work of the World War by the Bureau of Plant Industry" (123 pages), describing the work in connection with military operations and in connection with increasing the food and fiber supply of the world as well as of the United States. Other papers in this office are: "Call of the Great War," by David Fairchild, a mimeographed circular of 5 pages of propaganda for new food facilities; a memorandum concerning the appointment of a Committee on Seed Stocks, with an inventory taken by it, 64 pages; and a circular entitled "Special Instructions for Achievement Clubs," 2 pages.

The **Office of Soil Fertility** has a report which it prepared relative to the production of metol for photographic purposes, a report to the Medical Supply Board on the production of mannite, and a report (4 pages), to the United States Food Administration on the partial substitution of nitrate of soda for sulphate of ammonia in sugar crop production.

The **Office of Drug, Poisonous, and Oil Plant Investigations** has several multigraphed circulars which were prepared primarily for use in efforts to meet the increased demand for information concerning certain products. Among them are:

Castor beans (March 25, 1918, 3 pages).
Camphor (November 23, 1917, 3 pages).
Notes on coconut oil pressing (March 19, 1918, 2 pages).
Liquidambar (May 18, 1917, 1 page).
Insect powder plants (July 28, 1919, 1 page).

The same office sent out questionnaires relating to the production of crude drugs in the United States, and the data thus assembled was tabulated and placed on file.

The **Office of Sugar Plant Investigations** issued three circulars in mimeograph for public information in its field. They are: "Sorghum Sirup" (September, 1918, 4 pages); "Sirup-Sorghum Seed" (September, 1918, 1 page); "Improved Process for Use in the Preparation of Sugar Beet Sirup" (November, 1918, 1 page).

The **Office of Plant Diseases Survey** conducted several special surveys during the war and compiled special files of data on the diseases of cereals, especially wheat. The data are recorded on cards and arranged by crops, by States, and by counties. Summaries of the data were issued in mimeograph form in the "Plant Disease Bulletin." Estimates of annual losses from plant diseases, based on those made by pathologists in all parts of the country, were also issued.

A **Committee on Seed Stocks** was appointed which collected and disseminated information regarding stocks of seed available. Surveys were made of the seed stocks of important crops and from time to time, as the planting seasons approached, information was sent to dealers and farmers' organizations which enabled them to secure the seeds required with the least delay of time and effort. Emergency appropriations by Congress of $6,500,000 provided for the purchase and sale at cost of seed of feed and food crops. To meet the seed corn emergency which was very acute in the spring of 1918 as the result of unusually severe weather conditions during the preceding autumn and winter, the committee located and purchased large quantities of viable seed corn adapted to the regions in which the shortage existed, which were sold to farmers at cost. This was an important factor in the production of corn in 1918 in the States of Michigan, Ohio, and Illinois, and to a less extent in Wisconsin, North Dakota, and Iowa. Comparable activities related to the purchase and sale of stocks of seed of fodder and food crops. In the Southwest seed corn, cotton seed, and seed of sorghums and peanuts were purchased and sold; in the Northwest seed of oats, barley, and flax. The Committee on Seed Stocks coöperated actively with the Food Administration, the War Emergency Organization, the Grain Corporation, War Trade Board, Shipping Board, and the Seedsmen's War Service Committee, appointed by the seed trade. The Office of Seed Distribution distributed the following mimeographed papers for the committee:

Bean stocks reported by various dealers in Michigan (May 1, 1917, 2 pages).

Lists of firms or individuals known to have had seed stocks on hand during the last week in April: grain sorghums (May 10, 1917, 3 pages); sweet sorghums (May 10, 1917, 3 pages); pinto beans (May 10, 1917, 1 page); beans (May 10, 1917, 3 pages); buckwheat (May 31, 1917, 3 pages).

Circular letter to dealers relative to stock on hand of seeds of forage crops (June 8, 1917, 1 page).

List of firms or individuals known to handle seeds of the specific varieties: soy beans (June 10, 1917, 5 pages); beans (June 10, 1917, 4 pages).

List of county agents in the South in whose counties there is a surplus of winter oats (July 6, 1917, 3 pages).

Circular letter to dealers enclosing questionnaire as to varieties, quantities, and prices of seed grain "for sale this fall" (August 17, 1917, 2 pages).

Circular letter to dealers regarding details of drawing for samples of seed wheat (September 26, 1917, 4 pages).

Circular letter to all Seed Stocks Committees *re* report on location of domestic stocks of seed wheat, locates wheat stored and distributed by the Food Administration Grain Corporation (February 27, 1918, 1 page).

Circular letter to county agents *re* seed corn purchased and stored by the Department of Agriculture (April 22, 1918, 4 pages).

Supplemental information for county agents, referring to circular of April 22, 1918 (April 25, 1918, 3 pages).

Circular on war emergency seed corn reserve for late planting and replanting demands (April 26, 1918, 1 page).

Two special (unnumbered) circulars, issued by the Office of the Secretary before the declaration of war, with a view to increasing the world's food supply produced in the Southern States, were as follows:

Winter Wheat in the Cotton Belt, by Clyde E. Leighty (November 21, 1914, 6 pages).
Rye in the Cotton Belt, by Clyde E. Leighty (December 2, 1914, 4 pages).

To acquaint the agricultural leaders of the several States with the details of the program developed in 1917 five conferences were held in different sections of the country in which several bureau officials participated. Details of these conferences are contained in a typewritten report filed in the bureau entitled "Report on the Five Regional Conferences to Stimulate Wheat and Rye Sowing in the fall of 1917" (75 pages).

BUREAU OF ANIMAL INDUSTRY

Functions

The Bureau of Animal Industry, established by act of Congress in May, 1884, is primarily concerned with the promotion of the live stock and meat industries. It investigates the causes, prevention, and treatment of diseases of domestic animals; carries on work for the prevention and eradication of such diseases; conducts investigations and experiments in the dairy industry, animal husbandry, and the feeding and breeding of animals; and is charged with the administration of the federal meat inspection act.

War Activities

In connection with its inspection service, which was enlarged for the better protection of military meat from contamination, the bureau inaugurated a food-conservation movement in meat-packing establishments to eliminate waste, avoid the use of edible products for purposes other than food, and prevent the spoiling of meat from avoidable causes. Efforts to reduce losses of animal products from diseases and parasites were stimulated by war conditions. The Animal Husbandry Division coöperated with the States Relations Service and agricultural colleges in a campaign to increase the production of pork, poultry, beef, mutton, and wool. The Dairy Division stimulated the production of dairy products; conducted campaigns to reduce the loss of milk from spoiling; increased the utilization of skim milk and buttermilk in the form of cottage cheese and condensed skim milk; aided in the conservation of sugar by finding substitutes for a large portion of the cane sugar used in making ice cream; urged the construction of silos and the growing of legumes as means of conserving concentrated dairy feeds; effected a partial redistribution of dairy cattle to prevent a diminution in number from high prices of feed; and supervised the manufacture of waterproof glue from milk casein, an imported commodity prior to the war.

Publications

REPORTS

Report of the Chief of the Bureau of Animal Industry, 1917 (Washington, 1917, 63 pages). Meeting the food and war emergency, pig clubs, poultry clubs, utilization of dairy by-products.

Report of the Chief of the Bureau of Animal Industry, 1918 (Washington, 1918, 63 pages). Increase in animal products, combating animal diseases, the cottage-cheese campaign.

Report of the Chief of the Bureau of Animal Industry, 1919 (Washington, 1919). Progress in disease control, saving drouth-stricken cattle, stimulating production and utilization of dairy products, a substitute for a portion of the cane sugar in ice cream, casein for the manufacture of waterproof glue.

FARMERS' BULLETINS

798. *The Sheep Tick and its Eradication by Dipping,* by Marion Imes (May, 1917, 31 pages).

825. *Pit Silos,* by T. Pryse Metcalf and George A. Scott (June, 1917, 14 pages).

834. *Hog Cholera: Prevention and Treatment,* by M. Dorset and O. B. Hess (August, 1917, 32 pages).

850. *How to Make Cottage Cheese on the Farm,* by K. J. Matheson and F. R. Cammack (August, 1917, 15 pages).

855. *Homemade Silos* by Helmer Rabild and K. E. Parks (issued July 21, 1914; revised September, 1917, 55 pages).

873. *Utilization of Farm Wastes in Feeding Live Stock,* by S. H. Ray (August, 1917, 12 pages).

874. *Swine Management,* by George M. Rommel and F. G. Ashbrook (issued August 17, 1904; revised September, 1917, 38 pages).

876. *Making Butter on the Farm,* by William White (September, 1917, 23 pages).

889. *Back-Yard Poultry Keeping,* by Rob R. Slocum (November, 1917, 23 pages).

909. *Cattle Lice and How to Eradicate Them,* by Marion Imes (February, 1918, 27 pages).

913. *Killing Hogs and Curing Pork,* by F. G. Ashbrook and G. A. Anthony (December, 1917, 40 pages).

920. *Milk Goats,* by Edward L. Shaw (February, 1918, 36 pages).

935. *The Sheep-Killing Dog,* by J. F. Wilson (February, 1918, 32 pages).

957. *Important Poultry Diseases,* by D. E. Salmon (March, 1918, 48 pages).

976. *Cooling Milk and Cream on the Farm,* by J. A. Gamble (May, 1918, 16 pages).

DEPARTMENT OF AGRICULTURE BULLETINS

576. *The Manufacture of Cottage Cheese in Creameries and Milk Plants,* by Arnold O. Dahlberg (September 27, 1917, 16 pages).

584. *The Control of Hog Cholera, with a Discussion of the Results of Field Experiments,* by A. D. Melvin and M. Dorset (October 13, 1917, 18 pages).

585. *A Guide for Formulating a Milk Ordinance* (October' 18, 1917, 4 pages).

610. *Fish Meal as a Feed for Swine,* by Frank G. Ashbrook (December 7, 1917, 10 pages).

661. *The Manufacture of Casein from Buttermilk or Skim Milk,* by Arnold O. Dahlberg (April 9, 1918, 32 pages).

744. *Cooling Milk and Storing and Shipping It at Low Temperatures,* by James A. Gamble and John T. Bowen (January 17, 1919, 28 pages).

747. *The Economical Use of Fuel in Milk Plants and Creameries,* by John T. Bowen (January 9, 1919, 47 pages).

80. *Disposal of City Garbage by Feeding to Hogs* (December, 1917, 8 pages).

122. *Labor Saving in Live-Stock Production* (October 16, 1918, 14 pages).

YEARBOOK

"How the dairy cow brought prosperity in the wake of the boll weevil," by L. A. Higgins (1917, pp. 303-310).

"Sheep and intensive farming," by F. R. Marshall (1917, pp. 311-320).

"Breeding horses for the United States Army," by H. H. Reese (1917, pp. 341-356).

"Butterfat and Income," by J. C. McDowell (1917, pp. 357-362).

"Pig clubs and the swine industry," by J. D. McVean (1917, pp. 371-384).

"Better poultry through community breeding associations," by J. W. Kinghorne (1918, pp. 109-114).

"How dairying built up a community," by J. C. McDowell (1918, pp. 153-168).

"The rediscovery of an old dish," by Herbert P. Davis (1918, pp. 269-276).

"Live stock and reconstruction," by George M. Rommel (1918, pp. 289-302).

"Live-stock drought relief work in 1919," by George M. Rommel (1919, pp. 391-405).

Records

There is no segregation of the war-time records of the Bureau of Animal Industry, but all records of the bureau are classified and filed according to a decimal system, and a printed *Outline*, or index, facilitates the location of particular papers. Among the general heads in the classification are: meat inspection, animal diseases, animal husbandry, and dairy division. Under "dairy division" are such subjects as dairy statistics, circular letters with answers attached, special reports, feeds, silos and silage, ice cream, casein, milk, cream, butter, cheese, and eggs.

In the department library are the following mimeographed papers.

"Substitutes for a part of the cane sugar in ice cream," by S. H. Ayers, O. E. Williams, and U. T. Johnson (3 pages).

"Milk-plant letter No. 39 relative to the utilization of by-products in the dairy business" (May, 1917, 1 page).

Meat production, consumption, exports, imports, etc., for the calendar years 1914 to 1918, inclusive (7 pages).

"The Bureau Range Finder," a reflection of current public opinion regarding activities of the Bureau of Animal Industry, based on the press, correspondence, and kindred sources (2 pages, prepared weekly since December, 1918).

BUREAU OF MARKETS

The Bureau of Markets originated in a clause of the agricultural appropriations act of March 4, 1913, appropriating fifty thousand dollars for the acquisition and diffusion of useful information on subjects connected with the marketing and distributing of farm products. The Office of Markets and Rural Organization was established under the agricultural appropriations act of March 4, 1915, and this office became the Bureau of Markets July 1, 1917.[1]

Functions

As originally organized, shortly before the outbreak of the war, the Bureau of Markets functioned along three main lines: (1) investigation and demonstration; (2) service, including the diffusion of information; (3) administration of statutory regulations. Its investigations were in the fields of marketing and distributing farm products, of food supplies, of rural organization, of cotton standards, and of grain standardization. Its information was diffused in the form of market reports in the first nation-wide market news service ever inaugurated and in the form of bulletins of various kinds. Its regulatory work consisted in the enforcement of acts of Congress relative to cotton futures, grain standards, warehouses, and standard containers.

War Work

During the war the Bureau of Markets functioned chiefly as an organization for effecting a more efficient distribution and conservation of food products. With the assistance of the States Rela-

---

[1] On July 1, 1922, the Bureaus of Markets and Crop Estimates were consolidated with the Office of Farm Management to form the Bureau of Agricultural Economics.

tions Service and the Bureau of Crop Estimates it made four surveys to ascertain the quantities of food, food materials, and feeds in the country in order that their distribution and consumption might be more intelligently directed. The Bureau operated fifty-two market stations and established a market news service for the following commodities: (1) live stock and meats; (2) dairy and poultry products; (3) grain, hay, and feeds; (4) fruits and vegetables. It assisted in the organization and advised in the operation of coöperative purchasing and marketing, encouraged marketing with motor trucks as a factor in the solution of transportation problems caused by the war, and when the supply of burlap sacks had been cut off by war conditions it demonstrated the advantages of handling grain in bulk. The bureau demonstrated to growers and handlers of fruits and vegetables that loss from decay and deterioration in transit might be reduced by more careful handling, and it effected an improvement in the construction of refrigerator cars and storage houses. It further promoted conservation by a food-products inspection service and by a campaign to reduce losses in marketing cotton seed and its products. By coöperative investigations, the means of preventing losses of wheat and other grains from grain dust explosions at mills and elevators was discovered, the cause of cotton-gin fires was ascertained. When the supply of linen for airplane wings had failed there were conferences with the Bureau of Standards and other government agencies, and the Bureau of Markets met the emergency by producing a cotton fabric for a substitute. When the supply of silk was short it produced a very different cotton fabric as a substitute for balloon silk. Other war activities of the Bureau of Markets were: seed reports, cold storage reports, honey reports, grain-grading, distribution of nitrate of soda, regulation of stockyards and live-stock dealers, and the investigation of foreign markets.

Publications

REPORTS

Report of the Chief of the Bureau of Markets, 1917 (Washington, 42 pages). Seed marketing investigations; food supply investigations; daily market reports on locally grown truck products; weekly market reviews; quarterly reports on the supply of wool.

Report of the Chief of the Bureau of Markets, 1918 (Washington, 39 pages). War program; food supply investigations; food survey; fertilizer survey; coöperative purchasing and marketing; city marketing and distribution; transportation and storage; motor transportation of farm products; preservation of fruits and vegetables in transit and storage; marketing dairy products; marketing cotton seed and its products; cotton testing; market news service; seed reporting service; food products inspection service; purchase and distribution of nitrate of soda.

Report of the Chief of the Bureau of Markets, 1919 (Washington, 35 pages). Food surveys; preservation of fruits and vegetables in transit and storage; marketing dairy products; marketing cotton seed and its products; contraction of market news services; purchase and distribution of nitrate of soda; supervision of stockyards and live-stock dealers.

Farmers' Bulletins

792. *How the Federal Farm Loan Act Benefits the Farmer,* by C. W. Thompson (January, 1917, 12 pages).

802. *Classification of American Upland Cotton,* by D. E. Earle and Fred Taylor (July, 1917, 28 pages).

809. *Marketing Live Stock in the South,* by S. W. Doty (April, 1917, 16 pages).

830. *Marketing Eggs by Parcel Post,* by Lewis B. Flohr (August, 1917, 23 pages).

919. *The Application of Dockage in the Marketing of Wheat* (November, 1917, 12 pages).

922. *Parcel Post Business Methods,* by C. C. Hawbaker and John W. Law (February, 1918, 20 pages).

930. *Marketing Butter and Cheese by Parcel Post,* by Lewis Flohr and Roy C. Potts (May, 1918, 12 pages).

979. *Preparation of Strawberries for Market,* by C. T. Moore and H. E. Truax (May, 1918, 27 pages).

1032. *Operating a Coöperative Motor Truck Route,* by H. S. Yohe (February, 1919, 24 pages).

1050. *Handling and Loading Southern New Potatoes,* by A. M. Grimes (May 1, 1919, 18 pages).

Department of Agriculture Bulletins

547. *Coöperative Purchasing and Marketing Organizations among Farmers in the United States,* by O. B. Jesness and W. H. Kerr (September 19, 1917, 82 pages).

558. *Marketing Grain at Country Points,* by George Livingston and K. B. Seeds (July 28, 1917, 45 pages).

667. *Car-Lot Shipments of Fruits and Vegetables in the United States,* by Paul Froehlich (June 8, 1918, 196 pages).

682. *A Study of Prices and Quality of Creamery Butter,* by G. P. Warber (July 15, 1918, 24 pages).

688. *Marketing Berries and Cherries by Parcel Post,* by C. C. Hawbaker and Charles A. Burmeister (May 18, 1918, 17 pages).

690. *Marketing Practices of Wisconsin and Minnesota Creameries,* by Roy C. Potts (July 23, 1918, 15 pages).

709. *Reports of Storage Holdings of Certain Food Products,* by John O. Bell and I. C. Franklin (November 20, 1918, 44 pages).

729. *Suitable Storage Conditions for Certain Perishable Food Products* (July 24, 1918, 10 pages and chart).

764. *Factors Influencing the Carrying Qualities of American Export Corn,* by E. G. Boerner (July, 1919, 99 pages).

770. *Motor Transportation for Rural Districts,* by J. H. Collins (January 29, 1919, 32 pages).

776. *Cold Storage Reports, Season 1917-1918,* by John O. Bell (March, 1919, 44 pages).

792. *Reports of Storage Holdings of Certain Food Products during 1918,* by John O. Bell (July 25, 1919, 80 pages).

DEPARTMENT OF AGRICULTURE CIRCULARS

96. *Sugar Supply of the United States: Its Extent and Distribution on August 31, 1917* (January 31, 1918, 55 pages).

97. *The Supply of Lard in the United States: Its Extent and Distribution on August 31, 1917* (February 28, 1918, 32 pages).

98. *The Supply of Canned Salmon in the United States: Its Extent and Distribution on August 31, 1917* (February 28, 1918, 13 pages).

99. *Commercial Stocks of Miscellaneous Cereal and Vegetable Foodstuffs in the United States on August 31, 1917:* Corn, Corn Food Products, Beans, Rice, Rolled Oats, Sirup and Molasses, Vegetable Oils, and Vegetable Fats (February 28, 1918, 28 pages).

100. *Commercial Stocks of Wheat and Flour in the United States on August 31, 1917* (February 28, 1918, 37 pages).

101. *Commercial Stocks of Miscellaneous Animal Food Products in the United States on August 31, 1917:* Hams, Bacon and Shoulders, Salt Pork, Salt Beef, Salt Fish, and Condensed Milk (February 28, 1918, 19 pages).

104. *Commercial Stocks of Fertilizer and Fertilizer Materials in the United States as Reported October 1, 1917* (February 28, 1918, 12 pages).

YEARBOOK

"Teamwork between the farmer and his agent," by C. E. Bassett (1917, pp. 321-325).

"The service of cold storage in the conservation of foodstuffs," by I. C. Franklin (1917, pp. 363-370).

"Coöperative marketing—where? when? how?" by C. E. Bassett and O. B. Jesness (1917, pp. 385-393).

"Cattle loans and their value to the investor," by Charles S. Cole (1918, pp. 101-108).

"Some effects of the war upon the seed industry of the United States," by W. A. Wheeler and G. C. Edler (1918, pp. 195-214).

"Following the produce markets," by G. B. Fiske (1918, pp. 277-288).

"The farmer and Federal grain supervision," by Ralph H. Brown (1918, pp. 335-346).

"Government market reports on live stock and meats," by James Atkinson (1918, pp. 379-398).

"Cotton warehousing—benefits of an adequate system," by Roy L. Newton and James M. Workman (1918, pp. 399-432).

"How to use market stations," by G. B. Fiske (1919, pp. 94-114).

"Federal supervision of live-stock markets," by Louis D. Hall (1919, pp. 239-248).

"Why produce inspection pays," by H. E. Kramer and G. B. Fiske (1919, pp. 319-334).

"Selling purebred stock to South America," by David Harbell and H. P. Morgan (1919, pp. 369-379).

"The farmers' purchasing power, how organized," by J. M. Mehl (1919, pp. 381-390).

PERIODICALS

Food Surveys, April 29, 1918, to June 27, 1919 (2 volumes, 41 numbers). This periodical (monthly, and special numbers when occasion required) was published to make known the results of the food surveys which were undertaken to obtain such information concerning food and food materials as was thought necessary or desirable for the guidance of governmental agencies and the public in making plans for increasing production, for promoting efficient distribution, and for directing conservation and utilization.

Seed Reporter, November, 1917, to October 11, 1919 (3 volumes, 25 numbers). In this periodical information was published relative to: (1) seed crop movement; (2) receipts, shipments, imports, available supplies, demand, prices, quality, and commercial varieties of seeds; (3) seed-marketing and seed-crop studies; (4) crop estimates; and (5) operations of the Seed Stocks Committee.

The *Food Surveys* and *Seed Reporter* were succeeded, January 3, 1920, by the *Market Reporter*, a weekly periodical for the dissemination of marketing information relative to all important agricultural products.

Mimeographed Market Reports

The market news services on live stock and meats, dairy products, eggs, fruits and vegetables, grain, hay and feed, honey, and cold storage holdings were rendered in the form of mimeographed reports. The reports, begun or greatly expanded as war emergency measures, have for the most part been continued in the same or in modified forms. As issued and filed during the war they were as follows:

Live Stock and Meats

Daily Market Report on Meat Trade Conditions. February, 1917, to ———. Exhibits prices, supply, demand and trend of markets for fresh beef, veal, pork, lamb, and mutton in Boston, Los Angeles, New York, Philadelphia, Pittsburgh, San Francisco, and Washington.

Daily Report on Live-stock Loadings. July 30, 1917, to ———. Exhibits the number of cars of each kind of live stock loaded the day previous in the United States, classified by destinations, also tabulated by state origins for a number of large market centers.

Weekly Report of Meat Trade Conditions. January 4, 1918, to June 11, 1920. A Saturday review of market supplies, demand and prices of fresh beef, veal, pork, lamb, and mutton at Boston, Los Angeles, New York, Philadelphia, Pittsburgh, San Francisco, and Washington.

Weekly Live-Stock and Meat Trade News. December 4, 1917, to ———. Timely information pertaining specifically to potential supplies and market movements of live stock and meats, marketing methods, new restrictions and regulations affecting the marketing of live stock and meats.

Monthly Report on Live Stock at Stock Yards. January, 1917, to December 12, 1919. Exhibits (1) receipts of live stock during the preceding month and the cumulative receipts for the year to date of cattle, hogs, sheep, horses, and mules at some sixty stockyards representing more than fifty cities; (2) the number of cattle, hogs, sheep, horses, and mules shipped during the preceding month and the year to date from public stockyards representing more than fifty cities; (3) the number of cattle, hogs, and sheep shipped during the preceding month and the year to date from some thirty-five market centers for feeding and grazing purposes; (4) the total number of cattle, hogs, and sheep slaughtered during the preceding month and the year to date at more than fifty market centers.

Dairy Products

Daily Butter and Cheese Market Bulletins. February, 1918; subsequently incorporated in the *Daily Market Report.* Daily summaries of market conditions, receipts, shipments, supplies, cold storage movement, and prices of butter and cheese in New York, Boston, Philadelphia, Chicago, and San Francisco.

Weekly Butter Market Review. July 9, 1918, to ——. A summary of market conditions and receipts, shipments, supplies, cold storage movement, and prices of butter in New York, Boston, Philadelphia, Chicago, and San Francisco.

Weekly Cheese Market Bulletin. March 12, 1918, to ——. A survey of market conditions; receipts, shipments, and cold storage movement of cheese in New York, Boston, Philadelphia, Chicago, and San Francisco; a report of stocks in the hands of the wholesalers in those cities and in the hands of the dealers and in cold storage at primary markets in Wisconsin and New York State.

Monthly Dairy Product Report. November, 1917, to ——. Exhibits the quantity of butter, cheese, condensed milk, and other dairy products, including oleomargarine, manufactured in the United States, and the production for the corresponding month of the preceding year.

Monthly Report of Milk Prices. July, 1918, to ——. Exhibits the prevailing wholesale and retail prices of milk paid by the different classes of the trade and prices paid to producers in the larger and more important cities of the United States.

Eggs

Daily Egg Market Bulletin. February, 1918; subsequently incorporated in the *Daily Market Report.* Daily reports of market conditions, receipts, shipments, cold storage movement, and market supplies of eggs in New York, Boston, Philadelphia, and San Francisco.

Fruits and Vegetables

Daily Market Reports of Perishable Fruits and Vegetables. April 1, 1915, to ——. Issued from permanent market stations located in thirty-two of the larger cities of the United States and from numerous temporary field stations in various producing areas during crop movement. They contain: (1) telegraphic reports from the principal markets of the number of cars of each commodity unloaded daily, the origin of the commodities, prevailing jobbing prices, quality and conditions of receipts, marketing and weather conditions; (2) telegraphic reports from the railroads handling these crops of shipment from each State or district up to midnight of the night before; f.o.b. prices from the bureau's representatives in producing territory.

Weekly Car-lot Summary. May, 1917, to ——. Exhibits total number of cars shipped from each State by days and weeks as reported to the bureau telegraphically each day by the transportation companies.

Semi-weekly Summary of Car-lot Shipments. April 11, 1915, to ——. Exhibits car-lot shipments of sixty-one commodities not covered in the weekly summary, or of those upon which reports are discontinued for the remainder of the season. This report is based upon information sent in by the railroads by mail.

Market Reviews. April 14, 1917, to ——. The *Weekly Review,* issued on Tuesday, summarizes market conditions, current supplies, and prices of perishable fruits and vegetables. The *Week-end Review,* issued on Friday, covers the same subjects more briefly and is intended primarily for the press. The *Monthly Review,* issued to the press, summarizes market conditions and tendencies for the preceding four weeks.

Grain, Hay, and Feed

Weekly Market Letter. July 9, 1918, to September 27, 1919. Exhibits stocks, receipts, prevailing demand and prices of corn, oats, hay, and ground feed in the principal markets.

Cold Storage

Monthly Cold Storage Reports. December, 1916, to ——. Exhibit the storage holdings of apples, beef, butter, cheese, fish, lard, mutton, pork, and poultry.

Honey

Semi-monthly Market Report on Honey. June 29, 1917, to January 16, 1920. This report, issued during the heavy shipping season, exhibits the arrivals of honey on the markets at twelve important cities, as reported by the railroads during the preceding two weeks, and the range of jobbing prices for the different varieties and grades.

Wool Reports

The issue of the following wool reports was begun by the Bureau of Markets during the war and continued until taken over by the Bureau of the Census.

Quarterly Wool Stock Report. June, 1917, to ——. Exhibits the available supply of wool held by wool dealers and textile wool manufacturers in the United States at the close of each quarter of the calendar year. The stock is reported in pounds of grease, scoured and pulled wool, tops and noils, in all the generally accepted commercial grades.

Monthly Wool Consumption Report. January, 1918, to ——. Exhibits the total amount of wool in the United States which entered into the process of manufacture during the month in pounds of grease, scoured and pulled wool, in all the various commercial grades, also the amount of wool consumed in the principal textile manufacturing States.

Monthly Report of Wool Machinery. November, 1918, to ——. Exhibits number of active and idle machines in the United States and the number engaged in government work, as reported by wool manufacturers.

Miscellaneous Records

Of the miscellaneous records in the bureau files or in the department library, particular attention is directed to the following mimeographed papers.

The war work of the Bureau of Markets (April 28, 1919, 23 pages).

What the Bureau of Markets is doing to help in the war emergency (1918, 48 pages).

Publications issued by the Bureau of Markets prior to July 1, 1921 (May, 1922, 9 pages).

A descriptive list of periodical reports issued by the Bureau of Markets (October, 1918, 5 pages).

Reports on foreign markets for agricultural products, No. 1 (March 27, 1919, 29 pages).

A weekly project letter regarding federal grain supervision. February, 1918, to December, 1919 (about 10 pages in each issue). Among the topics are: Nashville falling in line on western wheat; appeal on Milwaukee wheat; new enterprise in Utah; grain men going into oil business; dissatisfaction over Sioux City grading; Galveston men like oats grade.

Food products inspection service, circulars 1 to 12, April 5, 1918, to November 1, 1919 (about 12 pages in each circular).

Food products inspection service, field notes 1 to 53. April 26, 1918, to October 25, 1919 (One or two pages in each number).

Table of packages per carload, May 15, 1917 (13 pages).

Annual report for the fiscal year 1919 of the projects under supervision of Wells A. Sherman (August 1, 1919, 40 pages). Market news service on fruits and vegetables; market surveys; methods and costs; wool division of the War Industries Board.

Revised method of determining dockage in wheat, recommended by the Department of Agriculture (July 31, 1918, 4 pages).

Some results of federal live-stock market supervision, by Louis D. Hall (May 14, 1919, 5 pages).

BUREAU OF CROP ESTIMATES

The statistical division of the Department of Agriculture became the Bureau of Statistics July 1, 1903; the Bureau of Statistics became the Bureau of Crop Estimates July 1, 1914; and the Bureaus of Markets and Crop Estimates were consolidated to become the Bureau of Markets and Crop Estimates July 1, 1921.

Functions

The Bureau of Crop Estimates was an agency during the war for furnishing statistical information of prime importance to other bureaus of the department, to the United States Food Administration, War Trade Board, War Industries Board, Council of National Defense, Federal Trade Commission, and Tariff Commission. It conducted investigations, collected and recorded statistics to keep these organizations informed on such matters as acreage and probable acreage of crops, shift in acreage due to war conditions, condition of crops, yield of crops per acre, consumption requirements, uses made of the wheat crop, prices on farms, prices at markets, number and value of live stock, exports and imports of agricultural products, probable deficiency of certain foods, financial condition of farmers, location of seed supplies, seed requirements, quality of seed, demand for farm labor, supply of farm labor, binder twine requirements, probable number of cattle to be fed, probable number of cattle to be grazed, slaughter of milch cows, probability of feeding more swine, supply of fertilizer, and demand for fertilizer.

Publications

The publications of the Bureau of Crop Estimates which relate to its war activities and contain much of the war-time information which it furnished are listed below.

REPORTS

Report of the Chief of the Bureau of Crop Estimates, 1918 (Washington, 1918, 14 pages). New significance given to the functions of the bureau by the war; estimate of the contribution of the farmers to the winning of the war.

Report of the Chief of the Bureau of Crop Estimates, 1919 (Washington, 1919, 11 pages). War organization of the bureau; work accomplished; demands for improved crop and live-stock reporting service.

Monthly Crop Report, 1917, 1918, and 1919 (Washington, 1917-1919, 3 volumes). Acreage, condition of crops, temperature and precipitation statistics, crop estimates, crop statistics, prices; estimated number of horses, mules, milch cows, other cattle, and swine; condition of farm animals and estimated losses; miscellaneous information relative to both crops and live stock.

DEPARTMENT OF AGRICULTURE BULLETINS

473. *Production of Sugar in the United States and Foreign Countries,* by Perry Elliott (February 12, 1917, 70 pages).

483. *Statistics of Fruits in Principal Countries: Production, Exports, and Imports for the United States and Foreign Countries,* by H. D. Ruddiman (February 14, 1917, 40 pages).

514. *Wheat, Yields per Acre and Prices, by States, 50 Years, 1866-1915* (February 13, 1917, 16 pages).

515. *Corn, Yields per Acre and Prices, by States, 50 Years, 1866-1915* (February 12, 1917, 16 pages).

594. *Geography of Wheat Prices: Summary of Conditions Affecting Farm Prices of Wheat in Different Parts of the United States,* by L. B. Zapoleon (February 21, 1918, 46 pages).

685. *Honeybees and Honey Production in the United States,* by S. A. Jones (June 20, 1918, 61 pages).

695. *Potatoes: Acreage, Production, Foreign Trade, Supply, and Consumption,* by George K. Holmes (October 16, 1918, 24 pages).

696. *Geographical Phases of Farm Prices: Corn,* by L. B. Zapoleon (September 26, 1918, 53 pages).

733. *Length of Cotton Lint, Crops 1916 and 1917,* by W. L. Pryor (September 6, 1918, 8 pages).

755. *Geographical Phases of Farm Prices: Oats,* by L. B. Zapoleon (March 19, 1919, 28 pages).

YEARBOOK

"Wool: production, foreign trade, supply, and consumption," by George K. Holmes (1917, pp. 401-424).

"Hides and Skins: production, foreign trade, supply, and consumption," by George K. Holmes (1917, pp. 425-446).

"Sugar supply of the United States," by Frank Andrews (1917, pp. 447-460).

"Statistics of grain crops, 1917" (1917, pp. 605-654).

"Statistics of crops other than grain crops" (1917, pp. 655-707).

"Statistics of live stock, 1917, and miscellaneous data" (1917, pp. 709-757).

"Imports and exports of agricultural products" (1917, pp. 759-799).

"Statistics of grain crops, 1918" (1918, pp. 449-506).

"Statistics of crops other than grain crops" (1918, pp. 507-586).

"Statistics of farm animals and their products" (1918, pp. 587-626).

"Imports and exports of agricultural products" (1918, pp. 627-665).

"Miscellaneous agricultural statistics" (1918, pp. 667-725).

"Three centuries of tobacco," by George K. Holmes (1919, pp. 151-175).

"Statistics of grain crops, 1919" (1919, pp. 509-567).

"Statistics of crops other than grain crops" (1919, pp. 568-643).

"Statistics of farm animals and their products" (1919, pp. 644-681).

"Imports and exports of agricultural products" (1919, pp. 682-721).

"Miscellaneous agricultural statistics" (1919, pp. 722-755).

BUREAU OF CHEMISTRY

The Bureau of Chemistry originated in an appropriation by Congress, August 12, 1848, for the chemical analysis of vegetable subjects produced and used for the food of man and animals in the United States. The Division of Chemistry, the oldest in the Department, was organized in 1866 and became the Bureau of Chemistry July 1, 1901.

Functions

The bureau is engaged in investigations relative to the chemistry of plant growth, the influence of environment on crops and plants, the preservation and utilization of food products, investigations relative to leather and tanning, investigations on the manufacture of dyes, on the manufacture of insecticides, on the manufacture of sugar and sirup, investigations in collaboration with other departments, and in the examination of foods and drugs necessary to its administration of the food and drugs act.

War Activities

The war activities of the bureau were chiefly coöperative. It assisted the United States Food Administration in conserving wheat and sugar by effecting the utilization of substitutes for wheat flour and substitutes for sugar used in soft drinks. It assisted in conserving fats and oils by promoting the use of vegetable oils for animal fats. It coöperated with the Department of Commerce in conserving tin plate needed for the preservation of fruits and vegetables. It assisted in the control and distribution of arsenic to prevent a shortage of insecticides. It assisted in reducing the loss of grain from grain dust explosions and in reducing the loss of cotton from fires in cotton gins. The chief of the bureau was a member of the Interdepartmental Ammonia Committee for the control of the production and distribution of ammonia.

Publications

REPORTS

Report of the Bureau of Chemistry, 1917 (Washington, 1917, 20 pages). Conservation of foodstuffs.

Report of the Bureau of Chemistry, 1918 (Washington, 1918, 24 pages). Coöperation with war agencies; conservation of foodstuffs; mill and elevator dust explosions and fires; sugars and sirups; oils and fats; insecticides.

Report of the Bureau of Chemistry, 1919 (Washington, 1920, 24 pages). Sugar, sugar derivatives, and sirup; oils and fats; grain-mill, elevator, and cotton-gin explosions and fires; leather and tanning.

FARMERS' BULLETINS

881. *Preservation of Vegetables by Fermentation and Salting,* by L. A. Round and H. L. Lang (August, 1917, 15 pages).

DEPARTMENT OF AGRICULTURE BULLETINS

635. *The Commercial Freezing and Storing of Fish,* by Ernest D. Clark and Lloyd H. Almy (March 9, 1918, 10 pages).

657. *A Wheatless Ration for the Rapid Increase of Flesh on Young Chickens,* by M. E. Pennington and others (May 2, 1918, 12 pages).

664. *The Prevention of Breakage of Eggs in Transit when Shipped in Carlots,* by M. E. Pennington and others (April 25, 1918, 31 pages).

681. *Grain-Dust Explosions,* by D. W. Dedrick, R. B. Fehr, and David J. Price (May 18, 1918, 54 pages).

701 *The Chemical Analysis of Wheat-Flour Substitutes and of the Breads Made therefrom,* by J. A. Le Clerc and H. L. Wessling (September 20, 1918, 12 pages).

706. *American Sumac: a Valuable Tanning Material and Dyestuff,* by F. P. Veitch and J. S. Rogers (July 26, 1918, 12 pages).

750. *A Method for Preparing a Commercial Grade of Calcium Arsenate,* by J. K. Haywood and C. M. Smith (October 5, 1918, 10 pages).

769. *The Production and Conservation of Fats and Oils in the United States,* by Herbert S. Bailey and B. E. Reuter (February 10, 1919, 48 pages).

YEARBOOK

"The peanut, a great American food," by H. S. Bailey and J. A. Le Clerc (1917, pp. 289-301).

DEPARTMENT OF AGRICULTURE CIRCULARS

Relation of dehydration to agriculture (January 25, 1919, 11 pages).

Explosions and fires in thrashing machines (1918, 6 pages).

The installation of dust-collecting fans for thrashing machines for the prevention of explosions and fires and for grain cleaning, by H. E. Roethe, Jr., and E. N. Bates (May, 1918, 11 pages).

The utilization of the potato, by H. C. Gore (1918, 11 pages).

Formulas for sugar-saving sirups (1918, 5 pages).

Malt sirup for candy (4 pages).

Preparation of sirup from sweet potatoes (2 pages).

Report of an egg conference, May 15 and June 1, 1918 (8 pages).

Save lives and food and property (1918, 2 pages).

OFFICE OF FARM MANAGEMENT

The Office of Farm Management originated in the Bureau of Plant Industry in 1904, was transferred to the Office of the Secretary in 1915, became the Office of Farm Management and Farm Economics in 1919, was made an independent office in 1920, and in 1922 was merged with the Bureau of Markets and Crop Estimates to form the Bureau of Agricultural Economics. During the war the office directed its attention chiefly to the shortage of farm labor, means of increasing crop production, and to a continuation of its study of wheat production. It urged a fuller use of farm machinery, appealed to the urban population to assist in harvesting crops, and, in coöperation with the Department of Labor, effected an improvement in the distribution of agricultural labor.

Publications

FARMERS' BULLETINS

838. *Harvesting Hay with the Sweep-Rake, a Means by Which Eastern Hay-Growers may Save Labor,* Arnold P. Yerkes and H. B. McClure (June, 1917, 12 pages).

877. *Human Food from an Acre of Staple Farm Products,* by Morton O. Cooper and W. J. Spillman (October, 1917, 11 pages).

904. *Fire Prevention and Fire Fighting on the Farm,* by H. R. Tolley and A. P. Yerkes (January, 1918, 16 pages).

905. *Ways of Making Southern Mountain Farms More Productive,* by J. H. Arnold (August, 1918, 28 pages).

924. *A Simple Way to Increase Crop Yields,* by H. A. Miller (February, 1918, 24 pages).

943. *Haymaking,* by H. B. McClure (April, 1918, 31 pages). Ways of saving time and labor and reducing costs.

956. *Curing Hay on Trucks,* by H. B. McClure (May, 1918, 19 pages).

963. *Tractor Experience in Illinois, a Study of the Farm Tractor under*

Corn-Belt Conditions, by Arnold P. Yerkes and L. M. Church (June, 1918, 30 pages).

981. *Farm Practices that Increase Crop Yields in Kentucky and Tennessee,* by J. H. Arnold (November, 1918, 38 pages).

986. *Farm Practices That Increase Crop Yields in the Gulf Coast Region,* by M. A. Crosby (June, 1918, 28 pages).

987. *Labor Saving Practices in Haymaking,* by H. B. McClure (June, 1918, 20 pages).

989. *Better Use of Man Labor on the Farm,* by H. R. Tolley and A. P. Yerkes (June, 1918, 15 pages).

991. *The Efficient Operation of Thrashing Machines,* by H. R. Tolley (June, 1918, 16 pages).

992. *The Use of Machinery in Cutting Corn,* by H. R. Tolley (July, 1918, 16 pages).

1008. *Saving Farm Labor by Harvesting Crops with Live Stock,* by J. A. Drake (September, 1918, 15 pages).

1009. *Hay Stackers, How They may be Used in the East and South to Save Labor,* by H. B. McClure (January, 1919, 23 pages).

1023. *Machinery for Cutting Firewood,* by H. R. Tolley (January, 1919, 16 pages).

1035. *The Farm Tractor in the Dakotas,* by Arnold P. Yerkes and L. M. Church (March, 1919, 32 pages).

1042. *Saving Man Labor in Sugar-Beet Fields,* by L. A. Moorehouse and T. H. Summers (June, 1919, 19 pages).

Department of Agriculture Bulletins

528. *Seasonal Distribution of Farm Labor in Chester County, Pa.,* by George A. Billings (April 13, 1917, 29 pages).

602. *Value of a Small Plot of Ground to the Laboring Man,* by W. C. Funk (March 5, 1918, 11 pages).

Yearbook

"The world's supply of wheat," by O. C. Stine (1917, pp. 461-480).

"A graphic summary of seasonal work on farm crops," by O. E. Baker, C. F. Brooks, and R. G. Hainsworth (1917, pp. 537-589).

"The thrashing ring in the corn belt," by J. C. Rundles (1918, pp. 247-268).

"Arable land in the United States," by O. E. Baker and H. M. Strong (1918, pp. 433-441).

"Farm practices in growing wheat," by J. H. Arnold and R. R. Spafford (1919, pp. 123-150).

"The horse power problem on the farm," by Oscar A. Juve (1919, pp. 485-495).

UNITED STATES WEATHER BUREAU

The United States Weather Bureau was established under a joint resolution of Congress, February 9, 1870, as a branch of the Signal Service of the War Department. It was transferred to the Department of Agriculture July 1, 1891, by an act of Congress approved October 1, 1890. During the war it was intimately associated with the meteorological section of the Signal Corps, U.S. Army, which coöperated with the French and the English in forecasting meteorological conditions on the Western Front. It also rendered various services to military organizations in the United States, but its importance for this survey is in its monthly reports of *Climatological Data for the United States by Sections* (Washington, 1917-1919).

BUREAU OF ENTOMOLOGY

The Bureau of Entomology was active during the war in guarding against the outbreak of insect pests ruinous or injurious to any of the staple crops and in measures to save stored grain, other food products, and lumber from loss or damage by operations of insects. A system of reporting insect outbreaks was organized, the result of which was an intimate knowledge of conditions almost from day to day of insect-pest increase over the whole United States. These conditions were made known to the economic entomologists of the country through circular letters, and coöperative measures were taken to hold crop pests in check. By conferences with chemists and insecticide manufacturers the problem of reduced quantity of arsenic was met, and by conservative use and better distribution the supply was made to cover the needs of the farmers, fruit growers, and gardeners. The bureau assisted the Quartermaster General's Department of the army by inspecting the enormous quantities of grain intended for shipment to Europe and gave advice as to fumigation and other treatment when such stored products were found to be infested with insects. It likewise inspected warehouses and mills in many parts of the country. Advice was given to representatives of the War and Navy Departments and to the United States Shipping Board relative to insect damage to lumber and stored wooden implements. Specialists sent out by the Beekeeping Section addressed thousands of beekeepers as to the need of more honey, with the result that the supply of this commodity for domestic consumption was much increased and exports of it to allied countries were ten times greater than at any period previous to the war.

Publications

FARMERS' BULLETINS

835. *How to Detect Outbreaks of Insects and Save the Grain Crops,* by W. R. Walton (June, 1917, 24 pages).

875. *The Rough-Headed Corn Stalk Beetle in the Southern States and its Control,* by W. J. Phillips and Henry Fox (October, 1917, 12 pages).

890. *How Insects Affect the Cotton Plant and Means of Combating Them,* by W. Dwight Pierce (December, 1917, 28 pages).

891. *The Corn Root-Aphis and Methods of Controlling It,* by John J. Davis (December, 1917, 12 pages).

908. *Information for Fruit Growers about Insecticides, Spraying Apparatus,* and *Important Insect Pests,* by A. L. Quaintance and E. H. Siegler (February, 1918, 99 pages).

940. *Common White Grubs,* by John J. Davis (May, 1918, 28 pages). Possibility of an outbreak in 1918.

950. *The Southern Corn Rootworm and Farm Practices to Control It,* by Philip Luginbill (May, 1918, 12 pages).

983. *Bean and Pea Weevils,* by E. A. Back and A. B. Duckett (September, 1918, 24 pages).

1003. *How to Control Billbugs Destructive to Cereal and Forage Crops,* by A. F. Satterthwait (January, 1919, 23 pages).

1037. *White Ants as Pests in the United States and Methods of Preventing Their Damage,* by T. E. Snyder (June, 1919, 16 pages).

YEARBOOK

"How weevils get into beans," by E. A. Back (1918, pp. 327-334).

Entomology and the War, by L. O. Howard (9 pages), is a reprint from *The Scientific Monthly,* February, 1919.

BUREAU OF BIOLOGICAL SURVEY

The Bureau of Biological Survey assisted in the conservation of food supplies by conducting campaigns against rats and other rodent pests, which destroy growing and stored food products; and against wolves, coyotes, and other predatory animals, which live to a great extent upon domestic flocks and herds.

Publications

FARMERS' BULLETINS

670. *Field mice as farm and orchard pests,* by David E. Lantz (June, 1915, 10 pages).

702. *Cottontail rabbits in relation to trees and farm crops,* by David E. Lantz (January, 1916, 12 pages).

869. *The muskrat as a fur bearer, with notes on its use as food,* by David E. Lantz (September, 1917, 22 pages).

896. *House rats and mice,* by David E. Lantz (October, 1917, 24 pages).

932. *Rodent pests of the farm,* by David E. Lantz (July, 1918, 23 pages).

YEARBOOK

"Coöperative campaigns for the control of ground squirrels, prairie dogs, and jack rabbits," by W. B. Bell (1917, pp. 225-233).

"The house rat: the most destructive animal in the world," by David E. Lantz (1917, pp. 235-251).

"Rabbit growing to supplement the meat supply," by Ned Dearborn (1918, pp. 145-152).

BUREAU OF SOILS AND OFFICE OF FERTILIZER CONTROL

In conformity with a proclamation of the President, issued February 25, 1918, the Office of Fertilizer Control was created in the Department of Agriculture to regulate, by licenses, the importation, manufacture, storage, and distribution of fertilizer ingredients. The Bureau of Soils coöperated with this office in determining the fertilizer requirements of the country and the available supplies of fertilizer ingredients.

With the abolition of the Office of Fertilizer Control shortly after the signing of the Armistice in 1918, the work of that office was transferred to the Bureau of Soils and was continued until the repeal of the Lever act in March, 1921. In its conduct of this work, and under the authority of the act referred to, the Bureau of Soils required the fertilizer manufacturers to submit for approval each spring and fall the figures upon which it was intended to base the selling price of their commodities, and in this way prevented the exaction of excessive profits.

Prior to the entry of the United States into the war the Bureau of Soils had carried its investigation of the fixation of atmospheric nitrogen to a point where it had already in operation a plant for the fixation of nitrogen, at that time the only Haber plant in operation in the country. The bureau was also operating a small plant for the oxidation of ammonia to nitric acid. These plants were put at the service of the War Department and thereafter, during the period of the war, active coöperation was maintained in the study of nitrogen fixation for the manufacture of suitable compounds for munitions and fertilizers.

In an endeavor to establish an American potash industry, the Bureau of Soils had for some years before the war been actively investigating sources of potash. With the advent of the war this work was promptly expanded and there was erected and placed in operation for experiment and demonstration a kelp products plant at Summerland, Calif. Here were worked out methods of producing not only potash salts but also absorbent carbons and iodine, both of especial value for war purposes. The plant was operated on a producing scale and made to yield a contribution to the country's potash supply.

Recognizing the desirability of the use of more concentrated fertilizers, through the use of which large amounts of car space could be saved and a reduction in freight charges effected, an investigation was made by the Bureau of Soils of a method for the volatilization of phosphoric acid by the pyrolytic process, and in conjunction with this a study was made of the preparation of concentrated fertilizer materials carrying the three principal fertilizer ingredients.

Publications

DEPARTMENT OF AGRICULTURE BULLETINS

699. *Analysis of Experimental Work with Ground Raw Rock Phosphate as a Fertilizer,* by W. H. Waggaman (October 16, 1918, 119 pages).

YEARBOOK

"The sources of our nitrogenous fertilizers," by Frederick W. Brown (1917, pp. 139-146).

"Phosphate rock our greatest fertilizer asset," by W. H. Waggaman (1917, pp. 177-183).

"Fertilizers from industrial wastes," by William H. Ross (1917, pp. 253-263).

"Atmospheric nitrogen for fertilizers," by R. O. E. Davis (1919, pp. 115-121).

717. "Importance of developing our natural sources of potash," by F. W. Brown.

733. "Conservation of fertilizer materials from minor sources," by C. C. Fletcher.

840. "Phosphorus in fertilizer," by W. H. Waggaman.

851. "Getting our potash," by W. H. Ross.

DEPARTMENT OF AGRICULTURE CIRCULARS

61. *Sources of American Potash,* by R. O. E. Davis.

Senate Document 410, 66th Congress, 3rd Session, is a statement of the fertilizer situation in the United States, by Milton Whitney.

BUREAU OF PUBLIC ROADS AND UNITED STATES HIGHWAYS COUNCIL

The United States Highways Council, consisting of the chief of the Bureau of Public Roads (chairman) and representatives from the War Department, Railroad Administration, War Industries Board, Fuel Administration, and Capital Issues Committee was formed in June, 1918, to coördinate the activities of government agencies in relation to the highways. The Bureau of Public Roads suspended most of its pre-war program, and the council and bureau, coöperating, were charged with the carrying out of the government's road-building program during the period of the war, a program which provided particularly for roads at and around the army cantonments and concentration points for war materials and for the improvement of roads necessary to facilitate movement from production points. After the war road building was promoted by a general distribution of road-building machinery, equipment, and supplies from the surplus war material of the army.

Publications

Report of the Director of the Bureau of Public Roads, 1918 (Washington, 1918, 20 pages). War work.

Report of the Chief of the Bureau of Public Roads, 1919 (Washington, 1919, 36 pages). War activities; distribution of surplus war equipment, supplies, and materials.

"Federal aid to highways," by J. E. Pennybacker and L. E. Boykin (1917, pp. 127-138).

"Electric light and power from small streams," by A. M. Daniels (1918, pp. 221-238).

PERIODICAL

Public Roads, a periodical issued by the Bureau from May, 1918, to December, 1921, contains the following articles:

"The U.S. Highways Council" (June, 1918, p. 2);

"Oil, asphalt, and tar supply" (June, 1918, p. 3);

"Work of the Bureau of Public Roads for the last fiscal year" (December, 1918, pages 6-48).

OFFICE OF INFORMATION

The Office of Information prepared and distributed the *Weekly News Letter,* conducted a *Special Information Service,* and issued a *Home Garden Series,* a *Canning-Drying Series,* and a *War Work Weekly.*

Weekly News Letter. This periodical, originally of three or four pages, was first issued August 13, 1913. During the war it was enlarged to eight, and, occasionally, to sixteen pages. As the official organ of the Department it was used to further agricultural campaigns and for the publication of official statements. Some of its leading articles during the war were: Food crops must be increased: war demands and world food shortage should be met by American farmers—efficient production imperative—what crops should be stressed and where (April 18, 1917); Raise more chickens, Farm labor problem (May 23); Food waste at home (June 20); Can and dry surplus fruits and vegetables (July 4); Save your own vegetable seed (July 11); Prepare now to store food crops for winter use (July 25); Saving of perishables (August 1); Billion bushels of wheat recommended for next year (August 15); Extension of Government's food production work (August 22); Nitrate of soda for fertilizers (October 10); Wage war on rodents (November 7); Problems of production, conservation and rural labor (November 29); Pork production for 1918: Department of Agriculture asks the States to increase swine 5 to 50 per cent—big corn crop will help (December 5); Secretary Houston reports year's gain on the agricultural front (December 12); Farm labor problem (January 2, 1918); Farmers to increase poultry production (January 9); Grow more spring wheat—increase food crops and meats (February 27); Policy and scope of Food Administration with relation to price fixing (March 6); City's part in solving farm-labor problem (March 13); Report of Advisory Committee of Producers: regulations adopted regarding food production measures—problems relating to seed, grain, fertilizers, equipment, labor, and live stock (April 17); Cottage cheese (April 24); Eat more rice, Potatoes back wheat (May 8); Let sweet clover bloom on wastes, increase honey and sugar supply (May 22); President places farm-implement industry under license system, Many ways to use honey as substitute for sugar (May 29); Soft-drink makers may save 50,000 tons of sugar by use of substitutes (June 5); President places stockyards and stock dealers under license system (June 26); War policy in road building (July 10); Business men's part in food production (July 17); All must help in clearing community of rodent pests, Keep canning, sugar or no sugar (July 24); The American system of agricultural education and research and its rôle in helping to win the war, Wheat yields increased by using right kind of seed (August 28); Cut wood, sell it, burn it—help save coal (October 9); Advantage of motor trucks shown in farming reports, War spirit drives forward in boys' and girls' clubs (October 30).

Special Information Service. This was an illustrated weekly news service under four departments of two columns each, in which were discussed problems of food production and conservation, especially as they related to the urban population and small producers. The four departments were: (1) Our Part in Feeding the Nation; (2) Helping the Meat and Milk Supply; (3) A Bird in the Hand (poultry); (4) The Housewife and the War. The service was inaugurated in October, 1917, and was furnished to more than seven thousand newspapers. It was continued in slightly different form after the war.

Home Garden Series. This was issued early in the season of 1918 to give advice to home gardeners on farms and in cities as aid to them in producing supplies of home-grown foods.

The Canning-Drying Series was intended to promote the saving of food produced in the home gardens.

War Work Weekly. This six-page weekly, issued in mimeograph, was established in May, 1918, to inform newspapers and agricultural journals regarding the results and progress obtained by the department's workers and its coöperating forces in the States in war emergency activities.

Department of Agriculture in the War, by Dixon Merritt (mimeographed, 208 pages), gives an account of the war work of each bureau and special war agency of the Department.

AGRICULTURAL ADVISORY COMMITTEE

The Agricultural Advisory Committee was composed of twenty-four representatives of agricultural and live-stock production. It assembled in Washington March 28, 1918, remained in session until April 4, and held another session August 5-8, 1918. For its proceedings and recommendations see (1) *Report of Advisory Committee of Agricultural and Live-Stock Producers in Consultation with the Department of Agriculture and the Food Administration, Sitting in Washington March 28 to April 4, Inclusive* (Washington, 1918, 32 pages); (2) Stenographic Report of the Proceedings of the Agricultural Advisory Committee of the U.S. Department of Agriculture and the U.S. Food Administration (multigraphed, 137 pages); (3) Statement, U.S. Department of Agriculture, Regarding Recommendations of Agricultural Advisory Committee at Its Meeting in Washington March 28 to April 4 (mimeographed, May 27, 1918, 44 pages); (4) Minutes of the Agricultural Advisory Committee, August 5-8, 1918 (mimeographed, 17 pages).

AGRICULTURAL COMMISSION TO EUROPE

The Agricultural Commission to Europe was appointed by the Secretary of Agriculture in August, 1918, to ascertain conditions of European agriculture as they had a bearing upon agriculture in the United States during the continuance of the war, and also to ascertain the outlook for agriculture during the period of reconstruction. For its findings see *Report of Agricultural Commission to Europe: Observations Made by American Agriculturists in Great Britain, France, and Italy for the United States Department of Agriculture* (Washington, 1919, 89 pages).

DEPARTMENT OF COMMERCE[1]

THE Department of Commerce dates its establishment as a separate entity, for the promotion of the commercial and industrial interests of the United States, from the act of Congress of March 4, 1913, creating the Department of Labor; but the organic act under which it operates is that of February 14, 1903, establishing the Department of Commerce and Labor. At the outbreak of the war the Department was organized in the following divisions: Office of the Secretary, Bureau of Foreign and Domestic Commerce, Bureau of Standards, Bureau of the Census, Bureau of Fisheries, Bureau of Lighthouses, Steamboat Inspection Service, Bureau of Navigation, Coast and Geodetic Survey.

OFFICE OF THE SECRETARY

Functions

Besides directing the work of the other divisions of the Department the Secretary of Commerce was a member of the Council of National Defense and of the War Trade Council, and chose his representative to serve as a member of the War Trade Board. He coöperated with the Commercial Economy Board of the Council of National Defense in a campaign against waste and subsequently organized the Waste Reclamation Service. He joined with the Secretary of Labor in calling a conference to provide for the proper manning of merchant vessels. He established the Industrial Board to stabilize prices as a means of expediting the process of commercial readjustment. He organized the Industrial Coöperation Service for the standardization of products, to search for outlets for waste products, to promote the commercial development of new products, and to minimize business abuses. An assistant to the Secretary investigated the problem of inland water transportation.

Publications

Annual Report of the Secretary of Commerce, 1917 (Washington, 1917, 291 pages). Measures for promoting foreign trade; commercial

---

[1] The material for this section was assembled by Dr. James A. Robertson of the Department of Commerce.

waste; commercial use of the waterways; provision for proper manning of merchant vessels; review of the work of the divisions.

Annual Report of the Secretary of Commerce, 1918 (Washington, 1918, 157 pages). Development of waterways; review of the work of the divisions.

Annual Report of the Secretary of Commerce, 1919 (Washington, 1919, 246 pages). Use of motion pictures in industry; development of waterways; Industrial Board; Industrial Coöperation Service. Waste-Reclamation Service; new fish food; review of the work of the divisions.

Standardization in the Construction of Freight Ships (Washington, 1916, 16 pages). An argument for standardization by a consulting engineer.

Advisory Conference on the Subject of Making Passenger Vessels More Secure from Destruction by Fire, held in the Office of the Secretary of Commerce May 3, 1916 (Washington, 1916, 63 pages). A discussion by representatives of the shipbuilding industry.

Proceedings of a Conference on Automatic Sprinklers on Vessels, held in the Department of Commerce May 22, 1916 (Washington, 1916, 34 pages).

Establishment of Load-Line Regulations. Proceedings of a conference held in the Office of the Secretary of Commerce September 27, 1916 (Washington, 1916, 54 pages).

Inland Water Transportation, by Walter Parker (Washington, 1917, 11 pages). A report to the Secretary of Commerce in favor of inland water transportation as a war measure and as essential to the development of an adequate and economic system of transportation for the promotion of domestic and foreign commerce after the war.

Inland Waterway Terminal Development, by Walter Parker (Washington, 1918, 10 pages). A report to the Secretary of Commerce.

Waste Reclamation: Organization, Functions, and Objects of the National and Local Service (Washington, 1919, 19 pages).

Report of an Investigation of the Akron Industrial Salvage Co. (Washington, 1919, 20 pages). Reviews progress of an experiment in waste reclamation dealing with the waste of the home, the store, and the factory.

Records

The unpublished records of the Secretary's Office consist of correspondence relative to administrational matters, wide in scope during the war, but treated as confidential, and of mimeographed or multigraphed circulars to the departmental units relative to the food conservation campaign, Liberty loan campaigns, and other war activities.

BUREAU OF FOREIGN AND DOMESTIC COMMERCE

Functions and Organization

The Bureau of Foreign and Domestic Commerce, a consolidation of the Bureau of Manufactures and the Bureau of Statistics, was created by the legislative, executive, and judicial appropriation act of August 23, 1912, to promote commerce and manufacturing by collecting and distributing information for the use and benefit of commercial interests. During the war the bureau gathered information relative to industrial and trade conditions both in the United States and in foreign countries; discharged functions for which the War Trade Board was subsequently created; assisted the War Trade Board in the control of export trade for the conservation of the resources of the country and in preventing the enemy from obtaining American supplies; coöperated with the War Trade Board and the United States Shipping Board in the utilization of available tonnage to the best advantage and in procuring raw materials and other supplies essential to the conduct of the war; directed the Tin-Plate Conservation Committee for the conservation of the food supply through preference in tin plate to packers of perishable foods until the perishable crop had been packed and by measures for increasing the supply of tin plate; adjusted differences arising between business houses and government war agencies, and differences arising from restriction on trade with foreign countries; aided in the reduction of freight-car shortage; and obtained priority in the manufacture and delivery of raw materials, prior to the creation of the General Munitions Board. After the armistice was signed the bureau supplied producers and exporters with information relative to the needs of people in foreign countries and the best means of satisfying them. The bureau operated in several divisions: Statistics, Research, Foreign Tariffs, Trade Information, Latin American, Far Eastern, District Offices, Foreign Service, Export Licenses, and Editorial.

Division of Statistics. From this division statistics were obtained by the War Trade Board for use in licensing imports and exports;

by the United States Food Administration for guidance in conserving food and stimulating food production; by the Bureau of Markets, Department of Agriculture, to determine the imports and exports of agricultural raw products; by the United States Shipping Board to ascertain the available vessel tonnage, vessel movements, port facilities, imports and exports by articles, by countries, and by customs districts. They were used by the Council of National Defense, the War Industries Board, and the United States Fuel Administration in the study of various problems. To meet the demand of the several war organizations for more up-to-date statistics than those in the monthly reports the division, in coöperation with the Bureau of Customs Statistics of the Treasury Department at New York, issued confidential reports three times a month, or for each period of ten days.

Research Division. Compilations of the imports and exports of many commodities of various countries were furnished by this division to special war agencies, regular government offices, trade organizations, and business concerns. Instruction was given by its staff to employees of special war agencies as to the best method of using and interpreting foreign statistical publications. Information was given by letter and by oral statement as to the production and consumption of various commodities in various countries, including the United States. Statements were compiled relative to the financial, economic, and commercial situation and development in foreign countries. Various economic studies and surveys were made, and some of these were published. Such reconstruction matters as foreign investment opportunities were given attention.

Division of Foreign Tariffs. This division reported on the trade restrictions in belligerent and certain neutral countries, prepared a confidential memorandum for the State Department on a plan for the control of exports of Russian foodstuffs, compiled statements for the War Trade Board and the United States Shipping Board on embargoes and import prohibitions in foreign countries, analyzed the Brest-Litovsk Treaty, and collected data for use in the consideration of reconstruction problems.

Division of Trade Information. The Division of Trade Information furnished information and suggestions as to the sources of names of American firms, and assisted the War Department in arranging for that department to use the bureau in disposing of surplus war supplies and property. The division also rendered assistance to American firms and individuals who desired to locate domestic sources of merchandise formerly imported from one of the Central Powers.

Latin American Division. The general purpose of the Latin American Division is the promotion of United States trade with all countries and colonies south of the United States, and from the economic data which was accumulated in the pursuit of this purpose was derived information needed in numerous war activities involving Latin American affairs. Here was information for the War Department relative to petroleum resources, nitrate, drug plants, castor beans, mahogany, coconuts, cohune nuts, cinchona bark, and quinine; for the Geological Survey relative to nitrate, petroleum, zinc, manganese, platinum, coal, tin, antimony, and tungsten; for the Food Administration relative to sisal, sugar, bananas, cereals, and coffee; and for the Federal Reserve Board relative to the exchange situation in Latin American countries. The division assisted the Shipping Board in determining the extent to which ship service between the United States and Latin America might be curtailed in order to supply tonnage for trans-Atlantic troop and munition movements, and it advised the War Trade Board with reference to the granting of licenses for export to South America.

Far Eastern Division. This division has jurisdiction over economic and trade matters in China, Japan, India, Siam and neighboring countries, the Philippines, East Indies, Straits Settlements, and Australia. During the war it translated certain Japanese documents for the Bureau of War Trade Intelligence, assisted the War Trade Board in economic research, assisted the War Industries Board in research relative to available supply of rum, assisted the Shipping Board in procuring information relative to ship subsidies in Japan, and made suggestions as to routes for trans-Pacific steamship service.

Division of District Offices. Besides the headquarters of this division in Washington, district offices were maintained in New York, Boston, Chicago, St. Louis, New Orleans, San Francisco, and Seattle, and coöperative offices were maintained by the chambers of commerce or other organizations in Philadelphia, Cincinnati, Dayton, Cleveland, Chattanooga, Portland, Ore., and Los Angeles. Prior to the establishment of the War Trade Board, October 12, 1917, these offices constituted the principal agency of the Exports Administrative Board for the administration of the exports-control system, and until the close of the war they assisted the War Trade Board, the War Industries Board, the Food Administration, the Fuel Administration, and the Railroad Administration in enforcing restrictive measures regarding trade. They acted as intermediaries in assisting business houses to adjust their manufacturing and business operations to the regulations of the various departments of the government; published and explained war regulations both of the United States and of foreign countries, by means of letters, conferences, addresses, and press announcements; made special investigations in cases from which difficulties arose in connection with foreign shipments, and settled or adjusted the dispute. During the period of reconstruction they responded to demands from American business men for advice and assistance relative to new markets and placed foreign business men in touch with American merchants.

Foreign Service Division. Of foreign service there are two branches: (a) that performed by commercial attachés and (b) that performed by trade commissioners or special agents.

The (a) commercial attachés centered their attention during the war on important economic developments, and reliable information regarding Germany was at a premium. Besides serving the Department of Commerce they acted as representatives of the War Trade Board, the Shipping Board, the War Industries Board, and the Food Administration, performed special missions for other Departments, and coöperated with representatives of the allied governments. They assisted in procuring raw materials and supplies for the army, the navy, and essential industries. Among these materials were optical glass, platinum, manganese, and tin. The commercial attaché in London made a study of the British war organization, assisted in the handling of Swedish iron ore and Norwegian molybdenum contracts, and coöperated with the American Chamber of Commerce in London in studying developments in the British paper manufacturing industry and the development of substances for textiles. The commercial attaché in Paris organized and operated the American office of the Inter-Allied Contingent Commission, aided in the purchase of supplies in France for the American forces, and made reports on French industrial reconstruction. The commercial attaché at the Hague represented the War Trade Board in the Inter-allied Joint Council, aided the American minister in carrying out the agreements that had been made with the Dutch government, and conferred with the Defense Blockade Council in Paris with reference to the general and financial blockade administration and the shipping of foodstuffs to Germany under the Brussels agreement. The commercial attaché in Copenhagen acted as expert adviser to the War Trade Board on continental trade, aided in the negotiation of the commercial agreements made with the Scandinavian countries, and furnished various confidential reports relative to peace conditions in those countries. The commercial attaché in Russia negotiated through the American embassy for the release of Russian commodities that were needed in the United States. The commercial attaché in Japan paid special attention to the cultivation of international good will and assisted in bringing about an agreement between the Japanese and United States governments whereby delivery of Japanese ships was arranged in return for shipments of steel. The commercial attaché in Buenos Aires had full charge, for the War Trade Board, of enemy-trading matters, suggested and assisted in the formation of the Allied Chamber of Commerce of Buenos Aires, and by his reports to the Shipping Board enabled that body to provide vessels with which to move cargoes that were urgently needed in the United States for war purposes. The commercial attaché at Lima acted as chairman of a subcommittee of the Allied Conference of Ministers in Lima, a body which was formed at his suggestion to consider matters of common war interest. Both commercial attachés in South America were particularly active in efforts to create a favorable atmosphere toward the United States and the Allies and to counteract German influence.

Shortly after the United States entered the war the (b) trade commissioners or special agents abroad were instructed to give particular attention, in addition to their regular work of investigating foreign markets, to special features of interest in connection with the government's war program. They responded by procuring information, conveyed in written reports or in personal interviews, relative to the status of foreign concerns with respect to enemy trade, foreign sources and market conditions of minerals and other materials essential to war industries, economic developments in Germany, German activities in Latin America, enemy propaganda in various countries, the effects of the war and the blockade on conditions in Scandinavia, port facilities and freight conditions in South America, Japanese mineral resources, lumber supplies available in Scandinavia, lumber trade in Russia, commercial and political conditions in Finland, crude rubber resources, railroad conditions in China, etc.

Division of Export Licenses. This division was created July 9, 1917, to exercise the control over exports that was vested in the Secretary of Commerce by executive order of June 22, 1917. It was succeeded, August 21, 1917, by the Exports Administrative Board.

Publications

The bureau has put forth several publications which tell of its war-time operations or which are essential to a study both of the effects of the war upon the foreign commerce of the United States and of the processes of reconstruction. A complete list of those for the war period is contained in the *Catalogue of Bureau Publications. A Review of Information Available to Manufacturers and Exporters in Bulletins Issued by the Bureau of Foreign and Domestic Commerce* (Washington, 1922, 55 pages). A select list follows.

Annual Reports and Trade Statistics

Annual Report of the Chief of Bureau of Foreign and Domestic Commerce . . . for the Fiscal Year ended June 30, 1917 (Washington, 1917, 77 pages). Review of the year's foreign trade; organization for licensing exports; tin-plate conservation; trade investigations by commercial agents; war work in the district offices.

Annual Report of the Chief of Bureau of Foreign and Domestic Commerce . . . June 30, 1918 (Washington, 1918, 93 pages). Review of the year's foreign trade; war work of special agents; war work of commercial attachés; war work in district offices; preparation for promoting after-war trade.

Annual Report of the Chief of Bureau of Foreign and Domestic Commerce . . . June 30, 1919 (Washington, 1919, 82 pages). Review of the year's foreign trade; war-time activities; reconstruction activities.

Monthly Summary of Foreign Commerce of the United States, July, 1916 (Washington, 1916, 92 pages). The same title for each succeeding month to June, 1920. These summaries exhibit quantity and value of imports and exports by articles and principal countries.

Quarterly Statement of Imported Merchandise Entered for Consumption in the United States and Duties Collected thereon during the Quarter ending September 30, 1916 (Washington, 1917, 58 pages). The same title for each succeeding quarter to June 30, 1920. The statements exhibit either the quantity or value, or both, of each imported commodity.

Foreign Commerce and Navigation of the United States for the Year ending June 30, 1916 (Washington, 1917, 950 pages, 15 tables, and commodity index). The same title for each succeeding year to 1920; the calendar year is the period covered after June 30, 1918.

COMMERCE REPORTS

Commerce Reports, published daily by the Bureau of Foreign and Domestic Commerce from January 2, 1915, to August 31, 1921, and weekly since September 5, 1921, are one of the most important sources of information relative to the effect of the war on the foreign commerce of the United States and will be useful in the reconstruction period. The material relates to general industrial, economic, and financial conditions, and especially to tariff and foreign market conditions affecting the principal commodities exported from the United States. It was sent in from all parts of the world by American consuls, commercial attachés, special foreign agents, and the bureau's district offices.

SPECIAL AGENT SERIES

This series consists of monographs on special industries and special phases of commerce. They were prepared by the special agents abroad and by others. The following numbers in the series, all published by the Government Printing Office, are within the scope of this survey.

96. *Dyestuffs for American Textiles and Other Industries,* by Thomas H. Norton (1915, 57 pages). Shows limited extent of the domestic manufacture

and the general dependence upon foreign-made dyes. All factors connected with the creation of a self-contained independent American coal-tar chemical industry are given.

107. *Cotton Goods in China,* by Ralph M. Odell (1916, 242 pages). Why American trade declines; American opportunities, American methods unsatisfactory.

110. *By-Products of the Lumber Industry,* by H. K. Benson (1916, 68 pages). Wood distillation, tannin extract, wood pulp.

111. *Dyestuff Situation in the United States, November, 1915,* by Thomas H. Norton (1916, 19 pages).

112. *Lumber Markets of the East Coast of South America,* by Roger E. Simmons (1916, 121 pages). Uses of various woods; the import trade.

113. *Central America as an Export Field,* by Garrard Harris (1916, 229 pages). Specific commercial openings in each country.

114. *Navigation Laws: Comparative study of principal features of the laws of the United States, Great Britain, Germany, Norway, France, and Japan,* by Grosvenor S. Jones (1916, 190 pages).

115. *Cotton Goods in the Straits Settlements,* by Ralph M. Odell (1916, 57 pages).

116. *Markets for Machinery and Machine Tools in Argentina,* by J. A. Massel (1916, 64 pages). The machinery trade; absence of machinery manufacturing in Argentina.

117. *Lumber Markets of the West and North Coasts of South America,* by Roger E. Simmons (1916, 149 pages).

118. *Markets for Machinery and Machine Tools in Peru, Bolivia, and Chili,* by J. A. Massel (1916, 88 pages). Adverse factors in American trade, factors in development of American trade.

119. *Government Aid to American Shipping, a study of subsidies, subventions, and other forms of state aid in the principal countries of the world,* by Grosvenor M. Jones (1916, 265 pages).

120. *Cotton Goods in the Dutch East Indies,* by Ralph M. Odell (1916, 55 pages). American cotton goods not imported, kinds of cotton goods imported.

121. *Artificial Dyestuffs used in the United States,* by Thomas H. Norton (1916, 254 pages). Artificial colors manufactured in the United States, classification of artificial dyestuffs imported during the fiscal year ended June 30, 1914.

122. *Development of an American Linen Industry,* by W. A. Graham Clark (1916, 23 pages). Flax production in the United States, flax growing and preparation for mill, flax manufacturing, linen bleaching and finishing.

123. *Cotton Goods in Ceylon,* by Ralph M. Odell (1916, 39 pages). Features of the market, cotton goods imported from the United States.

124. *Cotton Goods in British India: Part I—Madras Presidency,* by Ralph M. Odell (1916, 50 pages).

125. *Markets for Agricultural Implements and Machinery in Argentina,* by Frank H. von Motz (1916, 86 pages). Agricultural conditions, details of the market.

126. *Textiles in Cuba,* by W. A. Tucker (1917, 56 pages). Cotton-goods market, woolen-goods market.

127. *Cotton Goods in British India: Part II—Bengal Presidency,* by Ralph M. Odell (1917, 88 pages). Japanese and American goods, obstacles to American trade.

128. *Electrical Goods in Cuba,* by Philip S. Smith (1917, 40 pages).

129. *The Danish West Indies, Their resources and commercial importance,* by H. G. Brock, Philip S. Smith, and W. A. Tucker (1917, 68 pages).

130. *Wearing Apparel in Japan,* by Stanhope Sams (1917, 134 pages). American trade relations with Japan, necessity for meeting Japanese tastes.

131. *South American Markets for Fresh Fruits,* by Walter Fischer (1917, 163 pages). Fruits imported from the United States, future of American grapefruit sales, general outlook for American fruits.

132. *Markets for Paper, Paper Products, and Printing Machinery in Cuba and Panama,* by Robert S. Barrett (1917, 44 pages).

133. *Markets for Boots and Shoes in Cuba,* by Herman G. Brock (1917, 46 pages). Popularity of American shoes, requirements of the Cuban market.

134. *Electrical Goods in Porto Rico,* by Philip S. Smith (1917, 16 pages).

135. *Market for Boots and Shoes in Porto Rico,* by Herman G. Brock (1917, 28 pages).

136. *Pilotage in the United States: Summary of laws and regulations relating to pilotage in the several States,* by Grosvenor M. Jones (1917, 102 pages).

137. *Textiles in Porto Rico and Jamaica,* by W. A. Tucker (1917, 31 pages).

138. *Cotton Goods in British India. Part III—Burma,* by Ralph M. Odell (1917, 52 pages). General survey of the market, prospects for American trade in Burma.

139. *Markets for Construction Materials and Machinery in Cuba,* by W. W. Ewing (1917, 61 pages).

140. *Markets for Agricultural Implements and Machinery in Brazil,* by Frank H. von Motz (1917, 59 pages). Success of American makers, American prices satisfactory.

141. *The West Indies as an Export Field,* by Garrard Harris *et al.* (1917, 378 pages). Discusses the industrial, financial, and commercial conditions on each of the islands.

142. *Markets for Agricultural Implements and Machinery in Chile and Peru,* by Frank H. von Motz (1917, 48 pages).

143. *Paper, Paper Products, and Printing Machinery in Peru, Bolivia, and Ecuador,* by Robert S. Barrett (1917, 77 pages).

144. *Markets for Construction Materials and Machinery in Venezuela,* by W. W. Ewing (1917, 57 pages). Specific building activities, particular materials and equipment.

145. *Markets for Boots and Shoes in Jamaica,* by Herman G. Brock (1917, 24 pages).

146. *Markets for Agricultural Implements and Machinery in South Africa,* by Juan Homs (1917, 231 pages). South African agriculture, markets for particular lines of equipment, trade methods.

147. *Electrical Goods in New Zealand,* by R. A. Lundquist (1917, 47 pages).

148. *South American Markets for Dried Fruits,* by Walter Fischer (1917, 35 pages).

149. *Cotton Goods in British India: Part IV—Bombay Presidency,* by Ralph M. Odell (1917, 132 pages). Survey of cotton-goods trade, trade of the United States.

150. *Commercial Laws of Switzerland,* by Archibald J. Wolfe, supplemented and revised by Robert P. Shick and Phanor James Eder (1917, 52 pages).

151. *Shoe and Leather Trade in New Zealand,* by C. E. Bosworth (1917, 31 pages).

152. *Market for Boots and Shoes in Peru,* by Herman G. Brock (1917, 89 pages). Importance of the Peruvian market, position of American goods, factors affecting American trade.

153. *Chilean Market for Paper, Paper Products, and Printing Machinery,* by Robert S. Barrett (1917, 72 pages).

154. *Electrical Goods in Ecuador and Peru,* by Philip S. Smith (1917, 51 pages).

155. *Electrical Goods in Australia,* by R. A. Lundquist (1918, 64 pages).

156. *Railway Materials, Equipment and Supplies in Australia and New Zealand,* by Frank Rhea (1918, 164 pages).

157. *Cotton Goods in British India: Part V—Summary of Trade; Part VI —Cotton Manufacturing,* by Ralph M. Odell (1918, 57 pages).

158. *Textile Markets of Bolivia, Ecuador, and Peru,* by W. A. Tucker (1918, 106 pages).

159. *Shoe and Leather Trade in Australia,* by C. E. Bosworth (1918, 39 pages).

160. *Construction Materials and Machinery in Colombia,* by W. W. Ewing (1918, 75 pages). Specific building activities, particular materials and equipment, commercial practices and requirements.

161. *Shoe and Leather Trade in the Philippine Islands,* by C. E. Bosworth (1918, 23 pages).

162. *Colombian Markets for American Furniture,* by Harold E. Everley (1918, 34 pages). Special factors influencing trade, methods of entering markets, market for particular kinds of furniture.

163. *Paper, Paper Products, and Printing Machinery in Argentina, Uruguay, and Paraguay,* by Robert S. Barrett (1918, 165 pages).

164. *Textile Market of Chile,* by W. A. Tucker (1918, 52 pages).

165. *Tanning Materials of Latin America,* by Thomas H. Norton (1918, 32 pages). Woods, barks, leaves, roots, bulbs, fruits, and seeds.

166. *Agricultural Implements and Machinery in Australia and New Zealand,* by Juan Homs (1918, 195 pages).

167. *Electrical Goods in Bolivia and Chile,* by Philip S. Smith (1918, 94 pages).

168. *Wearing Apparel in Chile,* by W. A. Tucker (1918, 75 pages).

169. *Investments in Latin America and the British West Indies,* by Frederic M. Halsey (1918, 544 pages). Port and harbor improvements, railway development, industries, public utilities, government finances.

170. *Motor Vehicles in Japan, China, and Hawaii,* by Tom O. Jones (1918, 75 pages). Position of the American motor car, roads.

171. *Brazilian Markets for Paper, Paper Products, and Printing Machinery,* by Robert S. Barrett (1918, 77 pages).

172. *Electrical Goods in China, Japan, and Vladivostok,* by R. A. Lundquist (1918, 197 pages).

173. *Shoe and Leather Trade of China and Japan,* by C. E. Bosworth (1918, 37 pages).

174. *Markets for Boots and Shoes in Chile and Bolivia,* by Herman G. Brock (1918, 192 pages). Position of American goods, methods open to American manufacturers, needs for better grades of footwear.

175. *Construction Materials and Machinery in Chile, Peru, and Ecuador,* by W. W. Ewing (1919, 205 pages). Specific building activities, particular materials and equipment.

176. *Furniture Markets of Chile, Peru, Bolivia, and Ecuador,* by Harold E. Everley (1919, 165 pages). Market for particular kinds of furniture, trade methods.

177. *Boots and Shoes, Leather and Supplies in Argentina, Uruguay, and Paraguay,* by Herman G. Brock (1919, 182 pages). Requirements of the market, conduct of trade.

179. *Boots and Shoes, Leather, and Supplies in Brazil,* by Herman G. Brock (1919, 59 pages).

180. *Far Eastern Markets for Railway Materials, Equipment and Supplies,* by Frank Rhea (1919, 339 pages). Markets in China, Japan, Korea, Manchuria, and the Philippine Islands.

181. *Jewelry and Silverware in Cuba,* by S. W. Rosenthal (1919, 78 pages). Character of the trade, American opportunity.

182. *The Lumber Market in Italy and Reconstruction Requirements,* by Nelson Courtlandt Brown (1919, 184 pages). Foreign lumber requirements, special features affecting imports of lumber, opportunities for developing trade in American lumber.

183. *Furniture Markets of Argentina, Uruguay, Paraguay, and Brazil,* by Harold E. Everley (1919, 165 pages).

184. *Electrical Goods in Argentina, Uruguay, and Brazil,* by Philip S. Smith (1919, 133 pages).

186. *Chinese Currency and Finance,* by A. W. Ferrin (1919, 57 pages).

187. *Jewelry and Silverware in Chile, Bolivia, and Peru,* by S. W. Rosenthal (1919, 115 pages). The market and its opportunities.

188. *Construction Materials and Machinery in Argentina and Bolivia,* by W. W. Ewing (1920, 192 pages).

189. *Construction Materials and Machinery in Uruguay,* by W. W. Ewing (1920, 59 pages).

191. *Farm Implements and Machinery in France and North Africa,* by H. Lawrence Groves (1920, 36 pages).

192. *Construction Materials and Machinery in Brazil,* by W. W. Ewing (1920, 96 pages).

193. *British Industrial Reconstruction and Commercial Policies,* by Fred W. Powell (1920, 88 pages). Effects of the war, raw materials, power, quantity production, and standardization.

Miscellaneous Series

The publications of this series are monographs dealing with various commercial subjects relating to foreign and domestic trade.

They were prepared in the bureau or by its representatives in the United States and foreign countries. Particular attention is directed to the following, all of which were published by the Government Printing Office.

33. *Ports of the United States:* Report on terminal facilities, commerce, port charges, and administration at sixty-eight selected ports, by Grosvenor M. Jones (1916, 431 pages).

34. *The Men's Factory-Made Clothing Industry:* Report on the cost of production of men's factory-made clothing in the United States (1916, 300 pages).

35. *Export Trade Suggestions* (1916, 141 pages). Extracts from reports of American consular officers and data from other sources dealing with the promotion of American trade.

36. *The Shirt and Collar Industries:* Report on the cost of production of men's shirts and collars in the United States (1916, 178 pages).

37. *The Cotton-Spinning Machinery Industry:* Report on the cost of production of cotton-spinning machinery in the United States (1916, 99 pages).

39. *Peruvian Markets for American Hardware,* prepared under the supervision of the commercial attaché at Lima (1916, 64 pages). Part I, general review of conditions; part II, markets for particular lines of hardware.

40. *Consumption Estimates* (1916, 12 pages). Statistical tables showing production, imports, exports, and amounts available for consumption each year from 1865 to 1915, of corn, wheat, cotton, sugar, coffee, tea, liquors, wines, wool, coke, coal, iron, steel, tin, pulp-wood, and flaxseed.

41. *Markets for American Hardware in Chile and Bolivia,* by Verne L. Havens (1916, 190 pages).

42. *Australian Markets for American Hardware,* by William C. Downs (1916, 105 pages).

43. *Markets for American Hardware in Argentina, Uruguay, and Paraguay,* prepared under the supervision of the commercial attaché at Buenos Aires.

44. *Trans-Pacific Shipping,* by Julean Arnold and M. D. Kirjassoff (1916, 30 pages). Deals with Pacific shipping as it was affected by the war with special reference to the growth of Japanese merchant marine.

46. *Russian Market for American Hardware,* by Henry D. Baker (1916, 111 pages).

47. *Brazilian Markets for American Hardware,* prepared under the supervision of the commercial attaché at Rio de Janeiro (1916, 89 pages).

48. *Markets for American Hardware in Germany, the Netherlands, and Scandinavia,* by Erwin W. Thompson (1917, 126 pages).

49. *Markets for American Hardware in France, Algeria, and Morocco,* prepared under the supervision of the commercial attaché at Paris (1917, 61 pages).

50. *Far Eastern Markets for American Hardware,* prepared under the supervision of the commercial attaché at Peking (1917, 145 pages).

51. *Lumber Markets of the Mediterranean Region and the Near East,* by Raphael Zon (1917, 31 pages).

52. *Wholesale Prices of Leading Articles in United States Markets, January, 1914, to December, 1916* (1917, 14 pages).

53. *The Cane Sugar Industry: Agricultural, manufacturing, and marketing costs in Hawaii, Porto Rico, Louisiana, and Cuba* (1917, 462 pages).

54. *Canned Goods: Modern processes of canning in the United States, general system of grading, and description of products available for export,* by A. W. Bitting with the coöperation of the National Canners' Association (1917, 79 pages).

55. *Markets for American Hardware in Italy, Spain, and Portugal,* prepared under the supervision of the commercial attaché at Paris (1917, 109 pages).

56. *Consumption Estimates* (1917, 12 pages), cf. no. 40, above.

57. *German Foreign-Trade Organization,* by Chauncey Depew Snow (1917, 182 pages). Merchant shipping, government assistance to foreign trade, private and semipublic trade associations, study and cultivation of foreign trade and foreign markets.

58. *International Trade and Merchandising Methods,* by Edward Ewing Pratt (1917, 19 pages).

59. *Methods of Computing Values in Foreign Trade Statistics,* by J. J. Kral (1917, 23 pages).

60. *The Glass Industry:* Report on the cost of production of glass in the United States (1917, 430 pages).

61. *Commercial Organizations of the United States* (1917, 116 pages). A list giving the address of the secretary of each organization, number of members, annual income, and date of annual meeting.

62. *Argentine Markets for Motor Vehicles,* by David Beecroft (1917, 27 pages).

63. *Trade of the United States with the World, 1916-1917* (1918). Part I, imports of merchandise into the United States by countries and principal articles (112 pages); part II, exports (317 pages).

64. *Wholesale Prices of Leading Articles in United States Market, January, 1916, to December, 1917* (1918, 14 pages).

65. *German Trade and the War: Commercial and industrial conditions in war time and the future outlook,* by Chauncey Depew Snow and J. J. Kral (1918, 236 pages).

66. *Furniture Imports of Foreign Countries: Quantities, values, and sources of furniture imported by countries whose transactions exceeded $500,-000 in value, 1913 and 1918,* by Edward Whitney (1918, 31 pages).

67. *The Export Lumber Trade of the United States,* by Edward Ewing Pratt (1918, 117 pages). Defects of present system of marketing lumber abroad; development of the export lumber trade.

68. *Wearing Apparel in Argentina,* by Lew B. Clark (1918, 158 pages).

69. *Wearing Apparel in Bolivia,* by William Montavon (1918, 84 pages).

70. *The Conduct of Business with China* (1919, 47 pages). Deals primarily with the methods by which business with China is best carried on.

71. *Wearing Apparel in Brazil,* by William C. Downs (1918, 64 pages).

72. *Consumption Estimates* (1918, 14 pages).

73. *Economic Reconstruction* (1918, 74 pages). An analysis of main tendencies in the principal belligerent countries of Europe with statistics of production, consumption, and trade in important foodstuffs and industrial raw materials.

74. *Wearing Apparel in Peru,* by William Montavon (1918, 64 pages).

76. *International Trade in Footwear other than Rubber,* by Edward Whitney (1919, 93 pages). Import statistics of boots and shoes for countries whose imports exceeded $300,000 in value and export statistics of countries whose exports exceeded $3,000,000 in value, 1908 and 1913.

77. *Statistics of Austro-Hungarian Trade, 1909 to 1913,* by J. J. Kral (1919, 64 pages).

78. *Trade of the United States with the World, 1917-1918* (1919): Part I, imports of merchandise into the United States by countries and principal articles (112 pages); part II, exports (346 pages).

79. *International Trade in Cement,* by Edward Whitney (1919, 76 pages). Statistics of exports and imports for 1908, 1913, and the latest available year.

80. *Wholesale Prices of Leading Articles in United States Markets, January, 1917, to December, 1918* (1919, 14 pages).

81. *Selling in Foreign Markets,* by Guy Edward Snider (1919, 638 pages). Selections from published statements of business men and reports of experts on methods employed in export trade.

82. *Chemicals and Allied Products Used in the United States,* compiled by E. R. Pickrell (1919, 194 pages). Imports by quantities, values, and countries of origin during the fiscal year 1913-1914 and statistics of domestic production.

86. *Brazil: A study of economic conditions since 1913,* by Arthur H. Redfield and Helen Watkins (1920, 99 pages).

88. *The Economic Position of Argentina during the War,* by L. Brewster Smith, Harry T. Collins, and Elizabeth Murphy (1920, 140 pages).

90. *The Economic Position of Switzerland during the War,* by Louis A. Rufener (1919, 88 pages).

91. *Economic Aspects of the Commerce and Industry of the Netherlands, 1912-1918,* by Blaine F. Moore (1919, 109 pages).

92. *Stowage of Ship Cargoes,* by Thomas Rothwell Taylor (1920). Stowing to secure maximum weight and volume; stowing to secure maximum speed and minimum cost.

95. *Consumption Estimates* (1919, 14 pages).

96. *The Economic Position of the United Kingdom, 1912-1918,* by William A. Paton (1919, 160 pages).

97. *Training for Foreign Trade,* by R. S. MacElwee and F. G. Nichols (1919, 195 pages).

98. *Training for the Steamship Business,* by R. S. MacElwee (1920, 49 pages).

106. *Trade of the United States with the World, 1918-1919* (1920): Part I, imports of merchandise into the United States by countries and principal articles (103 pages); part II, exports (456 pages).

No number. *Saving of Waste Paper Material* (1916, 8 pages).

No number. *Substitutes for Tin Cans* (1917, 4 pages).

TARIFF SERIES

32. *Import Duties on Textiles in South America: Part I, Argentina* (1916, 34 pages).

34. *Tariff Systems of South American Countries* (1916, 308 pages).

35. *Commercial Travellers in Latin America* (1916, 42 pages).

Records

The bureau maintains a central correspondence file in which are preserved all incoming letters, carbons of replies thereto, carbons of letters originating in the bureau, and some economic reports. The material is indexed but is regarded as confidential.

Each division maintains its own file, where, in addition to carbons of its most important outgoing letters, are preserved reports and clippings. There is a file of consular reports in the Editorial Division, and a file of reports of foreign representatives in the Foreign Service Division. In the regional divisions the reports of consuls and bureau representatives are supplemented by reports and statistics from other sources, and by clippings from foreign and domestic periodicals. Here, too, are some economic studies of foreign countries, by the Military Intelligence Division and by the War Trade Board. The foreign-tariffs file in the Division of Foreign Tariffs, is the most complete in the United States.

The mimeographed and multigraphed material of the war period consists of preliminary statistical reports showing the trade of the United States with foreign countries, commodity bulletins, special and confidential circulars, and press releases. A few titles will show the character of the more important of the reports:

Chinese Market for American Machinery. Far Eastern Division. October 5, 1918.

Indian Industries and American Trade. Far Eastern Division. November 2, 1918.

The War and Brazilian Foodstuffs. Latin American Division. October 31, 1918.

The War and Chilean Foodstuffs. Latin American Division. November 7, 1918.

BUREAU OF STANDARDS

The Bureau of Standards had its genesis in a Senate resolution of May 29, 1830, which directed the Secretary of the Treasury to have an examination made of the weights and measures in use at the principal customhouses. It was formally established in the Treasury Department by act of Congress of March 3, 1901, was transferred to the Department of Commerce and Labor July 1, 1903, and has been a bureau of the Department of Commerce since the separate establishment of the Department of Labor in 1913.

Functions

The bureau is charged with the custody of the standards of measurement, constants, quality, performance, and practice, involving their care and preservation and the varied researches necessary to maintain their constancy; the comparison of the standards used in scientific investigations, engineering, manufacturing, commerce, and educational institutions, with the standards adopted or recognized by the government; the construction, when necessary, of standards, their multiples and subdivision; the testing and calibration of standard measuring apparatus; the solution of problems arising in connection with standards; the determination of physical constants and properties of materials, when such data are of great importance to scientific or manufacturing interests, and are not to be obtained of sufficient accuracy elsewhere; and such other investigations as are authorized or directed by Congress.

Organization

For the discharge of its scientific and technical functions the bureau is organized in the following divisions:

Division of Weights and Measures, in charge of matters pertaining to standards of length, mass, time, and density, whether they arise in connection with the precision standards used in scientific investigation, the master standards of manufacturers, or the ordinary weights and measures of trade.

Electrical Division, in charge of electrical problems, whether in connection with electrical standards of measurement, electrical constants, the electrical proportion of materials, or the performance of electrical equipment.

Division of Heat and Thermometry, in charge of heat standards, the testing of heat measuring apparatus, the determination of heat constants, and investigations pertaining to quality or performance where heat measurement is the essential and predominating factor.

Optical Division, in charge of work involving spectroscopy, polarimetry, color measurement, principles of optical instruments, and the measurement of the optical properties of materials.

Chemical Division, in charge of chemical standards and questions arising in connection with chemical work generally, especially in the industries.

Division of Engineering Physics, in charge of investigations relating to mechanics, sound, and the properties of matter, the testing and development of engineering instruments, experimental development and testing of aeronautic instruments, and aerodynamical testing and research.

Structural Engineering and Miscellaneous Materials Division, in charge of the investigation, testing, and preparation of specifications for miscellaneous materials, such as the metals and their alloys, stone, cement, concrete, lime, clay products, paints, oils, paper, textiles, and rubber.

Metallurgical Division, dealing with questions pertaining to the manufacture, specifications, testing, and use of the metals and their alloys.

Division of Ceramics, concerned with problems in connection with clays and clay products, glass manufacture, refractory materials, and vitreous enameled ware.

War Work

Ordinarily the Bureau of Standards occupies a position with respect to the manufacturing interests of the country analogous to the position which the bureaus of the Department of Agriculture occupy with respect to the agricultural interests. During the period of hostilities the bureau devoted its time and energy primarily to military problems, yet never before had the industries called upon it to such an extent for advice and scientific data as they did during the war. Many questions arose out of the manufacture of equipment and material of a military nature, and requests for advice and assistance came from manufacturers, from the War Industries Board, and from various commissions having to do with the production and commercial aspects of the war. The bureau coöperated with such organizations as the Aircraft Board, Emergency Fleet Corporation, National Research Council, War Industries Board, United States Railroad Administration, American Red Cross, Construction Division of the War Department, Engineer Corps, Motor

Transport Corps, Quartermaster Corps, Signal Corps, Ordnance Department, and several bureaus of the Navy Department in selecting from the great mass of ideas submitted, those which appeared to possess actual value. The war brought about a rapid and intensive application of the results of scientific research and a study of the effect of this upon the industries of the country may well begin with a survey of the war work of the Bureau of Standards. This fell into two categories, (1) the conduct of investigations and experiments, and (2) the supply of information.

Investigations and experiments were made by the bureau alone or in coöperation with the army and navy, other branches of the government, or private concerns, relative to the following subjects: aeronautic instruments, aeronautic power plants, aircraft construction, aircraft materials, airplane dopes, balloon gases, calibration of testing machines, chemical investigations, chromatic camouflage and chromatically concealed insignia, coke ovens, concrete and cement, concrete ships, electric batteries, electric blasting apparatus, electric tractors and trucks, electrical inductance method for location of metal bodies, gages, illuminating engineering, inks and ink powders, invisible signaling, invisible writing and the means for its detection, leather, magnetism, manila rope, medical supplies, metallurgy, physical tests of metals and metal structures, natural gas, optical glass and optical instruments, ordnance, paper, photography, protective coatings, radio communication, radiometry, radium, rubber, safety standards for military industrial establishments, searchlights, sound-ranging apparatus, sound transmitted through the earth, submarine detection, telephone problems, textiles, timepieces, toluol recovery, wheels (artillery, truck, and airplane), and X-rays.

The information furnished was of three types according to whether it was intended for (1) the bureau's own staff and its coöperating organizations, for (2) other scientific and technologic workers, or for (3) general dissemination. In every line of investigation experiments were followed up by the information service, which employed the most convenient or suitable mode of communicating their results—by direct conference, by memorandum, by letter, by mimeographed material, or by printed report. Some of the results of experiments are regarded as confidential.

Publications

The publications of the bureau, issued by the Government Printing Office, consist of scientific papers, technologic papers, circulars,
and miscellaneous publications. A descriptive list of all except the
annual reports is contained in Circular No. 24 (6th ed.), entitled,
Publications of the Bureau of Standards (1922, 182 pages). Particular attention is directed to the following:

MISCELLANEOUS

46. *War Work of the Bureau of Standards* (1921, 299 pages). Describes the war-time investigations "which seem most likely to result in
permanent benefit not only to the military departments, but also to the
industries and public."

38. *Annual Report of the Director Bureau of Standards to the Secretary of Commerce for the Fiscal Year ended June 30, 1918* (1918, 206
pages). Relation of the bureau's work to the public, to the government
service, to work for military purposes in connection with weights and
measures, to optical glass, to durability of concrete in sea water, etc.

40. *Annual Report of the Director Bureau of Standards . . . June
30, 1919* (1919, 293 pages). Relation of the bureau's work to the public, to industries, to the government, and to the military services during
the war.

21. *Metric Manual for Soldiers* (1918, 16 pages).

SCIENTIFIC PAPERS

318. *The Application of Dicyanin to the Photography of Stellar Spectra,*
by Paul W. Merrill (1918, 19 pages).

319. *Instruments and Methods used in Radiometry:* III, *the photoelectric
cell and other selective radiometers,* by W. W. Coblentz (1918, 30 pages).
Deals with the application of certain physical and chemical properties of
matter as a means of quantitatively measuring radiant energy.

326. *Electrical Oscillations in Antennas and Inductance Coils,* by John M.
Miller (1918, 20 pages). An application of the theory of circuits with uniformly distributed inductance and capacity to the oscillations in antennas and
induction coils.

333. *Optical Conditions accompanying the Striae which appear as Imper-
fections in Optical Glass,* by A. A. Michelson (1919, 5 pages).

334. *New Forms of Instruments for showing the Presence and Amount of
Combustible Gas in the Air,* by E. E. Weaver and E. E. Weibel.

337. *Constitution and Metallography of Aluminum and its Light Alloys with Copper and Magnesium,* by P. D. Merica, R. G. Waltenberg, and J. R. Freeman (1919, 14 pages).

338. *Some Optical and Photoelectric Properties of Molybdenite,* by W. W. Coblentz and H. Kahler (1919, 30 pages).

341. *Airplane Antenna Constants,* by J. M. Cork (1919, 15 pages).

342. *Reflecting Power of Stellite and Lacquered Silver,* by W. W. Coblentz and H. Kahler (1919, 3 pages).

343. *Location of Flaws in Rifle-Barrel Steel by Magnetic Analysis,* by Raymond L. Sanford and William B. Kouwenhoven (1919, 12 pages).

347. *Heat Treatment of Duralumin,* by P. D. Merica, R. G. Waltenberg, and H. Scott (1919, 46 pages).

363. *Preparation and Reflective Properties of some Alloys of Aluminum with Magnesium and with Zinc,* by R. G. Waltenberg and W. W. Coblentz (1920, 6 pages).

Technologic Papers

93. *Glasses for Protecting Eyes from Injurious Radiation,* by W. W. Coblentz and W. B. Emerson (2nd ed., 1918, 25 pages).

117. *Toluol Recovery,* by R. S. McBride, C. E. Reinicker, and W. A. Dunkley (1918, 60 pages).

119. *Ultra-Violet and Visible Transmission of Eye-Protective Glasses,* by K. S. Gibson and H. J. McNicholas (1918, 60 pages).

125. *Viscosity of Gasoline,* by Winslow H. Herschel (1919, 18 pages).

132. *Mechanical Properties and Resistance to Corrosion of Rolled Light Alloys of Aluminum and Magnesium with Copper, with Nickel, and with Manganese,* by P. D. Merica, R. G. Waltenberg, and A. N. Finn (1919, 11 pages).

137. *Coking of Illinois Coal in Koppers Type Oven,* by R. S. McBride and W. A. Selvig (1919, 51 pages). A report of a test which demonstrated that some Illinois coals can be coked in Koppers type oven without radical change in operating methods for producing coke for use in blast furnaces.

139. *Some Tests of Light Aluminum Casting Alloys: the effect of heat treatment,* by P. D. Merica and C. P. Karr (1919, 31 pages).

143. *A Study of the Deterioration of Nickel Spark-Plug Electrodes in Service,* by Henry S. Rawdon and A. I. Krynitsky (1920, 16 pages).

144. *Properties of American Bond Clays and their use in Graphite Crucibles and Glass Pots,* by A. V. Bleininger (1920, 52 pages).

145. *Direct Determination of India Rubber by the Nitrosite Method,* by John B. Tuttle and Louis Yurow (1919, 16 pages).

147. *An Apparatus for Measuring the Relative Wear of Sole Leathers, and the results obtained with leather from the different parts of a hide,* by R. W. Hart and R. C. Bowker (1919, 10 pages).

150. *Physical Tests of Motor Truck Wheels,* by Charles P. Hoffman (1920, 61 pages).

151. *Load Strain-Gage Test of 150-Ton Floating Crane for Bureau of Yards and Docks, U.S. Navy Department,* by Louis J. Larson and Richard L. Templin (1920, 34 pages).

152. *Investigation of Compressive Strength of Spruce Struts of Rectangular Cross Section and Derivation of Formulas Suitable for use in Airplane Design* (1920, 43 pages).

176. *Slushing Oils,* by Percy H. Walker and Lawrence L. Steele (1920, 23 pages).

182. *Effect of Repeated Reversal of Stress on Double Reinforced Concrete Beams,* by W. A. Slater, G. A. Smith, and H. P. Mueller (1920, 51 pages).

CIRCULARS

27. *The Testing and Properties of Optical Instruments* (2nd ed., 1918, 41 pages).

68. *Public Utility Service Standards of Quality and Safety* (1917, 8 pages). Standards for electric service, standards for gas service, standard methods of gas testing, national electrical safety code, electrolysis mitigation.

69. *Paint and Varnish* (1917, 85 pages). Information compiled for those interested in the use of paint and varnish.

74. *Radio Instruments and Measurements* (1918, 330 pages). Covers the fundamental theory of radio and the more important instruments, measurements, and formulas employed in radio work performed in the laboratories of the Bureau of Standards.

75. *Safety for the Household* (1918, 127 pages). Describes the seriousness of household hazards from fire, gas, electricity, and lightning, the nature of such hazards, and the precautions necessary to safety.

76. *Aluminum and its Light Alloys* (1919, 120 pages). Describes the physical properties of aluminum and discusses the effect of temperature, manufacturing operations, and impurities upon these properties.

77. *The Table of Unit Displacement of Commodities* (1919, 67 pages). Number of pounds of material per cubic foot when packed for shipment; number of cubic feet of space required for a ton; manner of packing.

78. *Solders for Aluminum* (1919, 9 pages). Discusses the use, serviceability, method of application, and composition of solders of aluminum. The circular was issued after extensive investigation during the war for the special use of the army.

79. *Electrical Characteristics and Testing of Dry Cells* (1919, 44 pages). A brief historical review of the development of the dry cell and the theory of the reactions which take place in it.

80. *Protective Metallic Coatings for the Rustproofing of Iron and Steel* (1919, 34 pages).

81. *Bibliography of Scientific Literature relating to Helium* (1919, 21 pages). Prepared at the request of the War Department.

Several reports describing work performed by the Bureau of Standards for the National Advisory Committee for Aeronautics are published in the fourth and fifth *Annual Reports* of that Committee (Washington, 1920), and in *Gas Age* (November 15, 1917) is a report by the bureau on the "Relation of the Gas Industry to Military Needs."

Records

The bureau maintains a central filing system and has an accurate check for the location of each letter. Besides correspondence the records of the Information Section and the divisions contain special reports (in part confidential) and scientific and technologic data that were assembled in the course of investigations and experiments. The technical data on radio subjects, for example, cover the following: principles of radio waves and apparatus, scientific and commercial data, radio organizations, instructional material, standard symbols and terminology, bibliographies, applications of radio to various purposes, and various technical subjects covered in laboratory work. The records for safety standards, compiled for the War and Navy Departments, cover such subjects as the following: building construction, crane construction, elevators, fire appliances and equipment, toilets, washrooms and locker rooms, power plants and prime movers, power transmission on apparatus, machine guarding, remote-control apparatus, head and eye protection.

Among reports are:

The compressibility of hydrogen.
The effect of oxygen on balloon gas.

The influence of water vapor hydrogen upon the lifting power of the gas.

A series of separate reports relative to aeronautic power plants.

Tables of temperature corrections for altitude instruments and altitude corrections for air speed indicators computed.

Report on testing methods and apparatus to be used in testing, made for manufacturers of aeronautic instruments.

Report on fire-retarding paints, made for the Bureau of Yards and Docks, Navy Department.

A general report of the Radio Laboratory, dated December, 1918, with regard to radio work performed for the Navy Department.

Report on the Roberts coke oven, May 23, 1918.

Report on Koppers oven installation.

Report on protective coatings.

Special report on storage batteries.

Five reports relative to investigations of the generation of hydrogen by the ferrosilicon process.

Nine reports relative to lists of acetylene generators.

"Fundamental Principles of Natural Gas Production, Service, and Conservation, with Special Reference to the Natural Gas Situation at Louisville, Ky.," presented August 20, 1918. This was later published as No. 7 of the *Mineral Industries of the United States* series of the National Museum.

Specifications for glasses for soldiers and engineers to provide protection against glare from snow.

Various rubber specifications.

Report on searchlights, made to Engineer Corps, January 23, 1918; and another to the American Physical Society, April 23, 1919.

Extension of the telephone system in the District of Columbia, prepared for the Postmaster General and submitted in April, 1919.

There are several mimeographed or multigraphed circulars called "Communications" that were issued by the Gage Section during or soon after the war.

BUREAU OF CENSUS

Prior to 1900 the Census Office was established each decade to take and publish the decennial census. Under act of Congress, March 6, 1902, the office was made permanent July 1, 1902. It was transferred from the Department of the Interior to the Department of Commerce and Labor July 1, 1903, was named Bureau of the Census at that time, and became a bureau of the Department of Commerce March 4, 1913.

Functions and Organization

The chief function of the bureau is to take, compile, and publish the decennial census, which covers the subjects of population, agriculture, manufactures, mines and quarries, oil and gas wells, forestry and forest products. This work is begun at the beginning of the last fiscal year of the decade and is completed three years later. During the seven years intervening between the thirteenth and fourteenth decennial censuses the bureau was collecting cotton statistics quarterly, monthly, and semi-monthly; tobacco statistics, quarterly; financial statistics with regard to States and financial and general statistics with regard to cities having a population of 30,000 or more, annually; statistics of manufacturers and electrical industries for each five year period; and statistics with regard to wealth, public indebtedness, taxation, transportation by water, and fisheries for each ten year period. Other statistics collected by the bureau are less pertinent to this survey.

During the period of the war the bureau was organized in nine divisions, an Administrative Division and the following eight statistical divisions: Population, Vital Statistics, Manufactures, Agriculture, Cotton and Tobacco, Statistics of Cities, Geography, Revision and Results.

War Work

Under act of Congress of August 7, 1916, the bureau collected and published statistics for the years 1915 and 1916 relative to raw and prepared cotton linters, cotton waste, and hull fiber consumed in the manufacture of guncotton and explosives, and absorbent and medicated cotton.

During the period in which the United States was engaged in the war the Division of Manufactures assisted in the mobilization of economic resources for military purposes in the following ways: (1) taking a census, for the Council of National Defense, of the production and capacity of plants engaged in the manufacture of nitric acid, a census of the production and capacity of establishments manufacturing sulphuric acid and materials used in making acids and explosives, and a census of the distribution of cannon powder, mobile artillery powder, small arms powder, trinitrotoluol, picric acid, ammonium nitrate, and military guncotton; (2) making a canvass, for the Federal Reserve Board, showing the production of dental gold by States, and the amounts and values representing the gross consumption and exportation of this commodity; (3) taking a census, for various war agencies, of production, consumption, and stocks on hand of such war materials and commodities as iron and steel, wool machinery and woolen manufactures, kapok, jute, silk, leather stocks, boots, shoes, other manufactured leather goods, antimony, and graphite crucibles; (4) preparing a list of shipbuilding establishments for the United States Shipping Board; (5) preparing data, for the United States Fuel Administration, showing the kinds and quantities of coal consumed by establishments using 100 tons or more per annum, and whether such establishments generated electricity for power.

The Division of Agriculture took a census, for the War Industries Board, of commercial greenhouses, embracing such items as area, value of products, and quantities of fuel, fertilizers, insecticides, and fungicides used.

The Division of Population prepared, for the Provost Marshal General, estimates of population and of registrants and a classification of occupations. The allocation of enlistments in the army was made by the Division of Manufactures. The allocation of Naval and Marine Corps enlistments was made by the Division of Revision and Results. Information determining the ages of registrants was furnished for the Department of Justice and local registration boards by the Geographer's Division.

In February and March, 1918, the bureau prepared a number of tables for the use of the Railroad Wage Commission in connection with the adjustment of the wages of railroad employees by the United States Railroad Administration.

Publications

The publications of the Bureau of the Census are listed in a *Circular of Information concerning Census Publications, 1790-1916* (Washington, 1917, 124 pages), and a supplement entitled *Census*

Publications Available for Distribution by the Bureau of the Census (Washington, 1921). Particular attention is directed to the following:

The Story of the Census (Washington, 1916, 38 pages). A history of of the bureau.

Annual Report of the Director of the Census to the Secretary of Commerce for the Fiscal Year ended June 30, 1917 (Washington, 1917, 43 pages). Organization, functions.

Annual Report of the Director of the Census . . . June 30, 1918 (Washington, 1918, 28 pages). War work.

Census of War Commodities: Iron and Steel Products (Washington, 1919, 16 pages). Statistics collected from 10,494 establishments.

Census of War Commodities: Statistics of Leather (Washington, 1918, 11 pages). Shows amount and distribution of leather on hand May 31, 1918.

Census of War Commodities: Textile Fibers (Washington, 1919, 16 pages). Wool, silk, jute, and kapok.

Census of War Commodities: Antimony and Graphite Crucibles (Washington, 1918, 10 pages).

Cotton Production and Distribution, Season of 1916-1917, Bulletin 135 (Washington, 1918, 144 pages). Production by States; prices; ginning; consumption; exports and imports; fiber consumed in explosives and absorbent cotton.

Cotton Production and Distribution, Season of 1917-1918, Bulletin 137 (Washington, 1918, 133 pages).

Cotton Production and Distribution, Season of 1918-1919, Bulletin 140 (Washington, 1919, 133 pages).

Cotton Production and Distribution, Season of 1919-1920, Bulletin 145 (Washington, 1920, 135 pages).

Stocks of Leaf Tobacco, 1917, Bulletin 136 (Washington, 1918, 44 pages). Production, prices, consumption, exports, and imports.

Stocks of Leaf Tobacco, 1918, Bulletin 139 (Washington, 1919, 46 pages).

Stocks of Leaf Tobacco, 1919, Bulletin No. 143 (Washington, 1920, 54 pages).

Estimates of Population for the Several States and the District of Columbia, for Counties, and for Cities of over 30,000, Made by the Bureau of the Census . . . in Pursuance of and for the Purpose Mentioned in Section 2 of an Act of Congress "To Authorize The President to Increase Temporarily the Military Establishment of the United States," Approved May 1, 1917 (Washington, 1917, 24 pages).

Estimates of Population by the Census Bureau Based upon the Regis-tration of June 5, 1917, for Use in Apportionment of the Forthcoming Draft (Washington, 1917, 28 pages).

Financial Statistics of States, 1917 (Washington, 1918, 129 pages). Total and per capita receipts of States from revenues; total and per capita payments of States for expenses, interest and outlays; total value of state properties; total and per capita indebtedness of States; total and per capita assessed valuation of property subject to taxation.

Financial Statistics of States, 1918 (Washington, 1919, 123 pages).

Financial Statistics of States, 1919 (Washington, 1920, 119 pages).

Financial Statistics of Cities Having a Population of Over 30,000, 1917 (Washington, 1918, 373 pages). Scope the same as that of the state statistics.

Financial Statistics of Cities Having a Population of Over 30,000, 1918 (Washington, 1919, 357 pages).

Financial Statistics of Cities Having a Population of Over 30,000, 1919 (Washington, 1921, 355 pages).

Municipal Markets in Cities Having a Population of Over 30,000, 1918 (Washington, 1919). Emergency distribution of food, due pri-marily to the high cost of living; community markets.

Transportation by Water, 1916 (Washington, 1920, 230 pages). Steam vessels, unrigged craft, sailing vessels, schooner barges, ferry-boats, yachts, and fishing craft; character of ownership, construction, tonnage, valuation, propelling power, freight, passengers, idle vessels.

Electric Railways, 1917 (Washington, 1917, 177 pages). Track and rolling stock, power equipment, traffic, capitalization, financial opera-tions.

Special Tables of Mortality from Influenza and Pneumonia in Indi-ana, Kansas, and Philadelphia, Pa. (Washington, 1920, 181 pages). Covers the period from September 1 to December 31, 1918.

The publications of the fourteenth decennial census, covering population, agriculture, manufactures, mines and quarries, com-prise *Bulletins, State Compendiums, Final Reports,* and an *Ab-stract.* The *Bulletins* are classified as: (1) general bulletins, giving general results for the county as a whole, by States, and where ap-plicable by the larger cities; (2) state bulletins giving for each State detailed results of the census in each of its four main branches; (3) special bulletins presenting additional data and discussion re-garding certain selected topics of which only the more general sta-tistics are published in the advance bulletins. Each *State Compen-*

dium contains all the bulletins relative to one State. The *Final Reports* consist of general analyses of results relative to the country as a whole. The *Abstract* is a summary of the principal statistics in each of the four main branches of the census.

BUREAU OF FISHERIES

The Bureau of Fisheries originated in a joint resolution of Congress of February 9, 1871, which provided for the appointment of a Commissioner of Fish and Fisheries to investigate the cause of the alleged diminution of fisheries and the feasibility of remedial measures. The organization created by the commissioner was recognized by Congress in June, 1878, as the United States Fish Commission. The commission became the Bureau of Fisheries of the Department of Commerce and Labor July 1, 1903, and as such was allocated to the Department of Commerce when a separate Department of Labor was created March 4, 1913.

Functions

The functions of the Bureau of Fisheries within the scope of this survey are: (1) propagation of useful food fishes, including lobsters, oysters, and other shell fish, and their distribution to suitable waters; (2) inquiry into the cause of decrease of food fishes in lakes, rivers, and coast waters of the United States; (3) study of the waters of the coast and interior in the interest of fish culture; (4) investigation of the fishing grounds of the Atlantic, Gulf, and Pacific coasts to determine their food resources and to promote the development of the commercial fisheries; (5) study of the methods of the fisheries and of the preservation and utilization of fisheries products; (6) administration of the salmon fisheries of Alaska; (7) administration of the law for the protection of sponges off the coast of Florida; (8) advice or assistance to state commissioners in the drafting of state fisheries laws; (9) collection and compilation of statistics of fisheries.

War Activities

During the war the efforts of the bureau were concentrated more than ordinarily upon the conservation, utilization, and increase of the economic resources of the fisheries. Investigations and experiments were made to determine the causes of souring and rust of salt fish in warm climates, to develop methods of smoking fish as a means of utilizing them for food, to develop methods of canning surplus fish in the home, to determine the nutritive value of neglected or little used fishery products with a view to encouraging their consumption, to develop methods of preserving or curing fishes occurring in large quantities but not utilized economically, and to produce agar-agar and sizing material from sea weeds, the latter as a substitute for gum and similar substances, the importation of which was curtailed or entirely cut off by war conditions.

To effect the utilization of fishes normally neglected and wasted, fisherman were provided with the necessary markets or instructed in the methods of curing. The public was informed, through publications and demonstrations, of the qualities of these fishes and of the best methods of preparing them for the table. In pursuance of this work agents of the bureau were placed in the field to increase production, eliminate waste, and utilize all fish caught, to give practical and direct assistance in caring for catches, to supply direct information as to location of potential markets, to create markets in new localities, particularly those most advantageously situated in respect to transportation facilities, to direct supplies of fish to regions inadequately or uneconomically supplied, and to assist wholesale and retail dealers in selling stocks of fish ordered on the bureau's suggestion. Particularly effective was the placing of instructors in Alaska in 1917 and 1918 to demonstrate the Scotch method of curing herring, and the utilization of part of the vast catches of menhaden for the production of stock and poultry food instead of solely for fertilizer.

In the field of fish culture encouragement was given to landowners to utilize local water supplies for growing food fish for domestic use, and the rescue of fishes imperilled by the drying up of overflowed lands along the Mississippi River was increased.

Publications

Annual Reports

Report of the United States Commissioner of Fisheries for the Fiscal Year ended June 30, 1916 (Washington, 1917, 114 pages). Covers the operations of the Bureau of Fisheries. Particularly important is the report of investigations relative to commercial fisheries.

Report of the United States Commissioner of Fisheries for the Fiscal Year 1918 (Washington, 1920, 94 pages). Modification of scientific work on account of the war, experiments relative to the preservation of fishery products, utilization of fish waste and waste fish, home canning of fish.

Report of the United States Commissioner of Fisheries for the Fiscal Year 1919 (Washington, 1921, 57 pages). Increasing production and consumption of fishery products, increasing the use of waste products of fisheries, development of aquatic sources of leather.

Economic Circulars

The publication of the circulars in the list below was a part of the government program for effecting food conservation and increase during the war. They were issued by the Government Printing Office and given a wide distribution.

23. *The Sablefish, alias Black Cod, an introduction to one of the best and richest of American food fishes, with recipes for cooking it,* by H. F. Moore (1917, 6 pages).

25. *The Burbot: a fresh-water cousin to the cod,* by H. F. Moore (1917, 4 pages).

26. *The Bowfin: an old-fashioned fish with a new-found use,* by R. E. Coker (1918, 7 pages).

27. *A Practical Small Smokehouse for Fish: How to construct and operate it,* by J. B. Southall (1917, 1st ed., 7 pages; 2nd ed., 12 pages).

28. *Preserving Fish for Domestic Use,* by H. F. Moore (1917, 2 pages).

29. *Why and How to Use Salt and Smoked Fish: sixty-one ways of cooking them,* by H. F. Moore (1917, 8 pages).

30. *Possibilities of Food from Fish,* by H. F. Taylor (1917, 4 pages).

31. *The Carp: a valuable food resource; with twenty-three recipes,* by H. F. Taylor (1917, 7 pages).

32. *The Whiting: a good fish not adequately utilized,* by H. F. Moore (1917, 4 pages).

33. *The Eulachon: a rich and delicious little fish,* by H. F. Moore (1917, 4 pages).

34. *Skates and Rays: interesting fishes of great food value, with twenty-nine recipes for cooking them,* by H. F. Moore (1918, 7 pages).

35. *Sharks as food, with thirty recipes,* by Lewis Radcliffe (1918, 8 pages).

36. *Fish Roe and Buckroe, with eighty-five recipes,* by Lewis Radcliffe (1918, 11 pages).

37. *How the Angler May Preserve His Catch,* by W. C. Kendall (1918, 7 pages).

38. *Whales and Porpoises as Food, with thirty-two recipes,* by Lewis Radcliffe (1918, 10 pages).

Records

The records pertinent to this survey consist of correspondence, memoranda, and scientific and practical studies. Much of the correspondence during the war period had to do with the bureau's conservation program. Among mimeographed and multigraphed records are memoranda on the following subjects: Norwegian method of canning sardines; Scotch method of curing herring; the Norwegian cure of herring; pickling sablefish; preparation of hides of sharks for the tanner; salt atkafish; canning alewives, roe and buckroe; time required to soften the bones of various fishes by canning in pressure cookers; use of whale meat for food; and preparation of fish eggs for food.

BUREAU OF LIGHTHOUSES

Functions and Organization

The Bureau of Lighthouses, successor to the United States Lighthouse Board, was organized July 1, 1903. In time of peace the bureau is charged with the establishment and maintenance of aids to navigation along the seacoast and on practically all the important navigable rivers and lakes of the country. It is organized in three operating divisions: Marine Engineering, Naval Construction, and Hydrographic. For administrative purposes the country is divided into nineteen lighthouse districts, each of which is in charge of a Superintendent of Lighthouses. Each district has one or more lighthouse depots and supply vessels or tenders. At a general depot on Staten Island general supplies are obtained, certain special apparatus manufactured, and various kinds of technical work performed.

During the war the bureau functioned primarily as an agency of national defense. By executive order of April 11, 1917, thirty lighthouse tenders were transferred to the War Department, and fifteen lighthouse tenders, four light vessels, and twenty-one light stations were transferred to the Navy Department. The tenders transferred to the War Department and one additional tender were subsequently transferred to the Navy Department. The tenders thus transferred continued the maintenance of aids to navigation and officers of the Lighthouse Service coöperated with the naval and military authorities in matters of navigation as well as coast defense. The vessels of the Lighthouse Service laid the defensive submarine nets, removed them after the armistice was signed, laid mines, placed buoys and marks for military uses, and acted as lookouts and reporting stations. By breaking ice in rivers and harbors they assisted in keeping navigation open for coal and other war materials. Certain aids on the Great Lakes which are usually removed in the late autumn were left in position until heavy ice had formed, in order to assist the merchant fleet. Officers of the Marine Engineering Division assisted the United States Shipping Board in matters respecting the design and sea trials of various types of vessels. Aid was rendered the War Industries Board with respect to the standardization and allocation for iron and steel chains for the different activities of the government requiring such material. The Commissioner of Lighthouses served as the representative of the department on the Wage Adjustment Board in New York Harbor.

Publications

Annual Report of the Commissioner of Lighthouses to the Secretary of Commerce for the Fiscal Year ended June 30, 1917 (Washington, 1917, 101 pages). Aids to navigation, coöperation with other branches of the government in the prosecution of the war.

Annual Report of the Commissioner of Lighthouses . . . 1918 (Washington, 1918, 83 pages). Aids to navigation, war activities, statistics.

Annual Report of the Commissioner of Lighthouses . . . 1919 (Washington, 1919, 99 pages). War activities, aids to navigation, saving of life and property.

The United States Lighthouse Service, 1923, by John S. Conway, Deputy Commissioner of Lighthouses (Washington, 1923, 111 pages). National defense activities, aids to navigation, history and growth of the service, fog signals, buoys, river lighting, lighting of bridges, saving of life and property.

Records

The manuscript records of the Bureau of Lighthouses consist of correspondence, instructions, reports, and administrative and miscellaneous papers. Many of the reports sent in were confidential during the duration of the war but the ban of secrecy has now been removed.

STEAMBOAT-INSPECTION SERVICE

The Steamboat-Inspection Service originated in an act of Congress of July 7, 1838, which provided for the inspection of the hulls and boilers of steam vessels. It developed under several minor amendments and two important acts of August 30, 1852, and February 28, 1871; was transferred from the Treasury Department to the Department of Commerce and Labor July 1, 1903, and since 1913 has been a bureau of the Department of Commerce.

Functions and Organization

The service is charged with the inspection of vessels, the inspection of boilers in federal buildings, the licensing of the officers of vessels, and the administration of the laws relating to vessels and their officers for the protection of life and property. At the head of the service is the Supervising Inspector General. Under him are ten supervising inspectors. Under the supervising inspectors are forty-six boards of local inspectors, each board consisting of an inspector of hulls and an inspector of boilers. The supervising inspectors and local boards are located in the principal cities. The ten supervising inspectors with the Supervising Inspector General form the Board of Supervising Inspectors, and this body makes the regulations for the government of the service. Blue prints or drawings of water-tube and coil boilers used in vessels of the United States merchant marine are passed upon by the Board of Supervising Inspectors, while designs of marine boilers of other types are passed upon by the local inspectors having original jurisdiction. Material that is subject to tensile strain if used in the construction of marine boilers is tested by an inspector. Inspectors of hulls attend to the examinations of the hulls of vessels and of life-saving equipment, such as life preservers, lifeboats, life rafts, and davits. Each member of a crew of a merchant vessel and every lifeboatman is required to have a certificate relative to his seamanship.

War Work

During the period of the war the Steamboat-Inspection Service, in close coöperation with the War Department, the Navy Department, or the United States Shipping Board, attended to the following matters: (1) inspection of vessels on the Great Lakes to frustrate possible intrigue or conspiracy before the United States entered the war and subsequently for protection against alien enemies; (2) guarding vessels passing through the Cape Cod Canal in order to prevent any action being taken "designed to result in the stoppage of the canal"; (3) inspection of interned German and Austrian vessels, reports of which were rendered to the United States Shipping Board; (4) inspection of vessels for the United States Shipping Board, in coöperation with the American Bureau of Shipping, with Lloyd's, and with all classification societies doing business in the United States; (5) licensing of watch officers of foreign built ships admitted to American registry without regard to the citizenship of such officers, under the act of Congress, August 18, 1914, "to provide for the admission of foreign built ships to American registry for the foreign trade, and for other purposes"; (6) aid to the navigation and engineering schools for watch officers that were established by the Recruiting Service of the United States Shipping Board, by examining the experience and other qualifications of applicants, in the Great Lakes region and on the seaboard, for admission; (7) inspection of steel plate for marine boilers and lowering the requirements; (8) investigation of alleged disloyalty of licensed officers. The Supervising Inspector General was a member of the Ship Protection Executive Committee of the United States Shipping Board, and several of the supervising inspectors served on committees having to do with war problems.

Publications

Annual Report of the Supervising Inspector General, Steamboat-Inspection Service, to the Secretary of Commerce for the Fiscal Year ended June 30, 1917 (Washington, 1917, 42 pages). War conditions and war measures.

Annual Report of the Supervising Inspector General . . . 1918 (Washington, 1918, 38 pages). War activities.

Annual Report of the Supervising Inspector General . . . 1919 (Washington, 1919, 43 pages). Reconstruction.

Amendments of Steamboat-Inspection Rules and Regulations (Washington, 1917, 20 pages), and *General Rules and Regulations: Ocean and Coastwise* (Washington, 1918, 205 pages), reflect war influence.

Records

With the exception of a few papers in the offices of the Supervising Inspectors the manuscript records of the service are preserved in a general file at headquarters in Washington. Those pertinent to this survey consist of general and special correspondence, reports, instructions, card records, and mimeographed or multigraphed circulars. Particular attention is directed to the correspondence in February and March, 1917, relative to the "necessity for the exercise of all possible precautions" against intrigue or conspiracy on the Great Lakes; to papers relative to the admission of foreign built ships to American registry under act of August 18, 1914; to the card record of inspection of vessels; and to such circulars of instruction as were issued relative to emergency war measures.

BUREAU OF NAVIGATION

The Bureau of Navigation, created as such by act of Congress of July 5, 1884, was transferred from the Treasury Department to the Department of Commerce and Labor July 1, 1903, and since 1913 has been a bureau of the Department of Commerce.

Functions

The functions of the Bureau include supervision of merchant seamen, except in so far as special duties are assigned to the Steamboat-Inspection Service or the Public Health Service; decision of questions relating to the issue of registers, enrolments, and licenses of vessels, and the filing of these documents; preparation and publication of lists of vessels of the United States; decision of disputed questions relating to the movements of vessels engaged in foreign trade at or from ports of the United States; supervision of laws relating to the admeasurement, letters, and numbers of vessels; decision of questions relating to the collection and refund of tonnage taxes; enforcement of special navigation and steamboat-inspection laws and those governing radio communications.

War Work

Through its control of entry and clearance of vessels in coöperation with the Treasury Department it was within the province of the bureau so to regulate the movements of merchant vessels as to prevent or restrict violations of the neutrality laws. Its investigations of alien enemy ownership, subsequent to the entry of the United States in the war, resulted in the seizure of several vessels by the Alien Property Custodian and the British Admiralty. In the joint supervision, exercised by the bureau and the Customs Service, of the signing on and discharge of seamen, there was effected the necessary control of the personnel of officers and crews for the elimination of alien enemies. Confidential weekly and monthly statements by the bureau to the War and Navy Departments relative to merchant vessels suitable for transport, coast defense, and auxiliary military service have been continued since the armistice for commercial purposes.

Publications

The following publications are of prime importance for a study of shipping and shipbuilding during the war.

Annual Report of the Commissioner of Navigation to the Secretary of Commerce for the Fiscal Year ended June 30, 1918 (Washington, 1918, 237 pages). Changes in trade since 1914, gains and losses during the war, statistical comparison of American merchant marine of 1917 and 1918, vessels built during the fiscal years 1917 and 1918.

Annual Report of the Commissioner of Navigation . . . 1919 (Washington, 1919, 216 pages). General conditions, growth of American shipbuilding, marine losses, war losses.

Annual List of Merchant Vessels of the United States . . . for the Year ended June 30, 1915 (Washington, 1915, 482 pages). Tonnage, dimensions, date and place of building, and home port are given for each vessel.

Annual List of Merchant Vessels of the United States . . . 1918 (Washington, 1919, 532 pages).

Annual List of Merchant Vessels of the United States . . . 1919 (Washington, 1920, 542 pages).

American Documented Seagoing Merchant, Gas, and Sailing Vessels of 1000 Gross Tons and Over (Washington, 1918, 12 pages). This was confidential during the war. It was issued as of date December 1, 1917. A note attached to a volume in the Bureau of Navigation in which the above list and monthly lists of a similar and expanded character are bound, to and including July 1, 1919, is as follows: "It appeared first in March, 1917, as a typewritten statement, and was followed in December, 1917, by the first printed number in this volume. It has since been issued monthly." Of the first typewritten lists only about six copies were made. The last number marked "Confidential" was that of June 1, 1919. In 1923 it was still a monthly publication.

Steel-Ship Building in the United States on July 1, 1916 (Washington, 1916, 13 pages).

German and Austrian Vessels in the Ports of the United States, a statement prepared by the Bureau of Navigation and published as Senate Document No. 722, 64th Congress, 2nd Session.

Records

The manuscript records include general correspondence, instructions, memoranda, special reports, and mimeographed or multigraphed circulars. Among the special reports are lists of interned vessels and lists of vessels destroyed at sea. Alien officers on American merchant ships, the inspection and measurement of foreign built ships, and seamen's certificates of nationality are some of the matters relative to which mimeographed circulars of instruction were issued.

UNITED STATES COAST AND GEODETIC SURVEY

The Director, most of the staff, and five vessels of the United States Coast and Geodetic Survey were transferred to the Army and Navy during the war.

DEPARTMENT OF LABOR AND WAR LABOR ADMINISTRATION[1]

Organization and Development

THE Department of Labor was established in 1913, when the former Department of Commerce and Labor was resolved into two separate departments, to promote the welfare of the wage earners of the United States. Prior to the war, four bureaus had been established, namely, the Bureau of Labor Statistics, the Bureau of Immigration, the Bureau of Naturalization, and the Children's Bureau, while a Division of Conciliation exercised the powers of mediation in labor disputes which were vested in the secretary by the act creating the department. Within nine months after the United States had entered the war, four war emergency services were established, the United States Boys' Working Reserve, the United States Public Service Reserve, the United States Employment Service, and the President's Mediation Commission.

During the early months of the war industrial relations were handled for the government separately by the War Department, the Navy Department, the Shipping Board, the Emergency Fleet Corporation, the Fuel Administration, and other federal agencies. The resulting industrial confusion made evident the need of a more uniform method of dealing with labor problems and particularly for some central agency to supervise labor in war production. Following the consideration of the problem in informal conference between the productive departments of the government and the Council of National Defense, the President, by executive order of

[1] The material for this part of the volume was compiled by Laura A. Thompson, librarian, Department of Labor. The library of the Department of Labor contains practically all the publications listed hereunder, besides a collection of labor journals and periodicals of the war period, much mimeographed material issued by various government offices, miscellaneous periodical articles and newspaper clippings relating to labor and the war, and two extensive mimeographed bibliographies on reconstruction compiled by the librarian. A convenient list of the department's publications is *Publications of the Department of Labor, June 15, 1921* (Washington, 1921, 30 pages).

January 4, 1918, appointed the Secretary of Labor to be War Labor Administrator. The Secretary appointed an Advisory Council and under his direction and that of the council a War Labor Administration was established with the following units: War Labor Conference Board, National War Labor Board, War Labor Policies Board, Bureau of Industrial Housing and Transportation, United States Housing Corporation, Division of Negro Economics, Information and Education Service, Investigation and Inspection Service, United States Training Service, Woman in Industry Service, and Working Conditions Service.

DEPARTMENT OF LABOR—PERMANENT ESTABLISHMENT

Records and Functions

All the permanent bureaus of the Department of Labor and the Division of Conciliation engaged in war emergency work. The files for the war period form part of the regular files of the bureaus and are not open for general inspection. This is true also of the records of the Employment Service and Women's Bureau, which have been continued as peace-time organizations. The general regulation of the department regarding access to records is as follows:

No account, letter, record, file, or other document or paper in the custody of the Department, or any bureau, office, or officer thereof, shall on any occasion be taken or withdrawn by any agent, attorney or other person not officially connected with the Department; no exception will be made without the written consent of the Secretary.

Copies of accounts, letters, records, files, and other documents or papers shall not be furnished to any person except with the written consent of the Secretary. Such written consent will be granted only to such persons as may have a personal material interest in the subject matter of the papers or at their request.

The Secretary of Labor directs the collection and dissemination of statistics relating to the conditions of labor and the products of labor, collects and publishes information regarding labor interests and labor controversies in the United States and other countries, appoints commissioners of conciliation in labor disputes, is charged with the enforcement of immigration laws and naturalization laws, and supervises matters pertaining to children. During the war he was a member of the Council of National Defense and chairman of the President's Mediation Commission. With the aid of an Advisory Council and the War Labor Conference Board he formulated the national war labor program and directed the administration of that program.

Publications

The Fifth Annual Report of the Secretary of Labor for the Fiscal Year ended June 30, 1917 (Washington, 1917, 159 pages). Contains a statement relative to mediation in each of numerous labor disputes under war conditions, reviews the war work of the United States Employment Service, mentions special studies of the Bureau of Labor Statistics with reference to the war, and discusses war-time naturalizations.

Sixth Annual Report of the Secretary of Labor . . . June 30, 1918 (Washington, 1918, 231 pages). Mediation in labor disputes; War Labor Administration (Advisory Council, National War Labor Board, War Labor Policies Board, Women in Industry Service, Bureau of Industrial Housing and Transportation, Information and Education Service, Training and Dilution Service, Investigation and Inspection Service, Working Conditions Service, Division of Negro Economics); special war activities of the Bureau of Immigration; special Americanization work of the Bureau of Naturalization; woman labor for war industries.

Seventh Annual Report of the Secretary of Labor . . . June 30, 1919 (Washington, 1919, 304 pages). Mediation in labor disputes; War Labor Administration; war activities of the United States Employment Service and the Bureau of Immigration; importation of laborers for war necessities.

Eighth Annual Report of the Secretary of Labor . . . June 30, 1920 (Washington, 1920, 269 pages). Contains a historical review of the Department of Labor prior to 1920 with special reference to war-time activities.

Labor's Relation to the World War (Washington, 1918, 28 pages). Address by W. B. Wilson, Secretary of Labor, an appeal to labor as the determining factor in the war.

BUREAU OF LABOR STATISTICS

Functions

This bureau was especially concerned during the war with the gathering and classification of data bearing on war-time necessities and policies, such as wage rates and retail prices in communities affected by the expansion in industry, types of collective bargaining, industrial hazards from accident and disease and the employment of women in men's occupations.

Publications

The bureau printed its data currently in its *Monthly Review* (name changed to *Monthly Labor Review* with the July issue, 1918) and in special bulletins forming a "Labor as affected by the war series." The studies in the cost of living published by the bureau formed the basis of many of the wage awards of the various labor adjustment boards, while a series of pamphlets descriptive of different occupations was prepared for the Employment Service.

Articles in *Monthly Labor Review:*

"Protection of labor standards" (May, 1917, pp. 647-661). Includes texts of recommendations of the Council of National Defense and of its Committee on Labor issued in April, 1917, and of resolutions of the American Association for Labor Legislation.

"Maintenance of existing labor standards" (June, 1917, pp. 807-809).

"Methods of meeting the demands for labor" (September, 1917, pp. 74-84).

"Compulsory work laws and laws to prevent interference with employment" (September, 1917, pp. 113-115).

"Cost of Living in the District of Columbia" (October, 1917-April, 1918).

"Prices and cost of living" (October, 1917-December, 1921).

"Dope poisoning in the manufacture of airplane wings" (October, 1917, pp. 18-25; February, 1918, pp. 37-64).

"Plans for adjustment of disputes in shipyards and in loading and unloading ships" (October, 1917, pp. 26-29).

"Standards of labor in the manufacture of army clothing in the United States" (October, 1917, pp. 30-33).

"Labor policy of the War Department" (December, 1917, pp. 51-53).

"Wage increases in the navy yards" (December, 1917, pp. 103-109).

"Some considerations affecting the replacement of men by women workers" (January, 1918, pp. 56-64).

"Award of board of arbitration in New York harbor wage adjustment" (January, 1918, pp. 230-233).

"Risk and avoidance of T N T poisoning" (February, 1918, pp. 13-35).

"Adjustment of shipbuilding disputes on the Pacific coast" (March, 1918, pp. 67-76). Includes texts of agreements and wage scales.

"Industrial and agricultural labor and the next army draft" (April, 1918, pp. 105-108).

"Women street railway employees" (May, 1918, pp. 1-22).

"Labor award in the packing-house industries" (May, 1918, pp. 115-127).

"Recent awards of the Shipbuilding Labor Adjustment Board" (May, 1918, pp. 127-142).

"Order of Director General of Railroads fixing wages of railroad employees" (June, 1918, pp. 1-21). Includes text of order promulgated May 25, 1918 (General order No. 27); (for supplementary orders see September, 1918, pp. 131-134; October, 1918, pp. 130-139; February, 1919, pp. 163-166; and June, 1919, pp. 145-164).

"Labor turnover of seamen on the Great Lakes" (June, 1918, pp. 46-53).

"New York harbor employees" (July, 1918, pp. 1-21).

"Association of harbor boat owners and employees in the port of New York" (August, 1918, pp. 45-62).

"Training of women for war work: a bibliography" (August, 1918, pp. 164-171).

"New York harbor wage adjustment" (September, 1918, pp. 1-26).

"Labor adjustment and the payment of bonuses at coal mines" (September, 1918, pp. 186-188).

"Emergency suspensions and variations of labor laws" (September, 1918, pp. 266-270).

"Classification of war industries to facilitate distribution of labor and materials" (October, 1918, pp. 28-34).

"Adjusting wages to the cost of living" (November, 1918, pp. 1-5).

"Organization of production committees at bituminous coal mines" (November, 1918, pp. 36-38).

"Proposed legislation on reconstruction in the United States" (November, 1918, pp. 48-53). This is one of numerous articles in this and subsequent numbers of the *Review* on reconstruction in industry.

"Wage situation in anthracite and bituminous coal districts" (November, 1918, pp. 166-170).

"Problem of the crippled man in industry" (December, 1918, pp. 18-30).

"New wage adjustment in shipbuilding industry" (December, 1918, pp. 197-212).

"Relation of cost of living to the public health: a standard minimum of health budget" (January, 1919, pp. 1-10).

"Method of applying wage increases to pieceworkers interpreted by Director General of Railroads" (January, 1919, pp. 167-171; February, 1919, pp. 150-153).

"Growth of employee's representation and collective bargaining" (March, 1919, pp. 153-162).

"Work of Woman's service section, United States Railroad Administration" (March, 1919, pp. 209-212).

"Influence of the war on accident rates in machine building" (April, 1919, pp. 12-22).

"Labor provisions in the Peace treaty" (August, 1919, pp. 27-39).

"A study of rents in various cities" (September, 1919, pp. 9-30).

"Summary of increased cost of living, July, 1914, to June, 1919" (October, 1919, pp. 1-8).

"Basic rates of wages in government arsenals [1914-1919]" (October, 1919, pp. 126-130).

"National Industrial Conference, Washington, D. C." (November, 1919, pp. 40-49).

"The bituminous coal strike" (December, 1919, pp. 61-78).

"The steel strike" (December, 1919, pp. 79-94).

"The strike of the longshoremen at the port of New York" (December, 1919, pp. 95-115).

Bulletins:

No. 244. *Labor legislation of 1917* (430 pages).

No. 257. *Labor legislation of 1918* (169 pages).

No. 265. *Industrial survey in selected industries in the United States, 1919* (509 pages).

No. 269. *Wholesale prices, 1890 to 1919* (205 pages).

No. 270. *Retail prices, 1913 to December, 1919* (498 pages).

No. 277. *Labor legislation of 1919* (409 pages).

No. 283. *History of Shipbuilding Labor Adjustment Board, 1917-1919* (107 pages).

No. 287. *History of the War Labor Board* (334 pages).

BUREAU OF IMMIGRATION

Functions

The Bureau of Immigration, as its principal war functions, had the care of certain interned aliens, supervised measures for maintaining the provisions of the seamen's law, enforced passport regulations, assisted in the enforcement of the espionage, trading with the enemy, and sabotage acts, and controlled the importation of laborers for war necessities. The employment work begun by its Division of Information was taken over by the Employment Service as a separate organization in January, 1918.

Publications

Annual Report of the Commissioner General of Immigration . . . 1917 (Washington, 1917, 231 pages). Brief review of the bureau's part in the war, a statement relative to the war emergency work of the Division of Information, and statistics of immigration.

Annual Report of the Commissioner General of Immigration . . . 1918 (Washington, 1918, 322 pages). Contains an account of the Bureau's most important war activities and discusses the subject of importation of labor for war necessities. Appendix I contains statistics of immigration; Appendix III contains the text of the report of the conference of steamship interests and the various seamen's unions held in Washington in August, 1917, at the call of the Secretary of Commerce and the Secretary of Labor acting jointly.

Annual Report of the Commissioner General of Immigration . . . 1919 (Washington, 1919, 412 pages). Contains a summary of the bureau's activities for the enforcement of travel-control regulations and of activities in connection with the importation of laborers for war necessities. Appendix I contains statistics of immigration; Appendix III contains a brief report on seamen's work.

Annual Report of the Chief of the Division of Information, 1918 (Washington, 1919, 30 pages). Historical sketch of the origin and early development of the Employment Service.

BUREAU OF NATURALIZATION

The war work of the Bureau of Naturalization had to do principally with facilitating the naturalization of aliens in the military and naval services of the United States and with the Americanization of the foreign-born.

Publications

The *Annual Reports of the Commissioner of Naturalization* for 1917, 1918, and 1919 (Washington, 1917, 1918, 1919; 79 pages, 71 pages, 111 pages), contain but little material pertinent to this survey other than a statement relative to military naturalization (*Report* for 1919) and accounts of the coöperation of the bureau with the public schools in Americanization activities.

CHILDREN'S BUREAU

Functions

During the war the Children's Bureau was primarily concerned with conserving, so far as possible, peace-time standards of life and labor for children and mothers, particularly the keeping of children in school as a safeguard against child labor and illiteracy, and assuring adequate living incomes to the families of men in the military service.

Publications

Annual Report of the Chief, Children's Bureau, to the Secretary of Labor, 1917 (Washington, 1917, 50 pages). Contains a "Brief wartime program" and an account of "Studies of child welfare in the warring countries and their bearing upon war conditions in the United States."

Annual Report of the Chief, Children's Bureau . . . 1918 (Washington, 1918, 27 pages). Measures of the President and the War Labor Policies Board with regard to child labor; program for "Children's Year."

Annual Report of the Chief, Children's Bureau . . . 1919 (Washington, 1919, 32 pages). Results of "Children's Year"; "Children's Year" follow-up; effects of the child-labor clause in government contracts.

Governmental Provisions in the United States and Foreign Countries for Members of the Military Forces and their Dependents, by S. Herbert Wolfe (Bureau publication No. 28, Washington, 1917, 236 pages). This is a study that was undertaken for the purpose of securing suggestions for a system of soldiers' compensation in the United States which was regarded as "basic to the consideration of child welfare in war time."

Children's Year Leaflets:

No. 3. *Children's Year Working Program* (12 pages).

No. 7. *Back-to-School Drive* (8 pages).

No. 8. *Suggestions to Local Committees for the Back-to-School Drive* (8 pages).

No. 10. *Advising Children in Their Choice of Occupation and Supervising the Working Child* (14 pages).

No. 13. *The States and Child Labor* (46 pages).

Children's Year Follow-up Series:

No. 3. *Every Child in School: a Safeguard against Child Labor and Illiteracy* (15 pages).

No. 4. *Children's Year: a Brief Summary of Work Done and Suggestions for Follow-up Work* (20 pages).

Records

The files of the bureau contain the records of the inspections made in connection with war contracts under the ruling of the War

Labor Policies Board that all government contracts should meet the minimum requirements of the federal child labor act which the Supreme Court declared unconstitutional June 3, 1918. A report on these "Special inspections of establishments engaged in war production" is printed in Bureau publication No. 78: *Administration of the First Federal Child-Labor Law* (Washington, 1921, pp. 133-161).

DIVISION OF CONCILIATION

The act creating the Department of Labor gave the Secretary "power to act as mediator and to appoint commissioners of conciliation in labor disputes whenever in his judgement the interests of industrial peace may require it to be done." The number of disputes calling for government mediation increased enormously with the beginning of the war, and during the war the division functioned as the Labor Adjustment Service in the war labor administration of the Department of Labor. Reports of its activities appear in the *Monthly Labor Review* and in the *Annual Reports* of the Secretary of Labor. The files for the war period form part of the permanent files of the service.

DEPARTMENT OF LABOR—EMERGENCY SERVICES

UNITED STATES BOYS' WORKING RESERVE

Functions

The Boys' Working Reserve was organized in April, 1917, for the purpose of mobilizing boys over sixteen and under twenty-one years of age for war work, chiefly in food production, but also in the manufacture of war-essential material. It was organized in three units: (1) agricultural, (2) industrial, and (3) vocational, and had branches in every State. From January, 1918, to June, 1919, it functioned as a division of the United States Employment Service.

Publications

Booklet of Information (n.p., n.d., 15 pages). Organization of the service, its operations, accomplishments, and plans.

Boy Power (monthly, November, 1917, to June, 1919). The official bulletin of the organization.

Making Boy Power Count (Washington, 1919, 8 pages).

"United States Boys' Working Reserve" is a particularly informing article in the *Monthly [Labor] Review* (June, 1917, pp. 991-993). An address on the same subject by H. W. Wells, associate director of the Reserve, is printed in the *Journal* of the National Education Association, October, 1918, pp. 113-115.

UNITED STATES PUBLIC SERVICE RESERVE

Functions

This agency was organized, June 14, 1917, by the Secretary of Labor, for the registration of adult male citizens who desired to offer their services to the government either with or without compensation, to work either directly on government enterprises or in enterprises engaged in service for the government. It became, in January, 1918, the recruiting arm of the United States Employment Service in securing labor for war industries.

Publications

The *Annual Reports* of the Director General, United States Employment Service, 1918 and 1919 (Washington, 1919), contain brief reviews of the activities of the Public Service Reserve.

The *U.S. Employment Service Bulletin* (January, 1918-February, 1919), contains items relative to the Public Service Reserve.

"Functions of the United States Public Service Reserve and Its Relation to the United States Employment Service" is the subject of an address by its director, William E. Hall, printed in the *Report of Proceedings of the National Labor Conference, Washington, June 13-15, 1918* (Washington, 1918, pp. 15-19).

"Plans of the U.S. Public Service Reserve to put the right man in the right job in war work requiring skilled labor" is the subject of an article in the United States *Official Bulletin* (January 28, 1918, p. 4).

The purpose of the agency and plan of operation are set forth in the *Monthly [Labor] Review* (September, 1917, pp. 77-79).

Records

The records of the agency were to a large extent of temporary value. Such material as has been preserved forms part of the files of the United States Employment Service.

UNITED STATES EMPLOYMENT SERVICE

Functions

A public employment service originated in 1907 in the Division of Information of the Bureau of Immigration. It developed rapidly after the outbreak of the war in Europe in 1914 and on January 3, 1918, was, by departmental order, established as the United States Employment Service, a distinct unit in the office of the Secretary of Labor. It absorbed, as divisions, the Public Service Reserve and the Boys' Working Reserve, and there were besides a Farm Service Division, a Women's Division, a Division of Stevedores and Marine Workers, a Mining Division, and a Negro Division. The United States was divided into thirteen districts each having a number of employment offices. Each district was in charge of a superintendent and there was a federal director in each State. By presidential proclamation, dated June 17, 1918, the Employment Service was made the central recruiting agency for unskilled labor needed in all war industries. After the signing of the armistice the service was engaged in finding employment for discharged soldiers and civilian war workers.

Publications

Annual Report of the Director General, U.S. Employment Service . . . 1918 (Washington, 1919, 59 pages). A summary of activities of the Public Service Reserve, Boys' Working Reserve, Farm Service Section, Women's Division, Skilled Labor Section, and Unskilled Labor Section.

Annual Report of the Director General, U.S. Employment Service . . . 1919 (Washington, 1919, 174 pages). War activities (pp. 5-17); post-war activities (pp. 17-24).

Annual Report of the Director General, U.S. Employment Service . . . 1920 (Washington, 1920, 43 pages). Soldier and sailor placements (pp. 17-18); farm and harvest work (pp. 18-22); status and future of the U.S. Employment Service (pp. 40-43).

U.S. Employment Service Bulletin (weekly, January 28, 1918, to

February 28, 1919). Contains information relative to labor and labor conditions throughout the United States.

Report of Proceedings of the National War Labor Conference (Washington, 1918, 91 pages). This was a conference of district superintendents and state directors of the Employment Service, held in Washington, June 13-15, 1918, to discuss employment problems, particularly the recruiting and distribution of unskilled labor.

Directory of Placement Offices, U.S. Employment Service (Washington, 1919, 24 pages). Indicates the location of the various U.S. Employment Service offices in each State.

National Labor Recruiting Program (Washington, 1918, 4 pages). Contains text of recommendations of the War Labor Policies Board and statement by the President regarding the recruiting of civilian workers for war industries.

In *Hearings*, June 18-20, 1918, before the subcommittee of the Senate Committee on appropriations on the sundry civil appropriation bill, 1919, H.R. 12441 (Washington, 1918), is a statement by John B. Densmore relative to the work of the U.S. Employment Service, of which he was the Director General (pp. 134-155).

Articles in the *Monthly Labor Review:*

"Federal employment work of the Department of Labor" (September, 1917, pp. 80-84).

"How the United States Employment Service is mobilizing workers" (May, 1918, pp. 191-205).

"Activities of the United States Employment Service" (July, 1918, pp. 133-137).

"Federal employment service and demobilization of the army and of war workers" (January, 1919, pp. 119-125).

"Reconstruction activities of the United States Employment Service" (February, 1919, pp. 117-123).

"Review of the activities of the United States Employment Service, compiled from articles in the United States Employment Service *Bulletin*" (April, 1919, pp. 140-145).

"The U.S. Employment Service in relation to the Demobilization of Labor," article by Nathan A. Smyth, Assistant Director General of the Service, in *Proceedings of the Academy of Political Science* (February, 1919, pp. 179-187).

The library, Department of Labor, has a mimeographed copy of *Weekly Reports on Labor Conditions* issued by the U.S. Employment Service from November, 1918, to June, 1919, and also a typewritten copy of the *Manual of the United States Employment Service.*

THE PRESIDENT'S MEDIATION COMMISSION

Functions

This body was appointed by the President September 19, 1917, to act as his personal representative in investigating, composing differences, allaying misunderstandings, and ascertaining the real causes of labor's discontent in the copper districts of Arizona, the oil fields of California, and the timber districts of the Northwest. Subsequently the Commission visited Chicago where a strike in the meat-packing establishments was threatened. It made two reports.

The text of the President's memorandum to the Secretary of Labor, naming the members of the Commission and defining its duties, is printed in the *United States Official Bulletin* (September 21, 1917, p. 1).

Publications

President's Mediation Commission. Report on the Bisbee Deportations to the President of the United States, November 6, 1917 (Washington, 1917, 7 pages). Reprinted in full in the *Monthly [Labor] Review* (January, 1918, pp. 13-17).

Report of the President's Mediation Commission to the President of the United States (Washington, 1918, 21 pages). Contents: mediation of specific difficulties; disputes in Arizona copper districts; California oil fields dispute; Pacific coast telephone dispute; unrest in the lumber industry of the Pacific Northwest; packing industry dispute; causes of labor difficulties; recommendations. This report, accompanied with recommendations for removing the causes of unrest, is reprinted in full in the *Annual Report of the Secretary of Labor, 1918* (pp. 11-28). An account of later work of administrators constituted to adjust differences is contained in the *Annual Report of the Secretary of Labor, 1919* (pp. 20-24, 42-43).

"Adjustment of Labor Difficulties in Arizona Copper Region," article in *Monthly [Labor] Review* (December, 1917, pp. 53-57).

In the Matter of the Arbitration of Six Questions concerning Wages, Hours, and Conditions of Labor in certain Packing House Industries, by Agreement Submitted for Decision to a United States Administrator ([Chicago, 1918], 15 pages). Contains the wage award issued by the administrator; it is reprinted in the *Monthly [Labor] Review*, May, 1918, pp. 115-127.

WAR LABOR ADMINISTRATION

ADVISORY COUNCIL

An advisory council, composed of men and women representative of employers, wage workers, and the general public, was appointed by the Secretary of Labor in January, 1918, to assist him, as War Labor Administrator, in formulating the war labor program and in organizing an adequate administration. The general plan involved not only a reorganization and extension of the existing organizations within the Department of Labor so as to make them suitable for war-emergency purposes, but it also provided for additional services and a means by which they could be brought into proper administrative relations with bureaus in other departments. The memorandum submitted by the council and the chart of organization showing the relationships of the proposed services to existing agencies in other Departments are printed in the *Annual Report of the Secretary of Labor, 1918* (pp. 95-97).

WAR LABOR CONFERENCE BOARD

On January 28, 1918, upon the advice of the Advisory Council, the Secretary of Labor provided for the creation of a War Labor Conference Board to be composed of a group of five representative employers nominated by the National Industrial Conference Board, and a group of five officers of national labor unions nominated by the American Federation of Labor, each group to select a representative of the public to serve alternately as chairman. On March 29, 1918, the War Labor Conference Board, thus constituted, submitted a unanimous report recommending the creation of a National War Labor Board to be composed of the same number of members and to be selected by the same agencies as the War Labor Conference Board. It further set forth in this report the principles and policies that should govern the relations between workers and employers in war industries for the duration of the war. This important report is printed in the *United States Official Bulletin* (April 1, 1918, pp. 1 and 7), and in *Government Organization in War Time and After*, by W. F. Willoughby (New York, 1919, pp. 227-231).

Publications

"Labor Program of the Department of Labor" by William B. Wilson, Secretary of Labor, in *Proceedings of the Employment Managers' Conference,* Rochester, N. Y., May 9-11, 1918, published as *Bulletin* No. 247, Bureau of Labor Statistics (Washington, 1919, 160-171), briefly reviews the evolution of the war labor policy.

American Labor and the War, by Samuel Gompers (New York, 1919, 377 pages). Part I, addresses, 1914-1918: labor and the war; labor and national unity; labor's function in war time. Part II, labor's official war record written at labor conventions, 1914-1918. [Unofficial.]

Labor Problems and Labor Administration in the United States during the World War, by Gordon S. Watkins (Urbana, 1920, 247 pages). Economic reorganization and the labor problem; attitude of American labor toward the war; labor conditions in relation to production; analysis of recent industrial unrest; decentralized labor administration; coordination in labor administration. [Unofficial.]

The following articles relative to the War Labor Conference Board appeared in the *Monthly Labor Review:*

"Uniformity in Federal labor policy" (February, 1918, pp. 77-81).
"War Labor Conference Board" (April, 1918, pp. 103-105).
"Organization of the war labor administration completed" (August, 1918, pp. 63-71).

NATIONAL WAR LABOR BOARD

Functions

The National War Labor Board was appointed by the Secretary of Labor in accordance with the recommendation of the War Labor Conference Board of March 29, 1918, and was formally constituted by proclamation of the President of April 8, 1918. Its powers and duties were defined in the proclamation as follows:

The powers, functions, and duties of the National War Labor Board shall be to settle by mediation and conciliation controversies arising between employers and workers in fields of production necessary for the effective conduct of the war, or in other fields of national activity, delays and obstructions in which might, in the opinion of the National Board, affect detrimentally such production; to provide, by direct appointment or otherwise, for committees or boards to sit in various parts of the country where controversies arise and secure settlement by local mediation and conciliation; and to summon the parties to controversies for hearing and action by the

National Board in event of failure to secure settlement by mediation and conciliation.

The principles to be observed and the methods to be followed . . . in exercising such powers and functions and performing such duties shall be those specified in the . . . report of the War Labor Conference Board dated March 29, 1918 . . .

The National Board shall refuse to take cognizance of a controversy between employer and workers in any field of industrial or other activity where there is by agreement or Federal law a means of settlement which has not been invoked.

The board continued to function for some months after the armistice but was practically discontinued at the close of the fiscal year in June, 1919. On August 12, 1919, it held its final meeting and formally dissolved.

Publications

National War Labor Board (*Bulletin* No. 287, Bureau of Labor Statistics, Washington, 1922, 334 pages) is a publication of fundamental importance for a study of the work of the board. It is a history of its formation and activities accompanied by the more important documents, and contains a summary and analysis of its awards.

Report of the Secretary of the National War Labor Board to the Secretary of Labor for the twelve months ending May 31, 1919 (Washington, 1920, 149 pages). Origin of cases; execution of awards, hearings by board and examiners; administration of awards. Appendix I is a special report on public utility cases (pp. 35-48); Appendix II is an analysis of the awards (pp. 51-115).

National War Labor Board Docket. A compilation of the actions of the National War Labor Board, 1918-1919 (Washington, 1919, 5 volumes).

Title page, table of contents, and some of the docket numbers are typewritten, other docket numbers are autographed from typewritten copy, the remainder are printed.

Contents:—Vol. 1. Docket Nos. 1-150; Bulletins 1 and 2; letter from the President of the United States to manufacturers at Bridgeport, Conn., September 17, 1918; letter from the President of the United States to striking employees at Bridgeport, Conn., September 13, 1918; rulings of the National War Labor Board in the Bridgeport award; organization and by-laws for collective bargaining committees instituted by the National War Labor Board for Bridgeport, Conn. Vol. 2. Docket Nos. 151-409. Vol. 3. Docket Nos. 410-770. Vol. 4. Docket Nos. 771-1160. Vol. 5. Analysis of awards by R. P. Reeder; proclamation of the President; principles and rules of procedure; organization and practice; memorandum report of the secretary as to the work of the board for twelve months ending May 31, 1919; index to docket Nos. 1-1160.

Aims and Purposes of the National War Labor Board (Washington, 1918, 15 pages). A bulletin of the board; consists of statements by Frank P. Walsh, joint chairman, printed in the New York *World* and St. Louis *Post Dispatch*, May 19, 1918.

Proclamation of the President of the United States Creating the National War Labor Board; Its Functions and Powers; Principles Governing Industry; Methods of Presenting Complaints and Procedure (Washington, 1918, 11 pages).

Principles and Rules of Procedure (Washington, 1919, 16 pages).

Memorandum on the Eight-Hour Working Day for the members of the National War Labor Board, submitted by the Secretary, July 20, 1918 (Washington, 1918, 104 pages). Part 1, recent application of the eight-hour day; Part 2, application of the federal eight-hour law in war time; Part 3, effect of the reduction of hours upon output in various industries.

Memorandum on the Minimum Wage and Increased Cost of Living for the members of the National War Labor Board, submitted by the Secretary July 12, 1918 (Washington, 1918, 148 pages). Part 1, digest and critical analysis; Part 2, budgetary studies and statements relating thereto.

In Re National War Labor Board, by League for Industrial Rights (New York [1918], 231 pages). [Unofficial.]

Part 1, principles and functions; Part 2, digest of decisions; Part 3, extracts from brief submitted by manufacturers in Bridgeport case. Supplement No. 1: Part 1, digest of additional decisions; Part 2, summary of required standards and recommendations of the War Labor Policies Board relating to the employment of women. Supplement No. 2: Part 1, digest of additional decisions; Part 2, rulings of the National War Labor Board in the Bridgeport award; Part 3, memorandum on manufacturer's appeal from examiners' ruling in Bridgeport case; Part 4, organization and by-laws for collective bargaining committees in Bridgeport, instituted by the National War Labor Board.

The Western Union and the War Labor Board (New York, 1918, 40 pages). Prime facts and steps taken; reasons for the company's position; War Labor Board report; attitude of the Post Office Department on the same problem. [Unofficial.]

Organization and By-Laws for Collective Bargaining Committees, instituted by the National War Labor Board for Bridgeport, Conn.

(Bridgeport, n.d.; reprinted in *Monthly Labor Review*, May, 1919, pp. 192-200).

War-Time Strikes and Their Adjustment, by Alexander M. Bing (New York, 1921, 329 pages). A recital of the labor difficulties which occurred during the war and an account of the mediating agencies created to adjust them. [Unofficial.]

Articles in the *Monthly Labor Review*:

"National War Labor Board—its purposes and functions" (May, 1918, pp. 54-58).

"President sustains National War Labor Board's decision in telegraph dispute" (July, 1918, pp. 21-22). Contains text of President's letter to the telegraph companies.

"Basic eight-hour day and minimum wage involved in decisions of National War Labor Board" (August, 1918, pp. 72-75).

"Awards and decisions of the National War Labor Board" (September, 1918, pp. 27-37; October, 1918, pp. 19-28; November, 1918, pp. 29-36; January, 1919, pp. 31-37; April, 1919, pp. 246-255).

"National War Labor Board umpire's decision in Employees *vs.* Worthington Pump and Machinery Corporation" (February, 1919, pp. 259-265).

Records

The records of the National War Labor Board are in the custody of the Secretary of Labor and are readily accessible to the Conciliation Service. For the most part they are in their original filing cases. The docket group, which forms the main part of the files, is arranged by docket number, with a card index to the cases, also an index by trade and occupation. Here are filed under the docket number the original documents in each case with copies of complaints, awards, etc. There are in addition two book records: (1) the appearance docket in which was kept a chronological record of the steps relating to the status of each case from its inception, either by original complaint, or by reference from some other governmental department; (2) the permanent docket which sets forth in detail all the actions described in the appearance docket, all awards and orders of the board, hearings, resolutions of the board, and other matters necessary for a full and complete record of each day's business.

A complete file of all awards and decisions, arranged by docket and number, has been made by the Department of Labor Library and bound in five volumes (see above, under *Publications*). With them is bound all other material issued in connection with each case and an analysis of awards made by Robert P. Reeder.

The Library of Congress and the Department Library have each a mimeographed copy of a "Summary of Awards of the National War Labor Board upon Rights to Organize, Women in Industry, and Hours of Labor," by Robert P. Reeder (60 pages). The Library of Congress has a volume of sixty-one mimeographed reports —November 20, 1918, to March 4, 1919—relative to the National War Labor Board that were prepared from press clippings by the Division of Information and Files.

WAR LABOR POLICIES BOARD

Functions and Publications

As recommended by the Advisory Council, the War Labor Policies Board was organized by the Secretary of Labor, May 13, 1918, to harmonize the policies of the numerous government bodies dealing with matters affecting labor. It was made up of representatives from the Department of Labor, War Department, Navy Department, Department of Agriculture, War Industries Board, Shipping Board, Emergency Fleet Corporation, Food Administration, Fuel Administration, and Railroad Administration. Its principal function was to determine, directly for war industries and indirectly for non-war industries, questions involving the distribution of labor, wages, hours, and working conditions. Among its problems were, elimination of labor turnover, adoption of uniform standards governing working conditions, granting exemptions from the draft on industrial grounds, standardization of wages, prevention of profiteering, employment of women, and child labor. The execution of the board's decisions, in so far as they affected war industries, was left to the departments or other government agencies represented in its membership. In non-war industries its decisions were given effect through the machinery of the War Industries Board which controlled the flow of raw materials to all industries.

After the signing of the armistice the War Labor Policies Board was concerned with devising means for after-war industrial adjustment. It was responsible, too, for the preparation of fourteen pamphlets for the Peace Conference on international labor standards and the labor situation in several European countries. The board was discontinued in March, 1919.

For the functions and recommendations of the War Labor Policies Board in various matters see the *United States Official Bulletin;* May 17, 1918, p. 13 (functions) ; June 15, 1918, p. 10 (wages) ; June 25, 1918, p. 4 (wage standards) ; July 1, 1918, p. 11 (wage regulation) ; July 5, 1918, p. 24 (standardization of labor) ; July 13, 1918, p. 3 (child labor) ; July 17, 1918, pp. 10, 13 (employment of women), p. 12 (stabilization of wages) ; July 20, 1918, p. 15 (child labor) ; July 22, 1918, p. 15 (changing wages) ; July 25, 1918, pp. 12, 15 (plan for wage standardization) ; September 30, 1918, p. 15 (employment of women) ; November 13, 1918, p. 8 (labor adjustment problem).

Articles in the *Monthly Labor Review:*

"Organization and functions of the War Labor Policies Board" (July, 1918, pp. 23-27).

"Standardized contract clause for government purchases" (November, 1918, pp. 38-40).

"Conference of state labor officials, Washington, D. C., September 30 and October 1, 1918" (November, 1918, pp. 40-46). This conference was called by the War Labor Policies Board to discuss effective coöperation in carrying out the war labor program.

Wages and the War, by Hugh S. Hanna and W. Jett Lauck (Cleveland, 1918, 356 pages). A summary of wage movements from 1911 to 1918. [Unofficial.]

The War Labor Administration, by William L. Chenery (Washington, 1918, 15 pages), is a pamphlet of which about one-half relates to the work of the War Labor Policies Board. It contains the clauses adopted by the board for introduction into war contracts.

Records

The records of the War Labor Policies Board have, for the most part, been transferred to the War Department. A file of the minutes of the meetings of the board, together with the minutes of the Conference Committee of Labor Adjustment Agencies, is in the custody of the Bureau of Labor Statistics. The newspaper clippings collected by the board, a file of the Daily Digest of Labor, and some general papers prepared by the staff of the board are in the Department of Labor Library.

BUREAU OF INDUSTRIAL HOUSING AND TRANSPORTATION; UNITED STATES HOUSING CORPORATION

Organization and Functions

One of the most pressing problems of the war labor administration was that of housing the large numbers of workers that gathered in the industrial centers far in excess of housing facilities. The Bureau of Industrial Housing and Transportation, Department of Labor, was organized in February, 1918, to handle the problem. Congress, by acts of May 16, June 4, and July 8, 1918, made $100,000,000 available "for the purposes of providing housing, local transportation and other general community utilities for such industrial workers as are engaged in arsenals and navy yards and in industries connected with and essential to the national defense, and their families." The act of June 4 empowered the President to create a corporation or corporations to take charge of the work. The President, by executive order of June 18, 1918, vested full authority in the matter in the Secretary of Labor. The United States Housing Corporation, organized by the Secretary of Labor, was incorporated July 9, 1918, under the laws of New York, primarily to facilitate the acquisition of land, the purchase of materials, and the construction of houses; and with the exception of certain minor matters this corporation took over the work previously begun by the Bureau of Industrial Housing and Transportation.

The Housing Corporation was organized under a general manager in thirteen divisions: Fiscal, Legal, Surveys and Statistics, Home Registration and Information, Industrial Relations, Operating, Transportation, Town Planning, Architectural, Engineering, Construction, Requirements, and Real Estate. The functions which it performed in the pursuit of its policy were: (1) to make available to the utmost such housing facilities as were found by careful investigation to exist in or near the communities in question; (2) to link up, through improved transportation, the places where labor was needed with the places capable of housing it; (3) to stimulate, aid, and encourage private capital to undertake building operations; (4) to avoid or reduce housing congestion by aiding in the distribution of labor and in the placing of war contracts; (5) to construct and operate houses, apartments, and dormitories.

In October, 1918, a Commission on Living Conditions was appointed by the Secretary of Labor as an adjunct to the housing service. Its function was to learn where bad living conditions were a factor in retarding war production and to devise ways and means of improving such conditions. It adapted its plans to post-war conditions and was continued until June 30, 1919.

Publications

Report of the United States Housing Corporation, December 3, 1918 (Washington, 1919, 126 pages). Organization and activities; reports of divisions are contained in appendices.

Report of the United States Housing Corporation (Washington, 1919-1920, 2 volumes, 915 pages). How the housing of labor affected the production of war essentials; history and organization of the United States Housing Corporation; general policies; measures adopted to prevent needless construction; acquisition of land; management of the properties; report of Commission on Living Conditions; housing shortage; investigating the trouble; municipal utilities. Appended to this report is a "Selected Bibliography of Industrial Housing in America and Great Britain during and after the War," prepared by Theodore Kimball (19 pages).

Standards recommended for Permanent Industrial Housing Developments (Washington, 1918, 15 pages). Standards for nine types of houses which were adopted by the Bureau of Industrial Housing and Transportation in consultation with the secretary of the National Housing Association.

To Provide Housing for War Needs: Hearings before the House Committee on Labor on H.R. 9642, February 11, 1918 (Washington, 1918, 58 pages).

Housing Facilities for War Needs, Hearing before the Senate Committee on Public Buildings and Grounds on H.R. 10265, April 10 and 11, 1918 (Washington, 1918, 65 pages).

Operations of the United States Housing Corporation, Hearings before a Senate Subcommittee on Public Buildings and Grounds Pursuant to Senate Resolution 371, December 6-17, 1918 (Washington, 1918, 291 pages).

United States Housing Corporation, Hearings before a Senate Subcommittee on Public Buildings and Grounds Pursuant to Senate Resolution 210, August 7-November 17, 1919 (Washington, 1919, 680 pages). *Report* of the Committee (45 pages).

An Investigation of Housing Conditions of War Workers in Cleveland, by the Committee on Housing and Sanitation, Cleveland Chamber of Commerce, and the United States Home Registration Service (Cleveland, 1918, 46 pages).

Preliminary Report on a Survey of Industrial Housing and Transportation in the Southeastern District and Indiana Steel Towns, by the Home Registration Service Committee, Illinois State Council of Defense ([1918], 29 pages). Issued by authority of the United States Housing Corporation.

Articles in the *Monthly Labor Review:*

"Housing by the United States Department of Labor" (February, 1919, pp. 246-252).

"Adjustment of rent profiteering cases by the Department of Labor" (March, 1919, pp. 283-285).

"Lessons from housing developments of the United States Housing Corporation," by Frederick Law Olmsted (May, 1919, pp. 27-38).

Records

The reference library of the Housing Corporation, with its files of copies of instructions to field officers and others, news clippings, photographs and plans of the different housing projects, and collection of building codes, has been transferred to the Department of Labor Library.

DIVISION OF NEGRO ECONOMICS

Functions

The Division of Negro Economics was established by the Secretary of Labor May 1, 1918, to advise the department on matters relating to negro wage earners and to outline and promote plans for greater coöperation between negro wage earners, white employers and white workers in agriculture and industry, particularly during the war emergency. It organized coöperative committees of white and colored citizens in States and localities where problems of negro labor arose, conducted an educational campaign to promote good feeling among the races as well as to secure coöperation of white and colored workers in the war-labor program of the department, and appointed a staff of negro field workers to assist both in effecting better racial labor relations and in mobilizing and stabilizing negro labor for winning the war. It was discontinued as a separate division in July, 1921.

Publications

The Negro at Work during the World War and during Reconstruction (Washington, 1921, 144 pages). The principal report by the division of its organization and operation. It deals with negro migration, white and negro workers in basic industries, contains several statistical tables, ten state reports, the texts of the constitutions of three state committees, and includes a survey of women in industry made by the Women's Bureau from December, 1918, to June, 1919.

Negro Migration in 1916-1917 (Washington, 1919, 158 pages). Reports of negro migration from Mississippi, Alabama, Georgia, South Carolina, and North Carolina, and a report on the negro migrant in the North. The publication was issued by the Division of Negro Economics although the reports were compiled before the establishment of that division.

INFORMATION AND EDUCATION SERVICE

Functions

The Information and Education Service was organized as a part of the war labor administration under a provision of the sundry civil appropriations act of July 1, 1918. Its function was to disseminate information among employers and wage earners concerning the work performed by the various branches of the Department of Labor and to stimulate the morale of workers and employers. This work was performed through the press, public speakers, motion pictures, posters, and by the organization of government committees composed of employers and employees in industrial plants. During the war it operated through the following divisions: Educational, Information, Economics, Industrial Plants, and Poster. After the signing of the armistice the Division of Public Works and Construction Development was added to stimulate the construction of public works and to gather and distribute information of use to industry in changing from a war to a peace basis. The Information and Education Service was responsible for the sending of the Employers Industrial Commission to Europe in the winter of 1918 for a study of labor matters, particularly the attitude of European employers toward adjustments of labor disputes and the methods and plans of the governments for allaying labor unrest. It also brought about, under the direction of the Secretary of Labor, the conference of governors and mayors held at the White House in March, 1919. The service was discontinued June 30, 1919.

Publications and Records

Report of the Information and Education Service, by Roger W. Babson, Director General (Washington, 1919, 47 pages). Part I, the war period, from July 1, 1918, to the signing of the armistice; Part II, reconstruction period, from the signing of the armistice to June 30, 1919.

Report of the Employers' Industrial Commission of the United States Department of Labor on British Labor Problems (Washington, 1919, 37 pages) is essentially an appendix to the above, as is also the following.

Proceedings of the Conference with the President of the United States and the Secretary of Labor of the Governors of the States and Mayors of Cities, March 3, 4, and 5, 1919 (Washington, 1919, 352 pages).

Economics of the Construction Industry (Washington, 1919, 263 pages). Data compiled by the Public Works and Development Division with a view to stimulating construction by enabling investors to determine what building investments were likely to be profitable. The data are classified under the following heads: (1) Decrease in the purchasing power of money; (2) Cost and supply of construction materials; (3) Labor and wages in the construction industry; (4) Sources and supply of capital for the construction industry; (5) Rents and land values; (6) Deferred construction.

The more important of several pamphlets and leaflets issued by the service are:

Points for War-Labor Speakers (1918, 30 pages).
Human Relations in Industry (1918, 10 pages).
Employment Questions (1918, 14 pages).
The Labor Outlook for 1919 (1919, 15 pages).
Prices during the War and the Readjustment Period (1919, 10 pages).
How Much Will Prices Fall? A Symposium of Statements by Some of America's Leading Men (1919, 8 pages).
Suggestions for Own-Your-Home Campaigns (1919, 46 pages).
Build It Now (1919, 15 pages).
Is the Cost of Construction High? (1919, 8 pages).
Tentative Draft of a Bill to Promote Home Building (1919, 27 pages).

When the Information and Education Service was discontinued its files were transferred to the Bureau of Labor Statistics, but they are of slight value.

INVESTIGATION AND INSPECTION SERVICE

This service was organized, under a provision of the sundry civil appropriations, or war labor administration act of July 1, 1918, as a central inspection agency for the various branches of the department, with a view to making quick investigations of acute industrial situations and reporting the facts promptly to other divisions of the government authorized to deal with them. To some extent its functions overlapped those of the Bureau of Labor Statistics but a cooperative working agreement between the two was arranged which provided that the Investigation and Inspection Service should undertake the briefer investigations needed to secure information for immediate use. It did not make investigations on its own initiative but only on requests from the office of the Secretary, the Division of Conciliation, the Employment Service, the Division of Negro Economics, the Bureau of Immigration, the Training Service, the Women in Industry Service, and the Working Conditions Service. Extensive investigations were made also for the War Industries Board and the Ordnance Department of the Army. The service was discontinued at the close of the fiscal year 1919.

Most of its investigations were of a confidential nature and the only report of an investigation by it that has been published is one entitled *Circular of the Investigation . . . relative to the Wages Paid to Seamen on American and Foreign Vessels Trading in American Ports*, which was submitted to the Senate Committee on Commerce, 66th Congress, 1st Session (Washington, 1919, 15 pages).

The records of the Investigation and Inspection Service were transferred to the Bureau of Labor Statistics, but they are of little value.

UNITED STATES TRAINING SERVICE

Functions

The United States Training Service, originally named the Training and Dilution Service, was provided for by the war labor administration act of July 1, 1918, and was organized July 16, 1918, to secure information respecting the best methods used in various plants for training persons to do skilled work, to ascertain what industries and particular plants were in need of larger numbers of trained workers, to determine the special types of employment in which training appeared to be most needed to meet the war emergency, to bring about the adoption by employers of the most practical and useful methods of training, and to make surveys of the war industries in order to determine occupations within such industries where the available supply of skilled workers was so limited as to necessitate the introduction of less skilled workers.

The service operated in three divisions: (1) Planning, (2) Administrative, and (3) Training. The Training Division supervised a field service by districts, twelve in number, coterminous in each instance with those into which the country was divided by the Ordnance Division of the War Department; and the district superintendents were instrumental in promoting the organization of training departments in numerous industrial establishments. A Dilution Division to effect the promotion of skilled workers and the employment of less skilled workers in their places was about to begin operations when the signing of the armistice made its services unnecessary. The other divisions of the service were discontinued June 30, 1919.

Publications

The Training Service issued twenty-six numbered *Bulletins* (Washington, 1919) as follows:

1. *How to Start a Training Department in a Factory* (24 pages).
2. *A Successful Apprentice Toolmaker's School* (8 pages).
3. *British Methods of Training Workers in War Industries* (68 pages).
4. *Training Employers for Better Production* (29 pages).
5. *Training Labor for Peace Time* (12 pages).
6. *Labor Turnover and Industrial Training* (7 pages).
7. *Industrial Training and Foreign Trade* (12 pages).
8. *Some Advantages of Industrial Training* (12 pages).
9. *Seven Million Candidates for Training* (15 pages).
10. *A Business Man's Experience with Industrial Training* (12 pages).
11. *Efficient Training in a Large Plant* (13 pages).
12. *How Training Departments Have Bettered Production* (24 pages).
13. *Industrial Training in Representative Industries* (15 pages).

14. *Training in Industrial Plants* (30 pages).
15. *Training in the Paper-Box Industry* (75 pages).
16. *Training in the Men's Suit and Overcoat Industry* (83 pages).
17. *Training Workers in the Women's Cloak, Suit and Skirt Industry* (83 pages).
18. *Industrial Training in the Overalls Industry* (57 pages).
19. *Training for Shirt Makers* (59 pages).
20. *Training in the Rubber Industry* (75 pages).
21. *Training in the Shoe Industry* (61 pages).
22. *Courses of Instruction in Piano Making* (65 pages).
23. *Outline Courses for Instruction in Lithography and Photolithography* (23 pages).
24. *Industrial Training for Foundry Workers* (68 pages).
25. *Courses of Instruction for Workers in Cotton Mills* (64 pages).
26. *The Foreman* (79 pages).

WOMAN IN INDUSTRY SERVICE

Functions

The Woman in Industry Service was organized July 9, 1918, to secure information on all matters relating to women in industry and to put such information into useful form, to develop in the industries of the country such policies and methods as would result in the most effective use of women's services in production for the war and at the same time prevent their employment under injurious conditions, to coördinate work for women in other divisions of the Department of Labor and in industrial service sections of other departments of the federal government, and to coöperate with state departments of labor for bringing about united action by the States in national problems relative to women's work. The service organized a Council of Women in Industry which was composed of women representing every division of the Department of Labor and other federal departments having organized work related to problems of women in industry, and this body, meeting weekly, discussed such subjects as safeguards to be established in new occupations, the enforcement of state labor laws, the regulation of night work under war conditions, the recruiting and training of women workers, etc. A Committee on Hazardous Occupations was appointed by the service to direct work for determining the occupations in which women might be employed safely as well as practical measures for eliminating danger. The Woman in Industry Service was made a permanent bureau, the Women's Bureau, by act of Congress approved June 5, 1920.

Publications and Records

First Annual Report of the Director of the Woman in Industry Service for the fiscal year ended June 30, 1919 (Washington, 1919, 29 pages). Material relative to the Council of Women in Industry; recruiting women for new occupations; standards governing the employment of women in industries; hazardous occupations; the problem of night work; state labor laws during the war; wages and industrial relations; wages after the war; the federal government as an employer of women; displacement of women workers.

Second Annual Report of the Director of the Women's Bureau . . . June 30, 1920 (Washington, 1920, 12 pages). Woman's part in American industries during the war; effect on the employment of women of laws regulating their hours of work; general industrial conditions for women in the United States.

Several *Bulletins* have been issued each year. Nos. 1 to 20 (Washington, 1918-1922) are as follows:

1. *Proposed Employment of Women during the War in the Industries of Niagara Falls, N. Y.* (1918, 16 pages).
2. *Labor Laws for Women in Industry in Indiana* (1918, 29 pages).
3. *Standards for the Employment of Women in Industry* (1919, 7 pages). Printed also as an appendix to the first *Annual Report* of the director.
4. *Wages of Candy Makers in Philadelphia in 1919* (1919, 45 pages).
5. *The Eight-Hour Day in Federal and State Legislation* (1919, 19 pages).
6. *Employment of Women in Hazardous Industries in the United States* (1919, 8 pages).
7. *Night-Work Laws in the United States* (1919, 5 pages).
8. *Women in Government Service* (1920, 37 pages).
9. *Home Work in Bridgeport, Connecticut* (1920, 35 pages).
10. *Hours and Conditions of Work for Women in Industry in Virginia* (1920, 32 pages).
11. *Women Street Car Conductors and Ticket Agents* (1921, 90 pages).
12. *The New Position of Women in American Industry* (1920, 158 pages). Section I. The New Position of Women in American Industry. Section II. Statistics of Women's Industrial Employment during and after the war. Section III. Results of Substitution of Women on Men's Work during and after the War.
13. *Industrial Opportunities and Training for Women and Girls* (1920, 48 pages).

14. *A Physiological Basis for the Shorter Working Day for Women* (1921, 20 pages).

15. *Some Effects of Legislation Limiting Hours of Work for Women* (1921, 26 pages).

16. *State Laws Affecting Working Women* (1921, 51 pages).

17. *Women's Wages in Kansas* (1921, 104 pages).

18. *Health Problems of Women in Industry* (1921, 11 pages).

19. *Iowa Women in Industry* (1922, 73 pages).

20. *Negro Women in Industry* (1922, 65 pages).

In the unpublished records of the Woman in Industry Service are minutes of the meetings of the Council of Women in Industry and of the Committee on Hazardous Occupations besides correspondence with labor officials in the States.

WORKING CONDITIONS SERVICE

Functions

The Working Conditions Service, established in July, 1919, was directed by the Secretary of Labor to examine into working conditions in war industries to determine standards of conditions which should be maintained in those industries, to adopt rules embodying such standards and explaining them, to determine the best means of securing the adoption and maintenance of the standards, and to cooperate with state authorities in these matters. It was organized in three divisions: (1) Industrial Hygiene and Medicine (the personnel of which was detailed from the United States Public Health Service), to improve the health and efficiency of industrial workers; (2) Labor Administration, to open a channel through which the best employment policies and practices of the country might pass into more general usage; (3) Safety Engineering, to reduce injury in industry. The service was discontinued June 30, 1919.

Publications

Report of the Working Conditions Service for the fiscal year ended June 30, 1919 (Washington, 1919, 35 pages). Describes the scope, functions, and activities of the service.

Treatment of Industrial Problems by Constructive Methods (Washington, 1919, 15 pages). Discusses the work of each division of the Working Conditions Service.

Employment Management, Employment Representation, and Industrial Democracy (Washington, 1919, 15 pages). Discusses welfare or shop committees, employers' unions, danger of misconceptions of employees' representation, the labor problem, personal relations, economic relations, technical problems.

Seven mimeographed *circulars* of the Division of Labor Administration treat of centralized employment departments, industrial medical service, absenteeism, absentee record forms, plant organs, labor relations, and Americanization.

INTERSTATE COMMERCE COMMISSION

Organization and Functions

THE Interstate Commerce Commission was created by section 12 of the act of February 4, 1887, to regulate commerce. Originally there were five members and the duties of the commission were chiefly to inform itself with regard to the management of the railroads, and to investigate complaints and report its findings. Prior to the war, the membership was increased to seven and the commission was charged with the enforcement of acts to promote the safety of travellers and employees, with the determination and enforcement of rates, and with making a physical valuation of railroad property.

Early in the war period the car-shortage situation became so acute as to demand an investigation by the commission, and the outcome of this was the act of May 29, 1917, which vested in the commission broad powers for the regulation of car service. In August of the same year, its membership was increased to nine. On December 5, 1917, the commission transmitted to Congress a special report with reference to transportation conditions as affecting and affected by the war (*Thirty-Second Annual Report*, pp. 4-9) in which stress was laid on the need of unification of the operation of railways during the period of the war. Three weeks later the President issued a proclamation establishing federal control over the railroads, to take effect December 28, 1917.

During the period of federal control the commission coöperated with the Railroad Administration. It was authorized by the federal control act of March 21, 1918, to hear complaints with regard to the reasonableness of rates and was directed to ascertain the average annual operating income for a three-year period, from July 1, 1914, to July 1, 1917, called the "test period," in order to establish a basis for the compensation to be paid the carriers for the use of their property by the government. Members of the commission conducted investigations at the request of the Director General of Railroads, and served on the committee which drafted the standard compensation contract provided for in the federal control act, while the services of the bureaus of statistics, tariffs, carriers' accounts, valuation, and car service were also utilized by the Railroad Administration.

Shortly after the armistice the prevailing opinion of the members of the commission, expressed in a statement to the Senate Committee on Interstate Commerce, was that the railroads should be returned to private ownership with a "broadened, extended, and amplified governmental regulation." Following this recommendation Congress passed the transportation act of February 8, 1920, under which private operation was resumed March 1, and by which the powers and duties of the commission, its membership increased to eleven, were greatly enlarged. The provisions of that act which are relevant to this survey made it the duty of the commission to certify as to the reimbursement of carriers for the use of carrier property by the government during federal control, as to deficits incurred by roads not under federal control, and as to the guarantee of a certain minimum income for six months succeeding the termination of federal control.

The commission is organized to function as a whole, in five divisions of three or more commissioners each, and through twelve bureaus. Division 1 directs the work of the Bureau of Valuation; Division 2 disposes of applications for the suspension of rates and fares; Division 3 disposes of cases not orally argued which are not allotted to a commissioner or reserved by the commission; Division 4 has charge of applications for security issues, and certifies as to the reimbursement of carriers for the use of their property during federal control, for the income guaranteed for the first six months after federal control, and for defraying deficits of carriers not under federal control; Division 5 directs the work of the Bureau of Car Service. Besides the Bureaus of Valuation and Car Service there are the bureaus of Finance, Accounts, Statistics, Informal cases, Traffic, Law, Inquiry, Service, Safety, and Locomotive inspection. The Bureau of Finance is charged primarily with the administration of those provisions of the transportation act which relate to applications made to issue railroad securities; the construction of a new railroad or the extension of an old one; the acquisition of control by one railroad over another; the collection of one-half the annual net income of a railroad in excess of six per cent of its value, and the making of loans to railroads. The Bureau of Accounts has been charged with the determination of the operating income of railroads for the three years ended June 30, 1917, and other items necessary to an adjustment of financial matters arising from federal control. The Bureau of Statistics receives and examines statistical reports from railway corporations, prepares monthly statements relative to operating revenues and operating expenses, and compiles wage statistics needed for the adjustment of wages, also accident statistics.

Publications

Thirty-First Annual Report of the Interstate Commerce Commission, December 1, 1916 (Washington, 1917, 298 pages). The annual reports of the commission contain a survey of its activities, statistical summaries, and a list of points decided in reported cases. The report for 1917 discusses transportation conditions arising from the war and tells of measures taken to relieve the acute situation with regard to car shortage.

Thirty-Second Annual Report of the Interstate Commerce Commission, December 1, 1918 (Washington, 1918, 188 pages). Tells of the transition to federal control and of the modifications of the commission's functions under federal control.

Thirty-Third Annual Report of the Interstate Commerce Commission, December 1, 1919 (Washington, 1919, 266 pages). Informing with regard to the return of the railroads to their owners.

Thirty-Fourth Annual Report of the Interstate Commerce Commission, December 1, 1920 (Washington, 1920, 291 pages). Informing with regard to the adjustment of matters arising from federal control and the enlarged functions of the commission. With regard to the reimbursement of deficits during federal control see the thirty-fifth and thirty-sixth annual reports.

Interstate Commerce Commission Reports, 1915-1922, Vols. 36-66 (Washington, 1916-1922). These volumes contain the reports of cases coming before the Interstate Commerce Commission, with the decisions of the commission. Each volume has a table of the cases reported therein, and a general table of the cases in Vols. 36-64 (July, 1915-December, 1921) has been printed as *Second Supplement* (Washington, 1922, 297 pages) of *Table of Cases and Opinions of the Interstate Commerce Commission.*

A few of the cases and decisions of the commission having an important bearing upon the general subject of this survey are noted below as illustrative of this class of material.

Car supply investigation. Submitted December 28, 1916. Decided January 18, 1917 (Vol. 42, pp. 657-706).

The fifteen per cent case. Proposed increase in freight rates in eastern, western, and southern territories. Submitted June 12, 1917. Decided June 27, 1917 (Vol. 45, pp. 303-355). Discussion of effects of the war on railway transportation.

Consolidated classification case. Submitted January 19, 1919. Decided July 3, 1919 (Vol. 54, 655 pages). Argument and report in favor of greater uniformity in freight classification.

Perishable freight investigation. Part I, protective service in transportation; Part II, cost of service and proposed charges. Submitted November 7, 1919. Decided February 4, 1920 (Vol. 56, pp. 449-671).

Ex parte 74. In the matter of the applications of carriers in official, southern, and western classification territories for authority to increase rates. Submitted July 6, 1920. Decided July 29, 1920 (Vol. 58, pp. 220-260).

Increased cost of railroad fuel, a report prepared in response to Senate Res. No. 412, December 27, 1920 (Vol. 61, pp. 761-781). Costs in 1919 compared with costs in 1920.

A tentative plan of the Commission for the consolidation of the railway properties of the United States into a limited number of systems, to which is appended a report to the Commission on the same subject by William Z. Ripley. August 23, 1921 (Vol. 63, pp. 456-600).

Thirty-First Annual Report on Statistics of Railways in the United States for the Year ended December 31, 1917, prepared by the Bureau of Statistics (Washington, 1919, 533 pages). This report and those for the years 1918 and 1919 are valuable for their tables relative to mileage, employees, equipment, valuation, traffic and operation, income, profits and losses, and receiverships.

Thirty-Second Annual Report on Statistics of Railways in the United States . . . December 31, 1918 (Washington, 1920, 807 pages).

Thirty-Third Annual Report on Statistics of Railways in the United States . . . December 31, 1919 (Washington, 1922, 819 pages).

FEDERAL TRADE COMMISSION

Functions

THE Federal Trade Commission was created by the act of September 26, 1914, replacing the former Bureau of Corporations of the Department of Commerce. Its normal functions are: (1) to prevent unfair methods of competition in commerce; (2) to investigate, and to compile information concerning the organization, business, conduct, practice, and management of corporations engaged in commerce; (3) upon direction of the President or by either house of Congress, to investigate alleged violations of the anti-trust acts by any corporation; (4) to investigate trade conditions in and with foreign countries which may affect the foreign trade of the United States; (5) under the export trade act of April 10, 1918, to receive statements and reports which associations engaged solely in export trade are required to file, and to investigate any acts of such associations in restraint of trade within the United States or in restraint of the export trade of any particular competitor.

Under the trading with the enemy act of October 6, 1917, and under executive orders issued in accordance therewith, the commission was charged with (1) the granting of licenses to apply for letters patent or the registration of copyright or trademark in an enemy country or in the country of an enemy ally, and (2) the licensing of the manufacture in the United States of articles controlled by enemy patents or trademarks. For the performance of these functions the commission was organized in five divisions: Administrative, Economic, Legal, Export trade, and Enemy trade.

Records and Publications

The records of the commission are regarded as confidential; the Federal Trade Commission act prohibits under penalty the making public of any information obtained by the commission, except by its authority or upon order of a court.

The administrative records are preserved in the Mail and Files Section of the Administrative Division. The Docket Section of the same division has custody of the records of complaints. These records are similar to those in the office of a clerk of court; they consist of applications for the issuance of complaints, correspondence, exhibits, and field or office reports relating to such applications, and the record of all formal proceedings. Each *Annual Report* of the commission contains an abstract of all proceedings disposed of during the year or pending at its close. The commission publishes its decisions: *Decisions, Findings, Orders,* and *Conference Rulings,* volume I, March 16, 1915-June 30, 1919 (1920, 631 pages), edited by Adrien F. Busick and Millard F. Hudson

The records of the administration of the export trade act of April 10, 1917, consist chiefly of the statements and reports which the export associations are required to file. The forms in which these are required to be made are printed among the exhibits in the *Annual Reports* of the commission for 1918, 1919, 1920, etc., which also contain, under the heading "Export Trade Division," accounts of the operation of the law and lists of the export associations which have filed statements. The commission has published, as "Foreign Trade Series No. 1," a pamphlet entitled *Discussion of and Practice and Procedure under the Export Trade Act* (Webb-Pomerene Law), 1919.

The records relating to enemy trade (*cf. Annual Reports,* 1918, 1919, 1920, under "Enemy Trade Division") consist of the following: (1) Records of licenses issued "to citizens of the United States and to corporations organized within the United States to make, use, and vend articles controlled by enemies or allies of enemies through patents, trademark, and copyright registration." The commission received 277 applications for such licenses and issued 71 licenses, which covered all but 62 of the applications. The licensees were required to file semi-annual statements with the commission "of the extent of the use and enjoyment of the license, and of the prices received from the sale or use of the subject matter of it." The most important of the licenses dealt with drugs, dyestuffs, certain kinds of machinery and apparatus, tooth paste, and operatic productions. (2) Records of licenses "to file and prosecute in the country of an enemy or ally of an enemy applications for patents or for registration of trademarks, prints, labels, or copyrights, or to pay any taxes, annuities, or fees in relation thereto." The authority to grant such licenses, vested in the commission by executive order of October 12, 1917, was revoked by order of April 11, 1918. During the interim about 1250 applications had been made and licenses issued. The pending applications, about 900 in number, were returned to the applicants. The authority to issue licenses was restored to the commission by executive order of November 25, 1919, and a blanket license was then issued. (3) Records of orders of secrecy regarding inventions issued under authority vested in the commission by the executive order of October 12, 1917. The purpose of orders of secrecy was to prevent the divulgation of any information respecting inventions which might be "detrimental to the public safety or defense, or might assist the enemy, or endanger the successful prosecution of the war." About 1300 orders of secrecy were issued relating to over 1000 inventions; they were lifted after the signing of the armistice. (4) Records of enemy control of corporations. Under authority of the Federal Trade Commission act, questionnaires were sent to about 600 corporations calling for such information (names of stockholders, etc.) as would reveal the real ownership or control of the corporation required to report. Questionnaires were also sent to all stockholders whose names were returned by these corporations. Any information secured in this way which revealed enemy interest was reported to the Alien Property Custodian, the War Trade Board, and other interested branches of the government.

The records of the Economic Division are most important from the point of view of this survey. The work of this division is described at some length in the *Annual Reports* for 1918, 1919, and 1920. The chief war-time function of the Economic Division and of the commission as a whole was the determination of costs of production and manufacture of the most important commodities. In the performance of this function the division served as a technical agent of those branches of the government which fixed prices. The division secured its cost data from special or periodical reports which it required from manufacturers and producers, and also from examinations of their books. Confidential reports, several hundred in number, were made by the division to other governmental agencies, chiefly to the special war organizations. They show, in many instances for different periods, both average costs and ranges of cost together with the aggregate quantities and percentages of a commodity which had been produced by various companies at or below various specific costs per unit. Lists of some 250 of the more important of these confidential reports are to be found in the *Annual Reports* for 1918 (pp. 29-30) and 1919 (pp. 38-42). The principal subjects of the war-time investigations of the division were coal, petroleum, mineral building materials, lumber and lumber products, paper, chemicals, raw cotton, wool and rags, boots and shoes, tobacco products, canned and dried foods, meat, grain trade, flour, farm operating equipment, and milk. The following list of confidential reports, selected from the lists printed in the *Annual Reports*, serves to illustrate this category of the records of the Economic Division.

Reports to the President

Cost of producing gasolene and fuel oil for June, 1917, September 7, 1917.
Report on cost of steel (second report), December 17, 1917.

Reports to the Department of War

Cost of duck on army order, December 19, 1918.
Cost of producing bleaching powder (two companies), January 9, 1919.
Cost of riprap stone (seven companies), January 25, 1919.
Cost of locomotive cranes (five companies), April 2, 1919.

Reports to the Department of the Navy

Costs of Boston lumber dealers, March 8, 1918.
Cost of producing "Grade A" zinc during 1917 and January-March, 1918, May 15, 1918.
Cost of steel wire rope, June 25, 1918.
Cost of producing sulphur, July 2, 1918.
Rail costs from ore to finished rails, July 20, 1918.
Cost of producing forged billets of company supplying Navy, August 9, 1918.
Cost of producing cast-iron pipe, November 29, 1918.
Cost of producing nickel and monel steel, year ending March 31, 1917, and July, 1917, November 30, 1918.
Cost of gasolene and fuel oil, first six months of 1918, and refinery investment and estimates covering the fiscal year ended June 30, 1918, December 26, 1918.

Reports to the War Industries Board

Preliminary report on steel costs, September 8, 1917.
Cost of producing sheet steel, November 17, 1917.
Cost of producing sole leather, July 12, 1918.

Cost of producing copper during months of May, 1918, and January-May, 1918, August 6, 1918.

Cost of producing hemlock lumber in Pennsylvania, April-July, 1918, August 12, 1918.

Cost of producing "Grade A" zinc, sheet and plate, April and May, 1918, August 17, 1918.

Cost of producing aluminum products first six months of 1918 and July, 1918, August 19, 1918.

Cost of six producers of chestnut wood extract, August, 1918.

Cost of coke, pig iron, and steel, November, 1917, and April-June, 1918, September 13, 1918.

Cost of production of steel (preliminary), September 17, 1918.

Cost of producing yellow pine lumber and timber—southern pine group—States of Alabama, Arkansas, Louisiana, Mississippi, and Texas, May, June, and July, 1918, September 17, 1918.

Cost of producing sulphuric acid, first six months and June and July, 1918, September, 1918.

Cost of producing yellow-pine lumber and timbers, Virginia-Florida group, July, 1918, September 20, 1918.

Cost of producing fir, spruce, and hemlock lumber in the States of Washington and Oregon, May, June, and July, 1918, October 8, 1918.

Tanning costs of upper leather, October 8, 1918.

Cost of producing Portland cement for seven months, 1917, and April-June, 1918, October 16, 1918.

Cost of producing gypsum wall board (one company), October 21, 1918.

Cost of cigarettes and tobacco (four companies), November 18, 1918.

Profits from tanning leather, November 9, 1918.

Profits of shoe manufacturers, November 20, 1918.

Wool dealers' profits, November 24, 1918.

Cost per pound of producing copper, August, 1918, also comparison with cost for the year 1917 and months March, April, May, June, and July, 1918, November 29, 1918.

Reports to the Fuel Administration

Actual yields from refining companies using large percentage of Gulf coast crude oil, March 19, 1918.

Cost of production of aviation gasolene, May 10, 1918.

Anthracite coal, cost of production tonnage of 99 companies, May 1917-1918, August 6, 1918.

Report showing in detail the costs of each coal operator in the central Pennsylvania field, by months, January-May, 1918, November 4, 1918.

Reports to the Food Administration

Cost of crushing cotton seed, July 16, 1918.

Cost of ginning cotton, July 16, 1918.

Table showing number of animals slaughtered by local wholesale slaughterers in 1916 and first six months of 1917, August 17, 1918.

Cost of canned salmon, October 29, 1918.

Report to the Department of Agriculture

Cotton textiles, December 14, 1918.

Reports to the Railroad Administration

Cost of producing locomotives on government order of company supplying Railroad Administration, August 20, 1918.

Cost of pig iron in June, 1918, in certain States, September 13, 1918.

Intercompany profits on rails, October 17, 1918.

Cost of production of special illuminating gas, December 24, 1918.

Reports to the Tariff Commission

Manganese ore in Phillipsburg, Montana, district, six months ending December 31, 1917, six months ending June 30, 1918, and three months ending September, 1918, December 24, 1918.

Manufacturing costs of open-hearth and bessemer standard steel rails, October, 1917-September, 1918, February 3, 1919.

Published cost reports. Just before the entry of the United States into the war the commission was directed by the President to make a comprehensive investigation of the food industries of the country, and as a means of preventing speculative excesses accompanying the rising prices following the close of the war similar investigations of other basic industries were undertaken. The results of these investigations have been published in a number of reports. The following is a list of such of them as seem pertinent to the present survey.

High cost of living, conference with delegates appointed by governors of States in re food and fuel supply and price, Washington, D. C., April 30 and May 1, 1917 (1917, 119 pages). Statements of the delegates regarding the work done in their various states for promoting the production and distribution of food. Organizations and surveys described in connection therewith.

Food investigation, report of Federal Trade Commission on canned foods, general report, and canned vegetables and fruits, May 15, 1918 (1918, 103 pages, 31 tables). Based on a study of books of important companies, canners, brokers, and wholesale grocers. Discusses conditions surrounding the industry, costs, profits, prices; activities of canners' associations; possible economies in manufacture and distribution. Covers years of 1916-1917.

Report of the Federal Trade Commission on canned foods, 1918; corn, peas, string beans, tomatoes, and salmon. November 21, 1921 (1922, 86 pages). Costs of canned foods during the war.

Food investigation, report . . . on canned foods; canned salmon (1919, 83 pages, 33 tables). Based on schedules sent all canners and on examination of the books of the most important. Report describes consumption, cost of production, and profits in salmon-canning, with recommendations for the protection of the industry from depletion and monopolization by rulings of the Food Administration.

Food investigation, report . . . on flour milling and jobbing (1918, 27 pages). Covers years 1912-1917, costs and profits of millers and distributors of wheat flour; marketing conditions and practices of millers and distributors of wheat flour (does not cover conditions and practices in the retail flour trade).

Food investigation, report . . . on meat-packing industry: Summary and Part 1 (1919, 574 pages); Part 2: Evidence of combination among packers (1918, 290 pages); Part 3: Methods of the five packers in controlling meat-packing industry, June 28, 1919 (1919, 325 pages); Part 4: The five large packers in produce and grocery foods (1920, 390 pages); Part 5: Profits of packers (1920, 110 pages); Part 6: Cost of growing beef animals; Cost of fattening cattle; Cost of marketing live stock (1920, 183 pages); Prepared by Farm Management Office, Animal Industry Bureau, and Markets Bureau.

Maximum profit limitation on meat-packing industry, 1919 (see Senate Doc. 110, 66th Cong., 1st Sess., 179 pages). Special investigation of the reasonableness of the maximum profit limitations fixed by the Food Administration; hearings before the Federal Trade Commission at Chicago relative to meat packers' profits, June, 1918; letters purporting to show disagreement between Herbert Hoover and chairman W. B. Colver as to the recommendations to be made; reports of expert accountants.

Food investigation, report . . . on private car lines: Part 1, General survey of private car lines; Part 2, Packer car lines and their relations to the public; Part 3, Nonpacker car lines (1920, 271 pages, 105 tables). Covers particularly the refrigerator transportation of meats and other perishable foods. Recommendations made to correct present irregularities of service and rates and to avoid monopolistic use of certain types of cars.

Food investigation, report . . . on wholesale marketing of food (1920, 268 pages). (1) Urgency of food problem and its proposed solution. (2) Present organization of the wholesale marketing system. (3) Conditions in the wholesale marketing of produce which make for losses. (4) Methods of handling wholesale food problem.

Report . . . on commercial wheat flour milling (1920, 118 pages, 35 tables). General survey of flour milling in the United States, and a discussion of changes in prices, costs, and profits, 1913-1918, based on data collected from the records of a small number of large milling companies producing a large part of the flour sold in the United States markets; milling situation on Pacific coast also discussed briefly.

Report of Federal Trade Commission on grain trade: Vol. 1, *Country grain marketing* (1920, 350 pages, 85 tables in text, 20 in appendix). A detailed description of the mechanism and methods employed in country marketing; purchase and sale of grains at country points; various conditions and circumstances affecting this trade. Deals principally with the processes of handling grains by various types of country elevators. Covers years 1912-1918.

Id., Vol. 2, *Terminal grain market and exchanges* (1920, 333 pages, 79 tables). Covers 17 markets, 10 of which, known as "primary markets," receive bulk of grain from local points in producing territory; describes growth and relative importance of these markets, and outlines the functions exercised and rules prescribed by these grain exchange associations.

Id., Vol 3, *Terminal grain marketing* (1922, 332 pages, 43 tables). Car-lot movement of grain, receiving and purchasing from country points, transportation and railroad terminal facilities, warehousing and storage at terminal points, merchandising and shipping business in terminal markets, operations of cash grain brokers, financing, the grain bulletin, scalping in the cash markets.

Id., Vol. 5, *Future trading operations in grain* (1920, 347 pages, 21 tables). Describes the technique of operations of future trading, including the facilities and machinery for it and such incidental references to purpose and functions as are necessary to an understanding of the technique.

Report of Federal Trade Commission on wheat prices for 1920 crop (1921, 91 pages, 16 tables). Data date back to 1911, but are chiefly for the year 1920. Investigation of dumping of Canadian grain, as complained against in October, 1920, by growers of North Dakota and adjacent regions.

Report of beet sugar industry in United States for five years ending with season of 1913-1914 (1917, 164 pages, 33 tables). The report deals chiefly with the costs and profits of growing sugar beets, the cost of manufacturing and marketing beet sugar, the profits in the manufacture and sale of beet sugar, and the relation between sugar beet growers and beet-sugar manufacturers.

Report of Federal Trade Commission on sugar supply and prices (1920, 205 pages, 53 tables). Covers 1919 and early 1920; conditions in the production and distribution of sugar; inquiry into prices and their reasonableness, existing supplies and causes of shortage; government policy in relation to 1919-1920 Cuban sugar crop.

Milk and milk products, summary (1921, 19 pages). Covers 1914-1918; information regarding the production, costs, prices, profits, various business practices in the milk and milk products industries during the war, and certain activities of the Food Administration in connection therewith. Covers the years 1914-1918. The report of which this is a summary has 234 pages.

Southern livestock prices (1920, 11 pages; same as Senate Doc. 209, 66th Cong., 2nd Sess.). Object, to determine whether or not producers of live stock in southern States were being discriminated against; includes (1) comparison of cattle and hog prices in southern with those in northern and western States; (2) similar comparisons for beef and pork products; (3) comparisons of quality; (4) comparisons of live-stock production and marketing methods in the south with those in north and west.

Commercial feeds, complete report (1921, 206 pages, 35 tables in text and 16 tables in appendix). Covers the years 1913-1920; the principal producing and consuming centers of animal feeds in the United States except Pacific coast; supply, fluctuation in price, extent of conversion of animal feeds; combinations or understandings between feed manufacturers, wholesale feed dealers, and retail feed dealers.

Report on fertilizer industry (1916, 269 pages; same as House Doc. 551, 64th Cong., 1st Sess., 74 tables, 6 diagrams). Describes conditions of production and sale of materials used in fertilizers. Also special study of wholesale price fluctuations and relation of wholesale prices to those paid by farmer.

Report . . . on causes of high price of farm implements (1920, 713 pages; 177 tables in text, 44 in exhibits). Covers the years 1914-1918, but with emphasis on 1916-1918; costs, prices, and profits of implement manufacturers; prices and profits of implement dealers; restraints of trade between manufacturers and dealers; situation of the farmer with respect to the prices paid for implements and his general economic position.

Report . . . on Anthracite and Bituminous Coal (1917, 420 pages, 69 tables; same as Senate Doc. 50, 65th Cong., 1st Sess. A summary giving the principal facts in answer to Senate Res. 51, 65th Cong., 1st Sess., and Senate Res. 217, 64th Cong., 1st Sess.). Production; cost; distribution; prices, in anthracite industry for fall and winter, 1916-1917. Bituminous coal industry referred to only incidentally.

Cost report of Federal Trade Commission: Coal, No. 1, Pennsylvania, bituminous (1919, 103 pages). This and the six following reports, Nos. 1-7, relate particularly to costs of coal during the war period.

Id., Coal, No. 2, Pennsylvania, anthracite (1919, 145 pages).

Id., Coal, No. 3, Illinois, bituminous (1920, 127 pages).

Id., Coal, No. 4, Alabama, Tennessee, and Kentucky, bituminous (1920, 210 pages).

Id., Coal, No. 5, Ohio, Indiana, and Michigan, bituminous (1920, 288 pages).

Id., Coal, No. 6, Maryland, West Virginia, and Virginia, bituminous (1920, 286 pages).

Id., Coal, No. 7, Trans-Mississippi States, bituminous (1921, 459 pages).

Preliminary report of the Federal Trade Commission on investment and profit in soft-coal mining. Part I, May 31, 1922; Part II, July 6, 1922 (1922, 222 pages). Important for the effects of the war on the industry.

Report on the price of gasolene in 1915 (1917, 224 pages, 37 tables in text, 39 in exhibits). Demand and supply; costs and margins; earnings, dividends, and quotations on the stocks of representative refining and marketing companies; inequalities in competition and price; retail price and margins.

Report on pipe-line transportation of petroleum (1916, 467 pages, 256 tables). Deals principally with pipe-line transportation of crude oil from the mid-Continent field (Kansas, Oklahoma, northern Texas, and northern Louisiana) to refineries or connecting pipe lines. Shows total investments and total earnings in the systems, investment in pipe lines, cost of transporting crude oil by pipe lines, charges and regulations imposed by owners on other shippers, excess of such charges over actual cost, and other phases of present conditions.

Advance in price of petroleum products, letter transmitting report in response to resolution directing commission to make immediate inquiry into cause of recent advance in prices of all petroleum products (June 1, 1920, 57 pages; same as House Doc. 801, 66th Cong., 2nd Sess.; 26 tables). Production, consumption, stocks, imports, exports, prices of petroleum products, chiefly in the United States, for years 1918-1920. Some tables cover 1910-1920. Discusses production in foreign countries, giving the probable nationality of the interests there in control. Recommendations for the relief of the situation of the United States in view of excess of present consumption over production.

Pacific coast petroleum industry, complete report, 1921. Two parts; covers the years 1914-1919. Part I: Production, ownership, and profits (276 pages, 61 tables). Sources of supply; effect on California production of oil, land withdrawals; organization and operation of large Pacific coast companies. Part II: Prices and competitive conditions (261 pages, 16 tables). Methods of marketing crude petroleum and petroleum products; distribution in domestic and export markets by large marketers; prices; competitive conditions.

Report on newsprint paper industry (1917, 162 pages, 32 tables; same as Senate Doc. 49, 65th Cong., 1st Sess.). Includes investigations of prices, costs, factors of supply and demand, and activities of manufacturers and jobbers; also recommendations for government supervision.

Book-paper industry, reports, 1917. Preliminary report, June 14, 1917 (11 pages, same as Senate Doc. 45, 65th Cong., 1st Sess.). Final report August 21, 1917 (125 pages, 34 tables). Increases in cost, price, and marginal profits, 1915-1916, and recommendations looking toward limitation of same.

Report on the Petroleum Industry of Wyoming (1921, 54 pages). The petroleum industry in the Rocky Mountain region; effects of the war.

Cost reports of Federal Trade Commission: Copper (1919, 26 pages, 14 tables). Report on cost of producing copper in the United States for 1918 and also in Canada, Mexico, Cuba, and South America; undertaken to assist the Price-Fixing Committee of the War Industries Board.

Report on woolen rag trade (1920, 90 pages, 21 tables). Information obtained at the request of the War Industries Board, for its use in regulating the prices of woolen rags. Includes relation of manufacture of shoddy to woolen rag trade; development of woolen rag trade; origin and kinds of commodities dealt in; nature of functions performed by various dealers; course of prices; profits of dealers; comprehensive classification of grades adapted to use in the trade.

Combed cotton yarns, complete report (1921, 94 pages, 96 tables, 11 charts). Covers chiefly the years 1913-1920; based on reports of 14 leading firms. Includes statement of costs and prices, showing that profits of 1916 and succeeding years were large enough to equal the total capital, including borrowed money required to conduct the business.

Report on leather and shoe industries, 1914-1918 (1919, 180 pages, 47 tables). Deals with the price of hides, general conditions in the hide market, the prices of certain kinds of leather, profits in the tanning industry, and cost of tanning certain staple leathers; cost of manufacturing shoes; cost and selling prices (wholesale and retail) of shoes; and general conditions in the hide, leather, and shoe business.

Shoe and leather costs and prices, complete report (1921, 212 pages, 66 tables in text and 37 in appendix). Based on schedules and on books of companies. Price trends of hide, leather, and shoes, 1913-1921, with special reference to prices, 1918-1919; production, consumption, and stocks of hides, leather, and shoes, 1918-1919; costs and profits per unit of production and with respect to total business of tanners, shoe manufacturers, shoe wholesalers and jobbers, and retailers, 1918-1919; general conditions in the hide, leather, and shoe industries.

Coöperation in American export trade (1916: Part I, 387 pages; Part II, 597 pages). Discussion of conditions developed by the war.

UNITED STATES TARIFF COMMISSION

Functions and Records

THE United States Tariff Commission was created by title VII of
the revenue act of September 8, 1916. Its chief function is the gathering of information on all phases of the tariff question for the use
of the President and committees of Congress. For each commodity
mentioned in the later tariff acts it gathers and records, in *Tariff Information Surveys*, a description of the commodity, its uses, methods
and processes of manufacture, divergencies between American and
foreign methods, conditions under which competition occurs between
products of foreign and domestic origin, the nature and sources of
supply of materials, domestic production and exports, imports, revenue from imports, the extent to which imports compete with domestic production, costs of manufacture in the United States and in
foreign countries, and references to sources from which further information may be obtained. Correspondence with manufacturers,
exporters, and dealers, and the proceedings of conferences held with
the representatives of certain industries are contained in auxiliary
files.

The commodities regarding which information was first gathered
were those that were most affected by the war, and the commission
particularly endeavored to secure all available data respecting disturbance to industries caused by the war and the conditions likely to
follow upon its close. In its annual reports the commission enu-
merates and briefly describes the work and publications completed
during the year under review.

Publications

The publications of the commission are: (1) annual reports, (2)
reports prepared for the consideration of problems arising from the
war, (3) tariff information surveys, which describe the industrial
and commercial conditions and tendencies in the production of commodities enumerated in the tariff act, (4) a tariff information series,
which is an outgrowth of the work on the tariff information surveys,
(5) special reports dealing with the commercial policies of the

United States and foreign countries. Particular attention is directed to the following:

First annual report of the United States Tariff Commission, 1917 (26 pages).

Second Annual Report, 1918 (118 pages).

Third Annual Report, 1919 (64 pages).

Fourth Annual Report, 1920 (64 pages).

List of principal subjects investigated and reported upon by the United States Tariff Commission (1921, 34 pages).

Subject index to tariff information surveys (manuscript) and reports (printed) (1920, 25 pages).

Dyes and other coal-tar chemicals (1919, 83 pages). A report to Congress recommending a revision of the tariff on dyestuffs to meet changes in the dye industry produced by the war.

The dyestuff situation in the textile industries (1918, 28 pages). A study of the effect of the shortage of dyestuffs on the textile industries.

Census of dyes and coal-tar chemicals, 1918 (1919, 103 pages). History of the dye industry in the United States since the beginning of the war, with statistics of imports and exports.

Cost of production in the dye industry, 1918 and 1919 (1920, 24 pages).

Silk and manufacture of silk (1918, 166 pages). Statistical tables; war disturbances; testimony of manufacturers.

Cotton venetians: import trade and domestic production (1919, 83 pages). Development of American trade in venetians prior to the war; future of the domestic venetian and its competitive strength after the war; government requisition of venetians for army use.

Cotton yarn: import and export trade in relation to the tariff (1920, 320 pages). Pre-war position of the United States as an exporter of cotton yarn; development of the yarn export trade during the war; outlook for retention of expanded export trade.

The wool-growing industry (1921, 592 pages). Wool control during the war; prices; wool growing in the United States; wool growing in foreign countries.

Agricultural staples and the tariff (1920, 190 pages). Changes effected by the war; comparison of conditions in Canada and the United States.

Costs of production in the sugar industry (1919, 55 pages). Pre-war conditions; war conditions; costs of specific items; relation of costs and prices.

Refined sugar: costs, prices, and profits (1920, 43 pages). Pre-war prices and profits; costs, prices, and profits during the war; government regulation of sugar.

Survey of the American bean industry (1920, 32 pages). Shortage during the war; competitive conditions.

Survey of the American peanut industry (1920, 32 pages). Production in the United States and foreign countries; conditions during the war.

Survey of the American cottonseed oil industry (1920, 26 pages). Substitutes and competing articles during the war.

Information concerning the domestic potato-product industries; potato flour, dried or dehydrated potatoes, potato starch, potato dextrine (1919, 28 pages).

The button industry (1918, 125 pages). Manufacture of buttons in the United States; button industry and trade in forcign countries; statistics; statements of manufacurers, importers and exporters.

The glass industry as affected by the war (1918, 147 pages). Pre-war trade; increase in the cost of materials; war disturbances in the supply of war materials; factors depended upon for holding export trade after the war.

Information concerning the potash industry (1919, 52 pages). Significance of potash in agriculture and in chemical industries; development of the industry during the war; detailed information concerning individual salts; wholesale prices.

Information concerning the pyrites and sulphur industry (1919, 31 pages). Summary of the pyrite and sulphur situation; domestic production; foreign production; imports; prices.

Information concerning zinc ore (1919, 45 pages). Effects of the war; domestic production; foreign resources and foreign production.

Information concerning tungsten-bearing ores (1919, 47 pages). Effect of the war upon the tungsten industry; competitive conditions.

Information concerning manganese ore (1919, 28 pages). Increased production in the United States during the war.

Information concerning the manganese industry (1919, 23 pages). Effects of the war upon the industry.

Information concerning graphite (1919, 28 pages). Domestic production; foreign production; imports; prices; competitive conditions; graphite producers by States (1917).

Information concerning optical glass and chemical glassware (1919, 35 pages). Establishment and development of the industries in the United States during the war; their status at the close of the war.

Information concerning scientific instruments (1919, 35 pages). The domestic industry; foreign production; competitive conditions; war developments.

The surgical instrument industry in the United States (1918, 54 pages). The American industry and foreign competition before the war; effects of the war upon the industry in the United States.

Industrial readjustments of certain mineral industries affected by the war (1920, 320 pages). Antimony; chromite; graphite; magnesite; manganese; potash; pyrites; sulphur; quicksilver; tungsten.

Interim legislation (1921, 33 pages). Discussion of tariff problems arising from the revenue exigencies of the war.

Depreciated exchange and international trade (1922, 118 pages). Rates of exchange; foreign and domestic prices of sundry commodities; wages in the United States, England, and Germany.

Information concerning American valuation as basis for assessing duties ad valorem (1921, 39 pages). Discussion of proposal to substitute home valuation for foreign market value of imported commodities as a means of preventing the "dumping" of inferior goods into the United States.

Japan: Trade during the war (1919, 147 pages). A study of the effect of war conditions upon the foreign trade of Japan, with particular reference to changes in the trade between Japan and the United States.

Summary of tariff information relative to H.R. 7456 (Fordney Bill), prepared pursuant to a request by the Senate Committee on Finance (1922, 1625 pages). Descriptive and economic data on commodities mentioned in the bill.

Commercial Policy in War Time and After, by William Smith Culbertson (New York, 1919, 479 pages). Surveys the influences of the war on American and foreign industrial conditions; discusses the various commercial problems of the United States; emphasizes the permanent changes caused by the war. [Unofficial.]

FEDERAL RESERVE BOARD

Functions

THE Federal Reserve Board is charged with the administration of the Federal Reserve banking system which was created by act of December 23, 1913, entitled, "An act to provide for the establishment of Federal Reserve banks, to furnish an elastic currency, to afford means of rediscounting commercial paper, to establish a more effective supervision of banking in the United States, and for other purposes." In supervising the Federal Reserve banks, the board directs the policy of the system as a whole, with special reference to the reserve, discount, and note-issue functions. During the war the board's chief concern was so to administer the system that it could meet the heavy demands and extraordinary conditions of war finance. As special war functions it took over control of security issues, foreign exchange, gold and silver, and the export of bullion, coin, and paper currency.

Publications

Fourth Annual Report of the Federal Reserve Board, . . . operations for the year, 1917 (Washington, 1918, 621 pages). Part I: discount policy in connection with war financing; war finance and banking; discount rates and war financing; curtailment of unnecessary credit. Part II, reports from districts: Boston, New York, Philadelphia, Cleveland, Richmond, Atlanta, Chicago, St. Louis, Minneapolis, Kansas City, Dallas, and San Francisco.

Fifth Annual Report of the Federal Reserve Board . . . 1918 (Washington, 1919, 913 pages). Effect of war financing upon the Federal Reserve banks; export of gold, bullion, and currency; regulation and control of foreign exchange; Capital Issues Committee; reports from districts.

Sixth Annual Report of the Federal Reserve Board . . . 1919 (Washington, 1920, 553 pages). Financial exigencies of the war; movement of the principal assets and liabilities of Federal Reserve banks; foreign trade and foreign credits; regulation and control of foreign exchange; exports of coin, bullion, and currency; reports from districts.

Federal Reserve Bulletin (Washington, 1915———). A monthly publication by the Federal Reserve Board. An *Index-Digest* to Vols. 1-6

(1915-1920) was published in 1921. For the years 1917 and 1918 particular attention is directed to the following topics:

"War loans to foreign countries" (January, 1917, Vol. 3, pp. 10-19).

"Collaboration with the Federal Trade Commission" (January, 1917, Vol. 3, pp. 21-23).

"Business conditions throughout the Federal Reserve districts" (February, 1917, Vol. 3, pp. 119-134).

"Investments in foreign loans" (April, 1917, Vol. 3, pp. 239-240).

"War financing" (May, 1917, Vol. 3, pp. 340-344).

"Foreign war loans" (May, 1917, Vol. 3, p. 349).

"German war loans" (May, 1917, Vol. 3, pp. 350-351).

"National banks and the war" (May, 1917, Vol. 3, pp. 351-352).

"The progress of inflation" (May, 1917, Vol. 3, pp. 375-377).

"Foreign exchange rates in belligerent, neutral, and silver-standard countries" (May, 1917, Vol. 3, pp. 404-406).

"Transactions with alien enemies" (June, 1917, Vol. 3, pp. 431-432).

"Coöperation of American Bankers' Association in connection with Liberty Loan" (June, 1917, Vol. 3, pp. 438-439).

"Export licenses in the foreign trade" (August 1, 1917, Vol. 3, pp. 582-585).

"Loans to cattle raisers" (September 1, 1917, Vol. 3, p. 659).

"Regulations governing export of coin, bullion, and currency" (October, 1917, Vol. 3, pp. 736-739).

"War-savings certificates" (December, 1917, Vol. 3, pp. 925-929).

"Credit needs of farmers" (December, 1917, Vol. 3, pp. 937-938).

"Changes in principal assets and liabilities of the New York clearing banks since April, 1917" (January, 1918, Vol. 4, p. 28).

"Capital Issues Committee of the Federal Reserve Board" (February, 1918, Vol. 4, pp. 77-79).

"Curtailment of unnecessary credit" (April, 1918, Vol. 4, pp. 260-263).

"War expenditures, war debts, and increase in note circulation of principal countries" (April, 1918, Vol. 4, pp. 267-284).

"Indexes of business conditions" (June, 1918, Vol. 4, p. 491).

"Work of the Capital Issues Committee" (June, 1918, Vol. 4, pp. 494-495).

"Control of coin, bullion, and currency movement" (June, 1918, Vol. 4, pp. 499-501).

"Movement of prices" (June, 1918, Vol. 4, pp. 504-505).

"Indexes of business conditions" (July, 1918, Vol. 4, pp. 597-600).

"Indexes of wholesale prices" (September, 1918, Vol. 4, pp. 810-812).

"Discount and interest rates prevailing in various cities" (September, 1918, Vol. 4, pp. 812-815).

"Loans for relief of banks and individuals in crop-raising sections of the West and Southwest" (September, 1918, Vol. 4, pp. 828-832).

"Conservation of productive power and credit" (October, 1918, Vol. 4, pp. 931-937).

"Condition of the savings institutions in the United States" (October, 1918, Vol. 4, pp. 952-954).

"Statement by War Trade Board relative to curtailment of less essential productive activities" (November, 1918, Vol. 4, p. 1078).

"Business conditions throughout the Federal Reserve districts" (December, 1918, Vol. 4, pp. 1220-1237).

UNITED STATES SHIPPING BOARD

Organization and Functions

THE United States Shipping Board was created by the shipping act of September 7, 1916, and was formally organized on January 30, 1917. It is a permanent establishment and its normal peace-time functions are: (1) the regulation of rates and practices of common carriers by water engaged in interstate and foreign commerce; (2) to encourage the development of a merchant marine and a naval auxiliary and reserve by constructive recommendations made upon the basis of investigations into such matters as comparative costs of shipbuilding and operation, systems of marine insurance, regulation of shipping, and methods of attracting investment in American shipping; (3) the acquisition by construction, purchase, lease, or charter of vessels, and their disposition, through sale, lease, or charter, for service in the merchant marine of the United States.

The war-time functions of the board were greatly extended by legislation and executive orders issued under authority thereof. They included the acquisition of vessels by requisition, commandeering, and seizure, the maintenance and operation of vessels, their assignment or allocation, and the regulation of shipping and shipbuilding, including wages and hours and conditions of labor. Other incidental and auxiliary functions were the improvement of port and terminal facilities, the building of drydocks and repair yards, the coördination of maritime with land transportation, the recruiting for the merchant service, the housing and transportation of shipyard employees, etc. Many of these war-time functions, especially the construction and operation of vessels, were performed by the United States Shipping Board Emergency Fleet Corporation, which was created by the board on April 16, 1917, under authority of section 11 of the shipping act of September 7, 1916.

A summary of the legislation affecting the Shipping Board is to be found in its *Second Annual Report* (December 1, 1918, pp. 13-16). A convenient compilation of laws, proclamations, and executive orders, revised to January 1, 1919, was published by the board: *The Shipping Act (as amended) and the Emergency Shipping Act with other laws relating to the Shipping Board and Emergency Fleet*

Corporation, with the Proclamations and Executive Orders pertaining thereto (Washington, 1919, 87 pages). A later edition, revised to July 1, 1920, is *Shipping Act and Merchant Marine Act, 1920, Suits in Admiralty Act, Emergency Shipping Legislation and other Laws, Proclamations, and Executive Orders relating to the Shipping Board and Emergency Fleet Corporation* (Washington, 1920, 151 pages). The board also compiled and published, April 1, 1919, *Appropriation laws of the Shipping Board and Emergency Fleet Corporation* (Washington, 1919, 26 pages).

The organization of the Shipping Board was subject to an almost constant process of development and modification during the war period. A series of organization charts in the files of the historian of the board shows the organization at various times. The chart of November, 1918, represents the fully developed war organization of the board, while that of April, 1919, is the most elaborate and complete. The *Second Annual Report* contains a good general account of the various divisions and their functions as of 1918. The more important offices and divisions for the purposes of this survey were as follows:

Shipping Board

Office of the secretary—where were preserved the minutes of the board, the weekly reports of divisions, the general files, and the files of the historian.

Division of planning and statistics—dealing with inventory and movement of vessels, studies of trade and commodities, studies of ocean freight rates and relative costs of operation, estimate of opportunities for employment of tonnage, etc.

Law division—handling all legal matters, except litigation, such as commandeering of vessels under construction, acquisition of Dutch vessels, negotiations for neutral tonnage, etc.

Marine and dock industrial relations—dealing with labor questions arising in the handling of ships, including loading and unloading.

National adjustment commission—for the adjustment of wages, hours, and conditions of labor, etc., of longshoremen.

Port and harbor facilities commission—for the preparation and distribution of information respecting the ports of the United States and of the world, and the survey and development of the port facilities of the United States.

Recruiting service—for recruiting and training officers and men for the merchant marine service.

Committee on assignment of vessels.

Ship protection committee—which passed on all protection devices for merchant vessels.

Ocean advisory committee—for the appraisal of requisitioned and lost vessels in order that just compensation might be made for them.

Division of regulation—for hearing complaints respecting rates and practices of common carriers by water.

EMERGENCY FLEET CORPORATION

Ship construction division—for the administration of ship contracts, the inspection of ship construction, and for general technical and engineering service.

Shipyards plant division—for the supervision of construction and maintenance of shipyard plants, drydocks, industrial plants, storage yards, etc.

Passenger transportation and housing division—for the supervision of the development of housing and transportation for shipyard labor and other employees.

Supply division—for the purchase of ship materials and parts.

Special staff—dealing with contracts, cancellations, claims, salvage, and industrial relations.

Division of operation—the operation and management of vessels directly and through private operators, including matters of construction and repair, commercial and foreign relations, personnel, employment, rates and claims, contracts, ship intelligence, allocations, etc. Under this was a field organization in districts as follows: New England, North Atlantic, Philadelphia, Baltimore, South Atlantic, Gulf, Great Lakes, Pacific Coast.

Publications

The majority of the publications of the Shipping Board and of the Emergency Fleet Corporation were educational, technical, or inspirational. There were, however, a large number which are of great value for the purposes of this survey, the more useful of which are listed below. The library of the Shipping Board has a collection of all the publications.

First Annual Report of the United States Shipping Board (December 1, 1917, 36 pages).

Second Annual Report of the United States Shipping Board (December 1, 1918, 212 pages). Contains summary of legislation, detailed account of organization, tables showing summary and classification of vessels under the jurisdiction of the board, etc.

Third Annual Report of the United States Shipping Board (June 30, 1919, 213 pages). Contains statistical tables showing changes in United States sea-going merchant marine during the World War, acquisitions, losses, etc.

Fourth Annual Report of the United States Shipping Board (June 30, 1920, 295 pages). Statistical tables, charts, etc.; chart showing gross tonnage of United States merchant marine, from April, 1917, to June, 1921.

Operations of the United States Shipping Board and United States Shipping Board Emergency Fleet Corporation from September 7, 1916, to January 1, 1921, by Joseph N. Teal (mimeographed, February, 1921, 29 pages).

Report of Director General Charles Piez to the Board of Trustees of the United States Shipping Board Emergency Fleet Corporation (April 30, 1919, 220 pages). Contains programs and statistics with regard to construction.

Report of E. N. Hurley, President of the U.S. Shipping Board Emergency Fleet Corporation to the Board of Trustees (August 1, 1919, 84 pages). Tells of construction and operating activities and offers a plan for future governmental policy regarding the merchant marine.

Report of Port and Harbor Facilities Commission of the United States Shipping Board (January 11, 1919, 86 pages). A survey of the capacity of such ports as were adequately provided with inland rail facilities to handle the requisite amount of shipping.

Report of the Committee on Classification and Rating of Vessels (mimeographed, 1919, 45 pages). Contains information for protection against fraud in the construction of vessels.

Register of Ships owned by the United States Shipping Board (February, 1919, 96 pages; 2nd ed., April, 1919, 121 pages; 3rd ed., July, 1919, 131 pages; 4th ed., January, 1920, 135 pages; 5th ed., August, 1920, 137 pages). Compiled by the Department of Shipping Information, Division of Operations.

Trade and Shipping between the United States and the Principal Regions of the World in 1914 and 1918 (1919-1920, 6 parts). These are published as numbered reports of the Division of Planning and Statistics. They show imports and exports in long tons and their shipping requirements in deadweight tons, and contain estimates of the probable cargo movement in 1919. The regions included are East Asian, South American, Middle American, Australasian, British Indian and East Indian, and West African.

Report of United States Shipping Board on vessels trading with the United States . . . These reports were prepared by the Division of Planning and Statistics and were issued monthly from November, 1918, to January, 1919. They contain tables of employment of vessels, their turn-around, space and weight employment, etc.

Control and Employment of Vessels Trading with the United States. Six reports of the Division of Planning and Statistics, issued monthly, March 1-August 1, 1919. They contain tables relating to vessels of 500 gross tons and over and also show status of the construction program of the Emergency Fleet Corporation.

Bulletins of the Department of Shipping Information, Division of Operations. These were printed periodically and circulated confidentially, in the following series:

"Ships in Port," showing arrival and clearance at American ports of ships in foreign trade.

"Exact Location of all Ships in which the Shipping Board is Interested."

"Assignment Chart," showing distribution of ships in various trades.

"Expected Deliveries of Steel and Wood Steamships."

"List of American Ships under requisition to the United States Shipping Board."

"Foreign Ships under Charter to the Shipping Board."

"Charters approved by the Chartering Committee of the United States Shipping Board."

"Deliveries of Steel Seagoing Steamships from Great Lakes Yards."

"List showing Ships removed from Owner's Service or assigned to Operating Companies."

Steamship Fuel Stations in Foreign Countries and Non-Contiguous United States Territories, compiled under the direction of W. O.

Scroggs (2nd ed., revised, September 1, 1919, 49 pages). This is a publication of the Division of Planning and Statistics; the first edition was issued May 1, 1919.

Terminal Charges at United States Ports. Report prepared under direction of C. O. Ruggles (February, 1919, 181 pages).

Ocean Rates and Terminal Charges, by Emory R. Johnson (Washington, 1919, 84 pages). Report of an investigation made by the Division of Planning and Statistics, in 1918; includes Requisition rates, Ocean charter and freight rates, Terminal services and charges, Costs and rates, Rate making and rate control by the Shipping Board, Rate regulation by the Shipping Board.

Discussion of conditions affecting ship production, with estimates of ship deliveries, steel and wood, April-December, 1918, by S. M. Evans (Washington, 1919, 52 pages).

Report of Conference held at Washington, D. C., on May 19, 1919, between Shipbuilders from Great Lakes, Atlantic and Gulf Coast Districts and United States Shipping Board Emergency Fleet Corporation (Washington, 1919, "confidential," 78 pages). Stenographic report of conference the purpose of which was "to discuss with the shipbuilders in what way the cost of ships (contracted for), where the keels have not yet been laid down, may be reduced in order to justify the board in asking Congress to appropriate the necessary money to complete these contracts."

Report of Conference held in Washington, D. C., on May 22, 23, 1919, between the United States Shipping Board Emergency Fleet Corporation and Representatives of Shipowners, Manufacturers, Bankers, and Farmers Association (Washington, 1919, "confidential," 143 pages). Stenographic report of discussion on best methods of promoting the American merchant marine.

History of the Shipbuilding Labor Adjustment Board, 1917 to 1919, by Willard E. Hotchkiss and Henry R. Seager (Bulletin of U.S. Bureau of Labor Statistics, No. 283, 1921, 107 pages). This board was not an organic part of the Shipping Board, but included a representative of that body. Its jurisdiction extended to disputes "concerning wages, hours, or conditions of labor in the construction or repair of shipbuilding plants or of ships in shipyards under the United States Shipping Board Emergency Fleet Corporation, or under said Shipping Board, or under contract with said corporation or with said board." It extended also to disputes in connection with work for the Navy Department in private shipyards.

Codification of the Shipbuilding Labor Adjustment Board Awards,

Decisions, and Authorizations, compiled by J. Caldwell Jenkins (1921, 341 pages).

Decision as to Wages, Hours, and other Conditions in Atlantic Coast, Gulf, and Great Lakes Shipyards (October 1, 1918, 27 pages). By the Shipbuilding Labor Adjustment Board.

Decisions as to Wages, Hours, and other Conditions in Pacific Coast Shipyards (October 1, 1918). By the Shipbuilding Labor Adjustment Board.

National Adjustment Commission, Chairman's Report for the Period ending December 31, 1918 (Washington, 1919, 174 pages). Mediation and decisions in disputes involving wages, and hours and conditions of labor of longshoremen. Report contains Rules of procedure, and Report of awards rendered.

Marine and Dock Labor, Work, Wages, and Industrial Relations during the Period of the War. Report of the Director of the Marine and Dock Industrial Relation's Division, United States Shipping Board, December 31, 1918. By Robert P. Bass, prepared by Horace B. Drury (Washington, 1919, 203 pages).

Report of Shipyard Employment Managers' Conference (1918, 62 pages). Held under the auspices of the Industrial Service Department, Division of Construction, Emergency Fleet Corporation, in Washington, D. C., November 9, 10, 1917.

Training of Shipyard Workers (1919, 88 pages). Report on the work of the Education and Training Section, Industrial Relations Division, Emergency Fleet Corporation. Tells of the plan and scope of training and contains statistical tables exhibiting costs and results.

Report of New England Shipbuilding Conference (1917, 52 pages). Held at Boston, October 1, 1917, under the auspices of the Industrial Service Department, Division of Construction, Emergency Fleet Corporation. Discussion of problems of wages, distribution of talent, shop instruction, etc.

Joint Shipping Industrial Conference held in Washington, June 4-5, 1919 (1919, 133 pages). Discussion of means of adjusting labor issues and promoting the efficiency and industrial harmony of the merchant marine.

Social Service in the United States Merchant Marine, by Alice S. Howard (1919, 15 pages). Report by the chief of the Social Service Bureau, U.S. Shipping Board Recruiting Service, on the welfare activities of the Bureau.

Emergency Fleet News. A weekly newspaper issued from February,

1918, to January, 1919, and distributed to shipyards, industrial plants, and office employees.

Building the Emergency Fleet, by W. C. Mattox (Cleveland, 1920, 279 pages). A historical narrative of the problems and achievements of the United States Shipping Board Emergency Fleet Corporation by the former head of the publications section of the corporation.

Records[1]

There was at no time a complete or even an approximate centralization of the records of the Shipping Board, although there was a "general file" in the office of the secretary. It is therefore necessary, in the case of many searches for information, to go to the divisional files. By a study of some general account of the board, as, for instance, that in the *Second Annual Report*, an understanding of the functions of the various divisions may be obtained and this will serve to indicate the particular place in the board's records where desired information is likely to be found.

OFFICE OF THE SECRETARY

Minutes. The Secretary's office preserved the verbatim reports of the proceedings of the board and the Emergency Fleet Corporation, and has all the minutes of the board together with excellent indexes to them. Originals of reports and various documents submitted to the board were kept by the secretary. Some of this material is regarded as confidential.

Historian's files. Though no history of the board was contemplated, the functions of the historian were extensive. The main burden of this office was to maintain comprehensive informational files covering all phases of the activities of the board and to prepare the annual report to Congress. In addition, a number of special tasks were performed, such as drawing up organization charts, preparing material for the Historical Branch of the General Staff, writing many reports covering special phases of the board's work, preparing bibliographies, compiling the policies and precedents of the board, studying the participation of merchant ships in the war, coöperating with the Historical Branch of the navy and the Naval

---

[1] This report on the records of the Shipping Board was prepared in 1920 by Professor J. G. Randall, who was historian of the Board in 1918-1919.

Consulting Board, handling part of the secretary's and chairman's correspondence, and writing articles from time to time for publication. The current routine of the office included the examination of many sources in the preparation of summaries for the informational files. No particular key to these files is necessary, for everything is topically classified and the topics are arranged alphabetically.

Weekly Reports. In the secretary's office there may also be found a complete set of weekly reports covering the activities of the various sections of the board and of the Emergency Fleet Corporation, assembled and compiled by the historian. The most inclusive are those of the Division of Planning and Statistics and of the Marine and Dock Industrial Relations Division. Every part of the board's organization was expected to present a weekly report.

General Files. As the records of the board were not fully centralized, the "general files" contain only a part of them; even so, they are of great volume, since they include the correspondence of the chairman, commissioners, secretary, and other officers of the board, reports submitted to the chairman, inter-office memoranda, and similar material. There is an arrangement of out-going letters by date as well as a topical classification. The more important topics are as follows:

Transshipments.
Correspondence touching adjustments, shipments, collisions, claims, damages, etc.
Enemy interned ships.
Newspapers, publications, advertisements.
Shipbuilding materials.
Policy regarding operation and ownership of the American merchant marine.
Cancellation of shipbuilders' contracts.
Relations with the Treasury Department, State Department, War Department, etc.
Relations with Great Britain.
Exhibition trip to South America.
Correspondence touching legislation.
Requisitioned Dutch ships.
Congressional investigations.
Charter hire and rates of passenger and cargo ships.
Steamship companies.
Shipbuilding companies.

Passenger and freight service to South America.
Foreign agencies of the Board.
Requisitioning of ships.
Agency agreements.
Inspection, classification, and rating of vessels.
Insurance.
Transfer of registry.
Strikes and labor troubles.
Liner service.
Port and harbor facilities.
Bunkering.
Sale of ships.
Appropriations.
Freight rates.
Weekly reports.
Correspondence with foreign countries.

MARINE AND DOCK INDUSTRIAL RELATIONS DIVISION

Files. The report of this division on its work has been noted in the section on publications, above. Its files are grouped under the following headings:

A. Analysis of Work: duties, methods of work, organization of crews, etc.
C. Cost of Living.
D. Directory: addresses, lists of people, time tables, etc.
Df. Definitions.
E. Employment: demand, supply, employment policies and methods, special problems.
Ee. Employees' Associations.
Er. Employers' Associations.
G. Government Agencies.
I. Insurance, Benefits, Pensions: compensation for loss of effects, injury, and death.
L. Legislation, Judicial decisions, Administrative acts.
M. Miscellaneous.
R. Relations—Employers and Employees: conferences, strikes, constitution of industry, policies and attitudes of labor, employers, and government.
T. Training.
V. Vessels and their operation: tonnage, traffic, charters, finance, methods of operation, etc.
W. Wages and working rules: rules governing subsistence, overtime, etc.
We. Welfare: health, sanitation, living quarters and conditions, food, recreation, effect of work and occupation on worker.

DIVISION OF PLANNING AND STATISTICS

The student of economic history will find the records of the Division of Planning and Statistics very useful. The large personnel of the division included many highly qualified research experts, and their attention was concentrated upon vital problems of tonnage conservation. The origin and functions of the division were thus explained in the *Second Annual Report* of the board (pp. 74-76).

In order to act upon the best scientific guidance in the conservation and maximum utilization of tonnage for essential war purposes, the Shipping Board on May 13, 1917, ordered that information should be compiled as to the needs for tonnage of the various commodities coming into the United States, and that data should be gathered showing the supplies of each kind of article available for shipment and for use in the United States, the vessels engaged in such trades, and similar facts.

By the end of 1917 it became evident that considerable tonnage must be diverted from commercial to military use and that such as remained in trade must be utilized to maximum efficiency for the carrying of such commodities as are most essential to the Nation under war conditions.

This program required the close coöperation of various governmental agencies, especially the War Trade Board, the Shipping Board, the War Industries Board, the War and Navy Departments, the Department of State, the Treasury Department, and the Food Administration. Since the departments directly concerned were the War Trade Board, which has authority by its licensing system to prohibit or restrict imports, and the Shipping Board, which controls the tonnage, a Division of Planning and Statistics was established by the Shipping Board on February 11, 1918, to secure the necessary information, and the director of this division was made a member of the War Trade Board.

The duties of this division are to keep a record of the movements and characteristics of ships and to plan voyage schedules so that the Board may use all ships to the limit of capacity; to obtain from available figures and through the advice of experts and business men, knowledge of the commodities imported, their essential uses, substitutes, possible sources of supply, and their relation to the prosperity of this and other nations, so that the ships left in commercial service after the Army needs are satisfied might be assigned by the Board to the most essential trade routes. The services of statistical experts were engaged for the Board as well as experts familiar with commodities, sources of supply, trade routes, and shipping.

The statistics compiled on ships and their movement cover a wide variety of facts. The division has on file special information derived from the sources concerning the number and types of vessels, their age, draft, size, cargo capacity, speed, motive power, material of construction, number of decks,

holds, hatches, fuel consumption, etc. Records are kept of the daily movements of ships in all parts of the world, of the dates and ports of entry
and departure, and the tonnage employed in the different trade regions.
Charts and diagrams are prepared to show the assignment of vessels to
given trades, the length of voyages and stays in port, the performance of
vessels engaged in carrying specified commodities, etc.

Files. The above account will serve to indicate the general character of the records of the division, but because of their importance, and
also in order to illustrate the methods of filing in use for the records
of many of the war administrations a considerable section is here reproduced from the "Subject Classification" of the division files.

030 Organizations of interest to Shipping Board
031 History
032 Aircraft production and training
033 National Shipping Associations
035 Lists of data available in other organizations
037 Railway transportation
    .1 Tunnels
    .2 Car ferry
    .3 Electric railways
038 Army organization
    .1 Requirements—discussion on
040 Education
044 Education for foreign trade
045 Training for shipping service
    .4 Shipping Board merchant marine
060 Statistical Abstracts
080 War Service Agencies
    .1 Executive orders creating and specifying authority
    .2 Optical industries
081 War Trade Board
    .01 Censorship notes.
    .02 Personnel
    .03 Activities reports
        .031 Research Bureau
        .037 Tabulation and Statistics Bureau
    .04 General instructions
    .05 Journal
    .06 Data in files
        .061 Research Bureau
    .1 Minutes (not analytical excerpts; these are filed by sub-
        ject)
        .19 Correspondence

.2   Confidential digest of news for Chairman
   .25 Daily digest of news and comment
.3   Cablegram section, methods and developments
.4   Foreign representation
   .42 News letter (Confidential)
.5   Organization
   .56 Bureau of Research
   .57 Tabulation and Statistics Bureau
.6   Coöperation in work of other boards
   .61 Division of information
.8   Current news of war boards

082 Review of war service agencies
083 War News
  .1   Munitions and offensive devices
     .12 Tanks
     .13 Gas
        .131 Gas defense
  .2   Submarines
     .25 Submarine destroyers, etc.
  .3   Pay of army
  .4   Custody of prisoners
  .5   German and pro-German press
  .6   War indemnities
  .7   Economic condition of warring countries
     .76 Political situation of warring countries
  .8   Labor and the war
  .9   Reconstruction

084 A.M.T.C. Material
087 War Labor Policies Board
088 After-the-War Plans
  .1   Peace Conference
  .2   Shipping plans
  .3   France
  .4   Great Britain's industrial plans
  .5   German industrial plans
     .52 German shipping plans
     .54 German merchant marine
  .6   Industries

089 War Industries Board
  .1   Personnel
  .3   Commodity organization
  .5   Charts of organization
  .7   Statistical Division
     .71 Weekly staff conferences
     .72 Activities reports

.9 Conservation Division
    .91 Monthly reports
    .92 Minutes of division meetings

095 Reports of Shipping Board
  .01 Surveys, comparisons with other organizations, etc.
  .1 Ship construction
  .2 Chartering committees
  .3 Division of operations
  .4 Legal information on and by Shipping Board
    .41 Creation of Shipping Board
  .6 Industrial service
  .9 Allied plans—other than A.M.T.C.

097 Intra-Shipping Board organizations

098 Publicity of Shipping Board
  .1 Press release
  .2 Convention speeches, etc.
  .6 Posters
  .9 Correspondence, suggestions, etc.

099 Information on Division of Planning and Statistics
  .2 Tonnage inventory
    .25 Material in files
  .3 Weekly reports
  .5 Charts of organizations, etc.
    .51 Library organization
  .6 Bibliographies—data in files, lists, etc.

100 Personnel

.   .   .   .

200 Ships and Shipping
201 Marine dictionaries
  .5 Navy magazines
202 Registers and rating schemes for vessels
  .8 Newspaper clippings and copy registering vessels
204 Shipping efficiency
  .9 Correspondence
205 Lists of vessels awarded official numbers (*e.g.* Weekly List of Navigation Bureau)
  .5 Tables showing tonnage of these vessels
  .9 Correspondence
206 Losses of U.S.
  .1 Enemy action
  .2 Marine risk
  .3 Abandonment
  .4 Sales
    .49 Correspondence

.5 Reconveyance to former owners
    .51 Requisitioned vessels
.7 Tonnage balance between losses and gains
.9 Correspondence

207 Commissioner of Bureau of Navigation reports (Commerce Department)
.5 Steamboat inspection service
    .51 Pilot rules

208 Standards of suitability and suitability tables
.1 Troop transports
    .11 Tonnage for A.E.F.
.2 Cargo transports
    .21 War zone
    .22 Ocean service outside war zone
    .23 Coastwise service only
.3 Tanker transports
.4 Refrigerating ships
.5 Sailing vessels
.6 Steamers
    .64 Trade regions
.7 Barges
.9 Correspondence *re* suitability

209 General correspondence on shipping

210 Lists of completed and accepted vessels (both requisitioned and contract wood and steel vessels)
.6 Licenses and applications for licenses for vessels
.9 Correspondence

211 Lists of completed and accepted steel vessels (both requisitioned and contract)
.5 Schedules for completion of steel vessels
.9 Correspondence

212 Lists of completed and accepted wood vessels (composite and concrete, incl.)

215 Ship movements
.1 U.S. to —— (alph. by destination)
    .11 Vessels clearing foreign
.2 Reports on vessels entering foreign
.4 Assignments
.5 Position of vessels
.6 Delays and causes for delays

216 Pilot and sailing directions

217 Steamship companies

218 Steamship lines
.1 Passenger trade

219 Mail—Schedule of ships carrying mail

220 Tonnage
    .1 Tonnage owned by U.S.S.B.
    .3 Measurements of vessels
        .33 For Panama Canal
    .5 Conferences of tonnage staff
    .7 Ballast
        .74 Minerals as ballast
    .8 Conservation of shipping and tonnage
    .9 Correspondence
221 Space requirements of merchandise: stowage
    .6 Packing methods
    .8 Dunnage
222 Government assurances
    .1 Wheat
    .5 Hides, leather, skins, fur skins, etc.
223 Cargo reports (General)
    .1 Additions to and revision of commodities for which reports
       are required
    .2 Cargo reports, special forms for
        .28 Owner forms
    .3 Periodical tables from cargo reports
    .4 Outgoing
        .41 Special reports on the basis of cargo reports in which
           vessel is not named
        .42 Special reports on the basis of cargo reports in which
           vessel is named
    .5 Reports on commodities made up from cargo reports
    .6 Cablegrams on cargoes of designated commodities
        .61 Ships sailing (in ballast)
        .67 Ship movement cablegrams (no cargo mentioned)
        .69 Correspondence *re* cabling
224 Estimated requirements and studies on requirements of tonnage
    .1 Tonnage savings, tables, etc.
    .5 Trans-Pacific tonnage requirements, estimates, etc.
225 Tonnage of individual vessels (alphabetical by vessel)
226 Bunkering priorities and requirements
    .5 Requirements of fuel for bunkering
    .9 Correspondence
227 Lighterage
    .8 Newspaper clippings
    .9 Correspondence
229 Special kinds of merchant ships (tonnage)
    .1 Tankers
        .19 Correspondence on tankers

       .2 Sailing and steamships
          .21 Sailing tankers
          .22 Steamships
230 Vessel control
       .1 Assignments to army
       .2 Assignments to other nations (alph.)
       .3 Assignments to navy
       .4 Assignments to relief
231 Transports for troops and supplies
       .1 Needs for (Press and articles)
       .8 Cablegrams on tonnage required
232 Blockades and internment and seizure
233 Transfers to and from U.S. flag
234 General ship control of S.B.
       .6 Caribbean committee—vessel control
       .7 Tonnage inventory section—reports on vessels controlled by S.B.
       .9 Correspondence
235 Vessels chartered to special individuals (not necessarily by War Department)
       .1 Lists of charterers
       .2 Approvals and disapprovals
       .3 Alphabetical file of charters by vessels
       .4 Charter form by name of firm
          .41 Charter parties
       .5 Chartered to S.B.
       .6 Agreements between S.B. and companies chartering *re* cargoes, etc.
       .8 Charter agreements with other nations
          .83 War risk insurance
236 Tonnage exchange
       .6 Rates by land
237 Sale
238 Rates for transportation
       .1 By water
       .2 Insurance against marine risk
       .5 Agency fees
       .6 Rates by land (freight)
240 Tonnage requirements specifications
       .2 Shipping Board, P. and S. Division
       .9 Correspondence
241 Tonnage requirements for U.S. imports from—
       .6 Allocation of shipping for this need
          .69 Correspondence

242 Tonnage requirements by localities
   .3 Distribution of tonnage by ports
   .6 Allocation of shipping for other countries' needs
   .9 Correspondence
243 Studies of tonnage required in parallel or comparative routings
250 Acquisitions
   .1 Surveys, estimates, etc., of potentially available tonnage
251 Construction and delivery
   .04 E.F.C. Summary of employment in shipyards
      .041 Steel
      .042 Wood composite and concrete
         .0422 Concrete alone
      .043 Fabricated
   .1 Steel
   .2 Wood, composite and concrete
   .3 Machinery
      .31 Turbine
      .35 Engines
      .38 Trade catalogs of shipbuilding machinery
   .4 Contractors
   .5 Delivery estimates
      .51 Steel
         .511 E.F.C. lists, alphabetically by yards for special yards
      .52 Wood
   .6 Launching
      .61 E.F.C. lists
   .7 Reconveyance
   .8 Clippings
   .9 Yards and plants for shipbuilding
      .901 Shipbuilding policy
      .903 Warehouses
      .905 Smaller shipyards: building of lighters, tugs, barge hulls, trawlers, etc.
      .92 Labor in shipyards
      .96 Ways and berths
         .961 Steel ships
         .962 Wood ships
252 Steel vessels building, contracts
253 Requisitioned vessels
   .1 Steel
   .2 Wood, composite, etc.
   .7 Reconveyance
   .8 Of foreign vessels (alphabeted by country)

254 Charter (Building contracts for chartered vessels)
    .8 Foreign vessels
255 Commandeering
    .5 Auxiliary, coastwise and smaller vessels commandeered
256 Repairs
257 Purchase of ships
    .8 Foreign vessels
    .86 Japan
258 Negotiations and contracts with foreign countries for shipbuilding, American account
    .6 Japanese shipbuilding contracts
        .62 Shipbuilding material for Japan
    .7 Chinese shipbuilding contracts
259 Disposition
260 Ports and port facilities
    .1 United States
        .13 Southern (surveys, etc.)
            .131 Working papers
    .2 Far East
        .21 Japan
        .24 Persia
    .3 Mediterranean
    .4 French
    .5 British
    .6 South America
    .7 Statistics of trade of certain ports and general descriptions
        .71 Carloads of traffic at
    .8 Africa
261 Port designation for import licenses
    .3 Official numbers assigned to ports by W.T.B.
262 Tables of distances to ports and from ports
263 Study of port receipts (F. H. Dixon collection)
    .1 Goods in customs storehouses
    .2 Examination and search of vessels in port for cargoes, etc. (alphabeted by country)
    .3 Goods in transit
    .5 Ready for export at ports (cumulation of freight waiting shipment)
    .6 Import distribution
264 Coal bunkering, oil bunkering and repair stations (bunkering facilities) speed and fuel of ships
    .3 Coal and coaling stations
        .313 Southern ports
    .5 Oil
    .7 Repair

265 Harbors, docks, etc.
266 Canals
    .3 Panama
        .31 Tolls
    .4 England
267 Port Code
270 Requisitioned vessels
    .02 Wood
    .1 Program of S.B. as to requisitions
    .2 Rates on requisitioned vessels
        .22 Wood
272 Steel requisitioned vessels
273 Wood requisitioned vessels
280 Foreign vessels
    .08 Interpretation and definitions as to the nationality of vessels
    .1 South American
        .12 Brazil
    .2 France
    .3 Denmark
    .4 Great Britain
        .44 Great Britain, merchant marine
            .445 Shipping of Great Britain's merchant marine
    .5 Germany
        .54 German merchant marine
    .6 Japan
        .64 Japanese merchant marine
    .7 Greece
        .74 Greek merchant marine
    .8 Norway
        .84 Norwegian merchant marine
            .845 Shipbuilding of merchant marine
    .9 Correspondence *re* ship information
281 Applications for licenses
283 Chartered to America
285 Allied and neutral
286 Losses of foreign vessels
    .3 Danish
    .4 Great Britain
    .5 Germany
    .6 Japanese
    .8 Norwegian
290 Shipping inquiries on special companies
291 Inquiries on special vessels
292 Earnings

294 Inquiries *re* shipping facilities between U.S. and—
    .5 South Africa

295 Inquiries *re* shipping facilities to and from certain ports and countries

297 Inquiries on vessel acquisitions from special sources (*e.g.*, State of Washington)

300 Commodities

301 Exports (Lists of, on different commodities; Specific commodity goes with the subject)
    .4 Initial file (alphabeted by commodity)

302 Investigative methods, questionnaires, etc.
    .1 Necessary imports, estimates, requirements, etc.
        .18 Donald Scott's requirements memoranda and notes
    .2 Classifications
        .25 Industries (and manufacturers—manufactured articles)
        .27 Geographical classification for commodities studies
        .29 Correspondence
    .4 Minerals
        .41 Committee on imports and exports
    .5 Conferences on commodities
        .59 Correspondence
    .7 Classification of countries for imports and exports
    .9 Correspondence

303 General plans *re* work of commodity sections

304 Stocks and productions census (alphabeted by subject)

305 Miscellaneous army requirements, supplies, and Q.M.
    .3 Rations
    .4 Army uniforms
    .5 Contracts for purchase of army and navy supplies
        .52 Advance payments
    .6 Specifications on imported goods

306 Miscellaneous navy requirements

307 Commodity specifications and requirements by government agencies
    .5 Food Administration commitments
        .59 Correspondence
    .7 Index plan

308 Special commodities on other bases than cargo reports

309 Control of the commodities
    .2 Control of industries

310 Combined lists of minerals and non-minerals (alphabeted by source)
    .1 Compilations from ten-day reports

.11 Ten-day report summaries covering imports of 88 designated commodities by port of entry (customs district), and country of origin

.12 Consolidated monthly reports on *idem*

.17 Status at the end of each ten-day period as to the import of these designated commodities compared for the schedule of 1918

.2 Tables, Lists of vessels made up from ten-day reports

311 Priorities

.2 Minerals

.3 Non-minerals

.4 Preferential list for passage through canals, etc.

.5 Production and manufacture, Priorities in

.6 Export priority list

.7 Imports from—, Priorities on

.9 Correspondence

.   .   .   .

380 Current U.S. production literature

388 Foreign production

390 Conservation recommendations and methods

.2 Minerals

.25 Coal and fuel in general

.4 Foodstuffs

.45 Meat

.5 Laws

391 Delivery systems

392 Publishing business

393 Reduced consumption

400 Foreign Trade

401 Report of Department of Commerce

402 Steamship facilities

403 Commercial treaties

404 Disputes as to authority in deciding questions of license, etc.

407 Navigation clauses

410 Exports and imports of U.S. and trade of U.S. with foreign countries

.05 Foreign trade magazine

.5 Comparison U.S. foreign trade with that of another country

.9 Correspondence

411 U.S. Customs Service

.2 Collector of Customs

.9 Correspondence in general of customs collectors (alphabeted by port)

412 Special agents series of Bureau of Foreign and Domestic Commerce

414 Trade promotion with neutrals
415 Trading with the enemy and enemy trading lists
    .3 Violations
    .5 Alien property custodian—ship
    .9 General correspondence
416 General trade restrictions
    .7 General trade restrictions—Allocation
418 American firms' branch offices in neutral countries
    .2 Export licenses from central office
    .3 Licenses to trade with the enemy
420 Imports of U.S.
    .1 Survey by commodities
        .15 Mineral commodities
    .2 Survey by trade regions
        .21 Countries
    .4 Foodstuffs
        .46 Breadstuffs
    .6 Consumption
        .66 Survey by commodities
421 Tariff on imports
423 Import licenses
424 Import of non-essentials
425 Required by Food Administration and other deciding agencies
    .1 Necessary imports (alphabeted by country of source)
    .5 General list of essential imports; also balance sheet of necessary imports and balance to be lifted
        .51 Non-mineral
        .52 Minerals
        .59 Correspondence
426 Restricted imports
    .05 Relaxation of import restrictions
    .1 Foreign embargo on export
        .11 Canada
    .2 Broken freight contracts
    .3 Minerals
    .4 Non-minerals
        .49 Correspondence
    .5 Revenue reductions
    .6 Temporary
    .7 Violations
    .8 Definitions and interpretations
        .81 Canada
        .89 Correspondence
    .9 Correspondence about work on subject

.4 United Kingdom
.41 England
470 Exports (alone) of other countries (alphabeted by country)
.2 Far East
.3 By commodities
.338 Rubber
.4 United Kingdom
.41 England
.5 Netherlands
.51 Holland
.6 Spain
471 Canada to U.S.
480 Foreign trade of special countries (both imports and exports), alphabeted by locality
.1 Economic conditions
481 Agricultural prospects as bases of foreign trade
482 Markets
486 Foreign control of trade (*i.e.*, combined imports and exports)
.4 British control of trade
490 Allied shipping agreements to supply war needs
.1 Program making committee for allied imports
.11 War Trade Board participation
.3 Munitions Council
491 Miscellaneous
.2 Committee of Restrictions of Food Supplies and Commerce of the Enemy
.29 Correspondence
492 Agreements between Allied countries to supply minerals
493 *Idem* to supply non-mineral raw materials
494 *Idem* to supply foodstuffs
.4 Agreements of Great Britain and U.S. to furnish foodstuffs
495 *Idem* to supply manufactured goods
496 *Idem* to supply agricultural products
.2 Agreements to furnish grain
.26 Agreements to furnish cereals
497 *Idem* to supply miscellaneous chemicals
500 Banking and Finance
507 Accounting
.1 Cost accounting
508 Credit
.1 Trade acceptances
510 American
.1 Treasury Department
.6 Federal Reserve Board
.8 Revenue

511 Income Statistics
518 War Finance of U.S.A.
    .6 Agreements with other countries (alphabeted by countries)
520 Foreign
    .1 National Mon. Commission reports
521 Japanese finance
    .1 Japanese financial relations to China
522 Chinese finance
523 France's finance
524 Great Britain's finance
    .3 Canada
525 Germany's finance
    .8 German war finance
600 Trade Arrangements
  610 Domestic governmental direction
  611 Price Control
    .5 Market reports, etc.
    .6 Price-fixing committee
    .7 Price Section summaries
       .723   Iron and steel
       .725   Coal
       .7287 Non-ferrous metals
       .7315 Rags
       .734   Lumber
       .738   Rubber
       .75   Price Section Charts
       .7530 Paper
       .75   Building material
       .754   Hides, skins, and leather
       .76   Price Section reports
       .76   Textiles and fibers
       .77   Chemicals and explosives
       .774   Fertilizers
    .9 Correspondence
  612 Minimum wage and wage control
  620 Railroad Administration and regulations
  650 Agreements with foreign countries
  651 Allied war arrangements
    .1 Reciprocity with neutrals
    .2 Franco-American bureaus
    .6 Boycott
  653 German and anti-Ally agreements and German agreements *re* shipping
  655 Ex-German vessels
    .2 Safe conducts

.5 German agreements with neutrals

.9 Correspondence

700 Statistical Methods

  702 Conferences

    .1 Staff conference of Planning and Statistics Division

    .3 Reports of conference of statistical group of War Industries Board, War Trade Board, and Shipping Board

    .5 Conference to form a coöperative statistical bureau

  703 Methods of filing statistical data

  705 Lists of statistical data in files

  706 Coöperative schemes

    .1 War Trade Board; War Industries Board; Shipping Board

    .2 Clearing House on Statistics

    .4 War Trade Board and other organizations, relating to A.M.T.C. material

    .7 Census Bureau coöperating with Shipping Board

  707 Supplies

  708 Terminology

  710 Criticism and discussion of methods

    .2 Shipping

    .3 Commodities

    .4 Foreign trade

      .43 Export studies

    .9 Of special organizations

  711 Discussion of 10-day data as compiled

  713 Graphic methods on shipping situation

  714 Metric system as applied to shipping

  715 Computers' work

  718 Statistical work about Emergency Fleet Corporation production; supplies, costs, employment, etc.

    .9 Correspondence

  719 Inter-departmental and outside memoranda. Correspondence of statistical service section about details

  720 Tonnage inventory. Shipping inventory

    .3 Inter-departmental correspondence on how to furnish and develop information; methods of coding for files, etc.

    .9 Correspondence, inter-office memoranda, etc.

      .91 Reports of data sent from Tonnage Section to E. F. Gay's office and other agencies

  721 Master file

    .9 Correspondence on

  724 Methods of tabulation on repair work

    .9 Correspondence on

  730 Commodity section

  731 Cargo reports

732 Original ten-day report
    .1 Monthly reports
    .9 Correspondence *re* above
733 Methods of taking trade censuses

EMERGENCY FLEET CORPORATION

The Division of Operations was that portion of the Emergency Fleet Corporation which was responsible for the operation of ships under government ownership or control. Its duties covered every phase of vessel management, and its vast daily business involved relations with other government departments, foreign governments, and many private shipping concerns. Besides the general office located in the Shipping Board building at Washington, there was an extensive field force of district and local agents reaching into every port. For the period of the war, the "General Files" (*i.e.* the records contained in one great filing office) are fairly complete for all the activities of the division. After the war, on account of the reorganization and rapid expansion of the division, departmental files were maintained in addition to the central files. In January, 1920, the "general files" were abolished for future material, all the records being thenceforth kept by the departments of the division, but the then existing general files were kept intact. These voluminous records cover the movement and history of every vessel owned, requisitioned, or controlled by the board, as well as a vast amount of business touching the operating end of the board's activities. Besides a general topical arrangement of material, the correspondence is arranged chronologically and also topically, and a special file under each particular ship is kept. Special mention should be made of the Department of Shipping Information of the Division (at one time called the "Department of Maritime Intelligence") which performed important statistical work. This work did not consist of research bearing upon tonnage problems such as was conducted by the Division of Planning and Statistics, but rather took the form of tabulations of data covering each particular ship, indicating the number and type of the ships, the assignment and allocation of vessels, the amount, season, and importance of the commerce in which they were engaged, and similar information.

The following are some of the more important titles indicating material to be found in the records of the Division of Operations:

Powers, duties, and functions of the Division of Operations
New York Managing Agency
Shipping Control Committee
Chartering Committee
Ship Protective Committee
Foreign agencies
Radio operators and apparatus
Pay and bonus to crews
Recruiting and education
Coastwise trade
Coastwise permits
Port facilities
Ships general (alphabetically arranged according to last name)
Danish ships
Dutch ships
French sailing vessels (exchange with United States)
Neutral tonnage, control of
Norwegian ships
Russian ships (Russian Volunteer Fleet)
Scandinavian sailing vessels
Swedish ships
German ships in U.S. ports and in foreign ports
Wooden ships
Protection of ships (armament and armed guard, Ship Protection Committee, Devices for protection against submarine, etc.)
Requisitioning of ships
Sale of ships to the Shipping Board
Assignments to managers and operators
Ship movements, general (statistical information)
Ship supplies and equipment, general
Coal (relations with Fuel Administration, bunkering contracts, shortage of coal handling devices, etc.)
Fuel oil
Bunkering stations
Marine insurance
Labor and labor affairs
Foreign governments, relations with

The Division of Construction was located in Philadelphia and had charge of the enormous task of emergency shipbuilding. The organization of the division was very elaborate and was constantly changing, being greatly reduced after the war. Important statistics regarding construction were received and published by the Division of Planning and Statistics in Washington. Besides ships and shipbuilding the records of the division for the war period cover finance and accounting, supplies, labor affairs, etc. A series of file headings indicating their character would fill a hundred pages. The war time records are for the most part considered obsolete and have been transferred to Washington.

FEDERAL BOARD FOR VOCATIONAL
EDUCATION

Functions

THE Federal Board for Vocational Education was created by Section 6 of the Smith-Hughes act of February 23, 1917, entitled, "An act to provide for the promotion of vocational education, to provide for coöperation with the States in the promotion of such education in agriculture and the trades and industries, to provide for coöperation with the States in the preparation of teachers of vocational subjects, and to appropriate money and regulate its expenditure." By this act financial aid is given to the States in the work of vocational education and the work is directed and supervised by a Federal Board. The members of the board are the Secretary of Agriculture, the Secretary of Commerce, the Secretary of Labor, the United States Commissioner of Education, and three citizens appointed by the President, one of them representing manufacturing and commercial interests, one representing agricultural interests, and one representing labor. The directing function of the board is derived from its obligation "to make, or cause to have made studies, investigations, and reports, with particular reference to their use in aiding the States in the establishment of vocational schools and classes and in giving instruction in agriculture, trades and industries, commerce and commercial pursuits, and home economics." The supervising function is derived from its authority to approve or disapprove plans of state boards with regard to kinds of vocational education, kinds of schools and equipment, courses of study, methods of instruction, qualifications of teachers, and plans of training teachers—an authority which has its sanction in the board's obligation annually to "ascertain whether the several States are using, or are prepared to use, the money received by them in accordance with the provisions of this Act."

Shortly after the board was organized appeals were made to it by the War Department and by the United States Shipping Board for assistance in training skilled workmen, and until the close of the war the Federal Board coöperated with state boards in training men for service in the more essential war industries. When the vocational rehabilitation of disabled soldiers and sailors became a problem of the board, the Bureau of War Risk Insurance, and other organizations, Congress passed the vocational rehabilitation act of June 27, 1918, which made it the duty of the board to furnish vocational rehabilitation to every person disabled while serving in the army or navy. An amendment of July 11, 1919, transferred the responsibility for determining the eligibility of disabled men for training and for maintenance from the Bureau of War Risk Insurance to the board, but when, by the Sweet act of August 9, 1921, the Bureau of War Risk Insurance was transformed into the independent Veteran's Bureau the board was relieved of its vocational rehabilitation work. In the meantime, by an act of June 2, 1920, provision was made for vocational rehabilitation of persons disabled in industry, the States to bear one-half the expense of the training and the Federal Board to determine who were entitled to it.

Organization

The organization of the board has varied with developments and changing functions. In 1920, while the vocational rehabilitation of disabled soldiers, sailors, and marines was still one of its functions, there were at headquarters the members of the board, a secretary, a chief clerk, an editor and statistician, and an executive staff, consisting of a director and three assistant directors, each of whom was chief of a division. The divisions were: (1) the Vocational Education Division, for the promotion of vocational education in the States; (2) the Rehabilitation Division, for vocational rehabilitation and return to civil employment of disabled soldiers, sailors, and marines; (3) the Industrial Rehabilitation Division, for the vocational rehabilitation and return to employment of persons disabled in industry or otherwise.

The Vocational Education Division embraced four services: industrial education, agricultural education, home economics education, and commercial education, and for purposes of administration and supervision the country was divided into four regions: North Atlantic, Southern, Central, and Pacific.

The Vocational Rehabilitation Division embraced the central office at Washington, fourteen district offices, and more than one hundred local offices. In the central office were the assistant director, a chief of the training service, a chief of the industrial relations service, a chief medical officer, a legal officer, a superintendent of allowances, a statistician, and an eligibility officer. The last of these assigned eligibility officers to districts and was responsible for their general supervision. Each district office was administered by three or more assistant district vocational officers who were heads of sections: (1) assistant district vocational officer in charge of training; (2) assistant district vocational officer in charge of industrial relations and local offices; (3) assistant district vocational officer in charge of cooperation. There were also a medical officer and his staff, an eligibility officer, and an adjustment board. Each local office was in charge of a supervisor and one or more assistants, and was responsible for the induction of eligibles into training, for remitting their subsistence pay, for supervision and control of their training, and for securing employment for them.

Publications

Annual Report of the Federal Board for Vocational Education, 1917 (Washington, 1917, 32 pages). Training conscripted men, training men for skilled labor in the shipyards, vocational reëducation of disabled soldiers and sailors, studies and investigations in progress, allotment of funds to states.

Second Annual Report of the Federal Board for Vocational Education, 1918 (Washington, 1918, 172 pages). Summary of progress, war problems, war training, vocational rehabilitation of disabled soldiers and sailors, home economics, statistical tables.

Third Annual Report of the Federal Board for Vocational Education, 1919 (Washington, 1919). Vol 1, Vocational Education (256 pages); Vol. 2, Vocational Rehabilitation (56 pages).

Fourth Annual Report of the Federal Board for Vocational Education, 1920 (Washington, 1920, 542 pages). Section II, Vocational rehabilitation and return to civil employment of disabled soldiers, sailors, and marines.

The Vocational Summary, May, 1918-July, 1921. A small monthly magazine published by the Federal Board for Vocational Education to inform the public regarding its activities in vocational education, vocational rehabilitation of disabled soldiers, sailors, and marines, and industrial rehabilitation.

Bulletins. From September, 1917, to June, 1922, the board published

76 bulletins containing chiefly the results of its researches. Special attention is directed to the following:

1. *Statement of Policies* (32 pages; rev. ed., 1922, 98 pages).

2. *Training Conscripted Men for Service as Radio and Buzzer Operators (International Code) in the United States Army* (15 pages).

3. *Emergency Training in Shipbuilding, Evening and Part-time Classes for Shipyard Workers* (71 pages).

4. *Mechanical and Technical Training for Conscripted Men (Air Division, U.S. Signal Corps)* (47 pages).

5. *Vocational Rehabilitation of Disabled Soldiers and Sailors. A Preliminary Study* (112 pages).

6. *Training of Teachers for Occupational Therapy for the Rehabilitation of Disabled Soldiers and Sailors* (76 pages).

7. *Emergency War Training for Motor-Truck Drivers and Chauffeurs* (75 pages).

8. *Emergency War Training for Machine-Shop Occupations, Blacksmithing, Sheet-Metal Working, and Pipe Fitting* (48 pages).

9. *Emergency War Training for Electricians, Telephone Repairmen, Linemen, and Cable Splicers* (31 pages).

10. *Emergency War Training for Gas-Engine, Motor-Car, and Motor-Cycle Repairmen* (79 pages).

11. *Emergency War Training for Oxy-Acetylene Welders* (86 pages).

12. *Emergency War Training for Airplane Mechanics* (59 pages).

13. *Agricultural Education—Organization and Administration* (43 pages).

15. *The Evolution of National Systems of Vocational Reëducation for Disabled Soldiers and Sailors* (319 pages).

16. *Emergency War Training for Radio Mechanics and Radio Operators* (75 pages).

17. *Trade and Industrial Education—Organization and Administration* (125 pages).

18. *Evening Industrial Schools* (55 pages).

19. *Part-Time Trade and Industrial Education* (52 pages).

21. *The Home Project as a Phase of Vocational Agricultural Education* (43 pages).

25. *Ward Occupations in Hospitals* (58 pages).

46. *The Turnover of Labor* (60 pages).

AMERICAN NATIONAL RED CROSS

Organization

A RED Cross War Council of seven members was appointed by the President May 10, 1917, and to this body was delegated, by the executive committee of the American National Red Cross, full control, management, and administration of Red Cross affairs connected with, or incident to, operations arising out of the war. Its chairman was the chief executive officer of the Red Cross during the period of the war or until the resignation of the council March 1, 1919. Serving the council in an advisory capacity were the Woman's Advisory Committee, the National Committee on Red Cross Medical Service, the National Committee on Red Cross Nursing Service, a Committee on Coöperation, and an Insurance Advisory Committee.

The headquarters organization at Washington, D. C., embraced ten departments, each with several bureaus: (1) Department of Military Relief, with bureaus of medical, sanitary, camp, construction, motor, and canteen service; (2) Department of Civilian Relief, with bureaus of information, delayed allowances and allotments, after-care of discharged disabled soldiers, training for home service, camps and camp sites, health resources for home service, and home service correspondence; (3) Department of Nursing, with bureaus of enrollment of Red Cross nurses, field nursing service, public health nursing, instruction and nurses aids, dietitian service, and nursing survey; (4) Department of Development with bureaus of chapter organizations and membership extension, junior membership and school activities, chapter production, entertainments and benefits, conservation, sales for interned allied prisoners, and special campaigns for funds and membership; (5) Department of Law and International Relations, with bureaus of prisoners' relief, communication, foreign relations, insurance, and cables; (6) Department of Supplies, with bureaus of stores, purchase, invoices, and transportation; (7) Department of Publicity, with bureaus of general publicity news, and literature; (8) Department of Foreign Relief, representing the Red Cross commissions to France, Italy, Great Britain, Belgium, Serbia, Palestine, Switzerland, Roumania, Greece, and Russia; (9) Department of Accounts; (10) Department of Personnel.

To meet the growth of Red Cross activities within the United States the country was divided into Red Cross Divisions—Atlantic, Central, Gulf, Lake, Mountain, New England, Northern, Northwestern, Pacific, Pennsylvania, Potomac, Southern, and Southwestern, each of which had an organization similar to that at the national headquarters, directed by a division manager who received general directions from the general manager at Washington. A fourteenth division had charge of activities in the territorial and insular possessions and in foreign countries not within the theaters of war. Within each division was a group of chapters which, under the supervision of the division organization and largely through committees, performed nearly all the Red Cross work within the United States. During the period of the war the number of chapters increased to a total of 3,742.

Publications

The American National Red Cross Annual Report, for the year ended June 30, 1918 (1919, 178 pages). Reorganization on a war basis and report of operations.

The American National Red Cross Annual Report . . . June 30, 1919 (1919, 303 pages). Adjustment of the war program and transition to a peace program.

The American National Red Cross Annual Report . . . June 30, 1920 (1920, 242 pages). Reorganization for a peace program; problems of adjustment and reconstruction.

Home Service and the Disabled Soldier or Sailor, by the Director General, Department of Civilian Relief, American Red Cross (1918, 106 pages). Principles and program, treatment, training, employment, compensation, public opinion, after-care, medical problems.

Handbook of Information for Home Service Sections, by the Director General, Department of Civilian Relief, American Red Cross (1918, 114 pages).

The Red Cross Bulletin (beginning March 31, 1917, 5 volumes). Issued by the Bureau of Publications for the dissemination of news to the chapters and their members.

The Work of the American Red Cross during the War, a Statement of Finances and Accomplishments for the Period July 1, 1917, to February 28, 1919 (Washington, 1919, 90 pages). Summary of financial operations, membership and war drives, work in the United States, work in France, work elsewhere overseas.

The Work of the American Red Cross; Report by the War Council of appropriations and activities from outbreak of war to November 1, 1917 (Washington, 1917, 144 pages). Summary of organization and operations of all services and details of expenditure of appropriations.

The Work of the American Red Cross; No. 2; Financial statement of Red Cross War Fund, March 1, 1918 (Washington, 1918, 127 pages). Details of the various activities through which the war fund was distributed.

The Work of the American Red Cross; No. 3; a statement of its war-time activities throughout the world (Washington, December 1, 1918, 67 pages). Summary of Red Cross war service from its inception to the armistice.

The American Red Cross in the Great War, by Henry P. Davison, Chairman of the War Council of the American Red Cross (New York, 1919, 303 pages). War Council, divisions and chapters, production of chapters, supplies and transportation, motor corps service, canteen workers, hospital ships, home service, the disabled soldier, Junior Red Cross.

Records

Each of the 3742 chapters of the Red Cross was asked in 1919 to prepare a history of its war achievements. About 2000 chapters responded and their histories range in size from two pages to a book of four hundred pages. A copy of each is kept in the archives at national headquarters, a second copy is in the division files, and a third is retained by the chapter. As the local chapters of the Red Cross during the war took part in almost every movement concerned with winning the war, the chapter history is, to a large extent, a history of the community during the war period.

Other records—chapter, division, and national headquarters—consist mainly of general correspondence and case correspondence, that is, letters about a soldier or soldier's family, and regarding allotments, allowances, insurance, casualties, the welfare of the family, etc.

COUNCIL OF NATIONAL DEFENSE

Functions

THE Council of National Defense was established as an advisory body by a clause in the army appropriations act of August 29, 1916, to coördinate industries and resources for the national security and welfare, to create relations which would render possible the immediate concentration and utilization of the resources of the nation, or, more specifically, to direct investigations and make recommendations to the President and the heads of executive departments relative to such matters as the mobilization of military and naval resources, the increased production of materials essential to the support of armies and the maintenance of the civilian population, the utilization of inland waterways, the development of sea-going transportation, the coördination of military, industrial, and commercial requirements, especially with regard to transportation; to furnish data as to amounts, location, methods, and means of production; and to give information to producers and manufacturers relative to the classes and quantities of supplies needed by the military and other services of the government. The council was formally organized in October, 1916, but its permanent organization was not effected until March, 1917.

For several months following the entry of the United States into the war, during the period of transition from a peace basis to a war basis, the council endeavored to bring to bear the intelligence and effort of American industrial and professional life upon such problems as the following: (1) the development of new sources of supply of raw materials and of finished products; (2) the coördination of purchases of supplies for executive departments of the government; (3) the introduction and adoption of standardized specifications in the manufacture of munitions; (4) the coöperative organization of transportation; (5) the formulation of an aircraft program; (6) the rendering of assistance to business in meeting the demands of war without impairing the essential service of trade; (7) the organization of the coal industry for increased production and more effective distribution; (8) the direction of the activities of the several States; (9) the organization of the leaders of American labor, of representative employers, and of civic and industrial leaders for the effective enlistment of the labor forces of the country; (10) the organization of the medical, engineering, and other professions for war service; (11) the promotion of scientific research; (12) the direction of the efforts of women.

Several of the most important war agencies of a later date originated in the council during this early period, and as they became independent or separate establishments they reduced in a notable way the functions of the council itself.

During the latter part of the war the principal activities of the council were the direction of the state, county, and municipal councils of defense, the direction of the war activities of women, the study of reconstruction problems, the promotion of a more efficient use of the highways for transportation purposes, and the consideration of general policies.

With the exception of the Reconstruction Research Division the council practically ceased to function June 30, 1919. That division continued active until April 1, 1920, when it was transformed into a research staff. Although the law by which it was created was not repealed there was no appropriation for the maintenance of the council subsequent to June 30, 1921.

Organization

The members of the council were the Secretary of War, chairman, the Secretary of the Navy, the Secretary of the Interior, the Secretary of Agriculture, the Secretary of Commerce, and the Secretary of Labor. There was an Advisory Commission of seven members, each of whom was chosen for his special knowledge of some industry or public utility, his development of some natural resource, or other special qualification. The director of the council was director of the Advisory Commission. It was the duty of the council to provide for the work of the commission to the end that the commission's special knowledge might be developed by suitable investigation, research, and inquiry and made available in conference and report for the use of the council.

During the period of transition from a peace basis to a war basis both council and commission organized a number of boards, divisions, sections, and committees, which, their duties and jurisdictions at first only vaguely prescribed, were the origins of separate war agencies or parts of such agencies. Among such were the Aircraft Production Board, Commercial Economy Board, Munitions Standards Board, General Munitions Board, War Industries Board, Statistics Division, Stored Materials Division, Industrial Inventory Section, Industrial Service Section, Inland Traffic Section, Automotive Transport Committee, Coöperative Committee on Cars, Interdepartmental Committee, Committee on Coal Production, Committee on Emergency Construction, Committee on Engineering and Education, Committee on Housing, Committee on Inland Water Transportation, Committee on Raw Materials, Minerals, and Metals, Committee on Shipping, Committee on Storage Facilities, Committee on Supplies, Committee on Telegraphs and Telephones, and Committee on Transportation and Communication.

The more permanent divisions of the Council were: the State Councils Section, the Woman's Committee, the Field Division, the Committee on Labor, the Medical Section, the Highways Transport Committee, the Department of Science and Research, and the Reconstruction Research Division.

State Councils Section. A council of defense was created in every State in the Union either by appointment by the governor or by act of the legislature. In most instances this was done at the suggestion of the Council of National Defense, and the State Councils Section was created to (1) guide the growth and work of the state councils; (2) afford to each of them the benefit of the experience of the others; (3) act as the communicating agency to bring the Council of National Defense and the other federal departments and war administrations in touch with the state councils; and (4) make the services of the state councils fully available to the federal government. As the recognized agency of the national council each state council was requested to (1) create and direct local councils of defense; (2) centralize and coördinate the war work of the State; (3) inaugurate independent activities for state defense work; and (4) assist the national council, the federal departments, and the war administrations in their various programs relative to military affairs, publicity, production and conservation of food and fuel, labor, transportation, industry, financial activities, and health.

Woman's Committee. The Woman's Committee was appointed

April 21, 1917, to coördinate and centralize the organized and unorganized forces of women throughout the country. It was organized in eleven departments as follows:

(1) State Organization, to direct the organization of the women of each State into state, county, city, and town units and to promote coördination between these and the councils of defense.

(2) Registration for Service, to direct the registration of women for voluntary service so as to procure definite information as to what service the women of the country were able and willing to render.

(3) Food Production and Home Economics, to coöperate with the Department of Agriculture in efforts to increase food production, conserve food, and promote general household thrift.

(4) Food Administration, to further the program of the United States Food Administration by bringing it to the attention of as many women as possible and by educating them with regard to its provisions.

(5) Women in Industry, to interpret to the women of the country the policy of the government regarding the maintenance of standards for women in employment, chiefly in coöperation with the Women in Industry Service of the Department of Labor.

(6) Child Welfare, to labor for the enforcement of child labor laws, full schooling for all children of school age, proper recreation for children, public protection of maternity and infancy, and mother's care for elder children.

(7) Maintenance of Existing Social Service Agencies, to give stimulus and support to efforts to maintain peace-time standards of social service activities.

(8) Health and Recreation, to coöperate with the Commission on Training Camp Activities in providing for the protection of health and for facilities for recreation in camps and camp vicinities for men in military and naval service, and for young women as well.

(9) Educational Propaganda, to further the general understanding of the more important questions involved in the war by means of addresses at state, county, and community meetings, by the distribution of literature, by pageants, by parades, and through the regular school channels.

(10) Liberty Loan, to assist in the sale of Liberty bonds and war savings stamps.

(11) Home and Foreign Relief, to assist the Red Cross and other war-relief agencies.

Field Division. This division was created in August, 1918, to amalgamate the State Councils Section and the Woman's Committee into a single connecting link between the council, the other federal departments and administrations on the one hand, and the state councils and state divisions of the Woman's Committee on the other, and further to unify the war work of the men and women of each State. The division was organized in eight sections: (1) Federal Agencies Section; (2) Organization and Information Section; (3) News Section; (4) Child Conservation Section; (5) Americanization Section; (6) Speakers' Section; (7) Field Section; and (8) Office Management Section.

Committee on Labor. The business of this committee was to formulate policies with regard to labor, to promote coöperation in regard to the conservation and welfare of the workers in the industries, and to suggest means of adjusting employment problems without interruption of industry. It was organized with several subcommittees, such as (1) the National Committee on Welfare Work, with a section on housing and a section on Industrial Training for the War Emergency; (2) the Committee on Women in Industry; (3) the Committee on Maintenance of Labor Standards; (4) the Committee on Foreign-Labor Relations; (5) the National Committee on Wages and Hours, etc. Close coöperation with the United States Food Administration was effected by the assistant to the chairman of the Committee on Labor through service as head of the Division of Labor of the Food Administration.

Medical Section. This section directed efforts to arouse the interest of women in nursing as a profession, enrolled physicians for war service in the Medical Reserve Corps and the Volunteer Medical Service Corps, was instrumental in standardizing essential medical and surgical supplies, assembled the necessary data for the classification of all hospitals in the United States, and conducted a campaign for the medical care and sanitation of industrial workers.

Highways Transport Committee. The highways transport committee was appointed in November, 1917, to increase and render more effective all transportation over the highways as a means of strengthening the transportation system and relieving the railroads. Its program provided for assistance to the War Department in the operation of its motor-truck convoy service to save freight cars; assistance to the Railroad Administration to reduce terminal congestion by developing "store-door delivery"; the establishment of return-load bureaus to eliminate the running of empty vehicles; the development of rural motor express routes from agricultural areas to consuming centers or shipping points; the encouragement of the removal of snow from the main highways; and, during the reconstruction period, a study of economic phases of highway transport dealing with the short haul and problems arising out of competition on the part of various forms of transportation, due to the entrance of the motor truck into commercial life. In July, 1918, the country was divided into eleven districts, each with a regional chairman.

Department of Science and Research (National Research Council). In April, 1916, the National Academy of Sciences offered to the President of the United States its services in organizing the scientific resources of the country. The offer was accepted and the Academy created the National Research Council comprising the chiefs of the technical bureaus of the army and navy, the heads of government bureaus engaged in scientific research, and scientists in educational institutions and research foundations. By a resolution passed February 28, 1917, the Council of National Defense requested the Research Council to coöperate with it in matters pertaining to scientific research for national defense, and from that date the Research Council served as the Department of Science and Research. During the period of transition from a peace basis to a war basis the work of the Research Council was performed as advisory agent of the Signal Corps, through membership in the General Munitions Board, in coöperation with the Naval Consulting Board, and by a number of committees, such as the military committee and committees on foreign service, navigation and nautical instruments, medicine and hygiene, chemistry, engineering, physics, and agricultural research. By executive order of May 11, 1918, the National Research Council was established on a war basis with duties defined as follows:

1. In general, to stimulate research in the mathematical, physical, and biological sciences, and in the application of these sciences to engineering, agri-

culture, medicine, and the useful arts, with the object of increasing knowledge, of strengthening the national defense, and of contributing in other ways to the public welfare.

2. To survey the larger possibilities of science, to formulate comprehensive projects of research, and to develop effective means of utilizing the scientific and technical resources of the country for dealing with these projects.

3. To promote coöperation in research at home and abroad in order to secure concentration of effort, minimize duplication, and stimulate progress; but in all coöperative undertakings to give encouragement to individual initiative as fundamentally important to the advancement of science.

4. To serve as a means of bringing American and foreign investigators into active coöperation with the scientific and technical services of the War and Navy Departments and with those of the civil branches of the government.

5. To direct the attention of scientific and technical investigators to the present importance of military and industrial problems in connection with the war and to aid in the solution of these problems by organizing specific researches.

6. To gather and collate scientific and technical information at home and abroad in coöperation with governmental and other agencies and to render such information available to duly accredited persons.

For the discharge of these duties the following divisions were organized: (1) Division of General Relations, with a section on industrial research and a section to promote the coöperation of educational institutions and the research committees in the several States with the Research Council and with the other research agencies of the government; (2) Military Division; (3) Division of Engineering; (4) Division of Physics, Mathematics, and Geophysics; (5) Division of Medicine and Related Sciences; (6) Division of Chemistry and Chemical Technology; (7) Division of Geology and Geography; (8) Division of Agriculture, Botany, Forestry, Zoölogy, and Fisheries.

Reconstruction Research Division. This division, created February 3, 1919, undertook four tasks: (1) to ascertain what conditions in the United States most demanded readjustment and offered the largest opportunity for activities of reconstruction; (2) to discover what activities were planned or carried on in the States, and by the federal government, by foreign governments, and by voluntary agencies for meeting the problems of readjustment and reconstruction; (3) to collect and study the opinions of the leaders in thought, of prominent men of affairs, and of conferences and congresses for aid in the formulation of reconstruction policies; (4) to act as a clearing house of information for state councils of defense, state reconstruction boards, or other state agencies active in readjustment.

Publications

First Annual Report of the Council of National Defense, for the fiscal year ended June 30, 1917 (Washington, 1917, 130 pages). Creation and organization of the Council and Advisory Commission. Activities of boards, sections, and committees.

Second Annual Report of the Council of National Defense . . . June 30, 1918 (Washington, 1918, 275 pages). Activities of the numerous boards, sections, and committees.

Third Annual Report of the Council of National Defense . . . June 30, 1919 (Washington, 1919, 160 pages). Analysis of duties and functions, organization charts, State Councils Section, Woman's Committee, Field Division, National Research Council, Medical Section and General Medical Board, Committee on Labor, Highways Transport Committee, and Reconstruction Research Division.

Fourth Annual Report of the United States Council of National Defense . . . June 30, 1920 (Washington, 1920, 108 pages). Finances, organization, activities, and records.

Industrial America in the World War, by Grosvenor B. Clarkson (Boston and New York, 1923, 573 pages). The author was secretary, and later director, of the Council of National Defense and of the Advisory Commission, and the book contains first-hand information relative to those bodies. [Unofficial.]

A Tribute and a Look into the Future, by Grosvenor B. Clarkson (Washington, 1919, 15 pages). A statement of the work of the state and territorial councils of defense and the state and territorial divisions of the Woman's Committee throughout the war.

The Nation at War, by James A. B. Scherer (New York, 1918, 285 pages). A record of the personal experience of a field agent of the State Councils Section, Council of National Defense, and an attempt to give the reader some general idea of what the state councils did as a whole. [Unofficial.]

An Analysis of the High Cost of Living Problem (Washington, 1919, 23 pages). Prepared under direction of Grosvenor B. Clarkson by the Reconstruction Research Division. It comprises a summary of findings, statistical facts regarding the high cost of living, and a discussion of the causes of the high cost of living and of remedial measures.

Report of the Woman's Committee, Council of National Defense, Covering a Year's Activities to April 21, 1918 (Washington, 1918, 54 pages). A report on the organization of the committee and the work of each of its departments.

The Woman's Committee, United States Council of National Defense, an Interpretative Report, April 21, 1917, to February 27, 1919, by Emily Newell Blair (Washington, 1920, 150 pages). Creation of the committee; relationship to federal departments; relationship of state divisions to state councils; departments of work; special work; achievements of state divisions; where the armistice found the committee; post-armistice period.

American Women and the World War, by Ida Clyde Clarke (New York, 1918, 545 pages). The Woman's Committee; state organizations; war relief organizations; food conservation; child welfare; health and recreation; patriotic education; the Liberty loan; women in industry; the Red Cross. [Unofficial.]

Agencies for the Sale of Cooked Foods without Profit, a Survey of Their Development with Particular Reference to Their Social and Economic Effect (Washington, 1919, 75 pages). Prepared by Iva Lowther Peters under the direction of the Food Production and Home Economics Department of the Woman's Committee. A review of pre-war experiments in communal feeding, national kitchens in Great Britain, and the American situation.

The Committee on Labor published the following:

Committee on Labor: Organization of the Committee, Scope and Objects, Preliminary Activities, Outline of Plans of Subcommittees, Membership List (Washington, 1917, 20 pages).

British Labor's War Message to American Labor (Washington, 1917, 100 pages; Senate Doc. 84, 65th Cong., 1st Sess.). Addresses and discussions at a meeting of the Committee on Labor held in Washington, D. C., May 15, 1917.

How the Shortage of Skilled Mechanics is being Overcome by Training the Unskilled (Washington, 1918, 63 pages). A review of intensive training provided by each of several large manufacturing companies.

Sanitation of Rural Workmen's Areas with Special Reference to Housing (Washington, 1918, 35 pages). A report by a committee on welfare work of the Committee on Labor; housing wage earners in labor camps; permanent housing.

Code of Lighting for Factories, Mills, and Other Work Places (Washington, 1918, 26 pages). A report of the Divisional Committee on

Lighting, Section on Sanitation, Committee on Welfare Work, Committee on Labor.

Requirements and Standards upon Heating and Ventilation (Washington, 1919, 22 pages). A report of the Divisional Committee on Heating and Ventilation, Section on Sanitation, Committee on Welfare Work, Committee on Labor.

Women Workers in the Philadelphia Naval Aircraft Factory, by the subcommittee on Women in Industry (1918, 47 pages). The labor force; processes of manufacture; training women for aircraft production; wages and hours.

The Medical Section published one report:

Report of the Chairman of the Committee on Medicine and Sanitation (Washington, 1918, 46 pages). Survey of hospitals and sanatoria; plans for cantonments and camp sites; reconstruction of maimed and crippled; child welfare; industrial medicine and surgery; nursing.

The Highways Transport Committee published five bulletins (Washington, 1918-1919) :

1. *Return-loads bureaus to save waste in transportation* (6 pages).
2. *The rural motor express to conserve foodstuffs and labor and to supply rural transportation* (6 pages).
3. *Return loads to increase transport resources by avoiding waste of empty vehicle running* (4 pages).
4. *Address by . . . Secretary of Commerce at conference of regional chairmen of the Highways Transport Committee* (8 pages).
5. *Address by . . . Secretary of the Interior at conference of regional chairmen of the Highways Transport Committee* (8 pages).

This committee also published the *Organization, Administration, and Operation of the District, County, and Community Committees of the State Highways Transport Committees of the State Council of Defense* (Washington, 1918, 6 pages).

The publications of the National Research Council are rather technical for the purpose of this survey. Attention is directed only to its second *Annual Report* (Washington, 1918, 27 pages), its third *Annual Report* (Washington, 1919, 74 pages), and to three of its *Bulletins* (Washington, 1919-1920) :

1. *The National importance of scientific and industrial research* (43 pages).
2. *Research laboratories in industrial establishments of the United States of America* (86 pages).
4. *North American forest research* (145 pages).

The Reconstruction Research Division published *Readjustment and Reconstruction Information* (Washington, 1919). Part I, Readjustment and Reconstruction Activities in Foreign Countries (188 pages) ; Part II, Readjustment and Reconstruction Activities in the States (371 pages).

Among a number of circulars and small publications issued by subordinate units of the council are the following:

Community circulars, 1, 2, 3, and 4 (Washington, 1918) relative to the development of community councils.

Two circulars (Washington, 1918) relative to the activities of the Field Division.

Industrial fatigue, preliminary report of Divisional Committee, on Industrial Fatigue, Section on Sanitation, National Committee on Welfare Work, Committee on Labor (Washington, 1918, 13 pages).

Manufacture and loading of high explosives, a report of Divisional Committee on Industrial Diseases, Poisons and Explosives, Section on Sanitation, Committee on Welfare Work, Committee on Labor (Washington, 1918, 19 pages).

Suggestions for the utilization of . . . proposed uniform highway traffic regulations and directions, submitted by the Highways Transport Committee (Washington, 1919, 4 pages).

MIMEOGRAPHED MATERIAL

The Library of Congress has a mimeographed copy of each of the following:

Directory of Auxiliary War Organizations, prepared by the Division of Statistics (November 1, 1917, 133 pages). Organization, functions, personnel, and other data relative to each auxiliary war agency that had been established when it was compiled.

A Report from the Director of the Council of National Defense and of its Advisory Commission to the Chairman of the Council (May 28, 1917, 48 pages). A statement of the organization and accomplishments of the council, commission, boards, sections, and committees.

Report on Organization and Activities of State Councils of Defense, by the State Councils Section (June 18, 1917, 49 pages). Letters and bulletins; state organization; committees; local organization; finances; coördination of clubs and societies; military establishment; relief; home defense; aliens; transportation; industrial activities; engineering activities; labor; supply and conservation of food.

Reconstruction Information (January 23, 1919, 99 pages). Extracts and digests of articles in official and private periodicals concerning readjustment and reconstruction activities in foreign countries.

Daily Digest of Reconstruction News (December 12, 1918, to February 17, 1921, 13 volumes). A daily chronicle in digest form of executive proclamations and orders, legislative enactments, departmental statements, reports and other material emanating from federal bureaus and offices, together with a résumé of news items bearing upon scientific, economic, and industrial problems in the United States and foreign countries.

Records

The Council of National Defense ceased to function June 30, 1921, and on the following day its records together with those of the War Industries Board and of the Committee on Public Information were transferred to the office of the Assistant Secretary of War in conformity with an executive order of April 21, 1921. Subsequently those of the Highways Transport Committee were transferred to the Bureau of Public Roads, Department of Agriculture, pursuant to the provisions of section 3 of the post roads act of November 9, 1921.

Council and Advisory Commission. The minutes of the meetings of the council and of the Advisory Commission, December 6, 1916, to February 21, 1921 (4 volumes), constitute an important body of records, especially for the early period of the war. Here, too, are records, indexed by agencies and by topics, of the activities of federal agencies, and of private organizations, and records containing information gathered by private organizations.

State Councils Section. Information upon which the decisions of this section were based was furnished principally by the state councils, but was also obtained from printed reports, magazines, and clippings. All this material is arranged in duplicate files, by States and by subjects. Particularly important records are:

(1) Bulletins, general letters, weekly information circulars, and circulars on general topics, issued by the section, many of them being requests from federal departments, or special war bureaus for certain activities to be undertaken by the state councils.

(2) Reports prepared by the section covering the responses of state councils to particular queries or proposals.

(3) Monthly questionnaires.

(4) Weekly memoranda prepared for the use of the section, reviewing the activities of the States.

(5) Minutes and reports of state council meetings.

(6) Minutes of the first and second state council conference.

(7) Annual and final reports by state councils.

Woman's Committee. The records of this committee comprise general correspondence with the state divisions, circulars issued by the committee, bimonthly reports of the state divisions, and weekly memoranda prepared for the use of the committee from information received concerning the state divisions.

Committee on Labor. The minutes of the meetings of this committee are preserved in one bound volume. Other records comprise the general correspondence of the committee and its subcommittees; reports of subcommittees; data relative to compensation, housing, and training for war emergency; and news clippings relative to labor conditions.

Medical Section. Such records of this section as are pertinent to this survey consist of correspondence filed under the following subjects; state activities, hospital matters, nursing, hygiene and sanitation, child welfare, Red Cross, and standardization.

Highways Transport Committee. The records of this committee consist almost wholly of its correspondence with regional chiefs, state committees, chambers of commerce, good-roads organizations, manufacturers, motor industries, and motor truck operators.

Reconstruction Research Division. There are records in this division under each of the following subjects:

Administrative reorganization

Aliens in public service

Americanization

Assistance for families of service men

Assistance for service men

"Back-to-School" drive

Bar examinations for service men

Bonuses for service men

Boys' Working Reserve

Building activity

Business re-adjustment

"Buy Now" campaign

Centralization of power in the Executive

Clearing house for social needs

Chain of wayside inns on highways

Coal at reduced prices

Commission on Public Welfare

Committee on Public Safety

Committee on Readjustment

Community councils

Community houses

Community organization

Community welfare

Compensation to state employees

Coöperation for price reduction

Coöperative distribution

Cotton acreage

Demobilization committees
Demobilization of service men
Development plans
Dismissal of women war workers
Education of returned service men
Employment
English language at public meetings
English language in schools
Farm and Industrial Council
Food production
Food control
Food situation
Foreign languages in schools
Foreign trade
High cost of living
Highways
Home for disabled service men
Home building
Home bureaus
Home gardens
Housing accommodations
Industrial-economic survey
Information service for returned
service men
Labor participation in business man-
agement
Labor standards for women
Land reclamation
Loans to service men
Marketing products
Minimum wage law
Moratorium for service men
Motor transport service
Organization for sheep production
Payments to war work organizations
Pensions for service men
Port facilities
Preference to service men in land en-
tries
Preference to returned service men in
public employment
Price fixing
Probation officers to coöperate in
post-war problems
Profiteering, public works

Reconstruction Association
Reconstruction Board
Reconstruction campaign
Reconstruction Commission
Reconstruction Committee
Reconstruction Conference
Reconstruction Congress
Reconstruction Convention
Reconstruction expenditures
Reconstruction legislation
Reconstruction measures
Reconstruction plans
Reconstruction policies
Reconstruction problems
Reconstruction progress
Reconstruction recommendations
Rehabilitation of disabled service
men
Reinstatement of returned service
men in retirement system
Revolutionary organizations
Revolutionary propaganda
Rights and privileges of service men
and their families
Roadside markets
Rural planning
School gardens
Shipbuilding
Shipping lines
State ownership of business enter-
prises
State supervision of transportation
Street improvement
Stimulation of food production
Tax exemption for service men and
for their widows
Trade with Russia and Siberia
Use of government harbor improve-
ments for commerce
Utilization of war materials
Veterans' Welfare Commission
Vocational education
Vocational reëducation for disabled
service men
Wage scales and hours of labor

War Veterans' Association

Wasteful services

Water resources

Welfare Commission

Welfare councils

Welfare of returned service men

Woman's Committee

Workingmen's and Soldiers' Council

Committee on Coal Production. The records of the activities of this committee, which were curtailed by the establishment of the United States Fuel Administration and terminated February 25, 1918, comprise minutes of its meetings, correspondence with coal-producing companies and railroads with regard to the movement of coal from the mines, and correspondence with the United States Geological Survey and other coöperating agencies.

Committee on Transportation and Communication. This committee was dissolved December 26, 1917, by the creation of the United States Railroad Administration. Its records include correspondence of the committee and its subcommittees, and particularly requests for priority allotments of cars.

Committee on Supplies. This committee was transferred to the Quartermaster Department of the Army in January, 1918. A record of its activities prior to that date is contained in correspondence with the Quartermaster Department and with firms submitting bids on equipment and subsistence. Records of contracts are listed by commodities.

WAR INDUSTRIES BOARD

Evolution and Dissolution

THE War Industries Board had its genesis in the Committee on Industrial Preparedness of the Naval Consulting Board which in 1916 listed, described, and classified some 27,000 of the more important industrial establishments of the country. In the meantime potential provision for industrial mobilization was made in section 2 of the army appropriation act of March 29, 1916, which established the Council of National Defense. In January, 1917, a member of the advisory commission of this council was authorized to continue his consultations with the leaders in the steel and metal industries for the purpose of determining how their resources could be got together so as to be operated as a unit. A month later, at a joint meeting of the council and advisory commission, a resolution was passed which provided for the calling of a series of conferences with the leading men in each industry fundamentally necessary to the defense of industry in the event of war, at which conferences these men should be asked to organize themselves so as to deal with the council through one man or through a committee of not more than three men. Pursuant to this resolution each member of the advisory commission was made chairman of a committee, the other members of which, designated by the chairman, were from either governmental or civil life, or both. Three of these committees, subsequently merged in whole or in part into the War Industries Board, were the Committee on Raw Materials, Minerals, and Metals, the Committee on Munitions, Manufacturing, and Industrial Relations, and the Committee on Supplies. By a resolution adopted March 31, 1917, the council created the General Munitions Board, composed of representatives of the army, navy, and advisory commission, to coördinate the buying for the several departments, to assist in the acquirement of raw materials and manufacturing facilities, and to make recommendations as to precedence of orders. The new board appointed committees the functions of which interfered with the functions of the advisory commission. Reorganization became imperative, and after considering the matter for six weeks the council, on July 8, 1917, voted to establish the War Industries Board.

The duties of the new board were defined in general terms as follows:

The board will act as a clearing house for the war-industry needs of the government, determine the most effective ways of meeting them, and the best means and methods of increasing production, including the creation or extension of industries demanded by the emergency, the sequence and relative urgency of the needs of the different government services, and consider price factors and, in the first instance, the industrial and labor aspects of problems involved and the general questions affecting the purchase of commodities.

The full exercise of these functions meant that the War Industries Board should be as supreme in industry as the army and navy were in war, but, like the council by which it was created, it was as yet only an advisory body. Its weakness from this position developed until, in the face of a demand for a reconstruction of the central war control, the President, by a letter of March 4 and an executive order of May 28, 1918, made it independent of the council and endowed it with ample executive authority emanating from his powers as commander-in-chief of the army and navy.

After the signing of the armistice the War Industries Board rapidly removed its restrictions on industry. The chairman tendered his resignation the 29th of November, and an executive order of December 31, 1918, directed that the board should dissolve January 1, 1919, save and excepting for the winding up of its affairs and the inventorying of its records and effects by a liquidating officer; that the Price Fixing Committee should continue to function until the expiration of all periods for the operation of fixed prices; that the Wool Division should be transferred to the Bureau of Markets, Department of Agriculture, for the settlement of claims; and that the Division of Planning and Statistics should be transferred to the War Trade Board. The liquidating officer completed his work July 22, 1919, and on that day the records in his custody were, by executive order, turned over to the Council of National Defense.

Functions

The War Industries Board, when established as a separate administrative agency, was charged with the task of procuring an adequate flow of materials for the War Department, the Navy Department, the Emergency Fleet Corporation, and the Railroad Administration; with the task of providing for the military needs of the allies; with the task of providing commodities required by neutrals in exchange for materials essential to the United States; and, in alliance with the Food, Fuel, and Labor Administrations, with the task of providing for the country's civilian needs. These tasks were performed mainly by stimulating and expanding the production of those materials essential to the war program and by depressing and curtailing the production of those things not of a necessary nature. Commodities of which there was or was likely to be a deficit were allocated, their increased production was encouraged by price-fixing, and their orderly flow into channels most conducive to the purposes of the war was regulated by priority rulings. The demands of the government, of the allies, and of the public were analyzed, measured, and often restrained. The extent to which and the manner in which the supplies could meet the requirements were ascertained so far as possible in order to determine what action should be taken.

In the board's charter, contained in the President's letter of March 4, 1918, its functions are stated as follows:

(1) The creation of new facilities and the disclosing, if necessary, the opening up of new or additional sources of supply;

(2) The conversion of existing facilities, where necessary, to new uses;

(3) The studious conservation of resources and facilities by scientific, commercial, and industrial economies;

(4) Advice to the several purchasing agencies of the government with regard to the price to be paid;

(5) The determination, wherever necessary, of priorities of production and of delivery and of the proportion of any given article to be made immediately accessible to the several purchasing agencies when the supply of that article is insufficient, either temporarily or permanently;

(6) The making of purchases for the allies.

Organization

Subsequent to its reorganization in March, 1918, the board was composed of a chairman, vice-chairman, the priorities commissioner, chairman of the price-fixing committee, the commissioner of finished products, a representative of the army, a representative of the navy, chairman of the labor division, the steel administrator, a technical adviser, a general counsel, and a secretary. The functional divisions of the board were the Requirements Division, Conservation Division,

Labor Division, Priorities Division, Price Fixing Committee, and the Allied Purchasing Commission.

Chairman. The duties of the chairman as prescribed in the President's letter of March 4, 1918, were as follows:

(1) To act for the joint and several benefit of all the supply departments of the government.

(2) To let alone what is being successfully done and interfere as little as possible with the present normal processes of purchase and delivery in the several departments.

(3) To guide and assist wherever the need for guidance or assistance may be revealed; for example, in the allocation of contracts, in obtaining access to materials in any way preëmpted, or in the disclosure of sources of supply.

(4) To determine what is to be done when there is any competitive or other conflict of interest between departments in the matter of supplies; for example, when there is not a sufficient immediate supply for all and there must be a decision as to the priority of need or delivery, or when there is competition for the same source of manufacture or supply, or when contracts have not been placed in such a way as to get advantage of the full productive capacity of the country.

(5) To see that contracts and deliveries are followed up where such assistance as is indicated under (3) and (4) above has proved to be necessary.

(6) To anticipate the prospective needs of the several supply departments of the government and their feasible adjustment to the industry of the country as far in advance as possible, in order that as definite an outlook and opportunity for planning as possible may be afforded the business men of the country.

The chairman was vested with the ultimate decision of all questions except the determination of prices, the other members of the board acting in a coöperative and advisory capacity. In the determination of prices he was governed by the advice of the price fixing committee.

Requirements Division. The vice chairman of the board was chairman of this division. The other members were: the chairman and the technical adviser of the board, the priorities commissioner, the commissioner of finished products, the chairman of the conservation division, the director of the chemicals division, the director of the steel division, the chief of the non-ferrous metals section, two representatives each of the army and the navy, and one representative each of the allies, the Department of Commerce, the Emergency Fleet Corporation, the Railroad Administration, the Food

Administration, the Fuel Administration, the Capital Issues Committee, the Marine Corps, and the Red Cross.

The division was charged with the duty of effecting such a distribution of those materials and supplies of which the production was less than the demand that they might be utilized, so far as practicable, by those industries that were most essential to the war; with the development of new sources of production; and, wherever feasible, with the conversion of existing facilities to more essential uses.

Most of the work was done through commodity sections established for the various raw materials or finished products that required investigation or allocation. Each of these commodity sections, with a chief and representatives of the army, navy, Emergency Fleet Corporation, Railroad Administration, and other governmental agencies, studied the particular commodity intrusted to its care and determined whether allocation was necessary, and if so, how the material should be allotted among the several departments of the government and the extent to which manufacturers and others, whether making war supplies or not, should be supplied. Each commodity chief was the government agent for dealing with the industry or industries for which his section was responsible, and centered in him was the task of gathering, chiefly by means of questionnaires, information about such industries as were in the province of his section.

Relative to resources and industrial conversions the division gathered information covering: (1) existing facilities for meeting direct and indirect war needs, in both raw materials and finished products; (2) the extent to which those facilities were occupied with unfilled orders and the extent to which they could take on additional orders; (3) if overloaded, the feasibility and extent of expansion necessary to relieve such overloading, or in the alternative the extent of transferring the overload to other facilities; (4) existing facilities not employed on war work, but capable of undertaking such work; (5) facilities whose production was curtailed because of war conditions and the extent to which they were susceptible of conversion for the production of war needs; the existence of available labor, of new sources of supply of raw materials, of unused power facilities, of available transportation facilities, etc., which might be available to relieve congestion or the overloading of facilities in other districts. For procuring this information the country was divided into twenty regions, in each of which an organization effected by chambers of commerce and other business men's organizations familiar with local conditions coöperated with a regional adviser, appointed by the War Industries Board, in making a thoroughgoing survey of industrial resources.

A special survey of power plants was made to determine the expediency of uniting through transmission lines, groups of independent plants in congested districts in order to secure the benefit of diversity and increase the potential power of the groups. Close contact was maintained with the War Finance Corporation in matters pertaining to the necessity or desirability for the expansion of power plants and the discouragement or prevention of new construction which would not contribute directly or indirectly to the winning of the war. A survey of existing and potential facilities to supply the direct and indirect war requirements of the country was pending when the armistice was signed.

Conservation Division. This division took over the conservation work of the Commercial Economy Board of the Council of National Defense. Its functions were performed in part by the chairman of the division and nine associates and in part by the chiefs of the commodity sections. The conservation programs both of the division and of the commodity sections were for the purpose of determining in each industry the uses to which labor, materials, equipment, and capital were put which could be dispensed with so that they could be released for more essential uses. To this end activities were particularly directed to the accomplishment of: (1) the reduction of the number of styles, varieties, sizes, and colors of manufactured commodities and especially the elimination of styles and varieties of articles which violated the principle of economy; (2) the elimination of certain adornments; (3) the substitution of articles and materials which were plentiful for those which were scarce and difficult to produce; (4) the reduction of the consumption of commodities for unimportant purposes; (5) the reduction of the waste of materials in manufacturing processes; (6) an economy in the use of samples for selling purposes; (7) an economy in packing and delivery.

Labor Division. The chairman of this division represented the

War Industries Board on the War Labor Policies Board, was a member of the committee of the latter board on the relation of military to industrial man power, was a member of the Price Fixing Committee of the War Industries Board, was chairman of the United States War Industries Badge Board, and a member of the pennant-award committee of the Emergency Fleet Corporation. He was constantly in touch with the officers of the American Federation of Labor and the general officers and representatives of the various unions whose members were employed in war industries. Within his division of the War Industries Board he organized the War Prison Labor and National Waste Reclamation Section with a membership as follows: the chairman of the executive committee of the National Committee on Prisons and Labor; the chief of the Office of Farm Management, Department of Agriculture; a representative of the Reclamation Division, United States Army; the Commissioner of Immigration, Department of Labor; the secretary of the union label trades department, American Federation of Labor; the assistant director of research, Federal Board for Vocational Education; the Assistant Secretary, Department of Commerce; a representative of the navy; and a representative of the adjutant general's office. The section operated along the following lines: (1) securing coöperation of government and organizations in reclamation of man power and waste material; (2) utilization of the labor of prisoners; (3) reeducation by vocational training of crippled soldiers and sailors, together with those injured in industry to enable them to become self-sustaining; (4) organization and direction of a national waste reclamation system with the county as a unit; (5) standardization of industries and occupations in penal institutions for producing materials; (6) national road work system for prisoners; (7) development of war prisoners' division in the army; (8) induction into industry and agriculture of discharged or paroled prisoners; (9) army and navy waste reclamation; (10) development of camp gardens.

Priorities Division. The Priorities Division was administered by a priorities commissioner assisted by a Priorities Board, a Priorities Committee, a Labor Section, and a Non-war Construction Section. The priorities commissioner was a member of the War Industries Board, a member of its Requirements Division, and chairman both of the Priorities Board and the Priorities Committee. The other members of the Priorities Board were the chairman of the War Industries Board and representatives of the army, navy, Shipping Board, Railroad Administration, Food Administration, Fuel Administration, War Trade Board, War Labor Policies Board, and Allied Purchasing Commission. The other members of the Priorities Committee were representatives of the army, navy, Shipping Board, Railroad Administration, engineering, and business.

The province of the Priorities Division was wholly within those industries in which the production or supply was short of the demand. Within that province it determined the proportions of any given article which were to be made accessible to the various and varying demands for it as well as the sequence in which materials should be manufactured and orders filled. The priorities commissioner was charged with the final decision in all priority matters, this authority having been delegated to him by the chairman of the War Industries Board. The Priorities Board formulated general plans for the coördination of the military and industrial programs. It defined those activities that were to be accorded preferential treatment because of their war or civilian importance, and certified its classifications to the Fuel Administration, the Railroad Administration, the Employment Service, and the industrial advisers to district draft boards for use and guidance in distributing fuel, furnishing transportation and labor, and passing on cases of industrial and occupational deferment. The Priorities Committee determined priorities in production, and to this end each member specialized in one or more of the commodities or purposes for which priorities in production were granted. The Labor Section coöperated with the Labor Division of the War Industries Board, the United States Employment Service, the War Labor Policies Board, and other governmental agencies dealing with labor problems, in rendering assistance in the administration of priorities in labor. The Non-war Construction Section had charge of a program, inaugurated as a war measure, to effect the deferment of all building construction that was not needed for war purposes or that was not, for any other purpose, clearly in the public interest.

Price Fixing Committee. The chairman of the Price Fixing Committee was a member of the War Industries Board. The other members were the chairman of the War Industries Board, the chairman of the Labor Division, the chairman of the Federal Trade Commission, the chairman of the Tariff Commission, the Federal Fuel Administrator, one representative each of the army and the navy, and an ex-governor of Virginia.

Particular prices were fixed during the war for aluminum, cement, copper, cotton fabrics, cotton linters, hides, leather, hemp, lumber, platinum, rags, sand, gravel, crushed stone, steel, wool, and zinc. Usually the prices (maximum prices) were fixed by agreement after a study of costs by the Federal Trade Commission. The prices were fixed both for the government and the public when government purchases were so large as to disturb market conditions, but if there was no promise of market disturbance the prices, as fixed, were only the maximum prices which the government should pay.

Allied Purchasing Commission. Through the Secretary of the Treasury, representing the United States, arrangements were made with the governments of Great Britain, France, Italy, Belgium, Russia, and Serbia by which all purchases made by these governments in the United States should be handled through or with the consent of a commission to be known as the Allied Purchasing Commission. As originally constituted, August 27, 1917, the members of the commission were members of the War Industries Board, and by the President's letter of March 4, 1918, reorganizing the board, the commission was made a component part of it, with the chairman of the board chairman of the commission.

Fifty-seven commodity sections supplied the functional divisions with indispensable statistical and expert information, were an important medium of communication with the industries and purchasing agencies, and directed the enforcement of the board's regulations. Contact with the industries was further facilitated by more than two hundred and fifty war service committees under the supervision of the United States Chamber of Commerce. Each committee represented an industry or branch of an industry and when occasion required the various units composing a particular industry joined in appointing some one committee to act as spokesman in negotiating with the government.

Division of Planning and Statistics. This division, operating in six sections, served chiefly as a central statistical bureau. (1) The Section on Price Statistics, working in close coöperation with the Price Fixing Committee, prepared a number of special reports. The work of the section was expanded immediately after the armistice and in 1919 its studies were published in a series of fifty-seven bulletins under the general title, *History of Prices during the War*. (2) The War Contracts Section collected some information on war contracts and deliveries and issued some bulletins based on partial returns. (3) The Section on War Industries Abroad searched foreign publications and foreign official documents for such information as would be of interest to the board. (4) The Editorial Section issued a series of bulletins for the information of war agencies relative to the status of the supply program and changes in the industrial conditions affecting it. (5) The Commodity Statistics Section assisted the commodity sections in tabulating and charting data. In some instances it organized and installed a complete statistical service for a commodity section. In other instances it coöperated in establishing joint statistical offices representing commodity sections of the board and other war agencies. (6) The Questionnaire Section was charged with the task of affording relief to manufacturers from the growing burden of answering questionnaires. An order of August 12, 1918, required that all questionnaires sent out by any branch of the board should first be submitted to the section. A special service of the division was the preparation for the President of a conspectus of progress in the accomplishment of the supply program, with weekly supplements.

Publications

American Industry in the War, a Report of the War Industries Board, by Bernard M. Baruch, Chairman (Washington, 1921, 421 pages). An official record of the activities of the board with explanations of the principles and policies by which it functioned, together with a discussion of the place occupied in the war by each of the leading industries. The numerous appendices contain lists of the war service committees and of their personnel, and much documentary and statistical material.

Industrial America in the World War, by Grosvenor B. Clarkson (Boston and New York, 1923, 573 pages). The author was appointed secretary of the Council of National Defense in March, 1917, and subsequently became the director of that body. His volume is a review of the evolution, organization, and operation of the board and its divisions. [Unofficial.]

The United States War Industries Board, an Outline of the Board's Origin, Functions, and Organization (Washington, 1918, 52 pages). Contains an organization chart.

Members of the War Industries Board Organization (Washington, 1919, 39 pages). Part I lists the members alphabetically, with position in the board and former business of each stated opposite his name. Part II lists the members by States and cities.

Directory of the War Industries Board (Washington, 1918, 46 pages). Part I, the board and its main divisions; part II, commodity and miscellaneous sections; part III, alphabetical personnel section; part IV, alphabetical commodity and materials sections; part V, clearance schedule.

Rules and Regulations of the Priorities Division, September 21, 1917, to December 20, 1918, are contained in a series of sixty circulars, and these are preserved in a bound volume in the Library of Congress.

Schedule of Maximum Prices, Hides, and Skins (Washington, 1918, 23 and 28 pages) is the title of two pamphlets issued by the Hide, Leather, and Tanning Materials Section. The one contains the schedule of prices for August, September, and October, 1918; the other, the schedule for November and December, 1918, and January, 1919.

The fifty-seven price bulletins prepared by, or in coöperation with, the Division of Planning and Statistics and published under the general title of *History of Prices during the War* are as follows:

1. *Summary,* by Wesley C. Mitchell (96 pages).
2. *International Price Comparisons,* by Wesley C. Mitchell, Margaret L. Goldsmith, and Florence K. Middaugh (395 pages).
3. *Government Control over Prices,* by Paul Willard Garrett, Isador Lubin, and Stella Stewart (834 pages). Part I, the problems that led the government into price control; part II, the administration of price controls during the war: the Food Administration, the Fuel Administration, the War Industries Board, the War Trade Board, the War Department, the Navy Department, the Department of Agriculture, the Federal Trade Commission, and the basis for determining a fixed price.
4. *Prices of Foods,* by Murray S. Wildman (19 pages).
5. *Prices of Clothing,* by John M. Curran (20 pages).
6. *Prices of Building Materials,* by Homer Hoyt (19 pages).
7. *Prices of Chemicals,* by F. E. Breithut (31 pages).

8. *Prices of Feed and Forage,* by Lloyd W. Maxwell (21 pages).

9. *Prices of Wheat and Wheat Products,* by Paul E. Peltason (22 pages).

10. *Prices of Corn and Corn Products,* by Harry F. Bruning (19 pages).

11. *Prices of Oats, Rice, Buckwheat, and their Products,* by Harley R. Willard (23 pages).

12. *Prices of Barley, Hops, Rye, and their Products,* by Lloyd W. Maxwell (17 pages).

13. *Prices of Sugar and Related Products,* by Frank F. Anderson (23 pages).

14. *Prices of Vegetables and Truck,* by Murray S. Wildman (18 pages).

15. *Prices of Edible Vegetable Oils.* Anonymous (16 pages).

16. *Prices of Fruits, Nuts, and Wine.* Anonymous (15 pages).

17. *Prices of Spices and Condiments,* by Debora E. Wood (12 pages).

18. *Prices of Tea, Coffee, and Cocoa,* by Lloyd L. Shaulis (18 pages).

19. *Prices of Tobacco and Tobacco Products,* by Lloyd L. Shaulis (20 pages).

20. *Prices of Live Stock, Meats, and Fats,* by William A. Barber (44 pages).

21. *Prices of Poultry and Dairy Products,* by William A. Barber (35 pages).

22. *Prices of Fish and Oysters,* by Irma H. Hotchkiss (20 pages).

23. *Prices of Cotton and Cotton Products,* by James Harvey Rogers, Grace M. Fairchild, and Florence A. Dickinson (57 pages).

24. *Prices of Wool and Wool Products,* by Katharine Snodgrass (53 pages).

25. *Prices of Silk and Silk Products,* by Oscar B. Ryder (49 pages).

26. *Prices of Hides and Skins and their Products,* by A. E. James and L. B. Kagan (49 pages).

27. *Prices of Hatter's Fur and Fur Felt Hats,* by J. Linden Heacock (13 pages).

28. *Prices of Hair, Bristles, and Feathers,* by J. Linden Heacock (19 pages).

29. *Prices of Buttons,* by J. M. Curran (22 pages).

30. *Prices of Rubber and Rubber Products,* by Isador Lubin (35 pages).

31. *Prices of Paper,* by W. A. Averill (25 pages).

32. *Prices of Fibers and Fiber Products,* by Jane Coates (29 pages).

33. *Prices of Iron, Steel, and their Products,* by Walter W. Stewart (46 pages).

34. *Prices of Ferroalloys, Non-ferrous and Rare Metals,* by H. R. Aldrich and Jacob Schmuckler (92 pages).

35. *Prices of Coal and Coke,* by C. E. Lesher (115 pages).

36. *Prices of Petroleum and its Products,* by Joseph E. Pogue and Isador Lubin (55 pages).

37. *Prices of Matches,* by Mary L. Danforth (9 pages).

38. *Prices of Clay Products,* by Homer Hoyt (20 pages).

39. *Prices of Sand and Gravel,* by W. J. Kotsrean (8 pages).
40. *Prices of Quarry Products,* by Homer Hoyt (15 pages).
41. *Prices of Cement,* by Homer Hoyt (11 pages).
42. *Prices of Glass,* by Viva B. Boothe (11 pages).
43. *Prices of Lumber,* by R. C. Bryant (112 pages).
44. *Prices of Paints and Varnishes,* by Arthur Minnick (25 pages).
45. *Prices of Mineral Acids,* by H. L. Lewenberg (18 pages).
46. *Prices of Heavy Chemicals,* by H. L. Lewenberg (20 pages).
47. *Prices of Miscellaneous Inorganic Chemicals,* by W. B. Meldrum (24 pages).
48. *Prices of Fertilizers,* by H. L. Trumbull (21 pages).
49. *Prices of Soaps and Glycerin,* by H. L. Trumbull (20 pages).
50. *Prices of Essential Oils, Flavoring and Perfumery Materials,* by W. B. Meldrum (21 pages).
51. *Prices of Wood Distillation Products and Naval Stores,* by P. W. Carleton (16 pages).
52. *Prices of Natural Dyestuffs and Tanning Chemicals,* by P. W. Carleton (15 pages).
53. *Prices of Coal-Tar Crudes, Intermediates, and Dyes,* by Webster N. Jones and F. W. Cassebeer (32 pages).
54. *Prices of Drugs and Pharmaceuticals,* by W. Lee Lewis and F. W. Cassebeer (24 pages).
55. *Prices of Proprietary Preparations,* by W. Lee Lewis and F. W. Cassebeer (13 pages).
56. *Prices of Explosives,* by C. L. Fry (26 pages).
57. *Prices of Miscellaneous Organic Chemicals,* by Arthur Minnik (18 pages).

MIMEOGRAPHED MATERIAL

The Library of Congress has assembled a small body of mimeographed material which embraces the following.

Weekly Review. The nine numbers of this paper, issued each Tuesday from September 28 to November 23, 1918, by the secretary's office, constitute a volume of 97 pages. Each number contained an announcement of policies and a summary of the more important activities of the board, its divisions, and sections. The paper was primarily for confidential use within the offices of the board organization and for other departments of the government whose work brought them in contact with the board.

Advice Sheet. The advice sheet was devoted to information and instructions. It was issued, as occasion required, by the Requirements Division to the chiefs of the commodity sections. Numbers 1 to 45, only one of more than one page, were issued from May 24 to November 23, 1918.

Bulletins to Regional Advisors. These bulletins contained information relative to policies as well as requirements and occasional suggestions for the direction of industries. They were issued, numbers 1 to 39, by the Resources and Conversion Section of the Requirements Division from September 4 to November 16, 1918.

Industrial Conversions. Two reports, one dated July 6, 1918, and the other October 24, 1918, contain lists of industrial conversions from normal business to war work. Column 1 contains names and addresses, in column 2 the normal business of each is stated, and in column 3 the war-time conversion.

Office Review. Thirty-one numbers of this review, dated from February 28 to November 11, 1918, and making a volume of 214 pages, were issued through the office of the Executive Secretary, Priorities Division, to disseminate information that would be of assistance in administering priorities, to acquaint members of the board organization with the decisions reached in order to insure uniformity of action, to preserve for reference a concise, accurate record of the decisions and activities of the division, and to summarize and review the several *Office Bulletins.*

Office Bulletins. These bulletins constitute a body of rules and regulations of the Priorities Committee. Twenty-six of them were issued from December 27, 1917, to May 3, 1918.

Price-Fixing Bulletins. A series of thirteen bulletins, by the Price Section of the Bureau of Planning and Statistics, designed to keep interested persons informed concerning the price-fixing actions of the government. Each bulletin contains a condensed tabular statement and the detailed schedules of prices adopted by the various price-fixing agencies.

1. Non-ferrous Metals (August, 1918, 22 pages).
2. Rubber (August, 1918, 8 pages).
3. Chemicals and Explosives (September, 1918, 23 pages).
4. Rags (September, 1918, 20 pages).
5. Lumber and Building Materials (September, 1918, 54 pages).
6. Manganese (September, 1918, 6 pages).
7. Platinum Metals (October, 1918, 5 pages).
8. Textiles and Fibers (October, 1918, 49 pages).
9. Paper (October, 1918, 10 pages).
10. Iron and Steel (November, 1918, 8 pages).
11. Fuels (November, 1918, 35 pages).
12. Hides, Skins, Leather, and Tanning Extracts (December, 1918, 51 pages).
13. Food (December, 1918, 21 pages).

Wholesale Price Bulletins. These constitute another series of bulletins by the Price Section of the Bureau of Planning and Statistics. They contain wholesale market quotations by months, quarters, and years, 1913-1918, upon groups of commodities within which there was price regulation, and show the relation of war prices to pre-war prices.

1. Non-ferrous Metals (August, 1918, 23 pages).
2. Rubber (August, 1918, 12 pages).
3. Chemicals (September, 1918, 37 pages).
4. Rags (September, 1918, 20 pages).
5. Iron and Steel (November, 1918, 55 pages).

6. Building Materials (other than lumber) (November, 1918, 27 pages).
7. Cordage Fibers (November, 1918, 20 pages).
8. Fertilizer (November, 1918, 33 pages).
9. Wool and Woolen Goods (December, 1918, 44 pages).
10. Fluctuations of Controlled and Uncontrolled Prices (December, 1918, 54 pages).

Boots and Shoes (December, 1918), by the Price Section, is a bulletin of somewhat different content. Part I reviews the price regulations and other government control of boots and shoes in the United States during the war. Part II reviews the war-time control of the industry in Great Britain, France, Italy, Switzerland, Holland, Germany, and Austria Hungary.

A Comparison of Prices during the Civil War and Present War (November, 1918), by the same section, makes comparisons by single commodities and commodity groups, briefly discusses the economic factors affecting prices during the two wars, and summarizes what the comparison shows.

Records[1]

Each of the eighty-odd units of the War Industries Board kept its files in its own way, and there was no central file for the board organization as a whole. Some papers were filed alphabetically, others were filed numerically. Some units kept a subject file; others kept a combination of alphabetic, numerical, and subject files. In the alphabetic files sometimes the writer and sometimes the addressee supplied the file key. In the performance of their functions there was frequently a complicated inter-relation between finished products and raw materials, commodity units and functional units, and as a consequence of this inter-relation there was reference of correspondence from one unit to another until the papers constituting contributory evidence in a particular case were scattered through the files of many units. However satisfactorily the records may have operated while under the jurisdiction of the individual units, they became an incoherent mass of approximately 3,000,000 pieces when those units ceased functioning and the file operators had departed.

Prior to the dissolution of the War Industries Board the records of the Aircraft Production Board, of the Wood Chemicals Section,

---

[1] For a brief survey of the records of the War Industries Board see the fourth *Annual Report of the United States Council of National Defense* (Washington, 1920, pp. 74-88). Material for the survey which follows in this volume, as comprehensive as conditions would permit, was compiled, through the courtesy of officers of the War Department, by Miss Adelaide R. Hasse, who from 1919 to 1923 had charge of the organization of the records.

and of the Supplies Committee were transferred to different services of the War Department. Those of the Wool Division were transferred to the Bureau of Markets, Department of Agriculture, by the executive order of December 31, 1918, dissolving the board. In conformity with the same order practically all other extant records of the board were assembled in the custody of the liquidating officer, where they remained until July 22, 1918, when, by executive order, the President directed, "that all records and files of the War Industries Board now in the custody of the liquidating officer of the board be turned over to the Council of National Defense to be catalogued so that a permanent record can be made, particularly with regard to their bearing on Council of National Defense matters, and that a distribution of these records shall then be made to the permanent departments most directly interested in them." The Council of National Defense ceased to function June 30, 1921, and the following day the records of the board were placed in the custody of the Assistant Secretary of War in accordance with an executive order of April 21, 1921.

The problem of "cataloguing" or organizing the files "so that a permanent record can be made" involved mainly the effecting of such coördination that all the correspondence, reports, etc., concerning a given matter might be located by means of segregation and a card index.

General Administrative File

The administrative file, by far the most important of the board's files, contains a large body of records particularly pertinent to this survey. It includes minutes of meetings, rulings, questionnaires, form communications, bulletins, final reports, weekly and monthly reports, special reports, industrial surveys, reconstruction data, office memoranda, circulars, and other administrative matter issuing from divisions, sections, and committees.

Minutes of Meetings. The meetings for which minutes were kept number nearly 2000 and cover the period from February 4, 1917, to February 27, 1919. They were of two kinds: (1) unit meetings and (2) meetings with representatives of some trade or industry. The minutes of the General Munitions Board (April 4 to August 9, 1917) are in two volumes; those of the War Industries Board (August 1, 1917, to January 23, 1919) are in 5 volumes; and those of the Price Fixing

Committee (March 14 to February 27, 1919) are in 11 volumes. Trade customs, trade stimulation, conversion, fuel, and raw-material requirements were topics of discussion, and the meetings were a large factor in shaping the conclusions of the War Industries Board units relative to rulings. The minutes are card-indexed in triplicate: by originating unit, by date, and by subject.

Rulings. Other executive and administrative agencies published their war-time rulings, but those of the War Industries Board, with the exception of those of the Priorities Division, were not so much as assembled until after the close of the war. The administrative file now (1923) has a collection that is nearly complete.

Questionnaires. The questionnaires of the War Industries Board were chiefly for the purpose of gathering information relative to the consumption of raw materials in the manufacture of war essentials and facilities for such manufacture. About five hundred of them have been assembled and the returns to some of them are very bulky.

Form Communications. Many of these were not so perfunctory as the term implies. They consist of both letters and telegrams but telegrams are the more numerous. Some of them amounted, in effect, to allocations. Those sent out by the chief of the Machine Tool Section inaugurated the production of certain tools for war purposes, and they show which manufacturers were called upon for such production.

Bulletins. Besides the bulletins mentioned under mimeographed material in the Library of Congress are five series of commodity bulletins that were issued monthly: (1) Non-ferrous metals, August and September, 1918; (2) Minerals, November and December, 1918; (5) Textiles and fibers, October, 1918; (6) Lumber, August and September, 1918; (8) Rubber, August and November, 1918. Series 3, 4, and 7 were not issued. Two series of bulletins of a statistical nature were issued by the Joint Office on Chemical Statistics in which the War Department and Navy Department as well as the War Industries Board were represented.

Final Reports. Each major and minor unit of the War Industries Board submitted a final report of its activities and the contents of these reports constitute a body of material of prime importance.

Weekly and Monthly Reports. The great majority of units made reports of this nature. In effect, they are minutes, constituting a current record of activities. It is from these reports that the origin and conclusion of much of the unit activity can be traced.

Special Reports. There are special reports by various units that were based upon particular investigations, and there are special reports on various subjects by the several commodity sections that were made at the request of the functional divisions. Particular attention is directed to the following:

1. Power Reports by the Power Section. These exist in manuscript only, but have been used in the report by Colonel Charles Keller on *The Power Situation during the War* (Washington, 1921, 300 pages). A partial list of these reports embraces:

California: Great Western Power Co., Pacific Gas and Electric Co., San Joaquin Light and Power Corporation, Sierra and San Francisco Power Co., Southern California Edison Co.

Illinois: Central Illinois Public Service Co., East Saint Louis Light and Power Co., Power Situation of Peoria, Properties Owned and Controlled by Illinois Traction System.

Iowa: Power Situation of Keokuk.

Maryland: Power Situation of Baltimore and Vicinity.

Missouri: Laclede Gas Light Co., Union Electric Light and Power Co.

New England: Distribution of Steam, Electric, and Hydro-Electric Power in New England, New England Power Situation.

New York: Power Situation in the Niagara-Buffalo District, Power Situation at Utica and Adjacent Territory.

North Carolina and South Carolina: Carolina Power and Light Co., Carolina Gas and Electric Co., North Carolina Electrical Power Co., Southern Power Co., Yadkin River Power Co.

Ohio: Power Situation, Lima District.

Pennsylvania: Duquesne Light Co., Paupack Water Power Project, Philadelphia and Suburban Gas and Electric Co., Power Situation at Erie, West Pennsylvania Power Co.

2. Commodity Reports by the Division of Planning and Statistics:

(a) Mineral Balance Sheets. These were commenced as a monthly issue. They show for each mineral the 1917 deliveries, sources of supply, and the 1918 deliveries through July. They were actually issued only in October and November, 1918.

(b) Special Reports for the Price Fixing Committee. These are a series of twenty-nine special studies for the use of the committee only: (1) Sand and gravel; (2) Spruce lumber; (3) Packer hides; (4) Bleaching powders; (5) Chestnut extract; (6) Carbon tetrachloride; (7) Caustic soda; (8) Soda ash; (9) Sulphur; (10) Formaldehyde; (11) Nitric acid; (12) Acetic acid; (13) Fluorspar; (14) Wood alcohol; (15) Mohair; (16) Supplement to No. 13; (17) Iron and steel; (18) Southern pine; (19) Cotton manufactures; (20) Brick; (21) Quicksilver; (22) Douglas fir; (23) Wool grease; (24) Rags; (25) Rosin; (26) Turpentine; (27) Hemlock; (28) Lumber; (29) Wire rope.

(c) Miscellaneous Commodity Price Reports. Nineteen of these were issued at irregular intervals: (1) Casein; (2) Imported cigarette paper; (3) Light Mexican crude oil; (4) Hemlock lumber; (5) Side leather; (6) Egyptian cotton; (7) Tobacco, cigarettes, and snuff; (8) Soda nitrate; (9) Sea-island cotton; (10) Rags; (11) Flax seed; (12) Cocoanut; (13) Burlap; (14) Spruce; (15) Lumber; (16) Paper; (17) Wool and woolen goods; (18) Comparison of prices during the Civil War and present war; (19) Comparison of governmental fixed prices with current market quotations on price regulated commodities.

(d) Miscellaneous Series Reports. These consist of twenty-one reports on various studies: (1) Supply and requirements for commodities entering into the military program (the "Stettinius Report"). In this document sixty-five commodities are included and tabulated as to consumption from 1913 to 1917, inclusive, the situation in 1918 as to stocks, the military requirements of the United States and the allies, and the probable production. (2) Schedule of information requested from each country by the Program Committee on Paper. (3) Preliminary report on the automobile industry. This shows the extent to which the industry entered the war program and lists seventy-one articles other than automobiles that were produced for war purposes by automobile manufacturers. (4) Soft drink industry. (5) Memorandum regarding wrist watches purchased in Switzerland. (6) Organization of a thrift campaign. (7) Data on the Swiss Agreement. (8) Distribution of rosin. (9) Iron and steel requirements. (10) Finished products of iron and steel. (11) Second report of progress of subcommittee on non-essential industries. (12) Memorandum on naval stores. (13) Iron and steel production and requirements. (14) Production of building materials for civilian consumption. (15) Production of lumber for civilian consumption. (16) The Swiss Agreement. (17) Final memorandum on curtailment of industries. (18) Iron and steel products. (19) Cars and locomotives and the world situation. (20) Commodity Survey—chemicals, a comprehensive report covering ninety-one of the principal articles handled by the Chemical Division of the War Industries Board. (21) Report on the Demand for Labor.

3. Reports on Special Subjects by the Statistical Division (predecessor of the Division of Planning and Statistics). These reports are numbered 1 to 88 but only the following have been located: (13) On Locomotive Plants; (21) List of Iron and Steel Producers and Annual Capacity of Each; (25) Mineral Supplies of the Central Powers; (27) Minimum Necessary Imports of Copper and Quicksilver; (30) Do. of Lead, Zinc, Antimony, and Tin; (32) Do. of Molybdenum, Tungsten, Nickel, and Cobalt; (33) Do. of Abrasives, Fullers Earth, Clay, and Mineral Waters; (34) Do. of Nitrates, Fertilizers, Sand, Gypsum, Salt, Magnesite, Stone, and Lime; (54) Enemy Aliens in Munitions Factories; (62) Claims of Increased Wage Cost of Harness; (63) Quicksilver Situation; (65) Clothing Contracts; (69) Distribution of 2381 Firms Holding War Contracts; (70) Essential Articles Purchased by Army Corps; (71) Distribution of Outstanding War Orders for Trucks and

Automobiles Placed by the United States and the Allies; (74) Raw Materials Situation in the United States on December 28, 1917; (75) Conflict of Interest between the United States and the Allies in Mineral Raw Materials; (76) British Industries Converted to Meet War Needs; (77) Smokeless Powder Requirements and Probable Production; (78) Essential Industries in Great Britain during the War; (84) Industrial Conversion in France during the War; (85) Concerning War Contracts in France; (87) Woodworking Industries in England, France and Germany and Their Conversion to Meet War Needs; (88) British, French, and German Industries Converted to Meet War Needs.

4. Cost of Production or Operation Reports. These were based on studies for the War Industries Board by the Federal Trade Commission and other government agencies. Among the commodities covered are aluminum, alkaline chemicals, army duck, birch veneer, brick, building tile, cartridge cloth, cast-iron pipe, charcoal, chestnut-wood extract, cigarettes and tobacco, coke, pig iron and steel, copper, copper castings, cotton compression, cotton goods, cotton linters, cypress lumber, fir, gypsum, plaster board, hardware, hemlock lumber, leather, millwork, mohair, paper, pine, portland cement, sand, gravel and crushed stone, spruce lumber, steel rails, soda ash, sulphuric acid, wood chemicals, woolen goods, wool grease, and zinc.

5. Condition of Industry Report. This report was made pursuant to a notice of the Requirements Division of July 9, 1918, printed in its *Advice Sheet No. 25*. The notice was the result of a request emanating from the chairman of the War Industries Board and made at a meeting of commodity chiefs held July 8, 1918. It was desired that each commodity chief submit a report respecting the industry with which he was concerned as to its present condition, the present and prospective needs of the government, normal production, present stocks, prospective condition, and civilian needs. The chiefs of the following commodity sections responded: Acids and Heavy Chemicals, Artificial and Vegetable Dyes, Chain, Chemical Glass and Stoneware, Cotton Goods, Electrical and Power Equipment, Electrodes and Abrasives, Felt, Hardware and Hand Tools, Harness, Jute, Hemp and Cordage, Knit Goods, Medical, Mica, Military Optical Glass, Non-ferrous Metals, Paint and Pigment, Railway Equipment, Refractories, Tanning Materials, Technical and Consulting, Tin, Tobacco, Toluol, Vehicle, Agricultural Implements and Wood Products, and Woolens.

6. Status of Industry Report ("Legge Report"). In October, 1918, the chairman of the Requirements Division, Mr. Alex Legge, went abroad to confer with the members of the War Industries Board's Foreign Mission. Before his departure he requested each commodity chief to provide him with a report on the status of the industry with which he was concerned, in order that the members of the mission might have recent and complete information. The chiefs of forty-six of the commodity sections responded and their reports are quite specific as to the industrial situation. They comprise information on such factors as:

Capacity, production, uses, distribution, and shortage concerning the following: sulphuric acid, acetylene, ammonia, benzol, carbon dioxide, caustic soda, chlorine compounds, cyanamide, hydrogen, oxygen, rare gases, saccharine, toluol, xylol, creosote, ethyl alcohol, cobalt, chromite, ferrosilicon, manganese, molybdenum, tungsten, vanadium, zirconium, chemical glass, chemical stoneware, asbestos, magnesia, rutile, electrodes, abrasives, white arsenic, bromine, camphor, metallic magnesium, mica, shellac, varnish gums, rosin, flax seed, linseed oil, platinum, clays, fluorspar, sulphur, barium chlorate, glycerin, acetate of lime, wood alcohol, acetic acid, insecticides, chloroform, motor trucks, copper and brass manufactured products, terra cotta, asphalt, brick, gypsum, cement, chains, cotton linters, cotton goods, cranes, electric wire and cable, smokeless powder and guncotton, ammonium nitrate, nitrate of soda, T N T, felt, hides and skins, manila rope, kapoc, military optical glass, high-pressure cylinders, forgings, pig iron, shell steel, steel plates and sheets, structural steel, tin plates, tubes, barbed wire, wire rope, paper, pig tin, tobacco, wood products, wool, and woolens.

7. "Business as Usual" Report (October, 1918). When the "business as usual" charge was made Mr. Alex Legge asked the unit chiefs to provide him with reports with which to refute it. The chiefs of the following divisions and sections responded: Allied Purchasing Commission, Steel, Chemicals, Acids and Heavy Chemicals, Alkali and Chlorine, Artificial Dyestuffs, Chemical Glass and Stoneware, Coal-gas Products, Creosote, Electrodes and Abrasives, Ferro-alloys, Fine Chemicals, Platinum, Tanning Materials, Sulphur and Pyrites, Mica, Woolens, Technical, and Consulting.

8. Controlled Industries Report. The secretary of the War Industries Board, in August and again in October, 1918, issued a memorandum to commodity chiefs requesting them to provide him with copies of agreements made with industries and with a list of such industries under their particular jurisdiction as had been put on the control list. The chiefs of the following units responded: Crane, Hide, Leather and Leather Goods, Fine Chemicals, Finished Products, Medical, Building Materials, Felt, Hardware and Hand Tool, Harness and Saddlery, Inland Traffic, Military Optical Glass, Platinum, and Rubber. A mimeographed summary of the replies is filed with the report.

9. New Industries Report. At the request of the United States Chamber of Commerce, the director of the Bureau of Foreign and Domestic Commerce, Department of Commerce, called upon the various units of the War Industries Board, in November, 1918, for assistance in the preparation of a report on articles produced on a commercial scale in the United States which were not so produced prior to 1915. The chiefs of the following units responded: Dye, Automotive, Chain, Explosives, Military Optical Glass, Paint and Pigment, Vehicle, Agricultural Implements and Wood Products, Textile, Rubber and Rubber Goods, Hardware and Hand Tool, Industrial Gases, and Lumber.

10. Effect of the War upon Industries Reports. These are statements in

the nature of interviews, one for each of several industries, conducted for the Requirements Division.

11. A report by Rear Admiral Frank F. Fletcher, navy representative on the War Industries Board, on the functioning of the board with the Navy Department.

Industrial Surveys. These surveys comprise data, assembled by States and cities, exhibiting the capacity and producing equipment of some 30,000 plants. A summary tabulation of 18,654 firms, classified geographically and by equipment, contains such items as union or non-union shops, number of employees, enrollment of skilled labor, laboratory facilities, shipping facilities, and attitude toward possible future contracts. Several locality surveys comprise data relative to manufacturing and housing facilities and labor conditions. Among them are those of Atlanta, Ga., South Bend, Ind., Pontiac, Mich., Minneapolis, Minn., Niagara Falls, N. Y., Monroe, N. C., Akron, Cincinnati, Hamilton, Portsmouth, and Toledo, O., Portland, Ore., Erie and Wilkes-Barre, Pa., Charleston, S. C., Alexandria, Va., Seattle and Spokane, Wash., and Racine, Wis.

"Calder Resolution" Correspondence. On September 11, 1918, the chairman of the War Industries Board addressed a letter to the mayor of New York, suggesting that as a war expediency, the construction of new school buildings be postponed. The letter was the occasion of a resolution introduced in the United States Senate on September 13, 1918, by Senator Calder, challenging the authority of the board to issue orders affecting the building industry. The correspondence arising out of the incident is filed with the records of the chairman's office.

Reconstruction Program. Early in November, 1918, the chairman of the War Industries Board asked the chiefs of divisions and sections for expressions of opinion, respecting the functions of the board during the readjustment period. The heads of the following units responded: Chemicals, Acids and Heavy Chemicals, Alkali and Chlorine, Artificial Dyes and Intermediates, Fine Chemicals, Miscellaneous Chemicals, Automotive Products, Electrodes and Abrasives, Felt, Ferro-alloys, Finished Products, Chemical Glass and Stoneware, Coal-gas Products, Creosote, Conservation, Cotton Goods, Hardware and Hand Tool, Hide and Leather, Iron and Steel Scrap, Lumber, Medical, Mica, Military Optical Glass, Navy Department, Paint and Pigment, Planning and Statistics, Platinum, Priorities, Pulp and Paper, Refractories, Steel, Textile and Rubber, Tanning Materials, Technical and Consulting, Tobacco, Vehicle, Agricultural Implements and Wood Products, Resources and

Conversion, and the regional advisers at Boston, Philadelphia, Pittsburgh, Rochester, Cincinnati, Atlanta, Birmingham, Chicago, Milwaukee, St. Louis, and Seattle.

Office Memoranda. In the files of the secretary of the War Industries Board are twenty-three office memoranda of one or two pages each on the following subjects:

(1) August 19, 1918, coöperation between commodity sections and the Resources and Conversion Section; (2) August 26, organization and functions of the Facilities Division; (3) August 29, appointment of certifying officers for furloughing of labor and others engaged in important war work; (4) September 9, responsibility of section chiefs relative to prices; (5) September 10, registration for the draft; (6) September 13, applications for preferential treatment; (7) September 17, appointment of "space officer"; (8) September 18, conflict in times of meeting; (9) September 20, trade meetings; (10) September 23, requesting commodity section data; (11) September 27, digests of meetings and weekly reports; (12) October 2, controlled industries; (13) October 7, on commodity chiefs, meetings; (14) October 14, cancellation of meetings; (15) October 16, commodity chiefs, meeting; (16) October 25, *U.S. Official Bulletin;* (17) October 28, distribution of section minutes and weekly reports; (18) November 18, preservation of records; (19) November 22, photograph of executives of the War Industries Board organization; (20) November 25, record of personnel; (21) November 30, preservation of records; (22) Not located; (23) No date, final historical report.

Unit Files

Allied Purchasing Commission

Upon the termination of the Allied Purchasing Commission its official files were transferred to the Treasury Department, but a considerable quantity of material subsequently found in various unit files of the War Industries Board has been assembled in the administrative file and so far as feasible classified by commodity under each of the allied powers. Particular attention is directed to:

Minutes of meetings with representatives of the allied missions, the Priorities Committee, the United States Treasury, the War Trade Board, and certain commodity sections.

Circulars, Nos. 1 to 9.

(1) October 30, 1917. Forms of recommendation for use in handling allied orders (1 page).

(2) February 13, 1918. (Not located.)

(3) March 25, 1918. Forms of contracts (2 pages).

(4) May 13, 1918. Forms of contracts as related to export licenses (4 pages).

(5) May 15, 1918. Forms covering export shipments to allies (1 page).

(6) May 27. Instructions relative to procedure for handling applications of allies for permission to purchase (3 pages).

(7) August 24. Procedure to be followed in case of inquiries regarding price and delivery (2 pages).

(8) September 16. Outline of information pertaining to applications (8 pages).

(9) October 1. Change in procedure of handling applications of allies for permission to purchase (2 pages).

Schedules of contracts: Belgian, British, French, Italian, and Russian.

Memoranda.

Cost reports by the Steel and Hide and Leather divisions and by the Chain, Cotton and Cotton Products, Hardware and Hand Tool, Crane, Lumber, and Non-ferrous Metals sections.

Final report (4 pages).

Acids and Heavy Chemicals Section

Minutes of weekly meetings. June 27 to November 8, 1918.

Minutes of three meetings with trade representatives.

Minutes of three special meetings.

Minutes of three informal meetings.

Minutes of a meeting of a subcommittee.

Weekly reports. August 2 to December 3, 1918.

Condition of industry report (2 pages).

Requirements report (1 page).

Requirements and procurement report (1 page).

Status of Industry report (9 pages). Status of capacity, production, requirements, and distribution of sulphuric and nitric acid.

Business as usual report (1 page).

Effect of the war upon industry report (20 pages).

Reconstruction program report (1 page).

Final report (22 pages). Price-fixing policy, capacity survey of acid production, labor situation at acid plants, and future of the industry.

Alkali and Chlorine Section

Minutes of weekly meetings. July 3 to November 10, 1918.

Minutes of five meetings with trade representatives.

Questionnaires.

Weekly reports. August 2 to December 7, 1918.

Requirements report (2 pages).

Requirements and procurement report (1 page).

Status of Industry report (2 pages). Situation as to military requirements, shortages, etc., of caustic soda, bicarbonate of soda, carbon tetrachloride, liquid chlorine, bleaching powder, chemical lime, and potash.

Effect of the war upon industry report (20 pages).

Business as usual report (1 page).

Reconstruction program report (2 pages).

Final report (13 pages). The substance of this report is well covered in the final *Report of the War Industries Board* (pp. 166-170).

Artificial Dyes and Intermediates Section

Minutes of three meetings of the section. October 29 to November 26, 1918.

Minutes of three meetings with trade representatives.

Weekly reports. August 2 to November 23, 1918.

Condition of industry report (1 page).

Requirements report (4 pages).

Requirements and procurement report: "Section has no information upon which to draw for a report."

Business as usual report (1 page).

Effect of the war upon industry report (14 pages).

New industries report (3 pages).

Reconstruction program report (2 pages).

Final report (9 pages).

Automotive Products Section

Form communications.

Minutes of meetings of the section. September 6, 1918, to November 20, 1918.

Questionnaires.

Weekly reports. July 20 to November 27, 1918.

Requirements report (2 pages).

Status of industry report (16 pages).

Effect of the war upon industry report (16 pages).

New industries report (1 page).

Reconstruction program report (15 pages).

Final report (15 pages).

Brass Section

Form communications.

Minutes of meetings of the section. June 4 to December 2, 1918.

Minutes of meeting with trade representatives. August 29, 1918.

Rulings.

Weekly reports. August 31 to November 30, 1918.

Status of industry reports. October 21, 1918 (7 pages); October 26, 1918 (3 pages).

Effect of the war upon industry report (18 pages).

Final report (13 pages).

Building Materials Division

Agreements and correspondence relative to the disposal of surplus stocks.

Form communications.

Form letters to war service committees. August, 1918, to March, 1919.

List of commodities handled (1 page).

Minutes of some ninety meetings with trade representatives.

Questionnaires.

Rulings.

Summary tabulations.

Weekly reports. August 5 to December 31, 1918.

Report of the Specifications Section (4 pages).

Requirements report (1 page).

Condition of industry report (6 pages).

Effect of the war upon industry report (45 pages).

Final report (126 pages).

Chain Section

Diary and memoranda. June 6 to December 5, 1918.

Form communications.

Minutes of weekly meetings of the section. May 29 to November 27, 1918.

Minutes of twelve meetings with trade representatives.

Questionnaires.

Rulings.

Condition of industry report (2 pages).

Status of industry report (1 page).

Requirements report (1 page).

Special report on transmission chain (4 pages).

Effect of the war upon industry report (27 pages).

New industries report (1 page).

Final report (16 pages).

Chemicals Division

List of commodities handled.

Minutes of semi-weekly meetings of the division. May 28 to December 31, 1918.

Special reports.

Requirements report (1 page).

Business as usual report (1 page).

Status of industry report (4 pages).

Effect of the war upon industry report (19 pages).

Reconstruction program report (5 pages).

Final report (10 pages).

Chemical Glass and Stoneware Section

Minutes of meetings of the section. September 19 to October 30, 1918.
Questionnaires.
Weekly reports. August 2 to November 30, 1918.
Condition of industry report (3 pages).
Requirements report (2 pages).
Business as usual report (1 page).
Effect of the war upon industry report (20 pages).
Reconstruction program report (3 pages).
Final report (23 pages).

Clearance Committee

Circular letters.
Clearance list.
Clearance forms.
Memoranda.
Minutes of meetings. May 28 to July 3, 1918.
Weekly reports. September 24 to October 19, 1918.
Monthly reports. February to May, 1918.
Final report (6 pages).

Coal-Gas Products Section

List of commodities handled.
Weekly reports. August 2 and 9, 1918.

Cotton and Cotton Linters Section

Bulletins.
Form communications.
Minutes of meetings. June 5 to December 19, 1918.
Rulings.
Questionnaires.
Weekly reports. August 3 to December 7, 1918.
Monthly reports. September to November, 1918.
Condition of industry report (1 page).
Status of industry report (5 pages).
Requirements report (1 page).
Requirements and procurement report (1 page).
Effect of the war upon industry report (20 pages).
Final report (10 pages).

Cotton Goods Section

Form communications.
Digests of fourteen meetings with trade representatives.

Minutes of meetings of the section. June 11 to November 13, 1918.
Daily reports. April 1 to December 4, 1918.
Weekly reports. July 13 to November 23, 1918.
Requirements report (5 pages).
Status of industry reports. October 23, 1918 (2 pages); October 24, 1918 (2 pages).
Effect of the war upon industry report (17 pages).
Reconstruction program report (2 pages).
Final report (16 pages).

Crane Section

Circular letters.
List of commodities handled.
Rulings.
Minutes of meetings of the section. May 28 to November 26, 1918.
Minutes of three meetings with trade representatives.
Weekly reports. June 1 to December 14, 1918.
Monthly reports. June to August, 1918.
Requirements report (1 page).
Requirements and procurement report (2 pages).
Status of industry report (3 pages).
Effect of the war upon industry report (20 pages).
Final report (10 pages).

Creosote Section

Circular letters.
Minutes of meetings of the section. August 8 to October 26, 1918.
Weekly reports. May 17 to October 26, 1918.
Requirements report (1 page).
Business as usual report (1 page).
Status of industry report (1 page).
Effect of the war upon industry report (35 pages).
Reconstruction program report (2 pages).
Final report (5 pages).

Electrical and Power Equipment Section

Form communications.
Minutes of meetings of the section. June 21 to November 8, 1918.
Minutes of six meetings with trade representatives.
Questionnaires.
Weekly reports. July 9 to November 23, 1918.
Requirements and procurement report (1 page).
Condition of industry report (3 pages).

Status of industry report (6 pages).
Effect of the war upon industry report (71 pages).
Final report (20 pages).

Electric Wire and Cable Section

Form communications.
Minutes of meetings of the section. August 23, 1918.
Questionnaires.
Weekly reports. August 24 to November 23, 1918.
Status of Industry report (2 pages).
Effect of the war upon industry report (18 pages).
Final report (11 pages).

Electrodes and Abrasives Section

Circular letters.
Minutes of two meetings with trade representatives.
Weekly reports. August 2 to November 30, 1918.
Condition of industry report (2 pages).
Business as usual report (2 pages).
Status of industry report (4 pages).
Effect of the war upon industry report (23 pages).
Reconstruction program report (5 pages).
Final report (26 pages).

Emergency Construction Committee

Form communications.
Questionnaires.
Final report (47 pages).

Ethyl Alcohol Section

Weekly reports. October 18 to November 30, 1918.
Status of industry report (1 page).
Final report (3 pages).

Explosives Section

Minutes of meetings. August 16 to December 12, 1918.
Weekly reports. October 19 to November 23, 1918.
Status of industry report (8 pages).
Effect of the war upon industry report (22 pages).
New industries report (1 page).
Final report (2 pages).

Felt Section

Form communications.
Bulletins.
Minutes of meetings of the section. July 23 to December 3, 1918.
Minutes of six meetings with trade representatives.
Questionnaires.
Rulings.
Weekly reports. August 2 to December 6, 1918.
Requirements report (2 pages).
Requirements and procurement report (2 pages).
Condition of industry report (5 pages).
Status of industry report (2 pages).
Effect of the war upon industry report (9 pages).
Reconstruction program report (3 pages).
Final report (20 pages).

Hatters' Felt Department

Circulars.
Minutes of meetings and conferences with regard to condition of industry, August 14 to November 6, 1918.
Questionnaires.
Conservation pledge.
Rulings.
Weekly reports. August 22 to November 20, 1918.

Paper Makers' Felt Department

Circular letters.
Minutes of meetings and conferences with regard to condition of industry. August 19 to October 31, 1918.
Questionnaires.
Rulings.
Weekly reports. September 7 to November 21, 1918.
Reconstruction program report (1 page).

Ferro-alloys Section

Circular letters.
Minutes of meetings of the section. July 25 to November 14, 1918.
Questionnaires.
Weekly reports. August 22 to November 23, 1918.
Requirements and procurement report (2 pages).
Business as usual report (1 page).
Status of industry report (5 pages).
Effect of the war upon industry report (21 pages).
Reconstruction program report (2 pages).
Final report (7 pages).

Fine Chemicals Section

Minutes of Meetings of the section. October 2 to 16, 1918.
Weekly reports. July 30 to November 16, 1918.
Business as usual report (9 pages).
Status of industry report (2 pages).
Effect of the war upon industry report (9 pages).
Reconstruction program reports. November 8, 1918 (1 page); November 13, 1918 (2 pages).
Final report (4 pages).

Finished Products Division

Form communications.
Form letters regarding war service committees.
Office memoranda.
Minutes of meetings of the division. July 17 to October 2, 1918.
Weekly reports. September 14 to December 28, 1918.
Reconstruction program report (1 page).
Final report (2 pages).

Fire Prevention Section

Form communications.
Minutes of twelve meetings with trade representatives. First report of the fire apparatus and protective device industry (12 pages).
Weekly reports. August 24 to November 23, 1918.
Final report (37 pages).

Flax Products Section

Circular letters.
Weekly reports. August 24 to November 16, 1918.
Status of industry report (1 page).
Effect of the war upon industry report (18 pages).
Final report (4 pages).

General Munitions Board[1]

Form communications.
Minutes of meetings. April 13 to July 25, 1917 (2 volumes).
Questionnaires.
Weekly reports. May 19 to July 30, 1917.

[1] The predecessor, with the Munitions Standards Board, of the W.I.B.; only a small section of its records have been card-indexed.

Hardware and Hand Tool Section

Form communications.

Minutes of meetings of the section. June 1 to November 21, 1918.

Minutes of forty-two meetings with trade representatives. June 6 to October 24, 1918.

Questionnaires.

Conservation schedule.

Reports by members of the section. August 29 to November 23, 1918.

Weekly reports. August 16 to November 23, 1918.

Condition of industry report (3 pages).

Requirements report (1 page).

Requirements and procurement report (3 pages).

Status of industry report (4 pages).

Effect of the war upon industry report (38 pages).

New industries report (1 page).

Reconstruction program report (9 pages).

Final report (91 pages).

Hide, Leather, and Leather Goods Division

Form communications.

List of commodities handled.

Minutes of weekly meetings of sections. July 11 to November 21, 1918.

Minutes of twenty-two meetings with trade representatives.

Rulings.

Monthly reports. August and September, 1918.

Weekly reports. September to November, 1918.

Requirements report (1 page).

Status of industry report (10 pages).

Effect of the war upon industry report (31 pages).

Reconstruction program report (4 pages).

Final report (83 pages).

Belting Section

Form communications.

Weekly reports. September 13 to November 23, 1918.

Effect of the war upon industry report (7 pages).

Final report (3 pages).

Boot and Shoe Section

Weekly reports. September 28 to December 7, 1918.

Effect of the war upon industry report (18 pages).

Final report (7 pages).

Glove and Leather Clothing Section

Circular letters.

Minutes of a meeting of the section. November 25, 1918.

Weekly reports. October 4 to November 1, 1918.
Effect of the war upon industry report (25 pages).
Final report, including minutes of meetings (33 pages).

Harness and Personal Equipment Section

Weekly reports. September 21 to December 7, 1918.
Condition of industry report (2 pages).
Effect of the war upon industry report (31 pages).
Final report (2 pages).

Hides and Skins Section

Form communications.
Weekly reports. September 28 to November 30, 1918.
Condition of industry report (2 pages).

Sole and Belting Leather Section

Effect of the war upon industry report (12 pages).
Final report (32 pages).

Sole Leather Section

Form communications.
Effect of the war upon industry report (16 pages).
Final report (17 pages).

Upper Leather Section

Form communications.
Weekly reports. September 19 to November 30, 1918.
Effect of the war upon industry report (10 pages).
Final report (5 pages).

Industrial Inventory Section

Form communications.
Industrial inventory forms.
Industrial inventory summaries.
Weekly reports. September 1, 1917, to December 2, 1918.
Daily reports. October 1 to December 2, 1918.
Final report (8 pages).

Industrial Gases and Gas Products Section

Weekly reports. November 23 to December 6, 1918.
Requirements and procurement report (5 pages).
Business as usual report (2 pages).
Status of industry report (9 pages).
Effect of the war upon industry report (36 pages).
New industries report (1 page).
Reconstruction program report (2 pages).
Final report (8 pages).

Inland Traffic Section

Forms and Instructions.
Building program (64 pages).
Report for July, 1918.
Weekly reports. October 1 to December 2, 1918.
Status of industry report (6 pages).

Joint Office on Chemical Statistics

Circular letters.
Questionnaires.
Memoranda.
Weekly reports. June 21 to December 14, 1918.
Special reports (Propellants and Explosives Bulletins). July 5, 1918, to January 20, 1919 (353 pages).
Special report on sulphur statistics (6 pages).

Joint Office on Leather Statistics

Weekly reports. May 11 to November 28, 1918.
Special report, statistical (21 pages).
Final report (8 pages).

Jute, Hemp, and Cordage Section

Circular letters.
Minutes of meetings of the section. October 1 and 15, 1918.
Minutes of fourteen meetings with trade representatives.
Questionnaires.
Weekly reports. September 24 to November 23, 1918.
Condition of industry report (3 pages).
Requirements report (1 page).
Status of industry report (12 pages).
Effect of the war upon industry report (74 pages).
Final report (4 pages).

Knit Goods Section

Form communications.
Minutes of meetings of the section. August 1 to September 25, 1918.
Minutes of five meetings with trade representatives.
Questionnaires.
Rulings.
Weekly reports. July 23 to December 16, 1918.
Condition of industry report (2 pages).
Requirements report (1 page).
Status of industry report (2 pages).
Effect of the war upon industry report (30 pages).
Final report (9 pages).

Legal Section

Opinions.
Weekly reports. August 31 to November 23, 1918.
Final report (2 pages).

Lumber Division

Form communications.
Form communications with emergency bureaus.
List of commodities handled.
Minutes of weekly meetings of the division. September 9 to November 21, 1918.
Minutes of thirteen meetings with trade representatives.
Price schedules.
Recommendations.
Weekly reports. September 11 to November 16, 1918.
Requirements report (1 page).
Effect of the war upon industry report (32 pages).
New industries report (1 page).
Reconstruction program report (1 page).
Final report (46 pages).

Lumber Committee
(Council of National Defense)

Minutes of executive meetings. May 14 to June 1, 1917.
Minutes of three special meetings. July 26 to December 13, 1917.
Weekly reports. May 5 to July 28, 1917.

Lumber Section

Minutes of six meetings of the section. January 11 to May 10, 1918.
Recommendations.
Rulings.

Machine Tool Section

Chart showing dates of action taken by the section to secure steady flow of machine tools. Classified list of circular letters attached (17 pages).
Minutes of meeting of the section. August 3, 1918.
Questionnaires.
Weekly reports. July 23 to December 17, 1918.
Requirements report (1 page).
Status of industry report (4 pages).
Effect of the war upon industry report (34 pages).
Final report (18 pages).

Medical Industry Section

Form communications.
List of commodities handled.
Minutes of meetings of the section. June 21 to December 13, 1918.
Minutes of eight special meetings.
Minutes of eight meetings with trade representatives.
Questionnaires.
Rulings.
Condition of industry report (3 pages).
Requirements report (1 page).
Status of industry report (3 pages).
Effect of the war upon industry report (59 pages).
Reconstruction program report (4 pages).
Final report (32 pages; Exhibits A-V).

Mica Section

Form communications.
Minutes of special meeting. October 10, 1918.
Report of conference with importers. May 31, 1918.
Condition of industry report (17 pages).
Requirements and procurement report (2 pages).
Business as usual report (1 page).
Status of industry report (1 page).
Effect of the war upon industry report (12 pages).
Reconstruction program report (1 page).
Final report (5 pages).

Military Optical Glass and Instruments Section

Form communications.
Minutes of meetings of the section. July 29 to October 28, 1918.
Questionnaires.
Rulings.
Weekly reports. July 24 to December 15, 1918.
Monthly report. August, 1918.
Condition of industry report (1 page).
Requirements report (8 pages).
Requirements and procurement reports (4 pages).
Status of industry report (1 page).
Effect of the war upon industry report (15 pages).
New industries report (1 page).
Final report (11 pages).

Miscellaneous Section

Minutes of weekly meetings of the section. August 8 to November 29, 1918.
Minutes of eight meetings with trade representatives.
Requirements and procurement report (1 page).
Status of industry report (2 pages).
Effect of war upon industry report (7 pages).
Reconstruction program report (1 page).
Final report (11 pages).

Munitions Standards Board[1]

Circular letter.
Minutes of two special meetings. March 21 and April 18, 1917.

Nitrate Section

Effect of the war upon industry report (9 pages).
Final report (22 pages).

Non-ferrous Metals Section

Form communications.
Minutes of thirteen meetings with trade representatives.
Questionnaires.
Weekly reports. June 4 to December 7, 1918.
Condition of industry report (12 pages).
Requirements report (7 pages).
Requirements and procurement report (1 page).
Effect of the war upon industry report (39 pages).
Final report (23 pages).

Ordnance, Arms, and Ammunition Section

Minutes of meetings of the section. July 19 to August 29, 1918.
Weekly reports. August 17 to October 29, 1918.
Requirements report (1 page).
Status of industry report (2 pages).
Effect of the war upon industry report (15 pages).
Final report (28 pages).

Paint and Pigment Section

Bulletins.
Minutes of meetings of the section. July 1 to December 10, 1918.
Minutes of fourteen meetings with trade representatives.

[1] This board, with the General Munitions Board, was the predecessor of
the W.I.B.

Questionnaires.
Weekly reports. August 5 to December 19, 1918.
Requirements and procurement report (1 page).
Condition of industry report (1 page).
Status of industry report (5 pages).
Effect of the war upon industry report (29 pages).
New industries report (1 page).
Reconstruction program report (6 pages).
Final report (10 pages).

Platinum, Gold, and Silver Section

Circulars.
Form communications.
Waiver forms.
Questionnaires.
Rulings.
Weekly reports. August 10 to November 25, 1918.
Requirements and procurement report (1 page).
Business as usual report (2 pages).
Status of industry report (2 pages).
Effect of the war upon industry report (14 pages).
Reconstruction program report (1 page).
Final report (13 pages).

Power Section

Form communications.
Minutes of meetings of the section. June 4 to October 22, 1918.
Reports of special conferences with engineers and others. June 4 to October 22, 1918.
Questionnaires.
Rulings.
Weekly reports. August 19 to November 26, 1918.
Special power reports. June 6 to November 10, 1918.
Summaries of power reports.
Status of industry report (2 pages).
Effect of the war upon industry report (9 pages).
Final report (4 pages).

Price Fixing Committee

Circulars.
Form communications.
Minutes of meetings. March 14, 1918, to February 27, 1919 (11 volumes).
Office memoranda.
Resolutions and rulings.

Schedules.
Weekly reports. August 12 to November 29, 1918.
Final report (3 pages).

Priorities Division

Office bulletins.
Circulars.
Forms. Nos. 1 to 95.
Minutes of meetings of the division. May 28 to December 20, 1918.
Minutes of approximately 150 meetings with trade representatives.

Priorities Board

Form communications.
Memorandum on curtailed industries (4 pages).
Preference lists.
Questionnaires.
Weekly reports. September 24 to November 18, 1918.

Priorities Committee

Form communications.
Memoranda.
Rulings.
Weekly reports. September 28 to October 12, 1918.
Reconstruction papers.
Final report (24 pages).

Production Committee

Form communications.
Weekly reports.

Pulp and Paper Division

Form communications.
Minutes of meetings of the section. September 14 to 28, 1918.
Minutes of seven meetings with trade representatives.
Conservation pledge.
Questionnaires.
Regulations.
Weekly reports. June 29 to November 25, 1918.
Status of industry report (4 pages).
Effect of the war upon industry report (18 pages).
Reconstruction program report (3 pages).
Final report (193 pages).

Manufacturing Section

Questionnaire.
Regulations.
Final report (5 pages).

Newspaper Section

Questionnaire.
Regulations.
Reconstruction program report (3 pages).

Paper Economy Section

Questionnaire.
Regulations.

Periodical Section

Questionnaire.
Regulations.

Fiber Board and Container Section

Questionnaire.
Regulations.
Weekly reports. September 21 to October 28, 1918.

Railway Equipment and Supplies Section

Form communications.
Questionnaire.
Requirements and procurement report (2 pages).
Effect of the war upon industry report (32 pages).
Final report (25 pages).

Raw Materials Division

Form communications.
Questionnaire.
Rulings.
Minutes of meetings. August 21 to October 30, 1917.

Refractories Section

Circular letters.
Minutes of five meetings with trade representatives.
Weekly reports. July 28 to November 29, 1918.
Condition of industry report (2 pages).
Business as usual report (1 page).
Status of industry report (2 pages).
Effect of the war upon industry report (21 pages).
Reconstruction program report (2 pages).
Final report (9 pages).

Requirements Division

Advice sheets. Nos. 1 to 45.

Commodity lists.

Form communications.

Minutes of meetings with representatives of government organizations. March 29 to December 29, 1918.

Reply to inquiry relative to requirements of cotton duck and felt (7 pages).

Reports (Hatfield) from commodity sections to the Division of Planning and Statistics on requirements.

Special Requirements Committee

Minutes of meetings. September 14 to November 8, 1918.

Resources and Conversion Section

List of regional advisers.

Bulletins to regional advisers. Nos. 1 to 39.

List of bulletins issued.

Form letters to regional advisers.

Lists of daily requirements sent to regional advisers.

Lists of industrial conversions.

Minutes of a special meeting of regional advisers. July 18 and 19, 1918.

Minutes of six meetings in regions 1, 2, 4, 5, 9, and 14.

Regional maps.

Weekly reports. August 17 to November 16, 1918.

Reports from regional advisers.

Final reports from regional advisers.

Final report by the chief of the section (7 pages).

Rubber and Rubber Goods Section

Form communications.

Minutes of two meetings of the section. August 26 and October 4, 1918.

Conservation pledge.

Questionnaire.

Weekly reports. August 24 to December 7, 1918.

Requirements report (1 page).

Effect of the war upon industry report (18 pages).

Final report (10 pages).

Silk Section

Minutes of ten meetings of the section. August 14 to December 10, 1918.

Minutes of eight meetings with trade representatives.

Weekly reports. September 10 to December 14, 1918.

Effect of the war upon industry report (11 pages).

Reconstruction program report (1 page).
Final report (4 pages).

Statistics Division

Form letters.
Charts showing distribution of firms holding war contracts.
Special labor bulletins, Nos. 1 to 22.
Seven "Bulletins on War Contracts." January, 1918, to May, 1918.
Weekly reports. December 1, 1917, to May 28, 1918.
Weekly reports on raw materials. April 13 to May 25, 1918.
Weekly reports. (War Contracts Files Section.) November 12, 1917, to March 30, 1918.
First Annual Report. April 6, 1918 (46 pages).
Special reports. These are listed above under General Administrative File, Special Reports, 3. Reports on Special Subjects by Statistical Division.

Steel Division

Circular letters.
Conservation pledge.
Rulings.
Minutes of meeting with shell steel manufacturers. September 23, 1918.
Summary of reports of blast furnace operators at meeting held September 23 and 24, 1918.
Summary of reports regarding railroads at meeting held September 23 and 24, 1918.
Minutes of meeting with representatives of the pipe industry held September 24, 1918.
Minutes of meeting with manufacturers of steel plates to discuss production. September 26, 1918.
Minutes of meeting with representatives of the wire fence industry to determine the amount of steel to be allotted to the industry. October 7, 1918.
Proceedings of a conference with regard to the handling of applications for priority on steel and pig iron.
Weekly reports. October 5 and 12, 1918.
Weekly reports of subcommittees.
Requirements and procurement report (1 page).
Business as usual report (1 page).
Status of industry report (3 pages).
Effect of the war upon industry report (32 pages).
Reconstruction program report (3 pages).
Final report (3 pages).

Iron and Steel Scrap Section

Minutes of meeting of the section. November 6, 1918.
Weekly reports. November 1 and 6, 1918.

Reconstruction program report (1 page).
Final report (4 pages).

Pig Iron Section

Minutes of meeting to consider possibility of increasing production and possibility of improvement by stimulating the industry through the supply of fuel and labor, or such other action as might be determined by the War Industries Board. November 23, 1918.

Weekly reports. October, 1918.
Status of industry report (5 pages).
Effect of the war upon industry report (26 pages).
Final report (4 pages).

Warehouse Distribution Section

Circular letters.
Rulings.
Final report (3 pages).

Sulphur and Pyrites Section

Weekly reports. August 2 to November 30, 1918.
Requirements report (1 page).
Business as usual report (1 page).
Status of industry report (2 pages).
Report of the sulphuric and nitric acid situation (9 pages).
Final report (16 pages).

Tanning Materials and Vegetable Dye Section

Form communications.
Minutes of meetings of the section. October 16 to December 4, 1918.
Minutes of seven meetings with trade representatives.
Weekly reports. August 2 to November 30, 1918.
Condition of industry report (2 pages).
Business as usual report (3 pages).
Status of industry report (1 page).
Effect of the war upon industry report (24 pages).
Reconstruction program report (2 pages).
Final report (10 pages).

Technical and Consulting Section

Weekly reports. June 4 to December 14, 1918.
Condition of industry report (1 page).
Business as usual report (1 page).
Status of industry report (2 pages).
Effect of the war upon industry report (9 pages).
Reconstruction program report (1 page).
Final report (4 pages).

Textile and Rubber Division

Circular letters.
Minutes of nine section meetings. July 1 to November 11, 1918.
Minutes of five meetings with trade representatives.
Weekly reports. September 21 to December 7, 1918.
New industries report (1 page).
Final report (1 page).

Tin Section

Form communications.
Minutes of meetings of the section. July 3 and 10 and October 18, 1918.
Minutes of five meetings with trade representatives.
Questionnaires.
Weekly reports. September 25 to November 26, 1918.
Requirements report (2 pages).
Condition of industry report (3 pages).
Status of industry report (1 page).
Effect of the war upon industry report (26 pages).
Final report (14 pages).

Tobacco Section

Minutes of twenty-two meetings of the section. June 20 to December 9, 1918.
Minutes of forty-four meetings with trade representatives.
Pledge not to expand manufacturing facilities.
Weekly reports. August 24 to December 12, 1918.
Condition of industry report (5 pages).
Requirements report (1 page).
Status of industry report (2 pages).
Effect of the war upon industry report (14 pages).
Reconstruction program report (1 page).
Final report (2 pages).

Vehicle, Implement, and Wood Products Section

Circular letters.
Minutes of meetings of the section. August 1 to November 26, 1918.
Minutes of five meetings with trade representatives.
Conservation pledge.
Questionnaires.
Weekly reports. June 29 to November 23, 1918.
Condition of industry report (1 page).
Requirements report (1 page).
Status of industry report (2 pages).

Effect of the war upon industry report (23 pages).
New industries report (1 page).
Reconstruction program report (2 pages).
Final report (3 pages).

Wood Chemicals Section

Circular letters.
Inventories.
List of commodities handled.
Minutes of two meetings with trade representatives.
Questionnaires.
Requirements and procurement report (1 page).
Requirements report (2 pages).
Status of industry report (4 pages).
Effect of the war upon industry report (21 pages).
Reconstruction program report (1 page).
Final report (10 pages).

Wool Division

Domestic Wool Section

Regulations regarding the domestic clip.
Conference with representatives of the mohair industry to fix a price on fall clip of mohair. September 4, 1918.
Weekly reports. August 5 to December 6, 1918.
Requirements report (1 page).
Final report (2 pages).

Noils and Waste Section

Rulings.
Special report on control of noils and waste. September 26, 1918 (5 pages).

Woolens Section

Minutes of eleven meetings of the section. July 17 to December 11, 1918.
Minutes of thirty-two meetings with trade representatives.
Weekly reports. July 25 to December 21, 1918.
Requirements report (1 page).
Condition of industry report (3 pages).
Business as usual report (1 page).
Status of industry report (4 pages).
Effect of the war upon industry report (16 pages).
Final report (2 pages).

WAR TRADE BOARD[1]

Evolution and Dissolution

THE War Trade Board, a body which had to do with measures relating to export and import control, the fueling and provisioning of vessels leaving United States ports, and the control of trade with enemies and allies of enemies, was established by executive order of October 12, 1917. It replaced the former Exports Administrative Board, which, created by executive order of August 21, 1917, had replaced the Division of Export Licenses of the Bureau of Foreign and Domestic Commerce, a division which was organized in accordance with an executive order of June 22, 1917, vesting the administration of export control in the Secretary of Commerce. The War Trade Board ceased to act as a separate entity June 30, 1919, when it became, with greatly lessened personnel, the War Trade Board Section of the Department of State. When this, with the exception of its import control of dyes and certain drugs, chemicals, and coal tar products, had nearly ceased to function, it was abolished by act of Congress, approved May 27, 1921, and its personnel, books, documents, and other records relating to dye and chemical imports were transferred to the Treasury Department, where the Dye and Chemical Section of the Division of Customs was organized to administer the control provided for in that act. This Dye and Chemical Section was done away with by the substitution of the provisions of the tariff act of 1922 for those of the act of May 27, 1921, and the records relating to dye and chemical import control were transferred in part to the head office of the Customs Division of the Treasury Department in Washington and in part to the office of the appraiser of merchandise in New York.

For a study of the various steps leading to the creation of the War Trade Board, and of its functioning, records, and dissolution, the following documents are essential: (1) the espionage act, June 15, 1917 (40 *U.S. Statutes at Large*, p. 217), authorizing the President (Title VII) to control, by proclamation, exportations

---

[1] The data contained in this report on the War Trade Board were compiled by Dr. James A. Robertson of the Department of Commerce.

from the United States and from Possessions of the United States; (2) executive order of June 22, 1917, vesting the administration of export control in the Secretary of Commerce, and creating an Exports Council; (3) executive proclamation of July 9, 1917, prohibiting the exportation of certain commodities except under the conditions stated in the proclamation; (4) executive order of August 21, 1917 (effective August 27), establishing the Exports Administrative Board and amending the provision with regard to the functions of the Exports Council; (5) executive proclamation of August 27, 1917 (effective August 30), prohibiting exports of practically all commodities to enemy territory and to the European neutrals except under license, and considerably enlarging the number of commodities that were placed under control by the proclamation of July 9, when offered for export to countries other than the above; (6) the trading with the enemy act of October 6, 1917 (40 *U.S. Statutes at Large*, p. 411), making it unlawful, among other things, for any person in the United States, except with the license of the President, to communicate or have any form of business or commercial relations with an enemy or enemy ally, as those persons are defined in the act, and providing for the control, by executive proclamation, of importations into the United States and into the possessions of the United States; (7) executive order of October 12, 1917, creating the War Trade Board; (8) two executive proclamations of November 28, 1917: the first extending the list of commodities subject to export control when destined for export to countries other than European neutrals and enemy and ally of enemy countries; the second containing a list of commodities, the importation of which was prohibited except under license; (9) two executive proclamations of February 14, 1918, declaring respectively that all merchandise exports and imports to or from any other country whatsoever, except possessions of the United States, were made subject to license control; (10) executive order of August 20, 1918, adding a representative of the War Industries Board to the membership of the War Trade Board; (11) executive order of March 3, 1919, as amended by executive orders of May 12 and June 23, 1919, authorizing the transfer of the War Trade Board to the Department of State, and the order of the War Trade Board of June 30, 1919, accomplishing such transfer;

(12) executive proclamation of June 24, 1919, transferring the control of exportations and importations of wheat and wheat flour from the War Trade Board to the United States Wheat Director; (13) departmental (State) orders of July 1 and October 7, 1919, creating the War Trade Board Section and prescribing its powers and duties; (14) the emergency tariff act of May 27, 1921 (42 *U.S. Statutes at Large,* p. 9), abolishing the War Trade Board Section of the Department of State, transferring its personnel, books, documents, and other records relating to dye and chemical import control to the Treasury Department, and prescribing the conditions and the classes of commodities, importations of which were to be subject to such control.

Functions

The War Trade Board was composed of representatives of the Secretary of State, the Secretary of the Treasury, the Secretary of Agriculture, the Secretary of Commerce, the Food Administration, the Shipping Board, and the War Industries Board. The objects for which it functioned were: (1) the commercial isolation of the enemy by control of United States exports to and imports from the enemy, ally of enemy, and neutral countries of Europe; (2) the financial isolation of the enemy by control of financial and business transactions and communications with enemies and allies of the enemy throughout the world, as those terms are defined in the trading with the enemy act; (3) the conservation of domestic supplies through export and tonnage restrictions and by obtaining essential imports from the powers that were associated with the United States in the war and from neutrals; (4) the conservation of ocean tonnage by the exercise of control of the fueling and provisioning of vessels in United States ports, and by import restrictions and priority in export shipments; (5) the procurement of tonnage by commercial and tonnage arrangements with other countries and the coördination of war trade activities of the United States with those of the governments that were associated with the United States in the war.

In these matters, the War Trade Board acted practically as the executive of the President, the Food Administration, the Shipping Board, the War Industries Board, the Fuel Administration, and other government organizations engaged in the prosecution of the war. Control over exports and imports, the fueling and provisioning of vessels, and trading with the enemy was exercised by issuing, withholding, or refusing licenses, and that this control might be exercised intelligently continuous liaison and coöperation were required with both permanent government units and with the emergency establishment, as well as with various national trade councils and with representatives of the allied powers. Such contact was especially close with the Bureau of Foreign and Domestic Commerce, Federal Trade Commission, Division of Customs of the Treasury Department, various offices of the State Department, War Department, Navy Department, Department of Justice, and Post Office Department, the Food Administration, Wheat Director, Sugar Equalization Board, Shipping Board, War Industries Board, Fuel Administration, Alien Property Custodian, American Diamond Committee, American Iron and Steel Institute, Plumbago-Graphite Association, Rubber Association of America, Inc., Tanners' Council of the United States of America, Textile Alliance, Inc., United States Shellac Importers Association, the Interallied Shipping Control Committee in New York, Interallied Blockade Committee in London, and several large European trade organizations, with each of which specific arrangements for coöperation were made.

The board restricted its own activities to (1) the formulation of specific policies outlined in occasional communications from the President with respect to the conservation of resources and the financial isolation of the enemy; (2) the consideration and choice of ways, means, and regulations for putting those policies into effect; (3) the devising of methods for coördinating its activities with those of other war agencies of the United States and with those of the governments of the countries associated with the United States; (4) the making of supply and ocean transportation arrangements with the associated governments; (5) the negotiation and operation of commercial and tonnage agreements with neutral countries, especially those of Europe; (6) the negotiation and operation of arrangements for obtaining from abroad supplies for the use of the United States and associated governments for military purposes and for civilian consumption in the United States;

(7) the supervision and direction of an executive force under the secretary, of a legal force under the counsellor, and of the bureaus and other units of the organization.

Organization

A **Contraband Committee** assisted in the formulation of rules and regulations relative to licenses, audited export and import licenses, handled special cases in which questions arose as to whether exceptions should be made to the general rules, and cases in which evasions, violations, or attempts to evade or violate the board's regulations were charged or suspected. Not long before the armistice was signed the Contraband Committee was superseded by the Exports Executive Committee and the Violations Committee.

A Bureau of Administration, a Division of Information, and a Bureau of Branches and Customs constituted the board's *administrative agencies*. A Bureau of Research and Statistics, a Bureau of War Trade Intelligence, and a Bureau of Foreign Agents constituted the board's *agencies of investigation and research*. A Bureau of Exports, a Bureau of Imports, a Bureau of Transportation, and a Bureau of Enemy Trade constituted the board's *agencies of control.* A summary of the functions of each of these agencies follows:

The **Bureau of Administration** furnished the personnel, office equipment, supplies, and organization required to carry out the policy of the board.

The **Division of Information** was the medium through which publicity was given to the policies, announcements, rules, and regulations of the board, and through which general information of a miscellaneous character, particularly that obtained from government publications, articles in the daily press, magazines and other periodicals, and announcements and regulations of other war organizations was procured and distributed among the members of the board and the personnel of the several bureaus. A Publications Section edited and published in mimeographed, multigraphed, or printed form (1) *Daily Record,* a confidential bulletin of the board; (2) *Daily Digest of the Press;* (3) *War Trade Board News,* published in the interest of the members of the organization; (4) *War Trade Board Rulings,* daily; (5) *War Trade Jour-*

nal, monthly; (6) *Rules and Regulations of the War Trade Board*, Nos. 1 and 2; (7) *Directory of the War Trade Board*; (8) *Enemy Trading Lists*; (9) *Confidential Suspect List*; (10) *Cloaks List*. A Distribution Section distributed material to the board organization in Washington, the branch offices, the press, and the general public. The library of the board had a clipping service and a translation service, besides books and periodicals. A General Information Service gave personal attention to specific requests and to the examination of printed material for data of interest to the organization.

The **Bureau of Branches and Customs** had jurisdiction over and management of all branches, coöperative offices, and representatives of the War Trade Board in the United States, and was responsible to the board for the transmission to the branches of all rulings of the board or of its committees and bureaus that might affect the branches or be necessary for their successful operation. The bureau was also charged with the duty of transmitting the rulings of the board to the Customs Division of the Treasury Department, the Post Office Department, and the Railroad Administration, all three of which coöperated with the board in the exercise of control over exports and imports. The branch offices instructed exporters and importers as to the proper method of complying with the regulations and rulings of the board with reference to exporting, importing, and enemy trade. They also received, recorded, and considered applications for export and bunker licenses, and in some instances issued the licenses.

The **Bureau of Research and Statistics** was formed by combining two bureaus, (1) the Bureau of Research and (2) the Bureau of Tabulation and Statistics, which had functioned separately from the creation of the War Trade Board until November, 1918, when they were made two divisions of the Bureau of Research and Statistics.

The Division of Research, originally the Bureau of Research, conducted the investigations necessary (1) to answer requests of officers and members of the board and other government organizations for information of an economic nature, such as economic sources, production and consumption figures, trade movements of important materials and commodities, and (2) to facilitate the decision of questions as to whether domestic supplies of commodities were sufficient to admit of exportation, and if so, whether only for purposes incident to the prosecution of the war, or for private commercial purposes as well. The division kept in easily available form information on matters constantly before the board, and initiated investigations in anticipation of inquiries and in order to prepare reports of value to the board and other war agencies.

The Division of Tabulation and Statistics tabulated export and import data showing the export and import licenses granted and refused, the quantities and values of each commodity licensed for export and import, and the countries of destination or origin. It prepared serial and special tabulations for the use of the various bureaus of the board and other branches of the government, checked the use of licenses in order to detect different forms of abuse, such as overshipment, unauthorized shipments, and alteration of licenses, and supplied conversion and stowage factors of commodities for government statistical agencies.

The **Bureau of War Trade Intelligence** collected data and imparted information to the Bureau of Exports, Bureau of Imports, and Bureau of Transportation with respect to the enemy or non-enemy character or affiliations of applicants for license, consignors, consignees, and purchasers of United States goods abroad, referred to in various applications. It furnished information to the Bureau of Enemy Trade respecting applicants for license to trade or communicate with enemies or allies of the enemy, or persons as to whom there was reasonable ground to believe that they were engaged in dealing with enemies or enemy allies. It furnished information of interest to the State Department, the Secret Service of the Treasury Department, the Bureau of Investigation of the Department of Justice, the Military and Naval Intelligence Divisions of the War and Navy Departments, the Postal and Cable Censorship Boards, the Alien Property Custodian, the Shipping Board, and various intelligence agencies of the associated governments, from all of which information was also received.

The **Bureau of Foreign Agents** determined the need for War Trade Board representatives in foreign countries, employed men to serve in that capacity, instructed and informed them, received and distributed their reports, which contained information of various kinds desired by the board and its several bureaus, especially the Bureau of War Trade Intelligence. Besides procuring the information contained in these reports, the foreign agents represented the board at conferences and on various interallied committees, and assisted the board in its negotiations of commercial and shipping agreements with other countries.

The Bureau of Exports considered applications for licenses to export from the United States, and issued or refused such licenses. It administered the regulations adopted in the interests of conservation of the resources of the United States so far as such regulations were applicable to exportations, administered measures adopted to prevent exportations to the countries of the enemy, the countries of the enemy's allies, and territories occupied by their forces, and inaugurated conservation measures designed to restrict the licensing of exportations to neutral countries. It administered the provisions, so far as export features of them were concerned, relative to the rationing of supplies for the countries with which the United States was associated in the war, and for the neutral countries under the various commercial agreements with their governments. It administered the measures intended to facilitate the movement from United States ports of supplies for the associated governments, for United States forces abroad, and for certain relief organizations. The bureau maintained a corps of experts, known as trade advisers, who were specially versed in and kept themselves posted as to production and supply, and as to the manufacturing, transportation, and market conditions which affected the groups of commodities under consideration for license to export, and whose duty it was to pass on and advise with respect to applications for such licenses from the viewpoint of conservation. A corps of trade distributors was maintained to consider applications for license to export to the particular countries or groups of countries to which they were respectively assigned. It was also the duty of the trade distributors to see that ration limitations were not exceeded in the quantities licensed for export, and that compliance was had with restrictions respecting exportations of particular commodities and with conditions relat-

ing to reëxportation to the enemy from the country of destination
as well as with any other conditions that might be imposed as pre-
requisites to the granting of licenses to export to the countries in
their respective jurisdictions.

The Bureau of Imports administered the control measures
adopted to facilitate, through the licensing system, the conservation
of tonnage for transportation of essentials and for giving priority
to the procurement of such raw materials and commodities as were
needed in the United States for manufactures for, or use by, the
government, or such as were essential for civilian use. It allocated
certain of the essential imported materials or commodities when but
limited supplies could be procured from abroad or provided with
tonnage for import. It procured guarantees against reëxport from
the United States or diversion from certain uses when such guarantees were required by the country of origin. In cases in which
adequate supplies for government manufacture or use were of para-
mount importance, it enforced conditions under which the government could obtain option to purchase such quantities as were required of the imported commodity prior to sale or release to other
consumers. The bureau maintained a corps of trade advisers whose
duty it was, in connection with the administration of the measures
for the conservation of ocean tonnage, to reduce the quantity imported of certain commodities and materials, to enforce the prohibition against the import of certain non-essentials except under the
conditions and in the particular instances specified in the regulations, to adjust the licensing of importations so as to bring about
reductions in lengths of haul in order to increase the number of
voyages per year in certain lines of traffic, to cause goods on the
American side of the Atlantic to be imported into the United
States whenever practicable by sailing vessels or small steamers
unsuitable for trans-Atlantic service, and to procure the importation of various bulky materials in more concentrated form.

The Bureau of Transportation administered the measures for
controlling the fueling and provisioning of vessels. It prevented the
use of coal, fuel oil, and ship's stores, when purchased in the
United States or brought into United States ports from abroad,
for voyages for the delivery of cargoes destined either directly or

indirectly for the benefit of the enemy or the enemy's allies. It co-operated with the Bureau of Exports and the Bureau of Imports in the enforcement of measures for the conservation of tonnage.

The **Bureau of Enemy Trade** considered and acted on applications for licenses involving trading with, or on behalf of, or for the benefit of the enemy or the enemy's allies. It considered and acted upon applications for license to enter into, or consummate financial or other business transactions with persons, firms, or corporations throughout the world, known or believed to be enemies or allies of the enemy, within the meaning of those terms as used in the trading with the enemy act.

Publications

Report of the War Trade Board for the Period ended December 31, 1917 (Washington, 1918, 10 pages).

A report to the President by the chairman of the board. It outlines the functions of the several units of the board and contains a small amount of historical matter.

Report of the War Trade Board (Washington, 1920, 476 pages). A report to the President by the chairman of the board, June 30, 1919.

A most important document and essential to any study of the War Trade Board. It is divided into six parts: Establishment of the War Trade Board and delegation of powers to it; The war trade policy of the United States and the functions of the War Trade Board; The execution of the functions of the War Trade Board; The relaxation of war-time control over trade; The organization of the War Trade Board; Appendix, containing ten ex-hibits, as follows: Laws, presidential proclamations, and executive orders; History of import rulings; List of imports controlled by government agencies; List of imports controlled through trade associations; Commodities for which importers were required to furnish the government an option to purchase; List of allocated imports; Export conservation list; Export allocations of caustic soda, questionnaire; Appropriations and expenditures; Personnel of the War Trade Board. The text is accompanied by charts showing: exports from the United States to various foreign countries; the exports from and imports to the United States, of various commodities; tonnage; and the or-ganization of the War Trade Board as a whole and each of its subdivisions. This is one of the most important contributions to the economic history of the war that has been published by the government.

Journal of the War Trade Board (Washington, 1917-1919). Issued by the Division of Information of the War Trade Board, under different formats, and in 23 numbers, as follows: November 15, December 10, 1917; January 8, 21, February 1, 11, May 1, 1918; and beginning with June, 1918, monthly, without special date. The title and subtitle change, as does the size. Nos. 7 and 15 contain cumulative indexes, and indexes covering one volume only are contained in other numbers beginning with No. 8.

The purpose of this publication is stated as follows: "The Journal is intended to keep branch offices of the Board, Commercial Attachés, consuls, customs officials, industrial and commercial organizations, trade journals, exporters, importers, and the daily press informed concerning the administrative procedure of the War Trade Board." It contains official announcements of the board, War Trade Board Rulings, other statements authorized by the board during the period covered by each number, material relative to exports and imports, lists of commodities requiring export license, conservation lists, and other materials bearing on the special field of the board, published in order that exporters, importers, and shippers might carry on their work with full knowledge of the methods of procedure necessary. The *Journal* circulated in editions ranging from 25,000 to 45,000 for each number. One copy was sent to all individuals, firms, and corporations on the mailing list of the War Trade Board, including applicants for export licenses. A complete set is available in the Library of Congress and in other libraries.

Rulings and Regulations of the War Trade Board. Two parts: No. 1 has subtitle, *Official Information for Shippers, Exporters, Importers, and Commercial and Trade Organizations,* November, 1917 (Washington, 1917, 69 pages); No. 2 has subtitle, *Manual for Shippers* (Washington, 1918, 112 pages). No. 1 is a compilation of the regulations of the War Trade Board to November, 1917. No. 2 is a second edition of No. 1, together with some new regulations. Regulations issued later than the date of No. 2 were published in the *Journal of the War Trade Board.*

Rules and Regulations of the Bureau of Imports of the War Trade Board (Washington, 1918, 25 pages). Embraces various forms used in the bureau until they became obsolete.

Directory of the War Trade Board and Its Bureaus (Washington, 1917 and 1918, 4 editions: No. 1, December 19, 1917, 12 pages; No. 2, February 1, 1918, 19 pages; No. 3, May, 1918, 19 pages; September, 1918, 19 pages). After the 4th edition mimeographed sheets showing changes in personnel were issued about every two weeks.

Trading with the Enemy, Enemy Trading List (Washington, 1917 and 1918, three parts). Part 1 (1917, 28 pages), contains notes on the enemy trading list and the list; a supplement of 8 pages was issued January 15, 1918. Part 2 (March 15, 1918, 152 pages) superseded all previous lists, supplements and announcements. It has 17 supplements: (1) April 15, 1918, 6 pages; (2) May 1, 1918, 8 pages; (3) May 17, 1918, 16 pages, with cumulative index embracing the dates March 15 to May 17, 1918; (4) May 31, 1918, 20 pages; (5) June 14, 1918, 24 pages; (6) June 28, 1918, 29 pages; (7) July 12, 1918, 31 pages; (8) July 26, 1918, 37 pages; (9) August 9, 1918, 39 pages; (10) August 23, 1918, 40 pages; (11) September 6, 1918, 44 pages; (12) September 20, 1918, 47 pages; (13) October 4, 1918, 50 pages; (14) October 18, 1918, 51 pages; (15) November 1, 1918, 52 pages; (16) November 15, 1918, 54 pages; (17) November 29, 1918, 56 pages. Part 3 (December 13, 1918, 195 pages) has 2 supplements: (1) January 24, 1919, 12 pages; (2) February 7, 1919, 16 pages.

Export Conservation List, May 17, 1918 (Washington, 1918, 8 pages).

Export Conservation List. Effective October 15, 1918 (Washington, 1918, 19 pages). Contains additions and modifications from May 17, 1918, to October 15, 1918. Superseded all previous export conservation lists.

Export Conservation List. Effective December 6, 1918 (Washington, 1918, 14 pages). Contains additions and modifications from October 15 to December 6, 1918. Superseded all previous export conservation lists.

Export Conservation List. Modifications and Removals Not Previously Announced are Effective on This Date (Washington, 1918, 7 pages). Superseded all previous export conservation lists. This and the following list show the relaxation that began immediately after the signing of the armistice.

Export Conservation List. Modifications and Removals Not Previously Announced are Effective on This Date (Washington, 1918, 7 pages). Superseded all previous export conservation lists.

Control of Exportations and Importations under the Espionage and Trading with the Enemy Acts, by Edmund W. Van Dyke, is an unpublished compilation available only in galley proof (1920, 28 galleys). It shows what commodities were from time to time included in the export conservation lists and lists of restricted imports, and gives dates of inclusion in, and removals from, such lists.

War Trade Board. Bureau of Transportation. General Rules. No. 1. "Governing Granting Licenses for Lumber, Fuel, Port, Sea and Ship's Stores and Supplies" (Washington, n.d., printed on two sheets of paper letter size).

Coal-Tar Dyes for Which Import Licenses Were Granted during the Fiscal Year 1920, by Charles S. Hawes (Washington, 1921, 50 pages,

2 tables). Table 1 contains statistics relative to dyes licensed by classes; table 2 contains statistics of dyes licensed by brands.

The following agreements were published for the confidential use of the government and subsequently reprinted from the originals:

Memorandum between the War Trade Board of the United States of America and the Government of Switzerland relating to Exports from the United States to Switzerland. December 5, 1917 (Washington, 1918, 13 pages).

Memorandum of Agreement between the War Trade Board . . . and the Norwegian Government relating to Exports from the United States to Norway. April 30, 1918 (Washington, 1918, 13 pages).

Memorandum of Agreement between the British, French, and Italian Governments and the Swedish Government. May 29, 1918. Adhered to by the War Trade Board by a memorandum of May 29, 1918, set out therein (Washington, 1918, 46 pages).

Danish Agreement. Agreement between the War Trade Board and Danish Special Shipping Committee (Fragthavn), September 18, 1918; agreement between the War Trade Board and the Merchants' Guild of Copenhagen and the Danish Chamber of Manufacturers, September 18, 1918; letter from the chairman of the War Trade Board to the Minister of Denmark, September 18, 1918; letter from the Minister of Denmark to the chairman of the War Trade Board, September 18, 1918; letter from the chairman, September 21, 1918 (Washington, 1918, 43 pages).

Agreement between the Royal Netherlands Government and the British, French, and Italian Governments and the War Trade Board. November 25, 1918 (Washington, 1919, 11 pages).

Joint Agreement between the Governments of Great Britain, France, and Italy and the Netherlands Oversea Trust. Adhered to by the War Trade Board. December 17, 1918 (Washington, 1919, 13 pages).

Memorandum between the Governments of France and Great Britain and the War Trade Board and the Swiss Confederation. January 22, 1919 (Washington, 1919, 8 pages).

The Rationing and Tonnage Negotiations with Switzerland, by the Bureau of Research and Statistics, War Trade Board (Washington, 1919, 146 pages).

Export Trade Policy of the United Kingdom, 1913-1918 (Washington, 1918, 60 pages), by the Bureau of Research.

Stowage of Ship Cargoes (Washington, 1919, 69 pages), compiled in the Division of Tabulation and Statistics.

The following publications were either compiled by members of the staff of the War Trade Board and published by other branches of the government or were compiled jointly by the War Trade Board and some other government agency:

Government Control over Prices, by Paul Willard Garrett assisted by Isador Lubin and Stella Stewart (Washington, 1920, 834 pages). This is No. 3 of the bulletins, edited by Wesley C. Mitchell, which constitute a "History of Prices during the War." This particular bulletin was prepared and published by the War Trade Board in coöperation with the War Industries Board. It is a record and an analysis of price regulation exercised by the government during the war.

Stowage Factors for Ship Cargoes: Space Requirements of Commodities Packed for Overseas Shipment (Washington, 1919, 72 pages). The first edition was compiled by the Division of Tabulation and Statistics, War Trade Board, and published by the board. A revised edition was published the same year by the United States Shipping Board.

Stowage of Ship Cargoes, by Thomas Rothwell Taylor (Washington, 1920, 350 pages). This is an expansion of the preceding under the auspices of the Bureau of Foreign and Domestic Commerce, Department of Commerce.

Economic Aspects of the Commerce and Industry of the Netherlands, 1912-1918, by Blaine F. Moore (Washington, 1919, 109 pages). This is one of five economic studies of foreign countries during the war by the Bureau of Research and Statistics, War Trade Board, that have been published by the Bureau of Foreign and Domestic Commerce, Department of Commerce. The other four are:

The Economic Position of the United Kingdom: 1912-1918, by William A. Patton (Washington, 1919, 160 pages).

Brazil, A Study of Economic Conditions since 1913, by Arthur H. Redfield assisted by Helen Watkins (Washington, 1920, 99 pages).

The Economic Position of Switzerland during the War, by Louis A. Rufener (Washington, 1919, 88 pages).

The Economic Position of Argentina during the War, by L. Brewster Smith, Harry T. Collings, and Elizabeth Murphey (Washington, 1920, 140 pages).

Records

The records of the War Trade Board and of the organizations which preceded it were, with a few exceptions, transferred to the War Trade Board Section of the Department of State and have remained in the custody of that department since the War Trade Board Section was abolished in May, 1921. For the most part they are in the original vertical filing cases, of which there are more than 1800 four-drawer sections, and nineteen steel safes. They are described by their custodian, E. W. Van Dyke, in a typewritten memorandum entitled, "Records in the Files of the War Trade Board Section of the Department of State" (March 21, 1921, 47 pages).

An inventory of the records of each unit of the organization follows:

The Board

Minutes of the meetings of the board.

Certified copies of the proclamations, executive orders, and instructions under which it acted.

Instructions of the board to its subdivisions and its foreign representatives.

Regulations and press notices issued by the board from time to time.

Agreements made by the board with certain European neutral nations, together with correspondence and memoranda relative to the negotiations preceding the agreements.

Correspondence with the President and other government officials.

Correspondence and notes of conferences with the various war missions and diplomatic representatives of other governments in this country, and with representatives of the board abroad.

Cablegrams to and from foreign representatives and agents of the board, consuls of the United States, and other United States government officials stationed in foreign countries.

Reports and memoranda submitted to the board by officers of other war boards and departments of the government, also note of conferences with these officers.

Reports and memoranda submitted to the board by members of its own personnel.

Minutes of the meetings of the Inter-Allied Blockade Committee in London and of other foreign war organizations.

Miscellaneous papers and data bearing on the work of the board.

General Instructions (mimeographed or multigraphed). These were instructions given by the board itself to the Bureau of Exports or to that bureau and the other bureaus and offices as well. They were generally of a confidential nature, but public announcements were frequently based on them. They were issued during the entire period of the board's existence, generally after the board meetings and by and with the authority of the board. A few are in printed form. Many were instructions to the Bureau of Exports to issue licenses to export.

Special Instructions (mimeographed or multigraphed). These treated special matters of importance and were issued for the use of the several subdivisions of the board. Some of them were with regard to matters related to shipping. They numbered some 250 to 300.

Export Interpretative Rulings (mimeographed or multigraphed). These consisted of rulings by the board pertaining to exports. They were numbered serially to 300 or higher; some unnumbered.

Import Interpretative Rulings (mimeographed or multigraphed). These consisted of rulings by the board pertaining to exports. They were numbered serially from 1 (November 30, 1917) to 548 (October 1, 1919) or higher; some unnumbered.

War Trade Board Regulations (mimeographed or multigraphed). About 1000 in number, of which Nos. 1 (January 2, 1918) to 849 (May 3, 1919) are numbered serially. Those issued in 1917 were also numbered as of that year (No. 1-'17 (July 9) to No. 85-'17); a few were unnumbered. Some of these regulations were released to the press, while other were confidential in nature. Among them are certain documents of great importance, as, for instance, "The Commercial Agreement with Norway, of May 4, 1918." Those regulations to which publicity was given were issued through the *Journal of the War Trade Board*, the *United States Official Bulletin, Commerce Reports,* two pamphlets, and the daily newspapers.

Instructions to the Bureau of Enemy Trade (mimeographed or multigraphed). About 200. Not numbered serially.

Contraband Committee

Book of minutes of its decisions, and various records.

Bureau of Administration

Books, vouchers, correspondence; records of appointments, services, resignations, etc., of members, officers, and employees of the board; miscellaneous records.

Division of Information

Correspondence, mailing lists, official sets of the various publications of the board, instructions to bureaus and personnel, and mimeographed or multigraphed advance copies of announcements and regulations.

Daily record (mimeographed or multigraphed). Issued every working day morning, October 17, 1917, to June 30, 1919. Beginning with No. 48, the paper appeared under a special head which was changed slightly at a later date. This was the confidential bulletin of the War Trade Board and contained the official announcements of the board to the staff, announcements of bureau directors, matters pertaining to internal administration, and other data. As such it was the medium for the distribution among the several units of the board of the regulations which were to be released on the following day. No. 1, for example, contained the following: Additions to Conservation List; Complete Conservation List; and Complete List of Articles requiring License.

Daily Digest of News and Comment (mimeographed or multigraphed). Issued daily from April 27, 1918, to March 17, 1919. It appeared under a printed title and head as follows: "War Trade Board. Digest of News and Comment. This Digest published daily at noon, reflects only the sentiments of the newspapers and other publications quoted. Clippings quoted are on file in the Division of Information." This caption was later changed to "Daily Digest of the Press. Clippings quoted are on file in the Division of Information." The paper contained a summary of articles appearing in forty newspapers and more than two hundred technical and trade periodicals received in the War Trade Board, referring either directly to the activities of the War Trade Board or dealing with subjects of special importance to the members of the organization. The circulation reached 300 copies, of which 190 were within the board itself and 110 outside.

The War Trade Board News. Contained welfare and organization news which it was thought might be interesting and helpful to the employees. It was of slight importance and was discontinued before the War Trade Board was dissolved.

The Confidential Suspect List (mimeographed or multigraphed). This list, which was for consultation in the War Trade Board only and did not circulate outside, was issued confidentially by the Division of Information. It was, however, open for consultation by shippers and interested persons.

The Cloaks List (mimeographed or multigraphed). Issued confidentially by the Division of Information and used in much the same way as the Confidential Suspect List.

News clippings. Several file cases are filled with clippings made by the bureau's clipping service. Some of these are stored in the sub-basement of the State, War, and Navy Building.

Bureau of Branches and Customs

Instructions and interpretations forwarded from time to time to branch offices.

Reports from branch offices.

Memoranda and letters from branch offices.

Instructions received from the board.

Correspondence with other bureaus of the board.

Instructions to and correspondence with the Customs Division of the Treasury Department and individual collectors of the customs.

Correspondence with the traffic executive of the allied powers in the United States, and with various other beneficiaries of the general or blanket licenses which were issued by the board in special cases.

Correspondence with branch offices as to routine and details connected with their work.

Bureau of Research and Statistics

Correspondence, economic data and studies, memoranda, instructions, etc.

Record cards punched by means of tabulating machines for the period

September 1, 1917, to May 10, 1919, when such tabulations were discontinued; 12,378,356 cards showing export and import licenses granted and refused and actual exportations and importations, arranged by commodity groups and countries.

Daily and monthly tabulations: Daily report of licenses granted for exportation of foodstuffs to eleven country groups, showing quantities, values, and the number of licenses; Monthly reports of exportation of coal, showing countries, number of shipments, quantities and values; Daily report in detail of licenses granted for exportation to Mexico; Monthly report of licenses for exportation of arms and ammunition to Mexico; Monthly report of licenses granted for importation of certain groups of commodities from Russia; Monthly report of licenses granted for exportation to Argentina, Brazil, and Uruguay, showing quantities, values, value per ton, percentage of actual exportations to quantities licensed, stowage factors, value per cubic foot, etc. About 1000 of such tabulations were issued in 1918.

List of Data available in the Bureau of Research, War Trade Board, issued in mimeograph November 1, 1918 (84 pages). The list (No. 2739) is arranged alphabetically, beginning with "Abrasives," and ending with "Zinc." Its character may be seen from the following citations:

Abrasives. United States imports, 1917, monthly by countries and districts of entry.
Brazil. Imports of rice, 1911-1916.
Meat and Dairy Products. United States exports to Chile, Peru, and Bolivia, July, 1916-June, 1917.
Tungsten. From South China.
Zinc. U.S. Exports of spelter cast in pigs and slabs, produced from foreign ore, July, 1917-February, 1919 (by months).

Additions to List of Data available in the Files of the Bureau of Research and Statistics, War Trade Board (mimeographed). Supplement No. 1, November 1, 1917-February 1, 1918 (32 pages); contains only additions to the complete list issued on November 1, 1918. Much of the data noted in these lists is highly important. Some of it should, however, be checked back against the original sources in order to avoid inaccuracies.

Bureau of War Trade Intelligence

Various card records: *e.g.* (1) information taken from letters and written reports (about 1200 daily at the height of the activities of the bureau) and hectographed on 5 x 8 inch cards, of which about 600,000 had been accumulated when the bureau ceased to operate in April, 1919; (2) record of persons and concerns, the property or interests of whom were in question or had been taken over by the government.

Forms used in the bureau.

Correspondence, reports, and memoranda relative to the investigations of the bureau, and notes of oral information obtained by the personnel of the bureau in the course of the investigations.

Status and other reports and memoranda from the branch offices of the War Trade Board and its representatives and agents abroad.

Letters, comments, and reports relative to the information obtained from letters that had been intercepted by the several censorships.

Secret service reports, about 2500 in number, relative to the status of individual persons and concerns.

Inter- and intra-bureau correspondence.

Correspondence with branch offices of the War Trade Board.

Correspondence with other departments of the government, various intelligence services, Committee of Public Information, Federal Reserve Board, Federal Trade Commission, Alien Property Custodian, and other war organizations.

Correspondence with foreign diplomatic and consular officers in the United States, and war missions of the entente powers to the United States.

Enemy trading lists, compiled by the bureau.

Confidential consignors list, compiled by the bureau.

Suspect and Cloaks lists, compiled by the bureau.

Bureau of Foreign Agents

By departmental order No. 143, of July 1, 1919, after the Department of State had assumed control of the War Trade Board, the administration of the Bureau of Foreign Agents, together with its equipment and personnel, was placed under the direction of the chief of the Consular Bureau of the Department of State. The records of the Bureau of Foreign Agents are now, therefore, a part of the records of the Consular Bureau; but copies of most of the reports and of the cable correspondence with foreign representatives and agents are in the files of the secretary of the War Trade Board, of the Bureau of Enemy Trade, and of the Bureau of War Trade Intelligence.

Bureau of Exports

Applications for license, more than 3,000,000 in number; copies of the export licenses; notices of refusal to grant license.

Copies of the various forms used in the bureau.

Correspondence with applicants for export licenses.

Correspondence in the nature of inquiries and answers to inquiries relative to license requirements, procedure, and country and commodity regulations.

Memoranda and correspondence with, and report from, other departments of the government.

Statistical information, etc., with respect to various commodities with which the trade advisers and officers of the bureau were obliged to acquaint themselves in order properly to perform their duties in passing on applications for licenses.

Data, memoranda, etc., relative to the necessities of the neutral countries, their requirements in connection with manufactures for the allies, the rationing of their supplies, the possibilities of exchanges of commodities, the distribution of commodities exported from the United States, and the procuring from consignors abroad of guarantees against reëxport.

Correspondence with the Allied Provisions Export Commission and Wheat Export Company, organizations intrusted with purchases in this country for the allied powers.

Correspondence with, and data from, other war organizations and departments of the government with regard to the requirements of the government, and with regard to the conservation of commodities and materials, quantities available for export, available transportation facilities, etc.

In the latter part of 1917, following the institution of export control, approximately 425,000 applications for export license were considered; in 1918, more than 2,000,000 were considered, and more than 230,000 refused; in 1919, notwithstanding that relaxation of restriction was in progress, a very large number of applications were considered and licenses granted or refused. During 1918, about 50,000 letters were written monthly by the bureau.

Bureau of Imports

Applications for import licenses, approximately 210,000 in number, and official copies of the licenses and allocation certificates issued thereon.

Notices of refusal to grant import licenses.

Copies of the various forms used in the bureau.

Correspondence with respect to import licenses and the general work of the bureau.

Memoranda, reports, statistical data, etc., with respect to economic conditions and importations.

Reports and information received from, and correspondence with, the various commercial organizations with which the bureau coöperated.

Bulletins and announcements sent out, and forms used by coöperating organizations in their dealings in behalf of the War Trade Board as assignees and distributors.

The records of this bureau relating to importation of dyes and dyestuffs, synthetic organic chemicals, synthetic organic drugs, and coaltar products generally were transferred to the Dye and Chemical Section of the Treasury Department under section 501 of the emergency tariff act of May 27, 1921. Subsequently, under the tariff act of 1922, these records were transferred in part to the head office of the Division of Customs, and in part to the office of the appraiser of merchandise in New York.

Bureau of Transportation

Applications for bunker licenses, with official copies of the licenses granted and notices of refusal to grant license.

Copies of forms used in the bureau.

Correspondence with applicants for licenses.

Agreements, guarantees, and other evidences of obligation on the part of owners and masters of vessels to comply with the conditions imposed by the regulations with respect to chartering, destination of vessels, dunnage, approval, inspection, and supervision of cargoes, as to non-enemy ownership or interest.

Forms in which consignments of cargoes were to be made.

Records relative to enemy or non-enemy character of applicants of consignees.

Bureau of Enemy Trade

Applications for licenses, of which about 25,000 were considered, together with the official copies of licenses and notices of refusal to grant license.

Copies of forms used in the bureau.

Correspondence with applicants for license.

Reports from, and memoranda to the bureau, showing the action by the Bureau of War Trade Intelligence in connection with applications for license.

Memoranda and data used in the consideration of applications.

This bureau was merged with the Bureau of War Trade Intelligence in May, 1919, but the records of the two bureaus were not consolidated.

UNITED STATES FOOD ADMINISTRATION

Organization and Functions

THE United States Food Administration was organized on a voluntary basis in May, 1917, but its work was chiefly educational until its establishment by executive order of August 10, 1917, under authority of the act of the same date: "An act to provide further for the national security and defense by encouraging the production, conserving the supply, and controlling the distribution of food products and fuel." After the armistice its activities were greatly curtailed and after August 21, 1920, it ceased to exist.

The activities of the Food Administration were as follows: (1) educational campaign, to secure the voluntary coöperation of the people in carrying out the measures of the Food Administration; (2) measures of food conservation, the object of which was to save wheat, meat, fats, and sugar, in order to meet the needs of the allies and to provide against possible domestic shortage; (3) measures to reduce the cost of distribution and to eliminate profiteering by means of licensing and voluntary agreements; (4) measures to secure an equitable and adequate distribution of food by regulating the amount of sales and by controlling transportation; (5) coördination of purchases for the governments of the United States and of the allies, allocation of purchases among sailors, and direct purchases of certain staples, especially wheat and sugar; (6) measures to secure adequate production through the guarantee or stabilization of prices; (7) insuring an adequate supply of certain collateral commodities, such as jute bags, binder twine, arsenic, ammonia, tin, etc.

The Food Administration was organized in a central administration located in Washington, and in branch administrations in each State. The former was organized in various divisions: Cereals, Meats and fats, Vegetables and fruits, Sea food, Dairy products, Sugar, Enforcement of regulations, Exports and imports, Storage, Conservation, Railway transportation, Overseas transport, Distribution, Coördinated allied army and navy purchases, States relations, Licensing, Statistics, etc. The state administrations, under which were organized county and city administrations, had a wide range of administrative functions. There were also organized from time to time as need arose various boards, inter-departmental or inter-ally, and numerous committees of producers, dealers, and distributors, which acted in an advisory capacity or facilitated the work of the Food Administration.

Two corporations were created to act as agents of the Food Administration in purchasing and selling. The first of these, the Food Administration Grain Corporation, was organized by executive order of August 14, 1917, for the purpose of buying and selling wheat and controlling its price; on June 30, 1919, it was reorganized by executive order of May 14, 1919, under authority of the wheat control act of March 4, of that year, as the United States Grain Corporation under the control of the Wheat Director. When the United States Food Administration and the office of Wheat Director were abolished by executive order, August 21, 1920, the head of the United States Grain Corporation was designated its president and director. The other corporation was the Sugar Equalization Board, created, July 11, 1918, by executive authority, for the purpose of coöperating with the allies in the purchase of Cuban sugar and of controlling its distribution in the United States.

Publications

A convenient compilation of laws relating to the Food Administration is *Laws of the Sixty-Fifth and Sixty-Sixth Congresses relating to Food* (House Document Room, 1920, 152 pages). This contains also the executive orders and proclamations on the same subject and the food acts of 1906, 1912, and 1913 with the regulations for their enforcement.

Brief accounts of the operations of the Food Administration are contained in the reports, of which three have been printed. The first of these, *United States Food Administration, Report for the Year 1917* (House Doc. 837, 65th Cong., 2 Sess.) is exceedingly brief. More informing is the *Annual Report of the United States Food Administration for the Year 1918* (Washington, 1919), most of which (pp. 59-317), is devoted to the publication of the licensing regulations adopted by the administration, the most convenient form in which they have been printed. The final report of the Food Administration has not been printed but there has been privately printed by Herbert Hoover a *Preface to a Report of the United States Food Administration* (April, 1920), which contains a summary in fifty pages of the work of the administration. A manuscript "History of the Food Administration," in about 160 typed pages, by William Mullendore, has been prepared to serve as a complete record of the activities of the Food Administration, but has not been published and remains in the files. It deals with the organization and powers of the Food Administration and takes up in turn the regulation of each of the commodities under control.

A careful contemporary study is worthy of note: "The Wheat and Flour Trade under Food Administration Control, 1917-1918," by Wilfred Eldred in *Quarterly Journal of Economics* (XXXIII, pp. 1-70, November, 1918).

An unofficial and popular account of one of the most important divisions of the Food Administration has been published: *War Time Control of Distribution of Foods. A Short History of the Distribution Division of the United States Food Administration, its Personnel and Achievements* (New York, Macmillan, 1920, 164 pages), by Albert N. Merritt, a member of the staff of the Food Administration.

The Food Administration put forth from time to time a great number and variety of publications. The Division of Bibliography of the Library of Congress has issued in mimeograph a "Trial Check List of the Publications of the U.S. Food Administration" in which are entered 425 items. Most of these are educational in character, designed to be of service in the campaign for food conservation and to provide material for speakers, writers, teachers, and others. The following single publications and series are of value for the purposes of this survey:

Bulletin No. 6 (Washington, 1917, 32 pages). This was published in August, 1917; it contains the plans of the Food Administration for wheat, bread, and flour control and a detailed statement of the food problem of the country under the headings, Cereals, Food animals, Meats, Dairy products, Wool and leather, Sugar, Vegetables, and Fish and sea foods.

Policies and Plan of Operation: Wheat, Flour, and Bread (December 1, 1917, no imprint, 171 pages). This contains, among other, sections on the following subjects: Marketing the 1916 harvest, World supply of wheat for 1917, Problems in the 1917 harvest, Determination of a fair price for government purchase, Organization of the Grain Corporation, Organization of the Milling Division, Organization of the Wholesale and Retail Division, Organization of the Baking Division, Rules and regulations, Voluntary agreements.

Bulletin No. 12. A Wheat Conservation Program for the United States (Washington, February, 1918, 15 pages).

Reference Handbook of Food Statistics as relating to the War, by Raymond Pearl, chief of the Statistical Division of the Food Administration, and Esther Pearl Matchett (Washington, 1918, 124 pages).

General Index Numbers of Food Prices on a Nutritive Value Basis, by Raymond Pearl (U.S. Food Administration, August, 1918, 13 pages).

Production of Meat in the United States and its Distribution during the War, by Stephen Chase, in charge of Meat and Live-Stock Section, Statistical Division, U.S. Food Administration (Washington, 1918, 85 pages). This contains 81 statistical tables and 11 charts.

Weekly Bulletin, Nos. 1-32, August, 1917-March 30, 1918. Each number consisted of a group of releases compiled from trade and technical journals by the Trade and Technical Press Bureau of the Food Administration. The subjects chiefly treated are economies in food, fuel, power, and transportation. A set is in the Library of Congress.

Official Statement of the Food Administration, Nos. 1-9, June 6-December 16, 1918. Contains statistics and reports respecting exports, stocks, available and prospective supplies, etc.

Minutes of the Committee on Prices, August 17-30, 1917. This is a mimeographed volume containing the minutes of the meetings of the committee, H. A. Garfield, chairman, which fixed the price of no. 1 Northern spring wheat at $2.20. With the minutes are bound 54 appendixes, consisting of reports, statements, statistics, memoranda, etc., which were considered by the committee. The volume here described is in the Library of Congress among the publications of the Food Administration.

The Story of the United States Grain Corporation (42 Broadway, New York, April 5, 1920, 19 pages). A brief general account of operations.

Grain and Flour Statistics during the War, United States Grain Corporation, compiled by A. L. Russell, statistician (no imprint, 1919, 43 pages).

Supplement to Grain and Flour Statistics during the War, United States Grain Corporation, compiled by A. L. Russell (no imprint, 1920, 44 pages). These two publications consist of statistical tables based upon the reports required from licensed mills and elevators by the Milling Division of the Food Administration and by the Grain Corporation. The first of these publications contains 34 tables, among which are the following: Digest of mill reports, June 15, 1918; Pre-war flour production by States; Wheat movement, 1917-1918; Wheat stocks, 1917-1918; Wheat movement from farms, 1917-1918; Flour purchases by

Milling Division and by Grain Corporation; Distribution of flour purchases, export and domestic. Among the 49 tables in the *Supplement*,
are noted the following: Wheat movement by States from farms and
apparent farm disappearance for 1917-1918; Abstract of average
flour prices; Average wholesale bread prices; Average retail bread
prices; Exports of domestic merchandise; Export of foodstuffs during
the war; Wheat and flour exports and distribution, 1917-1920.

*Conference of Representatives of the Grain Trade of the United
States, Washington, D. C., August 15, 1917* (57 pages).

*Conference of the Representatives of the Grain Trade of the United
States, held under the Auspices of the United States Food Administration Grain Corporation, New York, April 30, 1918* (252 pages).

Official Statement of Wheat Director, Nos. 1-10, October 1, 1919-July
1, 1920 (New York). Statistical information.

*Conference of Trade Representatives with the United States Wheat
Director*, New York, June 10-11, 1919 (259 pages).

*A Statistical Survey of the Sugar Industry and Trade of the United
States, 1918 and 1919*, by J. Bernhardt (New York, U.S. Sugar Equalization Board, 1920, 113 pages). Tables and diagrams showing receipts
of sugar, destination of sugar, etc., based on the figures secured by the
Sugar Equalization Board.

Government Control of the Sugar Industry in the United States, by
J. Bernhardt (New York, Macmillan, 1920, 272 pages). This is an
account of the work of the Food Administration and of the Sugar
Equalization Board. It constitutes the exposition of the *Statistical Survey,* noted above.

Records[1]

The records of the Food Administration, including those of the
state organizations, have been preserved in filing drawers and boxes.
The following account deals with the groups of these records which
appear to have the greatest value for the present survey.

Statistical Bulletins. The Bulletins, issued in mimeographed form by
the Statistical Division, constitute probably the most valuable single
class of records. They were intended for the information of heads of
divisions and were regarded as confidential during the war. Each Bulletin has several pages and contains statistical information, with tables,

[1] This report on the records of the Food Administration was prepared by
Everett S. Brown, Ph.D., a member of the staff of the Food Administration
during its entire existence.

diagrams, etc. By way of illustration, among the contents of Bulletin 882, of March 22, 1918, are the following: Weekly report on wheat and flour, Summary of the movements and prices of wheat and flour for the week ending March 9, Visible supply of wheat in the United States, Distribution of stocks, Flour output at principal milling centers, Domestic exports of wheat, Imports of wheat and flour substitutes, World shipments of wheat and flour, Export commitments and export performance, with diagram, January-June, 1918. The total number of these Bulletins was 1641; they were numbered serially, but were grouped in subseries according to subject. The subjects covered, with the series numbers, follow:

Series	Subject
1	Wheat—General
2	Flour—General
3	Weekly report on wheat and flour
4	Monthly summary on wheat and flour
5	Corn—General
6	Weekly report on corn
7	Monthly summary on corn
8	Oats—General
9	Weekly report on oats
10	Monthly summary on oats
11	Barley—General
12	Weekly report on barley
13	Monthly summary on barley
14	Rye—General
15	Weekly report on rye
16	Monthly summary on rye
17	Hay—General
18	Weekly report on hay
19	Monthly report on hay
20	Potatoes—General
21	Weekly report on potatoes
22	Monthly report on potatoes
23	Sugar—General
24	Weekly report on sugar
25	Monthly report on sugar
26	Live Stock—General
27A	Weekly report on hogs
27B	Weekly report on cattle
27C	Weekly report on sheep and lambs
28	Monthly report on meat
29	Meat—General

Series	Subject
30	Monthly report on cold storage holdings
31	Eggs—General
32	Monthly report on eggs
33	Dairy Products—General
34	Weekly report on dairy products
35	Monthly summary on dairy products
36	Garbage—General
37	Monthly report on garbage
38	Exports and imports—General
39	Monthly report on exports
40	Monthly summary on exports
41	Crop report—General
42	Weekly report on foreign crops
43	Cotton and cotton products
44	Peanuts and peanut products
45	Canned Goods—General
46	Weekly report on canned goods
47	Beverages
48A	Prices—Monthly report on Canadian retail
48B	Canadian—General
48C	Monthly index numbers on English
48D	English—General
48E	Monthly report on cottonseed
48F	General
49	Nutritive values
50	Conversion units
51	Miscellaneous
52	Weekly summary of commodity reports
53	Weekly report on retail prices, preliminary.
54	Weekly report on retail prices, final
55	Weekly report on wholesale prices
56	Rice—General
57	Beans—General
58	Weekly report on vegetable oils
59	Monthly report on fish
60	Quarterly report on retail prices
61	Monthly report on wholesale dealers
62	Price histories
62A	Current prices for history bulletins
63	Monthly report on coffee
64	Relative prices on selected commodities

An index was made for every two hundred bulletins. In the first place, a cross-reference table gives the subject and series file numbers of the bulletins. Lists of tables follow, showing the (I.) Index of Weekly Bulletins; (II.-V.) Weekly Report on Foreign Food Situation containing data on condition of crops (II.), production (II.), acreage (III.), rations (IV.), and prices (V.) of foodstuffs in foreign countries; (VI.) Weekly Report on Retail Prices in the United States and Canada; (VII.) Weekly Report on Wholesale Prices; (VIII.) Nutritive Values, Relative Cost and Retail Prices; (IX.) Monthly Report on Cold Storage Holdings in the United States and Canada (containing imports, exports, and wholesale prices). An alphabetical subject list completed the index.

License Regulations. The Food Administration, under authority of the Food Control Act, issued regulations for the licensing of dealers in various food commodities. These regulations were changed from time to time, as necessity demanded. They were issued first in pamphlet form, then by mimeograph, and finally in loose-leaf form. Most, but not all, of these regulations will be found in the appendix to the *Annual Report of the United States Food Administration for the year 1918* (pp. 59-317). Complete sets were kept on file at the Food Administration building. The regulations were grouped under the following headings:

I. General: all licensees for the importation, manufacture, storage, and distribution of food commodities and feeds.

II. Special: wheat millers and manufacturers of mixed flours.

III. Special: elevators and dealers in wheat, rye, corn, oats, and barley; corn, oats, rye, and barley millers.

IV. Special: malsters; near-beer manufacturers.

V. Special: dealers in rough rice; rice millers and manufacturers of rice flour.

VI. Special: manufacturers and refiners of sugar.

VII. Special: canners of peas, tomatoes, corn, dried beans, salmon, sardines and tuna, and manufacturers of tomato catsup, tomato soup, and other tomato products; manufacturers of condensed, evaporated, or powdered milk.

VIII. Special: packers of dried fruits.

IX. Special: dealers and brokers in cottonseed and peanuts and cotton ginners; crushers, crushers of cottonseed, peanuts, soya beans, palm kernels, and copra; importers of peanuts, peanut oil, soya bean oil, palm-kernel oil, copra, copra oil, and palm oil, and dealers and brokers in such imported products; refiners of, and dealers and brokers in, cottonseed oil, peanut oil, soya bean oil, palm-kernel oil, and copra oil.

X. Special: manufacturers of oleomargarine and other butter substitutes.

XI. Special: wholesalers, jobbers, importers, and retailers of licensed non-perishable food commodities.

XII. Special: brokers and auctioneers of licensed non-perishable food commodities.

XIII. Special: manufacturers of bakery products.

XIV. Special: dealers in glucose, refiners' syrups, maple syrup, sorghum, cane juice syrup, centrifugal molasses, open-kettle molasses, West India molasses and black-strap molasses, and manufacturers and mixers of mixed syrups and mixed molasses.

XV. Special: distributors of fresh fruits and vegetables.

XVI. Special: distributors of fresh fish and frozen fish.

XVII. Special: salt-water fishermen.

XVIII. Special: distributors of poultry.

XIX Special: distributors of eggs.

XX. Special: manufacturers and distributors of butter.

XXI. Special: manufacturers and distributors of cheese.

XXII. Special: distributors of milk and cream.

XXIII. Special: cold-storage warehousemen.

XXIV. Special: feeding stuffs.

XXV. Special: directions regarding the use of tin and other containers in commodities listed.

XXVI. Special: orders applying to all public eating places.

XXVII. Special: general storage warehousemen; manufacturers of alimentary paste of breakfast cereals; manufacturers and dealers in lard substitutes.

Licensees and Reports from Licensees. The names of all licensees, alphabetically arranged, were kept in a card index, which is in the Food Administration files.

Every licensee was required to file reports with the Food Administration. In some commodities the reports were made weekly, in others, monthly or quarterly, and in a very few cases, semi-annually. Several hundred thousand reports are in the Food Administration files. Their prime object was to expedite the movement of commodities on a direct line from producer to consumer, in other words, to prevent unnecessary inter-trading, with consequent enhancement of the price. Since the reports disclosed costs and profits they were used as a basis for prosecutions in charges of profiteering, and were considered confidential.

Press Releases: (1) National. The real basis for the conservation drives of the Food Administration was public opinion. In order that the people might be kept informed as to what was desired of them, the Food Administration issued releases to the press of the country. These releases contained appeals for conservation, food statistics, information on the European situation, and, in fact, anything which would help to impress upon the people the need of saving food and how this could be accomplished.

Fourteen hundred national releases were issued. They cover the period between May, 1917, when Herbert Hoover arrived from Europe to assume charge, and March, 1919, when this phase of Food Administration activities was brought to a close. Sets of the releases, in mimeographed form are in the files and are a mine of information for the student of food problems in relation to the war. A subject index was prepared for every one hundred releases. Practically all of these press releases were published in the *Official Bulletin,* issued by the Committee on Public Information.

(2) **State.** Special material not incorporated in the national press releases was issued separately and sent to the Educational Directors in the States. These "stories" were more of the human-interest type, but frequently contained statistics and information of considerable value to the investigator. Seven hundred and forty such "stories" were released. As in the case of the national releases, a subject index accompanies each one hundred releases.

Press Clippings. As already stated, the Food Administration depended in large measure for its success upon public opinion. In order the more properly to interpret public opinion, a press clipping bureau was maintained. Here press clippings on food matters were received from all parts of the country. From them a daily digest was prepared and presented to Mr. Hoover and other officials of the Food Administration. The clippings were filed chronologically by a loose-leaf system in groupings by States, cities, and newspapers. A subject card index of food "stories" in the New York *Times* served as a guide for national "stories."

Correspondence: (1) **Master File of Letters.** It was a rule of the Food Administration that two carbon copies must be made of every outgoing letter. One copy was retained in the division file, the other went to the master file. In the latter file, therefore, is a copy of every official letter sent out by a member of the Food Administration. The library bureau automatic file system was used in filing these letters.

(2) **The Food Administrator's File.** All the official correspondence of Herbert Hoover as Food Administrator was preserved to be turned over to the government. This file includes letters received and copies of

letters sent; they are filed alphabetically under the name of the corre-
spondent, with frequent cross references to subject matter.

(3) **Division or Commodity Files.** As already noted, each division
chief preserved in his files a copy of every outgoing letter. These files
also contain letters received, as well as much valuable data pertaining
to the commodity or subject under control of the particular division.
The most important of these divisions are: Home Conservation, States
Administration, Grain and Flour (Grain Corporation), Alimentation,
Educational, Legal, Meats, Mexican Relations, Statistical, Canned and
Dried Goods, Distribution, Coördination of Purchase, Canadian Relations, Food Purchase Board, Sugar, Rail Transportation, Marine
Transportation, Labor and Consumers, Colleges, Perishable Foods, Li-
cense, Cottonseed and its Products, Collateral Commodities, Garbage
Utilization, Oil and Fats, Hotels and Restaurants, Enforcement, Whole-
salers and Retailers, Commercial Baking, Sugar Equalization Board.

(4) **Digest of Outgoing Mail and Summaries.** A "digest" of outgoing mail, combined with summary statements by chiefs of divisions was
maintained day by day for the use of the Food Administrator, and is in
effect a convenient guide to the master file and to the division files. The
original of this "digest" is now in the Hoover Collection of Stanford
University. The following notes were made from it while it was still in
Washington to illustrate the value of the material in the correspondence files; all dates are of 1917.

Food conservation: August 2, 1917, proposed course in food conservation
to be given in Washington; August 4, coöperation of editors of religious
publications; August 6, letters to Scandinavian churches and organizations
in North America requesting their coöperation; August 7, coöperation of
Jewish organizations.

State organizations: August 9, banks of Georgia will loan money to farmers
on the security of crops other than cotton; August 11, wheatless week in New
England; August 14, policy in choice of state representatives; August 17, desirability of decentralized form of organization in the States; October 23,
plans for establishing milk stations in Boston; October 31, publication of
sugar prices in Kentucky.

Exports, imports, and embargoes: August 1, licensing exports of wheat,
flour, corn, and oats; August 2, efforts to locate destination of each food
shipment from the United States; August 6, reports on food situation in
foreign countries to which export licenses are requested.

Grain and flour: August 1, coöperation of millers; August 7, large number
of suggestions received respecting abuses in the grain trade; August 13, grain
purchasing agents to be placed at terminal points to buy for mills and for
exports; August 15, seed wheat in Oklahoma and Texas.

Press: August 13, promise of coöperation from certain newspapers and publishing companies.

Canned goods: August 6, receipt of many letters offering to sell new kinds of preserved food: October 31, situation respecting beans.

Prices: August 3, reports of price raising conspiracy on the part of certain millers; August 11, suggestion that soldiers be used in harvesting crops.

Potatoes: August 1, anxiety of potato growers regarding policy of Food Administration; August 3, proposed campaign to induce people to eat more potatoes; August 11, potato flour factory at Idaho Falls.

Sugar: August 16, increase in price of sugar to refiners; October 15, supply of sugar for the army, supply of sugar for use in factory processes; October 19, difficulty of harvesting sugar beet in Utah.

Transportation: August 1, deflection of shipping to Gulf points; October 22, difficulties of corn shippers in Ohio.

Dairy products: August 15, lack of assistance to producers in Maryland; August 16, acuteness of milk situation in various localities; October 20, reports of waste of milk in certain creameries.

Commercial bread and baking systems: August 2, proposed campaign for standard bread loaf; August 9, gathering of statistics respecting production costs of bakeries, supply of ammonia.

State Files. It was the plan of the Food Administration to have a central policy determined by the office in Washington but to decentralize administration of the policy as widely as possible among the States. With this object in view, there was appointed a food administrator for each State and Territory. State and local matters were largely in their hands. At the close of the Food Administration the state records were shipped to Washington in wooden cases. An accompanying invoice shows the contents of each box.

For each State there is a history of its Food Administration, reports of investigators, miscellaneous reports, correspondence between the state administrator and the States Administration Division at Washington, correspondence between the state administrator and the county administrators, miscellaneous correspondence. In the contents of the history of one of the state administrations are the following subjects: organization and growth of the administration, food pledge campaign, sugar, state merchant representative, library director, milk and ice division, woman's committee, bakers' state service, negro director, hotel and restaurant director, home economics director, director of movies, director of home demonstration agents, secretary of college women, county food administrators, price interpretation committees, conservation campaigns, campaign to double canned products, limitation of the sale of candy, conservation of flour, and distribution of conservation literature.

Among the subjects contained in the invoices to records from the States are: county files, hog reports, license reports, women's files, home demonstration agents, milling division, Grain Corporation, price interpreting, weekly bakery reports, records of the home economics director, correspondence of the publicity director, newspaper clippings, histories of food administrators, bread, corn, cottonseed, coffee, cold storage, farms, fairs and exhibits, mill feeds, butter, eggs, cheese, licensed dealers, milk licenses, markets and marketing, meat and merchants, sheep, soap, food survey, hotels, zone committee, wheatless and meatless, correspondence of the field organizer, flour mill reports, cottonseed, and sugar statements.

UNITED STATES FUEL ADMINISTRATION

Organization and Functions

THE United States Fuel Administration was created pursuant to the act of August 10, 1917, "to provide further for the National security and defense by encouraging the production, conserving the supply, and controlling the distribution of food products and fuel," an act which authorized the President to regulate the production, sale, shipment, distribution, apportionment, and storage of coal, coke, natural gas, and the fuel products of petroleum, to license those engaged in those industries, to prescribe rules and regulations for the conduct of their business, to requisition their plants and their business, to fix the price of coke and of coal, and to determine what were reasonable profits in the oil business. By an executive order, dated August 23, 1917, the President delegated these powers to a United States Fuel Administrator and the administration functioned from September 1, 1917, to January 31, 1919, when its orders, with but few exceptions, were suspended. It was formally closed June 30, 1919, but its price-fixing functions were revived October 30, and it was not until December 13, 1919, that it ceased to exist.

The administration was organized in three divisions, Administrative, Distribution, and Oil, each with several bureaus; and there was a subordinate or coördinate administration in each State. On the advisory staff of the administrator was an Engineers' Committee which prepared analyses of coal-production costs, and a Bureau of Labor to adjust disputes between employers and employees. The units of the Administrative Division were the bureaus of prices, investigation, state organizations, production, education, conservation, traffic and transportation, and mine track; those of the Distribution Division were devoted to bituminous coal, anthracite coal, coke, statistics, state distribution, and gas plants; those of the oil division to oil well supplies, oil production, pipe lines, technology, lubricants and foreign requirements, domestic consumption, prices and licenses, oil conservation, natural gas, marine transportation, oil statistics, engineering, and special assignments.

In the **Administrative Division** the business of the Bureau of Production was to stimulate the coal output by appealing to the patriotism of the miners, by protecting mine labor from depletion through enlistment and solicitation by other industries, by promoting efficiency of operation through improvement of working conditions, and by supervising the plants producing power for the mines. The Bureau of Conservation labored to effect a saving of coal by increasing efficiency in steam production, by eliminating waste, by effecting economy in the use of power through such measures as "lightless nights," and by restricting coal consumption by non-essential industries. The Bureau of Traffic and Transportation supervised the distribution of cars and directed their movements to destination, when loaded, by the shortest and most economical routes. The Mine Track Bureau considered the advisability of opening new coal workings. The Bureau of Investigation analyzed monthly reports from some four thousand jobbers to determine their observance or violation of the orders of the Fuel Administration. The Bureau of Statistics compiled statistics of production, of factors limiting production, of distribution, conservation, and consumption, and of stocks of coke and coal, and presented them in periodical and special reports.

The primary function of the **Distribution Division** was to assure to essential consumers an adequate supply of suitable fuel. This it endeavored to accomplish by means of a budget specifying the amount of coal to be supplied to States, or other defined areas from particular producing districts, by controlling distribution direct to the army, railroads, war plants, etc., and by emergency orders for shipments of coal during a period of shortage in conformity with the preference list or instructions of the War Industries Board.

The **Oil Division**, with the assistance of the National Petroleum War Service Committee, stimulated the production of crude petroleum, increased and improved transportation facilities, regulated prices, and labored to effect such a distribution of petroleum products and natural gas, regardless of ownership, as would in the largest possible measure meet the requirements of all industries essential to the prosecution of the war.

Local fuel administrations were organized in each State, in New England, the Pittsburgh district, the District of Columbia, and Cuba, with a fuel administrator assisted by state, county, and city committees. The principal functions of the state administrations were: (1) to furnish the administration in Washington with reliable statistics relative to transportation, consumption, and storage, and with information regarding conditions peculiar to any locality; (2) to conduct publicity and educational campaigns; (3) to adjust disputes; (4) to initiate plans for conservation applicable to the locality and not inconsistent with the national program; (5) to investigate costs; and (6) to effect an equitable distribution, at fair prices, of the coal allotted to the State by the National budget. The supervision and the coördination of the activities of the several state organizations were, with the exception of those pertaining to distribution, vested in the Bureau of State Organizations of the Administrative Division, to which periodical reports were made, from which instructions were received, and with which occasional conferences were held. The Distribution Division had a district representative in each producing district to facilitate the shipment of coal in response to emergency orders or requests, to make equitable allotments of such orders among operators, and to keep the Fuel Administration in Washington informed of conditions in the district. If the district representative failed to procure the allotted amount of coal to a State, the state administrator appealed to the director of the Bureau of State Distribution.

Publications

The final report of the Fuel Administration is published in seven quarto volumes with varying titles:

Report of the Administrative Division, 1917-1919. Parts I and II, edited by George E. Howes (Washington, 1920, 1921, 428 and 316 pages). Part I contains the report of the Bureau of State Organizations, the final reports of the state and district fuel administrators, and lists of the members of the state and district fuel committees. Part II contains the final report (pp. 9-38) of Hon. Harry A. Garfield, U.S. Fuel Administrator, with six appendixes showing the organization and personnel of the Fuel Administration, and containing a memorandum on the fuel situation in Europe, and the proceedings of a conference held with the United Mine Workers of America. The rest of the volume is devoted to the reports of the various bureaus of the Administrative Division, and to the report of the Oil Division, by Mark L. Requa.

Report of the Distribution Division, 1918-1919. Parts I, II, III (Washington, 1918, 1919, 1919; 143, 124, and 871 pages). Part I is devoted to "The Distribution of Coal and Coke" by C. E. Lesher, a report which deals with the requirements of coal in 1918, the means of meeting those requirements, and the process of distribution. There are a large number of maps and diagrams which show the consumption and the movements of coal. Part II, by Wayne E. Ellis, is entitled "The Zone System." It contains the maps of the bituminous coal zones, and a large amount of documentary material consisting of the zone orders and their modifications. Part III is composed of tables of statistics by C. E. Lesher showing production, shipments, consumption, stocks, etc.

Final Report of the Business Manager to H. A. Garfield, United States Fuel Administrator, edited by Laurence Mitchell (Washington, 1920, 302 pages). Payroll and disbursements of the Fuel Administration; report of librarian.

Report of the Engineers' Committee (Washington, 1919, 194 pages). The report is in 31 pages, the rest of the volume being devoted to graphic charts showing the costs of production in the various districts, exports and imports of coal, and prices.

General Orders, Regulations and Rulings of the United Fuel Administration, including acts of Congress, executive orders and proclamations of the President pursuant to which the United States Fuel Administration was created . . . (Washington, 1920, 614 + 30 pages). Includes *Supplement,* January 1, 1919-March 20, 1920.

Fuel Facts (Washington, 1918, 64 pages). Fuel problems; increased production; efficiency distribution; conservation.

President's Prices for Coal and Modifications, showing dates when effective (Washington, 1918, 16 pages).

Coal Prices and Classification of Bituminous Coal Fields. August 21, 1917-January 1, 1918 (Washington, 1918, 64 pages).

Prices and Marketing Practises covering the distribution of gasolene and kerosene throughout the United States, by A. G. Maguire (Washington, 1919, 24 pages). A report on an investigation of prevalent trade policies in the distribution and marketing of these commodities.

Prices of Petroleum and Its Products during the War, by Joseph E. Pogue. An investigation made in coöperation with the Price Section, Bureau of Planning and Statistics, War Industries Board (Washington, 1919, 55 pages).

Bituminous Coal Zones, with modifications to July 1, 1918 (Washington, 1918, 15 pages). Details for zonal system of coal distribution.

Fuel Situation at the Beginning of Winter, 1918-1919, by Harry A. Garfield, October 26, 1918 (Washington, 1918, 8 pages).

A System of Accounts for Retail Coal Dealers. November 1, 1917 (Washington, 1918, 23 pages). The adoption of a uniform system of accounting is urged.

Increasing Coal Mine Efficiency, by Charles E. Stuart (n.p., n.d., 22 pages). A non-technical discussion of the subject.

Engineering Bulletins, United States Fuel Administration, Bureau of Conservation (Washington, 1918-1919, Nos. 1-6, 8 to 20 pages each). Boiler and furnace testing; boiler water treatment; saving coal in steam power plants; saving steam in industrial heating systems.

Records

By an executive order, dated July 22, 1919, the records of the Fuel Administration, contained in 628 steel file cases of four drawers each, were transferred to the Department of the Interior, where they subsequently became a part of the records of the Bureau of Mines. Nearly one-third of them are the records of the state organizations and the Bureau of State Organizations. In these state files are approximately 400 periodical reports from state administrators containing an account of what had been accomplished; a survey of the general coal situation within the State with particular mention of unusual situations and threatened shortages; data relative to coal production, prices at which coal was sold, profits to dealers, status of contracts between jobbers or operators and industrial plants, and conservation measures; also, transportation, consumption, and storage statistics. There are reports by local committees to a state administrator containing information relative to the supply of fuel in the community, fuel requirements of the community, and economy in the use of fuel. The bureau held occasional conferences with the administrators from all the States or from particular sections or districts, and reports of the proceedings of many of these conferences are in the files. Some two hundred general letters of instruction and advice by the Bureau of State Organizations, besides similar communications from other bureaus in Washington, are included in the general correspondence with state administrators, and to this correspondence there is a book index. Some of the unpublished final reports of the fuel administrators in the several States contain much that was not included in the published reports.

The volume of statistical tables in part III of the final report of the Distribution Division contains only such of the more important statistics compiled in that division as were most available for tabulation within the time allotted for the preparation of that report. Much material of this nature yet remains to be gleaned from the files, especially from the weekly reports of district representatives to state administrators showing the number of cars shipped into each State the preceding week, classified as follows: to railroads; to army, navy, and other departments of the federal government; to state and county departments and institutions; to public utilities, to retail dealers, to manufacturing plants on the preference list of the War Industries Board; to jobbers; to Lake pools; to tidewater pools. Here, too, are the weekly reports of jobbers relative to the coal distributed by them the preceding week. The monthly reports from jobbers, which were used by the Bureau of Investigation, have been transferred along with the other records of that bureau to the Federal Trade Commission.

The files of the United States Fuel Administrator, Assistant United States Fuel Administrator, and Bureaus of Labor, Production, Traffic and Transportation, Prices, Conservation, and Education are not voluminous but contain some informing letters and reports.

The following schedule shows the general classification of the files of the Fuel Administration as they were transferred to the Interior Department and receipted for on July 25, 1919 (reprinted from *Report of Administrative Division*, Part II, p. 12).

List of files, indexes, and records delivered to Interior Department

First floor:	Cases
General files, correspondence, and telegrams	50
Correspondence principally from States	266
Conservation	12
Educational	6
State organizations	15
Production	11

Publications 5
Personnel 11
Oil Division—Field 8
Business office:
    Mr. Mitchell's files (live) 5
    Mr. Steele's files (live) 11
                                               — 16
Disbursing office (live) 25

Second floor (east rooms):
Fuel Administrator 2
Legal Adviser 1
Assistant Fuel Administrator 3
Fuel Administrator (outer office) 2
Fuel Administrator (outer office), Indexes—4 drawer cabinets
Bureau of Prices 6
Bureau of Prices (also 1 safe containing records)
Engineers 1

West rooms:
Contents to be designated (supposedly Mine Track Committee) 2
Bureau of Labor 3

North corridor: Oil—General correspondence, except engineering 19

South corridor:
Legal, general correspondence 50
    Safe, containing 6 duplicate original order books, 2 volumes License Board proceedings, 1 file containing papers, Cleveland and Western Coal Co., and Wisconsin Coal and Dock Co. *v.* William K. Prudden, Federal Fuel Administrator for Michigan.
    One package loose correspondence sheets *in re* retailers' prices, etc.

Center corridor:
Distribution 109
Retail Adviser 1
Traffic and Transportation 4

Books: Number
Official photographic records 1
Official personnel list 1
Catalogue of Distribution Division in two volumes (made in triplicate) in all 6
Index of production files and production managers (Mr. James B. Neale's files) in duplicate 2
Index to the general files 1

UNITED STATES RAILROAD ADMINISTRATION

Organization

SECTION 1 of the act of August 29, 1916, making appropriations for the support of the army, empowered the President, in time of war, to take possession and assume control of any system or systems of transportation, and the United States Railroad Administration had its inception in a proclamation of the President, dated December 26, 1917, whereby federal control of the railroads was assumed two days later and a Director General of Railroads was appointed to exercise that control. The nature of the control was in a measure determined and regulated by the act of March 21, 1918, "to provide for the operation of transportation systems while under federal control, for the just compensation of their owners, and for other purposes."

The administration, at the head of which was the Director General with an assistant director general, was organized in eight divisions and seven regions. The divisions, the chief of each of which was a director, were as follows: Division of Finance and Purchase; Division of Capital Expenditures; Division of Operation, with a Car Service Section, a Troop Movement Section, and a Fuel Conservation Section; Division of Traffic; Division of Inland Waterways; Division of Public Service and Accounting; Division of Labor; Division of Law. The regions, each under a regional director, were Eastern, Allegheny, Pocahontas, Southern, Northwestern, Central Western, and Southwestern. It was the duty of each regional director to direct railroad operations in his territory so as to handle traffic "with the least congestion, the highest efficiency, and the greatest expedition." To that end he was to see that terminals were used to the best advantage and to effect such changes in routing traffic as would promote efficiency. Other administrative units in Washington were the Board of Railroad Wages and Working Conditions, the Joint Fuel Zone Committee, the Exports Control Committee and the Bureau of Suggestions and Complaints. The Railroad Administration terminated, except for accounting and liquidating purposes, with the return of the railroads to private ownership March 1, 1920.

Publications

The Library of Congress has a collection of the publications of the Railroad Administration, consisting mainly of reports, general orders, administrative circulars, bulletins, and addresses, with a typewritten copy of a subject index. Another collection, nearly complete, is in the library of the Superintendent of Documents. Particular attention is directed to the following:

Report to the President of the Work of the United States Railroad Administration for the First Seven Months of Its Existence, Ending July 31, 1918 (Washington, 1918, 32 pages).

Annual Report of W. G. McAdoo, Director General of Railroads, 1918 (Washington, 1919). Embraces reports, issued separately, by division and regional directors and includes sections on capital expenditures (4 pages); operation (62 pages); traffic (16 pages); inland waterways (10 pages); public service and accounting (7 pages); labor (27 pages); law (23 pages); Exports Control Committee, with regard to how freight cars can best be routed through the various ports (11 pages); bureau of suggestions and complaints (4 pages); Allegheny region (7 pages); Pocahontas region (19 pages); Southern region (27 pages); Northwestern region (8 pages); Central Western region (15 pages); Southwestern region (15 pages).

Annual Report of Walker D. Hines, Director General of Railroads, 1919 (Washington, 1920). Finance (42 pages); purchases (10 pages); capital expenditures (14 pages); operation (115 pages); traffic (23 pages); inland waterways (31 pages); public service (46 pages); labor (84 pages); law (22 pages); Central Coal Committee (32 pages); Automatic Control Committee (32 pages); Eastern region (40 pages); Allegheny region (20 pages); Pocahontas region (19 pages); Southern region (24 pages); Northwestern region (35 pages); Central Western region (19 pages); Southwestern region (35 pages).

Report to the President by Walker D. Hines, Director General of Railroads, for Fourteen Months Ended March 1, 1920 (Washington, 1920, 48 pages).

Report of Director General of Railroads covering period from Relinquishment of Federal Operation to End of Calendar Year 1921 (Washington, 1922, 25 pages).

Statements of W. G. McAdoo, Director General of Railroads, before the Senate Committee on Interstate Commerce (January 3 and 4, 1919, 124 pages). Discussion in favor of extending period of federal control.

Address of Walker D. Hines, Director General of Railroads, before the Joint Committee of Bankers' Associations of New England, June 21, 1919 (1919, 19 pages).

Address of Walker D. Hines, Director General of Railroads, before the National Association of Railway and Utilities Commissioners, October 15, 1919 (1919, 14 pages).

Public Acts, Proclamations by the President relating to the United States Railroad Administration, and General Orders and Circulars Issued by the Director General of Railroads to December 31, 1918 (Washington, 1919, 452 pages).

Proclamation by the President relating to the United States Railroad Administration and General Orders and Circulars Issued by the Director General of Railroads from January 1, 1919, to February 29, 1920 (Washington, 1920, 153 pages).

Circulars and bulletins issued by the several divisions and sections of the United States Railroad Administration from January 1 to December 31, 1918 (1919, 450 pages).

Report of the Railroad Wage Commission to the Director General of Railroads, April 30, 1918 (Washington, 1918, 150 pages).

Labor. Statement by President Wilson to Representatives of the Railway Employees' Department, American Federation of Labor, August 25, 1919, and Report of Walker D. Hines, Director General of Railroads, to the President, August 23, 1919 (1919, 8 pages).

Memoranda of Understandings in Connection with the Memorandum of the Director General, dated November 15, 1919, in respect to Conditions under Which Time and One-Half for Overtime Would Be Granted in Freight Service (Washington, 1920, 14 pages).

Number of Women Employed and Character of Their Employment; January 1, April 1, July 1, and October 1, 1918 (1919, 36 pages). The same for 1919 (1920, 34 pages).

Survey and Recommendations of the Committee on Health and Medical Relief (Washington, 1920, 84 pages). Results of investigations of complaints with regard to unsanitary condition of stations, cars, and shops which were referred to the committee by the Bureau of Suggestions and Complaints.

Decisions of Railway Board of Adjustment. July-September, 1919 (368 pages); October-December, 1919 (184 pages); January-March, 1920 (312 pages).

Railroads and Government, Their Relation in the United States, 1910-1921, by Frank Haigh Dixon (New York, 1922, 384 pages). The war period, pp. 107-210; the return to private operation, pp. 213-365. [Unofficial.]

WAR FINANCE CORPORATION

Functions

THE War Finance Corporation was created by the act of April 5, 1918, "To provide further for the national security and defense, and, for the purpose of assisting in the prosecution of the war, to provide credits for industries and enterprises in the United States necessary or contributory to the prosecution of the war, and to supervise the issuance of securities, and for other purposes." By this act Congress appropriated $500,000,000 for the capital stock of the corporation and vested it with authority to make such loans to banks, bankers, trust companies, savings banks, and building and loan associations as should enable them to render financial assistance to persons, firms, corporations, and associations engaged in business operations deemed necessary or contributory to the winning of the war, and, in exceptional cases, to make loans directly to a person, firm, corporation, or association. The maximum amount which it might loan to a bank, banker, or trust company was determined chiefly by the amount which the person or institution had, during the preceding year, loaned to those engaged in war work.

Although originally created solely as an agency to assist in securing the necessary labor and materials for a successful prosecution of the war and with a statutory provision that its powers should cease six months after the termination of the war, the corporation was authorized by the Victory Liberty loan act of March 3, 1919, to advance an aggregate of $1,000,000,000 to American exporters and American banking institutions for the purpose of financing the exportation of domestic products. The authority to make such loans was exercised until May, 1920. Operations were then suspended, but on January 4, 1921, Congress, "for the relief of the present depression in the agricultural sections of the country," passed a joint resolution directing the Corporation to resume activities "with the view of assisting in the financing of the exportation of agricultural and other products to foreign markets."

Publications

First Annual Report of the War Finance Corporation (Washington, 1918, 11 pages). Covers the period from May 20, 1918, when the corporation was authorized by the President to commence business, to November 30, 1918. Contents: advances to public utilities, advances to industrial enterprises, advances to cattle raisers, miscellaneous advances, crop-moving loans, rates of interest, transactions in government bonds, receipts and expenditures, monthly advances, applications for advances.

Second Annual Report of the War Finance Corporation (Washington, 1919, 13 pages). Contents: advances to bankers, public utilities, and railroads, miscellaneous advances, cattle loans, transactions in government obligations, War Finance Corporation bond issue, capital stock, amendments to War Finance Corporation act, assets, liabilities, receipts, disbursements.

Third Annual Report of the War Finance Corporation (Washington, 1920, 25 pages). Contents: railroads, cattle loans, export loans, transactions in government obligations, a tabulated statement exhibiting data relative to all advances made by the corporation, receipts, disbursements.

Fourth Annual Report of the War Finance Corporation (Washington, 1922, 42 pages). Contents: financing cotton exports, advances to coöperative associations, improvement in the cotton situation, other agricultural commodities financed, export financing alone not sufficient, the agricultural credits act, advances for agricultural purposes, agricultural loan agencies established, coöperation of state bankers associations sought, volume of business, the live-stock situation, the corn belt advisory committtee, helping the farmer through financing institutions, situation without parallel, tabulated statements.

Circular No. 1 of the War Finance Corporation (Washington, 1921, 6 pages). Regulations for making applications for loans.

CAPITAL ISSUES COMMITTEE

Functions

THE Capital Issues Committee was created by Title II of the War Finance Corporation act of April 5, 1918, "to supervise the issuance of securities." It was the function of the corporation to render financial assistance to industries the operations of which were necessary or contributory to the war; it was the function of the Capital Issues Committee to conserve financial resources, labor, and materials for the prosecution of the war by discouraging investment of funds in enterprises which would not "strengthen the industrial and military structure of the country for the purpose of the war."

The function was performed by investigating and passing upon proposed issues of securities in excess of $100,000. Although the act did not make it compulsory for firms and corporations to submit their proposed issues of securities to the committee or abide by its decisions, the committee controlled the situation and accomplished its purpose on a voluntary basis. Besides the central committee there were twelve district committees with headquarters at Boston, New York, Philadelphia, Cleveland, Richmond, Atlanta, Chicago, St. Louis, Minneapolis, Kansas City, Dallas, and San Francisco. Business was commenced May 17, 1918, was suspended December 31, 1918, and on August 30, 1919, the committee was directed by executive proclamation to close up its affairs and turn over to the Federal Trade Commission all the records, "including letters, correspondence, and testimony," in its possession. The records thus transferred to the Federal Trade Commission are regarded as confidential.

Publications

Report of the Capital Issues Committee (House Document 1485, 65th Congress, 3rd Session, 9 pages). Contents: review of activities from May 17, 1918, to November 11, 1918; tabulated statement relative to applications; extract from a report of one of the district committees.

Final Report of the Capital Issues Committee, February 19, 1919 (House Document 1836, 65th Congress, 3rd Session, 7 pages). Contents: review of activities from November 11, 1918, to December 31,

1918; tabulated statement relative to applications; personnel of each district committee.

Expenditures of the Capital Issues Committee, January 2, 1919 (Senate Document 328, 65th Congress, 3rd Session, 2 pages). Expenditures of the central Committee and of each of the district committees.

Capital Issues Committee: Rules and Regulations (Washington, 1918, 7 pages).

ALIEN PROPERTY CUSTODIAN

Functions

THE office of Alien Property Custodian was created by the trading with the enemy act of October 6, 1917, which authorized the President to appoint, and prescribe the duties of, an officer with power to receive all money and property in the United States due or belonging to an enemy, or ally of an enemy, and to hold, administer and account for the same. Any person having the custody or control of alien property was required to report it to this officer. An amendment of March 28, 1918, authorized the Alien Property Custodian to manage all property, other than money, taken into his custody by virtue of the trading with the enemy act as if it were his own. With the exception, however, of certain commodities named in an executive order of April 2, 1918, alien property was to be sold only at public sale and to the highest bidder. The office was organized in six bureaus: Administration, Investigation, Trusts, Sales, Law, and Audits.

Publications

Alien Property Custodian Report (Washington, 1919, 607 pages). A detailed report of proceedings during the calendar year 1918 and to February 15, 1919; particularly informing with regard to German property in the chemical, metal, fur, and textile industries.

Report of the Alien Property Custodian (Washington, 1922, 1062 pages). Part 1 contains the names of the attorneys employed by the Alien Property Custodian and a statement of the character of the work performed by each. Part 2 contains a descriptive list of the corporations that were seized.

Annual Report of the Alien Property Custodian for the Year 1922 (Washington, 1923, 133 pages). Corporation management, trusts, claims.

Bulletin of Information (Washington, 1918, 70 pages). Contains the executive orders and instructions issued under the trading with the enemy act, also details regarding the organization and functions of the office.

Bureau of Sales, Alien Property Custodian (n.p., 1920, 3 volumes).

States the order of sale and the terms and conditions of sale for each property that was sold.

List of the Number of Certificates of Stock, Voting Trust Certificates, Registered and Bearer Bonds of Companies incorporated in the United States of America and its possessions, in which right, title, and interest have been seized by the Alien Property Custodian . . . the Certificates or Bonds not being in his possession (Washington, 1920, 46 pages).

COMMITTEE ON PUBLIC INFORMATION

Functions

THE functions which the Committee on Public Information was originally expected to perform are stated in a letter to the President signed by the Secretaries of State, War, and Navy and dated April 13, 1917, as follows:

Even though the coöperation of the press has been generous and patriotic, there is a steadily developing need for some authoritative agency to assure the publication of all the vital facts of national defense. Premature or ill-advised announcements of policies, plans, and specific activities, whether innocent or otherwise, would constitute a source of danger.

While there is much that is properly secret in connection with the departments of the government, the total is small compared to the vast amount of information that it is right and proper for the people to have.

America's great present needs are confidence, enthusiasm, and service, and these needs will not be met completely unless every citizen is given the feeling of partnership that comes with full, frank statements concerning the conduct of the public business.

It is our opinion that the two functions—censorship and publicity—can be joined in honesty and with profit, and we recommend the creation of a Committee on Public Information.

The committee was created by executive order, of same day, with the Secretary of State, the Secretary of War, and the Secretary of the Navy as members, but with the direction of its activities vested in a civilian chairman. As its functions developed the committee supervised the voluntary censorship of the newspaper and periodical press in the United States, served as a central agency for releasing news of government activities, and conducted a world-wide campaign for the conquest and mobilization of public opinion and for the support of morale both in the United States and in the allied and neutral countries. The committee ceased to function June 30, 1919, and was discontinued by an executive order of August 21, 1919.

Organization

The committee was organized in two sections; Domestic and Foreign. The Domestic Section operated in fifteen divisions: News, Official Bulletin, Civic and Educational Coöperation, Syndicate

Features, Production and Distribution, Speaking, Four Minute Men, Film, Pictorial Publicity, Exhibits at State Fairs, Advertising, Service Bureau, Women's War Work, Work among the Foreign Born, and Business Management. The Foreign Section had three divisions, Wireless and Cable Service, Mail Service, and Picture Service.

Division of News. This division was a centralized medium through which the public was informed of the progress of the war by the President, the war-making branches of the government, the Departments of Justice and Labor, the Council of National Defense, the War Industries Board, the War Trade Board, the National War Labor Board, and the Alien Property Custodian. The division also acted as a reference bureau in matters of voluntary censorship.

Division of the Official Bulletin. In conformity with an order of the President the *Official U.S. Bulletin* was prepared and issued daily by this division from May 10, 1917, to March 31, 1918,

That there might be some official source to which the public could look for authoritative information as to the acts and proceedings vitally affecting their legal rights and obligations; that there might be put into print for all time a faithful record of the part played by the government of the United States in the World War; that the government departments might be relieved of the very considerable correspondence with persons desiring the character of information which properly should be published from day to day; and that this information should be disseminated throughout the Nation in an effective manner.

Division of Civic and Educational Coöperation. This division was formed to educate the public, through the medium of popular pamphlets and in other ways, relative to the reasons for which the United States entered the war, the country's war aims, the nature of American institutions, and other related subjects. The pamphlets were produced with the aid of historians, economists, and political scientists of colleges and universities and in coöperation with the National Board for Historical Service.

Division of Syndicate Features. The volunteer services of novelists, essayists, and short story writers were enlisted by this division to write articles for the newspaper and periodical press making clear why the United States was in the war, explaining the ideals for which the country was fighting, and telling the story of the war machine in its various phases.

Division of Production and Distribution. When the demand for the committee's literature had exceeded the capacity of the Government Printing Office the Division of Production and Distribution was organized to contract for printing and to direct special campaigns for a wider distribution of publications.

Speaking Division. In the face of growing confusion due to the great number of speaking campaigns that were being inaugurated throughout the country the Division of Public Speaking was established in September, 1917, to act as a national clearing house for such campaigns, to seek coöperation among speakers' bureaus, to prevent duplication of effort and overlapping of territory, to supply speakers from government departments, to concentrate the attention of speakers during special periods upon particular national needs, and to foster in all speakers a sense of the unity of the national purpose.

Division of Four Minute Men. This division was organized with a director, a national advisory council, state chairmen, and local chairmen. The Four Minute men were volunteer public speakers who addressed moving-picture audiences during intermissions. They were appointed by the local chairmen. Their subjects, accompanied with instructions and data, were assigned by the director of the division.

Film Division. The principal function of this division was to utilize the material of the photographic section of the Signal Corps in such a manner as to place before moving picture audiences an effective pictorial record of the war progress of the United States.

Division of Pictorial Publicity. This division was created April 17, 1917, to enlist the artists of the country for services in the production of posters, window cards, car cards, placards, and other forms of art appeal.

Division of Exhibits at State Fairs. Plans for these exhibits were prepared in coöperation with representatives of the War Department, Navy Department, Department of Commerce, Department of Interior, Department of Agriculture, and the Food Administration. The country was divided into six circuits, and for each of these a combined government exhibit was furnished by the Ordnance Department, Signal Corps, Medical Department, Quartermaster Corps, Corps of Engineers, Commission on Training Camp Activities, Navy Department, Department of Commerce, Department of Interior, Department of Agriculture, Food Administration, and Committee on Public Information. For five of the circuits there was also a motion picture exhibit.

Division of Advertising. Created by President Wilson "for the purpose of receiving and directing through the proper channels the generous offers of the advertising forces of the Nation," the Division of Advertising planned and handled campaigns for the Council of National Defense, U.S. Shipping Board, U.S. Food Administration, U.S. Fuel Administration, Department of War, Department of Labor, Department of Agriculture, Liberty Loans, Red Cross, and other war agencies.

Service Bureau. The Service Bureau was created, under the direction of the Committee on Public Information, by executive order of March 19, 1918, to make available, in a central office in Washington, complete information records as to the function, location, and personnel of all government agencies.

Division of Women's War Work. This division was established to give impetus to all movements connected with the work of American women in the war, chiefly by means of short stories, feature articles, and pictures.

Division of Work with the Foreign Born. This division functioned chiefly through American loyalty leagues and foreign language bureaus.

Foreign Section. The purpose of the Foreign Section was, by wireless, cable, mail, and picture services, to make known to the entire world the institutions, war aims, war effort, and military progress of the United States.

Publications

Complete Report of the Chairman of the Committee on Public Information (Washington, 1920, 290 pages). States the purpose and reviews the activities of each section, division, and bureau of the committee.

How We Advertised America, by George Creel (New York and London, 1920, 467 pages). The most comprehensive and authoritative record in a single publication of the activities of each division of the Committee, compiled, immediately after it had ceased to function, by its chairman. [Unofficial.]

"America's Fight for Public Opinion," by Guy Stanton Ford, director of the Division of Civic and Educational Coöperation, published in the *Minnesota History Bulletin* (February, 1919, 24 pages). [Unofficial.]

Official U.S. Bulletin, published daily by the Committee from May 10, 1917, to March 31, 1919. In this publication is to be found material indispensable to a thorough study of each and every war agency, for in it the Committee purposed to print every state paper, proclamation, and executive order; all statements, pronouncements, and addresses by the President; every order, pronouncement, and regulation issued by the heads of the executive departments and the heads of the War Industries Board, War Trade Board, U.S. Food Administration, U.S. Fuel Administration, U.S. Railroad Administration, U.S. Shipping Board, War Labor Board, Alien Property Custodian, and other war organizations; data relative to war contracts; texts of important laws; proceedings of the United States Supreme Court; a résumé of the proceedings of Congress, etc.

The *United States Bulletin,* which succeeded the *Official U.S. Bulletin,* was published privately twice a week from April 3 to June 2, 1919, and once a week thereafter until August 23, 1920.

Report of the Director of the Official U.S. Bulletin to the Chairman of Committee on Public Information (n.p. [1918], 51 pages). A statement relative to the material published in the *Bulletin* and views of officers and business men relative to the service it rendered.

The Division of Civic and Educational Coöperation issued the following pamphlets in three series (Washington, 1917-1918):

War Information Series

1. *The War Message and Facts behind it,* annotated text of President Wilson's message, April 2, 1917 (28 pages).

2. *The Nation in Arms,* by Franklin K. Lane, Secretary of the Interior, and Newton D. Baker, Secretary of War (13 pages).

3. *The Government of Germany,* by Charles D. Hazen (16 pages).

4. *The Great War: from Spectator to Participant,* by Andrew C. McLaughlin (16 pages).

5. *A War of Self-Defense,* by Robert Lansing, Secretary of State, and Louis F. Post, Assistant Secretary of Labor (22 pages).

6. *American Loyalty, by citizens of German descent:* C. Kotzenabe, Otto Kahn, F. W. Lehmann, Franz Sigel, Hans Russau, Leo Rassieur, and A. J. Bucher (24 pages).

7. *Amerikanische Bürgertreue, von Bürgern deutscher Abkunft* (23 pages, translation of No. 6).

8. *American Interest in Popular Government Abroad,* by Evarts B. Greene (16 pages).

9. *Home Reading Course for Citizen-Soldiers,* prepared by the War Department (62 pages).

10. *First Session of the War Congress,* by Charles Merz (48 pages).

11. *The German War Code Contrasted with the War Manuals of the United States, Great Britain, and France,* by George Winfield Scott and James Wilford Garner (15 pages).

12. *American and Allied Ideals: an appeal to those who are neither hot nor cold,* by Stuart P. Sherman (23 pages).

13. *German Militarism and Its German Critics, fully illustrated by extracts from German newspapers,* by Charles Altschul (45 pages).

14. *The War for Peace: the Present War as Viewed by Friends of Peace,* compiled by Arthur D. Call (45 pages).

15. *Why America Fights Germany,* by John S. P. Tatlock (16 pages).

16. *The Study of the Great War, a topical outline with extensive quotations and reading references,* by Samuel B. Harding (95 pages).

17. *The Activities of the Committee on Public Information* (20 pages).

18. *Regimental History of the United States Regular Army, chronological outline, 1866-1918,* prepared by the Adjutant General's Office (48 pages).

19. *Lieber and Schurz, Two Loyal Americans of German Birth,* by Evarts B. Greene (24 pages).

20. *The German-Bolshevik Conspiracy* (30 pages).

21. *America's War Aims and Peace Program,* compiled by Carl L. Becker (52 pages).

Red, White, and Blue Series

1. *How the War Came to America* (46 pages).

2. *National Service Handbook* (246 pages). Domestic welfare; European war relief; religious organizations, professional men, and women; financing the war; industry, commerce, and labor; agriculture and the food supply; the civil service; medical and nursing service; the army; the navy; aviation.

3. *The Battle Line of Democracy* (133 pages). A collection of patriotic prose and poetry relative to the World War.

4. *The President's Flag Day Address* (30 pages). Annotated to show the evidence of German plans respecting the United States.

5. *Conquest and Kultur: Aims of the Germans in their own Words,* compiled by Wallace Notestein and Elmer E. Stoll (160 pages).

6. *German War Practices: Part I, Treatment of Civilians,* edited by Dana C. Munro, George C. Sellery, and August C. Krey (94 pages).

7. *War Cyclopedia, a Handbook for Ready Reference on the Great War,* edited by Frederic L. Paxson, Edward S. Corwin, and Samuel B. Harding (321 pages).

8. *German Treatment of Conquered Territory,* being Part II of "German War Practices," edited by Dana C. Munro, George C. Sellery, and August C. Krey (64 pages).

9. *War, Labor, and Peace,* recent addresses and writings of President Wilson (43 pages).

10. *German Plots and Intrigues in the United States during the Period of Our Neutrality* (64 pages).

Loyalty Leaflets

1. *Friendly Words to the Foreign Born,* by Joseph Buffington (8 pages).

2. *The Prussian System,* by Frederick C. Walcott (8 pages).

3. *Labor and the War,* an address by President Wilson to the American Federation of Labor (15 pages).

4. *A War Message to the Farmer,* by President Wilson (7 pages).

5. *Plain Issues of the War,* by Elihu Root (15 pages).

6. *Ways to Serve the Nation,* a proclamation by the President, April 16, 1917.

7. *What Really Matters* (6 pages).

Preliminary Statement to the Press of the United States (Washington, 1917, 20 pages). Program for supervising the voluntary censorship of the press.

The German Whisper, by Harvey O'Higgins, associate chairman, Committee on Public Information (30 pages). Enemy activities to promote discord in the United States among sects and races, industrial and social classes.

Three bulletins issued by the Speaking Division (Washington, 1918) are as follows:

1. *Purpose and Scope of the Work of the Speaking Division* (4 pages).

2. *Hints for Speakers: the Issues of the War at a Glance* (7 pages).

3. *Ships, Ships, and yet More Ships—The Nation's Greatest Need* (7 pages).

A volume of Four Minute Men *Bulletins,* May, 1917, to December, 1918, comprises forty-six general bulletins of information and instructions, three army bulletins, four school bulletins to junior Four Minute men, and a historical number with summaries of the organization and activities of Four Minute men in each State.

War Work of Women in Colleges (1918, 11 pages) was prepared by the Division on Women's War Work. It is a summary review of college war courses, student war activities, and employment of college women in war work.

Records

The records of the Committee on Public Information were transferred to the Council of National Defense in August, 1919, and to the War Department in July, 1921. They are arranged by divisions and subdivisions and indexed. They consist mainly of correspondence, mailing lists, news releases, newspaper clippings, Four Minute men questionnaires, reports of activities of Four Minute men, and a card file giving information concerning the function, location, and personnel of each of the government agencies. The following summary description of them, reprinted from the *Fourth Annual Report of the Council of National Defense* (pp. 88-91), indicates their general character.

Advertising. Correspondence of the Committee on Public Information concerning the work of the division which gave to the various government departments an organized advertising service made up of the volunteer help of all the national advertising agencies in the United States, and advertising rates of foreign newspapers in the files of the Foreign Press Bureau.

Business management. Records and other documents pertaining to the business affairs of the committee, including account books, pay rolls, vouchers, financial reports, personnel lists, mailing lists, lists of coöperating periodicals, and an index to photographic sources.

Civic and educational coöperation. Correspondence and mailing lists of the division which prepared pamphlets on the war for worldwide circulation.

Educational work. Correspondence, mailing lists, lists of special articles, news releases, and newspaper clippings in connection with the work of the Civic and Educational Coöperation Division and the Syndicate Feature Division of the committee.

Films and photographs. Correspondence, leases with exhibitors, photographs, and records of films shipped abroad and of films censored, other records and papers relating to the distribution and exhibition of moving pictures and photographs for the education of the people in the United States and abroad concerning the purposes and progress of the government's war activities, and for the stimulating of recruiting and of patriotic interest in the war.

Foreign newspapers. Clippings from foreign newspapers and detailed information concerning the foreign press, including advertising rates.

Foreign organization of committee's activities. Correspondence with and reports of activities from special commissioners sent to foreign countries; statement of the organization of the Committee on Public Information in each South American country; and records and accounts of the services in foreign countries.

Four Minute men. Correspondence, lantern slides, reports of activities, personnel and mailing lists, questionnaires, and instructions concerning the purpose of the work of the division which had the management of the plan whereby over 15,000 volunteer public speakers addressed motion-picture theater audiences during intermissions.

Government directory. A government directory card file giving complete information concerning the function, location, and personnel of each of the government agencies; and correspondence relating to government information.

News for the foreign press. Releases, correspondence, photographs, clippings, and literature and other papers used in connection with the service of daily sending out, by wireless to Eiffel Tower, about 1000 words of current news which was relayed from France to other European countries; and the press service of sending abroad by mail feature articles dealing with American life and activities.

News releases. Correspondence relating to the coördination and control of the daily news of military operations given out by the army and navy and files of news releases.

Official United States Bulletin. Mailing and subscription lists and correspondence concerning the publication of the *Official United States Bulletin,* a daily periodical of government news.

Speaking campaign. Correspondence and other papers relating to the coördination of the efforts of the various national speakers' bureaus by the establishment of a clearing house for speaking campaigns by prominent speakers throughout the country.

War exhibits. Clippings, correspondence, and photographs concerning the establishment by the committee of war exhibits used by state fairs and other expositions throughout the United States.

Women's war work. Correspondence, news releases, pamphlets, and other papers relating to the establishment of a clearing house for information concerning the services which women could render during the war.

Work with the foreign born. Surveys of foreign born in industrial plants, schools, and fraternal organizations, Americanization registration cards, lists of local agencies for work with the foreign born, correspondence, news releases, and other papers pertaining to the work of distributing to foreign-speaking people in this country information of America's purpose in the war, and the part they were asked to take in that crisis.

Lists. The following lists, principally on 3″ by 5″ cards, each classified and arranged alphabetically or by topics, are on file among the records of the various divisions and subdivisions of the Committee on Public Information: universities, colleges, libraries, other educational institutions, public welfare associations, granges, state superintendents of schools, mayors, clergymen, Four Minute men, authors of special war articles, films exported, films censored, chambers of commerce, national trade organizations, commercial business houses, coöperating trade and business periodicals, newspapers, foreign-language newspapers, special war articles, persons killed and wounded in action, and various personnel, mailing, and subscription lists.

STATE WAR HISTORY COLLECTIONS

RECORDS of the war activities of States and minor civil divisions have been collected by historical agencies in nearly every State in the Union. In several States a war records commission, war history commission, or war historian was appointed for the purpose; in others, the state historical society, state library, or state university took charge of the work. In a few instances a history of a State's participation in the war is in preparation, and several county histories of a similar nature have been published. For a comprehensive survey of activities for the collection of state and county records and of plans for publication, see "The Collection of State War Service Records," by Franklin F. Holbrook (*American Historical Review,* October, 1919, pp. 72-78) ; and "American Historical Activities during the World War," edited by Newton D. Mereness (*Annual Report of the American Historical Association for 1919,* Vol. 1, pp. 204-294). Lists of state war publications for the years 1917-1920 are appended to the *Monthly List of State Publications* for December, 1919, and December, 1920, issued by the Library of Congress, Division of Documents (Vol. 10, No. 12, pp. 581-648; Vol. 11, No. 12, pp. 553-572). A summary mention of such records and publications for each State as are particularly pertinent to this survey follows.

ALABAMA

Records

The collection of war records in Alabama was undertaken by the director of the Alabama State Department of Archives and History who, in September, 1918, was appointed State War Historian of the Alabama Council of Defense. County organizations coöperated with the State Historian and at the same time preserved county records for local use. The collection in the State Department of Archives and History (Montgomery) comprises material relative to all the important activities in which Alabama participated in the war. Here are the records of the Alabama Council of Defense and from these the compilation of a history of the organization has been undertaken. Here, too, are reports of industrial plants, chambers of commerce, boards of trade, patriotic societies, and women's clubs. Other records are those of the local services of the Food Administration, the Fuel Administration, the United States Employment Service, the School Garden Army, the Red Cross, the War Camp Community Service, the Y.M.C.A., the Y.W.C.A., the Knights of Columbus, the Jewish Welfare Board, and the military establishments within the State. Besides files of Alabama newspapers the department has complete files of the *New York Times*, the Boston *Transcript*, and the *Washington Post*.

Publications

Report of the Alabama Council of Defense, Covering its activities from May 17, 1917, to December 31, 1918 (Montgomery, 1919, 117 pages). Woman's committee; food administration; school garden army; Four Minute men; labor; extension service.

Farm Labor, Live Stock, and Crop Survey of Alabama, made by the State Department of Agriculture and Industries, with the coöperation of the U.S. Department of Agriculture, State Department of Public Instruction, Alabama Extension Service, and State Food Administration (Department of Agriculture and Industries, *Bulletin*, Vol. 8, Serial No. 79, April, 1918, 75 pages).

Social Problems of Alabama, by Hastings H. Hart (Montgomery, 1918, 87 pages). A study of social institutions and agencies of the State as related to its war activities. Alabama's war work; the State Council of Defense; the labor problem.

Proceedings of the Alabama State Council of Defense, held in the Senate chamber, Montgomery, Alabama, June 1, 1917 (Montgomery, 1917, 29 pages). Address by the governor; reports of committees.

ARIZONA

The Arizona State Library, the University of Arizona Library, and the Arizona Historical and Archaeological Society have files of Arizona newspapers for the period of the war, and various organizations were urged to coöperate in preserving a record of their war activities.

Publications

The Arizona Council of Defense: Its Purposes and a Brief Statement of its Work, Accomplished and under Way (Phoenix, 1917, 20 pages).

Résumé of first report of executive committee; committee on production, conservation, and distribution of food supplies; committee on labor; committee on transportation; committee on scientific research.

A Record of the Activities of the Arizona State Council of Defense from formation, April 18, 1917, to dissolution, June, 1919 (n.p., 1919, 50 pages). Organization of the state council; activities of state and county councils; coöperative work against predatory animals.

"The University of Arizona and the War" (in *University of Arizona Record*, Vol. 11, No. 1, 19 pages). Extension Service; College of Mines and Engineering; Arizona State Bureau of Mines.

ARKANSAS

Records

The collection of war records in Arkansas was undertaken by the Arkansas Historical Commission, and one of the last acts of the Arkansas State Council of Defense was to deliver its records to the commission. An index to the entire war history collection of the State exhibits a wide range of subjects, *e.g.*, banks, boards of commerce, churches, daylight saving, draft, draft boards, farmers, food, Food Administration, food conservation, Fuel Administration, fuel conservation, industry, mining, profiteering, reconstruction, Red Cross, taxation, thrift, transportation, and woman's service.

Publications

Report of the Arkansas State Council of Defense, May 22, 1917, to July 1, 1919 ([Little Rock, 1919], 88 pages). Patriotic education; conservation work; welfare work; county food administrators.

CALIFORNIA

Records

A war history committee in California was organized in March, 1918, through the coöperation of the State Historical Survey Commission with the State Council of Defense. When the Council was dissolved, February 1, 1919, the work of the history committee was turned over to the committee on reconstruction, and subsequently, by action of the legislature, it was placed wholly in the hands of the war history committee of the State Historical Survey Commission. A history committee in each county was asked by the state committee "to prepare reports or contemporaneous histories dealing with local war activities, and to gather and compile such other statistical information as might relate to the part taken by their respective counties in the great conflict." The war history department of the California Historical Survey Commission suggested an outline, in fourteen divisions, for each county history as follows:

(1) Period before America's entrance into the war.
(2) Military, naval, and aviation activities.
(3) Agriculture and the food supply.
(4) Industry and labor.
(5) Commerce, transportation, and communication.
(6) War finance and revenue.
(7) Social, welfare, and relief agencies.
(8) Education.
(9) Religion in the war.
(10) Professional men and women in the war.
(11) Women in the war.
(12) War legislation and administration of government.
(13) Public opinion and the war.
(14) Post-war period.

In the state collection are the records of the State Council of Defense; report and records of the Food Administration; and thirty-four numbers of the *Official Food Bulletin*, April 2 to November 19, 1918. There is an index to the *Los Angeles Times* compiled by the Los Angeles County war history committee, working through the Reference Department of the Los Angeles Public Library.

Publications

Report of the Activities of the California State Council of Defense from April 6, 1917, to January 1, 1918 (Sacramento, 1918, 53 pages). County councils of defense; increased crop production; food conservation and waste prevention; farm labor; women's activities.

Report of Women's Committee of the State Council of Defense of California from June 1, 1917, to January 1, 1919 (Los Angeles, 1919, 223 pages). County committees; Americanization; food administration; home economics; women in industry.

Reconstruction Program, Women's Committee of the State Council of Defense of California (Los Angeles, 1918, 12 pages). Women in industry; child welfare; public health; education; Americanization; economic problems.

Report of the Committee on Petroleum, California State Council of Defense (Sacramento, 1917, 191 pages). Location and description of California petroleum fields; production of California petroleum; transportation of California petroleum; refining California oil; utilization of the products.

Observations on the Recent Agricultural Inquiry in California, by Thomas Forsyth Hunt, director of the University of California College of Agriculture (Berkeley, 1917, 20 pages). An appeal to farmers to increase food production.

California in the War. Addresses delivered at State War Council held under the auspices of the State Council of Defense, San Francisco, March 5-6, 1918 (Sacramento, 1918, 69 pages). Food; mobilizing the household; Americanization; industrial conditions of women; transportation; fuel.

California in the War. War addresses, proclamations, and patriotic messages of Governor William D. Stephens ([Sacramento, 1921], 90 pages).

The War and America. Bulletin No. 24, California State Board of Education (Sacramento, 1918, 72 pages). Problems of finance, food, and clothing; government and schools in war time.

"War emergency farm bureaus," "More wheat," "The utilization of idle lands for wheat," "Extending the area of irrigated wheat in California for 1918," "Money power and crop production," and "Advancing the cause of coöperative marketing" are titles of articles in a war emergency issue of the University of California *Journal of Agriculture* (October, 1917, Vol. 5, No. 1).

The War Service Record of the University of California, 1917-1918 (printed as No. 3, Vol. 20, July, 1918, of the *University of California Chronicle,* 171 pages).

COLORADO

Records

War records were collected in Colorado by the State Council of Defense, the University of Colorado, and the State Historical Society. The original records of the State Council of Defense and of the Women's Council of Defense are preserved by the State Historical Society. Duplicates of most of these records are in the library of the university. The history department of the university made clippings from more than one hundred newspapers and classified them under such heads as, food and fuel consumption, war gardens, Liberty loans, Women's Council of Defense, Red Cross, Knights of Columbus, and Y.M.C.A. The State Historical Society has copies of the draft lists, records of the Four Minute men in some parts of the State, replies to questionnaires by men and women in the service, and miscellaneous records.

Publications

War Council and Ways and Means Committee: Food Supply. Reports to the governor, by H. W. Cornell, director of organization, Ways and Means Committee, A. W. Grant, secretary of War Council, Gerald Hughes of the War Council, and W. H. Kerr, chairman Marketing Committee (n.p., 1917, 19 pages).

Council of Defense, Committee on Organization: Instructions for Organization of County Councils of Defense (Denver, 1917, 10 pages).

Fourth and Fifth Annual Reports of the Public Utilities Commission of the State of Colorado, 1916-1918 (Denver, 1919, 191 pages). The war and public utilities; federal control of railroads.

Students' Army Training Corps at the University of Colorado (University of Colorado *Bulletin*, Vol. 18, No. 8 (General Series No. 129, 1920, 5 pages).

The *Industrial Bulletin*, issued since 1915 by the Colorado Fuel and Iron Company, Denver, contains a record of the war activities of that corporation.

CONNECTICUT

Records

In the fall of 1918 the Connecticut State Council of Defense established a Department of Historical Records under the direction of the state librarian. Three days after the signing of the armistice the state librarian, as chairman of the Committee on Historical Records, requested each town committee, bureau, and department serving under the State Council of Defense to prepare for the library a report of its activities. In April, 1919, the general assembly passed an act creating in the state library a department of historical records "to collect, classify, index and install in the library all available material relating to Connecticut participation, public or private, in the world war and thus to establish a permanent and accessible record of its extent and character, such record to be as complete and comprehensive as possible and to cover not only the activities of the State, its subdivisions and agencies but also of Connecticut agencies of the federal government, organizations of private persons and of those individuals who were direct participants in the great struggle, whether as soldiers, sailors, aviators, or otherwise." This enactment, together with the activities of the librarian and his staff, has brought to the state library voluminous records relative to every phase of war activity. Particularly pertinent to this survey are those of the State Council of Defense; reports of war activities of cities, towns, and counties; state agricultural survey; state industrial survey; automobile census; data relative to food, fuel, housing, social conditions, health, and sanitation; and reports from industrial, commercial, and welfare organizations.

The Library of Congress has a collection of form records, bulletins, and miscellaneous papers of the Connecticut State Council of Defense.

Publications

Report of the Connecticut State Council of Defense (Hartford, 1919, 236 pages). Publicity; food supply; transportation; non-war construction; industrial survey; commercial economy; fuel conservation; man power and labor; Boys' Working Reserve; Woman's Division.

The *Bulletin* of the Extension Service, Connecticut Agricultural College, contains, May-November, 1917, the following numbers, published as a part of the program of the Connecticut Committee on Food Supply:

4. *Home Canning Bulletin* (8 pages).
5. *Farm Manure and Its Housing,* by B. G. Southwick and F. W. Duffee (22 pages).
6. *Clover,* by B. G. Southwick (11 pages).
7. *Studies from the Survey on the Cost of Market Milk Production,* by K. B. Musser, G. C. White, B. A. McDonald, and H. F. Judkins (28 pages).
8. *Poultry Farm Management.* The results of an intensive study of the management practised on forty-two representative poultry farms, on most of

which itemized accounts were kept, by R. E. Jones, I. G. Davis, and B. A. McDonald (16 pages).

9. *Home Cheese Making,* by H. F. Judkins and P. A. Downs (16 pages).

10. *A Plan for Short Term Farm Loans in Connecticut,* by G. C. Smith (8 pages).

11. *Home Curing of Pork,* by J. A. Simms (15 pages).

Training Opportunities for Connecticut Women, by Dorothy Weir. Published by the Woman's Division, Connecticut State Council of Defense (n.p., n.d., 119 pages). Current demands for trained women in applied art, commerce, household economics, trades, and professions.

Report on War Chest Practice, presented to Connecticut State Council of Defense by Henry M. Wriston (n.p., n.d., 157 pages). Structure of the war chest; the campaign; collections; disbursements.

DELAWARE

The Adjutant General has been engaged in the collection of data relative to the part played by the service men of Delaware. The collection by the State of records of the various war-time activities within its borders has been considered.

FLORIDA

Records

No organization was created in Florida for the collection of war records, but Professor James O. Knauss of the Florida State College for Women has located the following:

Records of the State Council of Defense consisting of the governor's correspondence relative to the council, minutes of a meeting of the council (February 15, 1918), and minutes of a meeting of the executive committee. Executive Office, Capitol, Tallahassee.

Annual reports of the State Labor Inspector (1917-1920). Executive Office, Capitol, Tallahassee.

Reports of individual banking institutions in Florida. Comptroller's Office, Capitol, Tallahassee.

Records of the Pensacola Shipbuilding Company, builder of ten ocean steamers for the government. Pensacola.

Records of the Pensacola War Camp Community Service. Pensacola.

The publishers of the following newspapers report possession of complete files for the period of the war:

Times-Union, Jacksonville
Saint Augustine Evening Record, St. Augustine
Orlando Sentinel, Orlando
Palm Beach Post, West Palm Beach
Miami Herald, Miami
The Miami Daily News, Miami
St. Petersburg Times, St. Petersburg
St. Petersburg Independent, St. Petersburg
The Tampa Daily Times, Tampa
The Daily Democrat, Tallahassee

GEORGIA

The Department of Archives and History of the State of Georgia was created by act of August 20, 1918, and this body has undertaken to collect casualty records, records of the State's attitude toward the war, records of local activities, and records relative to the effect of the war on the State's social, financial, educational, economic, and religious conditions. It has the records of the State Council of Defense; a small collection of newspaper clippings relative to boards of trade, chambers of commerce, Liberty loans, and woman's work; and some records sent in from the counties.

IDAHO

The Idaho Memorial Association, one purpose of which was to compile a history of Idaho in the World War, has a complete file of the bulletins issued by the Idaho State Council of Defense. Other source material relative to economic and social conditions during the war is to be obtained chiefly from files of Idaho newspapers.

ILLINOIS

Records

The State Council of Defense of Illinois appointed a War History Committee a few weeks before the armistice was signed. The committee appealed to all war organizations in the State to preserve their records, encouraged the organization of county war history committees, and ceased to function after the dissolution of the council in December, 1918. It was succeeded by the War Records Section of the Illinois State Historical Library, which was engaged from July 1, 1919, to July 1, 1923, in the collection of records and in the publication of a series of volumes relative to Illinois in the war. In its collection of records are:

(1) Records of the State Council of Defense, embracing minutes of meetings of the Council and of those of its thirty-seven subordinate bodies,[1] records of conferences, reports, and correspondence.

(2) The working files of the Woman's Committee, State Council of Defense, and of twenty of its subdivisions.[2]

(3) Reports of the U.S. Food Administration in Illinois, State and county.

(4) Reports of county fuel administrators.

(5) Numerous reports of industrial establishments, constituting an important body of records relative to industries in Illinois during the period of the war.

(6) A few reports of chambers of commerce.

(7) Files of the Illinois divisions of the U.S. Boys' Working Reserve and the U.S. Public Service Reserve.

(8) Minutes of the meetings of the General Advisory Board of the Illinois Free Employment Office, which acted with the U.S. Employment

[1] Twenty of these subordinate bodies were as follows: Advisory Committee on Coal for Public and Quasi-Public Institutions, Advisory Committee on Coal Production and Distribution, Advisory Committee of the Electrical Industry, Agricultural War Board, Commercial Economy Administration, Committee on Engineering and Inventions, Committee on Fuel Economies and Electric Railways, Cook County Auxiliary Committee, Farm Labor Administration, Food, Fuel and Conservation Committee, Food Production and Conservation Committee, Four Minute Men, Highways Transport Committee, Home Registration Service Committee (coöperating with U.S. Housing Corporation), Industrial Survey Committee, Labor Committee, Non-War Construction Bureau, Public Service Reserve Committee (coöperating with U.S. Employment Service), Seed Corn Administration, and Survey of Man Power Committee.

[2] These subdivisions were: Allied Relief Department, Americanization Department, Child Welfare Department, Courses of Instruction Department, Employment Department, Finance Department, Food Conservation Bureau, Fuel Conservation Department, Illinois Motor Corps, Organization Department, Publicity Department, Recreation for Girls Department, Registration Department, Social Hygiene Department, Social Service Department, Speakers Department, Thrift and Conservation Department, Volunteer Placement and Filing Department, War Information Department, and Woman's Land Army.

Service in operating employment offices throughout the State during the war.

(9) A file of *The Weekly News Letter* issued by the Illinois State Federation of Labor, and a file of the proceedings of the annual conventions of the federation for the years 1917-1919.

(10) Reports of each of the two Liberty loan committees for the 7th and 8th districts, in which Illinois lies.

(11) A small amount of material relative to the operations of the Capital Issues Committee and War Finance Corporation in Illinois.

(12) The files of the Illinois headquarters of the Four Minute men.

(13) Reports of educational institutions in the State relative to their war work, including accounts of Student Army Training Corps activities.

(14) Records of activities of social welfare and relief organizations.

(15) Bulletins and periodicals issued by military and naval establishments within the State.

(16) Unofficial narrative reports of local draft boards relative to their activities.

(17) Files of more than forty newspapers and periodicals.

Publications

Final Report of the State Council of Defense of Illinois (Chicago, 1919, 282 pages). A general report on the work of the council and a summary report of each of its committees.

Final Report of the Woman's Committee of the State Council of Defense of Illinois and the Woman's Committee of the Council of National Defense, Illinois Division (Chicago, 1919, 316 pages).

War Documents and Addresses, edited by Marguerite Edith Jenison, Secretary of the War Records Section, Illinois State Historical Library (Springfield, 1923, 522 pages). Public opinion and the war; mobilizing the State's resources for the war; mobilizing Illinois men for service; preserving law and order in the State; bringing war activities to a close; post-war legislation.

The War-Time Organizations of Illinois, edited by Marguerite Edith Jenison (Springfield, 1923, 508 pages). Chronology of Illinois war activities; cyclopaedia of state war agencies; military activities; war finance; food; fuel; welfare activities; public sentiment and morale; bibliography of publications relative to war activities in the State.

First Administrative Report of the Directors of Departments, State of Illinois under the Civil Administrative Code, for the year ended June 30, 1918 (Springfield, 1918, 672 pages). Agricultural conditions; labor situation; public welfare and the war; activities of the Department of Public Health; activities of the Department of Trade and Commerce.

Blue Book of the State of Illinois, 1919-1920 (Springfield, 1920, 680 pages). Contains some laudatory but useful articles: "Civilian achievements of Illinois in the war," by Samuel Insull (pp. 97-103); "Illinois capital in the war," by B. F. Harris (pp. 109-110); "Labor and the war," by John H. Walker (pp. 110-113); "The press of Illinois and the war," by John H. Harrison (pp. 113-115); "Illinois schools and the war," by Francis G. Blair (pp. 115-117); "The farmer and war," by H. E. Young (pp. 117-121); "The State University and the war," by Edmund J. James (pp. 121-125); "War work and the churches of Illinois," by Samuel Fallows (pp. 125-126).

Annual Report of the Illinois Farmers' Institute for the year ending June 30, 1918 (Springfield, 1918, 308 pages). Proceedings of the twenty-third annual meeting of the institute at Bloomington, February 19-21, 1918.

The University of Illinois College of Agriculture published the following Extension Circulars.

13. *War Bread Recipes* (August, 1917, 8 pages).

20. *The Use of Farm Labor during the War,* by W. F. Handschin and J. B. Andrews (March, 1918, 11 pages).

24. *Grow More Wheat in Illinois,* by W. L. Burlison and W. F. Handschin (July, 1918, 8 pages).

25. *War Time Suggestions for Home Economics Exhibits at County and Community Fairs,* by Mamie Bunch and Naomi Newburn (July, 1918, 16 pages).

Illinois Activities in the World War, by J. S. Currey (Chicago, 1921, 3 volumes).

Two bulletins of the University of Illinois are: (1) "Municipal War Work," by Robert Eugene Cushman (February 4, 1918, Vol. 15, No. 23, 16 pages); (2) "The College Man and the War," by Edmund Janes James (August 12, 1918, Vol. 15, No. 50, 10 pages).

For other publications see bibliography in Jenison's *War-Time Organizations of Illinois,* cited above.

INDIANA

Records

From the entry of the United States into the war until the signing of the armistice the Indiana State Library was appealing to local libraries, historical societies, and the counties to collect and preserve newspaper files and other records of war activities in Indiana. The State Council of Defense joined with the library in a request to each county council of defense for a final report of its activities. Immediately following the signing of the armistice the governor suggested to the members of the Indiana Historical Commission that they attend to the collection of records and compile an official war history of the State. The commission responded by organizing a war history committee in each county, by assembling records in the State Library for classification, cataloguing, and preserving, and by preparing plans for publication. Each county was urged to collect records of every organization that had carried on war activities, compile a report, and prepare a history for publication. The commission attended to the collection of records of the State Council of Defense, Food Administration, Fuel Administration, Liberty loans, churches, fraternal organizations, clubs, banks, and manufacturing companies. The publication of a history of the State Council of Defense together with the activities of the State Conscription Board in one volume, and a history of the Liberty loan and war savings campaigns in another volume were among its plans.

Publications

Report of the Indiana State Council of Defense for the year ending December 31, 1917 (n.p., n.d., 66 pages). Merchants' Economy Committee; Four Minute men; Committee on Communications; Employers' Coöperation Committee; Labor Committee; War Camp Community Service; Committee on Food Production and Conservation; Coal Production Committee.

Indiana War Conference, held under the Auspices of the Council of National Defense and the Indiana State Council of Defense, Indianapolis, December 13-14, 1917 (Indianapolis, 1917, 10 pages).

Report of the Woman's Section of the Indiana State Council of Defense, from October, 1917, to April, 1919 (Indianapolis, 1919, 141 pages). Reports of committees; reports by counties.

Indiana War Service Text-Book for Indiana High Schools, planned by the State Council of Defense (n.p., 1918, 151 pages). The schools and the war; war-time savings; reserve of man power; food production; necessity for food conservation.

The Speakers' Bureau of the State Council of Defense (Bulletin of the

Extension Division, Indiana University, March, 1920, Vol. 5, No. 7, 43 pages).

Financing the War, by Ray S. Trent (Bulletin of the Extension Division, Indiana University, November, 1917, Vol. 3, No. 3, 24 pages).

The War Purse of Indiana; the five Liberty loans and war savings and thrift campaigns in Indiana during the World War, by Walter Greenough (Indianapolis, 1922, 278 pages).

Proceedings of Indiana Conference on Reconstruction and Readjustment, called by Governor James P. Goodrich at the State House, Indianapolis, November 26, 1918 (Indianapolis, 1918, 83 pages).

IOWA

Records

From the day on which the United States entered the war the State Historical Society of Iowa pursued the policy of collecting records of the conflict chiefly for publications: (1) a series of twenty-four booklets under the title, *Iowa and War,* issued monthly from July, 1917, to June, 1919; and (2) a series of volumes under the title, *Iowa Chronicles of the World War,* the publication of which was begun in 1920. In 1918 the Society issued No. 8 of its bulletin of information series under the title, "Collection and Preservation of the Materials of War History—A Patriotic Service for Public Libraries, Local Historical Societies, and Local Historians." The Society has the files of about thirty newspapers. The Historical Department of the State Library has a collection of war records but they relate chiefly to individual soldiers and sailors.

Publications

Welfare Campaigns in Iowa, by Marcus L. Hansen (Iowa City, 1920, 320 pages; "Iowa Chronicles of the World War"). Y.M.C.A.; Y.W.C.A.; Knights of Columbus; American Library Association; Jewish Welfare Board; Salvation Army; war chest.

Welfare Work in Iowa, by Marcus L. Hansen (Iowa City, 1921, 321 pages; "Iowa Chronicles of the World War"). Social, recreational, educational, religious, and educational work at Camp Dodge; welfare work throughout the State.

The Red Cross in Iowa, by Earl S. Fullbrook (Iowa City, 1922, 2 volumes; "Iowa Chronicles of the World War"). Development of the

Red Cross organization in Iowa; financing local organizations; work of the women; canteen service; home service; camp service; nursing service.

Social Work at Camp Dodge, by Fred Emory Haynes (Iowa City, 1918, 77 pages; reprinted from *Iowa Journal of History and Politics,* October, 1918, Vol. 16, pp. 471-547).

The Food Administration in Iowa, by Ivan L. Pollock (Iowa City, 1923, 2 volumes; "Iowa Chronicles of the World War"). Coöperative organizations; educational and publicity activities; food pledge campaign; conservation of grain; price interpretation; regulations relative to wheat, flour, feeds, sugar, and perishables.

Iowa War Proclamations (Iowa City, 1918, 48 pages; "Iowa and War"). War proclamations issued by the governor of Iowa between April 6, 1917, and July 1, 1918.

First, Second, and Third Liberty Loans in Iowa, by Nathaniel R. Whitney (Iowa City, 1918, 44 pages; "Iowa and War").

The Sale of War Bonds in Iowa, by Nathaniel R. Whitney (Iowa City, 1923, 236 pages; "Iowa Chronicles of the World War"). Financial situation in Iowa at the beginning of the war; machinery for the sale of the bonds; the five campaigns; handling of reluctant buyers; record of Iowa in the bond sales.

Organized Speaking in Iowa during the War, by Bertha M. H. Shambaugh (Iowa City, 1918, 56 pages; "Iowa and War").

"How Iowa State Institutions are Helping to Win the War," by A. E. Kepford, in *Bulletin of Iowa Institutions under the Board of Control* (1918, Vol. 20, pp. 236-241).

"Going to College in War Times" (August 1, 1917, *Official Publication* No. 9, Vol. 16, of Iowa State College of Agriculture and Mechanic Arts).

KANSAS

Records

The Kansas State Historical Society has the correspondence of Governor Arthur Capper relative to the Council of Defense, draft and exemption boards, exemption requests and farm furloughs, Navy League, Red Cross, railroads, and slackers.

In the society's comprehensive newspaper collection is a bound file of every newspaper published in Kansas during the war, and volumes of clippings on the following subjects:

(1) Work of various organizations during the European war, 1914-1918 (1 volume).

(2) Work and workers of the Y.M.C.A. during the European war, 1914-1918 (1 volume).

(3) Work and workers of the Y.W.C.A. during the European war, 1914-1918 (1 volume).

(4) Liberty loans and War savings stamps (1 volume).

(5) Camp Funston and Fort Riley (2 volumes).

(6) Organization and work of the Military Sisterhood of Kansas during the European war (1 volume).

(7) Red Cross activities of different counties in Kansas during the European war, 1914-1918 (1 volume).

(8) Work and workers of the Salvation Army during the European war (1 volume).

Publications

History of the Kansas State Council of Defense, edited by Frank W. Blackmar (Topeka, 1921, 137 pages). Agricultural production; report of the Committee on Labor; report of the Committee on Priority; report of the Committee on Utilization and Economy; reports of activities in some of the counties.

Several *circulars* were issued by the Council. Eight of these are as follows:

1. *Plant only tested seed* (April 18, 1917, 3 pages).
3. *Canning instructions* (May 10, 1917, 16 pages).
4. *Home-made apparatus for drying fruits and vegetables* (May 19, 1917, 14 pages).
5. *List of inspected seed wheat* (July 3, 1917, 102 pages).
9. *Use of wheat-saving cereals* (March, 1918, 12 pages).
10. *One-dish meals* (March, 1918, 16 pages).
11. *Seed list* (March, 1918, 74 pages).
15. *County war organizations in Kansas* (December, 1918, 18 pages).

Report of the Woman's Committee of the Council of Defense for Kansas from July 6, 1917, to December 30, 1918 (Topeka, 1919, 60 pages).

Winning the War with Wheat, issued by the Seed Wheat Committee, Kansas State Council of Defense (Topeka, 1917, 8 pages).

Council of Defense Chronicle (Nos. 1-3, March, April, August, 1918).

Food, U.S. Food Administration, Wichita, Kansas, Walter P. Innes, administrator (Nos. 1-18).

We are at War (Safety Bulletin No. 2, State Department of Labor and Industry, Topeka, 1917, 16 pages).

KENTUCKY

Records

Records of war activities in Kentucky have been collected by the State Historian for the Kentucky Council of Defense and by a local historian in each of the counties. The work was begun with the appointment of the State Historian in September, 1918, and that it might be pursued to completion the legislature continued the council in existence until March, 1924.

The material collected and compiled for the State during this period is bound in twenty-one volumes and includes reports of state-wide work of the Kentucky Council of Defense, Liberty loan and war savings stamp campaigns, food administrator, fuel administrator, Red Cross, Y.M.C.A., Knights of Columbus, Jewish Welfare Board, women's clubs, schools, churches, and Four Minute men; a history of the Students' Army Training Corps; a history of each military establishment within the State; and records of activities of the selective service boards, American Protective League, War Camp Community Service, Y.W.C.A., Boy Scouts, and Boys' Working Reserve.

At the county clerk's office in each county is at least one volume of war records (Jefferson County, 34 volumes) relative to council of defense activities, Liberty loan and war savings stamp campaigns, food and fuel administrations, local draft boards, Four Minute men, the Red Cross, and other organizations.

Publications

State Conference on Kentucky Problems, held at University of Kentucky, Lexington, March 4-5, 1919, under the auspices of the Kentucky Council of Defense (Frankfort, 1919, 122 pages). Rural schools; community organization; commercial organizations; illiteracy; roads; the soldier on the land.

Final Report of the War Historical Work of the Kentucky Council of Defense (n.p. [1924], 15 pages).

LOUISIANA

Records

The Legislature of Louisiana made no provision for the collection of records of industrial and social activities in the State during the period of the war, and the Louisiana State Council of Defense undertook only the collection of personal records of soldiers, sailors, and marines.

Publications

Minutes of the Meeting of the Louisiana State Council of Defense . . . September 24, 1918 (Baton Rouge, 1918, 15 pages). Organization and activities of the Council.

Condition of Women's Labor in Louisiana, a report by Women in Industry Committee, Council of National Defense, New Orleans Division and Louisiana State Division (New Orleans, 1919, 139 pages). Wages and cost of living; hours and industrial fatigue; labor turnover.

A Brief History of Woman's Committee, Council of National Defense, New Orleans Division, by Isoline Rodd Kendall.

Louisiana in the War, by Herman J. Seiferth (New Orleans, 1920).

MAINE

Records

The State Library of Maine has the records of the Committee on Public Safety and a small body of papers relative to industrial and welfare organizations. The libraries of the Maine Historical Society, the University of Maine, Bowdoin College, Bates College, and Colby College, and the Portland and Bangor public libraries have data relative to local participation in the war.

Publications

Committee of One Hundred on Public Safety (n.p., n.d., 52 pages). Organization of the committee; activities; abstracts of the reports of the county committees.

Emergency War Measures enacted by the Seventy-Eighth Legislature of the State of Maine (Augusta, 1917, 27 pages).

MARYLAND

Records

The collection of war records in Maryland was commenced shortly before the armistice by the Historical Division of the Maryland Council of Defense, and to carry on the work after the dissolution of the council, the legislature created a War Records Commission. The program of the commission was comprehensive and in its collection are:

(1) Records of the Maryland Council of Defense.

(2) History of the food administration.

(3) History of the fuel administration.

(4) Replies to questionnaires addressed to leading establishments engaged in industry, commerce, and transportation.

(5) Histories, reports, and records of military and naval establishments, including Camp Meade, Camp Holabird, Aberdeen Proving Ground, Edgewood Arsenal, Curtis Bay General Ordnance Depot, Perryville Ammonium Nitrate Plant, Zone Supply and Port Storage Office, General Hospital No. 2 at Fort McHenry, Indianhead Naval Proving Ground and Powder Factory, United States Naval Academy, Naval Overseas Transportation Service, and Naval Gun Factory at Poole Engineering and Machine Gun Company plant.

(6) Reports of Liberty loans.

(7) Report and records of Four Minute men.

(8) Report and records of the American Protective League.

(9) Histories, reports, and bulletins of welfare and relief organizations.

(10) Records of war activities of educational institutions, including reports of Students' Army Training Corps at the colleges in the State.

(11) Reports from churches and other religious organizations.

(12) Clippings from Baltimore and county newspapers.

The Maryland Historical Society has complete files of the newspapers of Baltimore.

Publications

Report of the Maryland Council of Defense (n.p., 1920, 334 pages). Camp community work; housing problem; motor truck trains; Red Cross; Americanization; non-war construction; commercial economy; labor and employment; agriculture.

General Meeting of the Maryland Council of Defense and . . . the Women's Section, February, 1919 (75 pages). Contains a report of the women's section.

Milk Cost Survey for the Week November 26 to December 2, 1917. Maryland State College and Public Service Commission coöperating (Baltimore, 1917, 42 pages).

Biennial Report of the Maryland State College of Agriculture and the Maryland State Board of Agriculture (Vol. 16, No. 5, October, 1919, 160 pages). Contains report on the agricultural work conducted under the auspices of the Maryland Council of Defense in coöperation with the Extension Service.

Baltimore and the Draft, an Historical Record. Issued by authority of the District Board of Baltimore City and the twenty-four local draft boards; compiled by Wm. E. Bauer and John P. Judge, Jr. (Baltimore, 1919, 256 pages).

Report of the Baltimore Chapter of the American Red Cross (Baltimore, 1918, 31 pages).

Maryland Division of the U.S. Boys' Working Reserve. Report for summer and autumn season of 1918, by Frank B. Cahn, Federal State Director (Baltimore, 1918, 6 pages).

Maryland Manual, 1917-1918 (n.p., n.d., 294 pages). Contains the war laws of Maryland for the year 1917.

MASSACHUSETTS

Records

No special provision was made by the State for the collection and preservation of its war records until 1923, when the state legislature passed an act, approved May 17, creating a Commission on the History of Massachusetts in the World War, and this body has undertaken the collection of material relative to both military and civilian activities.

The Massachusetts State Library has the records, including the correspondence, of the Executive Committee and of the various subcommittees of the Massachusetts Committee on Public Safety. Here, too, are the files of the principal newspapers published in Massachusetts, particularly valuable, in the absence of other records, for the substance of the reports pertaining to industrial conditions.

Publications

The Story of the Massachusetts Committee on Public Safety, February 10, 1917-November 21, 1918, by George Hinckley Lyman (Boston, 1919, 600 pages). Labor controversies and arbitration; food administration; fuel administration; women's activities.

Report of Executive Committee to Massachusetts Committee on Public Safety, March 17, 1917 (20 pages).

Report of Executive Committee to Massachusetts Committee on Public Safety, November 1, 1917 (Boston, 1917, 27 pages). Settlement of labor controversies; food administration; fuel supply; mobilization of school boys for farm service.

Report of the Committee on Mobilization of High School Boys for Farm Service to the Executive Committee, Massachusetts Committee on Public Safety, October 1, 1917 (Boston, 1917, 60 pages).

Report of the Committee on Public Safety of Springfield to the Mayor and City Council of Springfield, Mass., December 1, 1918 (37 pages).

Executive Proclamations and War Legislation, Commonwealth of Massachusetts (Boston, 1917, 46 pages).

Messages to the General Court, Official Addresses, Proclamations, and State Papers of His Excellency, Governor Samuel Walker McCall, for the years 1916, 1917, and 1918 (458 pages).

Massachusetts Agricultural College in the War (May, 1921, M.A.C. Bulletin No. 4, Vol. 13, 203 pages). The Massachusetts Food Committee; war work of the Experiment Station; special war service directed by the Extension Service; war work of the students; Students' Army Training Corps.

Agriculture and the World War and After. Handbook No. 2. Massachusetts Agricultural College (June, 1917, 8 pages).

The *Extension Bulletin* for 1919, issued by the Extension Service, Massachusetts College of Agriculture, contains the following numbers:

17. *The Service of Extension Workers in Time of War.* An address by W. D. Hurd (7 pages).
20. *Seed Production in 1918,* by H. F. Tompson (May, 1918, 18 pages).
22. *Home Canning,* by W. W. Chenoweth (May, 1918, 28 pages).
24. *The Home Manufacture of Fruit Products,* by W. W. Chenoweth.

The Utilization of Forest Products in Massachusetts as Affected by the War, by Paul D. Kneeland (Boston, 1918, 14 pages).

The Quincy Community Produce Exchange, What One Community Has Done, issued by H. B. Endicott, Food Administrator of Massachusetts (10 pages).

Food Conservation Cottages on Boston Common. Board of Food Administration, State House (Boston, 1918, 28 pages).

Medical Report of Influenza, Camp Brooks, Corey Hill, Brookline, October 15, 1918 (40 pages).

MICHIGAN

Records

Records of Michigan's industrial and social activities for the winning of the war have been collected by county war boards and county historical societies under the direction of the Michigan Historical Commission, by the Detroit Public Library, State Library, the libraries of the University of Michigan and the colleges of the State, and by the public libraries of Grand Rapids, Saginaw, Kalamazoo, Houghton, and other cities. The records comprise reports and other material relative to agriculture, commerce, finance, war industries, labor, education, and public opinion; material relative to churches, welfare agencies, fraternal orders, banks, manufacturing and commercial establishments; and material relative to military and naval establishments within the State. The Michigan Historical Commission in coöperation with the Michigan War Preparedness Board has undertaken the preparation of a history of Michigan in the war.

Publications

In the *Michigan History Magazine* are the following articles:

"Michigan in the Great War," by Roy C. Vandercook (April, 1918, Vol. 2, pp. 259-269).

"The University of Michigan in the War," by R. M. Wenly (October, 1918, Vol. 2, pp. 690-701).

"Work of the War Preparedness Board," by Roy C. Vandercook (January, 1919, Vol. 3, pp. 76-80).

"Michigan Agriculture and the Food Supply during the War," by Mrs. Dora Stockman (October, 1919, Vol. 3, pp. 540-546).

"Michigan Federation of Women's Clubs and the Great War," by Mrs. Florence I. Bulson (October, 1919, Vol. 3, pp. 564-574).

"War Work of the American Red Cross in Michigan," by Sidney T. Miller (October, 1919, Vol. 3, pp. 584-597).

"The University of Michigan and the Training of her Students for the War," by Arthur Lyon Cross (January, 1920, Vol. 4, pp. 115-140).

"Report of War Work of the Daughters of the American Revolution of Michigan from April, 1915, to April, 1919," by Mrs. William Henry Wait (January, 1920, Vol. 4, pp. 193-242).

"The United States Boys' Working Reserve: Boy Soldiers of the Soil," by L. B. W. (January, 1920, Vol. 4, pp. 279-286).

"Michigan in the Great War," by C. H. Landrum (April, 1920, Vol. 4, pp. 478-484).

"Michigan War Legislation, 1917," by C. H. Landrum (October, 1920, Vol. 4, pp. 799-833).

"Michigan War Legislation, 1919," by C. H. Landrum (April, 1921, Vol. 5, pp. 228-267).

Michigan War Records, Bulletin No. 10 of the Michigan Historical Commission (Lansing, 1919, 30 pages). A plan for the collection and preservation of war records.

Prize Essays Written by Pupils of Michigan Schools in the War History Contest for 1918-1919, Bulletin No. 11 of the Michigan Historical Commission (Lansing, 1919, 22 pages). War activities of schools, towns, and counties.

Reconstruction in Michigan. Report to the Governor by the Michigan Reconstruction Committee (26 pages). Conservation and relief; agriculture; unemployment and housing; industrial relations; Americanization; health and child welfare; business readjustment.

MINNESOTA

Records

The Minnesota Historical Society was active in collecting local war records from the day the United States entered the war. At the suggestion of the society the Minnesota Commission of Public Safety, in October, 1918, created the Minnesota War Records Commission which was formally established by act of the legislature in April, 1919. The program of the commission included the collection by each county of all available records of war activities within its borders and the making of a state collection consisting of duplicates of parts of the county records, of records of state organizations, and of records of federal organizations operating within the State. Particular attention is directed to the following papers in the state collection:

(1) Statements of the state and county units of the U.S. Food Administration.

(2) Reports and correspondence of the Department of Home Economics of the State Agricultural College.

(3) Final report of the U.S. Fuel Administration in Minnesota.

(4) Reports on the war activities of the Minneapolis Civic and Commerce Association.

(5) A private collection relative to activities of the War Industries Board.

(6) Records of the Minnesota branch of the Woman's Committee of the Council of National Defense.

(7) A private collection relative to the organization of Saint Paul women for war work in the early days of American participation.

(8) Records of branch offices of the United States Employment Service in Minnesota.

(9) A statement of the war services of the Woman's Relief Corps.

(10) Accounts of the war activities of the University of Minnesota.

(11) Histories of county chapters of the American Red Cross.

(12) Records of the war council of the Y.M.C.A. in Minnesota.

(13) Records of the war council of the Y.W.C.A. in Minnesota.

(14) Records of the Jewish Welfare Board.

(15) Records of the Woman's Division of the American Patriotic League of Saint Paul.

(16) Records of the Minneapolis and Saint Paul offices of the War Camp Community Service.

(17) Records of the Boy Scout organization of Saint Paul.

(18) Records of the Americanization Committee of the Minnesota Commission of Public Safety.

(19) A voluminous collection of newspaper clippings.

Publications

Report of Minnesota Commission of Public Safety (Saint Paul, 1919, 319 pages). Food production and conservation; marketing; fish as food supply; production of iron ore; fuel; labor; Americanization. An appendix contains the by-laws and orders of the commission and excerpts from minutes of its meetings.

Minnesota in the War. Official bulletin of the Minnesota Commission of Public Safety, September, 1917, to February, 1919 (Vol. 1, Nos. 1-52; Vol. 2, Nos. 1-18).

A comprehensive history of Minnesota's participation in the World War is in preparation by the War Records Commission, but only volumes devoted to military history have as yet appeared (1925).

MISSISSIPPI

The collection and classification of records of war activities in Mississippi has been undertaken by the Mississippi Department of Archives and History.

MISSOURI

Records

The State Historical Society of Missouri has the records of the Missouri Council of Defense and files of Missouri newspapers during the period of the war. The society has not undertaken the collection of other records of industrial and social activities in the State during the war but the legislature has made provision for a history of Missouri in the war by the Adjutant General.

Publications

Final Report of the Missouri Council of Defense (n.p., n.d., 121 pages). Agriculture and food production; commercial economy; non-war construction.

A survey of Missouri's participation in the war is contained in a series of six articles on "Missouri and the War," by Floyd C. Shoemaker, in the *Missouri Historical Review* (October, 1917; January, April, July, October, 1918; July, 1919; Vols. 12, 13).

The Thirty-Eighth, Thirty-Ninth, Fortieth, and Forty-First *Annual Reports of the Bureau of Labor Statistics, State of Missouri* (Jefferson City, 1918-1921, 2 vols., 1754 pages), constitute a war-time industrial history of the State. Missouri as an agricultural State; manufacturing; mineral resources and metal output; revival of Mississippi River traffic; business associations; organized labor; free employment; women wage earners; high cost of living; state and municipal welfare work.

The *Annual Reports* (Year Book) of the Missouri State Board of Agriculture for the years 1917, 1918, and 1919 (Jefferson City, 1917-1919) contain statistical data on agriculture in Missouri during the war years, war-time economic conditions in the State, crop production, live-stock production, and food conservation.

The *Monthly Bulletin*, Missouri State Board of Agriculture, contains the following numbers:

Arms and Agriculture (Vol. 15, No. 4, 31 pages).
War-Time Farming in Missouri (Vol. 15, No. 8, 63 pages).
The Farmer and the War (Vol. 16, No. 1, 47 pages).
The New Patriotism (Vol. 16, No. 2, 15 pages).
Live Stock in War Time (Vol. 16, No. 3, 19 pages).

Farming on a War Basis, by O. R. Johnson, is Circular No. 31, Extension Service, College of Agriculture (Columbia, 1917, 20 pages).

An Educational Program for the War (September, 1917, 39 pages) was published by the Division of Rural Education, State Normal School, Kirksville.

MONTANA

Orders Made and Promulgated by the Montana Council of Defense . . . March 15 and April 22, 1918 (Helena, 1918, 7 pages). Utilization of the man power of Montana; the use of the German language.

NEBRASKA

Records

The Nebraska State Historical Society has the records of the State Council of Defense, including the Woman's Auxiliary, files of nearly all the Nebraska newspapers during the period of the war, and a large collection of letters written by men in the service both in the United States and overseas.

Publications

Are You Sorry You Came to This Country? An address to citizens of the United States of German birth or ancestry by C. J. Ernst. Published and distributed by the Nebraska State Council of Defense (1917, 12 pages).

Bridging the Atlantic. A discussion of the problems and methods of Americanization by Sarka B. Hrbkova. Issued and printed by the Nebraska State Council of Defense (1919, 32 pages).

NEVADA

Records

The Nevada Historical Society has for the war period copies of the telegrams from the governor's office, copies of the orders promulgated by the adjutant general, and files of Nevada newspapers. The state legislature has made an appropriation to enable the secretary of the society to prepare a history of the State's participation in the war.

Publications

Nevada War Gardens, by C. S. Knight. State Service Bulletin, College of Agriculture, No. 17 (1918, 8 pages).

A number of leaflets and bulletins on foods, live stock, and gardens were published by the Extension Department, University of Nevada, to promote war conservation and production.

NEW HAMPSHIRE

Records

The New Hampshire Committee on Public Safety appointed a state war historian in August, 1917, to write a history of the committee and of its eighteen subcommittees, and to compile the service record of the men and women of New Hampshire who were in the military or naval service of the United States and the allies. The collection of other records of New Hampshire's participation in the war was left to the New Hampshire Historical Society.

Publications

The New Hampshire Committee on Public Safety (Concord, 1922, 141 pages). Organization; keeping in touch with the towns; industrial survey; transportation; curtailment of non-war construction; Americanization.

Food Administration in the Granite State during the World War (Concord, 1919, 43 pages).

NEW JERSEY

Records

The collection of war records in New Jersey was undertaken by a War History Bureau which was created by the state legislature, in 1919, as an adjunct to the State Library. The bureau has replies to questionnaires relative to the State Council of National Defense, the National League for Women's Services, the American Protective League, the War Camp Community Service, the public schools, Liberty loan campaigns, money drives, municipal and war relief committees. Eight important reports prepared for the bureau are as follows:

(1) War work of the New Jersey Council of Defense from March 28, 1917, to November 23, 1918.

(2) History of the United States Food Administration in New Jersey from May 8 to December 31, 1918.

(3) The work of the Federal Fuel Administration in New Jersey.

(4) The New Jersey school report.

(5) The Selective Service Organization for the State of New Jersey.

(6) War Work in the Hospitals, 1917 to 1919.

(7) The Mercy Committee of New Jersey.

(8) The Women's Liberty Loan Committee of New Jersey, April 21 to May 10, 1919 (Victory Loan).

The State Library has the files of the Camden *Post-Telegraph*, Newark *News*, Newark *Star Eagle*, *State Gazette* (Trenton), and Trenton *Times*.

NEW MEXICO

Records

The State Historical Service of New Mexico was organized in August, 1917, to gather and compile the war records of the State. The service was interested chiefly in personal records, but it has the files of some sixty daily and weekly newspapers of the State during the period of the war and has prepared a preliminary history of New Mexico's participation in the war.

Publications

"War Work of New Mexico" in the *New Mexico Blue Book*, 1919 (Santa Fé, 1919, pp. 63-114). The State Council of Defense; agricultural operations; education and labor; women's part.

War Service of the University of New Mexico, University Bulletin No. 96 (Albuquerque, 1919, 47 pages).

Council of Defense. New Mexico War News, edited by Guthrie Smith; published weekly, 1917-1918.

NEW YORK

Records

Within a few days after the declaration of war on April 6, 1917, the Division of Archives and History sent circular letters to historical and patriotic societies, libraries, and public officials of towns, villages, and cities, requesting them to inaugurate the work of gathering records of war activities. The State Library sent a similar request to libraries throughout the State, and subsequently a War Records Bureau was organized in the Adjutant General's Office. The state legislature passed an act, April 11, 1919, providing for the appointment of a local historian in each town, incorporated village, and city, except the City of New York, whose duty should be to collect and preserve historical material under instructions from the State Historian, who is the director of the Division of Archives and History, and on April 19, 1919, the legislature adopted a resolution directing the State Historian to prepare a history of New York's participation in the war.

The War Records Bureau of the Adjutant General's Office has personal service records, and records of the military and naval establishments within the State.

The State Library has the principal state collection of public documents, books, and pamphlets, including special state reports relative to agriculture, manufactures, and commerce. It has a file of the "chief newspaper" of each county, and files of some of the newspapers published in the larger cities. The Division of Archives and History has the annual reports of the 750 local historians who were appointed under the law of April 11, 1919—reports which, in the estimate of the State Historian, "vary from remarkable documents to those of mediocre excellence."

The material collected by the local historians includes records of the output of establishments supplying war material, records of all organizations, both social and industrial, which were engaged in operations connected with the war, and newspaper clippings relative to the war activities of particular political units.

Publications

Report of the New York State Food Commission, October 18, 1917, to July 1, 1918, with a supplementary report for the four months ending November 1, 1918 (Albany, 1919, 151 pages). Methods of meeting the farm labor situation; women farm labor specialists; tractors; increasing pork production; increasing wheat acreage; war gardens; distribution and transportation; conservation; Food Council of Greater New York.

The Food Supply and the War: Report of the New York State Food Supply Commission (Albany, 1918, 31 pages). The Patriotic Agricultural Service Committee was appointed by the governor April 13, 1917; by an act of the legislature this committee became the New York State

Food Supply Commission which functioned from April 17 until October 15, when it was succeeded by the New York State Food Commission.

List of Creameries, Cheese Factories, Milk Stations, Condensing Plants and Powdered Milk Plants in New York State (Agricultural Bulletin No. 113, Division of Agriculture, Department of Farms and Markets, November, 1918, 62 pages).

Proceedings of Second Patriotic Sheep Meeting, Exhibition, and Sale. Held at Albany, N. Y., November 12, 13, and 14, 1918 (Agricultural Bulletin No. 114, Division of Agriculture, Department of Farms and Markets, December, 1918, 86 pages).

Census of the Agricultural Resources of New York. Census of 1917 taken by order of the New York Food Supply Commission, census of 1918 taken by order of the New York State Food Commission (Albany, 1919, 69 pages).

Report of the Executive Committee, Mayor's Committee [City of New York] *on National Defense* (November 21, 1917, 41 pages). Organization and activities.

The Mayor's Committee on National Defense (New York, 1918, 327 pages). A report by the director general on the functioning of the subcommittees of the Committee on National Defense, City of New York: Committee on Arts and Decorations, Committee on Associated Cities, Committee on Associated War Work, Committee on Building and Construction, Committee on Civic Finance, Committee on Civic Problems, Committee on Commerce, Committee on Domestic Supplies, Committee on Labor, Committee on Loyalty, Committee on National Activities, Committee on Retail Industries, Committee on Trades and Manufacturers, Committee on Transportation, Committee on Wholesale Industries, and others.

Bulletin of the New York State Industrial Commission (monthly, 1917-1919). Devoted in part to such matters as the labor market, women in industry, what women earn, and child welfare standards.

Eighth Annual Report of the Conservation Commission (Albany, 1919). Review of conservation during the war and discussion of conservation in the reconstruction program.

Wood Fuel, by W. G. Howard (Albany, 1918, 8 pages). *Bulletin* No. 16 of the New York Conservation Commission, published in coöperation with the United States Fuel Administration.

Preliminary Report of Reconstruction Commission on Demobilization . . . and Unemployment in New York City, April, 1919 (Albany, 1919, 6 pages).

Report of Reconstruction Commission . . . on Retrenchment and Re-

organization in the State Government (Albany, 1919, 419 pages). Present organization; proposed organization.

Report of Reconstruction Commission on Public Improvements in Progress . . . and Contemplated, April 14, 1919 (Albany, 1919, 28 pages).

Report of Reconstruction Commission on a Permanent Unemployment Program, June, 1919 (Albany, 1919, 17 pages).

Report of Reconstruction Commission on Business Readjustment and Unemployment, April 14, 1919 (Albany, 1919, 21 pages).

Report of the Housing Committee of the Reconstruction Commission, March 26, 1920 (Albany, 1920, 65 pages).

Report of the Committee on Education of the Reconstruction Commission in the matter of Americanization, May, 1919 (Albany, 1919, 7 pages).

NORTH CAROLINA

Records

The Secretary of the North Carolina Historical Commission was director of the Historical Committee of the North Carolina Council of Defense. In October, 1917, the committee issued a bulletin urging the collection of such records as official documents, resolutions, and reports of public meetings, resolutions, reports, and activities of social, labor, and religious organizations, records of the work of the American Red Cross and of women's war work, announcements and orders of transportation companies, public service corporations, mill factories, and other industrial corporations, price lists, quotations from local markets, and records showing the effect of the war on economic conditions, and on schools and colleges. Persons collecting such records were requested to send them to the Historical Commission for preservation. In a majority of the counties the committee had assistants who gave special attention to the matter. In 1919 the state legislature passed an act authorizing and directing the Historical Commission to employ a Collector of World War Records to continue the work and to prepare a history of North Carolina's participation in the war.

The Commission's records relative to industrial and social activities include the following:

(1) Records of the North Carolina Council of Defense.
(2) Records of several county councils of defense.

(3) Miscellaneous county collections.

(4) Voluminous records of the U.S. Food Administration in North Carolina.

(5) Records of the U.S. Fuel Administration in North Carolina.

(6) Records of Andrew B. Baggerly, Navy Yard, 1917-1920.

(7) Records of the Liberty loan campaigns.

(8) Reports of war camp community service in several localities.

(9) Reports from various women's organizations in North Carolina during the period of the war.

(10) Miscellaneous data relative to education in North Carolina, 1917-1920.

(11) Miscellaneous economic data collected from various sources.

Publications

The North Carolina Council of Defense, Plan of Organization (Raleigh, 1917, 15 pages).

Methods of Saving Wheat, Meat, Sugar, and Fat. Bulletin of the North Carolina State Normal and Industrial College (Greensboro, 1917, 32 pages).

In *After-the-war Information Leaflets* issued by the Bureau of Extension, University of North Carolina (Chapel Hill, 1918) are the following:

Reconstruction and Citizenship (14 pages).

Studies in the Social and Industrial Condition of Women as Affected by the War, by Mrs. T. W. Lingle (19 pages).

A Course on Americanization. Studies of the Peoples and the Movements that are Building up the American Nation, by Mrs. T. W. Lingle (62 pages).

NORTH DAKOTA

Records

A War History Commission was appointed by the governor in 1918 to collect records and prepare a history of North Dakota's participation in the war. The commission had the coöperation of most of the county superintendents in collecting records and in 1920 the legislature made a small appropriation for carrying on the work. In 1924 the work was reorganized and placed under the direction of the State Historical Society.

Publications

The Quarterly Journal of the University of North Dakota (October, 1919, Vol. 10, No. 1) contains the following articles.

"North Dakota's Contribution through the Liberty Loan," by Samuel Torgerson (pp. 17-22).

"The Work of the Welfare Organizations," by Howard E. Simpson (pp. 23-40).

"Home Service Work of the Red Cross," by Frank J. Bruno (pp. 47-56).

"The Work of North Dakota's Physicians and Nurses," by Dr. F. R. Smyth (pp. 57-60).

"The Work of the Institutions of Higher Education," by Orin G. Libby (pp. 61-80).

"The Public Schools and the War," by M. Beatrice Johnstone (pp. 81-83).

"Various Secondary War Activities of the State," by Vernon P. Squires (pp. 84-92). State council of defense; food production and conservation; fuel conservation; Four Minute men.

OHIO

Records

Ohio had no war history commission that was established by law, but in February, 1918, the governor appointed the Historical Commission of Ohio, composed largely of members of the historical profession in the State. The commission worked in coöperation with the Ohio State Archaeological and Historical Society and the Ohio State University. It appointed a chairman of the county branch in about three-fourths of the counties and issued a bulletin in which it stated its purpose to build up such a collection of war material, civilian and military, as would represent all activities of the people of the State with reference to the war. Each county chairman was directed to collect all such documents, reports, and other records as would be useful in showing how the war had affected the life of the community in all its aspects.

Particularly important material in the commission's collection, which is housed in the library of the Ohio State Archaeological and Historical Society, are:

(1) Accounts written by public officials of their activities in war service, for example, an account of the fuel crisis in Ohio during the winter of 1917-1918, by E. D. Leach, assistant state fuel administrator.

(2) Bulletins issued by war service organizations, for example, the *Ohio Food Bulletin*.

(3) Files of 139 newspapers representing most of the counties.

(4) Religious periodicals.

(5) Chamber of commerce publications.

(6) Agricultural periodicals.

(7) Labor papers.

(8) Trade papers.

Publications

A History of the Activities of the Ohio Branch, Council of National Defense: How Ohio Mobilized Her Resources for the War (Columbus, 1919, 205 pages). Industrial relations and employment; food supply and conservation; Woman's Committee; profiteering; fire prevention.

Utilization of Food Recipes, prepared by the Home Economics Department, Ohio State University, and issued by the Agricultural Division, Ohio Branch, Council of National Defense (44 pages).

Proceedings of the Mayor's Advisory War Board, City of Cleveland. April 9, 1917, to December 27, 1918 (487 pages).

"Ohio's Religious Organizations and the War," by Martha L. Edwards, in *Ohio Archaeological and Historical Quarterly* (April, 1919, Vol. 28, pp. 208-224).

"Ohio's German-Language Press and the War," by Carl Wittke, in *Ohio Archaeological and Historical Quarterly* (January, 1919, Vol. 28, pp. 82-95).

OKLAHOMA

Oklahoma had no war history commission, but the collection of records of the war activities of the State was undertaken by the University of Oklahoma. A summary account of those activities is contained in Bulletin No. 19 of the Oklahoma State Council of Defense, which, under the title *Sooners in the War*, is an official report of that organization from May, 1917, to January 1, 1919 (Oklahoma City, 1919, 88 pages).

OREGON

The Librarian of the Oregon State Library was appointed State Historian to direct the collection of Oregon war records. Circular letters of instruction were sent out from the headquarters, and on a series of blank forms county historians collected information relative to drives for funds, welfare service, local war achievements, war literature, and miscellaneous economic, social, and educational activities. In the *Oregon Voter*, published weekly in Portland, are a number of articles on such subjects as: food campaign; why give up wheat; Oregon's food response; spruce; Liberty loans; Oregon's war contributions; Red Cross; college war training. Other publications relative to Oregon's participation in the war consist of a few bulletins issued by the State Council of Defense, the University of Oregon, and the Oregon Agricultural College.

PENNSYLVANIA

Records

The Pennsylvania War History Commission was appointed in October, 1918, by the Pennsylvania Council of National Defense and Committee of Public Safety "to organize agencies designed to perpetuate the deeds, records, and achievements of the soldiers, sailors, marines, and of citizens and organizations of the Commonwealth active during the war with Germany and Austria, and to prepare, print, and publish a history of such deeds, records, and achievements." With the aid of county committees and the coöperation of several state officials, and by sending out more than 100,-000 form letters (copies in Library of Congress), the commission procured the following:

(1) Reports of nearly 1000 industrial establishments, ranging from a few paragraphs to fifty typewritten pages.

(2) Two hundred and twenty-six reports of agricultural organizations and county food administrators.

(3) Sixty-three reports relative to commerce and transportation.

(4) More than 1000 reports of banking institutions.

(5) Reports of the Third and Fourth Federal Reserve Districts.

(6) The minutes of the Capital Issues Committee of the Third Federal Reserve District.

(7) Histories and narratives describing the conduct of Liberty loan campaigns.

(8) Twenty-seven labor reports.

(9) Reports on public opinion.

(10) Records of the American Protective League.

(11) More than 200 reports of church congregations.

(12) Reports of social, welfare, and relief organizations.

(13) Reports of educational institutions.

(14) Data regarding the Students' Army Training Corps.

(15) Histories of military establishments within the State.

(16) Histories and reports of draft boards.

(17) Files of 75 newspapers for December, 1918, and January, 1919, and a few files for a longer period.

Publications

Outline of Departmental Activities of the Committee of Public Safety of the Commonwealth of Pennsylvania (Philadelphia, 1917, 24 pages).

An Outline of the Wartime Activities of the Pennsylvania Council of National Defense (1919, 55 pages). Food supply; civilian service and labor; publicity and education; Woman's Committee; Highways Transport Committee.

First Annual Report of the Treasurer, Pennsylvania Council of National Defense and Committee of Public Safety (1918, 16 pages).

Emergency Service of the Pennsylvania Council of National Defense in the Influenza Crisis. Report of the Vice-Director, Department of Medicine, Sanitation, and Hospitals (Philadelphia, 1918, 39 pages).

Report of the Fourth Annual Meeting of the Emergency Aid of Pennsylvania, December 5, 1918 (75 pages).

Handbook of the Legal Advisory Department, Pennsylvania Council of National Defense (Philadelphia, 1918, 53 pages).

Relationship of Labor and Industry and the Pennsylvania Committee of Public Safety in War Time. Bulletin of the Pennsylvania Department of Labor and Industry (1918, Vol. 5, No. 1, 176 pages). Reconstruction, rehabilitation, and reëmployment of the war injured.

Pennsylvania's Part in the National Plan for Rehabilitating and Placing in Industry Soldiers and Sailors Disabled in War Service. Bulletin of the Pennsylvania Department of Labor and Industry (1918, Vol. 5, No. 2, 124 pages).

Selected Young Men on Selected Farms and Liberty Camps. U.S. Boys' Working Reserve, Pennsylvania Division (Philadelphia, 1918, 16 pages).

Pennsylvania's Participation in the World War (Harrisburg, 1919, 22 pages). An outline, by the Pennsylvania War History Commission, for a state or county history of the war.

RHODE ISLAND

Records

The Rhode Island Historical Society has a series of scrapbooks in which are mounted chronologically all items in the *Providence Journal* relative to Rhode Island and citizens of Rhode Island in the war.

The State Library has a collection of clippings by the soldiers' and sailors' information bureau, state headquarters, of the Rhode Island draft. Histories of the State Council of Defense have been prepared by S. Ashley Gibson, histories of the Food Administration by Herbert O. Brigham and by J. Taylor Wilson, and a history of the Woman's Committee by Mrs. Albert D. Mead.

Publications

Food Products. Report of Governor Beeckman's Commission on Living Costs in Rhode Island (1917, 21 pages).

SOUTH CAROLINA

Publications

Report of South Carolina State Council of Defense for half year ending December 31, 1917 (Columbia, 1918, 36 pages). Activities and achievements; Woman's Council; county councils.

Annual Report of the South Carolina Council of Defense, December 31, 1918 (Columbia, 1919, 38 pages). Activities and achievements.

The South Carolina Handbook of the War, issued by the South Carolina State Council of Defense (92 pages). Part II, The voice of South Carolina; Part III, How you can help win the war.

War Service Gardens in South Carolina, by C. P. Hoffman and W. G. Crandall. Extension Bulletin No. 39, Extension Service, Clemson Agricultural College (1918, 17 pages).

More Grain to Win the War, by C. P. Blackwell. Extension Circular No. 16, Clemson Agricultural College (1918, 8 pages).

The War Program of the State of South Carolina, a report by Hastings H. Hart (New York, 1918, 61 pages). The mobilization of 1917; future program for the war; care of the convalescent soldier; child dependency and the war; public health and the war; prisoners and the war.

The University and the World War, by W. S. Currell. Bulletin No. 50, University of South Carolina (August, 1917, 14 pages). Women and the war; war and agriculture.

SOUTH DAKOTA

The legislature of South Dakota provided for a war history commission, but the State has been interested chiefly in securing the personal records of men in the military and naval service. The preparation of reports of activities of the several war agencies has been left to the department of history of the University of South Dakota.

TENNESSEE

Records

Tennessee had a Historical Commission from 1919 to 1923, but its duties were chiefly the collection of individual service records of Tennessee soldiers, sailors, airmen, and marines. When the commission was abolished its records were transferred to the Division of Library and Archives, Department of Education. Among them are the following:

(1) Report of the libraries of Tennessee in war activities.

(2) Partial report of college war activities.

(3) Report of dentists of Tennessee in the world war.

(4) Report of Federated Women's Clubs.

(5) Report of the Ladies Hermitage Association.

(6) Davidson County women in the world war.

(7) Report of the Nashville Section of the Council of Jewish Women.

(8) Report of Le Bien-être du Blessé.

(9) Report of the five Liberty loans.

(10) Report of the activities of Four Minute speakers of Davidson County.

(11) History of the American Legion in Tennessee.

(12) Report of Boy Scout war activities.

(13) Report of Girl Scouts of Memphis and Shelby County.

(14) Knox County in the world war.

(15) Report of activities of the Nashville Kiwanis Club.

(16) Newspaper clippings concerning Tennessee and Tennesseans in the world war.

TEXAS

Records

The Texas War Records Collection of the University of Texas, established by the Board of Regents in October, 1918, has state,

American, and foreign material. In the state section are the following:

(1) Records of the Texas Council of Defense.

(2) Records of the Food Administration in Texas.

(3) A few records of war industries.

(4) Records of Liberty loan campaigns.

(5) Records of social, welfare, and relief organizations such as the Red Cross, War Camp Community Service, Y.M.C.A., Y.W.C.A., Knights of Columbus, Jewish Welfare Board, and Salvation Army.

(6) Records of the Speakers' Bureau.

(7) Records of the State draft board.

(8) Records of three military camps conducted under the supervision of the University of Texas.

(9) Files of newspapers covering the several sections of the State.

UTAH

Records

The collection of war records in Utah was begun by a War Historian appointed by the State Council of Defense. It was continued by the Utah Historical Society under an act (1919) of the legislature which designated the society as the proper depository for all state historical material and appropriated funds to enable it to prepare a history of Utah's participation in the war.

Publications

State of Utah Council of Defense (1917, 12 pages). Appointment; organization; work accomplished.

Report of the Council of Defense of the State of Utah (Salt Lake, 1919, 72 pages). Food supply and conservation; labor; commercial economy; non-war construction; women's work; Americanization; reconstruction.

State Council of Defense, County Councils of Defense, U.S. Food Administration, and Allied Organizations. Bulletin No. 3, Council of Defense (1918, 28 pages).

VERMONT

An act of the legislature of Vermont, approved March 28, 1919, provided for the compilation of a history of Vermont's part in the war. An amendment, approved March 2, 1921, required the governor to appoint a commission of five persons to supervise the compilation and authorized the commission to employ a secretary or historian.

VIRGINIA

Records

The Virginia War History Commission was appointed by the governor in January, 1919, to collect records and prepare a history of Virginia's participation in the war. Lists of the material collected from January 1, 1919, to January 1, 1922, are printed in *Virginia Magazine of History*, 1921, Supplements 1-4 (144 pages). The more important of the Commission's records within the scope of this survey are as follows:

(1) History of the First Virginia Council of Defense, April 26, 1917, to January 31, 1918 (75 pages).

(2) History of the Second Virginia Council of Defense, February 8, 1918, to August 8, 1919 (226 pages).

(3) History of the Virginia Industrial Council of Safety (3 pages).

(4) Two histories of the Federal Food Administration in Virginia.

(5) History of Newport News Shipbuilding and Drydock Company in War Time (51 pages).

(6) History of Du Pont Dynamite Plant at Hopewell (15 pages).

(7) Two reports of Woman's Munition Reserve at Seven Pines.

(8) Reports of industrial plants in Richmond, Fredericksburg, and Charlottesville.

(9) Labor conditions in Richmond (5 pages).

(10) Report of the Petersburg Labor Board (4 pages).

(11) Effects of the war on labor groups (2 pages).

(12) Report of Virginia Division, Woman's Land Army of America (2 pages).

(13) History of the Agricultural Council of Safety (6 pages).

(14) Records and correspondence of the Agricultural Council of Safety.

(15) Reports and questionnaires relative to food production and agricultural activities from seventeen cities and counties of Virginia.

(16) Local Food Administration reports from seven Virginia communities.

(17) Food Conservation narratives and reports from five Virginia communities.

(18) Report of the Capital City Division, National League of Woman's Service (gardens) (10 pages).

(19) Reports relative to commerce and transportation.

(20) Financing the World War, with special reference to the part played by the Federal Reserve Bank of Richmond, the Fifth Federal Reserve District, and the citizens of Virginia, 1917-1919 (440 pages).

(21) Reports and questionnaires relative to Liberty loan campaigns.

(22) Reports from several cities and counties on the Four Minute men.

(23) Civilian activities in war time (125 pages).

(24) Pre-war narratives, giving views of local public opinion during the years 1914-1917, from forty-two cities and counties.

(25) War History, Medical College of Virginia (37 pages).

(26) Twenty-four reports from Virginia colleges and universities.

(27) Report of the American Library Association in Virginia during the War (10 pages).

(28) Reports from public and private schools.

(29) Attitude of the church toward the war (8 pages).

(30) Questionnaires and reports from more than three hundred churches.

(31) Social life of Richmond during the World War (8 pages).

(32) The effect of war on status and outlook of women (5 pages).

(33) Reports of Red Cross Chapters in one hundred and three Virginia communities.

(34) Experiences of a Red Cross Worker (30 pages).

(35) War Camp Community Service in Virginia, 1917-1920 (10 pages).

(36) History of the War Camp Community Service in Virginia (30 pages).

(37) Reports by cities on war camp community service.

(38) Twenty-four reports from patriotic and fraternal organizations.

(39) Seventeen Young Men's Christian Association reports.

(40) Report of the war work of the Boy Scouts of Richmond (38 pages).

(41) Thirteen United War Work organizations' reports.

(42) General report on Catholic war relief activities in Virginia.

(43) Local reports on Salvation Army, Boy Scouts, Girl Scouts, Knights of Columbus, Jewish Welfare, and Y.W.C.A.

(44) Numerous reports and historical sketches of military and naval establishments within the State.

(45) Story of the Draft in Virginia (20 pages).

(46) History of the organization and operation of the selective military service law in the State of Virginia (27 pages).

(47) Proclamations, addresses, and messages of Henry Carter Stuart, war governor of Virginia, February 1, 1914-February 1, 1918.

(48) Proclamations and appeals of Westmoreland Davis, war governor of Virginia, February 1, 1918-February 1, 1922.

(49) Political Contributions of Virginia (52 pages).

(50) Sketch of post-war activities in Virginia (23 pages).

(51) Scrap books of clippings from Virginia newspapers with topical arrangement: e.g. Economic conditions in war time (4 volumes) ; pre-war conditions and activities (6 volumes) ; Virginia churches in war time (2 volumes) ; Virginia schools and colleges in the war (1 volume) ; Virginia communities in war time (7 volumes) ; The Red Cross in Virginia (2 volumes) ; War work and relief organizations (3 volumes) ; Post war conditions and activities (1 volume). An index to these clippings is in process of publication.

Publications

The University of Virginia in the World War, by John S. Patton (1922, 71 pages).

"War Extension Service," in *University of Virginia Record*, Extension Series (November, 1917, Vol. 3, 40 pages).

Report of the Virginia Division, National League for Woman's Service, by Mrs. W. W. Sale (Richmond, 1918, 18 pages).

"After the War: a Symposium" in *The Southern Workman* (March, 1919, Vol. 48, pp. 134-140). Race relations after the war.

Virginia War History in Newspaper Clippings, Arthur Kyle Davis, editor (Richmond, 1924, lxx + 453 pages). An instalment of an index to the collection of clippings noted above.

WASHINGTON

Records

The collection of records in Washington was by county committees operating under the direction of a member of the historical department of the State University and the material collected by each committee was deposited in the most central library in the county.

Publications

Report of the State Council of Defense to the Governor of Washington, Covering Its Activities during the War (Olympia, 1919, 125 pages). Organization; activities; coördination of patriotic work, conservation of resources, publicity, and education.

"Western Spruce and the War," by Edmond S. Meany, in *Washington Historical Quarterly* (October, 1918, Vol. 9, pp. 255-258).

WEST VIRGINIA

Publications

West Virginia Legislative Handbook and Manual and Official Register, 1919, compiled and edited by John T. Harris (Charleston, 1919, 920 pages). Part III, pp. 443-698, is a report of West Virginia's war activities by those who directed them: State Council of Defense; Liberty loans; war savings; Food Administration; Fuel Administration; Public Service Reserve; women in the war; schools in the war; the Four Minute men; Red Cross work; allied war relief work.

A Suggested Program for the Executive State Council of Defense of West Virginia, by Hastings H. Hart (Charleston, 1917, 24 pages). Based upon a study of the institutions and resources of the State by Clarence L. Stonaker.

Report of Secretary, West Virginia State Council of Defense, on the Operation of the Compulsory Work Law for the Year ending June 19, 1918 (15 pages).

WISCONSIN

Records

The collection of war records in Wisconsin was first undertaken by the State Historical Society. Early in 1918 a war history commission was appointed by the State Council of Defense to coöperate with the society in carrying on the work, and under this coöperative arrangement a war history committee was organized in each county to collect records of the county's participation in the war for deposit in the courthouse or some centrally located library. In

1919 a War History Commission was created by the legislature to take over from the society the further direction of war history activities. This commission functioned until June 30, 1923, when its duties, together with its records, were retransferred to the society.

In the bulky mass of records that have been acquired are the following:

(1) Records of the state council of defense and of the county councils of defense.

(2) Data relative to prices of food commodities.

(3) A report on the work of the Fuel Administration in Wisconsin.

(4) Records relative to the Liberty loans.

(5) Red Cross records.

(6) Records of the war work of Dane County.

(7) Office records and correspondence of the Wisconsin Loyalty League.

(8) Office records and correspondence of the National League for Women's Service in Wisconsin.

(9) Office records and correspondence of the Four Minute men.

(10) Files of most of the daily and weekly newspapers issued in Wisconsin during the period of the war.

Publications

The *Wisconsin Blue Book, 1919* (Madison, 1919), contains a section (pp. 301-438) on Wisconsin's war activities: State Council of Defense, Food Administration, Fuel Administration, labor, the draft boards, educational institutions, Y.M.C.A., and the Red Cross.

Wisconsin in the World War, by R. B. Pixley (Milwaukee, 1919, 400 pages). Recounts the activities of the State Council of Defense, Food Administration, Fuel Administration, and women in war work.

State of Wisconsin, Messages to the Legislature and Proclamations of Emanuel L. Philipp, Governor, 1915-1921 (Milwaukee, 1920, 529 pages).

Report of the State Council of Defense, April 12, 1917-June 30, 1919 (Madison, 1919, 71 pages). Organization; activities; financial statements.

Report of the Milwaukee County Council of Defense, May 1, 1917, to January 1, 1919 (Milwaukee, 1919, 56 pages). Marketing; food conservation; emergency fuel sales; vacant lot gardens; war contracts; war supplies made in Milwaukee; Americanization.

Forward, published by the Wisconsin State Council of Defense (weekly from May 16, 1917, to June, 1918, and fortnightly from June to December 19, 1918).

Americanization. Speaker's Bureau, State Council of Defense, Bulletin No. 2 (Madison, 1918, 10 pages).

Why Workingmen Support the War, University of Wisconsin Bulletin No. 896 (9 pages).

Serving Wisconsin Farmers in War Time, by H. L. Russell and K. L. Hatch, Agricultural Experiment Station, Bulletin No. 294 (July, 1918, 32 pages).

War Prices and Farm Profits, by H. C. Taylor and S. W. Mendum, Agricultural Experiment Station, Bulletin No. 300 (March, 1919, 18 pages).

War and Business. Preliminary Announcement, Third Wisconsin Commercial and Industrial Congress (February 20-22, 1918).

Organization and Training of the Labor Supply in the Public Schools. Boys Council of Defense League, Bulletin, prepared by the State Department of Education (Madison, 1918, 29 pages).

Desirability of Vocational Education and Direction for Disabled Soldiers, by Elizabeth G. Upham, Bulletin 876, Extension Division, University of Wisconsin (Madison, 1917, 20 pages).

Report of Special Legislative Committee on Reconstruction, February 5, 1919 (Madison, 1919, 30 pages). Agriculture; marketing; labor; women in industry; social insurance; increased inheritance tax, higher tax on large incomes.

WYOMING

Records

A War History Committee of the Wyoming State Council of Defense appointed a chairman in each county to direct the local collection of war records and itself undertook the task of assembling a comprehensive state collection in which are the following:

(1) Price lists, advertisements, and other material pertaining to the economic or industrial effects of the war.

(2) Data showing changes in educational programs and institutions to meet the emergency.

(3) Records of Wyoming men and women who served with the Red Cross, Y.M.C.A., or other relief agencies.

(4) Correspondence of war relief agencies.

(5) Newspaper files.

(6) Pamphlets issued by national, state, and local agencies.

The Wyoming Historical Department, created in February, 1919, took over the records and continued the work of the committee.

Publications

Thirteenth Annual Report of the Dairy, Food, and Oil Commissioner, December 1, 1917 (61 pages). Food conservation; food control; spirit of universal service; thrift for war savings.

INDEX

Aberdeen, Md., housing, 65; meetings at, 67.

Aberdeen Proving Ground, history, 72; records, 457.

Abrams *et al*, case, 24.

Abrasives, imports, 350; report, 352.

Acetate of lime, report, 352.

Acetic acid, price report, 342; report, 352.

Acetylene, report, 352.

Achievement clubs, instructions for, 157.

Acids and heavy chemicals, condition of industry report, 351.

Acids and Heavy Chemicals Section, minutes of meetings, 355; reports, 355.

Adams, E. L., bulletin by, 153.

Administrative Division, Fuel Administration, functions, 412.

Advice Sheet, War Industries Board, 344.

Advisory Council, War Labor Administration, 240.

Advisory Tax Board, duties, 35.

Adjutant General's Office, records, 51-52.

Advertising, Division of, function, 432; records, 436.

Aeronautic instruments, investigations *re,* 207.

Aeronautics, U.S. National Advisory Committee for, 148, 211.

Agricultural Advisory Committee, membership, 185; proceedings, 185.

Agricultural Commission to Europe, appointment, 136, 186; functions, 186; report, 186.

Agricultural conditions, effect of the war on, 142.

Agricultural depression, relief measures, 14, 423, 424.

Agricultural experiment stations, work and expenditures, 140-141.

Agricultural implement industry, conservation, 63.

Agricultural implements, condition of industry report, 351.

Agricultural Production, 137, 138.

Agricultural products, hearing on bill to authorize an association of producers, 11.

Agricultural Situation for 1918, 137.

Agricultural staples and the tariff, survey, 274.

Agricultural statistics, 173, 463.

Agriculture, assistance to, 44; extension work, 140; under reconstruction, 142; and food supply, 442; reports, 460; documents, 467; records, 478.

Agriculture, Department of, significance of records of, xxxvi; technical studies, xxxviii; annual reports, xxxviii, 136; represented at hearings before committees of Congress, 7; war work, 64, 134, 184; monthly surveys, 64; relation to the Food Administration, 135; coöperation with the Council of National Defense, 138; publications, 136-138, 140-143, 147-149, 151-156, 160-163, 164-167, 172-173, 174-176, 177, 180, 181-182, 183-184; records, 138-139, 143-145, 347; activities affected by reduced appropriations, 139; coöperation with agricultural colleges and farmer organizations, 139; coöperation with the Food Administration, 142, 143; coöperation with the Treasury Department, 142, 143; represented on War Labor Policies Board, 245; cost report to, 267; coöperation of Woman's Committee of Council of National Defense with, 320; administration of price control, 342; advertising for, 432; coöperation with Committee on Public Information, 432; public exhibit, 432.

Agriculture, Secretary of, question of transferring war material to, 97; war program, 135-136; member of the Council of National Defense and War Trade Council, 136, 318; statements prepared under direction of, 137; member of Federal Board for Vocational Education, 310; represented on War Trade Board, 379.

Aicher, L. C., bulletin by, 153.

annual reports, 110; member of Council of National Defense, 318; member of Committee on Public Information, 429.

Navy Department, relation with Council of National Defense, 11; relation of State Department with, 28; monthly survey, 66; war activities of each of the several bureaus, 66; functions, 104-109; coöperation with the War Department, 105; Bureau of Ordnance, operations, 107; relations with War Industries Board, 108; medical department, 109; training, 109; publications, 110; records, 111; coöperation of Geological Survey with, 115; coöperation of Bureau of Mines with, 118, 121; coöperation of Forest Service with, 147; coöperation of Bureau of Entomology with, 178; coöperation of Bureau of Standards with, 207, 211, 212; coöperation of Bureau of Census with, 214; transfer of lighthouse tenders to, 220-221; coöperation of Steamboat-Inspection Service with, 223; coöperation of Bureau of Navigation (D. C.) with, 225; industrial relations, 227; represented on War Labor Policies Board, 245; cost reports to, 265; coöperation in the conservation of tonnage, 290; relations of War Industries Board with, 333, 353; administration of price control, 342; contact with War Trade Board, 380, 383; coöperation with Committee on Public Information, 431; public exhibit, 432.

Navy Ordnance Activities, 110.

Nebraska, reclamation fund from, 123; records and publications, 464.

Negro at Work during the World War and during Reconstruction, a report, 250.

Negro Economics, Division of, functions, 249; publications, 250; investigations for, 252.

Negro migration, reports *re,* 250.

Negro Women in Industry, 256.

Nellis, J. C., bulletin by, 149.

Nelson, John H., report by, 148.

Nevada, reclamation fund from, 123; records and publications, 464-465.

Newburn, Naomi, circular by, 450.

New England, supply of spruce, 104; ship-operations district, 282; geographi-

cal division of the Red Cross, 315; power reports, 349; wheatless week in, 408; fuel administration, 413.

New England shipbuilding conference, report, 286.

New England Telephone Company, case against, 24.

New Hampshire, records and publications, 465.

New Hampshire Committee on Public Safety, history, 465.

New Haven, Conn., Winchester Repeating Arms Company, report, 64.

New Jersey, gas proving grounds, 85; records, 465-466; newspapers, 466.

Newlin, J. A., bulletin by, 149.

New London, Conn., submarine base at, 105; anti-submarine experimental station, 106.

New Mexico, reclamation fund from, 123; records and publications, 466; newspapers, 466.

New Orleans, La., zone finance officer, 93; office of Bureau of Foreign and Domestic Commerce in, 190.

Newport, R. I., torpedo station at, 105; emergency hospital buildings erected at, 109.

Newport News, Va., port of embarkation, history, 59; port headquarters of Naval Overseas Transportation Service, 106.

Newport News Shipbuilding and Drydock Company, history, 478.

News, Division of, service, 430.

Newspaper print industry, investigation of, 12.

News print paper, price fixing, 101.

Newton, Roy L., article by, 167.

New York, Deutscher Liederkrantz, loyalty of, 20; Merchants Association in favor of food control, 20; zone supply office, 57; port of, historical data *re,* 59; medical supply depot, 60; Industrial Service Section, Army Ordnance, report, 65; district ordnance office at, 67, 72; Regional Advisor, Region No. 3, report, 68; zone finance officer, 93; charge to jury U.S. district court, northern district of, 100; equipment of navy yard at, 105; port headquarters of Naval Overseas Transportation Service, 106; market reports on live stock and meats in, 168; market reports on dairy products in, 169; of-

terprises in, 171; harvesting sugar beets in, 409; records and publications, 477.

Utilization of war materials, records *re,* 330.

Vacuum Oil Company, case against, 22.

Vanadium, report *re,* 352.

Vandercook, Roy C., articles by, 460.

Van Dyke, Edmund W., *Control of Exportations and Importations,* 388; description of War Trade Board records by, 391.

Varnish, prices, 344; report *re,* 352.

Vegetable gardens, bulletins *re,* 154, 155.

Vegetable-oil industry, licensing, 405.

Vegetable oils, prices, 343; reports, 404.

Vegetables, conservation of, 141; bulletins *re,* 154; preservation of, 175; prices, 343.

Vehicle, Implement, and Wood Products Section, reports, 351, 375-376; minutes of meetings, 375.

Veitch, F. P., bulletin by, 175.

Vermont, 477-478.

Vessels, automatic sprinklers on, 187.

Veterans' Bureau, successor to Bureau of War Risk Insurance, 38; vocational rehabilitation work transferred to, 311.

Veterinary Corps, 87.

Violations Committee, 381.

Virginia, possibilities of manganese ore in, 116; grains in, 154; hours and conditions of work for women in industry in, 255; cost of yellow-pine lumber report, 266; coal-cost report, 270; represented on the Price Fixing Committee, 340; records, 478-480; publications, 480; newspapers, 480.

Viscose Company, case of, 26.

Vocational rehabilitation, 311, 313.

Von Motz, Frank H., monographs by, 196, 197.

Wage adjustments, 221, 230, 231.

Wages, investigations *re,* xxxviii; in government arsenals, 232; standardization of, 245; action of War Labor Policies Board *re,* 246; of women workers, 255, 256; report *re,* 286; records, 305.

Wages and cost of living, 9, 243.

Wages and hours, 244, 245, 321.

Wages and the War, by Hanna and Lauck, 246.

Wage scales and hours of labor, records *re,* 330.

Wage situation in coal districts, 231.

Waggaman, W. H., bulletin by, 181; articles by, 181, 182.

Wait, Mrs. William Henry, article by, 460.

Walcott, Frederick C., loyalty leaflet by, 435.

Walker, John H., article by, 450.

Walker, Percy H., paper by, 210.

Wallace, case against, 27.

Walsh, Frank P., statements by, 243.

Waltenberg, R. G., papers by, 209.

Walton, W. R., bulletin by, 179.

War, Secretary of, member of Inter-Departmental Social Hygiene Board, 39; annual reports, 50; opinions of Attorney General affecting, 97; chairman of Council of National Defense, 318; member of the Committee on Public Information, 429.

Warber, G. P., bulletin by, 166.

Warburton, C. W., bulletin by, 154.

War Camp Community Service, records: headquarters, 52; Alabama, 440; Kentucky, 455; New Jersey, 465; North Carolina, 470; Texas, 477; Virginia, 479.

War charities, hearings on bill to regulate, 13.

War commodities, census of, 215.

War contracts, hearing *re,* 13; list of, 17; adjustment and cancellation, 59, 93; bulletins *re,* 69, 341; protection of the government from fraud in, 95; opinion of Attorney General *re,* 97; in France, 351.

War contracts act, report of claims adjusted under, 93.

War Department, *see* Contents, xi-xii; relation with State Department, 28; industrial relations, 51, 227; relations with War Labor Administration, 51; opinion *re* sale of an enemy-owned patent to, 99; participation in mail service, 102-103; coöperation of Navy Department with, 105; coöperation of Geological Survey with, 115; coöperation of Bureau of Mines with, 118, 121; coöperation of Bureau of Education with, 126; War Plans Division, 132; coöperation of Forest Service with, 147; coöperation of Bureau of Entomology with, 178; coöperation of Bureau of Soils with, 181; represented in the U.S. Highways Council, 182; coöperation of

OUTLINE OF PLAN
FOR THE
ECONOMIC AND SOCIAL HISTORY OF THE WORLD WAR

EDITORS AND EDITORIAL BOARDS

GREAT BRITAIN
Sir William Beveridge, K.C.B., *Chairman.*
Professor H. W. C. Davis, C.B.E.
Mr. Thomas Jones, LL.D.
Mr. J. M. Keynes, C.B.
Mr. F. W. Hirst.
Professor W. R. Scott, D.Phil., LL.D.
Professor James T. Shotwell, *ex officio.*

AUSTRIA-HUNGARY
Joint Editorial Board.
> Professor James T. Shotwell, *Chairman.*

> Editors, Austrian Series:
Professor Dr. Friedrich Wieser, *Chairman.*
Dr. Richard Riedl.
Dr. Richard Schüller.

> Editor, Hungarian Series:
Dr. Gustav Gratz.

> Editor, Public Health Series:
Professor Dr. Clemens Pirquet.

BELGIUM
Professor H. Pirenne, *Editor.*

1

FRANCE

Professor Charles Gide, *Chairman.*
M. Arthur Fontaine.
Professor Henri Hauser.
Professor Charles Rist.
Professor James T. Shotwell, *ex officio.*

GERMANY

Dr. Carl Melchior, *Chairman.*
Professor Dr. Albrecht Mendelssohn Bartholdy,
                              Executive Secretary.
Dr. Hermann Bücher.
Professor Dr. Carl Duisberg.
Professor Dr. Max Sering.
Professor James T. Shotwell, *ex officio.*

ITALY

Professor Luigi Einaudi, *Chairman.*
Professor Pasquale Jannaccone.
Professor Umberto Ricci.
Professor James T. Shotwell, *ex officio.*

THE NETHERLANDS

Professor H. B. Greven, *Editor.*

RUMANIA

Mr. David Mitrany, *Editor.*

RUSSIA

Editor, First Series:
Sir Paul Vinogradoff, F.B.A. (1921-1925).
  (Died, December 19, 1925.)

SCANDINAVIA

Professor Harald Westergaard (Denmark), *Chairman.*
Professor Eli Heckscher (Sweden).
Professor James T. Shotwell, *ex officio.*

LIST OF MONOGRAPHS

This list includes only those published and in course of preparation, and may be changed from time to time. The monographs fall into two main classes, those which may be said to constitute full numbers in the series, volumes of from 300 to 500 pages; and partial numbers or special studies of approximately 100 pages or less, which may ultimately be incorporated in a full volume along with others dealing with cognate subjects. Titles have been grouped to indicate the proposed volume arrangement, but this grouping cannot be regarded as final in the larger and more complicated series. It is the intention, however, to keep to the total number of volumes indicated.

Monographs already published are indicated by an asterisk, partial numbers by a double asterisk.

AMERICAN SERIES

*Guide to American Sources for the Economic History of the War, by Mr. Waldo G. Leland and Dr. Newton D. Mereness.

War-Time Control of Industry in the United States, by Professor Alvin S. Johnson.

War History of American Railways and War Transportation Policies, by Mr. Walker D. Hines.

Financial History of the War: Revenue Aspects of the Problem, War Taxation, etc., by Professor Thomas Sewall Adams.

War Controls in the United States, by Professor Edwin F. Gay.

(Other volumes to follow.)

TRANSLATED AND ABRIDGED SERIES

*The History of French Industry during the War, by M. Arthur Fontaine.

Agriculture during the War, by M. Michel-Augé-Laribé.

Rationing and Food Control, by M. P. Pinot.

War Costs: Direct Expenses, by Professor Gaston Jèze.

War-Time Finances, by M. Henri Truchy.

Effect of the War upon the Civil Government of France, by Professor Pierre Renouvin.

The Organization of Labor in the Invaded Territories, by M. Pierre Boulin.

"Mittel-Europa": The Preparation of a New Joint Economy, by Dr. Gustav Gratz and Dr. Richard Schüller.

War Government in Austria, by Dr. Joseph Redlich.

(Other volumes to follow.)

*Bibliographical Survey, by Miss M. E. Bulkley.

*Manual of Archive Administration, by Mr. Hilary Jenkinson.

*British Archives in Peace and War, by Dr. Hubert Hall.

War Government of Great Britain and Ireland (with special reference to its economic aspects), by Professor W. G. S. Adams, C.B.

*War Government of the British Dominions, by Professor A. B. Keith, D.C.L.

*Prices and Wages in the United Kingdom, 1914-1920, by Professor A. L. Bowley.

*British War Budgets and Financial Policy, by Mr. F. W. Hirst and Mr. J. E. Allen.

Taxation and War-Time Incomes, by Sir Josiah C. Stamp, K.B.E.
    Taxation during the War.
    War-Time Profits and Their Distribution.

The War and Insurance. A series of studies: Life Insurance, by Mr. S. G. Warner; Fire Insurance, by Mr. A. E. Sich and Mr. S. Preston; Shipping Insurance, by Sir Norman Hill; Friendly Societies and Health Insurance, by Sir Alfred Watson; Unemployment Insurance, by Sir William Beveridge; with an additional section of the National Savings Movement, by Sir William Schooling.

*Experiments in State Control at the War Office and the Ministry of Food, by Mr. E. M. H. Lloyd.

British Food Control, by Sir William Beveridge, K.C.B., and Sir Edward C. K. Gonner, K.B.E.

*Food Production in War, by Sir Thomas Middleton, K.B.E.

**The Cotton Control Board, by Mr. H. D. Henderson.

*Allied Shipping Control; an Experiment in International Administration, by Sir Arthur Salter, K.C.B.

General History of British Shipping during the War, by Mr. C. Ernest Fayle.

*The British Coal Industry during the War, by Sir Richard Redmayne, K.C.B.

The British Iron and Steel Industry during the War, by Mr. W. T. Layton, C.H., C.B.E.

British Labour Unions and the War, by Mr. G. D. H. Cole:
    **Trade Unionism and Munitions.
    **Labour in the Coal Mining Industry.
    **Workshop Organization.

*Labour Supply and Regulation, by Mr. Humbert Wolfe, C.B.E.

4

Effect of the War upon Public Health:

Public Health Conditions in England during the War, by Dr. A. W. J. Macfadden, C.B.

Health of the Returned Soldier, by Dr. E. Cunyngham Brown, C.B.E.

*Industries of the Clyde Valley during the War, by Professor W. R. Scott and Mr. J. Cunnison.

Rural Scotland during the War. A series of studies under the direction of Professor W. R. Scott. Scottish Fisheries, by Mr. D. T. Jones; Scottish Agriculture, with special reference to Food, by Mr. H. M. Conacher; The Scottish Agricultural Labourer, by Mr. J. S. Duncan; Scottish Land Settlement, by Professor W. R. Scott; Appendix. The Jute Industry, by Mr. J. P. Day; Introduction, by Professor W. R. Scott.

Wales in the World War, by Mr. Thomas Jones, LL.D.

Guides to the Study of War-Time Economics, by Dr. N. B. Dearle:

Dictionary of Official War-Time Organizations.

Economic Chronicle of the War.

Studies in British Social History (to be arranged).

Cost of the War to Great Britain (to be arranged).

AUSTRIAN AND HUNGARIAN SERIES

Austria-Hungary:

*Bibliography of Austrian Economic Literature during the War, by Professor Dr. Othmar Spann.

*Austro-Hungarian Finance during the War, by Dr. Alexander Popovics.

Military Economic History, a series of studies directed by Professor Dr. Friedrich Wieser, Generals Krauss and Hoen, and Colonel Glaise-Horstenau.

Conscription, etc., by Colonel Klose; Munitions and Supply, by Colonel Pflug. Others to follow.

Economic Use of Occupied Territories: Serbia, Montenegro, Albania, by General Kerchnawe; Italy, by General Ludwig Leidl; Rumania, by General Felix Sobotka; Ukraine, by General Alfred Krauss; Poland, by Major Rudolf Mitzka.

*'Mittel-Europa': the Preparation of a New Joint Economy, by Dr. Gustav Gratz and Dr. Richard Schüller.

Exhaustion and Disorganization of the Hapsburg Monarchy, by Professor Dr. Friedrich Wieser, with a section on the Disruption of the Austro-Hungarian Economic Union, by Dr. Richard Schüller.

Empire of Austria:

*War Government in Austria, by Professor Dr. Joseph Redlich.

Industrial Control in Austria during the War, a series of studies directed by Dr. Richard Riedl.

Food Control and Agriculture in Austria during the War, a series of studies directed by Dr. H. Löwenfeld-Russ.

*Labor in Austria during the War, a series of studies directed by Mr. Ferdinand Hanusch.

Austrian Railways during the War (Civil Control) by Ing. Bruno Enderes; Transportation under Military Control, by Colonel Ratzenhofer.

*Coal Supply in Austria during the War, by Ing. Emil Homann-Herimberg.

The Moral Effects of the War upon Austria, by Chancellor Dr. Ignaz Seipel.

The War and Crime, by Professor Franz Exner.

The Costs of the War to Austria, by Dr. Friedrich Hornik.

Kingdom of Hungary:

Economic War History of Hungary: A General Survey, by Dr. Gustav Gratz.

Effects of the War upon the Hungarian Government and People, by Count Albert Apponyi.

Hungarian Industry during the War, by Baron Joseph Szterényi.

History of Hungarian Commerce during the War, by Dr. Alexander von Matlekovits.

History of Hungarian Finance during the War, by Dr. Johann von Teleszky.

Hungarian Agriculture during the War, by Dr. Emil von Mutschenbacher; and Food Control in Hungary during the War, by Professor Johann Bud.

Social Conditions in Hungary during the War, by Dr. Desider Pap.

Public Health and the War in Austria-Hungary:

General Survey of Public Health in Austria-Hungary, by Professor Dr. Clemens Pirquet.

*The Effect of the War upon Public Health in Austria and Hungary. A series of studies by Drs. Helly, Kirchengerger, Steiner, Raschofsky, Kassowitz, Breitner, von Bókay, Schacherl, Hockauf, Finger, Kyrle, Elias, Economo, Müller-Deham, Nobel, Wagner, Edelmann, and Mayerhofer, edited with Introduction by Professor Dr. Clemens Pirquet.

*Effects of the War upon Textile Industries, by Professor Albert Aftalion.

Effects of the War upon Metallurgy and Engineering (to be arranged); and Effects of the War upon Chemical Industries, by M. Eugène Mauclère.

Effects of the War upon Fuel and Motive Power:
  Coal Industry and Mineral Fuels, by M. Henri de Peyerimhoff.
  *Hydroelectric Power, by Professor Raoul Blanchard.

Forestry and the Timber Industry during the War, by General Georges Chevalier; and War-Time Aeronautic Industries, by Colonel Paul Dhé.

Organization of War Industries, by M. Albert Thomas.

Labor Conditions during the War, by MM. William Oualid and M. C. Picquenard.

Studies in War-Time Labor Problems (2 volumes):
  Unemployment during the War, by M. A. Créhange.
  Syndicalism during the War, by M. Roger Picard.
  *Foreign and Colonial Workmen in France, by M. B. Nogaro and Lt.-Col. Weil.
  *Women in Industry under War Conditions, by M. Marcel Frois.

Effects of the War in the Occupied Territories:
  The Organization of Labor in the Invaded Territories, by M. Pierre Boulin.
  Food Supply in the Invaded Territories, by MM. Paul Collinet and Paul Stahl.
  Damage Inflicted by the War, by MM. Edmond Michel and Prangey.

Refugees and Prisoners of War:
  The Refugees and Interned Civilians, by Professor Pierre Caron.
  Prisoners of War, by M. Georges Cahen-Salvador.

Effects of the War upon Transportation:
  French Railroads during the War, by M. Marcel Peschaud.
  *Internal Waterways, Freight Traffic, by M. Georges Pocard de Kerviler.

Effects of the War upon French Shipping:
  Merchant Shipping during the War, by M. Henri Cangardel.
  French Ports during the War, by M. Georges Hersent.

Effects of the War upon French Commerce, by Professor Charles Rist.

French Commercial Policy during the War, by M. Etienne Clémentel.

Effects of the War upon French Finances:
  *War-Time Finance, by M. Henri Truchy.
  War-Time Banking, by M. Albert Aupetit.

8

Studies in Social History:
  Coöperative Societies and the Struggle against High Prices, by Professor Charles Gide and M. Daudé-Bancel.
  Effects of the War upon the Problem of Housing, by MM. Henri Sellier and Bruggeman.
Effect of the War upon Public Health:
  Public Health and Hygiene, by Dr. Léon Bernard.
  The Wounded Soldiers, by MM. Cassin and Ville-Chabrolle.
The Poilu: Documents from the Trenches, by Professor J. N. Cru.
Economic History of French Cities during the War:
  Paris, by MM. Henri Sellier, Bruggeman and Poëte.
  *Lyons, by M. Edouard Herriot.
  *Rouen, by M. J. Levainville.
  *Marseilles, by M. Paul Masson.
  *Bordeaux, by M. Paul Courteault.
  *Bourges, by M. C. J. Gignoux.
  *Tours, by MM. Michel Lhéritier and Camille Chautemps.
  Alsace and Lorraine, by M. Georges Delahache.
Effects of the War upon Colonies and Possessions:
  The Colonies in War-Time, by M. Arthur Girault.
  Effects of the War upon Northern Africa, by M. Augustin Bernard.
The Cost of the War to France:
  *War Costs: Direct Expenses, by Professor Gaston Jèze.
  The Costs of the War to France, by Professor Charles Gide.

GERMAN SERIES

Bibliographical Survey of German Literature for the Economic History of the War, by Professor Dr. A. Mendelssohn Bartholdy and Dr. E. Rosenbaum; with a supplementary section on The Imperial German Archives, by Dr. Müsebeck.
Effect of the War upon the Government and Constitution of Germany:
  The War Government of Germany, by Professor Dr. A. Mendelssohn Bartholdy.
  The Political Administration of Occupied Territories, by Freiherr W. M. E. von Gayl, Dr. W. von Kries, and Dr. L. F. von Köhler.
Effects of the War upon Morals and Religion:
  Effect of the War upon Morals, by Professor Dr. Otto Baumgarten.
  Effect of the War upon Religion, by Professor Dr. Erich Foerster and Professor Dr. Arnold Rademacher.
  Effect of the War upon the Young, by Dr. Wilhelm Flitner.
  The War and Crime, by Professor Dr. Moritz Liepmann.

9

Effect of the War upon German Finance:

The Effect of the War upon Currency and Banking (to be arranged).

German Public Finance during the War, by Professor Dr. Walter Lotz.

GREECE

Economic and Social Effects of the War upon Greece, by Professor A. Andreades.

ITALIAN SERIES

Bibliographical Survey of the Economic and Social Problems of the War, by Professor Vincenzo Porri, with an introduction on the collection and use of the documents of the War, by Comm. Eugenio Casanova.

The Economic Legislation of the War, by Professor Alberto De'Stefani.

Agricultural Production in Italy, 1914-19, by Professor Umberto Ricci.

The Agricultural Classes in Italy during the War, by Professor Arrigo Serpieri.

Food Supply and Rationing, by Professor Bachi; and Food Supply of the Italian Army, by Professor Gaetano Zingali.

War-Time Finances, by Professor Luigi Einaudi.

Cost of the War to Italy, by Professor Luigi Einaudi.

Currency Inflation in Italy and Its Effects on Prices, Incomes, and Foreign Exchanges, by Professor Pasquale Jannaccone.

*Vital Statistics and Public Health in Italy during and after the War, by Professor Giorgio Mortara.

The Italian People during and after the War: A Social Survey, by Professor Gioacchino Volpe.

*Social and Economic Life in Piedmont as Affected by the War, by Professor Giuseppe Prato.

THE NETHERLANDS SERIES

*War Finances in the Netherlands up to 1918, by Dr. M. J. van der Flier.

The Effect of the War upon Supplies and upon Agriculture, by Dr. F. E. Posthuma.

The Effect of the War upon the Manufacturing Industry, by Mr. C. J. P. Zaalberg.

11

The Effect of the War upon Commerce and Navigation, by Mr. E. P. DeMonchy.

The Effect of the War upon Prices, Wages, and the Cost of Living, by Professor Dr. H. W. Methorst.

The Effect of the War upon Banking and Currency, by Dr. G. Vissering and Dr. J. Westerman Holstyn.

The Effect of the War upon the Colonies, by Professor Dr. J. H. Carpentier Alting and Mr. de Cock Buning.

The Effect of the War upon the Housing Problem, 1914-22, by Dr. H. J. Romeyn.

War Finances in the Netherlands, 1918-22. The Costs of the War, by Professor Dr. H. W. C. Bordewyck.

Japanese Series

Influence of the War upon Production of Raw Materials in Japan, by Mr. Kobayashi.

Influence of the War upon Japanese Industry, by Mr. Ogawa.

Influence of the War upon Japanese Commerce and Trade, by Mr. Yamazaki.

Influence of the War upon Japanese Transportation, by Mr. Matsuoka.

Influence of the War upon Japanese Finance and the Money Market, by Mr. Ono.

Social Influence of the War upon Japan, by Mr. Kobayashi.

Rumanian Series

The Rural Revolution in Rumania and Southeastern Europe, by Mr. D. Mitrany.

Economic Consequences of the War in Rumania:

The Effect of the Enemy Occupation of Rumania, by Dr. G. Antipa.

The Effect of the War upon Public Health in Rumania, by Professor J. Cantacuzino.

The Effect of the War upon Rumanian Economic Life (to be arranged).

Rumanian War Finance, by M. Vintila Bratianu.

Russian Series

Effects of the War upon Government and National Finances in Russia:

Effects of the War upon the Central Government, by Professor Paul P. Gronsky.

State Finances during the War, by Mr. Alexander M. Michelson.

Russian State Credit during the War, by Mr. Paul N. Apostol.

Currency in Russia during the War, by Professor Michael V. Bernadsky.

Municipalities and Zemstvos during the War:

The Zemstvos in Peace and War, by Prince J. Lvoff.

Effect of the War upon Russian Municipalities, and the All-Russian Union of Towns, by Mr. N. I. Astroff.

The Zemstvos, the All-Russian Union of the Zemstvos and the Zemgor, by Prince Vladimir A. Obolensky and Mr. Sergius P. Turin.

The War and the Psychology of the Zemstvos Workers, by Mr. Isaak V. Shklovsky.

Effect of the War upon Agricultural Coöperation and Coöperative Credit, by Professor A. N. Anziferoff.

The Russian Army in the World War: a study in social history, by General Nicholas N. Golovine.

Rural Economy in Russia and the War, by Professor A. N. Anziferoff, Professor Alexander Bilimovitch, and Mr. M. O. Batcheff.

Effect of the War upon Landholding and Settlement in Russia, by Professor Alexander Bilimovitch and Professor V. A. Kossinsky.

Problem of Food Supply in Russia during the War, by Professor Peter B. Struve.

State Control of Industry in Russia during the War, by Mr. Simon O. Zagorsky.

Effects of the War upon Russian Industries:

Coal Mining, by Mr. Boris N. Sokoloff.

Chemical Industry, by Mr. Mark A. Landau.

Flax and Wool Industry, by Mr. Sergius N. Tretiakoff.

Petroleum, by Mr. Alexander M. Michelson.

Effects of the War upon Labor and Industrial Conditions:

Wages in War-Time, by Miss Anna G. Eisenstadt.

Changes in the Conditions and Composition of the Working Classes, by Mr. W. T. Braithwaite.

Effects of the War upon Trade and Commerce:

Internal Russian Trade during the War, by Mr. Paul A. Bouryschkine.

Russia in the Economic War, by Professor Boris E. Nolde.

Effects of the War upon Transportation in Russia, by Mr. Michael B. Braikevitch.

Effects of the War upon Education and Public Health in Russia:
  Elementary and Secondary Schools during the War, by Professor
    D. M. Odinez.
  Universities and Academic Institutions during the War, by Professor P. J. Novgorodzoff.
Social History of the Ukraine during the War, by Mr. Nicholas M.
  Mogilansky.
Vital Statistics of Russia during the War, by Mr. S. S. Kohn; and
  Russia in the World War; a historical synthesis (to be arranged).

SCANDINAVIAN SERIES

The Economic Effects of the War upon Sweden, a series of studies
  edited and with an Introduction by Professor Eli F. Heckscher.
  The Effect of the War upon the Life and Work of the Swedish People (General Introduction), by Professor Eli F. Heckscher.
  The Effect of the War upon Swedish Agriculture and Food Supply,
    by Mr. Carl Mannerfelt.
  The Effect of the War upon Swedish Industry, by Mr. Olof Edström.
  The Effect of the War upon the Working Classes, by Mr. Otto
    Järte.
The Effect of the War upon Swedish Finance and Commerce:
  The Effect of the War upon Currency and Finances, by Professor
    Eli F. Heckscher.
  The War and Swedish Commerce, by Mr. Kurt Bergendal.
Norway and the World War, by Dr. Wilhelm Keilhau.
The Economic Effects of the War upon Denmark, by Dr. Einar Cohn,
  with a section on Iceland, by Mr. Thorstein Thorsteinsson.

YUGOSLAV SERIES

Economic Situation of Serbia at the Outbreak and during the First
  Year of the War, by Professor Velimir Bajkitch.
Economic and Social Effects of the World War upon Serbia, by Professor Dragoliub Yovanovitch.
Economic and Social Effects of the War upon Yugoslavia (to be arranged).

14

PUBLISHERS

The publication of the monographs is being carried forward under the general direction of Yale University Press, in coöperation with other publishers in other countries. Each of the volumes as published is thus made available not only through the national publisher, but through each of the other publishers in other countries.

The following volumes are now ready, or will be ready shortly:

AMERICAN SERIES

Guide to American Sources for the Economic History of the War, by Mr. Waldo G. Leland and Dr. Newton D. Mereness.

TRANSLATED AND ABRIDGED SERIES

The History of French Industry during the War, by M. Arthur Fontaine.

AUSTRIAN AND HUNGARIAN SERIES

(In German)

Bibliographie der Wirtschafts- und Sozialgeschichte des Weltkrieges, by Othmar Spann.

Das Geldwesen im Kriege, by Dr. Alexander von Popovics.

Die Kohlenversorgung Osterreichs während des Krieges, by Emil von Homann-Herimberg.

Die Regelung der Arbeitsverhältnisse im Kriege, by Ferdinand Hanusch.

Die äussere Wirtschaftspolitik Osterreich-Ungarns, by Dr. Gustav Gratz and Professor Dr. Richard Schüller.

Osterreichische Regierung und Verwaltung im Kriege, by Minister A. D. Professor Dr. Josef Redlich.

Studien über Volksgesundheit und Krieg; eine Reihe von Monographien, verfasst von den Doktoren J. Bokay, B. Breitner, C. Economo, A. Edelmann, H. Elias, E. Finger, C. Helly, J. Hockauf, K. Kassowitz, C. Kirchenberger, G. Schacherl, J. Steiner, R. Wagner, unter der Leitung von Professor Dr. Clemens Pirquet.

15

16

French Series
(In French)

Bibliographie générale de la guerre, by Camille Bloch.

Le Problème du Régionalisme, by Professor Henri Hauser.

Le Contrôle du Ravitaillement de la population civile, by M. Pierre Pinot.

L'Agriculture pendant la guerre, by M. Michel Augé-Laribé.

Les Industries textiles, by M. Albert Aftalion.

L'Industrie française pendant la guerre, by M. Arthur Fontaine.

Les Forces hydro-électriques, by M. Raoul Blanchard.

Les Formes du gouvernement de guerre, by M. Pierre Renouvin.

La Main-d'oeuvre étrangère et coloniale, by M. B. Nogaro and Lt.-Col. Weil.

La Santé et le travail des femmes pendant la guerre, by M. Marcel Frois.

La Navigation intérieure en France pendant la guerre, by M. Georges Pocard de Kerviler.

Les Finances de guerre de la France, by M. Henri Truchy.

Les Dépenses de guerre de la France, by M. Gaston Jèze.

Le mouvement des prix et des salaries durant la guerre en France, by M. Lucien March.

Etudes d'Historie locale:

  Lyon, by M. Edouard Herriot.

  Marseille, by M. Paul Masson.

  Rouen, by M. J. Levainville.

  Bordeaux, by M. Paul Courteault.

  Bourges, by M. Claude-Joseph Gignoux.

  Tours, by MM. Michel Lhéritier and Camille Chautemps.

Italian Series

La salute pubblica in Italia durante e dopo la guerra, by Professor Giorgio Mortara.

Il Piemonte e gli effetti della guerra sulla sua vita economica e sociale, by Professor Giuseppe Prato.

The Netherlands Series
(In English)

War Finances in the Netherlands up to 1918, by M. J. van der Flier.

The publishers and selling agents for each of the countries are as follows:

AMERICA

Yale University Press, New Haven, Connecticut.

AUSTRIA-HUNGARY

Holder-Pichler-Tempsky A.-G., Vienna, Austria.

FRANCE

Les Presses Universitaires de France, 49 Boulevard Saint-Michel, Paris, France.

GERMANY

Deutsche Verlags-Anstalt, Berlin and Stuttgart.

GREAT BRITAIN

Oxford University Press, Amen House, Warwick Square, London, E.C. 4. England.

ITALY

La Casa Editrice Laterza, Bari, Italy.

Inquiries regarding the contents or price of any of the volumes should be addressed to the publisher for the country from which the inquiry originates.